ROUTLEDGE HANDBOOK
OF MARXIAN ECONOMICS

Most developed economies are characterized by high levels of inequality and an inability to provide stability or opportunity for many of their citizens. Mainstream economics has proven to be of little assistance in addressing these systemic failures, and this has led both scholars and students to seek alternatives. One such alternative is provided by Marxian economics. In recent decades the field has seen tremendous theoretical development and Marxian perspectives have begun to appear in public discourse in unprecedented ways.

This handbook contains thirty-seven original essays from a wide range of leading international scholars, recognized for their expertise in different areas of Marxian economics. Its scope is broad, ranging from contributions on familiar Marxist concepts such as value theory, the labor process, accumulation, crisis and socialism, to others not always associated with the Marxian canon, like feminism, ecology, international migration and epistemology. This breadth of coverage reflects the development of Marxian economic and social theory, and encompasses both the history and the frontiers of current scholarship. This handbook provides an extensive statement of the current shape and future direction of Marxian economics.

The *Routledge Handbook of Marxian Economics* is an invaluable resource for students, researchers and policy makers seeking guidance in this field. It is designed to serve both as a reference work and as a supplementary text for classroom use, with applications for courses in economics, sociology, political science, management, anthropology, development studies, philosophy and history.

David M. Brennan is Associate Professor of Economics at Franklin & Marshall College in Lancaster, PA, USA.

David Kristjanson-Gural is Professor of Economics and Senior Fellow of the Social Justice College at Bucknell University, PA, USA.

Catherine P. Mulder is Associate Professor of Economics and the Program Director at John Jay College—CUNY, USA.

Erik K. Olsen is Associate Professor of Economics at the University of Missouri—Kansas City and Research Fellow at the Rutgers University School of Management and Labor Relations, USA.

ROUTLEDGE HANDBOOK OF MARXIAN ECONOMICS

Edited by David M. Brennan, David Kristjanson-Gural,
Catherine P. Mulder and Erik K. Olsen

LONDON AND NEW YORK

First published 2017 by Routledge

2 Park Square, Milton Park, Abingdon, Oxfordshire OX14 4RN
52 Vanderbilt Avenue, New York, NY 10017

Routledge is an imprint of the Taylor & Francis Group, an informa business

First issued in paperback 2019

British Library Cataloguing in Publication Data
A catalogue record for this book is available from the British Library

Library of Congress Cataloging in Publication Data
Names: Brennan, David M., editor. | Kristjanson-Gural, David, editor. |
Mulder, Catherine P., editor.
Title: Routledge handbook of Marxian economics / edited by David M. Brennan,
David Kristjanson-Gural, Catherine P. Mulder and Erik K. Olsen.
Description: New York : Routledge, 2017. | Includes index.
Identifiers: LCCN 2016043505 | ISBN 9781138774933 (hardback) |
ISBN 9781315774206 (ebook)
Subjects: LCSH: Marxian economics. | Economic policy. | Social policy.
Classification: LCC HB97.5 .R658 2017 | DDC 335.4--dc23
LC record available at https://lccn.loc.gov/2016043505

ISBN: 978-1-138-77493-3 (hbk)
ISBN: 978-0-367-32176-5 (pbk)

Typeset in Times New Roman
by Integra Software Service Pvt. Ltd.

For our friend, mentor and colleague whose vision, wisdom
and dedication to Marxian economics made this handbook possible.
Stephen A. Resnick
October 24, 1938 – January 2, 2013

CONTENTS

CONTRIBUTORS

Jack Amariglio is Professor of Economics at Merrimack College, USA, and former editor of the journal *Rethinking Marxism*. He is co-author (with David F. Ruccio) of *Postmodern Moments in Modern Economics* and co-editor (with Joseph Childers and Stephen Cullenberg) of *Sublime Economy: On the Intersection of Art and Economics*.

Erdogan Bakir is Associate Professor of Economics at Bucknell University in Lewisburg, PA, USA. His research has appeared in the *Review of Radical Political Economics*, *Journal of Economic Issues* and *Science & Society: A Journal of Marxist Thought and Analysis*.

Fabian Balardini is Associate Professor of Economics at the Borough of Manhattan Community College in New York City, USA. He is the author of *Oil Price Cycles: A Theoretical and Empirical Investigation Using Marx's Theory of Value*, and his research has appeared in *Socialism and Democracy* and *Razon y Revolucion*.

Drucilla K. Barker is Professor in the Department of Anthropology and the Women's & Gender Studies Program at the University of South Carolina, USA. She is a radical, feminist economist whose research interests are globalization, feminist political economy, and economic anthropology. Her work ranges from examinations of the roles of gender, race and class in social valuations of labor, especially affective labor, to feminist accounts of the financial crises that characterize late global capitalism.

Suzanne Bergeron is Professor of Women's Studies and Social Sciences and Director of Women's and Gender Studies at the University of Michigan—Dearborn, USA. In the 1980s, she was an undergraduate student of Stephen Resnick's, whose keen interest in the topic of the Marxian political economy of the household inspired her to pursue graduate study on the topic. She has since published widely on the topic of gender, development and social reproduction.

Rajesh Bhattacharya is Associate Professor in the Public Policy and Management Group at Indian Institute of Management Calcutta, India. He has also taught at South Asian University, University of Calcutta and Presidency University. He obtained his Ph.D. in Economics from

University of Massachusetts, Amherst. His research areas include Marxian economic theory, political economy of development and Indian economic history.

David M. Brennan is Associate Professor of Economics at Franklin & Marshall College in Lancaster, PA, USA. His research has appeared in the *Cambridge Journal of Economics*, the *Review of Radical Political Economics, Feminist Economics* and *Rethinking Marxism: A Journal of Economics, Culture & Society*, among other publications.

Dick Bryan is Emeritus Professor of Political Economy at the University of Sydney, Australia. He currently works on the social significance of financial derivatives and their implications for theories of value.

Theodore Burczak is Professor of Economics at Denison University, USA. He is author of *Socialism after Hayek* (2006) and several other articles advancing progressive critiques of Hayek and Austrian economics.

Antonio Callari is the Sigmund M. And Mary B. Hyman Professor of Economics at Franklin and Marshall College, in Lancaster, PA, USA. His work has been on Marxian theory and on intellectual history.

Al Campbell is Emeritus Professor of Economics at the University of Utah, USA. His research work includes the functioning of contemporary capitalism, and the theory and practical experiments of alternative human-centered political economic systems.

Guglielmo Carchedi has worked as a social affairs officer at the UN in New York and as a professor at the University of Amsterdam up to his retirement. He is now Associate Professor at York University, Toronto, Canada. He is the author of numerous books and articles on epistemology, sociology and political economy.

Anjan Chakrabarti is Professor of Economics, University of Calcutta, India. His recent book is *The Indian Economy in Transition: Globalization, Capitalism and Development* (with Anup Dhar and Byasdeb Dasgupta). He is the recipient of the Dr V K R V Rao Prize in Social Science Research in Economics for the year 2008.

Brett Clark is Associate Professor of Sociology and Sustainability Studies at the University of Utah, USA. He is the coauthor of four books, including *The Tragedy of the Commodity, The Ecological Rift, The Science and Humanism of Stephen Jay Gould*, and *Critique of Intelligent Design*.

Hans G. Despain is Professor of Economics at Nichols College in Dudley, Massachusetts, USA. Professor Despain is the Chair of the Economics Department and the Chair of Nichols College Honors Program. His primary areas of research include Marxian political economy and the political economy of education.

Anup Dhar is Associate Professor, School of Human Studies and Director of the Centre for Development Practice, Ambedkar University, Delhi, India. His recently published books include *Dislocation and Resettlement in Development: From Third Word to World of the Third* (co-authored with Anjan Chakrabarti) from Routledge and *World* *of the Third and Global Capitalism* (co-authored with Anjan Chakrabarti and Stephen Cullenberg).

Paulo L. dos Santos is Assistant Professor of Economics at the New School for Social Research in New York City, USA. His research includes work on the social and macro-economic content of contemporary financial practices, finance and development, income distribution, mathematical methods in economic analysis, and the development statistical-mechanical approaches to the analysis of economic systems. His articles have appeared in *Economic Letters, Journal of Post-Keynesian Economics, Metroeconomica*, and *Historical Materialism*, among other journals.

Esra Erdem is Professor for Social Economics at Alice Salomon University Berlin, Germany. Her research on the political economy of migration and urban postcapitalist practices has appeared in *Rethinking Marxism, German Politics and Society, Revista de Economia Mundial* and *Acta Geographica*, among other publications.

Duncan K. Foley is Leo Model Professor of Economics at the New School for Social Research in New York City, and an external professor at the Santa Fe Institute, USA. He received the PhD in Economics from Yale University, and has taught at M.I.T., Stanford, and Barnard College of Columbia University. His interests in economics center on economic theory, political economy, the history of economics, mathematical modeling, and the founda-tions of statistical reasoning. Recent research includes work on modeling the mammalian brain clock, the economics of global warming, economics and thermodynamics, Marxian value theory, social coordination problems, and Bayesian approaches to theory choice.

Satyananda Gabriel is Professor of Economics and Finance at Mt. Holyoke College, USA. He is former director of education for the Urban League of Greater Portland, Oregon and former director of the Financial Services Academy in Portland, Oregon. As academic coordinator of the National Rural Fellows and Rural Development Leadership Network, he taught courses in alternative economic enterprises, including analysis of productive self-employment and collective enterprises. He supervised the Volunteers in Probation Program for Multnomah County (Oregon) Adult Corrections. He has also served as consultant for UNDP in Central America and on various Native American reservations in the U.S.

David Kristjanson-Gural is Professor of Economics and Senior Fellow of the Social Justice College at Bucknell University, USA. His research explores the role of demand in Marxian theories of value and price, Marx's methodology and the ethical and practical dimensions of worker self-directed enterprises, particularly as a means of solving poverty. His published work appears in *Rethinking Marxism, Research in Political Economy, Historical Materialism* and *The International Journal for Pluralism in Economics Education*.

Andrew Kliman is a professor emeritus of economics at Pace University, New York, USA. He is the author of two books, *Reclaiming Marx's "Capital"* and *The Failure of Capitalist Production*, co-editor (with Nick Potts) of *Is Marx's Theory of Profit Right?*, and editor of Lexington Books' series, Heterodox Studies in the Critique of Political Economy. His research on value theory, economic crisis theory, and other topics has appeared in journals such the *Cambridge Journal of Economics*, the *American Journal of Economics and Sociology, Capital and Class*, and *Marxism 21*, and in popular media.

Costas Lapavitsas is Professor of Economics at the School of Oriental and African Studies, University of London, UK. He has published widely and his most recent books include *Profiting without Producing* (2013) and *Against the Troika* (2015) with Heiner Flassbeck.

Stefano B. Longo is Associate Professor of Sociology at North Carolina State University, USA. He is the coauthor of *The Tragedy of the Commodity: Oceans, Fisheries, and Aquaculture*.

Terrence McDonough was Professor of Economics at National University of Ireland, Galway, until his recent retirement. He is also Honorary Professor of Political Economy at the University of Sydney, Australia. He has published in the areas of capitalist stages, globalization, environment, and Irish and American economy and history. He maintains an active interest in community and labor economics education.

Richard McIntyre is Professor of Economics and Political Science and chair of the economics department at the University of Rhode Island, USA. He is the author of *Are Worker Rights Human Rights?* (2008) and many academic and popular articles. He is the general editor of the *New Political Economy* book series published by Routledge.

Fred Moseley is Professor Emeritus of Economics at Mount Holyoke College, Massachusetts, USA. He has taught courses in Marxian Economics, History of Economic Thought, U.S. Economic History, and Macroeconomics. He has published numerous articles on Marx's logical method, especially with respect to the transformation problem, and his new book *Money and Totality: A Macro-Monetary Interpretation of Marx's Logic in* Capital *and the End of the 'Transformation Problem'* was published in October 2015.

Catherine P. Mulder is an associate professor of economics and the program director at John Jay College—CUNY, USA. She has published two books, *Unions and Class Transformation: The Case of the Broadway Musicians* and *Transcending Capitalism through Cooperative Practices*. She has also published articles in journals, most recently in *Rethinking Marxism*. Cathy is also the current president of the Association for Economic and Social Analysis.

Bruce Norton is Associate Professor and Economics Program Coordinator at San Antonio College in San Antonio, TX, USA. He has published articles in journals including *History and Theory, History of Political Economy, Rethinking Marxism: A Journal of Economics, Culture & Society*, the *Review of Radical Political Economics, Social Concept*, and the *Cambridge Journal of Economics*.

Erik K. Olsen is Associate Professor of Economics at the University of Missouri—Kansas City and Research Fellow at the Rutgers University School of Management and Labor Relations, USA. He holds a doctorate from the University of Massachusetts Amherst, a B.S. from Northeastern University, and has published widely with contributions in several fields of economics. Currently he is engaged in research on the effect of group or cooperative ownership and participatory management on firm structure, performance and survival.

Michael Rafferty is Associate Professor of International Business at RMIT University, Melbourne, Australia. He currently works on the social significance of financial derivatives, especially in relation to offshore financial centers and the valuation of intangible assets.

Elizabeth A. Ramey is an Associate Professor of Economics at Hobart and William Smith Colleges in Geneva, NY, USA. Her research interests include gender and economics as well as the political economy of food and agriculture. She recently completed a book: *Class, Gender and the American Family Farm in the Twentieth Century.*

Bruce Roberts is formerly Professor of Economics at the University of Southern Maine, USA. His articles on Marx and value have appeared in numerous journals and books.

David F. Ruccio is Professor of Economics at the University of Notre Dame, USA, and former editor (from 1997 to 2009) of the journal *Rethinking Marxism*. His books include *Development and Globalization: A Marxian Class Analysis, Economic Representations: Both Academic and Everyday, Postmodern Moments in Modern Economics, Postmodernism, Economics, and Knowledge*, and *Postmodern Materialism and the Future of Marxist Theory.*

Alfredo Saad-Filho is Professor of Political Economy at SOAS, University of London, UK, and was a senior economic affairs officer at the United Nations Conference on Trade and Development. He has published extensively on the political economy of development, industrial policy, neoliberalism, democracy, alternative economic policies, Latin American political and economic development, inflation and stabilisation, and the labour theory of value and its applications.

Maliha Safri is Associate Professor and Chair of the Economics Department at Drew University, USA. Her research has appeared in *Signs, Middle East Journal, Organization, Rethinking Marxism, Journal of Design Strategies*, and edited book collections such as the recent *Making Other Worlds Possible: Performing Diverse Economies*. She won a collaborative National Science Foundation grant for research on noncapitalist economies in NYC, and is currently at work on that project.

Claudio Sardoni is Professor of Economics at Sapienza University of Rome, Italy. After graduating in Statistics in Rome, in 1982 he obtained his PhD in economics at the University of Adelaide, under the supervision of Geoff Harcourt. Sardoni's main area of research is macroeconomics and monetary theory, with particular attention to the Keynesian and Post Keynesian traditions and their relationship with the Classical and Marxian approaches. On these topics he has published many articles, chapters in books and two books.

Sean Sayers is Emeritus Professor of Philosophy at the University of Kent, UK, and Visiting Professor of Philosophy at Peking University, China. He has written extensively on many areas of philosophy from a Hegelian-Marxist perspective. His books include *Marx and Alienation: Essays on Hegelian Themes* (2011), *Plato's Republic: An Introduction* (1999), *Marxism and Human Nature* (1998), *Reality and Reason: Dialectic and the Theory of Knowledge* (1985), and *Hegel, Marx and Dialectic: A debate* (with Richard Norman, 1980). He was one of the founders of *Radical Philosophy* (1972–), and he is the founder and Editor in Chief of the online *Marx and Philosophy Review of Books* (2010–).

Ian J. Seda-Irizarry is Assistant Professor in the Economics Department at John Jay College, City University of New York, USA. He obtained his Ph.D. in Economics from the

University of Massachusetts, Amherst. His research interests include Marxian economic theory, economic history, and the political economy of development in Puerto Rico.

Andrew B. Trigg is Senior Lecturer in Economics at The Open University, UK. He has published widely in journals and edited volumes; his 2006 monograph, *Marxian Reproduction Schema: Money and Aggregate Demand in a Capitalist Economy*, is published by Routledge.

Roberto Veneziani holds a Ph.D. in Economics from the London School of Economics and Political Science. He is Reader at the School of Economics and Finance, Queen Mary University of London, UK. His research interests include Marxian economics, egalitarian principles, distribution of resources between generations, sustainable development, and normative principles in economics. He is also interested in the history of economic thought and in political economy from a mathematical perspective.

Richard D. Wolff is Professor of Economics Emeritus at the University of Massachusetts, Amherst and Visiting Professor at The New School University, New York, USA. His recent work is posted at rdwolff.com and democracyatwork.info. His most latest book (2016) is *Capitalism's Crisis Deepens*.

PREFACE

Marxian economics is a vital and evolving paradigm with a rich history. In recent decades the field has seen tremendous theoretical development, revealed important empirical applications, and significantly broadened its scope. This handbook provides a contemporary account of the discipline through studies of many of its key concepts. Its scope is broad, ranging from familiar Marxian concepts, such as value theory, the labor process, accumulation, crisis and socialism, to others not always associated with the Marxian canon, like feminism, ecology, international migration and epistemology. This breadth of coverage reflects the growth of Marxian economic and social theory, and encompasses both the history and the frontiers of current scholarship.

This handbook contains thirty-seven original essays commissioned specifically for this book from scholars recognized for their expertise in different areas of Marxian economics. Contributors come from the Americas, Europe, Asia and Australia, and include many of the leading scholars in the field, as well as younger scholars who have made promising contributions. They were asked to both survey the debates that shaped the evolution of these ideas and to give a rigorous description of current thinking and practice. Of course, each author approaches their subject from his or her own perspective and this is evident in the essays. As editors, we believe it is important for contributors to be free to take a position, but each author was also asked to pursue their ideas in a non-polemical fashion. In addition to this, we endeavored to be inclusive of a variety of different approaches and solicited contributions from scholars with varied perspectives.

The intended audience for this handbook includes established scholars as well as students, activists and others who want to become better acquainted with these key concepts. Readers who are familiar with the topics included here will find concise discussions of the state-of-the-art as well as original contributions. Those who are less familiar with these topics will find accessible discussions of how current practice evolved from seminal contributions and scholarly debates. Our hope is that both types of readers will find this volume to be a valuable resource.

While each entry stands on its own merit and may be read independently, the reader will notice that they are arranged into sections. Each section builds on the foundation provided by concepts in the preceding section. For this reason some readers may find it helpful to read the entries in order to provide at the outset the theoretical and conceptual background necessary to appreciate the entries later in the volume. The final section contains entries describing the key ideas of a number of different schools of thought within Marxian economics.

As editors, we came to this book project at the invitation of the late Stephen Resnick who felt that a handbook showcasing both the history and the contemporary evolution of Marxian economics was badly needed. Many of the key concepts used in Marxian economics initially seem self-evident (e.g., value, labor, capital, crisis), but may have specific meanings and significance that are distinct from both everyday usage and from mainstream economics. Furthermore, the understanding of these concepts progresses over time. We believe this volume will help address these issues by providing accessible discussions of the rich history of debate that resulted in the current understandings of these topics. Both Stephen Resnick and his collaborator Richard Wolff were innovative and saw Marxian economics as evolving and developing while also deriving its central insights from its foundational texts. In this spirit we hope the present volume generates continuing engagement among scholars to continue the work of advancing Marxian scholarship with the goal of achieving a more just and equitable society.

ACKNOWLEDGEMENTS

The authors would like to thank the following individuals and institutions for their important contributions to this volume. We thank the contributors for their careful scholarship and their willingness to engage with contending approaches in order to provide an overview of and advance the Marxian literature. We wish to thank the people we have worked with at Routledge Publishers for their assistance and their patience, especially Emily Kindleysides for initiating this project, and Andy Humphries and Elanor Best who shepherded it to completion. We also thank those involved in helping edit the manuscripts, Karen Jows from Bucknell University, Tami Lantz from Franklin and Marshall, and Judith Chien, Ph. D. Several institutions supported this project including John Jay College—CUNY, a PSC-CUNY Research Grant, a grant from the Office of The Advancement of Research at John Jay College-CUNY, Franklin & Marshall College and Bucknell University, which provided a Publication Subvention Grant. We thank the worker cooperative, Twin Oaks Indexing, for producing the extensive index. The editors would also like to thank their families, friends and colleagues for all their support and patience. Finally, we would like to thank Stephen Resnick and Richard Wolff for inspiring generations of scholars to engage with the important insights of Marxian Economics.

PART I

Dialectics and Methodology

1

DIALECTICS AND OVERDETERMINATION

Antonio Callari

The dialectic refers to a *process* in which objects of interest (e.g., "capital," "society") are understood as developing through contradictions structured in relationship to an essence, a force which both sets things as they are (and appear) and yet propels them into a beyond (as they could be). Marx (1977, 103) wrote that he used a dialectical method he had extracted (removed from its "mystical [idealist] shell") from Hegel. Arguing the impossibility of divorcing Hegel's dialectic from his idealism, Althusser (1970) proposed overdetermination as an alternative materialist framework.

We begin with Hegel's dialectic before turning to Marx's use of it and then to overdetermination as it was proposed by Althusser and developed further, later, by Stephen Resnick and Richard Wolff.

Dialectics

Hegel

Before Hegel, as the idea of "progress" ("science," "history") was taking shape, Kant had posed a formidable challenge to any certainty regarding this progress. Considering "knowing" and "being" separate domains of existence, Kant had philosophically produced an unbridgeable gap between them: the unknowability of the "thing in itself." To answer Kant, German Idealism rejected his premise of the separateness of knowing and being. Hegel's dialectic became a way of thinking their "unity."

German Idealism initially theorized this unity unidirectionally: Fichte (subjective idealism) made being the product of knowing (the "I"), Schelling (objective idealism) made knowing the product of being. Similarly situating knowing and being as two poles (*one active* and *the other passive*) of existence, both Fichte and Schelling placed them in a relationship of *reflection*, with the active element completely shaping the passive one, the latter thus being conceived as the mirror image of the former. With being and knowing thus *philosophically* absorbing each other, neither Fichte nor Schelling could give to history or science a positive place in their philosophies. They both turned to "genius" ("intuition") as the guarantor of the sought-for certainty of knowledge. They both produced formal ("ideal") systems, in which particular ideas or practices out of the axes of these systems could only be thought of as misrepresentations and could as such be erased or repressed. Both Fichte and Schelling took political positions that Hegel found problematic, Fichte viewing society as "tyranny" (over the "I"), and Schelling supporting authoritarianism (to weed out the ignorance of the masses) (Lukács 1976).

Considering Fichte and Schelling unable to respond to Kant, Hegel produced a philosophical system in which *both* being and knowing were active. Lukács labels Hegel's idealism "absolute" not only because it included both "subjective" and "objective" domains, but also because the system he produced, by including them both as active elements, was greater than the sum of its parts: it made a place for elements that the separate idealisms of Fichte and Schelling could not accommodate *positively*. The codetermination of knowing and being required Hegel to include *as positive elements* of his philosophy all ideas that have practical effects on the world, even if/when they can (actually or potentially) be shown to be or to have been errors in some respect or another (compare with Schelling's attitude toward popular ideologies). Hegel's world thus has to be a *totality*, comprehending and treating as positive both elements of Truth/truths and Its/their limits. Of course, Hegel's philosophy remains "idealist" because of the presence of a (one) *source* directing the codetermination of knowing and being. This direction is necessary if the choreography of knowing and being is to result in the required (versus Kant) certainty. The term "idealism" happens to comport well with the content(s) Hegel gave to this source: Notion (Reason, Spirit). Philosophically, however, the term refers to the presumption of the existence of *one* source, irrespective of the content of that source (a postulate that everything derives from "Matter" is as much an idealism as a postulate that everything derives from "Notion"). As we will see, only the existence of such *a* source could philosophically guarantee the unity of knowing and being Hegel was constructing.

Hegel laid out the "dialectical" (versus "formal") logic necessary for his system in his *Logic*: Part I is the Objective Logic (dealing separately with "Being" and with "Essence"); Part II is the Subjective Logic (dealing with knowledge, the Notion) (Blunden 1997). The part on Essence is "by far the most important part" of the entire *opus* (Engels 1940, 26). Essence both has a structured relationship to the world as it is, and contains aspects that propel it (the world) into some other state (and, eventually, into an absolute unity of knowing and being). "Essence" is what makes existence not a state, but a process, history.[1]

Hegel's dialectic has been summarized with a few fundamental laws. Engels (1940, 26) lists them as: 1) the "transformation from quality into quantity *and vice-versa*" (emphasis in original), illustrating the iterative process through which a quality (an entity, e.g., capital) undergoes quantitative accumulations that, at some point (when the contradictions within it break its unity—see note 2 below), precipitate its transformation into another quality (e.g., capital moving from manufacturing, to machinery, to centralization, to socialization)—this law summarizes the nature of Being; 2) "the interpenetration [unity, in other renditions] of opposites," pointing to the contradictory nature of being[2]—this law summarizes the nature of Essence; and 3) "the negation of the negation," which Engels argued was the "the fundamental law for the construction of the whole [Hegelian] system," speaking to the stage-structure of transcendence (see note 1 for the repeated transitions in the master-slave narrative). All three laws are important, but, for reasons that should become clear later, we will pay more attention to the second, the "interpenetration of opposites," and to one of its manifestations in particular, the *interpenetration of content and form*.

In Hegel's *master-slave narrative*, we saw that "content" (i.e., the being-and-knowledge of equality), although essence could be presumed always to push it beyond itself, could "exist" only in a particular form at a particular stage of the development of Spirit (i.e., the religious form in the stage of feudalism). The part of essence within the content that was yearning for more concrete determinations of equality could not exist *per se*, since the real being of equality was only given in its religious *form*. That part of the essence, therefore, cannot be discovered in the realm of ideas (that would have presupposed a sufficiency of thought Hegel could not accept), or in a logical analysis of the form in itself. It rather has to be discovered through an analysis of *concrete ways* in which the form imposed its logic on the content *and* of the fault lines (contradictions) *in these ways*. It is the task of theoretical work to discover, through analysis and synthesis,[3] these fault lines and to deduce from them the essence pointing to the next phase of history.

We note, in conclusion, that the parts of the *Logic* have a circular relationship. In describing the world, we do not go *from* being *to* essence *to* ideas; or *from* ideas *to* essence *to* being; or even *from* essence *to* being on the one hand, and to ideas on the other. Rather, Being (universal, particular), Essence (unity of opposites, form and content), and Notion (abstract and concrete) coexist and codetermine each other in their structures (e.g., the codetermination of content and form). We can thus enter Hegel's circle of existence at any point, move along its circumference, and return to the point of entry. But it is also important to note that this circle of Hegel does have a center (the search for certainty, the unity of knowing and being), which totalizes (captures every concreteness within) the space it defines by rotating a radius uniformly around itself. The owl of Minerva spreads its wings only at dusk, but it also always finds its perch at the center of the world.

Marx's Use of the Dialectic

We focus here on *Capital* (Marx 1977) and the work that, beginning in 1857 (Marx 1973), led Marx to it.[4]

When thinking of Hegel's influence in *Capital*, contradiction comes to mind most readily. In fact, Marx starts by highlighting the dual nature of the commodity (use and exchange value) so as later to be able to theorize all the potential contradictions of that duality. We however begin our discussion of Marx's relationship to the dialectic with the categories of content and form. When Marx wrote that, in the beginning chapter on value, he "coquetted with the mode of expressions peculiar to [Hegel]" (1973, 33), he had in mind "content and form" (the substance of value and the form of value in exchange) as well as "quality and quantity" (value and exchange value). Indeed, the two pairs mutually constitute each other.

It is instructive to trace the path that leads Marx to give prominence to the content-and-form relation. Marx (1973) sets out to work on his comprehensive critique of political economy (*Grundrisse*) on the occasion of the 1857 economic crisis *and* of an inadequate (in his mind) "socialist" response to that crisis, the Proudhonist Darimon's proposal for a "free credit" monetary reform of capitalism (Negri 1984). A decade earlier, Marx (1963) had criticized Proudhon's own concentration on money (as the presumed source of economic instability and injustice). He criticized as dilettantish Proudhon's use of the Hegelian idea of contradiction as a simple "opposition" of good (represented by labor as the source of value) and evil (represented by the corrupting force of money), and condemned, as petty bourgeois, his proposal to resolve the contradiction one-sidedly (on the side of money, with "labor notes"). In 1857, Marx is confronting the one-sided Proudhonist schematism again.

Marx pays attention to the category of *form* immediately as he starts writing the *Grundrisse* (within 10 pages, in the printed edition). "Proudhon and his associates," he writes, "never even raise the question [of 'the relation of circulation to the other relations of production'] in its pure form.... Whenever it is touched upon, we shall pay close attention"

(Marx 1973, 123).[5] Marx's intention to "pay close attention" to this question "in its pure form" means that he is visualizing a definite (pure in itself) space on which to fix the connection between production and circulation. Arguably, it is here that we can "see" Marx making an initial connection with the Hegelian category of *form* and taking a step toward the possibility of a grammar of content and form for his critique of Proudhonism.

Marx found a grammar of content and form also useful in his criticism of classical political economy. When he wrote to Engels that Hegel's *Logic* "had been of great use" to him in "discover[ing] some nice arguments," he gave his "complete demoli[tion of] the theory of profit as hitherto propounded" as the example (Marx and Engels 1983, 248; letter of January 16, 1858)—a clear reference to his invention of the concept of surplus value. It is not difficult to "see" how it is Hegel's form-and-content relation that gave Marx (who already had the general form-and-content relationship in mind as a result of his engagement of Darimon) the idea of *conceptually splitting* profit into two related but separate modes, the mode of substance and the mode of form. In Hegel, as we saw, content is both given by form (does not exist other than in its form) and yet different from it (it contains, as we have seen essence do, both the form and a surplus to the form). A sympathetic sensitivity to this relationship could thus easily have suggested to Marx the analytical task of coming up with a concept (on the side of content/substance) that both included and was different from (larger than) "profit." The concept, of course, needed its own distinct measure (as labor-value) in relation to the separate money-form measure of profit (price of production). The concept only needed a name: surplus value.[6]

Marx found the content-and-form relation useful in yet a third way. Hegel's essence could not be known in advance of an investigation of the concrete and contradictory ways in which it found embodiment in the world (see notes 1 and 3). Marx deplored the dilettantish Hegelianism of his "utopian" rivals who thought that essence (the determining force) could be known philosophically, prior to a thorough investigation of its concrete manifestations. In addition to criticizing Proudhon thus (see above), Marx derided Lasalle for his attempt to derive money directly (i.e., ideally) from its function as a medium of exchange (as "the unity of affirmation and negation," as an example of "the transformation of all things into their opposites"), without paying attention to the concrete ways of this function (letters to Engels of February 1, 1858 and February 25, 1859 [Marx and Engels 1983]). In contrast to Proudhon and Lasalle, Marx repeatedly prided himself (as Engels repeatedly praised him) for his "scientific" mode of investigation, his extensive analyses of concrete relations as a condition of his abstractions.[7] Hegel's form-and-content relation formalized Marx's appreciation of scientific work in a way that exposed the philosophical dilettantism of his adversaries, and this too must have carried weight in his decision to formulate his work as an application of the Hegelian method (in its inverted form, of course).

We can see the entire architecture of *Capital* (four volumes) through the lenses of the content-and-form relationship. Marx sets up the analysis in the first chapter of Volume I, where, after introducing the commodity as containing within its unity the duality of use and exchange value (thus laying out the possibility of crisis at the very beginning)[8] and after defining the terms of its measure (socially necessary labor-time), he moves directly to discuss the content (substance of value) and form (the form of value in exchange) relation. It is the grammar of content-and-form that allows Marx to define the specific mode of being of social labor in capitalism (the money form), and to do so in a way that would then enable all the concrete investigations that the remainder of *Capital* documents. These include 1) finding the motive force of capitalism (in Hegelian terms, the essence propelling itself beyond itself, the M – C – M' relation)—in chapters 2 and 3 of Volume I; 2) analyzing the forms (absolute and relative), mechanisms (capitalist accumulation, reserve army) and conditions (primitive accumulation) of the production of surplus value—in the remainder of Volume I; 3) analyzing the concrete processes of circulation and distribution associated with *these* forms, mechanisms and conditions—in Volumes II and III; and, last but not least, 4) analyzing the modes of knowing corresponding to real forms of being of social labor and of surplus value—respectively, in the section on commodity fetishism and in Volume IV (*Theories of Surplus Value*). It is in these concrete investigations, of course, that Marx finds the actualities of the contradictions (in both knowing and being) that the initial simple duality of the commodity (use and exchange value) could only posit potentially. The overall architecture of the work has a remarkable resemblance to the architecture of Hegel's *Logic*.

Overdetermination

Althusser (1970) proposed the approach of overdetermination in order to distance Marxist theory from Hegel, and from the Hegelian contradiction in particular, in connection with the question of a revolutionary conjuncture. Althusser looked to 1917 (Lenin) for an example of good thinking about revolutionary conjunctures. His own political conjuncture, however, was defined by the question of what Marxist theory needed to be in the 1960s (and beyond), after the grammar of Soviet Marxism, and the inadequacy of the concept of ideology associated with it, were showing themselves to be poor guides for a more effective practice of politics.

Althusser (Chapter 5 of Althusser and Balibar, 1970) argued that Marxism had become characterized by essentialism, a habit (enabled by the Hegelian concept of contradiction, as tension emanating from *within* an essence conceived as *a unity* of two opposites)[9] of reducing "society" to the expression of an essence. He saw a tendency for Marxist theory to reduce itself to two theoretical variations of essentialism, economism and humanism. In both, the dynamics of society are explained in terms of the operative dichotomous contradiction (forces and relations of production, or alienation), with the concrete relations of society being recognizable only as manifestations of *that* contradiction.[10] Althusser argued that Marxism needed a different theoretical apparatus, one capable of understanding the concrete relations of society in terms of whatever specificities they possessed on their own—the revolutionary conjuncture, as Lenin had learned, was visible in the conjunction of these specificities. He proposed "overdetermination" as such an apparatus. He received attention from Marxists who felt some need for a framework capable of addressing critical problems-issues-agencies-sites they were confronting in their times (e.g., race, gender, post-coloniality, governmentality, culture-ideology-desire) in a way that recognizes both the effects of class and the independent effects of these problems-issues-agencies-sites in the concrete relations of society.

Althusser borrowed the term overdetermination from Freud, who used it while developing the psychoanalytic method of free association in the interpretation of dreams (Freud 1938). Effective (i.e., enabling an identification of the source of patient symptoms; creating, we could say, a psychoanalytic revolutionary conjuncture) interpretation of the meaning of dreams could come only through the method of free association (i.e., there was no fixed point from which to deduce this meaning) because dream narratives were produced by the unconscious working to repress consciousness of the symptom-source, via processes of displacement and condensation. Overdetermination is the name Freud gave to the unstructured processes of condensation and displacement through which the dream images are constituted in the relationship between the unconscious and the preconscious. Thus not recognizable in the dream narrative, the source of the pathos could only be accessed by having the analysand freely disassociate the narrative's images from the narrative's logic and focus on the separate concretenesses of the images: it was, then, in the free association of these separated images with the analysand's tenuous memory bank that the path could be found to the source of the pathos. Althusser had been looking for a Marxism that no longer relied on a narrative certainty and took instead to investigating the concrete conditions of revolutionary conjunctures. It is easy to see him becoming attracted by the Freudian suggestion, then, that what is given to consciousness (the "dream" narrative for psycho-analysis, the narrative of "society" for Marxism) is an overdetermined effect, and that the way out of pathology (psychic in one case, social in the other) was therefore through an engagement with the polyvalent associations ensconced in the separate concretenesses (images for dream interpretation, sites and practices for social analysis) of being.

To place overdetermination within Marxism, Althusser (and his collaborators) had to theorize, again and differently, certain specific parts of the theory. Thus Althusser found himself re-theorizing "ideology" materially (Althusser 1971) and, later, materialism itself as "aleatory." Similarly, Etienne Balibar found himself re-theorizing the relation between forces and relations of production (in Althusser and Balibar 1970). But Marx's texts themselves also had to be rethought. If the concretenesses of the world could no longer be read as *manifesta-tions* (reflections) of the essence and its dichotomous contradiction, Marx himself could no longer be read as *revealing* that essence and contradiction. He had to be read, instead, as an instance of partisan (on the part of workers, theorized as a class, and on the part of revolutionary change) theoretical intervention in the world. This explains why Althusser attempted to understand *Marx*, not from the standpoint of an already known concept of surplus value, but from the standpoint of his *search for that concept* in the course of his theoretical struggle with political economy (in Althusser and Balibar 1970).

Now, we saw that Marx found Hegel "of great use" in just this search, his invention of the surplus value concept. There could thus seem to be a discrepancy between Marx's appreciation and Althusser's negation of Hegel. This appearance of discrepancy is created by a striking parallelism between the deficiencies Althusser was criticizing in official Marxism and the deficiencies Hegel had criticized in Fichte and Schelling: the deficiencies, political and philosophical, inherent in any schematic approach to the certainty of knowledge. And the appearance of discrepancy is further heightened by the fact that both Hegel and Althusser manufacture their remedies for these deficiencies from the same raw material, concreteness/es.

The discrepancy, however, disappears if we look at matters from the perspective of the broadly different philosophical frameworks within which Hegel and Althusser operated. Hegel had operated within the framework of a search for certainty. A century later, Althusser was operating within a quite different framework, when the idea of certainty had become profoundly shaken by both philosophical and political considerations. In this context, what matters is not just Hegel's and Althusser's similar regard for the concrete but *also* the broader framework within which that regard is ensconced. It is this difference in frameworks that explains Althusser's attack on Hegel on just those points where his (Hegel's) concretes are structured into a certainty producing centered totality, on the idea of essence and essentialist theoretical practices, on the idea of contradiction as a duality (the thing, any thing, and *its* other) structured into a unity, and on the idea of history as a process with *a* beginning and *an* ending.[11]

Althusser's call for a framework of overdetermination can be understood as an attempt to take any Marxist attention to the concrete out of the mystical shell of essentialism. Marx had argued that he had used a dialectic extracted from the dialectics of the mystical shell of idealism. Althusser (1970, 89–94) argued that the extraction requires more than the inversion by which the development of the contradictory unity of forces and relations of production takes the place of Hegel's Spirit. It requires detaching the concrete from the center that essence requires. It thus requires a radical reconstruction both of the interpenetration of knowing and being that had characterized Hegel and of the analytical tendencies of Marxism insofar as it found itself bound to the architecture of *that* particular interpenetration. Althusser made the call for that detachment and took a number of steps, by himself and with others, toward that detachment. But it was within the school of *Rethinking Marxism*, and particularly in the work of Stephen Resnick and Richard Wolff, that the interpenetration of knowing and being and the analytical tendencies of Marxism received the thorough reconstructions Althusser had suggested.

Resnick and Wolff (1987) took the interpenetration of knowing and being significantly beyond Althusser's initial proposal. While Althusser's initial formulation had remained tied to some notion of the economy and class as a determining Subject, even if only "in the last instance" (perhaps the only way available at the time to assert a Marxist "interpretation" of the world), Resnick and Wolff developed overdetermination as a framework for conceiving society and history as the processes "without a subject" toward which Althusser himself increasingly moved after 1970. They conceived of overdetermination as a process in which concretenesses reign over any abstractions (economy, society, or even class, or gender, or race, or governmentality) that would pretend to bind them into a structure (or even into independent substructures to be constituted into one), around a center (or even centers). In Resnick and Wolff, these abstractions remain part of the discourse, but they do so only as tools in the narrative process and as having effects in shaping behavior, but they are scrupulously deprived of any real separate being in themselves and thus of the ability to be determining, even "in the last instance."

In this conception, in fact, the interpenetrations that give us the world are not so much between knowing and being as they are among practices (actions, activities), shaped as these are by thoughts/ideas/identities, more or less coherently coordinated around "named" processes (economic, cultural, political, psychic), within sites (factories, households, corporate centers, government bureaus, schools, etc.). These practices, processes and sites have no "being" in themselves: any site is constituted in relations with practices, processes and other sites, and it does not exist other than through these relations; and the same mode of constitutivity and non-being applies to processes and practices (Resnick and Wolff 1987, 24). The interpenetration of overdetermination is not a mutual interaction of separate entities (qualities, beings), not the case that an X and a Y interact. It is rather a process by which entities, an X and a Y, get their beings only through the overdetermined (and hence uncentered) process of mutual constitutivity. Overdetermination does not require that the presence of separate entities (e.g., capital, the corporation, the household, the state, capitalism) be denied. What it does require is that this presence be never taken for granted, as a given or as something that has the ability to reproduce itself out of its own essence and force. What it requires is that the presence always be taken, in its being or in its reproduction, as something to be explained, and this not only in a way that does not presume the outcome but that, in explaining the outcome, makes clear the possibility of a different outcome (including, of course, the elements of a revolutionary conjuncture).[12]

In the perspective of overdetermination, what Marx did was to think of the ways in which something called "capitalism" would have to be pulling a variety of practices, processes, and sites together if a certain set of class relations (capitalist surplus value relations) was to be said to exist. There is nothing in this conception (and in this lies its main axis of opposition to, or at least contrast with, Hegelian formulations) that requires one to think of capitalism in essentialist terms (in the terms of center and of totality suggested by Hegelian habits)—in terms, that is, that reflect an inherent power of capital to reproduce itself (the accumulation drive working in specific ways) and to totalize the entire space of the world (all sites, practices and processes) at the service of that power. That essentialist conception left little or no space for Marxist theory to recognize and engage the complexity of the class process in relation to all other processes in "society" in the initial mode of production and in the mode of reproduction of that process, but also in the modes of resistance to it, and most importantly, in the mode of a revolution against it.

Space does not allow me to go into any details about the concrete ways in which Resnick and Wolff themselves and their collaborators (too many to mention here), have filled in the space for analysis defined by the contours of overdetermination as Resnick and Wolff drew them. They have addressed issues of Marxist theory;[13] subjectivity and desire (for a revolution against capital); gender and race in relation to class; development; labor history; the intersection of capitalist class processes with other class processes and non-class processes; knowledge; communism as a horizon of difference; and others. It will have to suffice for me to say that all of this work produces a narrative of capitalism as a decentered totality, pointing to the decentered modes of its reproduction—asking us to understand that capitalism reproduces itself not by virtue of any power of its essence, but by virtue of a project, complexly determined and complexly carried out (i.e., overdetermined and overdetermining) to manage the decenteredness of life, and asking us to understand as well the decentered nature of any revolutionary conjuncture creating the possibility for something else.

Notes

1 Marcuse (1954) provides an outline of the master-slave narrative which Hegel (in his *Phenomenology of Spirit*) offered as the history of the march of Spirit toward a unity with itself. Once Spirit posits the world as *its other*, "essence" propels it (through the concrete struggles of humans for knowledge *and* freedom) toward a state of unity with Spirit. It does so, however, in stages, not in one moment. Initially, empty of knowledge of nature and society, humanity creates slavery. Dialectically, thereafter, slavery creates the notion of freedom as *its* negation: the slave embodies the part of the essence that yearns to an "other" world (the master embodies the part of essence that corresponds to the world as it is). It is slaves who are in an objective position (being) to develop the subjective side (knowing). They develop knowledge both of nature (the thinking necessary for work: abstract thinking, mathematics, theory/principles, practice/applications, etc.) and of society (applying the idea of principles, generalized from the thinking about work and nature, allows slaves to invent the idea of freedom—out of their very lack of it). This, however, represents only one stage in history, in the march of Spirit and of the world toward a state of full unity. The notion of freedom emerging out of slavery is not yet one with the fullness of Spirit. Emerging, in the only way it can out of slavery, in the one-sided form of an "idea," it gives rise to a one-sided (on the side of knowing) civilization of religion, feudalism. Although it represents progress vis-à-vis slavery, feudalism limits the scope of spirit to the realm of religion, and keeps it from finding the full concreteness it yearns for in the world of nature and society (freedom of politics, of commerce, of science, of production). The age of religion thus reproduces, though *at a higher stage*, the master-slave relationship. Here, absolute monarchy embodies the part of the essence that corresponds to the world as it is; it is the rising bourgeoisie that embodies the part of essence that yearns to an "other" (fuller in its various concrete determinations of being) world. Hence the age of citizenship, of science, of commerce, the modern world (and, in some formulation, the *end of history*).

It is worth noticing that this narrative *begins* with Spirit positing as "its other" a bare, undeveloped, undetermined state of the world. In contrast to Kant and Schelling, Hegel could not present the world as just "there" to be "recognized." He needed the recognition to emerge from a process that began with "no-thingness." Had he posited an initial being with any concreteness, he would have faced the problem of how to guarantee knowledge of that concreteness, and he would then have seen his system collapse into Schelling's. However, it is important *also* to realize that if the process beginning with nothingness was to result in the full-of-concreteness unity of knowing and being that Hegel needed, *this beginning* had to be posited by a force (what Hegel called Spirit) containing within itself *both nothing (abstraction) and everything (concreteness)*. (We will see that this is relevant to Marx's beginning with the "commodity.") Fundamentally, Hegel's essence is this combination of nothing and everything, abstraction and concreteness. History and science are, then, nothing but processes through which the initially empty abstraction is progressively filled with increasing (wider and/or deeper) levels of concreteness.

2 The quantitative accumulations precipitate the contradictions within the qualities. Hegel's contradiction is different from the contradiction (antinomy) of formal logic. The Hegelian contradiction is a condition of tension *within* an entity, not a condition of opposition between different entities. Being a condition of "being," it is a matter of oppositions in the world, not of opposition of mental images and definitions—a *contra*-diction, not a contra-*diction*.

3 Lenin (1972, 220) included "the union of analysis and synthesis" in his own list of the most important laws of the dialectic.

4 Marx's relationship to Hegel in these writings received considerable attention in Rosdolsky (1992). Bellofiore, Starosta and Thomas (2014) and Moseley and Smith (2015) are products of a more recent wave of interest in the influence of Hegel on Marx. For a reading of the *Grundrisse* (Marx 1973) in a non-Hegelian, and even anti-Hegelian, key, see Negri (1984 and 2014).

5 On the same page, Marx described Darimon's idea of free-credit as "only a hypocritical, philistine and anxiety-ridden form of saying: property is theft." And he continued: "Instead of the workers *taking* the capitalists' capital, the capitalists are supposed to be compelled to give it to them" (emphasis in the original).

6 This does not address either the mathematical form Marx gave to the relationship between surplus value and profit (the transformation procedure) or the necessary complementary concept of labor-power. It does however explain the very possibility for Marx to think of the problem of "profit" in terms of such a relationship. It also explains how Marx came to think of including interest and rent as additional expressions of surplus value (if one, then more than one).

Murray (2015) also discusses the connection between Marx's concept of surplus value and the concepts of Hegel's *Logic*. Our discussion focuses on the relation of mutual constitutivity between content and form and does not presuppose that Marx comes to confront the problem of "profit" with an already constituted concept of surplus value. Murray's discussion focuses on a relationship of expression between essence (surplus value) and a form of "appearance" (profit), which seems both to presume that Marx's has a concept of surplus value to begin with and to tic Marx unnecessarily to a concept of essence as the source of appearances (content as the source of form).

7 The issues were political as well as philosophical. Marx worried about the often authoritarian, or even reactionary, politics that the abstract schematisms of dilettantish idealism tended to allow or, worse, produce. He sharply criticized both Proudhonists and Lasalleans in this vein.

8 Recall that the *beginning* has strategic value in Hegel.

9 The dichotomous nature of the Hegelian contradiction is necessitated by Hegel's idea that essence posits difference not simply as otherness but as *its* otherness. This was the necessary condition of the unity of knowing and being Hegel was producing—the price that had to be paid for Hegel's history to have, philosophically, a beginning and an end (see note 1).

10 Althusser mentioned Gramsci as an exception. But Gramsci, he thought, had not theorized the conditions for his own exception.

11 Of course, this is not to say that more Hegel-engaging Marxists did/do not recognize problems with the association of Marxism with a structure of essence and the certainty (teleology) tendencies it can produce. According to Buchanan (2010, 129), "Fredric Jameson insists" on linking the dialectic with "a scandal of the unexpected," but makes clear that Jameson's "surprise" is a surprising

revelation of essence and so it does not open up a non-essentialist horizon. Gert Reuten (2015) introduces an element of contingency and "underdetermination" in the Marxian dialectic, but it seems to me that "underdetermination" suggests a horizon of determination, whereas overdetermination rejects the horizon in principle.

12 Laclau and Mouffe (1985) had applied the concept of overdetermination exclusively to the nature of identity (i.e., the irreducibility of identity to any fixed place in society), thus problematizing the concept of a "subject." Resnick and Wolff developed the notion more broadly, to refer to the nature of being (ontology) as well of knowing (epistemology)–for a discussion of the different political frameworks (anchored or not anchored in "class") of these two absorptions of the concept of overdetermination, see Özselçuk (2009). Resnick and Wolff (1987, 25–30) address the question of subjectivity through the concept of an entry-point (subjects are differentiated exactly by the entry-point they adopt) and situate this very concept only generally consistently with the framework of overdetermination (a subject's adoption of an entry-point is an overdetermined effect). Özselçuk and Madra (2005) and Chakrabarti, Dhar, and Cullenberg (2012) use a Lacanian framework to produce an explicit outline of a process of subject formation consistent with the framework of overdetermination.

13 Wolff and Resnick (2012) themselves produced a reconceptualization of the analytical categories of value, surplus value, prices, distribution, crises, and reproduction and transformation in a way that took them out of an essentialist framework.

References

Althusser, L. 1971. "Ideology and Ideological State Apparatus." In *Lenin and Philosophy and Other Essays*, 85–126. New York and London: Monthly Review Press.

——. 1970. *For Marx*. Trans. by B. Brewster. New York: Random House.

Althusser, L. and E. Balibar. 1970. *Reading Capital*. Trans. by B. Brewster. London: New Left Books.

Bellofiore, R., G. Starosta, and P. Thomas, eds. 2014. *In Marx's Laboratory*. Chicago: Haymarket Books.

Blunden, A. 1997. "The Meaning of Hegel's Logic." https://www.marxists.org/reference/archive/hegel/help/mean.htm (accessed May 1, 2016).

Buchanan, I. 2010. *Dictionary of Critical Theory*. Oxford: Oxford University Press.

Chakrabarti, A., A. Dhar, and S. Cullenberg. 2012. *World of the Third and global Capitalism*. Kolkata: Worldview Publications.

Engels, F. 1940. *Dialectics of Nature*. New York: International Publishers.

Freud, S. 1938. "The Interpretation of Dreams." In *The Basic Writings of Sigmund Freud*, 181–468. New York: Random House.

Laclau, E. and C. Mouffe. 1985. *Hegemony and Socialist Strategy*. London: Verso.

Lenin, V. I. 1972. *Collected Works*. Vol. 38, *Philosophical Notebooks*. Moscow: Progress Publishers.

Lukács, G. 1976. *The Young Hegel*. Cambridge, MA: MIT Press.

Marcuse, H. 1954. *Reason and Revolution*. 2nd ed. New York: The Humanities Press.

Marx, K. 1963. *The Poverty of Philosophy*. New York: International Publishers.

——. 1973. *Grundrisse*. New York: Random House.

——. 1977. *Capital*. Vol. I. New York: Random House.

Marx, K. and F. Engels. 1983. *Collected Works*. Vol. 40. New York: International Publishers.

Moseley, F. and T. Smith, eds. 2015. *Marx's Capital and Hegel's Logic: A Reexamination*. Chicago: Haymarket Books.

Murray, P. 2015. "The Secret of Capital's Self-Valorization 'Laid Bare': How Hegel Helped Marx to Overturn Ricardo's Theory of Profit." In *Marx's Capital and Hegel's Logic: A Reexamination*, F. Moseley and T. Smith, eds., 189–213. Chicago: Haymarket Books.

Negri, A. 1984. *Marx Beyond Marx: Lessons on the Grundrisse*. Massachusetts: Bergin & Garvey Publishers, Inc.

——. 2014. "Review of *Karl Marx's Grudrisse: Foundations of the Critique of Critical Economy 150 Years Later*, edited by Marcello Musto." *Rethinking Marxism* 26(3): 427–433.

Özselçuk, C. 2009. "Post-Marxism after Louis Althusser: A Critique of the Alternatives." PhD Dissertation, University of Massachusetts, Amherst.

Özselçuk, C. and Y. Madra. 2005. "Psychoanalysis and Marxism: From Capitalist-All to Communist Not-All." *Psychoanalysis, Culture, and Society* 10(1): 79–97.

Resnick, S. A. and R. D. Wolff. 1987. *Knowledge and Class.* Chicago: University of Chicago Press.

Reuten, G. 2015. "An Outline of the Systematic-Dialectical Method: Scientific and Political Significance." In *Marx's Capital and Hegel's Logic: A Reexamination*, F. Moseley and T. Smith, eds., 241–268. Chicago: Haymarket Books.

Rosdolsky, R. 1992. *The Making of Marx's Capital.* London: Pluto Press.

Wolff, R. D. and S. A. Resnick. 2012. *Contending Economic Theory.* Cambridge, MA: MIT Press.

2

EPISTEMOLOGY

Jack Amariglio and David F. Ruccio

Epistemology was a preoccupation of Karl Marx from his earliest writings, and it has been a preoccupation of Marxists ever since. While epistemology is understood philosophically to refer to "the theory of knowledge," and most often as the conceptualization of what constitutes "truth" or at least the justification for apparently organized thoughts, in Marxism, as in most other philosophical and scientific traditions, there are too many strands or variants to permit a single concept of what counts as a "theory of knowledge." Likewise, there are a variety of putatively Marxist positions regarding the veracity of any knowledge claim and/or its disciplined, organized exposition. It is indeed possible to pluralize, so as to speak about different Marxist or Marx-inspired "theories of knowledge." But, in this entry, we focus less on epistemology as the ascertainment of theoretical truth and more as a general questioning about knowledge. This questioning inquires into the object of knowledge (the known); the "subject" of knowledge (the knower); its form and content; the social processes or practices through which knowledge is produced (or, in a different language, its "causes"); and its manifold, reverberating effects.

Object of Knowledge

What is to be known? What do Marxists take as the object(s) of a knowledge production process? Marxists have generally agreed that the material world, and especially that which is created or transformed by human effort or labor, is the primary—perhaps the only proper—object of knowledge. François Laruelle (2015, 5) comments that the different elements of the material world that Marxism takes as an object, from "nature" to the mode of production, are always assumed to have a certain universality. There are some Marxists who follow Friedrich Engels's resolute attempt (1940) to establish a broad-ranging, universal "dialectics of nature." Toward this end, Engels pursues Marx's famous, self-proclaimed inversion of Hegel's dialectics of the unfolding through time of Reason or The Idea (Marx 1977, 103), and Engels projects it into the realm of the natural world, as both Marx and he understood it vis-à-vis an avid familiarity with the natural sciences of their time. Marx and Engels regarded their dialectical materialism—separately and together—as enabling them to see homologies between their own "scientific" work and that of the established methodological, material practices in chemistry, biology, physics, astronomy, and more. They believed that their dialectical method was the principal means of constructing an epistemological position and a practice of truth-seeking about the economic and class structure of capitalism. Engels thought that dialectical elements of knowledge-building might be extended to these "hard" sciences as well. Thus, for example, in both *Anti-Dühring* (1934) and the *Dialectics of Nature* (1940), Engels applies to "nature" an epistemological stance first announced by Marx. For Marx, basic Hegelian conceptions of cause, effect, movement, and trajectory—for example the transformation of quantity into quality (1977, 423) or "the negation of the negation" (1977, 929)—can be employed to grasp the complexity of the materially grounded (capitalist) social world (Ollman 1992). Engels, following Marx's hints on the topic, calls for a unification of theory about theory (or knowledge about knowledge), denoted by and deployed through the application of a universal method of experimentation. This method, in his view, would facilitate the formulation of truths about the experienced, material world. Lenin (1927) would later authorize this same stance regarding Marx's scientific method.

Yet, Marx's own materialist epistemological position—which engaged with, but also sharpened itself against, Hegel's "idealism" and Feuerbach's incomplete, abstract, universalizing materialism (see also Lenin 1977)—prioritized the tasks of exposing, excavating, and/or uncovering the generalizable realities of human production and reproduction, and not all "nature" per se. As Marx opens his notebooks (the *Grundrisse*) in preparing *Capital*: "The object before us, to begin with, *material production*" (1973, 83). In the processes of material production and reproduction, humans make and remake themselves (Marx 1964), though not in a manner of their direct choosing or independent will, as Marx (1971, 20) warns us. Marx comments periodically in his writings on the nature of nature, or, rather, the sundry forms of differentiated material existence—inert or vital—that we presume exist prior to, independent from, and/or "outside" of human endeavors. This mute nature, though, can be apprehended and, often, bent—sometimes with great resistance—to human purposes through the application of intellectual and manual labor (see Sohn-Rethel's [1978] Marxist distinction between the labors). As Marx states in the *Grundrisse*, "nature builds no machines" (1973, 706); instead, machinery, electrical energy, all technologies of converting or concentrating natural power, are "organs of the human brain, created by the human hand: the power of knowledge objectified." Stiegler (2015) calls Marx's analysis here an "organology of knowledge" (135).

Importantly, Marx criticizes naturalizing social processes and attributing the qualities and capacities of human energy and labor-induced sweat to "things." As Marx argues in the first chapter of *Capital*, under capitalism, things are mainly, but not exclusively, equated to or are stamped from their birth as commodities. As a privileged object of knowledge, things live vexed lives, and in different schools of Marxian thought, knowledge of their troubled existence is interpreted dissimilarly. Some, like Georg Lukács (1971), perceive the job of Marx's knowledge-producing historical materialism to be meticulously unearthing the truth—though a complex dialectical method consisting of "mediations"—about the curious thingness of capitalist social life. This social life is covered over by and buried within deep strata of dense mystification and a pervasive "false consciousness": an ideological mindset that Marx linked to what he termed the "fetishism of commodities" (Marx 1977, 163–177; Cole 2014 argues that Hegel was Marx's primary inspiration for this discussion). Further inspired by Theodor Adorno, Max Horkheimer, Herbert Marcuse, Walter Benjamin, and others identified as the "Frankfurt School" (Arato and Gephardt 1982), contemporary Marxists have followed this Lukácsian demystificatory line of thought to describe and also condemn the capitalist "cultural industries" that proliferate commodity fetishism in all its many guises and make true knowledge of capitalism difficult at best.

For many Marxists, commodification breeds illusion, artifice, and deceit; it hides from view the real social relations of exploitative labor and production that are its source. Demystification—de-reification—puts things right in the sphere of knowledge, as capitalist commodities ultimately can be viewed as carriers of labor-produced and -denominated value (Bewes 2002). True, and potentially revolutionary, knowledge admits that commodified things have social effects but it insists on social causation that puts labor first and the results of that labor after. As Marx argued, the lived ideology of commodity fetishism "inverts" that causation, and it is a primary goal of Marxian political economy to stand this perceived chain of determination on its head. Marx's critique of commodity fetishism, from this standpoint, shows the "real abstraction" (Finelli 1989, Toscano 2008) that stands behind the concrete "use values" that are created with exchange—and exchange-value—in mind. To many Marxists, the objective of distinctively Marxian knowledge production is to move from one-sided, depthless abstraction to the many-sided, stratiform concrete, which, in capitalism, is the "real world" of commodity relations, a material universe structured first and foremost by class-exploiting productive activity.

Yet, in recent years, "thingness" has been reconceived such that, after all, commodities are themselves thought to have a "social life." Following the work of the anthropologist Arjun Appadurai (1986), some Marxists and related theorists (Lamb 2011, Freedgood 2006, Brown 2004) have opened up inquiries into the coming in and out of the commodity chain or circuits—or playing multiple roles within one circuit—which suggests that "knowing commodities" and the labor processes that give rise to and are imbued as value within them is more complicated than the portrait painted in "commodity fetishism." Even more recently, theorists associated with what is known as "object-oriented ontology" (Harman 2011, Bogost 2012) or "speculative realism" (Meillasoux 2008, Gratton 2014) have pushed "taking things seriously" even further. For speculative realists and "vibrant materialists," knowledge is an imposition and a mistake if it treats things as silent and also only effective and experiential if humans act on them or set them in motion; all ontology and epistemology after Kant is "anthropocentric" (Bennett 2010, Coole and Frost 2010). Things are only seen from the standpoint of human praxis. A promising engagement may soon arise (see Bennett 2015 for some opening thoughts) between Marxists dedicated to human-centered materialist epistemology—seeing knowledge as deriving from and directed by human manual and mental labor—and "speculative realists."

In the pursuit of knowledge of the concrete-real, many Marxists read things strategically or "symptomatically" for what these objects essentially connote. And what things connote (other than the objects found in untouched nature) is the process of production through which they were first brought into being and/or altered. Items that persist through time are the consequence of past labor expended. The things of the past can be studied directly for clues about their original constitution, and this study is often archival or archaeological in character.

The "reading" involved in comparing purportedly mute objects still in existence with documentation about the conditions under which they were produced is, at bottom, an archaeological practice. This knowledge-producing practice can be understood in the Foucauldean sense of genealogical work. Indeed, many Marxists from the 1960s on have reread Marx's epistemological positions through Michel Foucault's "archaeology of knowledge" (1972, 1997; see also Barrett 1991, Montag 1995, Escobar 2011, Ryder 2013). These readings emphasize the importance of epistemological ruptures, moments in which the norms of ascertaining and justifying "truth" shift irrevocably. And this idea of shifting truth norms is likewise true for Marxists who, sometimes as an alternative to the more

Continental philosophic language that one finds in Foucault, turn to the notions of "paradigm shifts" and scientific revolutions promoted by the philosopher of science Thomas Kuhn, or to Paul Feyerabend's view (1975, Bhaskar 1975) that the history and practice of science defy codification in particular methodological rules or consistently practiced transdiscursive norms of knowledge creation.

An archaeological knowledge-producing process can also refer to the specific disciplinary practice of archaeological digs, the interpretation of which involves discovering and deciphering grids of *in situ* natural objects (including previous life) or wholly fashioned, human-produced things: artifacts. Indeed, there is a field of Marxist archaeology (among others, see Saitta 1994, 2005, McGuire 1992, Childe 1936) in which unearthed things are read dynamically through thick interpretations of the class-inflected strata that surround and include these human-made artifacts.

While Marxist knowledge production has the material world, and frequently the sub-realm of manufactured things, as its primary object (Castree 1995), Marx hammers away about the impact ideas and ideation have on concrete social relations—while simultaneously locating ideas and their production within the realm of the real (Kain 1986). Marx rails against the supposed realm of "pure thought" (Marx and Engels 1970, 39). Indeed, ideas arise and are transmitted materially. They can only be voiced, heard, shared, written, and so on via concrete human activity and with the aid of associated labor-produced technologies. Without ideation (in the *Grundrisse* [1973, 101] Marx refers to the "thinking head"), the world would remain mute, echoless and meaningless to humans, and this despite our tactile experience of it. Subjecting idealist conceptions about the thought process to an all-encompassing, unyielding ("ruthless") critique will show, in the "last instance," that talkers and listeners are all engaged in the labor of discourse. And it is through such discourse that they configure "the real" in thought—although, of course, to Marx this configuration can predictably be done wrong.

Marx's critique of "idealism" as a false or mistaken epistemological stance can be found in his discussions, scattered throughout his writings, about demystification. In these passages, Marx specifically exposes the "ghost-walk" (Marx 1972, 830) of the "enchanted, perverted, topsy-turvy world" (830) that is imagined by political economists within bourgeois society. In Marx's view, classical political economy only partially defuses, and too often abets, this mystification; in its inconsistencies and frequent theoretical errors, it too is haunted by the "bourgeois standpoint" (830).

The "mature" Marx's description in *Capital* of the fog of exchange that characterizes commodity fetishism—capital's prevalent ideological mystification—can be referred back to his earlier attacks on universalist and dematerialized dogmas of all kinds, and that includes incipient forms of socialist thought. His insistence on dialectical materialism as a method for producing verifiable truth is also an attempt to heal an imagined rift, a disjunction, within knowledge and the known. On one side of this divide stands the "real world," as it is realized at a moment in time and created by human labor. On the other stands a mist-enwrapped world of pure or "abstract" ideas, transcendent across time and place, though often enough directing historical human (and super-human) events and destinies. The role of Marxism (at least among its schools that perceive this division) is to reveal the underlying truth of existing social relations. In this sense, Marxism is a knowledge machine, a means of production in the "thought-concrete," through which the historically based truth of human productive relations—with its focus on class and the violent constitution and rending of each epoch's social fabric (a violence unleashed primarily on the bodies of workers)—is laid bare. The truth may yet set us free.

For some, Marxism's epistemological stance is derived directly from the experiences of workers in capitalism who, for perhaps the first time for laborers down through many class-divided millennia (or at least since humans' "original" communal existence), are capable of shedding ideological untruths, and who can fully grasp the basis of social life via their shared thinking as a class "for itself." For others, though, Marxism delineates a practice of knowledge production that is not merely descriptive or simply a mirror, or the instinctual experience, of a preferred class "the subject of history." In this view, Marxism is primarily a disciplined, formal discourse available to all, but featuring labor and laboring as the points of departure, transit, and arrival, that weaves itself in thought through a multiplicity of contradictions and "overdeterminations."

One influential version of Marxism as a disciplined and disciplining (in the sense of providing an intellectual order over disparate thoughts), overdetermined discourse was developed by the Marxian political economists Stephen Resnick and Richard Wolff. Their work (1987) introduces the idea that Marxism, like other formal discourses, has an entry point through which its theoretical practitioners may construct an unparalleled knowledge. For Resnick and Wolff, Marxism's distinctive epistemological stance and its particular discursive "truths" result from "entering" discourse about the social world through its likewise distinctive concept of class. To "know" as a Marxist, therefore, is to know from the standpoint of class, in this case meaning to have "begun" one's investigation into the understanding of all things through the conscious utilization of class as an entry point, which also then serves as a guide and an end point. This notion of standpoint or entry point shares much in common with feminist epistemology (see Harding 1993, Smith 2004, Bakan 2012, Anderson 2015); likewise, black Marxist approaches (Robinson 2000, Kelley 2003), critical of the dominant white or Eurocentric Marxian voices, enter social theory with a proclaimed epistemological standpoint of either the intersection of race and class, or of race predominating (see also Young 2004).

For Marxists adopting Resnick and Wolff's view, class as entry point does not imply that all things—all social and economic processes—are manifestations or direct effects of class (see also Cullenberg 1996). It is merely (and strongly) that a distinctively Marxian knowledge about the world asks and answers questions through the lens of class—admittedly, one lens among many that social theorists may choose from (and, of course, that may choose them).

Subject of Knowledge

Turning to the "subject of knowledge," in *The German Ideology* (1970), Marx and Engels describe a human knower—a conscious, thinking being—as a product of the real historical moments of their lives. And, so, humans make history and seek and create knowledge through the practice of their labor. Marx's writings are replete with acknowledgements that humans produce knowledge, and that knowledge, in turn, as part of their conditions of existence, however "superstructural," partly produces them. So, at first blush, it might appear that Marx starts and stops with real, sensuous human individuals, joining together to create their material existence, and from there, humanity in general, as "the subject of knowledge," that is, the knower (or knowers) in epistemological inquiry. Though an advancement on Feuerbach, Marx might be thought, like his portrayal of Feuerbach, to regard knowledge "abstractly" rather than concretely.

But as many Marxian theorists since his time have remarked, Marx is a partisan, and his perspective on knowledge production, his epistemological stance, positions laborers—as a class, and only thereby individually—as possessing the ability to know the tangible world concretely, uniquely, and specifically (some would say "correctly") through their many acts of material production and their chronologically conjoint exploitation. Thus, workers are privileged by their labor, and their actual and potential knowledge of the forces and relations of production, to see the social world as a whole and their position within it. Some Marxists have gone so far as to advocate the exclusive veracity of "proletarian science," science that espies all material existence as corresponding to and stemming from the peculiar viewpoint of the proletariat or, relatedly, a suitably revolutionized peasantry (see Dominique Lecourt's superb 1977 study of Lysenkoism for a critique of one version of this tendency). Indeed, Marxists have often put forward the claim that no previous working class in history has been as propitiously positioned, by the sequence of all previous revolutionary transitions, such that they could consciously comprehend correctly and act upon an extant class-constituted social formation (Azad 2005). In this view, the proletariat is always capable of apprehending the totality of relations pertaining to their historical time and place. They can "know" the material world and the historical forces that gave rise to it like no other class in history.

Other contemporary offshoots of Marxism, like Stiegler (2010), come to the alternative conclusion that proletarianization—through the deskilling processes that Marx describes in *Capital*, the transfer of workers' knowledge to machines—is a process of losing knowledge, especially individual "know-how." Yet, though Frederick Taylor once described industrial workers "unfortunately" as "trained gorillas," Antonio Gramsci posited that these workers,

> have understood that 'trained gorilla' is just a phrase, that. . .the worker remains a man and even that during his work he thinks more, or at least has greater opportunities for thinking, once he has overcome the crisis of adaptation without being eliminated ... not only does the worker think, but the fact that he gets no immediate satisfaction from his work and realises that they are trying to reduce him to a trained gorilla, can lead him into a train of thought that is far from conformist.
>
> *(Gramsci 1988, 295)*

Marxists, from one standpoint, see the subject of knowledge to be the subject of history (Holland 1998 refers to this as Marx's "transcendental subjectivism"), and it is only from this privileged perch that knowledge can shake off its abstract philosophical (metaphysical) entrapment and, instead, become full, reliable, and liberatory. Yet, for some, the self-consciousness that workers are capable of possessing and utilizing in their quest to know the material world and the exploitative social relations under which they toil is not spontaneous. Nor is it capable of being spread throughout the working class or all society without the guidance of Marxism itself. In fact, Marx often ridicules the notion that thinkers, including proletarian autodidacts and self-conscious revolutionaries, can instruct the world to simply "open its jaws to let the roast partridges of absolute science fly into its mouth" (Marx 1978, 13). Instead, Marx's writings ensconce intellectual production based upon a dialectical materialist approach as constituting a necessary, though not sufficient, condition of existence for worker self-consciousness to break through and become scientific knowledge.

If producing class knowledge is the objective of Marxism, then the exploited class—in capitalism, wage workers engaged in "productive" labor, along with their non-working class allies and advocates—is the primary "knower" of concern of a Marxist epistemology. Epistemology, like all other theoretical discourses, is a battleground of competing ideas, and what distinguishes the standpoint from which "truths" are judged adequate or not to the concrete-real is the position within a broader class struggle that each standpoint actualizes. This is different from another Marxist view according to which there is a close correspondence among historical subjects, their class positions, and their ideas. In an alternative perspective, it is not the subjects themselves, imagined as seamless and contradiction-less wholes, who are the possessors of an advantaged, class-based knowledge. It is more that subjects, including productive laborers, are themselves (in)determined (there is always a subjective "lack" eluding complete closure) by class and other social and natural processes.

And, so, it is this complex positioning that takes the form of temporary, in flux, articulated subjective "unities"—one might say that the subject of knowledge is thus "decentered"—and this often-fragile, eradicable articulation affects any knower's ability to discern relative, class-modulated truths (it is into such an articulated space of decentered political subjects that Ernesto Laclau and Chantal Mouffe 1985 interject the Gramscian analytic of "hegemony"). Indeed, within Marxian schools, there has long been an interest in problematizing "the subject" based on an engagement with Freudian psychoanalytic theory. And this questioning of the cohesion or coherence of subjects, especially under capitalism, has had implications for the way knowledge is constructed and disseminated by such inherently conflicted subjects (Eyers 2015). If subjectivity, or better, subjectivation—suturing the many gaps and fissures of subjects—is always a psychic balancing act, which also consistently fails, then it is unclear what kind of knowledge can emanate from or interject into any knowing agent. What becomes of the Nietzschean "will to know" when subjects are enslaved, often joyfully, to their passions and when their passions are chained to their slavery (Lordon 2014)? In recent years, there has been a school of Marxism that considers questions of agency and psychical balance from the standpoint of the French Freudian theorist Jacques Lacan (see Žižek 1989, 1997, Copjek 1994, Özselçuk and Madra 2007, Madra forthcoming). In this relatively new Marxian tradition, there is an emphasis on passion, pleasure, desire, and fantasy in constituting subjectivity. Thus, it is possible to see the knower as always engaged in knowing through or against desire; the question is, what remains of the idea of "truth" in the face of inescapable desire or pleasure or fantasy?

Finally, more radically, following a line of reasoning and critique opened up by the French Marxist philosopher Louis Althusser (1971, Resch 1992), perhaps knowledge has no guiding subject, whether fissured, incomplete, or whole; in Jean-Pierre Dupuy's words (2009)—in reflecting on the effects of the cybernetic revolution—knowledge production may now (if not in the past) involve "subjectless processes" (155–56), that is, "knowledge without a subject" (157) (see also Smith 1985).

Content and Form of Knowledge

Turning now to the content and form of inquiry, epistemology traditionally addresses concerns regarding truth claims, that is, how humans know and "justify" what they claim to know and what distinguishes non-knowledge (usually categorized as "beliefs") from knowledge. Marxism has a long history of following the modernist project of cordoning off "ideological" non-truths from those statements that are justified either by/through practice and/or that proceed from and epitomize the application of a "scientific method." Marxism has long debated ideology versus science (see Amariglio 1987 on Althusser's distinction between them; see also Rossi-Landi 1990 and Kitching 1994), and many Marxists have turned back to Marx to find support for their positions that either Marx indeed inaugurated a new science (Murray 1988) or that Marxism has repeatedly failed to banish ideology from its precepts and methods. This failure is often portrayed as a result of Marxism's misguided adoption of classical epistemological positions and procedures, including that of "positivism." In this latter view, Marxism has yet to achieve its own scientific status; to do so requires the stripping away of that which is pre-scientific or ideological and, in its place, discovering/uncovering—"reading"—the particular epistemological norms implicit in Marx's method in his writings, especially *Capital*. In this reading, truth is relative to and primarily contained within the discourse that produces it, and the norms of veracity and justification that are peculiar to Marxism are not replicated or found in other discourses, though they may share some general characteristics with scientific exploration *sui generis*.

As in other modernist scientific discourses, truth is occasionally equated with "certain knowledge" within Marxism. Marx gives credence, in part, to this association in his writings. To take one example, in recounting the biblically inflected story of "the master spinner" in volume 1 of *Capital* (1977, 725–730), Marx, in a rhetorical flourish, perhaps, makes a claim for revealed truth. About some specific truths that *Capital* puts on display, often in a show trial, Marx says, "we know perfectly well." And that knowing, we come to understand, is the outcome of his exhaustive study of capitalist class exploitation and of the thieving expropriation of surplus-value from its original creators. For Marx, if we choose to read him this way, knowing exploitation is not through following an obfuscated discursive path; in fact, as he exclaims, it is "quite otherwise." The singular process of Marxian knowledge production, through contradictions exposed and exploded, leads to knowing with clarity and precision.

While attributing to Marx a mostly successful quest for "certain knowledge" has its historical roots in the always-uphill struggle to establish a Marxist perspective amidst the so-called (capitalist-accented) "marketplace of ideas," this slog, through the ups and downs of Marxism during the past 170 (give or take) years, also has been marked more recently by a different tendency: postmodernism. This postmodern or poststructuralist tendency toward truth (Anderson 1995) highlights a historically mandated and textually determined "uncertainty" or indeterminacy (on such indeterminacy, see Silverman's 2013 comments and Resnick and Wolff's response, also 2013), found through a reading of Marx's works, and from there, through Marxism's zigzag disquisitive history. Postmodern (and postcolonial) Marxists (Callari 1986, Resnick and Wolff 1987, Gibson-Graham 1996, Callari and Ruccio 1996, Ruccio and Amariglio 2003, Charusheela 2004, Bergeron 2006, among others), for example, frequently call attention to the "relativism" that they believe is Marx's main epistemological message and/or is exemplified in his texts. They underscore a different insight; from Marx's doctoral dissertation, Marx had a protracted interest in Epicurean philosophy and Lucretius, for whom inchoate matter is the true being of the world. In Lucretius, Marx not only found nascent materialism (as discovered in Spinoza), but he also found the idea of chance, which he emblematized as historical contingency. Marx's aleatory materialism (Callari and Ruccio 1996, Hardy 2014), for postmodern Marxists, also establishes an under-determination in the realm of knowledge; a discursive whole cannot close itself. Influenced by Jacques Derrida's conception of "deconstruction" (1967), postmodern Marxists insist that discourse is always marked by slippages, aporia, displacements, and deferments. For them, meaning is overdetermined and uncertain. A certain knower is thus a contradiction in terms.

In addition, if scientific discourse is not the mirror of nature, then there is an "ethical" dimension to all knowledge production. Cornel West (1989), utilizing Richard Rorty among other "pragmatist" philosophers, brings out the enduring, constitutive ethical and political aspects of how and what we know, and what we intend to do with this knowledge. As DeMartino (2016) and Diskin (2016) have also recently discussed, there is an ethical entailment in epistemological practices.

Another paramount aspect of Enlightenment and post-Enlightenment epistemological discourse has been the issue of "correspondence," that is, the question of whether or not the pursuit of truth is about thought being capable of creating a veracious account of the world outside the mind (in Marxism, see Ruben 1979, who finds a similar correspondence approach in Lenin 1927). Is true knowledge, as opposed to discourses of non-knowledge, a matter of thought conforming in essence to the real? In answering this question, this real is variously portrayed as existing prior to, independent of, and inexorably exterior to the mind. Yet, for some correspondence theorists, omnipresent, transcendent categories of the mind create a "real-in-thought" that can apprehend basic truths about that outer reality; there is an objective real to which thought should ultimately correspond, but it does not give itself up easily. In Marxism, for example, numerous theorists have pointed to Marx's distinction between essence and appearance and, from there, have attributed to Marx an epistemology of daedal extraction, or as Marx put it, discovering "the rational kernel within the mystical shell" (1977, 103). As Althusser notes, this process of extraction is often made equivalent to Marx's "inversion" of the Hegelian dialectic, Marx's claim to have saved dialectics from its mystified idealist past and present by standing Hegel on his head. Truth only emerges through hermeneutical practice, and it will only correspond to the real material world if this interpretive practice is correctly undertaken.

The form of epistemological questioning with Marxism often has a close relationship to its content. One version has it that Marx is engrossed with laying bare the "laws of motion" that animate all socioeconomic formations, and especially that of capitalism. Towards that end, Marxists claiming Marx as their inspiration dedicate themselves to applying Marx's science—his dialectical materialism (Paolucci 2007)—to any subject matter. Like other recognized, sanctioned sciences, such followers claim, Marx's method allows for the true uncovering of how the material world works, and, indeed, how knowledge of the law-like motion of matter through time and in specific locations is part and parcel of the Marxian approach to epistemology (this is essentially Lenin's summation [see 1930]).

Knowledge Production

The conceptualization of the production processes involved in making knowledge predictably varies with the different schools of Marxian thought. Several positions on knowledge production develop from a reading of Marx's brief exposition in the *Grundrisse* (1973, see also Stuart Hall's reading [2003] of Marx's 1857 "Introduction"). In his first notebook, Marx describes a knowledge-producing process that starts from the concrete as first perceived, then moves to abstraction, in which those elements of the initial concrete perceptions that are homologous are gathered together in a generality. But, not stopping there—as Marx accuses many others of doing—he moves on to the ultimate concrete, as he puts it, a concrete that is the rich result of its many determinations. As a unity-in-motion, it is the totality that can be grasped only by following this correct order in thinking. So, in this version, Marx announces the cognitive mechanism that permits truths to rise to the surface, as knowledge is produced that is accurate and reflecting its own procedural determinations.

Althusser provides another Marxist version of producing knowledge, claiming to "read" Marx symptomatically through his writings. This reading includes denoting the unsaids or "absent presences" that give meaning to what Marx indeed did say. In his discussion of what he called "theoretical practice" (Althusser and Balibar 1970, Hindess and Hirst 1975, Patton 1978, Althusser 1990, Sharp 2000). Althusser rejects the empiricist epistemological tendency to regard truth as there for the taking. Instead, Althusser describes a scientific process that is productive of knowledge through a scientific discourse's internal practices. Knowledge is not about finding essences in the real. Knowledge is not "objective" in this essentialist sense (Milberg and Pietrykowski 1994), and Marxism's epistemological stance is, or seeks to be, anti-essentialist (Resnick and Wolff 1987).

Truth, instead, is constructed in-house, that is, within a science that has relative autonomy from other sciences' norms and methods of finding truth. Marx's dialectical materialism is such a theoretical practice, Althusser contends. It contains its own epistemological norms as to what truth consists of and how such truth can be propagated for continued proliferation. Theoretical practice produces truths in the realm of the "concrete-in-thought," which is never adequate to, or a mirror of, the concrete-real that is always extrinsic to it but which is shaping it at all times (see Rorty 1979 for a non-Marxist criticism of knowledge mirroring nature). As Read (2005) states, "what defines science is less its specific content than its practice, the production of new objects of knowledge." In one rendition, Althusser (1970) describes in detail the transition from pre-scientific, perhaps ideological, concepts and "facts" (what he called "Generality I") to scientific knowledge (Generality III). Generality II, a middle term, is the process of production through the workings of a "problematic." The problematic is a framework that delineates particular problems that must be addressed. The problematic also elaborates the theoretical labor needed for this reading, the protocols of experimentation and testing required for detaching ideological elements from scientific knowledge, unique standards of proof, and so forth. There is also no transcendent, transdiscursive element— like mathematics—that confers scientific status to all other elements in the theoretical framework (Ruccio 1988). For Althusserians, knowledge is material, relative, conjunctural and overdetermined—all parts are needed in their intereffectivity in producing a science.

We note that Critical Realism, associated with Bhaskar (1975) and Alex Callinicos within Marxism (Bhaskar and Callinicos 2003; see also Brown, Fleetwood, and Roberts 2005), is another attempt to escape the confines of empiricist and rationalist epistemologies; critical realism expounds a notion of scientific knowledge production that presumes a hierarchically structured external reality. In this view, there is an underlying ontological real, a set of deep structures that determine surface reality, which must exist in order for the practice of science as they understand it to take place (see Ruccio 2009 for an appreciative critique of this tendency in economics).

And, for some Marxists, knowledge is always local (see Santamaria 1992), specific, and historical; as the material conditions of existence for theoretical discourse change, so will its internal elements. Some Marxists believe that a new stage in capitalism has appeared, one in which knowledge production, dissemination, and consumption have taken center stage. Cognitive capitalism, as its proponents call it (Vercellone 2007, Boutang 2012) is marked by the so-called "dematerialization" of work and by the rising importance of immaterial labor and immaterial assets. In this late capitalist era, knowledge production is thought to consist mostly of "information" or data rather than analytics. But, the resistance of Marxists to notions of "intellectual capital" and "intellectual property" that are rife in describing this era preserves the Marxist epistemological perspective that knowledge emanates from work, immaterial or not.

Effects of Knowledge

Finally, turning to the effects and effectivity of knowledge, once again, there are variations in Marxism on the purposes and actual consequences knowledge has on everything else around it. Clearly, all Marxists know well Marx's eleventh thesis on Feuerbach in which he admonishes that "the philosophers have only interpreted the world; the point is to change it" (in Tucker 1978, 145). Knowledge is a tool and a weapon, and the unique ideations that Marxism generates, its philosophical reflections, can and should take the form of class struggle in theory (Althusser 1976). Marxism thus conjoins theory and practice, and truth is practical and political at one and the same time. It follows that knowledge production is critical to political success, including the politics—struggles involving power (Foucault 1980, Stoddart 2007) and control—that also overdetermine the "pure" sciences. This Marxist view rejects the image of the pursuit of knowledge in any field as disinterested and neutral. From this standpoint, whether hitched closely or remotely to struggles in other areas of social existence, the conflict of ideas and contesting theories remains a fact of an organized thinking life. Into this mix, Marxism contributes its own science with its own point of view about the truths that matter and about the historical, conjunctural materiality of its own truth.

But another perspective on the way knowledge itself affects everything else is the Althusserian notion of "knowledge effects" (Althusser and Balibar 1970). Althusser put forward this idea to capture two ideas about the production of scientific knowledge. One is that knowledge is the result, an effect (and cause simultaneously) of a determinate production process: a material product (Althusser 2003). But, secondly, as result, knowledge is also a semblance, an artifice that exists only as the concrete-in-thought and not as "real knowledge," or the imaginary essence of a graspable, apparent object. The semblance of its existence is all knowledge has; it is no specter, but it is also no essential concrete-real. Following scientific procedures internal to its own problematic and thereby traversing, by partly transforming, the sprawling lifeworld of ideological discourse, it emerges as the only "real" that can be adequately known. As an effect, therefore, it blurs the lines drawn in classical epistemology between the real and thought; it is the theoretical coalescence of both (this exhibits Althusser's persistent Spinozism; see 2006). Knowledge effects reverberate throughout a social formation and are productive, in combination with other cognitive raw materials (including "everyday" representations [Ruccio 2008]), in their own right. For many Marxist epistemologists, knowledge is active and actionable, and its existence as material image/image of the material is one requisite condition for the revolutionary socioeconomic—especially class—change that Marx vehemently proposed.

References

Althusser, L. 1970. *For Marx*. Trans. by B. Brewster. New York: Vintage Books.
——. 1971. *Lenin and Philosophy, and Other Essays*. Trans. by B. Brewster. New York: Monthly Review Press.
——. 1976. *Essays in Self-Criticism*. Trans. by G. Lock. London: New Left Books.
——. 1990. *Philosophy and the Spontaneous Philosophy of the Scientists, and Other Essays*. Trans. by B. Brewster, J. H. Kavanagh, T. E. Lewis, G. Lock, and W. Montag. London: Verso.
——. 2003. *The Humanist Controversy and Other Writings*. F. Matheron, ed. Trans. by G. M. Goshgarian. London: Verso.
——. 2006. *Philosophy of the Encounter: Later Writings, 1978–1987*. F. Matheron and O. Corpet, eds. Trans. with an Intro. by G. Goshgarian. London: Verso.
Althusser, L. and E. Balibar. 1970. *Reading Capital*. Trans. by B. Brewster. London: New Left Books.
Amariglio, J. L. 1987. "Marxism Against Economic Science: Althusser's Legacy." In *Research in Political Economy*, P. Zarembka, ed. 10: 159–194. Greenwich, CT: JAI Press.
Anderson, E. 2015. "Feminist Epistemology and Philosophy of Science." In *The Stanford Encyclopedia of Philosophy*, Fall 2015 Edition, E. N. Zalta, ed. http://plato.stanford.edu/entries/feminism-epistemology/ (accessed July 18, 2016).

Anderson, W. T., ed. 1995. *The Truth About Truth: De-confusing and Re-constructing the Postmodern World*. New York: G. P. Putnam Sons.

Appadurai, A. 1986. "Introduction: Commodities and the Politics of Value." In *The Social Life of Things: Commodities in Cultural Perspective*, A. Appadurai, ed., 3–63. Cambridge: Cambridge University Press.

Arato, A. and E. Gephardt, eds. 1982. *The Essential Frankfurt School Reader*. London: Bloomsbury Academic.

Azad, B. 2005. "Marxism, Science, and Class Struggle: The Scientific Basis of the Concept of the Vanguard Party of the Proletariat." *Nature, Society, and Thought* 18(4): 503–533.

Bakan, A. B. 2012. "Marxism, Feminism, and Epistemological Dissonance." *Socialist Studies/Études Socialistes* 8(2): 60–84.

Barrett, M. 1991. *The Politics of Truth: From Marx to Foucault*. Stanford: Stanford University Press.

Bennett, J. 2010. *Vibrant Matter: A Political Ecology of Things*. Durham: Duke University Press.

——. 2015. "Systems and Things: On Vital Materialism and Object-Oriented Philosophy." In *The Nonhuman Turn*, R. Grushin, ed. Minneapolis: University of Minnesota Press.

Bergeron, S. 2006. *Fragments of Development: Nation, Gender, and the Space of Modernity*. Ann Arbor: University of Michigan Press.

Bewes, T. 2002. *Reification, or The Anxiety of Late Capitalism*. Verso: London.

Bhaskar, R. 1975. "Feyerabend and Bachelard: Two Philosophies of Science." *New Left Review* 94: 31–55.

Bhaskar, R. and A. Callinicos. 2003. "Marxism and Critical Realism: A Debate." *Journal of Critical Realism* 1(2): 89–114.

Bogost, I. 2012. *Alien Phenomenology, or What It's Like to Be a Thing*. Minneapolis: University of Minnesota Press.

Boutang, Y. M. 2012. *Cognitive Capitalism*. Cambridge: Polity Press.

Brown, A., Fleetwood, S., and J. M. Roberts, eds. 2005. *Critical Realism and Marxism*. London: Routledge.

Brown, B. 2004. *Things*. Chicago: University of Chicago Press.

Callari, A. 1986. "History, Epistemology, and Marx's Theory of Value." In *Research in Political Economy*, P. Zarembka, ed. 9: 69–93. Greenwich, CT: JAI Press.

Callari, A. and D. F. Ruccio, eds. 1996. *Postmodern Materialism and the Future of Marxist Theory: Essays in the Althusserian Tradition*. Hanover, NH: Wesleyan University Press/University Press of New England.

Castree, N. 1995. "The Nature of Produced Knowledge: Materiality and Knowledge Construction in Marxism." *Antipode* 27(1): 12–18.

Charusheela, S. 2004. "Postcolonial Thought, Postmodernism, and Economics: Questions of Ontology and Ethics." In *Postcolonialism Meets Economics*, E. O. Zein-Elabdin and S. Charusheela, eds. 40–58. London: Routledge.

Childe, V. G. 1936. *Man Makes Himself*. London: Watts & Co.

Cole, A. 2014. *The Birth of Theory*. Chicago: University of Chicago Press.

Coole, D. and S. Frost, eds. 2010. *New Materialisms: Ontology, Agency, and Politics*. Durham: Duke University Press.

Copjek, J. 1994. *Read My Desire: Lacan Against the Historicists*. Cambridge, MA: MIT Press.

Cullenberg, S. 1996. "Althusser and the Decentering of the Marxist Totality." In *Postmodern Materialism and the Future of Marxist Theory: Essays in the Althusserian Tradition*, A. Callari and D. F. Ruccio, eds. 120–149. Hanover, NH: Wesleyan University Press/University Press of New England.

DeMartino, G. 2016. "The Economist's Oath: On Economic Agency, Economic Theory, Pluralism, and Ecogenic Harm." *Rethinking Marxism* 28(1): 47–56.

Derrida, J. 1967. *Of Grammatology*. Trans. by G. Spivak. Baltimore: Johns Hopkins University Press.

Diskin, J. 2016. "Ethics and Epistemology in The Economist's Oath." *Rethinking Marxism* 28(1): 16–24.

Dupuy, J.-P. 2009. *On the Origins of Cognitive Science: The Mechanization of the Mind*. Trans. by M. B. DeBevoise. Cambridge, MA: MIT Press.

Engels, F. 1934. *Herr Eugen Dühring's Revolution in Science* [Anti-Dühring]. Moscow: Co-operative Publishing Society of Foreign Workers in the U.S.S.R.

——. 1940. *Dialectics of Nature*. C. Dutt, ed. and trans. New York: International Publishers.

Escobar, A. 2011. *Encountering Development: The Making and Unmaking of the Third World*. Princeton: Princeton University Press.

Eyers, T. 2015. *Post-Rationalism: Psychoanalysis, Epistemology, and Marxism in Post-War France*. London. Bloomsbury.

Feyerabend, P. 1975. *Against Method*. London: New Left Books.

Finelli, R. 1989. "Some Thoughts on the Modern in the Works of Smith, Hegel, and Marx." *Rethinking Marxism* 2(2): 111–131.

Foucault, M. 1972. *The Archaeology of Knowledge and the Discourse on Language*. Trans. by A. M. S. Smith. New York: Harper and Row.

——. 1980. *Power/Knowledge: Selected Interviews and Other Writings, 1972–1977*. Trans. by C. Gordon, L. Marshall, J. Mepham, and K. Soper. New York: Pantheon.

Foucault, M. and J. Faubion. 1997. *Aesthetics, Method, and Epistemology*. New York: New Press.

Freedgood, E. 2006. *The Ideas in Things: Fugitive Meaning in the Victorian Novel*. Chicago: University of Chicago Press.

Gibson-Graham, J. K. 1996. *The End of Capitalism (as we knew it): A Feminist Critique of Political Economy*. Cambridge, MA: Blackwell Publishers.

Gramsci, A. 1988. *A Gramsci Reader: Selected Writings*. Ed. by D. Forgacs. London: Lawrence & Wishart.

Gratton, P. 2014. *Speculative Realism: Problems and Prospects*. London: Bloomsbury.

Hall, S. 2003. "Marx's Notes on Method: A 'Reading' of the '1857 Introduction'." *Cultural Studies* 17(2): 113–149.

Harding, S. 1993. "Rethinking Standpoint Epistemology: What is 'Strong Objectivity'?" In *Feminist Epistemologies*, L. Alcoff and E. Potter, eds. London: Routledge.

Hardy, N. 2014. "Wolff, Althusser, and Hegel: Outlining an Aleatory Materialist Epistemology." *Rethinking Marxism* 26(4): 454–471.

Harman, G. 2011. *The Quadruple Object*. Winchester: Zero Books.

Hindess, B. and P. Q. Hirst. 1975. *Pre-Capitalist Modes of Production*. London: Routledge & Kegan Paul.

Holland, E. 1998. "Spinoza and Marx." *Cultural Logic* 2(1): 21–47.

Kain, P. J. 1986. *Marx' Method, Epistemology, and Humanism: A Study in the Development of His Thought*. Medford, MA: Springer.

Kelley, R. D. G. 2003. *Freedom Dreams: The Black Radical Imagination*. Boston: Beacon Press.

Kitching, G. 1994. *Marxism and Science: Analysis of an Obsession*. University Park, PA: Pennsylvania State University Press.

Laclau, E. and C. Mouffe. 1985. *Hegemony and Socialist Strategy: Towards a Radical Democratic Politics*. London: Verso.

Lamb, J. 2011. *The Things Things Say*. Princeton: Princeton University Pres.

Laruelle, F. 2015. *Introduction to Non-Marxism*. Trans. by A. P. Smith. Minneapolis: Univocal Publishing.

Lecourt, D. 1975. *Marxism and Epistemology: Bachelard, Canguilhem, and Foucault*. Trans. by B. Brewster. London: New Left Books.

——. 1977. *Proletarian Science?: The Case of Lysenko*. Intro. by L. Althusser. Trans. by B. Brewster. London: New Left Books.

Lenin, V. 1927. *Materialism and Empirio-Criticism*. New York: International Publishers.

——. 1930. *The Teachings of Karl Marx*. New York: International Publishers.

——. 1977. "The Three Sources and Three Component Parts of Marxism." In *Collected Works, Vol. 19*. 21–28. Moscow: Progress Publishers.

Lordon, F. 2014. *Willing Slaves of Capital: Spinoza & Marx on Desire*. Trans. by G. Ash. London: Verso.

Lukács, G. 1971. "Reification and the Consciousness of the Proletariat." In *History and Class Consciousness*. Trans. by R. Livingstone. Cambridge, MA: MIT Press.

Madra, Y. Forthcoming. "Process: Tracing Connections and Consequences." In *Marxism without Guarantees: Economics, Knowledge, and Class*, T. Burczak, R. Garnett, and R. McIntyre, eds. London: Routledge.

Marx, K. 1964. *The Economic and Philosophic Manuscripts of 1844*. Ed. and Intro. by D. J. Struik. Trans. by M. Mulligan. New York: International Publishers.

——. 1971. *A Contribution to the Critique of Political Economy*. Intro. by M. Dobb. Trans. by S. W. Ryazanskaya London: Lawrence & Wishart.

——. 1972. *Capital: A Critique of Political Economy, Vol. 3*, ed. by F. Engels. London: Lawrence & Wishart.

——. 1973. *Grundrisse: Foundations of the Critique of Political Economy*. 1973. Trans. with a Foreword by M. Nicolaus. New York: Vintage.

——. 1977. *Capital: A Critique of Political Economy. Vol. 1*. Intro. by E. Mandel. Trans. by B. Brewster. New York: Vintage.

——. 1978. "For a Ruthless Criticism of Everything Existing." In *The Marx-Engels Reader*, 2nd Edition. R. C. Tucker, ed. New York: W. W. Norton & Co.

McGuire, R. G. 1992. *A Marxist Archaeology*. San Diego: Academic Press.

Meillasoux, Q. 2008. *After Finitude: An Essay on the Necessity of Contingency*. London: Continuum.

Milberg. W. and B. Pietrykowski. 1994. "Objectivism, Relativism, and the Importance of Rhetoric for Marxist Economics." *Review of Radical Political Economics* 26(1): 85–109.

Montag, W. 1995. "'The Soul is the Prison of the Body': Althusser and Foucault, 1970–1975." *Yale French Studies*. 88: 53–77.

Murray, P. 1988. *Marx's Theory of Scientific Knowledge*. Boston: Humanities Press International.

Ollman, B. 1992. *Dialectical Investigations*. London: Routledge.

Özselçuk, C. and Y. Madra. 2007. "Economy, Surplus, Politics: Some Questions on Slavoj Žižek's Political Economy Critique of Capitalism." In *Did Somebody Say Ideology?: On Slavoj Žižek and Consequences*, F. Vighi and H. Feldner, eds., 78–107. Newcastle: Cambridge Scholars Publishing.

Paolucci, P. 2007. *Marx's Scientific Dialectics: A Methodological Treatise for a New Century*. Leiden: Brill.

Patton, P. 1978. "Althusser's Epistemology: The Limits of the Theory of Theoretical Practice." *Radical Philosophy*. Spring: 8–18.

Paynter, R. 2005. "Contesting Culture Histories in Archaeology and Their Engagement with Marx." *Rethinking Marxism* 17(3): 399–412.

Read, J. 2005. "The Althusser Effect: Philosophy, History, and Temporality." *Borderlands* 4(2).

Resch, R. P. 1992. *Althusser and the Renewal of Marxist Social Theory*. Berkeley: University of California Press.

Resnick, S. A. and R. D. Wolff. 1987. *Knowledge and Class: A Marxian Critique of Political Economy*. Chicago: University of Chicago Press.

——. 2013. "On Overdetermination and Althusser: Our Response to Silverman and Park." *Rethinking Marxism* 25(3): 341–349.

Robinson, C. 2000. *Black Marxism*. Foreword by R. D. G. Kelley. Chapel Hill: University of North Carolina Press.

Rorty, R. 1979. *Philosophy and the Mirror of Nature*. Princeton: Princeton University Press.

Rossi-Landi, F. 1990. *Marxism and Ideology*. Oxford: Oxford University Press.

Ruben, D.-H. 1979. *Marxism and Materialism: A Study in Marxist Theory of Knowledge*. Atlantic Highlands, NJ: Humanities Press.

Ruccio, D. F. 1988. "The Merchant of Venice, or Marxism in the Mathematical Mode." *Rethinking Marxism* 1(4): 36–68.

——. ed. 2008. *Economic Representations: Both Academic and Everyday*. New York: Routledge.

——. 2009. "(Un)real Criticism." In *Ontology and Economics: Tony Lawson and His Critics*, E. Fullbrook, ed., 263–274. London: Routledge.

Ruccio, D. F. and J. Amariglio. 2003. *Postmodern Moments in Modern Economics*. Princeton: Princeton University Press.

Ryder, A. 2013. "Foucault and Althusser: Epistemological Differences with Political Effects." *Foucault Studies* 16: 134–153.

Saitta, D. 1994. "Agency, Class, and Archaeological Interpretation." *Journal of Anthropological Archaeology* 13: 201–227.

———. 2005. "Marxism, Tribal Society, and the Dual Nature of Archaeology." *Rethinking Marxism* 17(3): 385–397.

Santamaria, A. S. de. 1992. "Economic Science and Political Democracy." In *Real-Life Economics: Understanding Wealth Creation*, P. Ekins and M. Max-Neef, eds., 10–20. London: Routledge.

Sharp, H. 2000. "'Is it Simple to be a Feminist in Philosophy?': Althusser and Feminist Theoretical Practice." *Rethinking Marxism* 12(2): 18–34.

Silverman, M. 2013. "'Overdetermined' or 'Indeterminate'?: Remarks on *Knowledge and Class*." *Rethinking Marxism* 20(3): 311–324.

Smith, D. E. 2004. "Ideology, Science, and Social Relations: A Reinterpretation of Marx's Epistemology." *European Journal of Social Theory* 7(4): 445–462.

Smith, S. B. 1985. "Althusser's Marxism Without a Knowing Subject." *American Political Society Review* 79(3): 641–655.

Sohn-Rethel, A. 1978. *Intellectual and Manual Labour: Critique of Epistemology*. Trans. by M. Sohn-Rethel. Atlantic Highlands, NJ: Humanities Press.

Stiegler, B. 2010. *For a New Critique of Political Economy*. Cambridge: Polity Press.

———. 2015. *States of Shock: Stupidity and Knowledge in the 21st Century*. Trans. by D. Ross. Cambridge: Polity Press.

Stoddart, M. C. J. 2007. "Ideology, Hegemony, Discourse: A Critical Review of Theories of Knowledge and Power." *Social Thought & Research* 28: 191–225.

Toscano, A. 2008. "The Open Secret of Real Abstraction." *Rethinking Marxism* 20(2): 273–287.

Tucker, R. C., ed. 1978. *The Marx-Engels Reader*, 2nd Edition. New York: W. W. Norton & Co.

Vercellone, C. 2007. "From Formal Subsumption to General Intellect: Elements for a Marxist Reading of the Thesis of Cognitive Capitalism." *Historical Materialism* 15: 13–36.

West, C. 1989. *The American Evasion of Philosophy: A Genealogy of Pragmatism*. London: Palgrave Macmillan.

Wolff, R. 1996. "Althusser and Hegel: Making Marxist Explanations Antiessentialist and Dialectical." In *Postmodern Materialism and the Future of Marxist Theory: Essays in the Althusserian Tradition*, A. Callari and D. F. Ruccio, eds. Hanover, NH: Wesleyan University Press/University of New England Press.

Young, R. J. C. 2004. *White Mythologies: Writing History and the West*, 2nd edition. London: Routledge.

Žižek, S. 1989. *The Sublime Object of Ideology*. London: Verso.

———. 1997. *The Plague of Fantasies*. London: Verso.

3

MARXIAN CLASS ANALYSIS

Richard D. Wolff

Concepts of Class

The concept of class poses profound problems for theory and practice. This is true across the academic disciplines and in the confused incoherence around "class issues" when concepts of class surface in economic, political and cultural discourses. Since 1945, the Cold War and its lingering effects prevented many discussions of social trends, events and crises from considering their class causes, components or consequences. For many, loyalty to capitalism and/or hostility toward its critics took the form of refusing to use concepts like class. The very idea of class when applied to the US or advanced capitalism anywhere was rejected with claims that it was outdated (since modern capitalism homogenized nearly everyone into a vast "middle class").[1] Many dismissed class analysis because it was "tainted by a lack of objectivity" (a quality that they located in the concepts they used instead of class). Only quite recently, following the 2008 global capitalist crash, have concepts of class resurfaced in many minds and therefore in much public discussion.

What might be called the return of the repressed discourse of class is problematic because there is no one concept of class. The word, like the concept, entails multiple, significantly different meanings among those who think and communicate using it. Only a small minority of users explicitly identifies and justifies which meaning it prefers. Most users think, speak and write as if the particular concept of class they use is the universally agreed concept. Because that is not the case, discourses using class categories are often confused and misunderstood. When the relation between class and social change arises as a practical matter, the problematic nature of class as a concept becomes historically urgent.

At least as far back as ancient Greece, people analyzed their own and others' societies by dividing populations into social subgroups according to their wealth and/or incomes. Much as they classified populations for some purposes according to gender, height, weight and age, for other purposes, such as understanding social conflicts, they could and did classify by wealth or income. Classes were the nouns applied to the subgroups derived from applying the verb *to classify*. Economic classifications generated the rich and the poor, the two polar classes. It was then a small step to subdivide populations into further subgroups located in the middle between the rich and the poor. Such subgroups—middle classes—held more wealth and/or received more income than those designated poor, but less than those designated rich.

Classifications into rich and poor presupposed some notion of private property to provide a boundary between one person's wealth and/or income and another's (much as age classifications presupposed some accepted way to measure and thereby differentiate each individual's age).

Ever since ancient Greece, many people analyzing societies have used that concept of class *defined in terms of owned wealth and/or income* to think, speak or write about social problems and to undertake actions for their solutions. Thus, for example, citizens, leaders, observers and so on might say that a society suffers from tension and conflict because of its particular divisions among rich, poor and middle classes. They might offer solutions entailing changed modes of distributing wealth and/or income or perhaps redistributing them after an initial distribution. Their class analyses and class-focused solutions—defined in terms of class qua property—represent what they believe to be useful, effective contributions to social betterment.

Another, equally ancient but quite different concept of class also still in wide usage defines it *in terms of power wielded over others*. People using this concept classify populations they scrutinize into those who give orders to others and those who take and follow orders from others. One is the powerful class while the other is the powerless class: the ruling class and the ruled. As with the property-based concepts of class, those who use power definitions of class also intersperse middle classes, members of society who took orders from some while giving orders to others. Now as for thousands of years many people make sense of the structures, changes, problems and solutions for societies by examining what they take to be their class structures: their organization into subgroups with more or less power over one another.

With two different concepts of class, class analyses could and did yield different understandings when applied to actual societies. Classifying populations according to who has and does not have property, including middle classes, yields different subgroupings from those resulting from classifications according to the power wielded (or not) over others. The social distribution of property is not identical to the social distribution of power. In any society, the individuals and subgroups who own the most property may or may not wield the most power, and so on. When thinkers and writers used the same term, "class analysis," while defining it differently, confusion could set in. When they were unaware of definitional differences and so did not acknowledge, identify or justify which definition they used, confusion was certain.

Periodically in human history, social revolutions took "class" seriously. Revolutionaries then undertook to change a society's class structure as a key, necessary component of the social transformation they sought. These transformations can be summarized as establishing equality and democracy. Revolutionaries committed to class-qua-property concepts focused on redistributing wealth and income or reorganizing how they were distributed initially. Their goal was a much more egalitarian distribution of wealth and income. In contrast, revolutionaries who conceived of class in terms of power rather than property focused on redistributing power and/or reorganizing how power was distributed initially. Their goal was a much more egalitarian distribution of power.

Not infrequently, class analyses worked with both property and power concepts, although rarely with much self-consciousness about the problems raised by two different definitions. Thus, for example, property theorists of class made the simplifying presumption that altering the social distribution of wealth and income would necessarily and correspondingly alter the social distribution of power. Similarly, power theorists of class could run the same determinist argument in the reverse direction: changing power distributions would necessarily alter the social distribution of property. Sometimes, analyses and activists made another, related and simplifying assumption, namely that those with wealth would also acquire power and those lacking either would likely also lack the other.

Across thousands of years of European history, class analyses rose and fell in their popularity and use for understanding social structures, changes, problems and solutions. Likewise the two basic definitions of class alternated in terms of which prevailed or, sometimes, how they were combined into composite definitions. Yet a certain insufficiency and failure dogged the class revolutions that punctuated European history, even when they "succeeded" in the sense that revolutionary forces defeated those who wished to avoid revolutionary change.

Despite the progress they achieved, their goals of egalitarian distributions of wealth and income and/or egalitarian distributions of power were never reached. For many, those failures provoked a fatalism that held the goals themselves as beyond human reach. Others questioned the thinking that had guided the revolutions. They asked whether something had been missed or misunderstood about social structures, changes, problems and solutions by successive revolutionary movements. If rectified, might that something enable revolutionaries finally to achieve their twin goals of equality and democracy?

Marx's New Concept of Class

Marx was one who asked such questions. In producing his answer, Marx generated another new and different concept of class even as he also made frequent use of the ancient property and power concepts of class inherited from previous generations of revolutionaries.

Marx believed that those generations had not achieved their basic goals of equality and democracy because they had not understood a basic process in all societies. That failure to understand had worked to undermine their revolutionary projects. By not understanding and therefore inadequately transforming that process, their revolutionary projects failed. Even when their revolutions achieved significant and socially progressive changes in property and power distributions, those did not progress to the levels of equality and democracy they had hoped and worked for. Often, the progressive changes they achieved could not be sustained beyond a few years. For Marx, the personally transformative example of such limitedly successful revolutions was the French Revolution. It overthrew feudalism but its goals of *liberté, égalité, fraternité* were not achieved.

Marx's *Capital* presented his analysis of the missed social process—basically the production and distribution of the surplus, as we shall show below. *Capital* explained how this class-qua-surplus process helped to shape the social distributions of property and power. The failures of previous revolutions (such as the French) to achieve genuine, sustainable equality and democracy emerge as consequences of their failure to recognize, understand and transform this class-qua-surplus process.

Even though Marx devoted much of his life to research and exposition of his new surplus conception of class, many readers and followers since have missed the originality of his new and different concept. They read his work instead as if it were an important new application of the old property and power concepts of class to analyzing capitalism. That is indeed one of Marx's contributions. However, to see only that misses the crucial importance of his new class-qua-surplus concept to both understanding and getting beyond capitalism. Marx's focus on the surplus thus carries over into our time too as a key component of critical social analysis demanding recognition and application.

Early in volume one of *Capital*, Marx identifies his new notion of class. He defines it as a distinct social process that occurs together with the physical labor process within the activity known as production. In production, workers labor—men and women use brains and muscle—to transform naturally occurring objects into useful products. They labor on raw material inputs with tools and equipment inside buildings, etc., with their means of production. But the labor process is not the same thing as the class process. The class process refers to a connection among the people engaged with the production activity that is different from the labor connection that generates a specific product.

Class, for Marx, refers to how, in production, a surplus gets produced. All human societies produce such surpluses. However, societies differ in how they organize the production and distribution of their surpluses. In Marx's view, there have always been subsets of populations in communities (from families through villages to whole nations) that have performed labor in the production of goods and services. Those subsets have always produced more output than they themselves consumed: the "surplus" output or simply the surplus. That surplus has then been distributed to other persons inside or outside the community.

The class structure of a community or society is, then, its distinct organization of the production and distribution of surplus. A specific subgroup of individuals is designated, consciously or unconsciously, by custom or deliberation, to produce the surplus (i.e., they produce more than they themselves consume). Those same or other individuals receive the surplus and distribute some or all of it to still others: recipients of distributed shares of the surplus. Each community or society designates which individuals can receive distributed shares of the surplus, consume them, and thereby live without themselves producing the surplus. Likewise, every society designates a subgroup to do work that does not itself produce a surplus but rather provides conditions for the labor of others who do produce the surplus. Such *enablers* of surplus production by others need to receive a distribution of the surplus produced by those others; that distribution provides the enablers with their own consumption and with the means for performing their enabling functions. For example, a person who keeps the necessary records of what surplus-producing laborers do is such an enabler; so too are the persons who clean up residues of production, who make sure the surplus-producers keep to their tasks, etc. Marx differentiated between "productive" workers (those who directly produced surpluses) and "unproductive" workers (the enablers who provided needed conditions for surplus production). Both productive and unproductive workers were needed for any class structure to exist and persist, but their relationship to surplus production was crucially different. One kind of worker produced the surplus while the other, the enabler, lived off distributions of that surplus.

The earlier pre-Marxian concepts of class (qua property or power distributions) had no place for such a surplus concept of class. When those pre-Marxian concepts were applied to understand and/or transform societies, the results were class analyses that did not recognize, know or use the surplus concept. Their social analyses and prescriptions did not take into account how the societies they scrutinized organized the production and distribution of surpluses. They were, in effect, blind to the existence and social effects of society's class (qua surplus) structure.

Marx's *Capital* introduced the class-qua-surplus analysis and advocated using it to transform society. He did so in the belief that past revolutionary projects for social equality, democracy and liberty were limited to pre-Marxian property and power concepts of class. Early revolutions could have done better and gone further had they also understood and applied the class-qua-surplus concept. Marx saw his own contribution to theory and revolutionary practice as precisely enabling that application.

Such application meant that revolutionary projects had henceforth to address and change how society organized the production and distribution of its surpluses. If the society's class-qua-surplus structure were not transformed, then egalitarian reforms in the distributions of property and power, if won by revolutionary struggles, would be insecure. They would likely be undone by the unchanged class-qua-surplus structure. To cite a modern example, the transformations of property and power distributions achieved by the 1917 revolution in Russia were eventually undone by the insufficiently changed organization of the surplus across the production sites of the Soviet Union.[2]

In *Capital*, Marx spelled out the change he sought in societies' class-qua-surplus structures, the change required to surpass the limitations of past revolutions. That change was from the past's exploitative class-qua-surplus class structures to the non-exploitative class structure Marx advocated. By exploitative, Marx explicitly explained a class structure in which the people who produced the surplus were different from the people who received and further distributed that surplus. In slave economic systems, slaves produced while masters received and distributed surpluses. In feudal economic systems, serfs produced the surpluses received and distributed by lords.

Marx's *Capital* explained that in capitalism, laborers in production—those whose brains and muscles directly converted raw materials and means of production into finished products—thereby added value to the values embodied in the raw materials and means of production used up in production. The "value added" by the direct laborers plus the value of used-up means of production equaled the value of the output. "Value" was the metric because, in the capitalist economy Marx was analyzing, products took the form of commodities, products that passed from their producers to their consumers by means of exchanges in markets. Exchange is what attaches value to the products of human labor if and when they pass from their producers to their consumers by way of markets.

For Marx and his value theory, the value of the capitalist product is simply the addition of two components. The first is the value carried over to—embodied in—the finished product from the used-up portion of the raw materials, tools and equipment. In effect, production relocated the values of the used-up means of production into the product. The second component is the value added by living labor as it worked, transforming raw materials by means of tools and equipment. Exploitation exists in capitalism, Marx showed, because the value added by direct laborers in their labor activity during production generally exceeds the value paid to the direct laborers for performing that labor activity.

In other words, a portion of the value added by labor in production is a surplus: the excess of the value added by the workers' labor over the value of the wage they receive. The capitalist who appropriates that surplus is the employer in the capitalist system: a person or persons usually other than the direct laborers who produce the surplus. The capitalist employer also distributes that surplus after having received or appropriated it. Thus the capitalist exploits the direct laborer (proletarian) much as the master exploited the slave and the lord the serf.

Capitalism did NOT liberate slaves and serfs from exploitation. Rather, it merely changed the form, the particular social organization, of continuing exploitation.

Equality and Democracy

Capitalist exploitation negates social movements toward egalitarianism. The exploitation makes production a conflict-ridden tension between the worker and the employer. The former's self-interest leads to demands for higher wages—to enhance and secure his/her standard of living—in exchange for the labor performed. The employer's self-interest seeks to extract more surplus from the direct laborers and pay the least possible to enablers. Usually, the disparity in resources brought to their conflicts favors the employers over the employees. Surpluses appropriated by employers tend to rise faster than real wages. This growing inequality ramifies throughout capitalist societies undermining whatever egalitarian tendencies might characterize their political and cultural aspects.

Of course, capitalism's inequality tendencies can interact with its other dimensions (e.g., capitalist cycles) to provoke political and cultural backlashes that reverse capitalism's inequalities. The reversals prove temporary because they are undone (reversal of the reversal) by capitalism's underlying tendencies toward inequality.[3] Thus, for example, the US left in the 1930s (CIO unionization drives, large socialist and Communist parties) forced a reversal of the extreme inequality built up in US capitalism before 1929. That reversal lasted to the 1970s, only to be then undone by capitalism's usual underlying inequality tendencies. The latter reasserted themselves precisely because the underlying exploitative class-qua-surplus structure of US capitalism had not been transformed by the left's social struggles and reforms of the 1930s or thereafter.

Similarly, capitalism's organization of the surplus directly contradicts democracy and undermines it too when, temporarily, democratic moments occur. The direct contradiction lies in the organization of typical capitalist enterprises, large, medium and small. A tiny subset of the persons involved with the enterprise usually owns and directs the enterprise; in corporations, for example, this subset comprises major shareholders and the boards of directors they select. The tiny subset can and virtually always does exclude the mass of employees from genuine participation in ownership or direction of the enterprise. The democratic logic—that persons affected by decisions have the right to participate in making them—is denied entry into the capitalist enterprise. In the US, the democracy celebrated at least formally in the political sphere is banished from the economic sphere.

This absence of democracy from the workplace, where adults spend most of their waking lives, undermines the capacity and often the desire of individuals for democracy in politics. At the same time, the inequalities generated by capitalism provide employers with the disproportionate financial resources to shape politics and culture to their liking as opposed to that of the largely excluded masses. The result in the US is mostly *formal* but little *real* political democracy. Periodic upsurges of democratic demands and even the occasional achievement of democratic reforms fail to last because the unchanged class-qua-surplus structure of capitalism works systemically against them.

Across *Capital*, Marx elaborates his class analysis of capitalism. In the first volume, his goal is to show how capitalism's surplus is produced and received/appropriated. In the second and third volumes, Marx explores how capitalists distribute the surpluses they appropriate from direct laborers. The surplus distributions are aimed primarily to secure certain conditions for the continuation of class exploitation and to provide means of production and consumption to the range of enablers of capitalist exploitation, its unproductive workers. These include supervisors who make sure direct laborers do their work, security guards who protect the enterprise, and an army of other enablers such as the secretaries, clerks, various managers, sales and purchasing personnel. This argument is spelled out in detail for the capitalist class process elsewhere.[4]

Capitalist production of the surplus positions and sustains the producing worker and the appropriating capitalist as its two poles. Capitalists' surplus distributions to unproductive enablers thereby secure their capitalist positions as the surplus appropriators and distributors. The production of the surplus enables its distribution and vice-versa. For Marx, the class structure of the capitalist system refers to its unique organization of the production and distribution of the surplus.

Of course, the class structure's reproduction is not assured or self-contained; it depends on its environment. The appropriators' surplus distributions merely try to secure the class structure's conditions of existence and its reproduction by shaping as many of its environment's dimensions as possible with the surplus available for those distributions. The surplus distributions may or may not succeed. Capitalists may not appropriate enough surplus to distribute the requisite quantities. There may be enough surplus, but the appropriators may divert too much to their own consumption or too little to secure one or another particular condition of existence of the class structure. How the surplus is distributed will shape the evolution of the class structure and thus the amount of surplus it generates. A class structure's continual changes can and eventually do include its transformation into another, different class structure.

The Class Structure of Communism

Aspects of the capitalist class structure and of class qua surplus as a concept become clearer when applied to a non-capitalist class structure and, in particular, to the communist class structure as envisioned by Marx. The difference between the two class structures is simple and straightforward. Communist class structures are defined by the absence of exploitation. The producers and appropriators of the surplus in a communist class structure are the same people, whereas in the capitalist class structure, they are different people. In an enterprise whose class structure is communist, the productive laborers collectively are also the appropriators of the surpluses they produce. It then follows that they are also the surplus distributors. The productive laborers displace the capitalists who literally disappear from the communist class structure.

Of course, such communist producers/appropriators/distributors of the surplus need to sustain the enablers of the production of the communist surplus, the communist form of "unproductive" workers. The distribution of communist surpluses defines two positions at its poles: the "productive workers" who are also the appropriators and distributors of the surplus at one pole, and the recipients of distributed shares of the surplus, the "unproductive" workers at the other pole. As in all class structures, the process of distributing the surplus is the object of struggle between distributors and recipients. However, the key difference separating the communist from all exploitative class structures is this: in the latter, the exploiting classes (slave masters, feudal lords and capitalist employers) interpose themselves between the productive and unproductive laborers. In the communist class structured enterprise, the productive and unproductive laborers remove the interposers and negotiate directly with one another to determine together both the size and the distribution of the surplus.

The significance of this difference is huge. First, capitalists are in the position of distributing portions of the surplus to themselves (as owners, shareholders and/or as top corporate executives). These portions are often—and for obvious reasons—large. The deep tendency toward inequality exhibited in and by capitalism is closely linked to who distributes its surpluses. The small minority that decides the distribution in capitalism serves itself and thereby worsens inequalities over time. The distribution of the surplus decided by productive and unproductive workers democratically acting together and without any capitalist interposer would likely be much less unequal.

Second, consider the example of a technical change in the methods of production available to an enterprise, a change that both enhances profitability but is also ecologically dangerous or toxic. The capitalist enterprise will likely choose to implement the change because the extra profit means there will be more to distribute. The capitalists making the decision are few and can finance escapes from the toxic consequences in terms of their living locations, etc. The communist enterprise will likely choose otherwise, since its collective decision-makers (productive and unproductive workers deciding democratically) will weigh the health risks and costs that they, their families and neighbors will have to bear if the toxic technology is used. One cause of ecological damage would be reduced by a class change from capitalist to communist class structures in enterprises.

Third, consider the example of moving production from a relatively high-wage to a relatively low-wage location. Capitalists have been doing that in large numbers for nearly half a century, leaving North America, western Europe and Japan for China, India, Brazil and so on. Capitalists made those choices for their enterprises because relocation enabled them to extract more surpluses. They used those additional surpluses to better secure their conditions of existence but also to pay themselves higher salaries, dividends, etc. Had their enterprises been instead organized as communist, their decision-makers (their productive and unproductive workers together democratically) would have evaluated relocation differently in terms of its impacts on them and on their communities. The alternative class structures with their different sets of decision-makers would have identified, counted and weighed costs and benefits differently. They would thereby have reached different conclusions and made different decisions. The massive relocation of capitalist enterprises since the 1960s would have been far, far less of a social phenomenon had communist class structures of enterprise played larger roles in our economies.

On a more general level, inside a capitalist enterprise, its governance—the process of defining and choosing among alternative courses of action in and by the enterprise—is undemocratic. In the corporate form of capitalist enterprise—the major form in our time—the board of directors makes the basic decisions of what, how and where to produce and what to do with the surplus. Boards of directors typically include twelve to twenty individuals elected by shareholders, or more accurately, by the few major shareholders (since elections assign one vote per share and share ownership is highly concentrated). The hundreds or thousands of corporate employees—the vast majority of persons working in those enterprises—are excluded from participating in the decisions made by the board of directors. Those employees depend on and live with the consequences of board decisions but have no role in making them.

The opposite is the case in a communist enterprise. There, the combined productive and unproductive workers collectively and democratically make the decisions assigned to boards of directors in capitalist enterprises. The democracy of enterprise governance intrinsic to the communist class structure supports and reinforces democracy in the politics of the larger society. Democratizing the enterprise—in class terms, converting it from a capitalist into a communist class structure—is a way of converting formal into real political democracy.

The Varieties of Class Analyses

The basic logic of class-qua-surplus analysis entails asking the same basic question wherever and whenever production occurs in any society. If, at any site in a society, human beings are using their brains and muscles to transform objects given in nature into what they or other human beings deem useful objects, then production is happening there. The following question then applies: is a surplus being produced at that site? If the answer is yes, class analysis follows. That is, the specifics of the production and distribution of the surplus are investigated to determine how they participate in shaping the economic, political and cultural aspects of the society in which the production occurs.

We may answer the class analytical question with a simple "no." Production can occur without the production of a surplus being involved. When someone walks through the woods and carves a piece of wood into a figurine that the carver gives to a nearby child, no surplus—and hence no class process—is involved. If, however, the carving in the woods is by a wage-receiving carver with a knife and raw wood provided by an employer who receives and sells the resulting figurines, a surplus is involved. Class analysis does then apply.

So far—and in the tradition of most economic analyses—we have limited discussion to the enterprise as the social site of production. Now we can relax that limit. Production occurs elsewhere at social sites such as the household and the state, among others.

In households over the last two centuries, as capitalist class structures have spread across enterprises, capitalist class structures have NOT similarly prevailed among households. Households certainly are sites of production. Raw foods are transformed by labor, tools and equipment into finished meals; unclean rooms and clothing are transformed into neat and clean residences and outfits, and so on. Moreover, the direct performers of the labors of cooking, cleaning, etc. produce more output than they themselves consume, a household surplus. It is possible to identify the appropriator and distributor of that surplus and hence to pinpoint the class structure of the household.

Across most US history, the traditional household displayed an internal class structure quite different from the capitalist class structure of most enterprises. Inside households, no wages or market exchanges or profits existed. Rather, elaborate customs and traditions, often sanctified by religious doctrines and rituals, specified who produced the surplus, when, where and how, and likewise who received/appropriated it. Traditional rules of home and family life likewise governed to whom (to which enablers) the appropriator distributed what portions of the household surplus in order to secure the conditions of existence of the household's class structure.

In traditional US households, the adult wife produced the household surplus, often helped by children when old enough to work. The husband appropriated the surplus and distributed it to others inside and outside the household in ways likewise sanctioned by traditions and religions. In these households, the surplus-performing wives were neither the slaves of their husbands nor their wage-earning employees. The wives were not equals in a communist class structured household sharing the surplus producing but also surplus appropriating positions inside households. Rather, the typical household class structure in the US most resembled the feudal class structure of medieval Europe.[5]

It follows that modern "capitalist societies" have a much more complex and variegated class structure than economic analyses and the adjective "capitalist" have usually recognized. Their households have often been the sites of very different, non-capitalist class structures. That means that individuals in those societies were engaged with, participated in and were shaped in part by multiple, different class structures. Class-qua-surplus analysis generates a much more complex, nuanced analysis of individuals and groups than merely locating them in relation to property and power distributions or locating them solely in relation to the particular surplus organization of enterprises.

The state may also be a social site of production and class. This occurs, for example, if and when officials of the state establish—as their state function—productive organizations in which surpluses are produced, appropriated and distributed. Popular language has often depicted these organizations as "state enterprises" precisely because they do what enterprises outside the state do. Thus state enterprises have become differentiated from "private" enterprises in recognition of what we here describe as production and class occurring in the state. In the US, for example, state governments own and operate state institutions of higher learning that produce and sell college and university credits to students; the federal government sells postal services and train services to the public; local governments sell transport services; and so on. In such state institutions, surpluses get produced, appropriated, and distributed. Such institutions include productive and unproductive workers. Unlike households, the class structures at the site of the state—in state enterprises—do largely replicate the capitalist structures found in private enterprises.

Class-qua-surplus analyses of the state have some provocative implications. For example, increasing the size and productive role of state enterprises, say at the expense of private enterprises, has nothing to do with any change in the society's class structure from capitalist to something non-capitalist, say "socialist." Such an argument misunderstands what class means or defines it in terms other than the organization of the surplus. Government enterprises can be, and in modern times often have been, capitalist in their class structures just as private enterprises have been. More government and less private production merely changes the site of capitalist class structures; it has not been a displacement of capitalism for an alternative system—at least so far as class qua surplus is concerned.

Only if the state enterprises were organized to produce and distribute surpluses in a different, non-capitalist way would the shift from private to state production also entail a shift from capitalist to non-capitalist class structures of production. If state enterprises were required to operate as communist class structures, for example, such that their productive workers would also function, collectively and democratically, as appropriators and distributors of the surpluses they produced, then the shift from private to state would coincide with a shift from capitalist to communist class structures of production.

Class and Income

The class-qua-surplus analysis of income is simple and straightforward. An individual obtains income by being a performer of surplus labor (and therefore paid a wage or salary for that performance) and/or by being a recipient of distributions of the surplus. The capitalist is merely a middle-person, someone who appropriates the surplus and then distributes it. Little income accrues to the capitalist per se (indeed, corporate boards of directors typically receive little pay for their services on such boards).

Productive workers who produce surpluses get wages, the non-surplus portion of the value added by their labor. Unproductive laborers also get wages, but those are portions of the surplus appropriated by capitalists from productive laborers. Capitalists then distribute such portions to unproductive laborers for securing certain conditions of existence of capitalist production. Class-qua-surplus analysis thus differentiates productive from unproductive wages. These are different payments for very different things, either for producing surplus or else for enabling others to produce surplus. Productive and unproductive laborers may or may not recognize, be conscious of their differences. They may think of themselves as nearly identical, say by focusing on their shared experience of being paid wages. Or they may differentiate themselves by the specific tasks they do such as white collar versus blue collar.

Class-qua-surplus analysis differentiates them otherwise, according to their very different relationship to the organization of the surplus. One produces it while the other enables that production in exchange for a distributed portion of the surplus. From the standpoint of class-qua-surplus analysis, concepts such as "the wage-earning class" or "the working class" are problematic. All wage-earners or workers are not occupants of the same class position. They divide into two different class positions that often generate different perspectives on how the economy and society function, different notions of what is to be done to improve and change the economy, and different social change strategies.

Of course, if the goal is to unify productive and unproductive workers into a combined social force, then class-qua-surplus analysis would entail the need to recognize and accommodate their class differences to construct and sustain that unity. Assuming the unity because they are all wage-earners, working class, etc. would not be strategically appropriate or likely very effective. Indeed, to head off such unity, capitalists and their ideological supporters have long stressed other differences among wage-earners (age, gender, race, skills, education, ethnicity, white versus blue collar, etc.). Just as constructing unity among them has required learning to recognize and accommodate the reality of those differences, it also requires doing likewise for their class-qua-surplus differences. Otherwise, efforts to build unity risk failure.

Relatively few individuals become rich from the wage or salary payments they earn as producers of surplus. Wealth accrues chiefly to those in a position to secure large portions of distributed surpluses from the surplus appropriators. Major shareholders thus secure wealth by receiving dividend payments. Top managers secure huge salaries and pay packages that are surplus distributions. Lenders and landlords obtain interest and rentals from appropriators of the surplus who secure access to money and land—conditions of their surplus appropriation—by distributing such portions of the surpluses they appropriate. Here lies another importance of private property, since that is what allows the owners of means of production (land, money, etc.) to withhold it from production. Those owners enable access to their means of production—so that production can occur—only if they get interest and rental payments from the surpluses appropriated and distributed in capitalist enterprises.

Because a communist class-qua-surplus structure effectively democratizes the enterprise, the productive laborers appropriate and distribute the surplus they produce. Who will receive what distributed shares of the surplus and for what purposes will be decided by negotiations between the collectives of productive and unproductive workers respectively. Far less unequal distributions will result than those that flow from the undemocratic surplus distribution decisions of major shareholders and boards of directors (who tend to give themselves the largest distributions).

Class Struggles

Marx's class-qua-surplus analysis crucially differentiates class struggles. First of all, the major focus is upon class as the object of struggle, not its subject. Given the complexities of class analysis discussed above, the notion of a "class" as a social actor is very problematical. Class-qua-surplus as the object of social struggles has a quantitative and a qualitative dimension. The quantitative dimension concerns (1) the size of the surplus produced and appropriated, and (2) the sizes of the portions of the surplus distributed to its various recipients. Social groups struggle over those quantitative dimensions. For example, productive workers struggle with capitalists over the size of the wages paid to them, the length of the working day, and other aspects of the production and appropriation of the capitalist surplus. To take another example, capitalists struggle with governments over the size of the portion of the capitalist surplus delivered to governments as taxes on profits. Class struggles over the quantitative dimensions of surplus production and distribution are a more or less constant feature of class structures, slave and feudal as well as capitalist.

Sometimes, accumulated political and cultural conflicts coalesce with economic conflicts to provoke struggles over the qualitative dimensions of class qua surplus. Then the object of struggle is, for example, a capitalist class structure for enterprises versus a non-capitalist class structure. In the United States today, a social movement embraces worker cooperatives as a preferred alternative to capitalist corporations. Much of that movement does not yet grasp the relationship between such a movement and Marx's definition of the class differences between these two alternative organizations of an enterprise's production and distribution of surpluses. Nonetheless, it represents an early stage in a class struggle over the qualitative dimensions of class.

Property, Power, and Surplus Conceptualizations of Class Today

Marx's class analytical focus on organizations of the surplus still contests with formulations that stress the alternative property and power concepts predating Marx. Countless definitions of class, often attributed to Marx or Marxism and stemming from left and right perspectives, are variations of the classic property and power definitions. These prevail in most statements by politicians, journalists and academics. Rarely do they exhibit much awareness of the multiplicity of class definitions; equally rarely do they bother to justify the particular definitions they use. Capitalism continues to be conceptualized chiefly as "private enterprise plus free markets" and differentiated from "socialism" or "communism" defined as "state-regulated or state-operated enterprises plus state-regulated or state-planned distributions of resources and products." The key dimensions of class are thus property (who owns enterprises) and power (who/what distributes inputs and outputs). The internal organization of the enterprise drops out of the prevailing public discussions altogether.

However, an increasing number of new and different conceptualizations of class closer to Marx's surplus concept are also emerging. They have been stimulated by two social changes. The first was the collapse of so many of the socialist economies built upon property and power definitions of class. Perceptions that they lacked genuine democratic participation eventually deepened into a recognition that the prevailing definitions of capitalism and socialism were lacking in fundamental ways. Rethinking those definitions returned many to Marx's writings and to the discovery there of class-qua-surplus arguments of the sort discussed above.

The second social change has been the global capitalist crisis of 2008 and its aftermath. Perceptions have grown that the old centers of capitalism in western Europe, North America and Japan are increasingly dysfunctional for most residents and that they are economically divided and decreasingly democratic. Criticisms of the neoliberal versions of private and market capitalism have proliferated. Such criticisms too have worked their way back to the Marxist tradition.

One interesting result of both social changes has been the rediscovery of cooperative economic forms. Cooperatives and theories and theorists associated with them were marginalized in popular and academic discourses during the Cold War. Cooperatives and their supporters, fearing to be associated with a demonized anti-capitalism, socialism, etc., kept very low profiles. Now they are resurfacing. Cooperative worker ownership of enterprises, cooperative worker self-management, workers' self-directed enterprises and still other pointedly non-capitalist firm organizations have become major organizing principles of critiques of contemporary capitalism and the construction of non-capitalist enterprises. Writers such as Gar Alperovitz and David Schweikart, while they make little direct use of or reference to Marx's class-qua-surplus theory, have focused their critiques of capitalism on the undemocratic internal workings of capitalist firms far more than traditional socialists did.[6] Similarly, Michael A. Lebowitz's work on Cuba's turn of its economic development strategy to focus far more than ever before on worker cooperatives reflects a rethinking of socialism that is also wending its way toward class-qua-surplus theory and practice.[7]

The group gathering around the website *democracyatwork.info* has been producing a growing body of work that uses and explicitly extends Marx's theory of the surplus and the class definition based thereon. It engages both the systemic critique of global capitalism's recent development and the formulation of an alternative to capitalism focused on transforming capitalist enterprises into workers' self-directed enterprises. Its goal is to return worker cooperative enterprises—understood in Marx's surplus-focused way—to center stage in strategies of social change.[8] Marx's new and different concept of class, like so much of Marx's work, is returning to the forefront of critical thinking as yet again capitalism hits the fan.

Notes

1 Revealingly, at the same time inside the USSR applications of class analysis were likewise banished on the parallel grounds of their irrelevance to the post-class structure of Soviet society.
2 See this argument made in detail for the entirety of Soviet history, in Resnick and Wolff 2002.
3 See Piketty 2014.
4 See Resnick and Wolff 1987, Chapter 3, and Wolff and Resnick 2012, Chapter 4.
5 See the detailed class analyses of households gathered in Cassano 2009. Note that if households were reduced to sites where no production was undertaken, where only consumption occurred, class-qua-surplus analysis would not apply.
6 See Alperowitz 2011 and Schweickart 2011.
7 See Lebowitz 2014.
8 See Wolff 2012 and Mulder 2015.

References

Alperovitz, G. 2011. *America Beyond Capitalism: Reclaiming Our Wealth, Our Liberty, and Our Democracy.* 2nd edition. Takoma Park, MD and Boston, MA: Democracy Collaborative Press and Dollars and Sense.

Cassano, G. ed. 2009. *Class Struggle on the Home Front: Work, Conflict, and Exploitation in the Household.* New York: Palgrave Macmillan.

Lebowitz, M. A. 2014. *The Contradictions of Real Socialism.* New York: Monthly Review Press.

Mulder, C. 2015. *Transcending Capitalism through Cooperative Practices.* New York: Palgrave Macmillan.

Piketty, T. 2014. *Capital in the Twenty-first Century.* Cambridge, MA: Harvard University Press.

Resnick, S. A. and R. D. Wolff. 1987. *Knowledge and Class: A Marxian Critique of Political Economy.* Chicago: University of Chicago Press.

———. 2002. *Class Theory and History: Capitalism, Communism and the USSR.* New York and London: Routledge.

Schweickart, D. 2011. *After Capitalism.* 2nd edition. Lanham, MD: Rowman and Littlefield.

Wolff, R. D. 2012. *Democracy at Work: A Cure for Capitalism.* Chicago: Haymarket Books.

Wolff, R. D. and S. A. Resnick. 2012. *Contending Economic Theories: Neoclassical, Keynesian and Marxian.* Cambridge, MA: MIT Press.

PART II

Analytical and Theoretical Topics

4

EXPLOITATION

Guglielmo Carchedi

Exploitation is the appropriation by capital of a share of the value produced by the laborers. Its origin is that the capitalists, as owners of the means of production, buy the laborers' labor power and force them to work for a time longer than the time the laborers need to produce the means of their own reproduction (wage goods). The labor needed to produce those wage goods is necessary labor; the time needed for the production of the wage goods is necessary time. The extra time is surplus labor, which is an extension of necessary labor. Since under capitalism value is labor performed by the laborers for capital, the subdivision of new labor into necessary labor and surplus labor is also the subdivision between the value of labor power and surplus value. Given that value (hours of labor) can become manifest only as money quantities, necessary and surplus labor become manifest as wages and profits.

Exploitation takes place first in production. As long as the commodities are not sold, value and surplus value are only a potentiality. They become realized when, after wages have been advanced by the laborers, the commodities incorporating the surplus value, are sold.

Exploitation depends on the one hand on the value of labor power and on the other on the length of the working day and the intensity of labor.

> The value of labour power is determined by the value of the necessities of life habitually required by the average laborer. The quantity of these necessaries is known at any given epoch of a given society and can therefore be treated as a constant magnitude.
>
> *(Marx 1967, 519)*

Different types of labor power (e.g. more or less skilled) have different values because the wage goods (both objective and mental) needed for the reproduction of labor power vary with the degree of skills required.

The value of labor power is given at any particular time. However, that value changes over time due to a number of factors, principally the relation between that value and the wage. The wage is agreed upon at the beginning of the production period, when labor is hired. But the wage is paid at the end of that period. During that period, the laborers must advance their own wage. This can be considered to be the money manifestation of the value of labor power, of the quantity and quality of (objective as well as mental) wage goods considered as socially necessary for the (different categories of) laborers. When a new period begins, the capitalists might enforce a lower wage. Then wages fall below the value of labor power. But if wages are each time lower than the value of labor power and this becomes the new standard of living of the laborers, the value of labor power falls. Then, the lower wage becomes the money manifestation of the new, lower value of labor power. Thus, the value of labor power and thus the rate of exploitation are co-determined by the power relations between capital and labor (Marx 1967, 522–3).

Under certain favorable (for labor) historical circumstances, some commodities that used to belong to the category of luxury goods might be considered necessities of life (wage goods), either because of the strength of the working class or because those luxuries can be produced more cheaply. If the period of time is sufficiently long, the value of labor power is not fixed but varies due to these factors. If these factors change, those luxuries of life that had entered the category of wage goods might re-enter the category of luxuries.

If the value of labor power is given (over a short period of time), exploitation is determined by three factors: the length of the working day (the longer the working day, the greater the quantity of value and surplus value), the intensity of labor (more intense labor creates more value and surplus value), and the productivity of labor (e.g. if productivity increases, the value contained in a given quantity of wage goods decreases, and with it first the real wage and then the value of labor power).

There is no exploitation yet when the laborers sell their labor power for a wage. The sale of labor power is a condition for exploitation. It is because the laborers must sell their labor power that the capitalists can force them to work for a time longer than that required for the reproduction of their labor power. This is radically different from neo-classical economics.

In neo-classical economics there is no exploitation in a well-functioning economy. Exploitation is due to the discrepancy between wages and the value of the marginal product. Since in the long-run labor and all other factors of production are paid according to their marginal productivity, exploitation is the manifestation of a self-correcting malfunctioning of the system rather than being, as in Marx, an essential element of it. The neo-classical view implies that the economy is or tends towards equilibrium, a proposition completely at odds with textual evidence in Marx and with empirically observable reality. The neo-classical view rests on the notion of *homo oeconomicus*, an ideological construction devoid of scientific content (see Carchedi, 2011, Chapter 2, Section 6).

Other authors, from a *neo-Ricardian perspective*, deny that exploitation is the appropriation by capital of part of the value created by labor. For example, G. A. Cohen (1979) argues that labor does not create value:

> if labor creates value, past labor creates value; and if past labor creates value, then past labor determines the value of the product. But the labor theory of value says that value magnitudes are determined by currently necessary labor time.

This is a gross distortion of Marx. The analysis of the capitalist production process in *Capital* I is crystal clear. Past labor creates new value *in the past*. This is the output of the past production process. It becomes the input of the present production process. The input's value is *transferred* to the value of the commodities presently made. Current labor determines the new value created *currently*. Thus the value of commodities is given by *both* past *and* current labor and not, as in Cohen's erroneous rendition, by *either* past labor *or* present labor.

Having rejected what he thinks the labor theory of value is, Cohen proceeds to assert that labor does not create value but only use values. These have value, but value is not abstract labor. This critique is based on the amputation of an essential element of Marx's theory, the distinction between concrete and abstract labor. For Marx, every moment of labor is both concrete labor (that which creates the use values) and abstract labor (that which creates value and surplus value). Cohen, and more generally the neo-Ricardian critique, ignores abstract labor. Therefore, it does not touch upon Marx's internal, logical consistency. What we have here is not Marx's theory but a different theory, which, moreover, is undermined by the incommensurability problem. This problem is that concrete labors are by definition different and that different concrete labors, lacking a common element that makes them comparable, cannot be compared (added, subtracted, etc.). The argument that money makes commensurable different incommensurable use values disregards that money is a representation of value. If money represented use values, it could not perform the commensurability function. To perform that function, money must represent abstract labor. Only abstract labor makes comparison possible. But the neo-Ricardian theorists deny its existence.

The value form approach too departs radically from Marx's notion of exploitation. Chris Arthur is the main representative of this view, Arthur distinguishes between two forms of exploitation, in production and in distribution. Consider exploitation in production first. Since the laborer works the whole working day for capital, exploitation" comprises the whole of the working day, not just the so-called "surplus labour time" (Arthur 2004, 55). Consequently, abstract labor does not produce value, only surplus value. For Arthur, value and surplus value are "posited" by capital in the act of exploitation and not created. But "to posit" is a metaphor, a verbal *escamotage* whose function is to hide the fact that value is indeed created. If value is not created by labor but "posited" by capital, value and surplus value are created not by labor but by capital. This is contrary to the very essence of Marx's theory. In any case, simple observation contradicts this view. If exploitation "comprises the whole of the working day," why should the capitalists incessantly try to reduce the necessary labor, i.e. wages, and lengthen the surplus labor, i.e. profits?

For Arthur the quantity of the value posited by capital can be measured, it is the socially necessary exploitation time (SNET). This is the socially necessary work of control and surveillance. But this implies a theoretical inconsistency. On the one hand, value can be measured by SNET, on the other value can be measured by the socially necessary labor time (SNLT) (Arthur 2004, 205).

The notion of exploitation in distribution is equally problematic. It "arises from the discrepancy between the new wealth created and the *return* to those exploited in production" (Arthur 2001, 33, emphasis added). But if value is "posited" by capital through the SNET, i.e. if the laborers do not create value, no wealth (value) can be returned to them. It must then be returned to capital, which "posits" value. At the end of the road, it is capital that is exploited by labor.

Contrary to the above-mentioned theories, the *Marxist feminist approach* has contributed important insights into the nature of capitalism and thus of exploitation. Marlene Dixon (1977) stresses that working women are super-exploited. First, when they enter the labor force, because they are, like male laborers, expropriated of surplus labor, and differently from male laborers because they are forced into de-qualified and low paid jobs. And even in this case, they are paid less than male laborers. Second, because of "the denial by capital of compensation for labor consumed in production and reproduction of labor power" within the nuclear family.

Fraad, Resnick and Wolff (1994, Chapter 1) make a powerful argument for the existence of what they call exploitation within the household. They define exploitation in terms of the appropriation by men of the use values generated by women's labor within the household.

This extension of the notion of exploitation to the appropriation of use values within non-capitalist production relations, while welcome to clarify a specific type of economic oppression, weakens indirectly the historical specificity of capitalist exploitation by using the same term for two radically different situations.

It is undeniable that women play a pivotal role in the reproduction of their partners' labor power and thus of their own labor power. It is also undeniable that they are subjected to oppression and subjugation while performing this reproductive domestic labor. And it is equally undeniable that they should be paid for this highly socially useful, indispensable labor. However, within the household they are not directly hired by capital and thus they are not exploited in the capitalist sense. Their exploitation (i.e. oppression) is not only of a different kind, it has also a different bearing on the reproduction of the capitalist system. To mention only one example, women's domestic exploitation (oppression) bears no relevance for a theory of crisis.

Marx's critics hold that exploitation cannot be measured in terms of labor time in the case of *mental production*. But it can. The profits realized in mental production can be divided by the wages paid to the mental laborers. This is the rate of exploitation in money terms. If this ratio is applied to the hours worked by mental laborers, we get the rate of exploitation of mental labor in terms of labor hours. The labor theory of value and thus exploitation is applicable not only to the production of objective commodities but also to the production of knowledge (Carchedi 2014).

References

Arthur, C. 2001. "Value, Labour and Negativity." *Capital and Class* 73: 15–39.
———. 2004. *The New Dialectic and Marx's* Capital. Leiden: Brill.
Carchedi, G. 2011. *Behind the Crisis*, Leiden: Brill.
———. 2014. "Old Wine, New Bottles and the Internet." *Work organization, labour and globalization* 8(1).
———. Forthcoming. "Crises and Marx's Law." In G. Carchedi and M. Roberts, eds., *The World in Crisis*. London: Zero Books.
Cohen, G. A. 1979. "The Labor Theory of Value and the Concept of Exploitation." *Philosophy & Public Affairs* 8(4): 338–360.
Dixon. M. 1977. "On the Super-Exploitation of Women." https://www.marxists.org/subject/women/authors/dixon-marlene/super-exploitation.htm (accessed September 29, 2016).
Fraad, H., S. A. Resnick, and R. D. Wolff. 1994. *Bringing It All Back Home: Class, Gender, and Power in the Modern Household*. London: Pluto Press.
Marx, K. 1967. *Capital*, Volume I. New York: International Publishers.

5

LABOR AND LABOR POWER

Erik K. Olsen

The distinction between labor and labor power is a basic concept in Marxian economics and one of the central points developed by Marx in volume one of *Capital*. It is an especially fruitful theoretical insight that has profound implications for understanding the origin of surplus value, absolute and relative surplus value, relations between capital and labor, the labor process, the evolution of production technology, the role of management and supervision in the capitalist enterprises, and macroeconomic dynamics. Early in volume one of *Capital* Marx distinguishes between the *capacity* or *potential* to labor and the *actual* amount of labor performed, and introduces the term "labor power" to distinguish the former from the latter (1967a, 167, 171). The distinction is clear: labor power is the capacity or potential to produce, labor is actual production. The relation between the two is described as "labor-power in use is labor itself" (177). The difference between labor and labor power arises because worker effort is variable and they may work at a pace or intensity below their capacity.

The distinction between labor and labor power exists in all forms of production, but is especially important in capitalist production because laboring occurs in the context of the exchange of labor power for a wage. The commodity workers bring to market is labor power, which capitalist producers purchase as an input into production. Once purchased labor power belongs to the employer, and they consume it by putting the worker to work under their direction (Marx 1967a, 175–6, ch. VII). But unlike other commodities, what the capitalist purchases exists only as potential, and the quantity of labor they actually receive by consuming their purchase depends on the degree to which the worker exerts herself in production. There is then a unique aspect of the purchase and consumption of the commodity labor power: the capitalist purchases something that exists only as potential and what they ultimately receive from their purchase depends on their ability to extract labor from labor power.

Marx discovers the unique aspects of the commodity labor power in the first draft of *Capital* (*Grundrisse*, 1973, 275). There, for the first time (Nicolaus 1973, 20–1, 44–7), he identifies the distinction between labor and labor power (though he had not yet begun to use this new terminology consistently), and emphasizes the unique aspect of this commodity exchange.[1]

> If we now further inquire how the exchange between capital and labor is different in content from simple exchange (circulation), then we find that ... *In the exchange*

between capital and labor, the (sale of labor power for a wage) *is an exchange, falls entirely within ordinary circulation; the* (extraction of labor from labor power) *is a process qualitatively different from exchange, and only by* misuse could it have been called *any sort of exchange at all.* It stands directly opposite exchange; essentially different category.

The extraction of labor from labor power is a "different category" from simple commodity exchange in that it involves a contest that depends on the relative strength, planning, organization, and guile of the exchanging parties *after* the commodities have been exchanged and the purchaser seeks to consume their purchase. The difference between them is the difference between the sphere of circulation, which Marx mockingly calls "a very Eden of the innate rights of man", and the "hidden abode of production" where conflict over the labor process is a driving force (1967a, 176). Frederick Taylor (1919, 10, 49–51), who famously used scientific methods to aid management in their efforts to extract labor from labor power, refers to this struggle evocatively as a "war" on the shop floor, and hence we have the contrasting images of the sale of labor power for a wage as a simple commodity exchange followed by a war between the exchanging parties over what that commodity will actually provide.

Formal Definitions

Marx's definition of labor power has conceptual rigor but also raises several measurement issues. Labor power has two dimensions to it, duration and capacity. The duration of labor power is easily measured in units of time, and monitoring the amount of time a worker puts in on a job is routine in most workplaces. The capacities that a worker brings to the job, on the other hand, are not easily observed or measured. It is relatively uncontroversial to propose that some set of capabilities exist in a human being, but they may be context dependent, mutable, and their extent may not be fully known even to the individual who possesses them. The knowledge and skill of a worker is likely increasing over their lifetime while at the same time their physical capabilities first increase then decline after a certain age. But despite these difficulties, the idea that at a point in time a worker possesses a set of capabilities that can be exercised is valid.

Let L_p represent the quantity of labor power purchased from an individual worker. This is defined as,

$$L_p = t\alpha \qquad (1)$$

where t is the units of time and α is an index (a unitless number) of this worker's capacity to perform the function for which they are hired relative to the population. If an employer draws a large number of employees from a population of workers with varying capacities they can expect that their labor force will reflect the average capacity of the population, in which case $\alpha = 1$ for this group of workers and L_p is simply a measure of duration.

A quantity of labor has three dimensions: duration, capacity, intensity. The first two dimensions are derived from its connection to labor power but the third results from the variability of worker effort levels. Indeed the critical distinction between labor and labor power is a consequence of the fact that worker effort levels are variable, and the actual amount of labor performed depends on the degree to which the worker exerts herself and exercises her skills and capabilities during the time period. In Marx's words, "Increased intensity of labor means increased expenditure of labor in a given time" (1967a, 524). Output, and hence the firm's profit, is maximized when the worker exerts maximal effort, but there are good reasons to expect that the worker chooses their effort level using criteria different from this. Marx (1967a, 331–2; 1972, 505) stresses an unavoidable "antagonism of interests" between the employer and the wage laborer, which is rooted in the worker's inclination to choose an effort level favorable to their own well-being rather than profit maximization of the firm. The wage relation means that the level of intensity a worker exerts on the job does not benefit them directly, as it would if they were an independent commodity producer, but rather benefits the employer in the form of higher profits. It is in the interest of the employer to increase the intensity of work, but it is the worker who bears the cost of this in the form of increased toil.[2] It is the variability of worker effort level coupled with the antagonism of interests between a capitalist employer and a hired laborer that makes the extraction of labor from labor power a ubiquitous problem in capitalism.

Following Bowles (1985),[3] designate the worker's effort level as l^* (measured in labor per hour), and the total amount of labor performed L is defined as,

$$L = l^* L_p \tag{2}$$

By isolating the distinct components of effort and duration of labor time definition (2) provides insight into several important points in Marxian economics.

Consequences of the Difference between Labor and Labor Power for the Capitalist Enterprise and Economy

The first and perhaps most basic theoretical consequence of the difference between labor and labor power is Marx's theory of the origin of surplus value. Explaining the source of surplus value (and hence profit) requires explaining how a capitalist entrepreneur can purchase a set of commodities as inputs into production, pay for them at their exchange value, and yet end up with output worth more than the cost of the inputs. Equivalents are exchanged, money for labor power and nonlabor means of production, but once consumed in production these inputs produce a commodity whose exchange value exceeds its cost of production. In consuming these inputs something more must be created. Marx calls this something more "Mehrwert," literally "more worth" or "more value" in English, and explains its origin this way:

> We are, therefore, forced to the conclusion that the change originates in the use-value, as such, of the commodity, i.e., in its consumption. In order to be able to extract value from the consumption of a commodity, our friend, Moneybags, must be so lucky as to find, within the sphere of circulation, in the market, a commodity, whose use-value possesses the peculiar property of being a source of value, whose actual consumption, therefore, is itself an embodiment of labor, and, consequently, a creation of value. The possessor of money does find on the market such a special commodity in capacity for labor or labor-power.
>
> *(1967a, 167)*

The consumption of labor power is the creation value because, by definition, it is the performance of (socially necessary abstract) labor that creates value. Since the cost of labor power is not determined by the amount of labor provided, it is possible for an employer to extract a quantity of labor that exceeds the cost of the labor power they purchase. Note, however, that in order for the consumption of labor power to provide more labor than was exchanged for it in the form of money both the duration L_p and intensity of work $l*$ must be sufficient to achieve an expansion of value. Furthermore, since the creation of surplus value (and hence profits) involves these two factors, increasing the production of surplus value does also. Increasing surplus value absolutely consists of increasing L_p without a concurrent increase in the total wage payment or offsetting reduction in work intensity. Increasing surplus value relatively involves driving down the cost of wage goods, thereby driving down the cost of the real wage, or increasing $l*$ so that more labor is provided per unit labor power. All of these are avenues for increasing surplus value and profits, but only one of them, increasing the level of effort $l*$, falls within the purview of this essay.

Increasing the Intensity of Labor

Marx notes[4] that capitalists' efforts to increase productivity by increasing the intensity of labor shapes the evolution of technology itself:

> it by no means suffices for capital to take over the labor-process in the form under which it has been historically handed down, and then simply to prolong the duration of that process. The technical and social conditions of the process, and consequently the very mode of production must be revolutionized, before the productiveness of labor can be increased.
>
> *(1967a, 315)*

This is an especially provocative insight in that it implies the techniques and methods of production are not autonomous technical phenomena independent of class relations, but rather are shaped by these relations.

The central place of conflict over the pace of work in capitalist enterprises was readily apparent in early inquiries into large-scale manufacturing establishments. Ure (1835), who studied manufacturing in the north of England six decades after Arkwright established his first mill in Cromford, concludes that Arkwright's celebrated accomplishment in creating a water-powered loom is a secondary achievement to his success in subordinating millworkers to factory discipline.

> The main difficulty did not, to my apprehension, lie so much in the invention of a proper self-acting mechanism for drawing out and twisting cotton into a continuous thread, as in the distribution of the different members of the apparatus into one co-operative body, in impelling each organ with its appropriate delicacy and speed, and above all, in training human beings to renounce their desultory habits of work, and to identify themselves with the unvarying regularity of complex automation. To devise and administer a successful code of factory discipline, suited to the necessities of factory diligence, was the Herculean enterprise, the noble achievement of Arkwright. Even at the present day, when the system is perfectly organized, and its labour lightened to the utmost, it is found nearly impossible to convert persons past the age of puberty, whether drawn from rural or from handicraft occupations, into useful factory hands. After struggling for a while to conquer their listless or restive habits, they either renounce the employment spontaneously or are dismissed by overlookers on account of inattention.
>
> *(15–16; quoted by Marglin 1974, 84–5).*

Ure correctly identifies the importance of overcoming the workers' resistance to this new way of working, but he underestimates the degree to which Arkwright's technological innovation—replacing handicraft techniques with water-powered continuous-flow production—itself serves to impose factory discipline on workers and enable the employer to dictate the pace of work. No longer in control of the labor process, the millworker is regulated by the machine. This distinguishes them from craft workers who regulate the pace of labor themselves and hence are able to choose what Ure takes to be a "desultory" pace of work rather than a pace that reflects the wishes of their employer.

Several authors have developed the basic insight that capitalist employers use the technique of production itself to gain control over the production process and increase the pace of labor. Marglin (1974) studies the impact of class relations on the evolution of capitalist methods of production from pre-capitalist ones. In this development guild and handicraft production first evolve into the putting-out system, large-scale workshops subsequently emerge during the period that Marx (1967a, 336, ch. XIV) refers to as the era of "manufacture" (*manufaktur*), and finally modern capitalist production techniques arrive with mechanization and machine pacing. Marglin argues forcefully that each step in this evolution is a consequence not of technological superiority but rather is designed to substitute capitalists' for workers' control of the production process (Marglin 1974, 84). For example, he points out that large-scale workshops characteristic of the period of manufacture employed the same basic equipment and techniques used in home-based production, but removing the workers from their homes and gathering them under a single roof made it possible to directly supervise and discipline workers, something that formerly had been impossible. An important difference between a weaver working in their own home as a contractor and one selling their labor power and working in a large workshop is that the hired worker can be told the pace at which they will work. Productivity increases not because of any change in the physical production process, but rather it increases because the wage worker must take direction while the independent producer is free to work at their own pace. Only in a most perverted sense can the ability to compel a worker to work harder with the same equipment be called a technological improvement. But once factories do emerge independent producers, whose products compete with those produced by wage workers, are compelled to quicken their pace or else cease to be competitive. The market brings the products of different private laborers into competition with one another and in so doing imposes the same harsh discipline on them all.

Braverman (1974) focuses primarily on the era after the emergence of capitalism and analyzes the forces driving the transformation of the labor process from the early period of industrial capitalism to modern production. He emphasizes Taylor's influence on industrial design during this period and finds three basic principles (112–21) driving this transformation: the "dissociation of the labor process from the skills of the workers," which has come to be called 'deskilling'; the separation of the conceptual aspects production from the execution of production; and the monopolization of knowledge about the production process in the hands of management. Together this ensemble of factors have the effect of changing the production process from something utilizing knowledge, methods and techniques developed by the direct producers themselves while engaged in independent craft or guild production, and hence under their control, to a routinized process under management control and requiring basic skills that can be acquired relatively easily. Gaining control over the labor process through these methods allows the capitalist employer to dictate the tempo and the outcome of production, makes individual workers relatively easy to replace, and eliminates wage premiums associated with skilled trades.

This transformation of the labor process also has important implications for the location choice of capitalist enterprises. Gordon (1977), Peet (1987) and Olsen (2010) all emphasize the importance of conflict between workers and capitalist employers in the choice of location and the use of relocation to increase management control of the workplace. Once employers no longer find it necessary to employ skilled workers with mastery of a particular craft, who may be localized in a particular area or region, it becomes possible to locate production wherever they find low wages and a ready pool of laborers. Firms and entire industries can become freed from the geographic areas that they were historically associated with, and with that comes freedom from the customary wages, rules, work norms, culture (including labor militancy), and expectations that are part of the social environment of these districts.[5] In this way the struggle over control of the labor process—ultimately driven by the pressure to extract labor from labor power—influences the geography of capitalist production itself, and should be recognized as an important aspect of the development of neoliberal capitalism and globalization.

Deskilling, the separation of conception from execution, and the monopolization of knowledge proved to be successful ways for capitalists to gain control of the production process, and thereby increase the extraction of labor from labor power. But these methods encountered limits to their effectiveness especially with the rise of widespread unionization in the 1930s. Edwards (1979, ch. 8) argues that unions gave workers a means to bargain over conditions in the workplace and limited employer's ability to use technical means to control every aspect of the production process. He finds that "technical control" utilizing the methods advocated by Taylor and identified by Braverman, which was widespread by the 1920s, was not in itself adequate to control production in the unionized workplace, and continuing efforts by management led to the emergence of "bureaucratic control" in the period after 1945. Edwards defines bureaucratic control as:

> embedded in the social and organizational structure of the firm and is built into job categories, work rules, promotion procedures, discipline, wage scales, definitions of responsibilities, and the like ... In its most fundamental aspect, bureaucratic control institutionalized the exercise of hierarchical power within the firm. The definition and direction of work tasks, the evaluation of worker performances, and the distribution of rewards and imposition of punishments all came to depend upon established rules and procedures, elaborately and systematically laid out.
>
> *(Edwards 1979, 131)*

But bureaucratic control, as identified by Edwards, did not replace technological control, it augmented it. One of the clearest manifestations of this growth of bureaucracy was the growth of supervisory and other nonproduction employees in capitalist enterprises over the postwar period. Gordon (1981; 1990; 1996, 46–51) consistently finds, using a range of different data sources and classifications of production/nonproduction or supervisory/nonsupervisory, that the size of the bureaucracy and the intensity of supervision in U.S. enterprises increased significantly in the period after 1947 before plateauing in the early 1980s.[6]

Edwards's conception of bureaucratic control and Gordon's empirical work on supervision also illustrate an important point made by Marx in *Capital*: that the supervisory and disciplinary functions of management (as distinct from its coordinating function) are also consequences of the antagonism of interests between labor and capital. Supervision and discipline are so ingrained in the capitalist workplace that it requires a historical perspective to recognize them as consequences of antagonistic production relations. Marx notes that the same antagonism of interests found in capitalism exists "in all modes of production based on the antithesis between the laborer, as the direct producer, and the owner of the means of production" (1967c, 384). He repeatedly points out the analogy between slavery and capitalism over this point (1967a, 332; 1967b, 382–90; 1972, 355, 507), and is scathing in his criticism of other economists for failing to recognize this similarity. In his analysis of the role of management in volume three of *Capital* (1967b, 382–90) he concludes that whenever production is based on antagonism between the direct producer and the owner of the means of production (as, for example, under slavery and capitalism) supervision and discipline become necessary to overcome worker's resistance in production. In his words: "The greater this antagonism, the greater the role played by supervision" (Ibid., 384). Marx also looks forward to emerging production relations for contrast, and notes that "In a cooperative factory the antagonistic nature of the labor of supervision disappears, because the manager is paid by the laborers instead of representing capital counterposed to them" (Ibid., 387).

Marx's conclusion that supervision and discipline are necessitated by the antagonism of interests between workers and their capitalist employers, coupled with his observation that this is eliminated in producer cooperatives, implies that there should be a reduction in the ratio of supervisory to production employees in worker-owned businesses. There is empirical support for this in Greenberg (1986), who studies plywood cooperatives in the Pacific Northwest of U.S. and finds that "The (worker cooperatives) are easily able to manage production with no more than two foremen per shift, and often with only one, whereas the (conventionally-owned plants) often require six or seven" (Greenberg 1986, 45–6).

The techniques to increase the intensity of labor considered thus far are largely changes to the firm itself. But from a Marxist perspective the enterprise always exists in a social context, both influenced by this context and influencing it at the same time. For example, Marx argues that during periods of rising unemployment "the pressure of the unemployed compels those that are employed to furnish more labor" (Marx 1967a, 640). The employed are compelled to increase their effort level because the threat of unemployment becomes both increasingly credible and costly for the worker. This is a remarkable insight that makes the labor extraction problem an important aspect of Marx's theory of cyclical dynamics (Marx 1967a, 612–40).[7]

The role that unemployment plays in disciplining labor leads Kalecki (1943) to be skeptical that a capitalist economy can maintain full employment.[8] He argues that unemployment is a persistent part of capitalism because without it the employer's most important disciplinary device—the ability to fire an employee—loses its effectiveness. Unemployment is then necessary in a capitalist economy to allow employers to successfully extract labor power from labor power and maintain their class positions. This point is developed formally by Bowles (1985). In Bowles's model the effort level a worker offers depends on both the cost of job loss and the level of surveillance or supervision by the employer, with the effort level positively related to both of these. The cost of losing a job depends on the probability of finding alternative employment if terminated, and is then inversely related to the level of unemployment. Since the cost of job loss is increasing with unemployment worker effort levels should be also.[9]

The evidence of whether labor productivity is countercyclical (rising during periods of decreasing output and rising unemployment), as is predicted by Marx's approach, is mixed for the U.S. economy. During the period from 1947 to the early 1980s the conventional measure of productivity (output per worker) appears to be largely procyclical, rather than countercyclical. But in the decades since the early 1980s it appears to be largely countercyclical. This does not, in itself, call the Marxian link between unemployment and worker effort into question, but rather suggests that "labor hoarding"—the willingness of a business to keep more workers on their payroll than is necessary to meet the current demand for their product—may have been one of the rewards used by management during the era of bureaucratic control. In this interpretation the emergence of countercyclical movements in labor productivity is a symptom of the decline of bureaucratic control in the 1980s and the growth of the more ruthless forms of industrial relations characteristic of the era of neoliberalism.

Conclusion

The difference between labor and labor power is a fundamental concept in both theoretical and applied Marxian economics. Because the exchange of labor power for a wage is a ubiquitous feature of capitalism the labor extraction problem, arising out of the difference between labor and labor power, is also. The consequences of this problem are widespread and profound. Indeed the basic features of capitalist enterprises and aspects of the macroeconomy are all shaped in important ways by the firm's need to overcome this problem in order to maximize the extraction of surplus value and profitability.

The effects of the labor extraction problem have only been partially explored, and there are a number of issues that could be usefully analyzed with more attention to this issue. I want to call attention here to two issues, but this is far from an exhaustive list. Consider first the question of the relationship between social relations and the productive forces in society. Cohen (2000 [1978], 134–5) and Cohen and Kymlicka (1988) express a strictly technological determinist position with admirable clarity and argue that (i) the forces of production develop autonomously and (ii) exert a deterministic influence over the remainder of the society, which conforms to these evolving forces. In contrast, the work considered in this essay suggests that the productive forces themselves are profoundly shaped by the prevailing social relations, and the relationship between them is characterized by reciprocal influence rather than autonomy and primacy/subordination. A second issue to consider involves progressive economic policy. The difference between labor and labor power, and the consequent labor extraction problem, make it possible to recognize the exchange of labor power for a wage as a social institution that is inferior to some form of collective worker ownership. Collective ownership eliminates the antithesis between the direct producer and the owner of the means of production, and thus offers the opportunity to eliminate the antagonism of interests at the root of the labor extraction problem. Advocates for progressive social change and policy makers have paid too little attention to this advantage from this form of enterprise.

Notes

1 Engels was the first to point out that Marx did not discover the labor/labor power distinction until the late 1850s (1976, 5–6). He considered this discovery so important that he posthumously revised some of Marx's early writings to include this distinction.

2 It is, of course, true that a worker might find their work intrinsically rewarding, but it is unlikely that will continue when their employer imposes an increased pace and intensity of work and transforms the labor process itself through mechanization and minute specialization. Whatever charm the work holds for the worker is not the objective of capitalist production, which is designed and initiated to produce profits, not job satisfaction.

3 See also Gordon (1981).

4 This idea is developed in some detail in section IV of volume one of *Capital* (Marx 1967a).

5 In economic geography Vernon's (1966) influential product cycle theory emphasizes changes associated with the introduction, maturation, and standardization of products to explain changing patterns of industrial location. He remarks that manufacturing processes that "receive significant inputs from the local economy, such as skilled labor" or "rely heavily on upon external economies" are less able to relocate in pursuit of lower production costs. What Vernon, and those influenced by his work, fail to recognize is that production technology is not static; the "standardization" of production involves decoupling it from local inputs and economies in order to achieve geographic mobility, and hence requires precisely the kind of changes emphasized by Braverman and subsequent Marxian literature.

6 Goldstein (2012) finds no such plateau in the 1980s. He shows managerial employment and wages increasing consistently from 1984–2002.

7 Goodwin's (1967) formalization of Marx's theory of cyclical dynamics assumes that labor productivity grows at an exogenously given rate. It is then only a partial representation of Marx's overall theory of cyclical dynamics.

8 See also Boddy and Crotty (1975), which builds on Kalecki's analysis of the political aspects of unemployment and Marx's analysis of cyclical dynamics (including the impact of unemployment on productivity) to develop their theory of a political business cycle.

9 The same basic dynamics are present in Bowles 2005, ch. 8, though in that version of the model the cost of job loss is replaced by the value of the worker's "fallback position."

References

Boddy, R. and J. Crotty. 1975. "Class Conflict and Macro-Policy: The Political Business Cycle." *Review of Radical Political Economics* 7(1): 1–19.

Bowles, S. 1985. "The Production Process in a Competitive Economy: Walrasian, Neo-Hobbesian, and Marxian Models." *The American Economic Review* 75(1): 16–36.

Braverman, H. 1974. *Labor and Monopoly Capital*. New York and London: Monthly Review Press.

Cohen, G. A. 2000. *Karl Marx's Theory of History: A Defense* (expanded edition). Princeton, NJ: Princeton University Press.

Cohen, G. A. and W. Kymlicka. 1988. "Human Nature and Social Change in the Marxist Conception of History." *Journal of Philosophy* 85(4): 171–191.

Edwards, R. 1979. *Contested Terrain*. New York: Basic Books.

Engels, F. 1976. "Introduction." In K. Marx, *Wage-Labour and Capital, Value Price and Profit*. New York: International Publishers.

Goldstein, A. 2012. "Revenge of the Managers: Labor Cost-Cutting and the Paradoxical Resurgence of Managerialism in the Shareholder Value Era, 1984 to 2001." *American Sociological Review* 77(2): 268–294.

Goodwin, R. 1967. "A Growth Cycle." In *Socialism, Capitalism, and Economic Growth*, C. Feinstein, ed., Cambridge: Cambridge University Press.

Gordon, D. M. 1977. "Class Struggle and the Stages of American Urban Development." In *The Rise of the Sunbelt Cities*, D. C. Perry and A. J. Watkins, eds. Beverly Hills, CA: Sage Publications.

——. 1981. "Capital-Labor Conflict and the Productivity Slowdown." *The American Economic Review* 71(2): 30–35.

——. 1990. "Who Bosses Whom? The Intensity of Supervision and the Discipline of Labor." *The American Economic Review* 80(2): 28–32.

——. 1996. *Fat and Mean*. New York and London: Martin Kessler Books, The Free Press.

Greenberg, E. S. 1986. *Workplace Democracy: The Political Effects of Participation*. Ithaca and London: Cornell University Press.

Kalecki, M. 1943. "Political Aspects of Full Employment." *The Political Quarterly* 14(4): 322–330.

Marglin, S. A. 1974. "What Do Bosses Do?" *Review of Radical Political Economics* 6(2): 60–112.

Marx, K. 1967a. *Capital*, Volume 1. New York: International Publishers.

——. 1967b. *Capital*, Volume 3. New York: International Publishers.

——. 1972. *Theories of Surplus Value*, Part 3. London: Lawrence & Wishart.

——. 1973. *Grundrisse*. London and New York: Penguin Books.

Nicolaus, M. 1973. "Foreword." In K. Marx, *Grundrisse*. London and New York: New Left Books.

Olsen, E. K. 2010. "Class Conflict and Industrial Location." *Review of Radical Political Economics* 42(3): 344–352.

Peet, R. 1987. "The Geography of Class Struggle and the Relocation of United States Manufacturing Industry." In *International Capitalism and Industrial Restructuring*, R. Peet ed. Boston: Allen & Unwin.

Taylor, F. 1919. *The Principles of Scientific Management*. New York and London: Harper and Brothers Publishers.

Ure, A. 1835. *The philosophy of manufactures: or, An exposition of the scientific, moral, and commercial economy of the factory system of Great Britain*. London: Printed by William Clowes and Sons, Stamford Street.

Vernon, R. 1966. "International Investment and International Trade in the Product Cycle." *The Quarterly Journal of Economics* 80(2): 190–207.

6

ABSTRACT LABOR

Bruce Roberts

In all social circumstances, material reproduction involves the generation and disposition of particular products (specific use-values, in appropriate quantities) by means of an allocation of available resources—natural and produced physical resources, but also, crucially, human labors. Each particular use-value is produced because a portion of available social labor takes the form of the specific activities it requires. So in all times and places, each qualitatively distinct use-value is inherently associated with a qualitatively specific cluster of human laboring activities.

When Marx takes capitalist social relations as his focus, he confronts further dimensions of social reproduction. Capitalist production is production *for* exchange: outputs are consciously and intentionally produced as commodities, produced *in order to be* exchanged, and thus production and exchange are interacting phases of the broader process of social reproduction. When outputs are produced as commodities, they are no longer simply *use-*values with particular characteristics, but also "bearers" of *exchange-*value since they are exchangeable in certain proportions with all other commodities. Commodities thus have a dual nature: as use-values, each is defined by the particular and unique qualitative characteristics that make it useful in consumption or production, but as exchange-values, those characteristics are irrelevant and all that matters is their common property of exchangeability: as an exchange-value, a commodity represents simply a quantitatively specific part of aggregate social output which, via exchange, can enable the acquisition of some other equal portion of that aggregate.

Given his focus on the social (class) relations of capitalism, Marx immediately poses this dual nature of commodities in relation to a parallel "two-fold character" of the labors engaged in their production.[1] On the one hand, as noted above, the commodity as a qualitatively specific use-value is associated with the qualitatively specific labor activities needed for that use-value: "the totality of heterogeneous use-values … reflects a totality of similarly heterogeneous forms of useful labour" (Marx 1976, 132). On the other hand, as a bearer of exchange-value, each commodity is qualitatively homogeneous yet quantitatively distinct, and so "as exchange-values they represent the same homogeneous labour, i.e., labour in which the individual characteristics of the workers are obliterated" (Marx 1970, 28). In Marx's terminology, the heterogeneous labors associated with the use-value dimension of commodities are *concrete* labors, unique and distinct; the homogeneous labor associated with the exchange-value dimension is instead *abstract* labor, human labor in general, abstracted from its various concrete forms. Concrete labors as such give the commodity its use-value, but those same concrete labors simultaneously represent the abstract labor that gives the commodity its *value*: as "congealed quantities of homogenous human labor, ... as crystals of this social substance ... common to them all, [the products of labour] are values—commodity values" (Marx 1976, 128). And value is the category with which Marx then proceeds to analyze the exchange-value relations established between commodities in the market.

As initially presented at the beginning of *Capital* 1 (prior to any mention of money), value is measured in units (hours) of abstract labor-time. As a magnitude, commodity value counts only the labor-time that is "socially necessary," the time required to produce "under the conditions of production normal for a given society and with the average degree of skill and intensity of labour prevalent in that society" (Marx 1976, 129). So differences (in skill, productivity, intensity, etc.) among the individuals producing any one specific commodity by performing a particular type of labor are disposed of by averaging, i.e., counting only labors done under average social conditions. All other dimensions of difference between concrete labors, including those presented by qualitatively different skills (i.e., "complex" rather than "simple" labors) are presumably accounted for in some fashion ("obliterated") through what Marx refers to as a "reduction" process that commensurates disparate individual labors and creates the homogeneous (abstract labor) unit of account for value.[2]

In several passages Marx says more about this reduction process through which concrete labors are homogenized as abstract labor, and his repeated invocation of the role of exchange within that process has proven to be an issue where different interpretations are possible. Marx writes (with emphasis added):

> The point of departure is *not* the labour of individuals considered as social labor, but on the contrary the particular kinds of labour of private individuals, i.e., labour which proves that it is universal social labour *only* by the supersession of its original character in the *exchange process*. Universal social labour is consequently not a ready-made prerequisite but an emerging result. ... on the one hand, commodities *must enter* the exchange process as materialised universal labour-time, on the other hand, the labour-time of individuals *becomes* materialised universal labour-time *only as the result of the exchange process*.
>
> *(Marx 1970, 450)*

> [T]he specific social characteristics of [producers'] private labours *appear only within* ... exchange. In other words, the labour of the private individual manifests itself as an element of the total labour of society *only through* the relations which the act of exchange establishes between the products, and, through their mediation, between the producers.... It is *only* by being exchanged that the products of labour acquire a socially uniform objectivity as values ...
>
> *(Marx 1976, 165–6)*

> The equalization of the most different kinds of labor can be the result only of ... reducing them to their common denominator, ... human labor in the abstract, and *only exchange brings about this reduction*, opposing the products of different forms of labor with each other on the basis of equality.
>
> *(Marx, quoted in Rubin[3] 1972, 148)*

It is *only the expression of equivalence* between different sorts of commodities which brings to view the specific character of value-creating labour, by *actually reducing* the different kinds of labour embedded in the different kinds of commodity to their common quality of being human labour in general.

(Marx 1976, 142)

Clearly Marx sees a relationship between the commensuration of heterogeneous commodities as equivalents in exchange and the commensuration of heterogeneous concrete labors that occurs when commodity value is expressed in terms of abstract labor. But the nature of the relationship has been differently interpreted. Is the relationship simply one of "reflection" or "expression," or is it more complex and causal?[4] Do the results of exchange simply "manifest" or "bring to view" quantitative relations *already determined* when labors are performed *in production*, or is exchange more deeply constitutive of *how* production labors "*count*," how they are weighted, in determining values? Or are there perhaps implications for the very possibility of quantitative measurement of value in terms of labor-time?

Some have argued that abstract labor can only be expressed in terms of money, and that therefore there is no need to pursue a reduction that would allow value to be expressed in a labor-time unit of account. Pursuing the method of "systematic dialectics," members of the loose-knit group of authors favoring the "value-form" approach (e.g., Reuten (1988), Reuten and Williams (1989), Arthur (2004)) seek to break from any "substance" conception of value, even that found in Marx. Labor is viewed as the source of value, but not its substance and not its measure: "only in the market is the product constituted as a commodity and the labour that produced it constituted as abstract labor in the form of money," and so "money as it appears in the market is the only expression of value. There are no pre-market value entities (such as labour-embodied in a Ricardian conception of value...)" (Reuten 1988, 53–4). Commodity producers of course anticipate the market's outcomes and make advance calculations (an "ideal precommensuration"), but "it is only the validation of labour and its products in the market that determines where and how much value(-added) is actualized" (Reuten 1988, 57). The market attaches a money measure to the commodity and so to the labors that are expressed in its value, and no other measure of the labors performed in production is necessary or even possible: "abstract labor ... is a category of the *social* process of validation (... not a category of the individual process of production...)" (Reuten 1988, 57).[5] This rejection of the very possibility of an abstract labor unit of account separates the value-form approach from the quantitative concerns present in other interpretations of value categories.

Most interpreters do understand abstract labor as a quantitative measure, the original unit for conceiving commodity value, but not all view the concept as useful. Critics of Marx's value theory are, not surprisingly, also typically critics of abstract labor as that theory's core quantitative concept—Steedman, for example, whose treatments of heterogeneous labors are an extension of his critique of Marxian value theory in *Marx After Sraffa*. Steedman argues that Marx follows (and, for consistency, *must* follow) the practice of the classical economists in aggregating heterogeneous concrete labors into a "quantity of labor" by using weights proportional to relative wages (Steedman 1985, 560). With the real wage bundle for each type of concrete labor-power taken as data, his reading of Marx implies that a uniform rate of exploitation (e) can be present only if the value added by the labor performed by each concrete labor type is proportional to the value of each wage bundle. This allows a classical-type "wage aggregation" quantifying heterogeneous labors on a common scale as abstract labor while also determining commodity values in Steedman's sense of the term, as the abstract labor expression for the concrete labors directly and indirectly embodied in the commodity[6] (Steedman 1980, 46–8).

But Steedman considers this an empty triumph:

> The concept of 'abstract labour' … is a metaphor for the fact that each specific labour is one part of the social division of labour. Apart from [this], the metaphor and the concept can be discarded at zero cost to Marx's theory.
>
> *(Steedman 1985, 573)*

And since this "neo-Ricardian" approach regards the calculation of commodity value as simply an unnecessary step in the derivation of competitive prices and profits, abstract labor is similarly redundant, a phrase with "no genuine explanatory content"—"just a pair of words" (Steedman 1985, 568, 573). Note that in this neo-Ricardian conception of abstract labor no reference is made to the exchange process—abstract labor is derived with reference solely to technical production conditions and the information on real wages taken as data.

A different quantitative understanding of abstract labor, similar in some respects to (even though deeply different from) the neo-Ricardian understanding, is the probabilistic approach of Farjoun and Machover (1983). They reject any "deterministic" relation between value and price, denying both the need for and realism of the imposition of a uniform competitive rate of profit as a part of price theory. Instead, they treat profit rates and price-value ratios as random variables, to be theorized in terms of their characteristic distributions rather than calculated from more basic data. Still, they recognize their own need to develop an empirically measurable and testable definition of the "labor content" of commodities, one independent of prices (so as to avoid any "deterministic" relation between value and price). Thus, they explicitly pose the question of how to aggregate the value added by different types of concrete labor. Marx's approach, they note, involves distinguishing "skilled" from "simple" labor, which requires the derivation of "skill coefficients" with which to weight different labor types. But Marx, they argue, did not present a method independent of prices with which to derive these coefficients (Farjoun and Machover 1983, 216), and the authors express skepticism that there is any such method available. However, their own probabilistic approach (treating price-value ratios as random variables) does not require any such calculation: "skill coefficients are not required by our probabilistic theory, nor can we see any reasonable way of determining them"; since "all we need is a consistent way of measuring the labour-content of commodities," they instead "opt for the egalitarian solution of the problem," in which the contributions to value of different types of labor "count on an equal basis, so that … a baker-hour [counts] as equal to a tool-maker-hour" (Ibid., 221, 215). Each measured hour of concrete labor is assumed to count, like any other, as an hour of abstract labor.[7] Farjoun and Machover regard this egalitarian method of calculation as both "appealingly simple" and "most consonant with the very notion of abstract labour" (itself regarded as "one of [Marx's] deepest insights" into a commodity economy) (Ibid., 215, 213). In the end, although they reject the perceived determinism of the neo-Ricardian conception of price-value relations, they nonetheless have in common with Steedman the premise that "labour-content is determined solely in the sphere of production," independent of prices and all other exchange phenomena (Ibid., 223–4).

Still another approach to quantifying abstract labor is exemplified by McGlone and Kliman (2004), operating from within the "temporal single system interpretation" (TSSI) of value theory. McGlone and Kliman read Marx on the "two-fold character" of labor as implying that "the labour of workers in capitalist production is *immediately* abstract as well as concrete" (McGlone and Kliman 2004, 141). This means for them that concrete labors as we observe and measure them are simultaneously abstract labor-time: "*clock-hours thus measure abstract labor*" (Ibid., 149, n. 4, emphasis in the original). Thus, while observed concrete labors are heterogeneous in many ways including skill complexity, for McGlone and Kliman it is still the case that "even though complex and simple labour create different amounts of value, ... complex and simple labour are both abstract labour" (Ibid., 136).[8] By thus "disentangling" the concept of abstract labor from the issue of skill complexity, they can then proceed to the latter issue, recognizing that "the reduction of complex to simple labour presupposes the separate and prior reduction of concrete to abstract labour" (Ibid., 139). The complex/simple issue is regarded as merely a "measurement problem, specifically an index number problem," one that perhaps presents "measurement difficulties" but is "trivial and unnecessary" to the larger project of Marxian value analysis.[9] Finally, having reduced complex abstract labor to simple abstract labor, the value created by an hour of work can be specified using Marx's definition of "socially necessary" labor: "each hour of work of a simple labour-power, working at average intensity and under average technological conditions ..., is one hour of abstract, socially necessary labour" (Ibid., 140). For McGlone and Kliman, "abstract, value-creating labour [is] the exact same real work as the concrete labour that produces use-values, and ... each hour of the one is likewise an hour of the other, given only that the work is socially necessary" (Ibid., 141). Thus, in this TSSI approach, "workers' labour in the capitalistic production process is made abstract by, and is abstract within, this [production] process" (Ibid., 135–6), and "no reference to exchange of the products is needed in order to determine either the abstract labour extracted from workers or the products' values" (Ibid., 142). Indeed, allowing any role for exchange in commensurating different labors is said to make labor-value analysis "devoid of significance" (Ibid., 135).

The views so far considered represent two broadly distinct positions. On the one hand, value-form theory stresses the crucial role of the exchange process in constituting abstract labor, but denies the possibility of a quantitative reduction permitting an abstract labor unit of account (i.e., a non-monetary measure). On the other hand, in their very different ways, the neo-Ricardian, probabilistic, and TSSI approaches all affirm the need for abstract labor as a quantitative measure but see that measure as determined within the production sphere in a way that excludes the exchange process from any constitutive role. In addition, though, there is a third broad position, affirming both the quantifiable abstract labor unit of account and the role (suggested in the quotations from Marx above) of the exchange process in commensurating concrete labors as abstract labor.

The early essays of Isaak Rubin (published in English only in 1972) emphasize Marx's repeated invocations of exchange when considering the concept of abstract labor. Rubin seeks to counter the then-prevalent "physiological interpretation" of abstract labor, insisting that abstract labor is a "social phenomenon" which "we must construct" as a social and historical category, yielding, in Rubin's phrase, "a sociological theory of abstract labor" (Rubin 1972, 135). Individual acts can be seen as social when they are viewed as parts of a broader whole, and so a private and individual act of labor "is social if it is examined as part of the total mass of homogeneous social labor or, as Marx frequently said, if it is seen in terms of its 'relation to the total labor of society'" (Ibid., 141). But "the equalization of labor is carried out through the equalization of things" (Ibid., 98). It is the exchange of disparate and dissimilar *use*-values (their commensuration as equivalent *exchange*-values) that allows them to be counted as parts of the whole product. At the same time, this process also accomplishes a second commensuration: although "the concrete labor of producers is not directly social labor but *private*, ... this private labor can become social only through its equalization with all other forms of labor, through the equalization of their products" (Ibid., 98, 141). Concrete labors, the private and particular acts of separate individuals, are commensurated in and through exchange as social, general, and universal labor, simply parts of a (homogeneous) social whole expressed in terms of abstract labor.

Rubin examines Marx's texts, stressing that "in later editions of *Capital*, Marx, with increasing sharpness, underlines the idea that in a commodity economy only exchange transforms concrete into abstract labor" (Rubin 1972, 148; see also endnote 2). He also explicitly seeks to counter the criticism that this amounts to the (un-Marxian) notion that abstract labor and value originate in the exchange sphere. Rubin understands Marx's invocation of exchange in this context as referring not to a "particular phase" distinct from and subsequent to the production phase but to exchange as "a social form of the production process" which "puts its specific imprint on the entire process of reproduction" (Ibid., 149). For Rubin, value originates in production labors, not exchange relations, but the "specific imprint" of exchange is what allows production labors to be counted on a common quantitative scale:

> in a commodity economy ... the equality of two amounts of abstract labor signifies their equality as parts of total social labor—an equality that is only established by means of the equalization of the products of labor. ... equality in the form of abstract labor is established through the process of exchange.
>
> *(Rubin 1972, 155)*

However, while for Rubin abstract labor is an explicitly quantitative concept, he does not present a formal quantitative treatment.

Krause (1982) invokes Rubin in developing his own quantitative approach. Krause was the first to present a systematic formal treatment of abstract labor as an "induced relation" derived from equivalence in exchange: if two commodities are market equivalents when taken in certain physical quantities (e.g., 20 yards of linen and 1 coat), this equivalence relation "results in the 'equating' of certain quantities of the various concrete labours expended in [the] production" of those physical quantities (Krause 1982, 94–5). "Concrete labour viewed in terms of this equivalence relation is designated abstract labour" (Ibid., 10). Crucially, though, Krause understands the induced relation in terms of *value*, i.e., the abstract labor expression for the concrete labors directly and indirectly embodied in those commodities, so that relative quantities of abstract labor embodied equal relative prices, an equality he refers to as "the fundamental relation" (Ibid., 90). Krause completes his system with what he calls the "standard reduction of labour" as a way of determining the reduction coefficients (abstract labor per unit of each concrete labor performed).[10] In combination, these elements of Krause's system guarantee the equality of relative prices and relative values, since value for Krause is understood as the abstract labor expression for concrete labors directly and indirectly embodied. In effect, Krause derives coefficients to count concrete labors as abstract labor in precisely the way needed to impose a uniform capital composition, a circumstance which eliminates the price-value deviations that Marx, in *Capital* 3 and beyond, regards as the general capitalist case. To Krause, this is his system's strength (it disposes of the need to engage in price-value transformation), but it brings with it some rather un-Marx-like results.[11]

The approach to abstract labor as an induced relation is most extensively developed by Roberts (2004, 2005, 2009), who, unlike Krause, begins from the premise that relative values and (capitalist) relative prices can and do systematically diverge. Hence, when equivalence is established in the market between commodities in particular proportions (20 yards of linen and 1 coat), this equates the concrete labors "contained in" the *exchange*-values of the commodities, rather than in their (generally different) *values*. Roberts focuses on passages from *Contribution to the Critique of Political Economy* (*CCPE*), where Marx examines the measurement of "the specific character of ... labour which is embodied in exchange-value," recognizing that when "regarded as exchange-values all commodities are merely definite quantities of congealed labour-time" (Marx 1970, 29–30). But the labor-time represented in exchange-value is explicitly *social* labor, and thus "equal" despite the heterogeneity of the various concrete labors performed. How is this accomplished? Marx answers by means of an analogy; concerning exchange-value as "the specific manner in which the social character of labour is established," he says:

> the effect is the same as if the different individuals had amalgamated their labour-time and allocated different portions of the labour-time at their joint disposal to the various use-values.
>
> *(Marx 1970, 32)*

Roberts (2004, 128) points out that individuals, as such, have only *concrete* (private, particular, individual) labors to dispose of; if they were to "amalgamate" those concrete labors, the result is the aggregate vector of concrete labors available "at their joint disposal"; if they were then to "allocate different portions" of that aggregate to particular commodities, each such portion would be a quantitatively distinct but *qualitatively identical* "share" of the total, a vector of labors "of uniform quality, whose only difference, therefore, is quantity" (Marx 1970, 30).

Marx here applies to the measurement of labors an analytical metaphor that appears regularly in his later work, that of an "aliquot part" economy, in which actual magnitudes (e.g., capitals or individual commodities, as well as labors performed) are replaced by equivalents derived by the same "amalgamate and allocate" procedure. As one among many possible examples, Marx writes:

> The average profit which a capital ... yields in a certain trade it yields not as the capital employed in this particular way, nor in the proportion, therefore, in which it produces surplus-value, but as an aliquot part of the aggregate capital of the capitalist class.
>
> *(quoted in Baumol 1974, 55)*

In this and many other cases, Marx poses competitive capitalism as enforcing results identical to those derived by first amalgamating (here, taking the "aggregate capital") and then allocating qualitatively uniform portions (an "aliquot part") of appropriate magnitude. Here, each capital's profit emerges as a redistributed share of aggregate surplus-value amounting to the surplus-value that would be generated by a capital of equivalent size but average composition; similarly, in the quotation from *CCPE* above, the same logic shows that individual acts of concrete labor become commensurable (as parts of commodities' exchange values) when each is replaced by a socially average composite of concrete labors taken in the same proportions as (because it is an aliquot share of) the social aggregate of concrete labors.[12]

Roberts combines Marx's "amalgamate and allocate" metaphor and the approach to abstract labor as an induced relation, developing a formal system in which actual inputs (commodities and concrete labors) are replaced by their aliquot share counterparts (a "standard technology"). The system has a determinate solution[13] in which (1) the vectors of concrete labor hours directly and indirectly embodied in commodities under aliquot part or standard technological conditions are proportional to each other (they all have the same "average" composition as the aggregate of concrete labors) and so can be added directly to express each commodity as a magnitude of homogeneous (abstract) labor; and (2) those magnitudes (the "average labor" directly and indirectly embodied) express the commodities' exchange values (or, in fully competitive capitalism, their production prices). This is precisely the "induced relation": the equality of use-values as equivalents in exchange also expresses (induces) the equality of the labors that are "contained in" their exchange values. In effect, extending Marx's aliquot part metaphor as a means of abstracting from the technological heterogeneity of actual production conditions in one stroke creates a viable (homogeneous) labor-time unit of account and applies it to the quantification of exchange value as "average labor embodied." Moreover, viewing the commodity as it appears in competition, "as a part, both really and conceptually, of production as a whole" (Marx 1971, 112–13), highlights the intimate connection between the dual nature of commodities and the "twofold character" of the labors that produce them: the expression of each use-value as an exchangeable (aliquot) part of the social product as a whole is simultaneously the expression of the concrete labors it contains as parts of the aggregate of social (abstract) labor. So, in this reading, price formation ("gravitational" adjustment of relative prices to levels expressing exchange equivalence) is inseparable from the formation of abstract labor as the homogeneous unit of measure for the labor content of commodities. Each is an aspect of a single process that simultaneously commensurates use-values as market equivalents and commensurates concrete labors as abstract labor, so that equivalents in exchange do indeed "contain" equal amounts of abstract labor (Roberts 2005, 155–6).

Like other variants of the Marxian tradition, Roberts sees value as *generated* in production, not exchange—its substance derives from labors performed, while the act of exchange, in and of itself, creates nothing (neither use-value nor value itself originates in the act of property transfer). But "universal social labour" is not immediately quantifiable in production—it is "not a ready-made prerequisite but an emerging result" (Marx 1970, 45). Hence, Roberts argues, like Rubin ("the equalization of labor is carried out through the equalization of things"), that value is only *measurable* (concrete labors are only commensurable as abstract labor) through the combined impact of production-*and*-exchange. In this reading of Marx, labors only become "labor" through the same market equivalences that turn use-values into "income."

Overall, there are clearly unsettled issues remaining for Marxists working in this area of value theory, particularly concerning the role (if any) for the exchange process in the determining the quantitative unit of account for value: is abstract labor determined fully in production, with exchange merely providing a visible expression or manifestation of quantitative relations determined prior to it, or do the concrete labors deployed in production become quantifiable as abstract labor only in the broader context of exchange, as the consequence of exchange equivalence?

Notes

1 Indeed, Marx referred to his treatment of "the two-fold character of labour" as one of "the best points in my book [*Capital* 1]," in a letter to Engels, August 24, 1867 (Marx 1987, 402).

2 Whether abstract labor should be approached through a single reduction encompassing all aspects of heterogeneity, or through a process with analytically distinct reductions (treating complex versus simple labor as a separate problem), has been a matter of dispute among interpretations; see below. The most extensive early discussion of complex and simple labor is Hilferding [1904] 1949.

3 The quoted passage is translated from the fetishism section of the French edition of *Capital*, vol. 1 [1872]; Rubin stresses that the final part of this sentence, containing the explicit reference to exchange, was inserted by Marx into the French edition as a conscious effort to clarify the meaning of the prior German editions.

4 As Rubin (1972, 147) recognized, the issue here "borders on a very serious and profound question of the relation between production and exchange. … On one hand, value and abstract labor must already exist in the process of exchange, yet on the other hand, Marx in several passages says that abstract labor presupposes the process of exchange."

5 Fred Moseley has much in common with this "value-form" group, including the insistence on the primary importance of measuring value magnitudes in terms of money. However, Moseley differs in that he does treat labor performed as measurable at the level of "the individual process of production"—he takes as data "the quantity of the current socially necessary labor-time (L) (in units of abstract labor hours)" (Moseley 2015, 31). But he never interrogates how the different concrete labors underlying his L are aggregated—with regard to the needed "reduction coefficients," he sees it as sufficient to note that "Marx simply took the reduction coefficients as given, as did Smith and Ricardo before him" (Moseley 1997, 3), so that concrete labors "are assumed to be converted" into abstract labor (Moseley 2015, 31)—and so Moseley, like the value-form group, has little to say about abstract labor as a unit of account.

6 The coefficients expressing abstract labor per unit of each concrete labor emerge from the (normalized) eigenvector derived from the matrix showing the various concrete labors directly and indirectly embodied in the wage bundles, with $(1/1 + e)$ as the corresponding maximal eigenvalue.

7 While this "egalitarian solution" dispenses with the need for skill coefficients, it actually goes further to dispense with any need to consider any and all *other* factors beyond skill differences that might differentiate concrete labors.

8 McGlone and Kliman's idiosyncratic usage of the term abstract labor here differs from that of other commentators (and arguably from Marx as well) since abstract labor hours in their sense are apparently not homogeneous: they note, for example, that "if the abstract labour of [weavers] is, on average, more or less complex than the abstract labor of [tailors]," then "the amounts of abstract labour extracted differ across industries" (McGlone and Kliman 2004, 140–1).

9 McGlone and Kliman, like Marx, present no "rule" for the quantitative reduction of complex to simple labor (their numerical example assumes that "one can somehow determine" the coefficients), but they suggest in passing that the reduction of complex to simple labor would use information on the training time necessary for creation of skilled labor-power; this approach to determining skill coefficients is dismissed by both Steedman ("impossible to take … seriously") and Farjoun and Machover ("we know of no reasonable way of determining them") (McGlone and Kliman 2004, 138–9).

10 The coefficients emerge from the left-hand eigenvector corresponding to the maximal eigenvalue of the matrix of input-output coefficients (commodity inputs per unit of output).

11 In addition to the imposition of definitional proportionality between prices and values, there are further issues: Krause must then derive wage rates consistent with those prices and the implied rate of profit, rather than, a la Marx, treating (real) wages as data describing the reproduction of labor-powers, determined presumably by factors including the state of class struggle.

12 "[A] 'socially average' hour of work is literally a composite hour incorporating all the various concrete labors in the proportions in which each type enters into the social aggregate … [and] the value created by such an average composite hour [can be] set equal to 1 (one abstract labor hour)" to define the unit for measuring value, with the scale for value added by living labor thus set by the aggregate of clock-hours of labor performed (Roberts, 2004, 118).

13 Determinate, using Marx's typical assumption of a uniform rate of exploitation *e*; that *e* is derived without reference to or prior solution for prices, from the usual data on production conditions and real wages, given only the "rule" for exchange equivalence (equal values changing hands in *Capital 1*, profit rate uniformity in *Capital 3*, etc.). Reduction coefficients for particular concrete labors then follow, along with values and prices (Roberts 2009, Appendix). Note that "value" here is understood in the sense of the term developed by "single system" interpretations (see "Value and Price," this volume).

References

Arthur, C. 2004. *The New Dialectic and Marx's* Capital. Leiden: Brill.

Baumol, W. 1974. "The Transformation of Values: What Marx Really Meant (An Interpretation)." *Journal of Economic Literature* 12(1): 51–62.

Farjoun, E. and M. Machover. 1983. *Laws of Chaos: A Probabilistic Approach to Political Economy.* London: Verso.

Hilferding, R. [1904] 1949. *Böhm-Bawerk's Criticism of Marx.* New York: Augustus M. Kelley.

Krause, U. 1982. *Money and Abstract Labour.* London: Verso.

Marx, K [1859] 1970. *A Contribution to the Critique of Political Economy.* New York: International Publishers.

——. 1971. *Theories of Surplus-Value*, Part 3. Moscow: Progress.

——. [1865] 1976. *Capital*, vol. 1. London: Vintage.

——. [1867] 1987. *Marx & Engels Collected Works*, vol. 42. London: Lawrence & Wishart.

——. [1872] 2012. *Le Capital*, vol. 1. Paris: Hachette Livre-BNF.

McGlone, T. and A. Kliman. 2004. "The Duality of Labour." In *The New Value Controversy and the Foundations of Economics*, A. Freeman, A. Kliman, and J. Wells, eds., 135–150. Cheltenham: Edward Elgar.

Moseley, F. 1997. "Marx's Concept of Abstract Labor: Substance or Form? A Critique of the 'Value-Form' Interpretation of Marx's Theory." International Symposium on Marxian Theory, Mexico City.

——. 2015. *Money and Totality.* Leiden: Brill.

Reuten, G. 1988. "Value as Social Form." In *Value, Social Form and the State*, M. Williams, ed., 42–61. London: Macmillan.

Reuten, G. and M. Williams. 1989. *Value-form and the State.* London and New York: Routledge.

Roberts, B. 2004. "Value, Abstract Labor, and Exchange Equivalence." In *The New Value Controversy and the Foundations of Economics*, A. Freeman, A. Kliman, and J. Wells, eds., 107–134. Cheltenham: Edward Elgar.

——. 2005. "Quantifying Abstract Labor: 'Aliquot Part' Reasoning in Marx's Value Theory." In *The Capitalist State and Its Economy; Democracy in Socialism*, P. Zarembka, ed., 137–169. Bingley: Emerald Group Publishing.

——. 2009. "Ricardo : Standard Commodity :: Marx : __?__." *Review of Political Economy* 21(4): 589–619.

Rubin, I. [1923] 1972. *Essays on Marx's Theory of Value.* Detroit: Black & Red.

Steedman, I. 1977. *Marx After Sraffa.* London: New Left Books.

——. 1980. "Heterogeneous Labour and 'Classical' Theory." *Metroeconomica* 32(1): 39-50.

——. 1985. "Heterogeneous Labour and Marx's Theory." *History of Political Economy* 17(4): 551–574.

7

MONEY

Costas Lapavitsas

Introduction

For several decades following the end of the Second World War the theory of money remained a relatively neglected part of Marxist economics, particularly within Anglo-Saxon Marxism which has gradually come to play a leading role in Marxist theory. This rather warped evolution of Marxist economics merits examination as a separate topic in the history of economic thought, particularly as monetary phenomena form such an integral part of Marx's oeuvre. Since the late 1970s, however, things have begun imperceptibly to change and a corpus of work has emerged which is a recognisable theory of money, although it does not yet constitute monetary theory in the full sense of the term.

This development reflects the transformation of capitalism during the last four decades: money and finance have assumed an extraordinary place in the operations of both economy and society since the 1970s. It is not surprising that a Marxist theory of money has gradually begun to emerge in that context. However, the more recent theoretical output will not be presented and discussed in this essay, partly because it still lacks the internal coherence that would allow for such a discussion. There is no doubt, nonetheless, that the gradually emerging theory is heavily based on Marx's own work on money, found mostly in *The Contribution to Political Economy*, *The Grundrisse*, and the three volumes of *Capital*.[1] This essay aims to make a positive contribution to the emerging theory by summing up Marx's distinctive approach to money, particularly in relation to fundamental writings from other theoretical traditions. References to selected recent developments in Marxist monetary theory will be made throughout.

More specifically, there are four fundamental issues in Marx's writings on money that provide the backbone for any Marxist theory of money. First, the presence and role of money in society in general; second, the logical and historical emergence of money; third, the forms and functions of money; fourth, the transformation of money into capital. A Marxist approach to money could be usefully outlined by considering these issues in turn.

The Presence and Economic Role of Money in Society in General

Money is prevalent in capitalist society, but it also is an ancient economic form frequently encountered in non-capitalist societies. Consequently, the question of its economic role has an inherent generality, which could be captured by counter-posing two general forms of organisation of the economic life of society, both of which were alluded to by Marx in *The Grundrisse*.[2]

First, society could allocate resources consciously on the basis of centralised power; along similar lines, society could distribute the final product on the basis of aggregate principles that could include command, custom, hierarchy, and tradition. In such a society money would play a marginal role and, at the limit, it could even be excluded altogether. The range of societies that could potentially fall into this category is very large: from the palace economies of the ancient Middle East to the socialist societies of the twentieth century. Second, society could allocate resources to economic tasks as well as distributing the final product through impersonal market processes, thus severely limiting the importance of unconscious processes. The role of money in a society of this type would be of critical importance, and nowhere more than in a capitalist society in which even labour power would be allocated through market processes.[3]

Thus, for Marx, the role of money in capitalist society is to be the unconscious and automatic organiser of economic life: money is the *nexus rerun* of capitalism.[4] Specifically, money allows for the accounting of available resources; for the commensuration of claims to the final product; and for the transfer of claims from the present to the future. The circulation of money facilitates the transfer of resources to those who wish to deploy them; its hoarding is a method of storing claims on resources, but also a means of effecting radical changes in resource allocation. Consequently, money accrues enormous social power in capitalist society.

This aspect of the Marxist theory of money is reminiscent of contemporary economic, sociological and anthropological theories that treat money, first, as a contrivance recording contributions to production and thus claims on goods; second, as an accounting device to render output measurable; and third, as a technical mechanism facilitating the transfer of resources; or even as a means of connecting current expenditure of resources to future claims on output.[5] However, for Marxist monetary theory, money's ability to operate in these ways is a result of the social relations that underpin markets. Money is never a mere technical device that solves economic and social problems, but always the crystallisation of social relations in societies pivoting on exchange.

Moreover, it is clear that the organising role of money is performed in a blind, automatic and essentially "foreign" way among participants in exchange. Money negates the conscious and "relational" mode of organisation of societies based on command, custom and hierarchy. It does not need prior networks of obligations and authority to bring about the necessary allocation and distribution of resources since it draws on the impersonal mechanisms of the market. It follows that societies which integrally contain both exchange and money could potentially break out of the tyranny of traditional obligations and custom; but the price they would pay would be the loosening of social links. Heavily monetised societies inevitably veer toward the cold calculation of monetary returns.

The issue that immediately arises at this point is, if money is so vital to certain types of society, how does it emerge? Is it a spontaneous response to society's intrinsic need for an organising medium, given the absence of conscious organisation? Marx provided a remarkable answer to this question.[6] Money is certainly a spontaneous outcome of exchange interactions, but it does not emerge within human societies; rather, it emerges where different societies meet and trade with each other. In the course of history, the internal affairs of human societies, including the allocation of resources, have tended to be organised through customary, hierarchical and generally "relational" mechanisms. Commodity exchange, and thus money, arose where different societies came into contact with each other; at those points "relational" mechanisms were weak, or altogether absent. In a profound sense, for Marx, both markets and money are external to human society, though they can certainly penetrate it, disrupting existing relations and creating new ones that incorporate money.

The Logical and Historical Emergence of Money

If money has an organic presence in certain types of society, what is the logical and historical process through which it emerges? One answer to this fundamental question was famously provided by Adam Smith, who contrasted barter to monetary exchange and concluded that barter would systematically break down as commodities would not necessarily be available in the right quantities, at the right time and at the right place to allow for desired transactions to take place.[7] Money, or a commodity that everyone would find acceptable, would increase the efficiency of transacting, and thus commodity owners would benefit if they carried some money when they went to market.

Smith's argument about the greater efficiency of monetary exchange compared to barter is, of course, indisputable, but tells us nothing about the emergence of money. For, where does this marvellous commodity that all would find acceptable come from, and through what processes? The gravity of this issue began to be realised only in the 1860s and 1870s, as the Classical School declined and was followed by Neoclassicism, the German Historical School and Marxism. They offered distinctive answers, all of which continue to shape contemporary theorisations of the emergence of money. It is also notable that Marx was the first great economist to tackle the question in depth.

The Neoclassical School treats capitalism as a collection of markets. Ideally, and as is assumed by general equilibrium analysis, markets are complete and foresight by participants is full. In that context, there is no room left for money: there is no reason for commodity owners to hold some of their wealth in a barren thing that could not even be consumed.

Quite naturally, therefore, the most powerful neoclassical argument on money's emergence was provided by Austrian neoclassicals, who typically reject general equilibrium analysis, focusing instead on the actions of economic agents. Carl Menger postulated that money is the spontaneous outcome of market interactions among commodity owners.[8] Commodities have "marketability," which is the ease of being exchanged with another, and which depends on the perception by other commodity owners. "Gifted" commodity owners ascertain the superior "marketability" of one commodity and through use increase that commodity's "marketability" until it dominates all others. This is an elegant argument, but it suffers from two weaknesses: first, the assumption that commodities inherently possess "marketability" is entirely arbitrary; and second, it treats money primarily as a means of exchange, which is a narrow way to analyse such a powerful and complex economic phenomenon.

The German Historical School treats capitalism as complex social system with a wealth of institutions, but has offered no theoretical view of its functioning. Money allows exchange to proceed, but also facilitates a broad range of other economic and social phenomena. Contrary to Neoclassicism, money was not seen as a spontaneous outcome of commodity exchange. The most coherent formulation of this approach was by Knapp who provided the foundations for the current of "chartalism."[9] For Knapp, money is the creation of non-market forces and processes which are typically associated with state power. The state is the creator of money, which is essentially a legal convention that allows for the accounting of value as well as for a range of other functions.

The German Historical School has ceased to exist but its legacy on money is still very much alive.[10] It is easy to see the appeal of a theory that stresses the broad functioning of money in capitalism, and even links money's emergence to the state. Money appears to be a fundamental aspect of all human societies as well as a key institution that is inherently linked to state power. In contemporary capitalism this approach seems particularly well-suited to explaining the role of the central bank in supporting monetary circulation. Its weakness, however, is apparent: an enormously prominent economic phenomenon is accounted for through the arbitrary power of the state. It is one thing to accept that the state and money are closely linked, but quite another to claim that money is inherently a creature of the state.

The Marxist School provided its own distinctive answer to the question. Indeed, Marx proudly claimed to have solved the "riddle of money."[11] Similarly to Neoclassicism, money was treated by Marx as a spontaneous outcome of interactions among commodity owners; but, like the German Historical School, Marx also saw money as relying integrally on social institutions and possessing a broad role in both economy and society. For Marx, money is the spontaneous and necessary encapsulation of social relations among commodity owners, a claim with two distinctive aspects.

First, money is an outcome of the contradictory unity of use value and exchange value in a commodity. As use values commodities are available for specific purposes, in specific quantities, times and places; i.e., they are particular. As exchange values commodities are entirely non-specific, highly divisible and in principle available at any place and time; i.e., they are general. In the course of exchange the particular aspect of the commodity continually contradicts the general and thus exchange breaks down. Money offers a resolution of this contradiction by detaching the general from the particular aspect of the commodity. Specifically, money represents exchange value for all commodities, and in relation to money all commodities become simply use values. The contradiction is thus overcome and direct exchange is replaced by monetary exchange. Nonetheless, the contradiction is also reproduced at a higher level as monetary exchange is prone to gigantic breakdowns.[12]

Second, and as is apparent from the first, a logical argument is necessary regarding the process through which the contradiction between use value and exchange value would be overcome. Marx developed this argument in the first chapter of *Capital* in connection with the evolution of the form of value. Thus, the form of value traverses four stages: the accidental, the expanded, the general and the money stage. In the first stage two commodity owners happen to come into contact and one (the active, or relative party) leads the interaction with the other (the passive, or equivalent party). In doing so the owner of the relative assigns rudimentary direct exchangeability to the equivalent. In other words, the action of the relative makes it possible for the equivalent to buy the relative. The emergence of money occurs as rudimentary direct exchangeability is generalised through the four stages of the form of value, eventually becoming universal and attached to a single commodity. Money emerges as the universal equivalent, or the independent form of value; it is the commodity than can buy all other commodities.[13]

Marx's logical derivation of money's emergence through the development of the form of value is an astonishingly powerful performance, although his argument is not watertight. There is a lot more to be said about the role of social institutions, customs and practices among particular societies – i.e., non-economic factors – in inducing the passage of the form of value through its various stages. Marx himself explicitly recognised that the passage to the final stage necessarily rests on the physical features and the customary uses of the leading money commodity, i.e., gold.[14] Thus, money's emergence is inextricably bound with the social and physical uses of particular commodities.

To sum up, for Marxist theory, money is an encapsulation of relations among commodity owners, a necessary outgrowth of market interactions. Money plays a pivotal economic and non-economic role in societies that integrally contain commodity exchange, but it is not the creation of non-economic forces, such as the state. Rather, money is a creature of commodity exchange, generated spontaneously and necessarily by commodity interactions. Specifically, money is the independent form of value, the commodity that can buy all others, which resolves the problems of direct exchange. As such, it delivers certain key functions in commodity exchange, while assuming a variety of forms.

Functions and Forms of Money

In the analysis of the functions and forms of money, Marxist economics comes close to having a monetary theory, for that is where the relationship between money, output, and prices is explored in some depth. Money is shown to have three fundamental economic functions that are closely related to the forms taken by it; the correspondence between function and form is of paramount importance in shaping money's impact on economic activity, thus providing a framework for monetary theory.[15]

The first function of money is to measure values and thus to account for prices. In several places in his work, Marx appeared to think that money is able to measure value because the money commodity contains value.[16] Thus, if a natural unit of commodity x contained, say, 6 hours of abstract labour, while a natural unit of the money commodity (perhaps a gram or an ounce), g, contained, say, 3 hours of abstract labour, the value of x would be expressed as $x/g = 2$ (natural units of the money commodity). Money in this connection would be acting as the measure of value, or more specifically, as the "extrinsic" measure of value in contrast to the "intrinsic" measure of value, which would, of course, be hours of labour.

If, moreover, each natural unit of the money commodity was conventionally divided into standard units defined, say, by the state – i.e., coins – money would function as a unit of account (or standard of price) in addition to functioning as measure of value. Assuming that each natural unit of g was divided into, for instance, 3 conventional units, each of which was called a dollar, \$, the value of x would be expressed as its money price, $p_x = x/_{g/3} = \$6$.

Simple and powerful as this account is, it appears to hinge entirely on the existence of a money commodity with its own value. If the money in use was actually valueless, this procedure would seem unable to measure and render into price the value of a commodity.[17] The implications would be profound, affecting the entire structure of Marx's theory of value. Not surprisingly, there has been considerable difficulty within Marxist economics with contemplating a world in which there is no evident function for a money commodity, such as contemporary capitalism. But the difficulty rests on a misapprehension, partly caused by Marx.

For one thing, and contrary to what Marx appeared to think, a unit of measurement does not, in general, have to possess the same substance as the entity it intends to measure. Thus, length is measured in standard metres, but these do not correspond to a conventional object that has, say, "one metre length." Rather, the standard metre is the distance covered by light in a vacuum in 1/299792458 of a second. That is, length is measured in terms of the speed of light and time. By analogy, commodity value does not need to be measured (and rendered into price) by a thing (i.e., money) that itself contains value.

Vital in this regard is the difference between ideal and real measurement of value. The example of measuring a commodity value given above would be an ideal measurement that would happen essentially in the mind. The real measurement of commodity value, on the other hand, would happen blindly and automatically through the repeated exchange of the commodity for money, eventually resulting in a market price. The money commodity (which contains value) would measure value in practice by being regularly and customarily exchanged for other commodities, rather than through an ideal division of the value content of a commodity on paper. The monetary problem would then be how the ideal would be related to real measurement of value. The point is, however, that the putative impossibility of value measurement by a valueless money would immediately be shown as a non-problem. Valueless money would be just as able as commodity money to perform the measuring function in practice, provided that it was generally accepted among commodity owners. The difference between commodity money and valueless money in this respect would refer to the relationship between the ideal and the real measurements, that is, to the range and stability of commodity price. To discuss this issue further it is necessary to move to the next function of money.

The second function of money is to act as means of exchange, or narrow means of circulation. Once again, the function of means of exchange must occur in practice, for which there must be regular and customary exchange of commodities for money. Furthermore, money as means of exchange would be naturally characterised by velocity and quantity. Marx was fully aware of the "equation of exchange" simply rendered as $M = TP/V$, where M is the quantity of money, V the velocity of money, and TP the total price of commodities exchanged.[18] However, he rejected the Quantity Theory of Money: the total price of commodities, TP, is not determined by the quantity of money, M; rather, the determination runs in the opposite direction. M, in other words, is the quantity of money necessary in the sphere of exchange which would be spontaneously provided through a process of hoarding and dishoarding of money, given the prices of commodities and money's velocity.

The function of means of exchange has major implications for the form of money. The most intuitive form of the money commodity as means of exchange is, of course, coin struck by the state. However, as it circulates coin is inevitably worn, i.e., it loses some of its material content, thus becoming a symbol of itself. In this way a path is opened for the state to issue proper symbols of the money commodity, which are typically cheap metallic coins, or valueless paper money, both based on state fiat. It is a historical fact that in the eighteenth century, as capitalism began to take root across Europe and North America, commodity money began to give way to valueless symbols of itself. Fiat money is an integral and fundamental aspect of mature capitalism to the present day; however, its functioning has become intertwined with credit money, as is shown below.

It is immediately clear that, as means of exchange, fiat money differs from commodity money in terms of its quantity. The quantity of commodity money is determined spontaneously through hoarding and dishoarding of money, given prices and velocity; in contrast, the quantity of fiat money is determined by the state. It follows that, if the state issued fiat money in excess of the amount necessary in circulation, the total price of commodities would have to rise, assuming that velocity remained constant. Marx accepted this pure version of the Quantity Theory of Money in the case of fiat money and under exceptional conditions.[19]

However, for Marx, the pathological rise in prices as a result of increases in the quantity of fiat money would be a reflection of the malfunctioning of money as measure of value. The true difference between commodity and valueless fiat money, in other words, is not that the latter cannot measure value, which it evidently can in practice. It is, rather, that the real accounting of value (the rendering of value into market price) by valueless money depends also on the quantity of money; by this token, it could even be manipulated by the state. To put it differently, although valueless money could certainly measure value, its rendering of value into price could be volatile and even arbitrary.

The third function of money, for Marx, is to act "as money," a truly distinctive function indicating the special place held by money in society. To be more specific, Marx subdivided the "as money" function into three: hoarding, means of payment and world money, each of which conveys different aspects of "money as money." In performing this composite function money is able to stand outside the process of exchange confronting it as the independent form of value and the material crystallisation of exchange relations. Money "as money" demonstrates its exceptional economic and social power, particularly in capitalist society.

The hoarding function is fundamental to Marxist monetary theory for a variety of reasons. Hoards of money are a necessary counterpart to circulating money; they act as pools that spontaneously regulate the quantity of money in circulation keeping it in line with commodity prices and velocity. Hoards of money also reflect the withdrawal of money from circulation and hence the withdrawal of aggregate demand from capitalist markets.[20] Finally, hoards of money represent concentrations of value in the monetary form which are potentially available for lending, i.e., they are latent money capital. Hoards of money, therefore, are a foundation of the credit system and of the provision of credit in a capitalist economy.

The payment function is equally fundamental and, for Marx, defines "broad means of circulation," thus opening the path for the analysis of credit. It is worth stressing that the Marxist theory of credit rests on the prior existence of money, i.e., it is a monetary theory of credit. Marx certainly had no truck with the idea that credit is the primary relationship among exchange participants, i.e., with a credit theory of money. Rather, credit relations emerge out of monetary relations. To be specific, money as the universal equivalent splits the act of sale, $C - M$, from the act of purchase, $M - C$, where C is commodity and M is money. Money is further capable of splitting the act of sale into the advance of the commodity against a promise to pay, $C -$ IOU, followed by the settlement of the promise to pay through the payment of money, IOU $- M$, where IOU is an instrument of indebtedness (promise to pay). The most fundamental form of credit is thus trade or commercial credit which thoroughly permeates, indeed underpins capitalist circulation. On the basis of trade credit more complex relations of credit also emerge which involve the lending of money.

By opening the way for credit relations, money also creates enormous room for its own evolution. Thus, the IOUs created in the course of credit transactions could begin to circulate as money, if there was sufficient trust and confidence in the issue's ability to honour the promise to pay. This is the foundation of credit money, which is a form of money that is clearly different from both commodity and fiat money. Credit money rests on a promise to pay that must be eventually settled, while commodity money and fiat money are not promises to pay but rather the final means of payment. Furthermore, and unlike fiat money, credit money is not a symbol of commodity money, even though it is also valueless. Rather, credit money is a privately created form of money that rests on the issuer's promise to pay and is typically generated when a private debt is created.

Credit money is the dominant form of money in advanced capitalism taking primarily the form of promises to pay by (or claims on) banks. Thus, the banks that usually issue credit money tend to hold the private debts of others against their own promises to pay on their balance sheets. For this reason, credit money has a protean character and does not need to have a corporeal existence but could be a book entry or an electronic signal.

The greatest transformation of credit money in advanced capitalism occurs through its systematic linking with state-issued fiat money via the central bank. Contemporary central banks are public institutions sitting atop the credit system and providing their own promises to pay as final means of payment. The promises to pay by contemporary central banks – both banknotes and deposits held by private banks – are not convertible into anything other than themselves. The state proclaims central bank money to be inconvertible legal tender, even though such money is created by the central bank as it makes loans to others. Contemporary legal tender is fiat money backed by the power of the state, not least as the central bank normally holds state instruments of debt against it.

Control over central-bank-issued fiat money in mature capitalism is a cornerstone of the state's ability to intervene in the sphere of finance and in the economy more generally. Command by central bank over the final means of payment allows it to influence interest rates, thus impacting on credit provision across the economy. Equally, it allows the central bank to provide liquidity, i.e., the final means of payment, in enormous volumes at times of crisis, thus preventing generalised collapses of the financial system. This is the basis of monetary policy in advanced capitalism.

Finally, the third subdivision of "money as money" is "world money," arguably the most complex, least developed and most innovative aspect of Marx's analysis of money in mature capitalism. For Marx, money in the world market is distinct from money in domestic markets. The world market is an anarchic entity without a unifying set of institutions supervised by a single state authority, and nor does it contain a structured credit system, though it certainly contains vast markets of finance. The world market is also the terrain for interaction among private capitals that are based in separate countries as well as among the states of these countries. There are payments and value transfers to be made among both enterprises and states which necessitate the use of a special form of money that could transcend national borders. This is "world money" to which all countries and private capitals must have access, if they wish to participate in the world market.

Marx claimed that as "world money" money would revert to the commodity form and become gold once again.[21] This is clearly a reflection of the institutional framework at the time of his writing, i.e., of the Gold Standard during the second half of the nineteenth century. The twentieth century has presented the remarkable phenomenon of certain national monies acting as quasi-world money, at times without even being convertible into a commodity money, or indeed into anything other than themselves. World money has become a partially managed form of money created by nation states. The benefits drawn by the states that could issue quasi-world money are substantial, including the ability to pay abroad by simply creating more domestic money, i.e., partly fiat money.

Money and Capital

The issue that remains for discussion is the connection between money and capital. Needless to say, money as an economic and social phenomenon long predates the emergence of the capitalist mode of production. For money to emerge and function it is enough to have broad commodity exchange rather than capitalist production and circulation, which involve absolute property over the means of production and the hiring of labour-power for wages by the capitalist class. At the same time, money remains the fundamental form of capital and it systematically becomes capital, when capitalist social conditions are prevalent. What, then, is the connection between money and capital?

A vital distinction in this regard is that between money operating simply as money and money operating as capital. For Marx, money is the natural starting and finishing point of the circuit of productive capital, summed up as $M - C \ldots P \ldots C' - M'$, where M is money, C are commodity inputs (means of production and labour power), P is production, C' is commodity output, and M' is money revenue.[22] Thus, money is the form in which capital normally commences its circuit as well as the form to which capital must return (plus profit). Money also provides the objective of the circuit in the form of profit, i.e. the increment of

M' over M. Money, finally, is one of the means of achieving that objective since it is deployed to hire workers and purchase means of production. The characteristic motion of money as capital, therefore, could be abbreviated to M – C – M'.

In contrast, the characteristic motion of money as plain money is best presented as C – M – C', i.e. as a summation of pure market transactions (or simple exchange) discussed in sections two and three of this essay. The motivating purpose of C – M – C' is merely the acquisition of different use values, which is facilitated by money. The difference between money operating as capital and money operating as plain money is, thus, striking.

The theoretical question then becomes: how and under what conditions does money begin to operate as capital? In the *Grundrisse*, Marx explored the possibility that money as capital could emerge out of money as money through the dialectical unfolding of the latter, particularly through the ability of money to stand aloof from circulation and indeed to rise above it.[23] This is not a persuasive approach for it contradicts the experience of history, and collapses the rich diversity of social factors necessary for the emergence of capitalism into the internal unfolding of the universal equivalent. In contrast, in *Capital* Marx rightly focused on the commodity labour-power as the defining feature of capitalism since it creates value and surplus-value.[24] Money could systematically become capital only if the social and historical conditions for the emergence of capitalism were satisfied including, above all, the formation of the capitalist and the working class.

That is not to deny that money could frequently become capital even under social and historical conditions that are not capitalist. This is clearly attested when money acts as commercial capital in pre-capitalist societies. It is even more vividly seen when money acts as the means of credit across societies. Thus, trade credit and even the plain lending of money are practices that could be found in a range of non-capitalist societies. The point is though, that in capitalist society mechanisms emerge which systematically collect money, transform it into capital and make it available for purposes of capitalist accumulation. This is precisely the content of the credit (and more broadly the financial) system.[25]

In sum, within mature capitalism, the transformation of money into capital is an integral and institutional process reflecting, on the one hand, the existence of wage labour and private property over the means of production and, on the other, the creation of social mechanisms that systematically turn money into capital. Even so, money continues to function also as plain money, for instance, in the expenditure of wage income by workers. The historical complexity of money's social and economic role is actually enhanced by its systematic transformation into capital.

Notes

1 Respectively, Marx (1970; 1973; 1976; 1978; 1981).

2 See, for instance, Marx (1973, 156–74). Marx's fundamental argument has been neatly summed up by Hilferding (1981, ch. 1).

3 The conceptual distinction between the "acatallactic" and the "catallactic" organisation of society and the corresponding role of money is fundamental to the Austrian School in economics, see, for instance, Mises (1998). It is also fundamental to Polanyi's analysis of capitalism (Polanyi, Arensberg and Pearson 1957).

4 See, for instance, Marx (1976, 228).

5 See, indicatively, Davidson (1978); Hart (1986); Kocherlakota (1998).

6 See Marx (1973, 223); see also, Marx (1976, 447–8).

7 See Smith (1904, vol. 1, ch. 5).

8 See, for instance, Menger (1892).

9 See Knapp (1924).

10 This is essentially the origin of the contemporary chartalist current of Modern Monetary Theory; see, for instance, Wray (2000).

11 See Marx (1976, ch. I, sec. 3).

12 See Marx (1970, 42–6).

13 See Lapavitsas (2005).

14 See Marx (1976, 162–3).

15 See Lapavitsas (1991).

16 See, for instance, Marx (1976, 192).

17 This partly explains the appeal of the concept of the Monetary Expression of Labour Time (MELT), developed separately and independently by Duménil (1980) and Foley (1982). Strictly speaking this work is not monetary theory proper but an attempt to tackle the perennial "transformation problem." Foley has, nonetheless, made an outstanding contribution to the revival of Marxist monetary theory (see, for instance, Foley 1983). The MELT is defined as the ratio of total money value added over total current living labour per period. It could thus be interpreted as the inverse of a kind of "value of money," and be deployed to express values into money in particular instances. For this reason the concept has been extensively deployed in the recent revival of Marxist monetary theory, see, for instance, Moseley (2005). It has also been deployed in monetary work produced by post-structuralist Marxism in the tradition of Stephen Resnick, for instance, Kristjanson-Gural (2008). The point to bear in mind is that the MELT is defined *ex post facto* as the ratio of two aggregate quantities resulting from completion of the circuit of total social capital. This is a very different "value of money" from the one traditionally deployed in monetary theory which is defined *prior* to the completion of the circuit and indeed plays a decisive role in setting aggregate prices.

18 See Marx (1976, 210–20).

19 See Marx (1970, 118–19).

20 See Lapavitsas (2000).

21 See Marx (1976, 240).

22 See Marx (1978, ch. 1).

23 See Marx (1973, 250–64).

24 See Marx (1976, ch. 6).

25 Discussed in Marx (1981, pt. 5).

References

Davidson, P. 1978. *Money and the Real World*. London: MacMillan.

Duménil, G. 1980. *De la valeur aux prix de production*. Paris: Economica.

Foley, D. 1982. "The Value of Money, the Value of Labor Power, and the Marxian Transformation Problem." *Review of Radical Political Economics* 14: 37–47.

——. 1983. "On Marx's Theory of Money." *Social Concept* 1(1): 5–19.

Hart, K. 1986. "Heads or Tails? Two Sides of the Coin." *Man* 21(4): 637–656.

Hilferding, R. (1981). *Finance Capital*. London: Routledge & Kegan Paul.

Knapp, G. 1924. *The State Theory of Money*. London: MacMillan.

Kocherlakota, N. 1998. "Money is Memory." *Journal of Economic Theory* 81(2): 232–251.

Kristjanson-Gural, D. 2008. "Money is Time: A Re-interpretation." *Review of Radical Political Economics* 17(1–2): 201–211.

Lapavitsas, C. 1991. "The Theory of Credit Money: A Structural Analysis." *Science and Society* 55(3): 291–322.

——. 2000. "On Marx's Analysis of Money Hoarding in the Turnover of Capital." *Review of Political Economy* 12(2): 219–235.

——. 2005. "The Emergence of Money in Commodity Exchange, or Money as Monopolist of the Ability to Buy." *Review of Political Economy* 17(4): 549–569.

Marx, K. 1970 [1859]. *Contribution to the Critique of Political Economy*, Moscow: Progress.

———. 1973 [1939]. *Grundrisse*, London: Penguin/NLR.

———. 1976 [1867]. *Capital*, Volume 1. London: Penguin/NLR.

———. 1978 [1885]. *Capital*, Volume 2. London: Penguin/NLR.

———. 1981 [1894]. *Capital*, Volume 3. London: Penguin/NLR.

Menger, C. 1892. "On the Origin of Money." *Economic Journal* 2: 239–255.

Mises, von L. 1998. *Human Action: A Treatise on Economics*. Auburn, AL: Ludwig von Mises Institute.

Moseley, F., ed. 2005. *Marx's Theory of Money: Modern Appraisals*. London: Palgrave Macmillan.

Polanyi, K., C. Arensberg and H. Pearson, eds. 1957. *Trade and Markets in Early Empires*. Glencoe, IL: Free Press.

Smith, A. 1904 [1776]. *The Wealth of Nations*. London: Methuen & Co. Ltd.

Wray, L. R. 2000. "Modern Money." In *What is Money?*, J. Smithin, ed., 42–66. London: Routledge.

8

VALUE AND PRICE

Bruce Roberts

Marx's discussions of value and price of course draw upon prior traditions in political economy, but they also represent the application of a more general materialist approach to the analysis of social class. The fundamental class-defining categories of necessary labor and surplus labor are applicable in all social circumstances, but the presence of capitalist commodity exchange forces particularization of those categories as part of a more elaborate accounting language with which to quantify and analyze exploitation and its consequences.

At the most general level, all societies produce outputs to meet various needs, combining non-human inputs (produced means of production, along with "nature") and various human efforts. Social production in all forms thus requires some pattern of performance of labors, allocating efforts to different tasks, but it also inevitably generates some pattern of appropriation of these products, a social distribution of output (inherently a pattern of appropriation of the labors performed in producing the outputs). There is no reason to expect these patterns ever to be the same: an individual's labors, if any, are sure to be qualitatively and quantitatively different from the labors that produce the products he/she acquires through social distribution outcomes. Understanding the differences but also the connections between the patterns of labor performance and labor appropriation is a task Marxism approaches through the organizing principle of class.

Even at this general level, labors performed and products produced can and should be understood as inextricably linked. The total/gross social product stands as the counterpart to *all* inputs, human and non-human, required to produce it, but if we analytically set aside both non-human inputs to production and the corresponding portion of total product that replaces those consumed physical inputs, the remainders also represent counterparts: the social *net product* (output beyond replacement) is associated simply with the *new labors* performed in production. Economic activity is thus a process of transforming human efforts, the various active labors that people engage in, into net outputs (sometimes but not always commodity outputs) that are the physical basis for social reproduction, the source of all consumption plus net investment. Whatever its apparent complexity and unique features, every economy *is* simply an ongoing process of transforming human labors into material rewards received. Non-labor inputs to production, in particular the physical means of production, are literally no more or less than that—the *means* by which society accomplishes this transformation.

Given this substantive social identity between the social net product and the labors performed in its production, Marx understands social distribution, which partitions the net product, as implicitly accomplishing a parallel partitioning of the aggregate labor that produced it. The terms "necessary labor" and "surplus labor," universally applicable to any social situation, provide the foundation for conceptualizing class:

> Assuming some form of social production to exist ... *a distinction can always be made* between that portion of labour whose product is directly consumed individually by the producers and their families and—aside from the part which is productively consumed—that portion of labour which is invariably surplus-labour, whose product serves constantly to satisfy the general social needs no matter how this surplus-product may be divided, ...[or] who may function as representative of these social needs.
>
> *(Marx 1967, 877–8, emphasis added)*

Division of net output between reproduction of labor performers and the residual surplus product is paralleled by a conceptual partitioning of aggregate new labor between corresponding necessary and surplus portions. And while satisfaction of "social needs" might be accomplished in a collectively conscious and direct way, historically it more often occurs via various mechanisms enforcing class exploitation.

Theorizing exploitation quantitatively is most challenging in the presence of systematic commodity exchange. In capitalism, access to produced commodities is mediated by markets in which every transaction simultaneously involves acquisition of a portion of social output by the buyer and the receipt of an income by the seller. Marxism's (unique) response is to count each commodity in *two* distinct though related ways. On the one hand, "value" accounting tallies flows of "doing," of labor performed: here, the number attached to each commodity measures the human labor "put in" to create each good. On the other hand, "price" accounting (more generally, a study of "value-form") tallies payments—revenue and income flows: each commodity's price expresses not the labor it takes to produce it but the labor it "brings in" in exchange, so that the heterogeneous social product is measured by the labor-time expressed in the (money) incomes generated by each sale. Marx employs both "countings" in labor-time terms because a crucial aspect of what capitalist class relations are to Marx is summarized in the fact that these two simultaneous measures are both different and related. Each commodity "counts" both as a fraction of the total stream of income deriving from the social product and as a fraction of the total doing involved in producing that total product, and typically the two measures differ, even though the total product considered alternately as a sum of payments and a sum of doings is still the same total product.

On this basis, Marxism derives some basic statements at the heart of the class analysis of capitalism. First, not all who receive incomes engage in performance of labor; it then follows that if some who do not engage in the "doing" of labor nonetheless receive payments allowing command over produced output, it must be the case that others who do engage in "doing" are receiving less than (an equivalent for) their full "doing." In Marx's simpler language, rewards to non-doers presuppose *"surplus labor."* Applied to the situations of the aged, the disabled, the very young, the point is obvious; applied to non-doers of a different sort—recipients of capitalist incomes reflecting ownership titles rather than labor performed—the point may be less obvious but no less inescapable. Non-labor incomes and the access to goods/services they provide presuppose the existence of surplus or *unpaid* labor and the corollary existence of a surplus product (output beyond that required to reproduce the performers of labor). When actual performers of labor are neither individual nor collective participants in appropriating such surplus labor, Marx called this *exploitation*.

Second, as noted, even though the total product considered as the sum of doings is identical to the total product considered as the sum of payments, this need not be so for individual commodities. Hence, a commodity's value (the total doing or congealed social labor-time it represents as an output of production) need not be identical to its price (the social labor time it represents in an equivalent exchange, paid in the form of money by the buyer). If so, then labor-time is *redistributed* by the act of exchange—the divergence between commodity values and prices enforces transfers of labor-time, including surplus labor, such that the labor-time represented by the incomes realized from the commodity's sale diverges from the labor-time originally performed to produce those incomes. In general, then, the capitalist distribution of income (and thus also the allocation of outputs purchased with those incomes) inherently presupposes *re*distributions of labor-time. And, incorporating the prior point, the profits of capital realized from sales represent a *redistribution* of the *unpaid* surplus labor-time of labor performers.

Marx, in fact, structures *Capital* to examine a sequence of such redistributive transfers, initially from performers of wage labor to employers who capture the revenue from the sale of output, but then subsequently, via market pricing, from less to more productive firms within each industry, from one industry to another based on inter-industry competition or monopoly power, to entities external to commodity production in the form of rents or interest on debt, to governments via taxes, and so on, layer upon layer. A capitalist economy distributes rewards through multiple and overlapping market and (sometimes) non-market redistributions of the labors, the paid and especially unpaid "doings," that make all income possible. Every distribution of income, and product, is thus simultaneously a *re*distribution of labor, and value, and Marx's theory of value with its juxtapositioning of the categories of value and price is the accounting language designed to make this understanding of class visible and quantifiable in a consistent fashion.

Summarizing the basic accounting claims that emerge from within this vision: given appropriate units for commensurating labors on a common scale (see "Abstract Labor," this volume) and for translating between labor-time and money measures, it should be the case that:

1   the value of total product equals the price of total product (whether both are measured in money terms or both directly in terms of labor-time);
2   the value added by performance of current labor equals, because it is the source of, the aggregate income represented by the social net product;
3   aggregate profit in the broad sense (income available to property ownership) expresses and thus equals unpaid surplus labor in the form of surplus-value (new value created by labors performed, net of payments made to performers of the labor that created that new value).

All three accounting relations must hold simultaneously to strictly sustain the vision of a capitalist economy as a class-structured site for multiple redistributions of unpaid as well as paid labor-time. Value is created by current labor, and value and surplus-value are then "conserved" even as they are redistributed via the pricing of commodities in exchange (of course, value may also be "destroyed" in various ways, though not as a consequence simply of normal commodity exchange).

Over the years since Marx, competing perspectives have emerged concerning the categories of value and price, perspectives that offer different conclusions as to whether, and to what extent, these statements can hold consistently and simultaneously, and why and to what degree it matters if some or all of these accounting claims are deemed inconsistent, or simply dropped as unnecessary.

Influenced by the Ricardian mathematician Bortkiewicz, much 20th-century commentary interpreted commodity value in a fashion that guarantees inconsistency among the three accounting relations. This traditional approach (Bortkiewicz 1907, Sweezy 1942, Seton 1957) sees Marx, like Ricardo, conceiving commodity value as determined strictly by the technical conditions of production: the ("dead") labor contribution from consumed means of production is expressed simply by the labor technically required to produce these elements of constant capital; adding the value added by ("living") labor-time performed by current workers yields output value. Later contributors (e.g., Pasinetti 1977, Steedman 1977) in this vein formalized this approach to values as "vertically-integrated labor coefficients": $\lambda = l [I - A]^{-1}$.[1] Values (λ) formalized in this fashion as physically-embodied quantities of labor are determined simply by technology (per-unit input coefficients, A and l), without reference to the scales of the various outputs, the conditions governing distribution and exchange, or even the form of the social relations of production. On the other hand, capitalist prices—conceived initially as exchange ratios between commodities—necessarily involve reference to the distribution of income (typically via a specification of wages in some form, often a "real wage bundle" of commodities needed to reproduce labor-power b) and the criteria for exchange (typically, a competitive rate of profit (r) on advanced capital); prices expressed on any absolute scale require some further normalizing constraint. This reading of Marx thus premises two distinct ("dual") systems of equations, a "value system" in which technological conditions alone determine the quantity of labor embodied in each output, and a separate "price system" in which additional information on distribution (e.g., b) allows determination of exchange ratios; a subsequent condition typically incorporating information on output levels (x) then allows prices to be "normalized" on some absolute scale so that value and price magnitudes can be aggregated and compared.

This "neo-Ricardian" (NR) approach to value allows only limited satisfaction of the accounting relations above—limited, due to now well-known inconsistencies arising from any scale normalization for prices in the presence of a competitive rate of profit. One can impose any particular scale constraint desired (enforcing, say, equality of aggregate values and prices), but in general this does not permit the satisfaction of other conditions (for example, equality of aggregate surplus-value and profit). Only under quite specific and restrictive assumptions is it possible to fulfill simultaneously all three accounting claims above.[2] To critics of Marx, this problem of inconsistency arises because of a deeper problem: reference to value and surplus-value is unnecessary if the question is simply to specify the price structure consistent with a competitive distribution of profit. If reference to value is redundant in that project, the point of basing analysis on an accounting in labor-time terms is itself undermined—the entire Marxian conception of exploitation based on the appropriation of surplus labor is called into question.

The neo-Ricardian critique has provoked various Marxian responses, all of which, in one way or another, emphasize the crucial contribution made by Marx's focus on labor as the source and substance of value and the basis for a class accounting of the quantitative dimensions of capitalism. In particular, though, the established conception of value embedded in the NR approach has become a watershed, a dividing point from which alternative approaches diverge. Three broad forms of response can be distinguished. Some commentators have *affirmed* the conception of value as labor directly and indirectly embodied on the basis of the existing technology, while defending the central importance of "labor-content" in understanding price phenomena, irrespective of the inconsistencies among accounting relations it entails. Others have effectively *abstained*, implicitly accepting the embodied-labor conception but directing attention elsewhere, in particular to the useful-ness of a labor-time accounting of the distribution of value-added. Still others have *rejected* that embodied-labor conception of value as a misspecification, instead affirming a different reading of value that allows consistency among the basic accounting claims.

Affirmation of the embodied-labor conception entails acceptance that not all the basic accounting relations can hold simultaneously. Some (e.g., Shaikh 1984) see this not as a problem but rather as a structural consequence of the "relative autonomy" of circulation; if the equality of aggregate price and aggregate value ("direct price") is presumed, the implied general deviation between total surplus-value and total profit then simply reflects the flow of the portion of surplus-value used for capitalist consumption out of the "circuit of capital" and into the "circuit of revenue" (with price-value deviations at the commodity level showing up in the aggregate as transfers between circuits that entail a loss or gain of actual profit relative to surplus-value ("direct profit")) (Shaikh 1984, 54). But these deviations are argued to be empirically rather small; referring to various studies, his own and by others, Shaikh (1998) finds that both cross-sectional and temporal variations in prices are highly correlated with variations in value. Value, he argues, thus dominates in the empirical *regulation* of prices, even though labor-embodied value does not consistently satisfy all of the theoretical accounting relationships implied by Marx's vision of capitalism.

The empirical correlation between embodied-labor values and prices is a central focus for others who reject the neo-Ricardian critique of value analysis for different reasons. Farjoun and Machover (F&M) (1983) argue for a probabilistic approach to price theory. Capitalist competition does indeed direct capital flows to areas of high profitability, but, they argue, this generates a tendency not for a uniform "equilibrium" rate of profit on capital but rather "a sort of dynamic equilibrium with a characteristic distribution of the various rates of profit among various capitals" (F&M 1983, 18). Dispensing with any requirement for profit rate unifor-mity allows a probabilistic approach not merely to rates of profit but also to prices as random variables. F&M pose unit price as a random variable related statistically rather than deter-ministically to the "labor content" of a commodity (effectively identical to the labor-embodied measure of value), justifying this with several Marx-like arguments about the centrality of labor. Empirical studies in this tradition (Cockshott and Cottrell 1998, Frohlich 2013) offer evidence that labor-content functions as a significant "attractor" for market price, to a degree roughly equivalent to that of production prices calculated in the neo-Ricardian manner. F&M argue that their approach leads to a "reconstructed" Marxian theory in which "labour value ... must play a central role"—the apparent "contradictions" in accounting "arise not from the notion of labour-value, but from the insistence on a deterministic connection between labour-values and individual ... prices and rates of profit" (F&M 1983, 137). Even without a fully consistent accounting structure of the sort that "deterministic" readings of capitalist competition seek, one can apparently still assert that "through the disorderly mechanism of competition, [the *surplus* labour-content created in the economy] is carved up among all firms, and appears as their profits" (F&M 1983, 156). Accounting consistency is downplayed as an overly "deterministic" concern, with empirical statistical applicability elevated instead as the crucial criterion.

A second, different response to the NR critique also stresses empirical applicability, although correspondence to macroeconomic data rather than statistical correlation is its focus. What is now commonly labeled the "new solution" (NS) approach[3] (Duménil 1980, Foley 1982, Mohun 2004) basically accepts the labor-embodied conception of value, but directs attention away from relationships involving commodity value (individual or aggregate), towards those describing distributive shares.

The broad Marxian vision described above presumes that current performance of labor creates the new value available to distribute as social net income; simultaneously, the portions of that income representing profit (initially encompassing all forms of property income) derive simply from redistributions of the surplus-value created by the surplus labor of current workers. The NS approach is able on its own terms to sustain the simultaneous validity and consistency of these two relationships; what allows this to hold, despite the NR critique, is a reinterpretation of surplus-value as the result of *unpaid* labor, where it is the payment for labor power, rather than the labor embodied in the commodities effectively received through that payment, that defines paid labor as distinct from unpaid labor.

To clarify: the new solution envisions two distinct accounting realms, a value realm with labor-time as the unit of account, and the price realm where magnitudes are measured in terms of money prices (**P**). These realms are of course related, and translation from one realm to the other occurs via a scalar often referred to as the "monetary expression of labor-time" or "melt" (m). The value created by new living labor can be expressed in money (as "money value added" MVA) by multiplying total hours worked (**lx**) by m. MVA is by definition the result of measuring the social net product with prices (**Py**), which in turn expresses the social net income available to distribute. Jointly, these imply that the melt (m) is = **Py/lx**, a definition quite deliberately based on the social *net* product (**y**).

Of course, MVA breaks down into total wages plus total profit. And total value added by new labor (whether measured in labor-time or money) breaks down into necessary labor plus surplus labor. The new solution then interprets surplus labor as unpaid labor in the following sense: total surplus labor expressed in money (and therefore also monetary surplus-value) equals MVA minus the money paid for total labor-power, i.e., (**mlx** – **Pblx**). Since this is definitionally identical to (**Py** – **Pblx**), which is total money profit, it follows that total profit equals total surplus-value, whether measured in money (**mlx** – **Pblx**) or directly as unpaid labor-time (**lx** –[**Pb**/m]**lx**), where **Pb**/m here expresses the "paid portion" of an hour worked (the money wage translated via m into a measure of paid labor; **Pb**/m is the wage share of social net income).[4]

This is clearly a break from the prior general understanding of surplus-value, since aggregate surplus-value in this NS sense is conceived without direct reference to the values of individual commodities. Yet, since commodity value is still conceived in the traditional labor-embodied sense, the neo-Ricardian critique is not fully bypassed: the monetary value of the *net* product ($m\lambda$**y**), derived from the new value added by living labor (**lx**), is indeed equal to the price of that net product (**Py**), but the monetary value of the total *gross* product ($m\lambda$**x**) does *not* equal its price (**Px**).

New solution authors regard this as a minor defect, outweighed by the perceived gain in terms of empirical applicability. While the new solution approach to "price" originated in response to the theoretical issues involving prices in the presence of a uniform competitive profit rate, the same accounting is possible using any actual market price vector; it is this that then allows, for example, the NS use of NIPA data in Marxian macro analyses. Still, that gain comes with a corresponding loss in terms of consistency with the broader Marxian theoretical vision. NS accounting is not capable of fully sustaining the vision of capitalist pricing as multi-layered redistribution of labor-time, since inequality of $m\lambda$**x** and **Px** means that aggregate labor-time accounting does not "add up": aggregate value is not conserved in the process of its redistribution via the pricing structure. As a result, while NS analyses regularly employ the concept of *surplus*-value or unpaid labor as the aggregate from which profit and the various distributions out of profit derive, they make very little use of the concept of *value* as distinct from price, either at the level of the individual commodity or at the aggregate level.

A third broad strain of thinking instead focuses on the importance of theoretical consistency, arguing for an understanding of value and price categories that does fully sustain the coherence of the overarching vision of capitalist pricing as the redistribution of paid and unpaid labor-time. While there is considerable diversity among the particular perspectives here, a common element is rejection of the traditional labor-embodied (λ) conception of commodity value in favor of an alternative specification with a broader set of determinants. These various approaches exemplify what some have called a "single system" (SS) interpretation, as distinct from the analytically separate or "dual" systems of value and price equations of the neo-Ricardian critique (and most other Marxian responses).

The original "single-system" interpretation was presented by Wolff, Roberts, and Callari (1982) and later developed by Roberts (1988, 1997, 2009).[5] WRC deliberately set aside the question of the melt and monetary measures of value and price variables, focusing instead on prices ($\mathbf{p}$) and profits ($\boldsymbol{\pi}$) denominated on the same scale and in the same labor-time units as value and surplus-value (given a value for the melt, however specified, monetary measures of prices and values are necessarily proportional to these labor-time measures, and have the same relationships). Market exchange values are understood to fluctuate around a "center of gravity" reflecting what Marx calls "equivalent" exchange. "Gravitation" here comes about because non-equivalent exchange will provoke adjustments to supply and demand, and the resulting price adjustments keep exchange ratios "tethered to" or centered on equivalence. Crucially, though, the particular "equivalence rule" defining that center of gravity depends on particular social circumstances—equivalent exchange is *not* simply assumed for all cases to require equal quantities of value changing hands (for example, behaviors that create pressures for a competitively equalized rate of profit enforce a social equivalence rule *different* from the value-equivalent exchange of *Capital 1*).

In general (i.e., outside the special circumstances assumed in *Capital 1*), the labor-time attached to a commodity in (equivalent) exchange will differ from the direct and indirect labor-time required to reproduce it, and the crucial premise of the SS interpretation is that, when this is the social norm, it is the former rather than the latter that carries forward as the *relevant* measure of its labor-content. This premise can be seen as broadening the narrower insight at the core of the New Solution. The NS accounts for *variable* capital and its contribution to output value by what is *paid* for labor-power (wages), yet constant capital is still tallied by the labor technically embodied in (required for the reproduction of) the commodities that are later productively consumed; in contrast, single-system approaches treat *both* constant and variable capital symmetrically: each is counted by the labor represented by the *payment* made for them, thus tallying them as the *paid labor* portions of output value.

So the SS specification of value ($\mathbf{v}$) for a competitive capitalist economy à la *Capital 3* differs from λ-value: $\mathbf{v} = \mathbf{pA} + \mathbf{l}$, or $\mathbf{v} = \mathbf{pK} + \mathbf{s}$ (where $\mathbf{K} = \mathbf{A} + \mathbf{bl}$, the commodity measure of consumed constant and variable capital). Clearly $\mathbf{v}$ and $\mathbf{p}$ are approached differently from the separate and distinct "dual" systems of the prior literature. Note, though, that despite appearances, this equation for value does *not* imply, as some have argued, that a solution for $\mathbf{v}$ in this sense requires a prior solution for $\mathbf{p}$ (see Roberts 2009); moreover, expressed here as production price $\mathbf{p}$ in terms of labor-time, price is not some causally different and dimensionally incommensurable measure alien to Marxian value accounting, but is instead, as Marx claimed, "a definite social manner of expressing the amount of labour bestowed upon an object" (Marx 1967, 82) (see Roberts 1997, where it is shown that production prices

p represent the labor embodied in commodities under technologically average or 'standard' conditions).

In this SS approach, values (**v**) and prices (**p**) emerge from the same social process of competitive production and exchange, and each reflects the *same* set of basic determining factors (technologies-in-use, output scales, distribution arrangements, along with the social form of equivalence relations—the ruling form of market competition). Values and prices are different as measures—one approaches the commodity as a consequence of the various flows of "doing" necessary to reproduce it, the other as a source of income representing a claim on a portion of the aggregate of "doings" expressed in the social product—but each can be derived from the same data without explicit reference to the other (Roberts 1997; 2009).

Given the **v**-value conception, all three accounting requirements noted above for the Marxian vision are satisfied here (**vx = px**, **lx = py**, and **sx = (l – pb)x = πx**); the conceptual consistency of these measures allows the labor-time accounts to "add up" in a way that conserves value as commodities move through (equivalent) exchange. In this SS approach, the presence of consistent measures of value and price makes visible the *class* nature of capitalist distribution: every distribution of commodities and revenue is inherently a *re*distribution of the (paid and unpaid) labor-time "bestowed upon" those commodities.

A similar but ultimately quite distinct "temporal" viewpoint emphasizes the time dimension in its SS analysis. The "temporal single system interpretation" (TSSI) (Kliman and McGlone 1988, Freeman 1995, Kliman 2007) is concerned not with the structure of equivalent exchange at each moment in time but with the effects produced by changes in the basic data that play out through time. Rather than seeking the particular set of price (and value) relationships which, when applied to *both* inputs and outputs, allows for exchange equivalence at each moment, TSSI takes the set of input prices as given (valuation of constant and variable capital inputs is treated as historical data, given when they enter the production process), and the resulting output prices are then derived based on current circumstances, with no expectation that the latter will match the former. The rate of profit derived is then differently specified from the rest of the literature, with its denominator expressing "capital" based on the *prior* (rather than current) period's reproduction cost of capital.

TSSI thus explicitly rejects the simultaneous treatment of price determination that is central to the SS approach in WRC and most other treatments of profitability as well (although, for any *given* set of basic data, the TSS solutions for values and prices follow a temporal sequence that converges to the same results as the WRC approach). TSS authors claim a greater textual fidelity to Marx, and see their treatment as validated by its congruence with other aspects of Marx's work, especially the Marxian tendency of the rate of profit to fall: TSSI authors vigorously argue that only the TSS approach to value and price guarantees the dynamic relation between rising labor productivity and falling profitability said to be Marx's signature conclusion (Kliman 2007).

A further variant of the SS approach, the "Macro-Monetary" interpretation (Moseley 2015), stresses Marx's focus on *money*-capital advances (the advance of "M" which becomes M′ after capitalist production and sale) and argues that constant and variable capital must be taken as predetermined money magnitudes already expressed in terms of the relevant set of prices. The stress on monetary measurement in this approach is so all-encompassing that the measure and even the concept of value as a quantity of social labor-time largely disappears as an analytical category, with only the quantity of current living labor employed (**l**) remaining as a significant variable not derived in or taken to be pre-given in money terms.

Despite specific differences, SS interpretations share a common premise that the constant capital component of output value is impacted by the payment conditions through which input commodities are acquired, rather than exclusively determined by technical production conditions. It is this different fundamental understanding of labor-time in relation to value that allows each of these single-system approaches to argue that Marx's vision stands up to the charge of accounting inconsistency.

And more generally, *all* the various responses to the NR critique understand and deploy the basic Marxian categories of value and price to defend the fundamental class-analytic insight concerning exploitation and its consequences: unpaid surplus labor performed by workers is appropriated as surplus-value and then redistributed complexly though market and non-market mechanisms.

Notes

1 Space constraints allow formal consideration of only the simplest case: single-product industries (no joint production) with no fixed capital, uniform turnover, and homogeneous labor, all of which is taken to be productive labor. A customary notation then defines: $\mathbf{A}$, matrix of commodity input coefficients per-unit output; $\mathbf{l}$, vector of labor input coefficients per-unit output; $\mathbf{b}$, vector of commodities required to reproduce each unit of labor-power (the "real wage bundle"); $\mathbf{x}$, vector of gross outputs produced; $\mathbf{y} = [\mathbf{I} - \mathbf{A}]\mathbf{x}$, vector of net outputs; λ, vector of commodity "value" understood as vertically-integrated labor coefficients; $\mathbf{P}$, vector of prices expressed in "money"; $\mathbf{p}$, vector of prices expressed in labor-time.

2 See Steedman (1977), or the summary in Roberts (1997); Steedman also enumerates other circumstances that critics see as sources of inconsistency or indeterminacy in Marxian categories (e.g., fixed capital, joint production, heterogeneous labor, etc.).

3 The label "new *solution*" reflects the initial focus on rebutting the NR critique of Marx's volume 3 "solution" for a general rate of profit via "transformation" of values into production prices, but the approach is more accurately understood as a Marxian accounting framework applicable whatever the form of pricing.

4 NS authors typically take as distributional data not a real-wage bundle $\mathbf{b}$ but a scalar wage in money terms w, where w takes the place of $\mathbf{Pb}$ in the above relations.

5 Recent extensions of this general approach include Kristjanson-Gural (2009) and Olsen (2013); Roberts (1997) takes up the more complex cases not formally considered here.

References

Bortkiewicz, L. von. 1952 [1907]. "Value and Price in the Marxian System." *International Economic Papers* 2: 5–60.

Cockshott, W. P. and A. Cottrell. 1998. "Does Marx Need to Transform?" In *Marxian Economics: A Reappraisal*, Vol. 2, R. Bellofiore, ed., 70–85. New York: St. Martin's Press.

Duménil, G. 1980. *De la valeur aux prix de production*. Paris: Economica.

Farjoun, E. and M. Machover. 1983. *Laws of Chaos: A Probabalistic Approach to Political Economy*. London: Verso.

Foley, D. 1982. "The Value of Money, the Value of Labor Power, and the Marxian Transformation Problem." *Review of Radical Political Economics* 14(2): 37–47.

Freeman, A. 1995. "The Psychopathology of Walrasian Marxism." In *Marx and Non-equilibrium Economics*, A. Freeman and G. Carchedi, eds., 1–28. Cheltenham: Edward Elgar.

Frohlich, N. 2013. "Labour Values, Prices of Production and the Missing Equalization of Profit Rates: Evidence from the German Economy." *Cambridge Journal of Economics* 37(5): 1107–1126.

Kliman, A. 2007. *Reclaiming Marx's 'Capital': A Refutation of the Myth of Inconsistency*. Lanham, MD: Lexington Books.

Kliman, A. and T. McGlone. 1988. "The Transformation Non-problem and the Non-transformation Problem." *Capital and Class* 35: 56–83.

Kristjanson-Gural, D. 2009. "Post-Structural Logic in Marx's Theory of Value." *Rethinking Marxism* 21(1): 14–33.

Marx, K. 1967 [1865]. *Capital*, Volume 3. New York: International Publishers.

Mohun, S. 2004. "The Labour Theory of Value as Foundation for Empirical Investigations." *Metroeconomica* 55(1): 75–95.

Moseley, F. 2015. *Money and Totality*. Leiden: Brill.

Olsen, E. 2013. "Similarities and Differences in Two Marxian Theories of Value." Working paper, University of Missouri, Kansas City.

Pasinetti, L. 1977. *Lectures on the Theory of Production*. New York: Columbia University Press.

Roberts, B. 1988. "What is Profit?" *Rethinking Marxism* 1(1): 136–151.

———. 1997. "Embodied Labor and Competitive Prices: A Physical Quantities Approach." *Cambridge Journal of Economics* 21(4): 483–502.

———. 2009. "Ricardo : Standard Commodity :: Marx : ___?___." *Review of Political Economy* 21(4): 589–619.

Seton, F. 1957. "The Transformation Problem." *Review of Economic Studies* 24(3): 149–160.

Shaikh, A. 1984. "The Transformation from Marx to Sraffa." In *Ricardo, Marx, Sraffa: The Langston Memorial Volume*, E. Mandel and A. Freeman, eds., 43–84. London: Verso.

———. 1998. "The Empirical Strength of the Labour Theory of Value." In *Marxian Economics: A Reappraisal*, Vol. 2, R. Bellofiore, ed., 225–251. New York: St. Martin's Press.

Steedman, I. 1977. *Marx After Sraffa*. London: New Left Books.

Sweezy, P. 1970 [1942]. *The Theory of Capitalist Development*. New York: Monthly Review Press.

Wolff, R., B. Roberts, and A. Callari. 1982. "Marx's (not Ricardo's) 'Transformation Problem': A Radical Reconceptualization." *History of Political Economy* 14(4): 564–582.

9

CAPITAL

Fred Moseley

The title of Marx's book is of course *Capital*, thereby clearly indicating the centrality of the concept of *capital* in his theory of capitalism. As Marx put it in the *Grundrisse*, the first draft of *Capital*:

> The exact development of the *concept of capital* [is] necessary, since it [is] the *fundamental concept of modern economics*, just as capital itself, whose abstract, reflected image [is] its concept …, [is] the *foundation of bourgeois society*.
>
> *(Marx 1973, 331; brackets in the text; emphasis added, including in the quotations below)*

In *Capital*, Marx introduced his central concept of capital in Part 2 of Volume 1, which is entitled "The Transformation of *Money* into *Capital*." Chapter 4 is entitled "The General Formula for *Capital*," and this general formula for capital is expressed symbolically as:

$$M - C - M' \qquad \text{where } M' = M + \Delta M$$

in which M represents the initial money capital advanced to purchase means of production and labor-power, C represents commodities, M' represents the final money capital recovered through the sale of commodities, and ΔM represents the increment of money that emerges at the end of this circuit.

In this chapter, Marx defined capital as follows:

> *More money* is finally withdrawn from circulation than was thrown into it in the beginning. The cotton originally bought for £100 is for example resold at £100 + £10, i.e. £110. The complete form of the process is therefore $M - C - M'$, where $M' = M + \Delta M$, i.e. the original sum [of money] advanced plus an increment [of money]. This increment or excess over the original value I call '*surplus-value*'. The value originally advanced, therefore, not only remains intact while in circulation, but increases its magnitude, adds to itself a surplus-value, or is valorized. And this movement converts it [money] into *capital*.
>
> *(Marx 1977, 251–2)*

We can also see from this passage that surplus-value is defined as ΔM, or the increment of money that emerges at the end of the circuit of capital. The production of surplus-value is the main purpose of capitalist production, and is the most important phenomenon to be explained by Marx's theory of capitalism (or any theory of capitalism). The general formula for capital focuses Marx's theory on this all-important question: where does the total ΔM come from and what determines its magnitude?[1] Most of Volume 1 is devoted to this central question for the economy as a whole.[2]

Later in the chapter, Marx summarized his definition of capital as follows:

> Value therefore now becomes value in process, *money in process*, and, as such, *capital*. It comes out of circulation, enters into it again, preserves and multiplies itself within circulation, emerges from it with an increased size, and starts the same cycle again and again. *M–M'*, *'money which begets money'*, such is the description of *capital* given by its first interpreters, the Mercantilists.
>
> *(Marx 1977, 256)*

In an earlier draft of this chapter in the *Manuscript of 1861–63*, Marx began with a very clear question, which is the main question that his theory is about: *How does money become capital?* (Marx and Engels 1988, 9).[3] And a few pages later, Marx presented a summary definition of capital similar to the passages from Volume 1 quoted above:

> Value (*money*) resulting from circulation as adequate exchange value (money), taking on an independent form [money], but entering again into circulation, preserving and multiplying (increasing) itself in and through it, is *capital*.
>
> *(Marx and Engels 1988, 12)*

Thus we can see that Marx's concept of capital is clearly and emphatically defined in terms of *money*, as *money that becomes more money*. This definition of capital in terms of money obviously also applies to the two components into which the initial money capital advanced is divided—*constant capital* (the initial money capital advanced to purchase means of production) and *variable capital* (the initial money capital advanced to purchase labor-power) (Marx 1977, Chapter 8). Algebraically, $M = C + V$, all in terms of money (C here refers to constant capital, not to commodities as in the general formula for capital). Marx's distinction between constant capital and variable capital follows from the labor theory of value, according to which variable capital (or rather the labor-power purchased with variable capital) is the only source of surplus-value and constant capital only transfers its previously existing money value to the price of the product.

One common interpretation of Volume 1 is that it is only about labor-times, not money or prices; i.e. that all the variables in Volume 1 refer to quantities of labor-time, and none refer to quantities of money (e.g. Sweezy 1942; Steedman 1977). According to this "two-system" interpretation, Marx's theory deals with money and prices only in the "price system" of Volume 3. Volume 1 is about the "value system," which is only in terms of labor-times. Even the quantities of *capital* (constant capital and variable capital) in Volume 1 are often interpreted to refer to quantities of labor-time (embodied in the means of production and means of subsistence, respectively).[4] I argue that this view is a fundamental misinterpretation of Volume 1, which loses sight of the essential *monetary nature of capital* in capitalist production and in Marx's theory of capitalism. Money is derived in the very first chapter of Volume 1 (Section 3), as the *necessary form of appearance of the substance of value which is abstract labor*, and from then on Marx's theory is about quantities of money that represent and thus are determined by quantities of labor-time. The core concept of Volume 1 is *capital*, and capital is defined in terms of *money* (that becomes more money). The main purpose of Volume 1 is to explain how this all-important *monetary* phenomenon happens.

Chapters 5 and 6 of Volume 1 argue that ΔM is possible (as a regular general feature of a capitalist economy) only because capitalists are able to purchase labor-power on the market and then utilize labor-power in production where it produces more value than it cost. Thus the existence of wage-labor is a necessary condition for ΔM and thus for capital.

Marx's concept of capital is sometimes interpreted as a "social relation." In my view, this formulation is only partially correct. I would say that capital is the process through which money becomes more money, but this process *requires* wage-labor, i.e. requires the social relation between capital and wage-labor as a precondition. So it is more correct to say that capital *requires* the social relation of wage-labor than to say that capital *is* a social relation. The latter formulation does not explicitly include the defining characteristic of Marx's concept of capital—money becoming more money.

Marx's concept of capital in term of money is very different from the concept of capital in neoclassical economics, which is defined in terms of heterogeneous *physical goods* – as quantities of material inputs to production (machinery, equipment, buildings, raw materials, etc.); i.e. "capital *goods*" in a production function. Thus capital is analyzed in neoclassical economics as "goods used to produce other goods," rather than as "money used to make more money," and this neoclassical concept is a general concept that applies to all types of modes of production, not just capitalism.

Marx criticized a similar general and physical concept of capital of the classical economists:

> Capital would be only a new name for a thing as old as the human race, since every form of labour, including the least developed ... presupposes that the product of prior labour is used as means for direct, living labour.
>
> *(Marx 1973, 258)*

Marx's concept of capital, on the other hand (money that becomes more money) is a historically specific concept that applies primarily to the capitalist mode of production.[5]

In Chapter 48 of Volume 3, Marx criticized a similar ahistorical concept of capital in the form of the "Trinity Formula": capital–profit, land–rent, and labor–wages. In this formula, capital is combined with land and labor, which are inputs to production in all modes of production. In this way, capital is itself implicitly assumed to also be an input in all modes of production, and in effect to be "only another name" for the physical means of production. Marx's main point in this chapter is that capital is *not* "only another name" for means of production; means of production function as a particular form of capital only within the capitalist mode of production.

> The first striking thing about this formula is that alongside capital, this form of an element of production belonging to a specific mode of production, ... we have ranked without further ado: the earth, on the one hand, and labour on the other, two elements of the actual labour process, which are material elements of any process of production and have nothing to do with its social form.
>
> *(Marx 1981, 955)*

The neoclassical definition of capital in terms of heterogeneous "capital goods" is the reason why neoclassical economics has an insoluble "aggregation problem"—because different kinds of physical means of production cannot be meaningfully added together. Marx's concept of capital, on the other hand, which is defined in terms of money, has no such "aggregation problem" because money is homogeneous by nature; there is no problem adding up quantities of money capital across the economy.

The Circuit of Money Capital

The expanded form of Marx's circuit of money capital is the well-known symbolic expression:

$$M - C...P...C' - (M + \Delta M)$$

where P stands for the production process. We can see that this circuit of money capital takes place in *two "spheres,"* the sphere of *circulation* and the sphere of *production*, and consists of *three phases*, consecutive in time: (1) the *advance* of money capital to purchase means of production and labor-power in the sphere of circulation, prior to production; (2) the *production* process, in the sphere of production; and (3) the *recovery* of money capital through the sale of commodities after production, again in the sphere of circulation.

Marx's circuit of money capital refers to a *real process*, which takes place in *real historical time*. Capital exists first in the form of money advanced in the sphere of circulation, then in the form of labor-power and the prices of the means of production in the sphere of production, then in the form of the prices of the commodities produced at the end of the production process, and then finally back again in the form of money recovered, including more money than was originally advanced at the beginning of this real historical process. This process takes a certain amount of real time from the advance of money capital to the recovery of more money capital. This temporal aspect of the circuit of money capital was succinctly expressed by Marx as follows: "*Before* production, we had a capital of *£500. After* production is over, we have a capital of *£500* plus a value increment of *£100*" (Marx 1981, 124).[6] Marx's theory explains how this all-important monetary phenomenon happens.[7]

The temporal nature of Marx's circuit of money capital is also evidenced by his emphasis throughout *Capital* on the distinction between the "old value" (or "transferred value") and the "new value" components of the price of commodities. "Old value" exists at the beginning of the circuit of money capital in the form of the initial money constant capital advanced to purchase means of production and in the form of the price of these means of production. This previously existing "old value" is transferred to the price of the output. The quantity of "transferred value" is determined by and cannot exceed the quantity of "old value" that previously existed. On the other hand, "new value" did not previously exist at the beginning of the circuit, but is instead the result of the labor in the current period, and hence is also the source of surplus-value or ΔM that is produced in the current period, and that comes to exist at the end of this period.

This circuit of money capital is the logical framework of Marx's theory of surplus-value. The main goal of Marx's theory is to explain how this all-important phenomenon happens, i.e. how the initial M at the beginning of this circuit becomes $(M + \Delta M)$ at the end of the circuit. The "general formula for capital" is *not* just incidentally introduced in Chapter 4 of Volume 1, and then plays no essential role in the rest of the theory; instead the expanded circuit of money capital is the general logical framework of Marx's theory for the rest of the three volumes of *Capital*. Marx summarized this general framework as follows in the Introduction to Part 7 of Volume 1:

> The transformation of a sum of *money* into means of production and labor-power is the first phase of the movement undergone by the quantum of value which is going to function as *capital*. It takes place in the sphere of circulation. The second phase of the movement, the process of production, is complete as soon as the means of production have been converted into commodities whose value exceeds that of their component parts, and therefore contains the value originally advanced plus a surplus-value. These commodities must then be thrown back into the sphere of circulation. They must be sold, their value must be realized in *money*, this money must be transformed once again into *capital*, and so on, again and again. This cycle, in which the same phases are continually gone through in succession, forms the *circulation of capital*.
>
> *(Marx 1977, 709)*

Keynes once referred to Marx's M – C – M' circuit of capital as a "pregnant observation," and Keynes agreed with Marx that the goal of entrepreneurs in not "more product," but is instead "more money," and that a theory of an "entrepreneurial economy" should be in terms of money variables, not real variables. (Keynes 1979, 81–82) Keynes did not seem to realize that Marx's M – C – M' circuit of capital is not just a "pregnant observation," but is instead the general logical framework for Marx's theory. Unfortunately, Keynes did not adopt Marx's M – C – M' framework in his own theory, but instead adopted an aggregate supply / aggregate demand framework, in which aggregate supply is essentially aggregate costs, and costs include the prevailing rate of profit as a given. Thus ΔM is hidden as a "cost" in Keynes' theory (as it is in most of neoclassical economics) and is transformed in effect into a part of M (!), and no explanation of the all-important ΔM is provided by Keynes' theory.

Marx's logical framework of the circuit of money capital is also very different from the framework of Sraffa's theory, which consists instead of a input-output matrix in terms of *physical* quantities, a labor input vector, and a system of simultaneous equations based on these physical givens.[8] Sraffa's logical framework is a 'circular flow of production,' by which is meant the circular flow of physical inputs and outputs, not the circular flow of quantities of money capital. Sraffa's theory is not a theory of ΔM, but is instead a theory of relative prices that reproduce the initial given physical quantities of inputs.

In order to compare Sraffa's logical framework with Marx's framework, Sraffa's framework could be represented symbolically as follows:

$$Q...P...C'$$

where Q stands for the physical quantities of means of production and quantities of labor.[9] The most striking difference of Sraffa's framework (compared to the Marx's framework) is the *complete absence of money*, especially the absence of ΔM, the most important characteristic of capitalist economies. The first phase of the circulation of money capital in the sphere of circulation—the advance of money capital to purchase means of production and labor-power—is missing altogether. It is as if no money capital is advanced in capitalism to purchase means of production and labor-power. But this is not the case; money capital is advanced in capitalism, in definite quantities, and this quantity of money capital advanced must be recovered before there can be any surplus-value (ΔM).

A controversial issue with respect to the circuit of money capital in Volume 1 is the following: do the quantities of money capital in Volume 1 refer in principle to the *actual* quantities of money constant capital and variable capital in circulation in the real capitalist economy that are equal (in long-run equilibrium) to the prices of production of the means of production and means of subsistence, *or* do the quantities of money capital in Volume 1 refer to *hypothetical* quantities of money capital that are proportional to the labor-values of the means of production and means of subsistence. The prevailing interpretation (e.g. Sweezy 1942; Steedman 1977) is the latter—that the quantities of money capital in Volume 1 are *hypothetical* quantities, which later have to be transformed from hypothetical quantities to actual quantities in Volume 3. I (and others) argue, to the contrary, that the quantities of money capital in Volume 1 are *actual* quantities of money capital from the beginning, i.e. from Chapter 4 of Volume 1.[10] The "general formula for capital" refers in principle to the actual quantities of money capital in circulation in the real capitalist economy. As Marx expressed this point at the end of Chapter 4:

> M – C – M ' is in fact therefore the general formula for capital, in the form in which it *appears directly* in the sphere of circulation.
>
> *(Marx 1977, 257)*[11]

The main purpose of Volume 1 is to explain how the actual M at the beginning of the circuit of capital becomes the actual M+ΔM at the end of the circuit, not to explain a hypothetical ΔM that would later have to be transformed into the actual ΔM in Volume 3.

These different interpretations of the circuit of money capital have important implications for the alleged "transformation problem" in Marx's theory. According to the "hypothetical" interpretation of the circuit of money capital in Volume 1, there is a transformation problem in Marx's theory because these hypothetical quantities must be transformed into actual quantities in Volume 3. And the critics argue that Marx "failed" to make this necessary transformation from hypothetical value quantities to actual price quantities in Volume 3. On the other hand, according to the "actual" interpretation of the circuit of money capital in Volume 1, *there is no transformation problem in Marx's theory*, because the quantities of money capital in Volume 1 are actual quantities from the beginning, and the same actual quantities of money capital (disaggregated) are taken as given in the Volume 3 theory of the division of the actual total ΔM (determined in Volume 1) into individual parts (equal rates of profit across industries, commercial profit, interest, and rent). For an extensive elaboration of this "actual" interpretation of the circuit of money capital, see Moseley 2016.[12]

A related issue is the following: in the case of technological change and the consequent change in the prices of means of production that occurs between the time constant capital is advanced to purchase means of production and the time the output produced with those means of production is sold (especially for long-lasting machines and equipment), should the magnitude of constant capital that is taken as given at the beginning of the circuit of money capital in the theory of ΔM be the *historical* costs of the means of production at which the means of production were purchased in the past *or* should the magnitude of constant capital be the *current* costs of the means of production at which the same means of production could be purchased today? The prevailing interpretation is that in this case constant capital should be valued at the current cost of the means of production. On the other hand, the Temporal Single System Interpretation of Marx's theory (commonly abbreviated as TSSI) argues that the constant capital should be valued at the original historical cost of the means of production (Kliman 2007). In my view, the textual evidence is strongly in favor of the current cost interpretation. For example, one of the counter-acting factors to the fall in the rate of profit discussed in Chapter 14 of Volume 3 of *Capital* is the "cheapening of the elements of constant capital":

> And related to what has been said is the *devaluation of existing capital* (i.e. of its material elements) that goes hand in hand with the development of industry. This too is a factor that steadily operates to stay the fall in the rate of profit …
>
> *(Marx 1981, 343)*

This controversy has important implications for the falling rate of profit, since it affects the magnitude of the constant capital in the denominator of the rate of profit, but it has no implications for the transformation problem, since the transformation problem has to do with the determination of prices of production in a given period of time, with technology and the prices of the means of production constant for this period.

All in all, I would say that the concept of capital and the circuit of money capital as the logical framework of Marx's theory have not received the attention they deserve in the Marxian literature, although this seems to be changing of late for the better, with emphasis on the monetary nature of Marx's concept of capital by Harvey (2010) and Heinrich (2004). It is hoped that going forward that Marxist economists will pay more attention to these key concepts in Marx's theory. The title of the book is *Capital*!

Notes

1 Marx once stated that, in the circuit of money capital, ΔM is the "most striking" feature which "leaps to the eye" (Marx 1978, 140).

2 Marx clarified in Chapter 5 (1977, 266–7) that his theory of ΔM in Volume 1 is in terms of industrial capital and abstracts from commercial capital and interest-bearing capital. In Volume 3, Marx further explained commercial profit and interest as deductions from the total surplus-value produced by industrial capital. These particular forms of capital provide further evidence that Marx's concept of capital is defined in terms of money since these particular forms are clearly quantities of money. These particular forms of capital are not discussed further here.

3 This volume contains a fairly complete draft of Parts 2–4 of Volume 1 of *Capital*, which has been published only in recent decades. It is very interesting and an important bridge between the first draft of Marx's theory of surplus-value in the *Grundrisse* and the final published versions. It was published for the first time in German in 1976 in the *Marx/Engels Gesamtausgabe* (MEGA), Volume II/3.1, and in English in 1988 in the *Collected Works of Marx and Engels*, Volume 30. After this draft of Volume 1, the rest of the *Manuscript of 1861–3* is mainly the *Theories of Surplus-Value* which had been previously published, but also contains a first draft of parts of Volume 3.

4 Unfortunately, Wolff, Roberts, and Callari, in their interpretation of the transformation problem (1984), adopt this interpretation of capital in terms of labor-time not only in Volume 1, but also in Volume 3.

5 The process $M \rightarrow M + \Delta M$ can also apply to non-capitalist economies (slavery, putting out system, usury), but Marx's theory is about this process in a capitalist economy.

6 See also Marx 1977, 256 and Marx and Engels 1988, vol. 33, 79 for similar "before … after" statements.

7 The "temporal single system" interpretation (TSSI) of Marx's theory (e.g. Kliman) has also emphasized that Marx's theory of the circuit of capital is in terms of real historical time.

8 Sraffa also assumed a given *wage share* of total income, which ranges from 0 to 1, and thus clearly is not the same as Marx's money variable capital advanced to purchase labor-power.

9 Sraffa (1960) has described this process as "the production of commodities by means of commodities" (the title of his book). However, it would be more accurate to describe it as "the production of commodities by means of *physical quantities*," since the physical inputs are not treated as commodities with already existing prices. Mark Blaug commented that Sraffa's theory should be called "The Production of Commodities Without Anything Called Capital" (Blaug 1996, 134); this would also be a good title.

10 Mattick 1991, Ramos 1998, and Moseley 2016.

11 Marx expressed the same point in the earlier draft of this chapter in the *Manuscript of 1861–3* mentioned above: "We first examined the form of capital in which it is directly presented or *appears for observation*" (Marx 1988, 20).

12 Wolff, Roberts, and Callari (1984) also argue there is no transformation problem in Marx's theory (i.e. that constant capital and variable capital are the same in the determination of both values and prices of production). However, as mentioned above, they define constant capital and variable as quantities of labor-time rather than as quantities of money.

References

Blaug, M. 1996. *Economic Theory in Retrospect*. Cambridge: Cambridge University Press.

Harvey, D. 2010. *A Companion Guide to Marx's* Capital. London: Verso.

Heinrich, M. 2004. *An Introduction to the Three Volumes of Karl Marx's* Capital. Translated by A. Locascio. New York: Monthly Review Press.

Keynes, J. M. 1979. *The Collected Writings of John Maynard Keynes*, Volume 29, *The General Theory and After: A Supplement*, edited by D. Moggridge. London: Macmillan.

Kliman, A. 2007. *Reclaiming Marx's Capital: A Refutation of the Myth of Inconsistency*. Lanham, MD: Lexington Books.

Marx, K. 1973. *Grundrisse*. London: Penguin Books.

——. 1977. *Capital*, Volume 1. New York: Random House.

——. 1978. *Capital*, Volume 2. New York: Random House.

——. 1981. *Capital*, Volume 3. New York: Random House.

Marx, K. and F. Engels. 1988. *Marx-Engels Collected Works*, Volume 30. New York: International Publishers.

Mattick, Jr., P. 1991. "Some Aspects of the Value-Price Problem." *International Journal of Political Economy* 21(4): 9–66.

Moseley, F. 2016. *Money and Totality: A Macro-Monetary Interpretation of Marx's Logic in* Capital *and the End of the 'Transformation Problem'*. Leiden: Brill.

——. Forthcoming. "Wolff and Resnick's Interpretation of Marx's Theory of Value and Surplus-Value: Where's the Money?" In *Marxism without Guarantees: Economics, Knowledge, and Class*, T. Burczak, R. Garnett, and R. McIntyre, eds. London: Routledge.

Ramos, A. 1998. "Value and Price of Production: New Evidence on Marx's Transformation Procedure." *International Journal of Political Economy* 28(4): 55–81.

Sraffa, P. 1960, *Production of Commodities by Means of Commodities: Prelude to a Critique of Economic Theory*. Cambridge: Cambridge University Press.

Steedman, I. 1977. *Marx After Sraffa*. London: New Left Books.

Sweezy, P. 1942. *The Theory of Capitalist Development*. New York: Monthly Review Press.

Wolff, R., A. Callari and B. Roberts. 1984. "A Marxian Alternative to the 'Transformation Problem'." *Review of Radical Political Economics* 16(2–3): 115–135.

10

THE CIRCUIT OF CAPITAL

Paulo L. dos Santos and Duncan K. Foley

Introduction

The Circuit of Capital is a conceptual tool first advanced by Marx (1893) to analyze the process of capitalist accumulation, its requirements, and potential contradictions. It is founded on consideration of the characteristic motion or metamorphoses experienced by capital value as it seeks self-expansion through the exploitation of wage-labor, which Marx schematized as,

$$M - C(lp, mp)...P...C' - M' \tag{1}$$

The circuit is opened as capital value in monetary form M is advanced as capital outlays that purchase input commodities C, including labor power and means of production. Those inputs are combined in productive processes P that result in the completion of output commodities C'. The circuit is closed as output commodities are sold, typically generating revenues M' that exceed the original capital outlay and realize capitalist profits. Those profits are grounded on the appropriation of surplus value, made possible by the fact that employed labor-power can typically contribute more value to output commodities than its own value. The capitalization of fractions of profits to support growth in the scale of the circuit is taken as the most general foundation for the accumulation of capital—i.e., economic growth.

Marx emphasized the significance of the fact that the movement of capital value through the various phases of (1) took place over concrete, historical time. Mobilized inputs only yield output commodities gradually, giving rise to what may be termed a *production lag*. Output commodities are sold over time, defining a *realization lag*. Earnings retained by capitalist enterprises are only gradually recommitted to capital outlays, defining a *finance lag*. The existence of time lags also ensures three different stocks of capital value accumulate in the circuit. The production lag ensures there are stocks of input commodities tied up in production; the realization lag ensures there are inventory stocks of unsold output; and the finance lag ensures there are stocks of capital in monetary form awaiting recommitment to the circuit.

Aggregate social capital is composed of myriad pulses of value traversing the circuit, so that at any given time a certain measure of value is engaged in each stage of the process.

The demand and supply for commodities may be considered in relation to individual circuits, resulting in a dynamic macroeconomic framework defined by the necessary relationships between time lags and the stocks and flows of capital value. Marx sought to use this broad approach to cast light onto issues like the supply and demand relationships between industries producing consumption and investment goods, the dynamic determinants of profitability in accumulation, and the formation of what is now called aggregate demand.

Foley (1982) codified the Circuit of Capital into a well-specified dynamic model of capitalist accumulation. This resulted in a distinctively broad analytical framework offering a deliberate, stock-flow-consistent account of the dynamic interaction between productive and consumption undertakings. Against this framework, most neoclassical, Keynesian, and Kaleckian aggregative models of accumulation may be understood as special cases of the Circuit of Capital. Foley's (1982) formalization has also been recently applied and extended to consider a range of important productive and financial developments that dynamically condition growth, profitability, and distribution in contemporary capitalism.[1]

The Framework

The Circuit of Capital consists of three flows of value—capital outlays, the value of finished output, and sales—and three stocks of value—productive capital, inventories, and financial or money capital. The flows of value are governed by five parameters—the markup on costs (which is defined by the rate of exploitation and the composition of capital), the proportion of profits recommitted to the circuit (called the *rate of capitalization* below), and the three time lags in the circuit—the production lag, the realization lag, and the finance lag.

In constructing a mathematical representation of the circuit it is easiest to make the simplifying assumption that the time lags in the circuit are simple delays. Hence, it will be assumed that a dollar advanced as capital stays in the production process for a given time period and then emerges all at once as finished product. A more general, but mathematically more complicated, approach to time lags allows value to flow gradually through different phases in the circuit.[2]

Let Z_t, P_t, S_t respectively represent flows of capital outlays, finished commodities (valued at cost), and commodity sales during time period t. Similarly, let Π_t, N_t, F_t respectively denote the stocks of productive capital; goods in inventory (valued at cost); and financial or monetary capital during that period. The composition of capital will be measured by the fraction k of capital outlays that is taken to purchase labor power. Profits represent a realization of a markup on costs $q = k\varepsilon$, where ε measures the rate of exploitation. The production, realization, and financial delays in the circuit will be given by T_p, T_r, T_f. Their sum defines the total *turnover time* of the circuit and is represented by τ.

The equations of the framework simply record the assumptions made about time lags and accounting conventions. The flow of finished output during a point in time will be equal to capital outlays undertaken T_p periods earlier,

$$P_t = Z_{t-T_p} \tag{2}$$

Along similar lines, sales taking place during a time period correspond to the output commodities completed T_r periods earlier. Sales generate revenues that represent both the recovery of production costs and profits,

$$S_t = (1+q)P_{t-T_r} \tag{3}$$

The fraction of total sales representing the recovery of production costs, and the fraction representing profits are respectively given by,

$$S'_t = \frac{1}{1+q} S_t \tag{4}$$

$$S'_t = \frac{q}{1+q} S_t \tag{5}$$

A fraction $1-p$ of profits is spent in capitalist consumption, ensuring p is a propensity to save profit income by the capitalist sector. If capital outlays draw exclusively on own funds, capital outlays will be,

$$Z_t = S'_{t-T_f} + pS''_{t-T_f} \tag{6}$$

The accounting rules relating balance sheets and income statements establish the laws governing changes in the stocks of value in the Circuit of Capital. For instance, the stock of productive capital is increased by capital outlays, which mobilize means of production and labor-power, and is decreased as finished output emerges from production. Using $\dot{Q}_t$ to denote the time rate of change of any stock Q_t, we have,

$$\dot{\Pi}_t = Z_t - P_t \tag{7}$$

In a similar fashion, inventories are increased by finished output flows and decreased by production costs recovered by sales, while the stock of financial or monetary capital is increased by sales revenues and decreased by capitalist consumption and capital outlays,

$$\dot{N}_t = P_t - S'_t \tag{8}$$

$$\dot{F}_t = S_t - (1-p)S''_t - Z_t = (1+pq)S'_t - Z_t \tag{9}$$

Equations (2)–(9) constitute the basic model of the Circuit of Capital.

Simple Reproduction

The simplest case of the model developed above to examine is the simple setting where all profits are consumed, leaving no funds to increase the scale of reproduction. Marx termed this case *simple reproduction*. As no profit capitalization takes place, enterprises only retain revenues corresponding to the recovery of production costs, ensuring that the scale of capital outlays (and of accumulation) is constant,

$$Z_t = P_t = S'_t \tag{10}$$

The model cannot establish how large these flows will be; all it can establish is that they will stay at whatever level they have once the economy "starts." It also establishes that capitalists consume the totality of profits, given by qS'_t.

The identities contained in (10) also ensure that the stocks of capital value described by (7)–(9) do not change along this accumulation path. As the length of time it takes value to flow through each one of these stocks is given by the respective fixed delays, it is possible to establish how large balance-sheet stocks must be. Since it takes exactly T_p units of time for value committed by capital outlays to production to emerge as finished output, the total stock of productive capital must be equal to $Z_t T_p$. By the same reasoning, and (10), it can be established that,

$$\Pi_t = Z_t T_p \tag{11}$$

$$N_t = P_t T_r = Z_t T_r \tag{12}$$

$$F_t = S'_t T_f = Z_t T_f \tag{13}$$

Total capital value in circulation X_t, which consists of the sum of these three stocks, is given by,

$$X_t = \tau Z_t, \tag{14}$$

It is now possible to turn formally to the dynamic determinants of growth, profitability, and distribution in simple reproduction. Obviously growth will be zero. The rate of profit ρ is given by the ratio of profit flows to total capital value in circulation. Formally,

$$\rho \stackrel{\text{def}}{=} \frac{S''_t}{X_t} = \frac{q S'_t}{\tau Z_t} = \frac{q}{\tau} \tag{15}$$

Marx put considerable weight on this relationship, which helps highlight oft under-appreciated dynamic determinants of the aggregate profitability of capital. Relationship (15) states that the rate of profit is determined by the input-cost markup and by the circuit's turnover time. The mark-up rate measures how much a unit of value expands in a single turnover in the circuit. The turnover time establishes how many turnovers take place during any given unit of time. The ratio in (15) thus measures by how much value committed to the circuit expands per unit of time—a natural dynamic measure of profitability. All factors determining the paces at which value travels through each phase of the circuit will thus directly condition profitability, alongside the rate of exploitation and the composition of capital.

Finally, the functional distribution of income may be measured by the ratio of profits to wages, denoted by ψ. In simple reproduction, this ratio will be given by,

$$\psi \stackrel{\text{def}}{=} \frac{S''_t}{k Z_t} = \varepsilon \frac{S'_t}{Z_t} = \varepsilon \tag{16}$$

As with profitability, the class distribution of income is shown here to have important dynamic determinants in the accumulation of capital. Distribution is obviously shaped by the rate of exploitation, given by the ratio of average unpaid to paid labor time in production. It is also conditioned by the ratio of the present, cost-accounted value of commodity sales and present capital outlays. This ratio conditions distribution because, as Marx was at pains to emphasize, profits and wages do not represent a sharing of output. Wages logically pertain to the opening of the circuit—the capitalist decision to produce. Profits pertain to the closing of the circuit—as output commodities are sold and their value, including surplus value, is realized.

The ratio in (16) has an intuitive interpretation as a measure of capitalist "animal spirits." Cost-accounted sales measure the past capital outlays that opened the individual circuits being presently closed by the sale of their outputs. The ratio thus provides a natural measure of the extent to which capitalist enterprises are effectively expanding the scale of the aggregate circuit. In simple reproduction this ratio will be one, ensuring that the rate of exploitation describes exhaustively the ratio of aggregate profits to aggregate wage flows. As is taken up below, this is not generally the case in the process of accumulation.

Expanded Reproduction with Say's Law

It is possible to relax the assumption that no capitalization of profits is taking place. This allows consideration of *expanded reproduction*, in which accumulation takes place at growing scales. For now, the assumption made above of a given realization lag will be maintained, ensuring that aggregate demand consistently allows the timely sale of output—i.e., that Say's Law holds. Instrumentally, expanded reproduction implies all flows and stocks are increasing at the same, unknown, exponential rate g. Along such evolutions, all stocks and flows Q_t will evolve according to $Q_t = Q_0 e^{gt}$. Note also that this means that $Q_{t-x} = Q_t e^{-gx}$. This ensures that ratios between any two stocks or flows remain constant along these evolutions. Exponential, expanded-reproduction evolutions may thus be interpreted as evolutions with commodity-market and monetary equilibrium, in the sense that aggregate ratios of sales to inventories, sales to productive capacity, and of financial and real holdings to total assets, remain constant.

A few substitutions involving the system outlined in section two make it possible to investigate the properties of expanded-reproduction evolutions of this kind. Because current sales depend on past production, and because past production depends on even earlier capital outlays, current sales may be related to the capital outlays that financed the production of commodities being currently sold. Formally, (2) and (3) ensure that,

$$S_t = (1 + q)Z_{t-(T_p + T_r)} \tag{17}$$

Present capital outlays are in turn financed by past retained earnings. By (4)–(6), this dependence may be expressed as,

$$Z_t = (1 + pq)S'_{t-T_f} \tag{18}$$

From (4), (17), and (18), it is possible to relate present capital outlays to their past values, casting light onto the dynamic evolution of the circuit,

$$Z_t = (1 + pq)Z_{t-\tau} \tag{19}$$

Since capital-outlay flows are assumed to evolve exponentially, this may be expressed as,

$$Z_0 e^{gt} = (1 + pq)Z_0 e^{g(t-\tau)} \tag{20}$$

Simple manipulation yields the system's rate of growth,

$$g = \frac{1}{\tau} ln[1 + pq] \tag{21}$$

A number of important insights about expanded reproduction in capitalist economies are contained in this equation. Both the markup and capitalization rates condition the rate of expansion of a capitalist economy. The expression $1 + pq$ measures the rate at which a unit of capital value self-augments during one turnover of the Circuit of Capital. It is conditioned by the extent to which social relations and the development of productive forces permit the exploitation of wage labor, and the measure to which the resulting surplus is effectively used to expand the scale of reproduction. As expected, the rate of growth of capital value in historical time is fully described by this measure divided by the circuit's turnover time.

It is possible to find expressions for the value of a few economically significant stock-flow ratios along exponential, expanded-reproduction paths under the present specification. To do this it is useful to normalize the system to the measure of productive capital outlays at time zero, so that $Z_0 = 1$. From this, (2), and (3) it is possible to establish the relative measure of output-commodity flows, sales and its two constituent parts along exponential, expanded-reproduction paths,

$$P_0 = e^{-gT_p} \tag{22}$$

$$S_0 = (1 + q)e^{-g(T_p + T_r)} \tag{23}$$

$$S_t' = e^{-g(T_p + T_r)} \tag{24}$$

$$S_t'' = qe^{-g(T_p + T_r)} \tag{25}$$

It is also possible to find the relative magnitude of the three stocks of capital value in the economy. For instance, along exponential evolutions the stock of productive capital must be growing at the same rate as the rest of the system. Thus, $\Pi_t = \Pi_0 e^{gt}$. But by (7) the time derivative of this must be equal to capital outlays minus commodity-output value flows,

$$\dot{\Pi}_t = g\Pi_0 e^{gt} = (Z_0 - P_0)e^{gt} \tag{26}$$

But since we have normalized the system to the steady-state measure of capital outlays, so that $Z_0 = 1$, and (22) tells us that $P_0 = e^{-gT_p}$, it follows that the value of productive capital relative to capital outlays is given by,

$$\Pi_0 = \frac{1}{g}(1 - e^{-gT_p}) \tag{27}$$

Following the same line of reasoning, it may be shown that,

$$N_0 = \frac{1}{g}(1 - e^{-gT_r})e^{-gT_p} \tag{28}$$

$$F_0 = (1 + pq)\frac{1}{g}(1 - e^{-gT_f})e^{-g(T_p + T_r)} \tag{29}$$

$$X_0 = pq\frac{1}{g}e^{-g(T_p+T_r)} \tag{30}$$

The rate of profit along exponential, expanded-reproduction paths will be given by the relative magnitude of profits divided by the relative measure of total capital value committed by enterprises,

$$\rho = \frac{S_0''}{X_0} = g\frac{qe^{-g(T_p+T_r)}}{pqe^{-g(T_p+T_r)}} = \frac{g}{p} = \frac{1}{p\tau}ln[1+pq] \tag{31}$$

Note that (31) is the Cambridge Equation establishing the equilibrium relationship between the rates of growth, profit, and capitalization. Note further that if pq is sufficiently near zero, this expression will be arbitrarily close to the measure of profitability in simple reproduction,

$$\rho \approx \frac{q}{\tau} \tag{32}$$

Finally, it is possible to consider the measure of the class distribution of income provided by the ratio of profits to wages along expanded reproduction paths, which as above is given by,

$$\psi = \varepsilon\frac{S_0'}{Z_0} \tag{33}$$

Unlike simple reproduction, positive growth in the scale accumulation by definition requires ongoing expansion of the scale of capital outlays. This means that at any point in time, present capital outlays are greater than the past capital-outlay commitments being presently recovered through sales. The exact relative measure of these asynchronous capital outlays shapes the aggregate class distribution of income over and above the rate of exploitation. Generally, this measure may be taken to capture the aggregate investment responsiveness of capital to sales.[3] In the dynamic, fixed-lag terms of the present Circuit-of-Capital framework, this will be given by,

$$\frac{S_0'}{Z_0} = e^{-g(T_p+T_r)} = (1+pq)e^{-\frac{T_p+T_r}{\tau}} = (1+pq)e^{\left(\frac{T_f}{\tau}-1\right)} \tag{34}$$

As should be expected, this ratio depends on the per-turnover growth in capital value made possible by the realization of profits and their capitalization. But it also depends on dynamic relationships defined by the three time lags in the circuit; specifically, on the share in total turnover time represented by the finance lag. Along exponential-growth paths, this share dynamically conditions the magnitude of capital outlays relative to sales. Shorter financial lags ensure this magnitude decreases, so that for a given pattern of consumption behavior by wage earners, they result in greater wage shares of aggregate income. Conversely, quicker production and realization lags will result, *ceteris paribus*, on greater profit shares of aggregate income.[4]

Demand-Driven Growth

Marx (1893) also used his discussions of the Circuit of Capital to investigate the problem of aggregate demand, seeking to locate the source of the money flows that allow the sale and of produced commodities at their value. The first insight this offers is that the money demand for produced commodities arises directly or indirectly from the Circuit of Capital itself. This point is also the basis of Keynes's analysis of aggregate demand, which can be situated within the analytical terms of the Circuit of Capital. This can be done by extending the framework developed above so that deliberate attention is given to the interactions between production, consumption, and balance-sheet decisions and the formation of aggregate demand. On these bases it is possible to obtain important insights concerning the dynamic relationships conditioning growth, profitability, and distribution in an expanding economy.

Aggregate demand in a closed, private economy may be divided into three exhaustive categories: demand by capital for means of production, demand by wage earners for consumption goods, and capitalist demand for consumption goods. While consumption demand may be interpreted to involve time lags between revenues and expenditures (in a manner analogous to the finance lags), analysis is greatly simplified if consumption out of wages is taken, like consumption out of profits above, as a given fraction of wage income.[5] Aggregate demand will then be,

$$D_t = (1 - k)Z_t + c^w k Z_t + (1 - p)S_t'' = (1 - k(1 - c^w))Z_t + (1 - p)S_t'' \tag{35}$$

where c^w is the marginal consumption propensity of workers. Aggregate demand funds sales, which by (4) and (5) may be decomposed into profits and recovered costs,

$$D_t = S_t' + S_t'' \tag{36}$$

Subtracting capitalist consumption from both sides of (36), and assuming that capital outlays are entirely financed from unconsumed capitalist revenues, as described in (18), it follows that,

$$(1 + pq)S_t' = (1 + pq)(1 - k(1 - c^w))S_{t-T_f}' \tag{37}$$

Along exponential, expanded-reproduction paths, this condition holds only if,

$$gT_f = ln[1 - k(1 - c^w)] \tag{38}$$

Since the finance lag is non-negative, this condition is only satisfied by negative rates of growth if workers save, that is, if $c^w < 1$. Even if workers consume all of their income, (38) holds only if the rate of growth and or the finance lag are zero. Positive growth sustained by the capitalization of profits appears impossible in this light, unless the finance lag is allowed to vanish to zero—which would correspond to a setting with an infinite velocity of money and arbitrarily illiquid positions for capitalist enterprises. Under a constant, positive finance lag, past retained earnings cannot support the growing scales of capital outlays necessary to ensure growth in the scale of profit capitalization—even before savings by workers are considered.

This apparent predicament for the accumulation of capital drew the attention of Rosa Luxembourg (1913), who based her analysis of imperialism on it. Seeking to provide a systematic, economic foundation in the accumulation of capital for the sharpening inter-imperialist rivalries of her time, Luxembourg argued that a closed capitalist system undergoing accumulation would always run into inadequacies of aggregate demand and as a consequence would be forced to seek external markets to realize its surplus production. Luxembourg was entirely correct in identifying a difference in Marx's system between aggregate demand and the needs of realization in any setting where a fraction of profits is being capitalized (and or workers save). But her argument that this provided an economic imperative for imperialist expansion which alone could ameliorate the problem was not convincing. Where do the external markets get the money to buy the surplus product of the capitalist system? If they get them from selling something to the capitalist system, they add as much as they subtract from aggregate demand.

Marx himself, at the very end of Volume II of *Capital* (1893, 522–3), proposes an alternative view, which was taken up by Bukharin's (1924) critique of Luxemburg. In a commodity monetary system, the monetary commodity does not need to be realized through sale. It is already value in monetary form. In such a setting it is possible to imagine a situation in which the output flows of this sector match exactly the desired "savings" of capitalists and workers. While logical, this argument is contrived. A more convincing argument is already latent in (38), which implies that if wage earners are willing and capable of consuming in excess of their income, positive rates of growth are possible. In such a setting, the demand for the capitalization of profits is ultimately accommodated indebtedness by wage earners.

More broadly, the development of credit systems and credit-monetary forms may be understood to offer a potentially flexible means of mediating the desire to accumulate capital value in monetary form by capitalists and wage earners, and the desire of some enterprises or some wage earners to spend in excess of their present revenues. Suppose that total capital outlays are financed through a combination of past retained earnings and present net borrowing, so that,

$$Z_t = (1 + v)(1 + pq)S'_{t-T_f} \tag{39}$$

Where v offers a measure of leverage supporting capital outlays. Following the same process leading to (37), but using the expression for capital outlays in (39) instead of (18), this yields,

$$(1 + pq)S'_t = (1 - k(1 - c^w))Z_t \tag{40}$$

The flows in the economy are fully described by (2), (4), (5), (39), and (40). Productive capital and inventories still evolve according to (7) and (8). Two more sets of specifications complete the model. First, characterizations of the evolution of the financial position of each sector are necessary. Under a simple credit-monetary financial system, a sector's financial position is exhaustively measured by its net monetary position, given by the sum of money holdings and debt obligations. Abstracting from interest flows, wage earners see their net monetary position evolve in line with their savings,

$$\dot{M}^w_t = (1 - c^w)kZ_t \tag{41}$$

The equivalent position for capital evolves according to retained earnings and capital outlays,

$$\dot{M}_t^c = (1 + pq)S_t' - Z_t \tag{42}$$

Note that by (40), $\dot{M}_t^c = -\dot{M}_t^w$, in line with the aggregate source-use identity this economy.

An important, second specification relates to the evolution of inventories and the scopes for aggregate demand to determine the economy's rate of growth. Demand in excess of inventories results in demand-pull inflation, not real output growth. Demand can only determine output or growth in settings where aggregate inventories are positive.

Expanded Reproduction with Demand Determination: Limits and Types

The model just outlined may be solved for exponential, expanded-reproduction paths. Their characteristics offer important insights into the interactions between aggregate demand, commodity production, and balance-sheet behavior that shape a capitalist economy's rate of growth, aggregate profitability, and income distribution. This includes a few useful conclusions that are unattainable on the basis of most conventional macroeconomic approaches.

As above, equations (39) and (40) define the system's demand-determined rate of growth,

$$g = \frac{1}{T_f} ln[(1 - k(1 - c^w))(1 + v)] \tag{43}$$

Which holds for all exponential evolutions along which inventories are positive, i.e., $N_t > 0$.

Using the measure of capital outlays to normalize the economy, it is possible to find expressions for the relative measure of all steady-state flows and stocks in the economy. Output flows will be given as in (22). The cost-accounted measure of sales can be established from (40),

$$S_0' = \frac{1 - k(1 - c^w)}{1 + pq} \tag{44}$$

The stock of productive capital will be as given by (27). In contrast, the measure of inventories is different under demand determination. Their evolution along expanded reproduction follows,

$$\dot{N}_t = e^{-gT_p} - \frac{1 - k(1 - c^w)}{1 + pq} \tag{45}$$

Which ensures that the steady-state inventory stock is,

$$N_t = \frac{1}{g}\left(e^{-gT_p} - \frac{1 - k(1 - c^w)}{1 + pq}\right) \tag{46}$$

The net monetary position of wage labor and capital will in turn be given by,

$$\dot{M}_0^w = \frac{1}{g}k(1 - c^w) = -\dot{M}_t^c \tag{47}$$

Adding up all assets and liabilities of capitalist enterprises yields their net worth,

$$W_0 = \frac{1}{g} \left(\frac{pq(1 - k(1 - c^w))}{1 + pq} \right) \tag{48}$$

A number of observations follow from (43)–(48). First, the expression for the economy's demand-determined rate of growth makes it clear that the "paradox of thrift" holds in the present framework. Lower measures of leverage in capital outlays and lower consumption propensities by wage earners, result, *ceteris paribus*, in lower rates of growth. In this important sense the present framework echoes one of the central conclusions of Keynesian approaches to the role of demand in setting output and growth. But it does so within analytical terms that explicitly account for the dynamic interplay between aggregate demand and productive undertakings. This helps broaden conclusions drawn on standard Keynesian bases.

This is most readily evident in the recognition that demand can only exert an independent influence on the real measure of output if inventories are positive. Formally, this requirement may be expressed for expanded-reproduction paths by using (46), which yields,[6]

$$g \leq \frac{1}{T_p} ln \left[\frac{1 + pq}{1 - k(1 - c^w)} \right] \tag{49}$$

This inequality defines the upper-bound for the economy's rate of growth. This constraint is defined not only by the savings behavior of wage earners, but also by two supply-side constraints—the production lag, which measures the dynamic pace at which inputs can be transformed into outputs, and the rate at which profits are capitalized to finance expansions in the scale of productive investment. Here the Circuit of Capital offers an explicit characterization of the dynamic, productive constraints that define the scopes within which aggregate demand may act as an independent determinant of the pace of economic activity.

The endogenous expression for the economy's rate of growth in (43) also points to a useful distinction between two broad types of changes that may boost the economy's rate of growth. Within the limits defined by (43) and (49), growth may be increased either by increasing the aggregate consumption propensity of wage earners, or by increasing leverage and the pace at which retained earnings are recommitted to capital outlays. The first possibility sees growth boosted by increases in measures of consumption by wage earners in the economy. This may be called "consumption-led growth." In the second possibility growth is boosted by increases in measures of capital outlays, in what may be broadly called "investment-led growth."

One important feature of this distinction that is suggested by the analytical terms of the Circuit of Capital is that the two types of growth generally have opposing effects on the distribution of income. In the present setting, the ratio of profits to wages is given by,

$$\psi = \varepsilon \frac{(1 - k(1 - c^w))}{1 + pq} \tag{50}$$

"Consumption-led" growth defined by comparatively higher consumption propensities by wage earners will exhibit comparatively greater profit shares in aggregate income. Conversely, increases in the relative measure of investment ushered by greater profit capitalization rates will result in comparatively higher wage shares.[7] In the Circuit of Capital, the relative measure of consumption and productive outlays in aggregate demand directly influences the aggregate distribution of income.

Consumption and investment undertakings will also shape the aggregate profitability of capital in settings of demand determination. Profitability in the present setting may be measured as the return on net worth, given by (44) and (48), from which it follows that,

$$\rho \stackrel{\text{def}}{=} \frac{qS_0'}{W_0} = \frac{g}{p} \tag{51}$$

As above, this is a simple statement of the Cambridge Equation, where growth is given by (43).

The Circuit of Capital distinctively shows that developments like greater leverage in capital outlays, quicker paces of recommitment of enterprise retained earnings to investment, and more aggressive consumption behavior by wage earners, etc. all contribute to growth according to their impact on the *measure* of aggregate demand—within the limits specified by (49). But each of those developments contributes to the class distribution of income according to its impact on the *composition* of aggregate demand.

Finally, the present specification points towards the financial or monetary requirements of expanded reproduction. Note that (43) implies that positive growth only takes place when,

$$\frac{v}{1+v} > (1 - c^w)k \tag{52}$$

In words, borrowing by enterprises must exceed savings by wage earners. Private-sector savings are insufficient to supply the volume of loans necessary to meet growing demand for money holdings. Growth requires a consistent, positive injection of means of purchase into the economy—i.e., monetary expansion. This need may be understood as a primary driver of the development of contemporary credit-monetary systems. The Circuit of Capital offers a distinctively useful basis on which to theorize the development of those systems, the contradictions they may throw up, and their relationship to the process of accumulation. As such, the Circuit of Capital may be usefully applied and extended further to provide systematic accounts of the social and macroeconomic content of contemporary capitalism and its distinctive financial practices and relations.

Notes

1 See Abeles (2013) for an application to the problems of contemporary open economies; Basu (2014) and dos Santos (2011) for consideration of the impacts of credit allocation; Jiang (2014) for a dynamic, agent-based model founded on the Circuit of Capital; and dos Santos (2014, 2015) for applications to the contemporary determinants of the functional distributions of income and wealth. A number of additional, interesting applications by other authors are currently in press.

2 The general, distributed-lag framework was first advanced in Foley (1982) and fully developed in Foley (1986a). Foley (1986b) set out the simplified, time-delay specification grounding the present discussion.

3 The theoretical significance and pertinence of these determinations to contemporary capitalism was first motivated in dos Santos (2014, 2015).

4 It is possible to express these two points in relation to important stock-flow ratios that are defined by the three time lags under consideration. Dynamic evolutions where capital is willing to maintain total asset positions that are less liquid, in that they hold greater measures of productive capital relative to money, will exhibit, *ceteris paribus*, higher wage shares. Conversely, evolutions with quicker paces

of production, higher rates of utilization of fixed capital, and tighter inventories will in turn exhibit comparatively higher profit shares.

5 For the purposes of the present discussion, this involves no loss of generality. For a general approach to Circuit-of-Capital frameworks with dynamic consumption lag processes, see dos Santos (2014).

6 The full expression of this constraint in terms of the exogenous variables under the current parametrization is given by $1 + pq > (1 + v)^{T_p/T_f}(1 - k(1 - c^w))^{1 + T_p/T_f}$.

7 In most general settings, cases of "investment-led" growth defined by higher measures of leverage in capital outlays and quicker paces of investment of enterprise retained earnings will also result in comparatively higher wage shares. This is not the case here only because the specification of consumption by wage earners implies that the capital-outlay elasticity of aggregate demand is exactly one. See dos Santos (2014).

References

Abeles, M. 2013. "Duncan Foley's Circuit of Capital Model for an Open Economy." In *Social Fairness and Economics: Economic Essays in the Spirit of Duncan Foley*, L. Taylor, A. Rezai, and T. Michl, eds., 228–253 New York: Routledge.

Basu, D. 2014. "Comparative Growth Dynamics in a Discrete-Time Marxian Circuit of Capital Model." *Review of Radical Political Economics*, forthcoming.

Bukharin, N. 1972 [1924]. "Imperialism and the Accumulation of Capital." In *Imperialism and the Accumulation of Capital*, K. Tarbuk, ed. London: Allen Lane, Penguin Press.

dos Santos, P. 2011. "Production and Consumption Credit in a Continuous-Time Model of the Circuit of Capital." *Metroeconomica* 62(4): 729–758.

———. 2014. "A Note on Credit Allocation, Income Distribution, and the Circuit of Capital." *Metroeconomica* 65(2): 212–236.

———. 2015. "Not 'wage-led' versus 'profit-led,' but investment-led versus consumption-led growth." *Journal of Post-Keynesian Economics* 37(4): 661–686.

Foley, D. 1982. "Realization and Accumulation in a Marxian Model of the Circuit of Capital." *Journal of Economic Theory* 28(2): 300–319.

———. 1986a. "Money, Accumulation and Crisis." *Fundamentals of Pure and Applied Economics* 2. London: Harwood Academic Publishers.

———. 1986b. *Understanding Capital*. Cambridge, MA: Harvard University Press.

Jiang, X. 2014. "Endogenous Cycles and Chaos in a Capitalist Economy: A Circuit of Capital Model." *Meteroeconomica* 66(1): 123–157.

Luxemburg, R. 1972 [1913]. "The Accumulation of Capital-An Anti-Critique." In *Imperialism and the Accumulation of Capital*, K. Tarbuk, ed., 45–150. London: Allen Lane.

Marx, K. 1967 [1893]. *Capital*, Volume 2. New York: International Publishers.

11

RENT

Fabian Balardini

The Theory of Rent in Marx

Marx presented his theory of rent in what are considered to be two of his most mature economic works: *Theories of Surplus Value* (henceforth, *TSV*) and *Capital*. In *TSV*, written during 1862–3, Marx investigated the historical development of the concept of rent by examining the related theoretical challenges, contributions of, and errors committed by previous thinkers. In *Capital*, written throughout the 1860s, 1870s, and early 1880s, the theory of rent was presented in a detailed manner within the context of what Marx calls the *general laws of value of commodities and of capitalist production*. In what follows, we present Marx's theory of rent based on these two major works. More specifically, we summarize his critique of earlier thinkers on the subject; provide a description of the fully developed theory of rent he advanced as a result of this critique; and finally present an overview of the various interpretations and debates of this theory that have been proposed within the Marxian economic tradition up through the first fifteen years of the 21st century.

Critique of the Physiocrats and Adam Smith

Marx began his analysis of rent in *TSV* by stating that "all economists share the error of examining surplus-value not as such, in its pure form, but in the particular forms of profit and rent" (Marx 1975, I: 40). Following this assessment, Marx began his investigation of the historical development of the concepts of surplus-value, profit, and rent by identifying the Physiocrats as the first thinkers to make significant contributions to our understanding of these economic categories. Writing in the early 1700's, the Physiocrats argued that agriculture is the sector of the economy where surplus-value is created, since "the sum total of the means of subsistence which the laborer consumes … is smaller than the sum total of the means of subsistence which he produces" (Marx 1975, I: 46).

Having defined surplus-value as the excess of use-values produced over and above the use-values consumed by agricultural workers, the Physiocrats defined rent as the appropriation of this surplus of use-values by landlords. Marx considered this a major theoretical advancement over the previous analysis conducted by thinkers known as Mercantilists, according to whom surplus-value was simply the excess of money profits resulting from unequal trade between nations.[1] However, Marx criticized the Physiocrats for reducing value to use-value and surplus-value "to material substance in general" (Marx 1975, I: 46), likewise for providing a feudal definition of surplus-value, as being "derived from nature and not from society; from man's relation to the soil, not from his social relations" (Marx 1975, I: 52). The theorizing of surplus-value as resulting from social relations and not nature was, according to Marx, Adam Smith's most important contribution. Smith argued that money profits (surplus-value) from selling commodities did not originate from the sale of commodities above their value, or as the result of unequal exchange, but rather from the selling of commodities at their values through exchange between equals. This argument implies that a commodity's surplus-value is included in its value, which in turn suggests that the surplus-value originates in production rather than in trade or exchange. For Smith the profit of a capitalist "originates from the fact that he has not paid for a part of the labor contained in the commodity, but has nevertheless sold it" (Marx 1975, I: 79).

In other words, Smith was able to move beyond the Physiocrats' feudal definition of value and surplus-value to correctly conclude that profit (surplus-value) is the appropriation (by the capitalist) of the unpaid labor of others (the workers).

Among Adam Smith's successors, David Ricardo was the only one to call for analyzing the determination of value as a function of labor-time as the starting-point of "the physiology of the bourgeois system—for the understanding of its internal organic coherence and life process" (Marx 1975, II: 166). Having argued that labor was the source of value, both Smith and Ricardo concluded that commodities sell at prices of production—equal to their values— that provide capitalist producers the average rate of profit on capital invested. Although Marx recognized that Smith and Ricardo succeeded in identifying labor as the source of the value and surplus-value of commodities, he criticized them for failing to understand that the values of commodities undergo a two-stage transformation, whereby commodities end up selling at prices not identical to their values.

In *TSV* and *Capital*, Marx presented a detailed analysis of this two-stage transformation of values into prices of production as part of the mechanism through which the total mass of surplus-value extracted from the working class is distributed among all capitalist producers. Marx held that this distribution of surplus-value is accomplished by capitalist producers engaging in a competitive struggle among themselves within each sector of the economy, which in turn results in an initial transformation of the individual values of commodities into a common market-value, and a subsequent transformation of market-values into prices of production that results from capitalist competition across different sectors of the economy. Smith and Ricardo's failure to analyze the transformation of individual values of commodities into a common market-value within sectors prevented them from theorizing what Marx called differential rent; similarly, their failure to analyze the transformation of market-values into prices of production prevented them from theorizing what Marx called absolute rent.

Before discussing Marx's theory of differential and absolute rent, it is important to review how Smith's successors faced the theoretical challenge of explaining rent within the context of a theory of value based on labor time. Marx described this challenge as consisting

> in showing how, after the equalization of surplus-value between the various capitals to give the average profit … there is still an excess part of this surplus-value leftover, a part which capital invested on the land pays to the landowner in the form of ground-rent.
>
> *(Marx 1981: 917)*

In other words, since rent represents an amount of money in excess of the average rate of profit that the "farmer-capitalist pays the landowner ... for permission to employ his capital in this particular field of production" (Marx 1981: 754), how are the farmer-capitalists expected to come up with this additional amount of money when the selling of their products only provide them enough money to realize the average rate of profit? In a detailed review of the literature, Marx analyzes the two different explanations to this puzzle provided by Smith's successors: 1) a theory or rent based on monopoly prices; and 2) the alternative theory of rent provided by Ricardo. Regarding the theory of rent based on monopoly prices, Marx stated that it

> presupposes the very phenomenon which is to be explained, namely, that in a particular sphere of production, the price of a commodity must carry more than the general rate of profit, more than the average rate of profit, and to this end must be sold above its value. It presupposes that agricultural products are excluded from the general laws of value of commodities and of capitalist production. It, moreover, presupposes this, because the peculiar presence of rent side by side with profit prima facie makes it appear so. Hence this is absurd.
>
> *(Marx 1975, II: 36)*

Critique of David Ricardo

Having noted the absurdity of a theory of rent based on monopoly prices, Marx then turned to Ricardo's theory of rent. According to Ricardo, population growth leads to an increase in the demand for agricultural goods. Since this demand is met by cultivating land of increasingly lesser quality, the price of agricultural goods is ultimately determined by the price of goods produced on marginal land. From this perspective, rent results when those producers working on the best land (and hence, with lower production costs) sell their agricultural goods at the (higher) price determined by agricultural goods produced on the worst land. In the process, they realize profits in excess of the average that landlords appropriate as rent. Marx identified a number of erroneous assumptions in Ricardo's theory of rent: first, that movement is always towards marginal land; second, that there exists a permanent state of excess demand in agriculture; and third, that agricultural goods always sell at a price equal to the value of goods produced on the worst land.

With respect to the first assumption, Marx argued that not all new land used to produce agricultural goods is of the worst quality, moreover, that the notion that movement is always towards the worst land is not historically accurate. Based on the historical evidence, Marx also disagreed with Ricardo's assumption that there exists permanent excess demand for agricultural products such as is always driving prices up. Here he noted the empirical evidence that, during the first half of the 18th century, the prices of agricultural goods actually declined due to excess supply (Marx 1975, II: 144). Ultimately, Marx's main disagreement with Ricardo was that the value of the product in any given sector is not equal to the individual value of the product produced on any particular type of land, but is instead equal to the common market-value for that sector, which is determined by the total quantity of agricultural products produced on all types of land required to satisfy demand:

> this law, that the market-value cannot be above the individual value of that product which is produced under the worst conditions of production but provides a part of the necessary supply, Ricardo distorts into the assertion that the market-value

cannot fall below the value of that product and must therefore always be determined by it.

(Marx 1975, II: 271)

For Marx the market-value of a commodity represents what he calls the socially necessary labor time: the labor time necessary to produce the quantity of the commodity required to satisfy society's need or demand. In agriculture, the market-value results from the total quantity of goods (supplied by competing capitalist producers working on all types of land) required to satisfy demand, and this market-value can only equal the value of the product produced on the worst land (as Ricardo argued) if the quantity of goods so produced corresponds to the amount necessary to satisfy demand. Put another way, if the quantity of goods produced on the worst land is not equal to the amount necessary to satisfy demand, or if this quantity is redundant because demand is already being satisfied by the goods being produced on the best land, then it is the latter, not the former, that will determine the commodity's market-value. In arguing that the price of an agricultural commodity always equals the individual value (or price) of the goods produced on the worst land, Ricardo effectively neglected the effects of capitalist competition and demand on the determination of a commodity's market-value.

Ricardo's insistence that goods produced on the worst land always determines the price (or value, since he assumed that the two were identical) of a commodity reflects, according to Marx, an inability to properly grasp the distinction, not only between price and value, but also between the market-value and individual value of commodities. Marx considered this theoretical point to be of such importance that he presented a long quantitative example in chapter 12 of *TSV* II, wherein he considered a number of possible scenarios in which the market-value of a commodity (coal) produced in a rent-bearing sector could fall below the individual value of the coal produced in the worst mine, in order to show that rather than playing the determinant role, as Ricardo would argue, production in the worst mine was instead determined by the intensity of competition among capitalist producers facing uncertain demand for their commodity. Marx also rejected Ricardo's assumption of a declining direction of production from the best to the worst land, arguing rather that the direction of production in rent-bearing sectors like agriculture would instead be ascending from the worst to the best land, if higher quality land is discovered and its product is required to satisfy demand. In this case, it is the best land that determines the market-value, and if the quantity supplied by it is large enough to cause the market-value to fall, then the worst land could be displaced from the market altogether.

In addition to criticizing Ricardo's failure to understand the transformation of individual values into a common market-value, Marx also criticized his failure to analyze the effect of landed property on the transformation of market-values into prices of production. Marx argued that the unrestricted flow of capital across sectors transforms market-values into prices of production, and that through this process, surplus-value is distributed among capitalist producers in accordance with the size of the capital they invested—what he called their advanced capital. In sectors with landed property, however, Marx argued that the flow of capital into these sectors faces a barrier, inasmuch as capital investment can only occur if the capitalists involved pay rent to landlords. As a result, landed property, by acting as a barrier to the otherwise free flow of capital investment, does not allow the transformation of market-values into prices of production. The transformation of the market-value of agricultural goods into prices of production, therefore, is unable to take place, with the result that these goods are sold not, at their price of production, but at their market-value.

Marx's Theory of Absolute and Differential Rent

Based on his devastating critique of Ricardo's theory of rent, Marx was able to provide what he called a theory of ground rent as the "form in which landed property is economically realized and valorized" (Marx 1981: 755). Marx identified two basic types of ground rent: an absolute rent, given by the difference between the value and the price of production of a commodity, and a differential rent, given by the difference between the market-value and the individual value of a commodity. Absolute rent is the rent paid for using even the worst land, and results from two factors: 1) the intervention of landed property, which acts as a barrier to the free flow of capital investment and thus prevents the transformation of a commodity's market-value into its price of production; and 2) the selling of a commodity at a value above its price of production, which implies that commodities produced in sectors bearing absolute rent have higher values than commodities produced in sectors without absolute rent. This implies that in sectors with absolute rent, more labor or variable capital is used to produce commodities than in sectors without rent.

Marx made the distinction between the amount of money spent on workers, or variable capital (v), and the amount of money spent on machines, equipment, and raw materials, or constant capital (c), and defined the relationship between the two as the organic composition of capital (c/v). Sectors with a high organic composition of capital are less labor intensive than sectors with a low organic composition of capital. This implies that sectors with absolute rent have a low organic composition of capital; products produced in such sectors require more labor (that is, they are labor intensive) and consequently have a higher value than products produced in sectors with a high organic composition of capital.

Using data on agriculture, Marx concluded that during the 1700's and 1800's, the introduction of technology in agriculture occurred at a slower pace than in industry, meaning that the organic composition of capital in agriculture was lower than in industry. However, he also noted that in the future, improvements in technology might well see the organic composition of capital in agriculture become equal to, or even greater than, the organic composition of capital in sectors without rent, such as industry. If that were to occur, then absolute rent in agriculture would disappear.

Marx also argued that as a result of the intervention of landed property, the production conditions determining excess profits (to be transformed into rent) in rent-bearing sectors are different than those determining excess profits in industry, since

> in industry it is always the most recently added, most productive capital that yields an excess profit by reducing average prices. In agriculture excess profit may be the result, and very often must be the result, not of the absolute increase in fertility of the best fields, but the relative increase in their fertility, because less productive land is being cultivated.
>
> *(Marx 1981: 755)*

In other words, Marx concluded that what distinguishes agriculture from industry is that, whereas excess profits in industry are obtained via cheaper production, in agriculture they are obtained via dearer production. As a result, the market-value of commodities produced in rent-bearing sectors tends to be determined by production conditions with lower productivity: "In connection with differential rent in general, it should be noted that the market-value is always above the total production price for the overall quantity produced" (Marx 1981: 799). Marx concluded that the intervention of landed property alters the formation of the market-value of all commodities produced in rent-bearing sectors, creating what he calls a false social (or market) value: "...where society, considered as a consumer, pays too much for agricultural products, this is a minus for the realization of its labor-time in agricultural production, but it forms a plus for one portion of society, the landowners" (Marx 1981: 800).

Marx defined differential rent as resulting from the difference between the market-value of a commodity and its individual value. All the commodities that are produced at an individual value below the market-value carry an excess profit, which is taken by the landlord in the form of rent rather than by the capitalist in the form of surplus profits. As discussed above, Marx's theory of differential rent was a consequence of his critique of Ricardo's inability to understand the transformation of individual values into a common market-value. Marx's point is that differential rent is the excess profit that originates as a result of capitalist competition within a sector, which gives rise to a market-value different from individual value; the difference is appropriated by landlords rather than by capitalists who are able to produce at higher productivity levels.

Marx's emphasis on the formation of market-value in rent-bearing sectors in line with the logic of capitalist competition present in sectors without rent, such as industry, is part of his critique of Ricardo's implicit assumption: that in rent-bearing sectors, there is no capitalist competition such that the price of agricultural goods is always determined by the worst land. In addition to critiquing Ricardo, Marx made a distinction between what he called differential rent of type I, which results from "the varying productivity of equal capital investments on equal land areas of different fertility" (Marx 1981: 812); and differential rent of type II, which results from the varying productivity of unequal capital investments on lands of equal area and fertility.

Marx was able to provide a logically consistent explanation of the economic category of rent as the economic valorization of landed property under capitalism. Landlords are able to take some of this surplus value in the form of absolute rent so long as they succeed in blocking capital investment in their sectors to the extent that the organic composition of invested capital becomes smaller than the composition of capital invested in sectors without landed property. Alternatively, landlords are able to appropriate a portion of this pool of surplus value in the form of differential rent so long as they succeed in imposing the payment of rent as a requirement for capitalist investment in their lands.

Although Marx placed special emphasis on landed property as a barrier to free competition and the movement of capital within and across sectors—which in turn gives rise to the conditions necessary for the formation of differential and absolute rents—Marx also held that landed property is subject to the capitalist mode of production, in the sense that landed property does not present any real threat to the reproduction of capitalism itself.

The Theory of Rent in Marxian Economics

Essentialist Interpretations

Today there is a general consensus among Marxists scholars that Marx defined rent as a class payment received by landlords from capitalist producers as a necessary condition for the production of commodities requiring access to the exploitation of lands or mines. A review of the Marxian economics literature on the theory of rent also reveals a surprising consensus, with the vast majority of authors adopting an interpretation of Marx's theory of rent that relies on a particular interpretation of Marx's theory of market-value. This dominant interpretation of Marx's theory of market-value states that, although in industrial sectors the market-value of commodities is determined by the average conditions of production, in the case of rent-bearing sectors—given the presence of landed property—the market-value of commodities is determined not by the average, but by the worst conditions of production. This theory of market-value determination leads to the also widely adopted interpretation of Marx's theory of rent stating that differential rent is determined by the conditions of production on the worst lands and mines.

The adoption of this view, which (as we saw above) Marx refuted in his critique of Ricardo, might be explained in part by a lack of interest and detailed research into Marx's own writings on rent, something that Ernest Mandel pointed out a few decades ago: "Marx's theory of rent is the most difficult part of his economic theory, the one which has witnessed fewer comments and developments, by followers and critics alike, than other major parts of his system" (Mandel 1990: 38).

This apathetic stance towards the understanding of rent at a time when the environmental destruction wrought by the capitalist system is fast becoming the most serious threat confronting human society is unacceptable to say the least. Such an interpretation can also be explained as a consequence of the essentialist and deterministic methodology used by the vast majority of Marxist economists, which emphasizes production conditions as the main determinant of value. Ironically, one of the first to offer this essentialist interpretation linking Marx's theory of market-value to Marx's theory of rent was Mandel:

> So long as, through increase in population and a lag in agricultural productivity, the demand for agricultural produce exceeds the supply, this price will remain determined by the value of the agricultural commodities produced under the worst conditions of profitability…The difference between this price and the price of production of the wheat produced on land with a higher productivity represents a differential rent which is taken by the landowner.
>
> *(Mandel 1962: 276).*

Mandel does correctly define the price of agricultural products as being determined by the worst production conditions, so long, of course, as demand for the product exceeds supply. However, 22 pages later, when again discussing the determination of the price of agricultural products, he says:

> According to Marx's theory of ground rent, it is in fact the demand for agricultural products which in the last resort determines the price of these products. This price is based on the value of the unit produced on the plot of land with the worst conditions of productivity (marginal price) where products find a buyer.
>
> *(Mandel 1962: 298)*

Essentially, Mandel contradicts himself: whereas initially he stated that the market-value of wheat was determined by the worst conditions of production "so long … as demand exceeds supply," 22 pages later he is claiming that, although demand seems to be the determinant of value, in reality it no longer matters, since he now implicitly assumes that the product of the worst land creates its own demand, inasmuch as it always "finds a buyer."

Mandel is, in fact, describing a particular state of the market, one that assumes that an excess of demand is the permanent state of the market in the agricultural sector, thus leading to the conclusion that the worst land always determines the market-value of agricultural products. Discussion or even acknowledgement of Mandel's contradiction is not only completely missing in the literature, most writers who came after Mandel have adopted the same interpretation, even placing greater emphasis on the role played by production conditions while neglecting the role played by demand in determining market-value. In Fine (1979), for example, the role played by demand in determining the market-value of commodities produced in rent-bearing sectors is completely ignored. Indeed, he is one of the first to argue that the determination of market-value of commodities in rent-bearing sectors undergoes a distortion compared to that of market-value in industrial sectors without rent. According to Fine:

> the market-value is not formed from the average of normal values, but by the worst method of production. This is not because the worst method is predominant, but because the intervention of landed property modifies the social formation of value in agriculture.
>
> *(Fine 1979: 250)*

However, instead of providing a clear explanation of the mechanism by which the intervention of landed property leads to market-values being "formed" by the worst method of production, Fine cites—in a puzzling manner—the following paragraph from *Capital*, which clearly describes Marx's own method:

> This is determination by market-value as it asserts itself on the basis of capitalist production through competition; the latter creates a false social value. This arises from the law of market value, to which the products of the soil are subject. The determination of market value of products, including therefore agricultural products, is a social act, albeit a socially unconscious and unintentional one. It is based necessarily upon the exchange value of the product, not upon the soil and the differences of its fertility.
>
> *(Marx 1981: 799)*

The distortion in the determination of market-values in rent-bearing sectors is also suggested by Itoh (1980). According to Itoh "…the marginal worst condition which is necessary to satisfy the social demand become the regulator of market value" (Itoh 1980: 89). Unfortunately, if Itoh had considered cases where production corresponding to the marginal worst condition might not be necessary to satisfy social demand, he would have concluded, as did Marx, that in those cases, the marginal worst condition cannot be the regulator of market-value. Shaikh (1990) provides an almost identical interpretation of the determination of market-value in rent-bearing sectors:

> it should be noted, incidentally, that while the shift of regulating conditions to one extreme or the other is precipitated here by 'extraordinary combinations' of supply and demand, this need not be the case when we consider technical change (in which the regulating conditions will be the best generally accessible methods of production) or production in agriculture and mining in which the regulating conditions are often the ones on the margin of cultivation and location, hence among the worst of the lands and locations in use.
>
> *(Shaikh 1990: 256)*

The assumption made by all of these authors of a permanent state of excess demand is once again explicitly stated by Mandel in his introduction to *Capital*, where he argues that in sectors where landed property prevent an influx of capital, "there is a long term preponderance of demand over supply. So the firms operating with the lowest productivity of labor in the branch still receive the average rate of profit (i.e., they determine the price of production, or the value, of the commodity produced in that branch)" (Marx 1981: 56).

Alternatively, if excess demand is not assumed, supporters of the view that the worst land always determines the market-value in rent-bearing sectors assume that the worst land's product is always necessary to satisfy demand. Yet as Marx argued against Ricardo, there may be cases when the supply from the best land makes the supply from the worst land, not only unnecessary, but even redundant. In such cases, it is the best land that determines both the market-value and the amount of differential rent to be appropriated by landlords.

Anti-essentialist interpretations

The essentialist interpretation of Marx's theory of market-value and rent described above has been challenged by a small but growing number of authors. Based on a detailed reading of Marx's writings, they argue that it is wrong to conclude that a particular condition of production (i.e., the worst land) should in and of itself determine the market-value of commodities without taking into account demand and other production conditions. Indart (1988), for example, argues that in sectors without rent:

> demand conditions establish what conditions of production are to become the value-determining ones, but their selection is from a given set of production conditions. It is in this sense that I see demand conditions as playing an indirect role in the determination of value.
>
> *(Indart 1988: 457)*

Horverak (1988) for his part provides a similar interpretation of Marx's theory of market-value:

> the market value of the commodities will now depend on whether there is correspondence between society's total demand for a commodity and the labor time spent on producing it... The scope of variation in the market value is set by the individual values: the market value can never be higher than the individual value of the commodity produced under the worst production conditions, or lower than the individual value of the commodity produced under the best conditions.
>
> *(Horverak 1988: 282).*

More recently, the dominant interpretation of Marx's theory of market-value has been criticized in a number of articles by Kristjanson-Gural (2005, 2009). In these articles, Kristjanson-Gural calls attention to the implicit essentialist methodology used in the dominant interpretation of Marx's theory of market-value, which contradicts what he persuasively shows to be Marx's own anti-essentialist approach. According to Kristjanson-Gural (2009), the Marxian tradition by failing to recognize Marx's anti-essentialist methodology has committed what he calls a diachronic error in their interpretation of Marx's theory of market-value, one that

> results from comparing logical claims at two different moments or levels of analysis without taking into account the different meanings and relationships between concepts that apply at each level.
>
> *(Kristjanson-Gural 2009:15)*

More specifically, this diachronic error has translated into a failure to understand how Marx developed the meaning of market-value through a step-by-step introduction of new contingencies into his analysis, likewise, how this concept relates to the relationship between value and exchange-value. By ignoring the steps Marx introduced in defining value in the first chapter of *Capital* volume I, where value is presented as resulting from a production process carried out by an individual capitalist, to the more developed concept of value as market-value in chapter 10 of *Capital* volume III, in the context of intra-industry competition, the Marxian tradition has failed to trace the logical development of the concept of value as socially necessary labor time.

Marx's step-by-step methodology gives rise to a very different interpretation of the concepts of market-value and socially necessary labor time; market-value becomes defined as the value of the commodity such as corresponds to the amount of labor time socially necessary in a dual sense: reflective of the average amount of time needed to produce the commodity and the amount of labor time needed to satisfy the existing social need, or demand, for the commodity.

In contrast to the dominant interpretation, an anti-essentialist interpretation finds no contradictions vis-à-vis Marx's presentation of market-value in chapter 10 of *Capital* volume III, wherein market-value is over-determined by both production and demand conditions: value is determined by the production process, while its magnitude is determined by demand vis-à-vis the spectrum of individual values ranging from the lowest to the highest individual value of commodities produced by competing capitalists seeking to satisfy the existing social need.

This anti-essentialist critique of the dominant theory of market-value in Marxian economics opens the door to an interpretation of Marx's theory of rent that enables us to better understand some of the most important features of the global capitalist system of the 21st century, wherein production and demand for primary commodities continue to play a crucial role in both advanced and emerging economies. Marxian economists need to rethink their understanding of market-value and rent by taking into account—rather than neglecting—a proper analysis of the brutal competition for profits that currently drives the behavior of producers operating on all types of land, likewise the determinants of the demand or social need of growing populations for these commodities.

Note

1 "In the Mercantile system, surplus-value is only relative—what one wins, the other loses: profit upon alienation or oscillation of wealth between different parties. So that within a country, if we consider the total capital, no creation of surplus-value in fact takes place. It can only arise in the relations between one nation and other nations." (Marx 1975, I: 66).

References

Fine, B. 1979. "On Marx's Theory of Agricultural Rent." *Economy and Society* 8(3): 241–278.

Horverak, Ø. 1988. "Marx's View of Competition and Price Determination." *History of Political Economy* 20(2): 275–297.

Indart, G. 1988. "Marx's Law of Market Value." *Science and Society* 51(4): 458–467.

Itoh, M. 1980. *Value and Crisis: Essays on Marxian Economics in Japan.* New York and London: Monthly Review Press.

Kristjanson-Gural, D. L. 2005. "Exchange, Demand and the Market-Price of Production: Reconciling Traditional and Monetary Approaches to Value and Price." *Rethinking Marxism* 22: 171–202.

——. 2009. "Poststructural Logic in Marx's Theory of Value." *Rethinking Marxism* 21(1): 14–33.

Mandel, E. 1962. *Marxist Economic Theory*, Volume 1. New York: Monthly Review Press.

——. 1990. "Introduction." In *The New Palgrave: Marxian Economics*, J. Eatwell, M. Milgate and P. Newman, eds. New York and London: W.W. Norton and Company.

Marx, K. 1975. *Theories of Surplus Value.* Part I and Part II. Moscow: Progress Publishers.

——. 1981. *Capital.* Volume 3. New York: Penguin Books.

Ricardo, D. 1973. *Principles of Political Economy and Taxation.* London and New York: Dutton.

Shaikh, A. 1990. "Market Value and Market Price." In *The New Palgrave: Marxian Economics*, J. Eatwell, M. Milgate and P. Newman, eds. New York and London: W.W. Norton and Company.

Smith, A. 1985. *An Inquiry into the Nature and Causes of the Wealth of Nations.* New York: Random House.

12

PRODUCTIVE AND UNPRODUCTIVE LABOR

Erik K. Olsen

The distinction between productive and unproductive labor is one of the more controversial ideas in economics. It can be traced to economic thought in antiquity,[1] has been part of modern economic thought since at least the 17th century, and features prominently in Physiocratic and classical political economy (Marx 1969, 176–82; Boss 1990). While this distinction is rejected by utilitarian economics, it remains a fundamental concept in Marxian economics despite sometimes heated debates within Marxism itself.[2] It is now associated most prominently with Marxist economics, though quite similar ideas can be found in other heterodox approaches, as in Veblen (1901) for example.

The literature on this topic demonstrates its continuing importance for Marxian economics. The productive/unproductive distinction can be clearly defined, is theoretically consistent, and provides a rigorous basis for empirical research. This distinction is also integral to Marxian theories of class and exploitation, and as such is an important aspect of Marxism's ethical critique of capitalism. A longstanding and growing literature documents the tremendous growth in unproductive activities in developed economies over the last century. But there is no consensus about what the consequences of this are for firm performance or aggregate dynamics, and this question represents one of the frontiers of Marxian economics.

Marx on Productive and Unproductive Labor

Marx develops a conception of productive and unproductive labor first briefly in *Grundrisse* (Marx 1993, 272–3, 305–6), and then subsequently through an extensive criticism of others in *Theories of Surplus Value* (1969, 152–300). Taking inspiration from Adam Smith he offers this definition:

> Productive labor, in its meaning for capitalist production, is wage-labor which, exchanged against the variable part of capital . . . , reproduces not only this part of the capital (or the value of its own labor-power), but in addition produces surplus-value for the capitalist. It is only thereby that commodity or money is transformed into capital, is produced as capital. Only that wage-labor is productive which produces capital.
>
> *(Marx 1969, 152)*

Marx retains this conception of productive labor in *Capital* with very little change.[3] When first analyzing the labor process he remarks that only labor engaged in the creation of a product is "productive labor," but also notes that in capitalism this criterion alone is not sufficient to determine whether labor is productive (1967a, 181). He returns specifically to this question again and gives this definition:

> Capitalist production is not merely the production of commodities, it is essentially the production of surplus-value. The laborer produces, not for himself, but for capital. It no longer suffices, therefore, that he should simply produce. He must produce surplus-value. That laborer alone is productive, who produces surplus-value for the capitalist, and thus works for the self-expansion of capital. . . . Hence the notion of a productive laborer implies not merely a relation between work and useful effect, between laborer and product of labor, but also a specific, social relation of production, a relation that has sprung up historically and stamps the laborer as the direct means of creating surplus-value.
>
> *(Marx 1967a, 508)*

These descriptions give two specific criteria for a Marxist definition of productive labor in capitalism. Assuming that production is viable and results in a surplus, productive labor satisfies two conditions:

1   It is production labor.
2   It is paid labor employed by capital.

Labor that does not meet both of these conditions is, by definition, unproductive.

These two conditions provide a theoretically rigorous and empirically useful definition, and together provide a common basis for most Marxist definitions of productive labor (compare, for example, Mohun 2003, 45; Shaikh and Tonak 1994, ch. 2; Resnick and Wolff 1987, 132–41; Foley 1986, 118–20; Howard and King 1985, 128–32). This definition involves two dimensions, a distinction between production and nonproduction activity, which is common to all economic theories, and a distinction between capitalist and non-capitalist production relations, which is of particular concern for Marxism. It is important to note that Marx's distinction does not attempt to assess whether a type of activity is useful or useless (by whatever criteria), or whether it is a "good" instead of a "bad," and it should also be noted that the difference between material and immaterial labor (or the distinction between goods and services) plays no part in this definition (Marx 1969, 156–60).[4] Rather the salient characteristics are whether an activity is *production* and whether it is *in the employ of capital*. These two criteria provide a relatively simple definition of productive labor, but they also require further specification of what production is, and what it means to be employed by capital.

Capitalist Employment

Much of the early part of volume one of *Capital* is devoted to developing a conception of capital. Marx refers to it as "self-expanding value" and notes that when money (value) is advanced for the purpose of making more money it becomes capital (Marx 1967a, 153). Marx's famous circuits of capital are designed to illuminate precisely this process, and, according to condition (2) above, only labor that enters into a circuit of capital is potentially productive labor. This potential is realized when condition (1) is also satisfied.

Employers advance capital to purchase labor power, and labor power exchanged for a wage from capital becomes (variable) capital. But not all producers sell their labor power, and not all wages are advances of capital. Peasants, artisans, and other self-employed persons produce and sell commodities, but they neither sell their labor power for a wage nor do they produce primarily by hiring others to do it for them. In Marx's assessment the productive/ unproductive distinction does not apply to this type of producer because they are outside of capitalist social relations.

> But what is the situation with independent handicraftsmen or with peasants who do not employ any workers, hence do not produce as capitalists? . . . they are *producers of commodities*, as always in the case of peasants . . . and I buy the *commodities* from them, . . . In this relation they meet me as sellers of commodities, not as sellers of labor, and this relation therefore has nothing to do with the exchange between capital and labor, hence it also has nothing to do with the distinction between *productive* and *unproductive labor*, which depends merely on whether the labor is exchanged for money as money or for money as capital. They therefore belong neither to the category of *productive workers* nor to that of *unproductive workers*, although they are producers of commodities. Their production is not subsumed under the capitalist mode of production.
>
> *(Marx 1994a, 141)*

The case of independent production for use, as in household labor, would similarly fall outside of capitalism and be neither productive nor unproductive. In contrast, Marx considers wage labor paid out of "revenue"—a term for the income of a capitalist used for personal consumption (Marx 1967a, 591; Marx 1969, 291)—unproductive because it includes the sale of labor power but this does not involve an advance of capital. In various places Marx works through numerous examples contrasting workers paid from revenue to perform personal services for a capitalist with workers paid from capital to produce these same services as a commodity for sale. The general principle that he derives from these examples is that unless labor is exchanged against capital it does not enter into a circuit of capital, creates no surplus value for a capitalist, and cannot be considered productive.

The employees of state agencies are another important case of workers who receive wage and salary income that is not paid from capital. State agencies perform government functions associated with what Shaikh and Tonak call the "maintenance and reproduction of the social order" (Shaikh and Tonak 1994, 60).[5] This includes functions of government at the national, state, and local level. These activities are primarily funded by revenues raised from taxation and the issuance of debt, and usually are not sold as commodities in markets. Marx's discussion of government officials and employees clearly indicates that, following Smith, he views them as unproductive, but his analysis is very limited.[6] In some cases he includes them with landlords, usurers, and rentiers, but in other cases he includes them with "ideo-logical classes" (Marx 1967a, 446) who, directly or indirectly, perform services for the industrial capitalist. In both cases these groups are paid out of the surplus value of the capitalist, which does not return directly to them in the form of a marketable product, and hence these payments are not advances of capital. Marx uses the term "*faux frais*" (literally "false costs," but interpreted variously as "overhead costs" or "incidental expenses") to refer to costs like this, and includes direct business taxes in this category of expenses (Marx 1967a, 220; 1967b, 421, 457). Unlike state *agencies*, Marx sees state-owned *enterprises* as poten-tially both engaging in production and operating with a capital stock (Marx 1975, 200;

1967b, 97). Hence they may be capitalist, and wage laborers at these enterprises may perform productive labor and create surplus value. This treatment carries over into the modern Marxist literature (Resnick and Wolff 1987, 231–74; Shaikh and Tonak 1994, 59).

Production and Nonproduction Activity

In *Capital* Marx refers to production as the labor process and describes it as "human action with a view to the production of use-values, appropriation of natural substances to human requirements" (Marx 1967a, 183–4). This presents production as deliberate human action to create goods or services able to satisfy human wants. But production takes a specific form under capitalist social relations. In this case it must not only satisfy some want or need, but must also be profitable. Profit gives the owner of capital an incentive to engage in production; usefulness or serviceability of the product is necessary but it is not a sufficient condition to induce capitalist production.

Production is a subset of human activities, shaped by but analytically distinct from nonproduction activities. This distinction is not uniquely Marxist. Stone and Stone (1961, 32) use the concept of a "production boundary" to define a set of production activities and differentiate them from nonproduction activities in the economy.[7] For Stone and Stone nonproduction activity consist of consumption, accumulation and international trade, but their taxonomy is only one of the many possible. The boundary between production and nonproduction activities and the classification of nonproduction activities are very basic theoretical issues with competing perspectives. The question of what is and is not production has a long history, and different positions in these debates help define competing paradigms in economics.[8] Indeed, much of the disagreement over productive and unproductive labor is fundamentally paradigmatic dispute over the location of the production boundary.

Marx's views are clearly grounded in classical political economy, and hence differ significantly from the current orthodoxy, which is strongly shaped by utilitarianism. Alfred Marshall, for example, that great popularizer of the utilitarian approach to economics, expresses this rather plainly when defining production:

> Man cannot create material things. When he is said to produce material things he really only produces utilities. In the mental and moral world indeed he may produce new ideas. But in the physical world, all the he can do is either to re-arrange matter so as to make it more useful, as when he makes a log of wood into a table; or to put it in the way of being made more useful by nature, as when he puts seed where the forces of nature will make it burst out into life. It is sometimes said that traders do not produce: that while the cabinet maker produces furniture, the furniture dealer merely sells what is already produced. But there is no scientific foundation for this distinction. They both produce utilities, and neither of them can do more: the furniture-dealer moves and re-arranges matter so as to make it more serviceable than it was before, and the carpenter does nothing more.
>
> *(Marshall 1890, 116)*

For Marshall, like Jevons before him (Brennan 2006), what economic activity produces is utility, and any activity that creates utility is production. He seems not to recognize that this pushes the production boundary back so far that it would include a utility-producing smile exchanged between passers-by on the street. A more recent contribution that also advocates an expansive production boundary is that of Becker, who is well aware that he pushes the production boundary back so far that it all but disappears and production comes to encompass the majority of human action (Boss 1990, 247–51). Becker (1965, 503–4) uses the concept of "productive consumption" to refer to activity typically interpreted as consumption (such as eating, sleeping, and "play") that he classifies as production. This leads him to conclude that "Not only is it difficult to distinguish leisure from other non-work but also even work from non-work" (Becker 1965, 504).

In contrast to these expansive views, very early in his economic work Marx (1973, 83–111) adopts a production boundary that defines distribution, circulation and consumption as non-production activities. This production boundary is made explicit by Marx's famous circuit of money capital, $M - C \ldots P \ldots C' - M'$, where M and M' represent quantities of money capital, C and C' quantities of commodity capital, either as input into production or output, and P is the transformation of capital inputs in production. While this is familiar, what is often overlooked is that production is only one moment in the circuit. The moments $M - C$ and $C' - M'$ represent circulation (the conversion of money into inputs and production output into money) and as such are nonproduction activities outside the production boundary.

In *Capital* Marx discusses nonproduction activities in some detail, with particular attention to circulation (1967b, chs 5, 6; 1967c, part IV), finance (1967c, part V), and land rental (1967c, part VI). In his analysis of circulation Marx notes that nonproduction activities are indeed necessary for capitalist production to take place, but this does not make them forms of production:[9]

> In the production of commodities, circulation is as necessary as production itself, so that circulation agents are just as much needed as production agents. The process of reproduction includes both functions of capital, therefore it includes the necessity of having representatives of these functions, either in the person of the capitalist himself or of wage laborers, his agents. But this furnishes no ground for confusing the agents of circulation with those of production, any more than it furnishes ground for confusing the functions of commodity capital and money-capital with those of productive capital. The agents of circulation must be paid by the agents of production. But the capitalists, who sell to and buy from one another, create neither values nor products by these acts, this state of affairs is not changed if they are enabled or compelled by the volume of their business to shift this function on to others.
>
> *(Marx 1967b, 126–7)*

It is worth considering precisely what circulation entails because, as Marx was well aware, production and circulation typically occur together and are not as easily separated as the circuit of money capital makes it appear. In practice circulation is typically the business of wholesale and retail trade enterprises, and involves several distinct processes: transportation, warehousing, marketing and the exchange of legal title to a commodity. In part these different activities are reflected in the final purchasers' price of a good, which can be decomposed into the producers' price, the wholesale and retail trade margins, and the transportation cost (Lawson, Bersani, Fahim-Nader and Guo 2002, 22). For Marx both transportation and warehousing are, within limits, aspects of the production process continued in circulation (Marx 1967b, 52–5, 136–52; see also Savran and Tonak 1999 and Tregenna 2009), and thus the practice of separating trade margins from transport costs is consistent with a Marxian decomposition of the activities of the trade sectors into production and nonproduction activities. The nonproduction activities of the enterprises in these trade sectors consist of marketing and the exchange of title, which *in themselves* create no good or service that enters into consumption, but rather are costly activities associated with the realization of produced commodities.[10] Market exchange is only one of the many ways, along with planning, lottery, potlatch, tradition, kinship networks, right of citizenship, etc., societies use to allocate produced goods and services to final consumers, and these are all alike in the sense that none of them are forms of production.

Of course one could reject this argument by simply assuming that trading activities are *per se* the production of services, and this is the convention taken in modern national accounts. But this is clearly a decision based on paradigmatic grounds, not on anything obvious or intrinsic about these activities. Consider, for example, an increase in the retail trade sector mark-up *ceteris paribus*. Current conventions in national income accounting would report this as an increase in *real* national income and product because they interpret the retail trade sector as producing a service, the output of which is measured by its total trade margin (Bureau of Labor Statistics 2012). Consequently, an increase in the retail trade margin is recorded as an increase in the production and sale of retail services, even if the total volume of goods passing to consumers remains unchanged. This is axiomatic for a conception of the economy that assumes all remunerated activities are production, but it cannot be defended on utilitarian grounds or any grounds other than a paradigmatic commitment to treating all remunerated activities symmetrically as production. This is a theoretical choice, nothing more. Similar examples abound. The private, market-based U.S. healthcare system spends significantly more on activities, like billing and coding, risk assessment and risk management, finance, advertising, etc., than government, non-market systems. These circulation activities are entirely separate from patient care but significantly increase the cost of providing it. And yet these costs are counted as part of the "output" of health care sector under current conventions in economic accounting.

Looking beyond circulation activities, for Marxism most supervision in the workplace is, like circulation, nonproduction activity, but it is nonproduction for a very different reason. Supervision becomes necessary when the interests of workers and their employers are contradictory or antagonistic. Marx notes that when labor is a "combined social process" involving a number of different laborers working together, coordination is necessary and "this is a productive job (Marx 1967c, 383)." However, he also notes that whenever production is based on antagonism between the direct producer and the owner of the means of production (as under slavery and capitalism) management must also involve supervision and coercion to ensure labor productivity (Marx 1967a, 330–2).

The antagonism of interests between workers and their employers is easy to identify. A worker's effort level is variable and the quantity of surplus they produce depends directly on work intensity. Work intensity is costly for the worker, requiring the exertion of energy and attention, but the profitability of the enterprise is directly a function of their effort level. Therefore, the effort level chosen by an unsupervised worker will certainly be less than what their employer would choose for them (see Chapter 5, "Labor and Labor Power," in this Handbook). Supervisory labor is then a consequence of this antagonistic or contradictory relationship, necessary in order to impose the employer's objectives on employees.

Supervision, in this case, is not necessary to produce, it is necessary to produce under capitalism because the conflicting incentives of worker and employer require it.[11] It makes little sense to think of coercive supervision when a worker works independently, as do peasants, the self-employed, etc., and, in Marx's estimation, it would not be necessary under communism either (Ollman 1977, 30). What is left then is that supervisory labor (as distinct from the labor of coordination) is nonproduction activity because it is necessitated by antagonistic social relations of production and the profit making imperative of capitalist production rather than anything intrinsic to a specific production activity. Instead of a productive input, coercive supervision consumes a portion of the surplus created in production (Marx 1972, 355). This contrasts with modern conventions, which recognize that principal-agent relations give rise to agency problems that require costly solutions, but, taking an expansive view of production, counts these solutions as production.

Space limitations prevent significant discussion here of the other two types of nonproduction activity discussed at length in *Capital*, finance and the rental of land. Marx never seriously entertains the question of whether these are production and simply accepts that they are not. The financial sector generates its income by taking deposits and lending money at interest, which is why Marx's circuit of interest bearing capital, M – M', contains neither production nor circulation (Marx 1967c, 391).[12] Land rental provides access to land and existing structures. Even though without them a market economy would be constrained, it is highly dubious to claim that these sectors produce a product (measured by sectoral income) rather than simply a claim on the output of the productive sectors.

Empirical Estimates

The empirical Marxist literature estimating unproductive labor stretches back at least to the 1920s, usually done as part of estimating of value aggregates for national economies.[13] This includes work on a number of different countries published in many languages, but the English-language literature focuses primarily on the U. S. and the discussion here reflects that orientation. Notable contributions to the development of Marxist empirical methods include Gillman (1958), Wolff (1977), and Moseley (1991). Shaikh and Tonak (1994) construct the methodology that is now standard for estimating productive and unproductive labor. This is described, analyzed in detail, and significantly updated by Mohun (2005, 2014) and Paitaridis and Tsoulfidis (2012). Olsen (2011) uses Shaikh and Tonak's basic theoretical approach to develop a Marxian social accounting matrix and emphasizes the class aspects of this work.

Shaikh and Tonak estimate productive and unproductive shares of total employment for the 1948–89 period (1994, Table F). They find that 85 percent of total employment growth in the U.S. economy over this period was unproductive, and that the unproductive share of total employment grew from 43 percent to 64 percent. Furthermore, they find that while a majority of unproductive labor is in nonproduction sectors, the increase in unproductive labor increased disproportionately because of growth in nonproduction employment in production sectors (trade, government, etc.).[14] Mohun (2005, 2006, 2014) and Paitaridis and Tsoulfidis (2012) present more recent estimates. Drawing general conclusions from these various estimates is difficult because they are not easily comparable. All of these estimates are ultimately based on the U.S. Input-Output and National Income and Product Accounts, supplemented by Bureau of Labor Statistics surveys, and these change significantly as a result of the transition from the older Standard Industry Codes (SIC) system of industrial classification to the current North American Industrial Classification (NAICS) system in the late 1990s and early 2000s. These changes are significant enough that data using the SIC system are not directly comparable with that using the NAICS system, and likewise the Marxian estimates using data collected with these different classification systems are not comparable. Differences in methodology, revisions to data sources, and the inclusion or exclusion of general government also gives rise to significant differences in results.

Despite their differences, these studies indicate that the long-term trend of a growing unproductive share of total employment, which Gillman (1958) first identified as beginning in the late nineteen-teens, persisted through the 1980s and then levelled off, but the growing share of wage and salary income going to unproductive workers continued unabated. The twentieth century U.S. economy is characterized by persistent growth in unproductive labor and a concomitant increase in the unproductive share of wage and salary income, with these trends diverging after 1990. Easy characterization of the U.S. experience is further compli-cated by Mohun (2014, 363–5), who shows that over the 1964–2010 period the increasing share of wage and salary income captured by unproductive labor went entirely to supervisory and managerial employees, while the share going to the "unproductive working class" remained constant. Mohun's analysis shows the importance of a Marxian class analysis that goes beyond a simple distinction between productive and unproductive labor and considers the composition of these broad class groupings. Characterizing unproductive labor as an undifferentiated group obscures important within-group differences.

Does the Distinction Matter?[15]

The Marxian classification scheme for productive and unproductive labor may be theoreti-cally consistent and provide a sufficient basis for empirical research, but the important question remains whether this distinction yields important insights for economic and social analysis. The importance of the finding that the U.S. economy added large numbers of unproductive laborers in the 20th century is called into question by the fact that it also grew robustly over much of this period. What precisely is the substantive research program motivated by the stylized fact of a growing class of unproductive laborers?

One consistent argument made by Marxist authors is that unproductive activities are simply a drag on economic performance because they consume surplus value and reduce profits, which interferes with accumulation and growth (Gillman 1958, 85; Moseley 1991, 153; Shaikh and Tonak 1994, 213; Paitaridis and Tsoulfidis 2012, 217–18). Baran (1957) and Baran and Sweezy (1966) take a somewhat different perspective and argue that unproductive activities are "waste" within the capitalist economic system, but this waste has an unintended benefit. They propose a tendency for the surplus to rise in the era of monopoly capitalism (Baran and Sweezy 1966, chs 3–4), potentially giving rise to a realization problem from a lack of effective demand. For them, growth of unproductive activities provides a necessary outlet for the expanding surplus and thereby supports the effective reproduction of the system.

There is support in Marx's writings for the idea that some unproductive activities are 'wasteful' in the sense of arising simply out of the antagonism inherent in capitalist social relations, or the ideological, policing, and public welfare functions necessary to maintain stability in an exploitative, class-divided society. But it is much more difficult to sustain the argument that Marx viewed all unproductive activities as simply burdening capitalist repro-duction and growth. Marx clearly argues that some unproductive activities may increase surplus value in capitalist production, thereby increasing profitability, and indeed in many cases this is precisely why an industrial capitalist is willing to pay for them.[16] For example, in analyzing circulation Marx (1967b; chs 5–6; 1967c, 279–80) argues that merchant's capital reduces the time of circulation M – C and C' – M', which reduces the turnover time of industrial capital and increases surplus value. Supervisory labor increases work intensity of productive laborers, and in so doing increases the rate of surplus value. Similar arguments can be made for other forms of nonproduction activity.

Some Marxists have pursued research along these lines. Gordon (1990; 1996, ch. 3) studies the growth of corporate bureaucracies in the postwar period, with particular emphasis on supervisory labor, and argues that U.S. corporations increasingly relied on a "stick" strategy of conflictual labor relations, in which workers receive low wages and little job security and must therefore be intensely supervised in order to produce efficiently.[17] Duménil and Lévy (2003, 2011) emphasize that the purpose of unproductive labor within enterprises is to maximize the profit rate, and focus attention on the growth of unproductive labor as a means that corporations use to increase profit beyond simply inducing productive workers to increase labor intensity.

Resnick and Wolff (1987, 187–91) were perhaps the first to stress the complex and contradictory role of unproductive labor in Marxian economic dynamics. They emphasize that capital accumulation is inversely related to growth in unproductive labor only if this growth leaves the Marxian rate of profit unchanged or declining. Since the effect of any expenditure of surplus value on an enterprise's rate of profit is highly contingent, so too is its effect on capital accumulation. Increasing expenditure on the internal bureaucracy of a firm, for example, could reduce total cost by reducing the cost of finance, purchasing, etc., thereby increasing profit, and potentially capital accumulation. But if this expenditure simply increases the compensation of employees without reducing total cost, profit and accumulation would be reduced rather than increased. This same contingency exists for almost any use of surplus by the enterprise.

Several authors have sought to establish the impact of unproductive labor by introducing it into models of economic growth. Wolff (1987, ch. 4) made the first sustained effort along these lines, but his work owes more to Baumol's two-sector (manufacturing, service) model of unbalanced growth and Solow's neoclassical growth model than it does to Marxism. In effect, Wolff adapts Baumol's theory of the differential rates of productivity growth between goods and service sectors to model the effect of unproductive activity on a capitalist economy. Dutt (1991) takes inspiration from Wolff's work and endeavors to develop an avowedly "neo-Marxist" two-sector model. But again the long-period dynamics are driven by differential rates of "productivity" growth in the two sectors (positive in the productive sector, zero in the unproductive sector), and the long-period dynamics are ultimately driven by something akin to "Baumol's disease." There is certainly something to be gained in Marxism by recognizing these Baumol-type effects, but it is just as certain that the effect of unproductive activity on Marxian dynamics cannot be limited simply to this.

More recent work introduces unproductive labor into Marxian models in a more complex way than has been done previously. Olsen (2015) and Vasudevan (2016) integrate unproductive labor into dynamic models of a capitalist economy, but unlike the Wolff-Dutt approach allow for these activities to potentially increase work intensity, reduce the turnover time of capital, or both. Olsen also introduces endogenous technological change resulting from ongoing transformation of the labor process and finds that, like Resnick and Wolff's firm-level analysis, at the aggregate level the effect of unproductive activities on economic performance is contingent. It may squeeze profits and reduce economy-wide growth or increase work intensity, reduce turnover time, and develop productivity-enhancing technological change, thereby increasing profitability and the rate of growth. Olsen's analysis of Shaikh and Tonak's (1994) data shows that both outcomes are observed at different points in the U.S. during the postwar period.

This emerging literature indicates that the Marxian perspective on unproductive labor is changing, and it raises important questions about precisely why it is called "unproductive." One answer is simply that Marx inherited this terminology from classical political economy. But this ignores another less obvious but more profound explanation: the productive/unproductive distinction is the basis for Marx's theory of class. In his mature economic works

Marx very clearly analyzes the relationship between different occupations and social groups by referencing their position relative to the production, appropriation and distribution of a surplus.[18] This requires a clear explanation of where surplus is created and how it subsequently circulates through the constellation of positions that constitute the class structure. In such a taxonomic system some produce surplus value, and hence are productive workers, while others receive the surplus value produced by others. Marx's analysis of the class structure of capitalism is then intimately linked to the productive/unproductive distinction because it is an integral part of his theory of the origin of surplus value. The Marxian ethical and moral indictment of capitalism as a historically-specific class system that exists and reproduces itself through the exploitation of workers is also based on the idea that workers who create surplus value by their labor in production neither receive nor control it (Resnick and Wolff 2005, 34; Henry 1975). But if all wage and salary employment is production, then surplus value production is ubiquitous and both Marxian class theory and its ethical implications are greatly circumscribed.

What is clear is that the Marxist productive/unproductive distinction has sufficient theoretical and empirical bases, and provides unique and provocative insights into a capitalist economy. Research using this distinction has only recently reached the point where it is possible to employ many of the methods common in social science research. Whether this emerging line of research will yield insights that transcends paradigmatic and political boundaries remains to be seen.

Notes

1 Aristotle (1988, book I, part X, 15) groups retail trade with usury as ways of making money from money, which he considers unnatural because money, in itself, creates nothing.

2 See Hunt (1979, 309, note 4) for a list of this literature within Marxism, but Hunt's treatment of the productive/unproductive distinction itself is not recommended. A more recent example is the exchange between Mohun (1996, 2002), Houston (1997) and Laibman (1999).

3 Gough (1972) provides significant detail of Marx's treatment of productive and unproductive labor in *Capital* and *Theories of Surplus Value*. See also Marx's *Economic Manuscript of 1861–63* (Marx 1994a, 121–46) and "Results of the Direct Production Process" (Marx 1994b, 442–52), both of which contain significant analyses of this topic. Gough did not have access to either of these texts.

4 This point is unambiguous (see, for example, Marx 1969, 158) but is an important source of confusion in the literature. Marx uses a variety of occupations throughout his work to illustrate the conditions under which they are productive or unproductive depending on the social circumstances of the labor process, including writer, schoolteacher, piano player, actor, musician, prostitute, clown, and singer, so it is difficult to understand how there could be any controversy over this issue.

5 See also Resnick and Wolff (1997, ch. 5; 2002) for a Marxist analysis of the state.

6 Marxists have generally accepted as a settled issue that government activities are unproductive, but few have analyzed this in detail. Among the few that do are Shaikh and Tonak (1994, 60) and Savran and Tonak (1999, 138), both of which argue that government functions are nonproduction activity. There are sufficient grounds in Marx's work to conclude that this is indeed his position (1969, 303–4).

7 Unlike the usage here, "production boundary" is often used to distinguish types of production included in national accounts from those, like illegal activities and household production for use, which are not. Following Stone and Stone (1961) this entry uses this term to distinguish between production and nonproduction.

8 Brennan (2006, 404) provides a very insightful analysis of the evolution of this idea from a feminist perspective and argues that the production boundary is "one of the most historically debated aspects of economic thought." Studenski (1958, 11–26) traces a four-century-long history of the

development of concepts of production and national income in economic thought, beginning in the 16th century. Studenski's work exhibits obvious erudition, but his treatment of Marx is badly misleading and borders on polemical. Studenski seems to mistakenly interpret Soviet national accounting, with its exclusive focus on material production, as an accurate expression of Marx's views. Boss (1990) also covers some of the more recent literature and, while no more sympathetic towards Marx than Studenski, does a significantly better job interpreting his work.

9 Boss (1990, 6–7) calls reasoning of this type an "input-output error" guilty of an "unproductiveness fallacy". She coins these terms but fails to provide convincing theoretical foundations, instead seeming to assume that anything "economically necessary" simply *must* be considered production, and hence to argue the converse is to advance a fallacy. But the Marxian position is that many nonproduction activities, like trading, civil governance, military, police, etc., are forms of social consumption, not production (Shaikh and Tonak 1994, 1–5).

10 Baran and Sweezy (1966, ch. 5) analyze circulation from a Marxist perspective with particular emphasis on marketing.

11 See Bowles (1985; 2004, 269–78) for a rational choice microeconomic analysis of the capitalist employment relation that derives the existence of nonproductive supervisory labor in competitive equilibrium.

12 Marx's views are, of course, significantly more sophisticated than this (Marx 1967c, part V). See Lapavitsas (2013, esp. ch. 6) for a modern analysis of the profits of the financial sector.

13 Shaikh and Tonak (1994, 161–72) provide a comprehensive survey this early empirical Marxian literature.

14 Mohun (2014, Tables 2 and 3) provides a comprehensive breakdown of productive and unproductive sectors by SIC and NAICS sectors. An appendix also contains a very useful description of data sources and in-depth discussion of methods.

15 This section draws from Olsen (2015).

16 It may seem contradictory to propose that unproductive activities may increase the production of surplus value and yet be considered unproductive. But these activities remain nonproduction, and hence unproductive, because the production boundary is established by function, not effect. Marx's position on this is discussed by Olsen (2015, 39).

17 Goldstein (2012) extends Gordon's analysis through the first decade of the 2000s.

18 See Chapter 3, "Marxian Class Analysis," in this Handbook, and Resnick and Wolff (1987, ch. 3). Wright (2015, viii, 9–11, 44–7) discusses varieties of Marxian class theory with particular emphasis on the issue of exploitation and class.

References

Aristotle. 1988. *The Politics*. Edited by Stephen Everson. Cambridge: Cambridge University Press.

Baran, P. A. 1957. *The Political Economy of Growth*. New York: Monthly Review Press.

Baran, P. A. and P. M. Sweezy. 1966. *Monopoly Capital*. New York: Monthly Review Press.

Becker, G. 1965. "A Theory of the Allocation of Time." *The Economic Journal* 75(299): 493–517.

Boss, H. 1990. *Theories of Surplus and Transfer*. Boston: Unwin Hyman.

Bowles, S. 1985. "The Production Process in a Competitive Economy: Walrasian, Neo-Hobbesian, and Marxian Models." *American Economic Review* 75(1): 16–36.

——. 2004. *Microeconomics: Behavior, Institutions and Evolution*. Princeton: Princeton University Press.

Bowles, S. and A. Jayadev. 2007. "Garrison America." *The Economists' Voice* 4(2): Article 3.

Brennan, D. M. 2006. "Defending the Indefensible? Culture's Role in the Productive/Unproductive Dichotomy." *Feminist Economics* 12(3): 403–425.

Bureau of Labor Statistics (U.S. Department of Labor). 2012. "Wholesale and retail Producer Price Indexes: margin prices." *Beyond the Numbers* 1(8): 1–4. Available at: http://www.bls.gov/opub/btn/volume-1/pdf/wholesale-and-retail-producer-price-indexes-margin-prices.pdf (accessed July 15, 2016).

Duménil, G. and D. Lévy. 2003. "Production and Management: Marx's Dual Theory of Labor." In *Value and the World Economy Today*, R. Westra and A. Zuege, eds. New York and Basingstoke: Palgrave Macmillan.

———. 2011. "Unproductive Labor as Profit-Rate-Maximizing Labor." *Rethinking Marxism* 23(2): 216–225.

Dutt, A. 1991. "Unproductive Activity and Stagnation: A neo-Marxian Model." *Review of Radical Political Economics* 23(1 and 2): 95–103.

Foley, D. 1986. *Understanding Capital: Marx's Economic Theory*. Cambridge, MA: Harvard University Press.

Gillman, J. M. 1958. *The Falling Rate of Profit*. New York: Cameron Associates.

Goldstein, A. 2012. "Revenge of the Managers: Labor Cost Cutting and the Paradoxical Resurgence of Managerialism in the Shareholder Value Era, 1984–2001." *American Sociological Review* 77(2): 268–294.

Gordon, D. 1990. "Who Bosses Whom? The Intensity of Supervision and the Discipline of Labor." *The American Economic Review* 80(2): 28–32.

———. 1996. *Fat and Mean*. New York: The Free Press.

Gough, I. 1972. "Marx's Theory of Productive and Unproductive Labour." *New Left Review* I/76: 47–72.

Henry, J. F. 1975. "Productive Labour, Exploitation and Oppression—A Perspective." *Australian Economic Papers* 14(24): 35–40.

Houston, D. 1997. "Productive-Unproductive Labor: Rest in Peace." *Review of Radical Political Economics* 29(1): 131–147.

Howard, M. C. and J. E. King. 1985. *The Political Economy of Marx*, 2nd edition. New York: New York University Press.

Hunt, E. K. 1979. "The Categories of Productive and Unproductive Labor in Marxist Economic Theory." *Science and Society* 43(3): 303–325.

Jayadev, A. and S. Bowles. 2006. "Guard Labor." *Journal of Development Economics* 79(2): 328–348.

Laibman, D. 1999. "Productive and Unproductive Labor: A Comment." *Review of Radical Political Economics* 31(2): 61–73.

Lapavitsas, C. 2013. *Profiting Without Producing*. London and New York: Verso.

Lawson, A. M., K. S. Bersani, M. Fahim-Nader, and J. Guo. 2002. "Benchmark Input-Output Accounts of the United States, 1997." *Survey of Current Business* 82: 19–43.

Marshall, A. 1890. *Principles of Economics* (1st edition). London and New York: Macmillan and Co.

Marx, K. 1967a. *Capital*, Volume 1. New York: International Publishers.

———. 1967b. *Capital*, Volume 2. New York: International Publishers.

———. 1967c. *Capital*, Volume 3. New York: International Publishers.

———. 1969. *Theories of Surplus Value*, Part 1. London: Lawrence & Wishart.

———. 1972. *Theories of Surplus Value*, Part 3. London: Lawrence & Wishart.

———. 1973. *Grundrisse*. London and New York: Penguin Books.

———. 1975. "Notes on Adolph Wagner." In *Karl Marx, Texts on Method*. Trans. and edited by T. Carver, 159–219. Oxford: Basil Blackwell.

———. 1993. *Grundrisse*. New York and London: Penguin Books.

———. 1994a. *Economic Manuscript of 1861–64*, in K. Marx and F. Engels, *Collected Works*, vol. 34, 7–247. New York: International Publishers.

———. 1994b. "Chapter 6: Results of the Direct Production Process." In K. Marx and F. Engels, *Collected Works*, vol. 34, 355–461. New York: International Publishers.

Mohun, S. 1996. "Productive and Unproductive Labor in the Labor Theory of Value." *Review of Radical Political Economics* 28(4): 30–54.

———. 2002. "Productive and Unproductive Labor: A Reply to Houston and Laibman." *Review of Radical Political Economics* 34(2): 203–220.

———. 2003. "Does All Labour Create Value?" In *Anti-Capitalism: A Marxist Introduction*, A. Saad-Filho, ed., 42–58. London: Pluto Press.

——. 2005. "On Measuring the Wealth of Nations: The US Economy, 1964–2001." *Cambridge Journal of Economics* 29(5): 799–815.

——. 2006. "Distributive Shares in the US Economy, 1964–2001." *Cambridge Journal of Economics* 30(3): 347–370.

——. 2014. "Unproductive Labor in the U.S. Economy 1964–2010." *Review of Radical Political Economics* 46(3): 355–379.

Moseley, F. 1991. *The Falling Rate of Profit in the Postwar United States Economy*. New York: St. Martin's Press.

Ollman, B. 1977. "Marx's Vision of Communism: A Reconstruction." *Critique* 8(1): 4–41.

Olsen, E. K. 2011. "Modeling the Economic Surplus in a SAM Framework." *American Journal of Economics and Sociology* 70(5): 1175–1207.

——. 2015. "Unproductive Activity and Endogenous Technological Change in a Marxian Model of Economic Reproduction and Growth." *Review of Radical Political Economics* 47(1): 34–55.

Paitaridis, D. and L. Tsoulfidis. 2012. "The Growth of Unproductive Activities, the Rate of Profit, and the Phase-Change of the U.S. Economy." *Review of Radical Political Economics* 44(2): 213–233.

Resnick, S. A. and R. D. Wolff. 1987. *Knowledge and Class*. Chicago: University of Chicago Press.

——. 2002. *Class Theory and History*. London and New York: Routledge.

——. 2005. "The Point and Purpose of Marx's Notion of Class." *Rethinking Marxism* 17(1): 33–7.

Rubin, I. I. 1973. "Productive Labor." In *Essays on Marx's Theory of Value*, I. I. Rubin, 259–275. Montreal and New York: Black Rose Books.

Savran, S. and E. Ahmet Tonak. 1999. "Productive and Unproductive Labour: An Attempt at Clarification and Classification." *Capital & Class* 22(68): 113–152.

Shaikh, A. M. and E. Ahmet Tonak. 1994. *Measuring the Wealth of Nations: The Political Economy of National Accounts*. Cambridge: Cambridge University Press.

Stone, R. and G. Stone. 1961. *National Income and Expenditure*. London: Bowes and Bowes.

Studenski, P. 1958. *The Income of Nations*. New York: New York University Press.

Tregenna, F. 2009. "Services' in Marxian Economic Thought." *Cambridge Working Papers in Economics* (0935), Faculty of Economics, University of Cambridge. Available at: http://www.econ.cam.ac.uk/research/repec/cam/pdf/cwpe0935.pdf (accessed July 15, 2016).

Vasudevan, R. 2016. "Financialization, Distribution and Accumulation: A Circuit of Capital Model with a Managerial Class." *Metroeconomica* 67(2): 397–428.

Veblen, T. 1901. "Industrial and Pecuniary Employments." *Publications of the American Economic Association*, third series, 2(1): 190–235.

Wolff, E. N. 1977. "Unproductive Labor and the Rate of Surplus Value in the United States, 1947–67." In *Research in Political Economy*, Volume 1, P. Zarembka, ed., 87–115. Greenwich: JAI Press.

——. 1987. *Growth, Accumulation, and Unproductive Activity*. Cambridge: Cambridge University Press.

Wright, E. O. 2015. *Understanding Class*. London and New York: Verso.

13

ALIENATION

Sean Sayers

Alienation is a pervasive feature of modern life. It is one of the few theoretical terms from Marxism that has entered into ordinary language. There it usually denotes a vague feeling of malaise or meaninglessness. In Marx, however, it has a precise meaning derived from Hegel's philosophy, and it plays a central role in Marx's economic and social thought. For Marx, alienation is a condition in which our own activities or products take on a form that is independent of us and act against us.[1] Moreover, it is not a merely subjective feeling or appearance, it is an objective social and historical condition.

The Politics of Alienation

Marx's discussion of alienation is most prominent and explicit in his early writings, particularly in the *1844 Manuscripts*, where the influence of Hegel's philosophy is most evident.[2] The place of these writings in Marx's work, and the relation of Marx to Hegel more generally, has long been controversial. Although Marx himself went out of his way to stress his allegiance to Hegel,[3] there was little recognition of this among his early followers. A mechanistic and economistic interpretation was common. In the Stalin period this was imposed as the Communist orthodoxy. Hegelian Marxists (such as Lukács, Korsch, Gramsci, Deborin, Ilyenkov, etc) were barely tolerated.

The *1844 Manuscripts* suffered a similar fate. These, and other early writings by Marx left unpublished at his death,[4] did not see the light of day for many years. The *1844 Manuscripts* first appeared in Moscow in 1932.[5] The Soviet authorities treated them with suspicion as juvenilia written when Marx was still excessively under the spell of Hegel, and before he had developed his 'mature' economic theory and the historical materialist approach. This was the attitude adopted by many other writers on Marxism as well who seldom referred to or discussed these works.[6]

Things changed rapidly with the 'thaw' that followed Stalin's death in 1953. Translations of the early works into English and other European languages began to appear, and they rapidly became the focus for criticism of the mechanistic and economistic form of Marxism that had been the Communist orthodoxy. They were hailed by a variety of 'humanist' Marxists in Eastern and Western Europe and America and by thinkers associated with the New Left, as evidence of a newly revealed humanist, ethical aspect of Marx's thought.[7]

These claims were also strongly disputed, most influentially by Althusser. Many were persuaded to refocus their attention away from the Hegelian and ethical themes in Marx's work and back onto its political, economic and historical ideas. However, in his zeal to expunge any traces of Hegelianism from Marxism, Althusser went to the opposite extreme. He argued that there was a radical 'break' – an 'epistemological break' – between the Hegelian, ethical ideas of Marx's early work centred on the concept of alienation, and his mature 'scientific' and materialist theory.[8] 'Humanism' became a term of abuse. From this perspective the concept of alienation has no place in an account of Marxist economics.

An equally strong hostility to the Hegelian themes in Marxism and to the concept of alienation (though on very different grounds) has been a defining feature of the school of analytic Marxism as well, which has been influential in the English speaking world in recent years.[9]

Now that the political dust has settled somewhat, it has become increasingly clear that the idea of a sharp break between Marx's early and later thought is untenable. Even Althusser himself abandoned it, and came to recognize that Hegelian themes are present in Marx's work throughout.[10]

As regards the idea of alienation, it is true that the term itself is used only rarely by Marx in his later work. However, the *concept* of alienation, as defined above, is a feature of Marx's thought throughout. This is clear from *Grundrisse*,[11] the first full draft of what was later to become volume one of *Capital*. This is a later work in which not only the concept but also the language of 'alienation' is used extensively. It is as it were the 'missing link' that makes clear that underlying Marx's shifting attempts to find suitable forms of expression for his ideas, there are deeper continuities in Marx's thought.[12]

Althusserian and analytical Marxism have dominated Marxist philosophy for the past fifty years, with the result that little attention has been paid to the theme of alienation, particularly in the context of Marxist economic thought. This is unfortunate. The attempt to understand Marx's philosophy without reference to Hegel leads to a seriously distorted picture both of Marx's early and later work. Alienation – even in the early works – is not a merely moral idea. It is at the centre of Marx's initial attempts to analyse capitalism in social and economic terms. Marx does not abandon this analysis as his thought develops. Rather, it is deepened and enriched and worked out in economic detail in Marx's later work.

Early Work

The most extended account of alienation in Marx's early works occurs in the section of the *1844 Manuscripts* devoted to 'estranged labour'. Indeed, labour is sometimes treated as the main or even as the sole area about which Marx uses the concept, but this is not the case. Marx identifies alienation in many areas of life, including religion, politics, and social and economic relations. In his earliest work, religion is the central example. 'Man makes religion, religion does not make man', says Marx,[13] and yet the gods that we have created appear to be independent beings, often judgemental and hostile.

Alienated Labour

From 1844 onwards, Marx's work focuses increasingly on economics. The *1844 Manuscripts* constitutes Marx's first extended attempt to get to grips with the work of the classical political economists, Adam Smith, James Mill, J. B. Say, etc. This represents a decisive turn in his thought. His notion of alienated labour is often taken to describe a purely subjective condition, a lack of satisfaction in work. Marx, however, uses the concept to analyse the ways in which – in capitalism – our own products take on an independent and hostile form.

Work is our 'species being' (*Gattungswesen*), the activity which distinguishes humans from other species. Other animals are driven by their individual appetites and instincts. For the most part, they satisfy their material needs immediately, by directly consuming what is immediately present to them. Humans, by contrast, are social beings who work to transform what is immediately present to satisfy their needs. Work is thus a distinctively human activity, a social activity, and it leads to self-development and self-realization. In labour man 'acts upon external nature and changes it, and in this way he simultaneously changes his own nature'.[14] In conditions of alienation, however, work is reduced to its 'animal' character-istics. It loses its distinctively human features and becomes a mere means to satisfy our individual material needs. These ideas originate directly from Hegel's philosophy; they are developed and given a critical dimension by Marx.[15]

Economic Relations

Mainstream economics regards work as an essentially individual activity to satisfy individual needs. Although it may take place within the context of relations with others, these are treated as purely contingent. For Marx, by contrast, human beings are essentially social. Work, as a human activity, necessarily occurs within a context of social relations. In the *1844 Manuscripts* and subsequently, Marx insists that in work we create not only a material product, we also produce and reproduce our social relationships.[16]

As the products of our labour we should be able to recognize our social and economic relations as a confirmation of our powers and abilities. In conditions of alienation, however, they become independent of us and opposed to us. Individuals are atomised and economic forces take on a life of their own, obeying their own quasi-objective laws. This is a further aspect of alienation: the alienation of 'man from man'.[17]

This is how both individuals and the economy are usually regarded in economics. However, individuals are not separate atoms; and economic laws, unlike natural laws, are social products, specific to particular forms of society. Mainstream economics thus presents what are the alienated features of a specific sort of society as though there are objective and universal economic forms. In this way, Marx's critique of political economy in this area parallels his critique of the economists' picture of labour.

Later Developments

Marx does not abandon these ideas in his later economic thought, rather he develops and extends them.[18] This is evident in his accounts of the concepts of abstract labour and the idea of fetishism which are central features of Marx's theory of value as it is presented in its finished form in *Capital*.[19] These concepts do not constitute a break but rather an elaboration and expansion of the ideas initially first sketched out in his early works under heading of 'estranged labour'.

Abstract Labour

According to the theory of value which is at the core of Marx's economic thought, a commodity has two aspects: a use value and a (exchange) value. Two kinds of labour go into its creation. In so far as work creates a use value (a product that meets needs), it is concrete labour. Different forms of concrete labour go to create qualitatively different products to meet different specific needs (carpentry is a different activity from shoemaking, and so on). But in so far as the product of labour is destined for exchange, the labour that goes into it creates something of value which can be equated with and exchanged for other things of equal value. According to Marx, this equivalence of value is achieved by equating the quantities of labour embodied in them. The labour involved in this value relation is what Marx terms 'abstract', 'homogeneous', 'social labour'.[20] Such abstract labour is a mere means to the creation of value, it is indifferent to its specific concrete quality.

The abstraction involved here is not merely conceptual, Marx insists, 'it is an abstraction which is made every day in the social process of production'.[21] It occurs only in conditions in which commodity production has become the prevalent form: i.e., in bourgeois society.

> Indifference towards specific labours corresponds to a form of society in which individuals can with ease transfer from one labour to another, and where the specific kind is a matter of chance for them, hence of indifference. Not only the category, labour, but labour in reality has here become the means of creating wealth in general, and has ceased to be organically linked with particular individuals in any specific form.[22]

The split between use value and value goes back to beginnings of exchange, but it grows and reaches its fully developed form only with the predominance of commodity production in capitalism.

> The product of labour is an object of utility in all states of society; but it is only a historically specific epoch of development which presents the labour expended in the production of a useful article as an 'objective' property of that article, *i.e.*, as its value.[23]

The social effects of the development commodity production were becoming apparent in ancient Athens, a city state whose wealth was founded on commerce and trade. In Plato and Aristotle's time the distinction between use value and value, concrete and abstract labour, was beginning to assert itself socially; but concrete labour, production for use, was still the predominant form of production.

Plato treats craft work (e.g., shoe making), and money making as two quite separate and distinct activities, and maintains that the 'proper' activity of the worker is to pursue his craft *and not* to make money.[24] Aristotle formulates the distinction between use value and value with great clarity, and regards the use value of a product as its 'proper' use.[25]

> Every piece of property has a double use … For example a shoe may be used either to put on your foot or to offer in exchange. Both are uses of the shoe; for even he that gives a shoe to someone who requires a shoe, and receives in exchanges coins or food, is making used of the shoe as a shoe, but not the use proper to it, for a shoe is not expressly made for purposes of exchange.[26]

Now, with the development of capitalism, commodity production has become the predominant form. Most production is not directly for use but for exchange. Exchange value predominates over use value; abstract labour predominates over concrete labour: i.e., labour which is a mere means to an end external to it predominates. We do not usually satisfy our needs directly through our work. Rather, work takes the form of wage labour: it is undertaken in order to earn a wage, and its product is robbed of all specificity, it is simply something of value, destined for exchange.

This is precisely the form of work that Marx analyses under the heading of 'alienated' or 'estranged' labour in the *1844 Manuscripts*. In his later work he gives an account of it under the heading of 'abstract labour'. This concept is developed fully in *A Contribution to the Critique of Political Economy* (1859) and subsequently in *Capital*, Volume I, specifically in the context of the theory of value (as outlined briefly above). This notion is just beginning to emerge in *Grundrisse* (1858): for example in the following passage where the connection between the earlier account of alienated labour and the later concept is clearly evident.

> The worker himself is absolutely indifferent to the specificity of his labour; it has no interest for him as such, but only in as much as it is in fact *labour* and, as such, a use value for capital. It is therefore his economic character that he is the carrier of labour as such – i.e. of labour as *use value* for capital; he is a worker, in opposition to the capitalist. This is not the character of the craftsmen and guild-members etc., whose economic character lies precisely in the *specificity* of their labour and in their relation to a *specific master*, etc. This economic relation – the character which capitalist and worker have as the extremes of a single relation of production – therefore develops more purely and adequately in proportion as labour loses all the characteristics of art; as its particular skill becomes something more and more abstract and irrelevant, and as it becomes more and more a *purely abstract activity*, a purely mechanical activity, hence indifferent to its particular form.[27]

Economic and Social Relations

Economic and social relations, too, take on an alienated form: a form which is independent and hostile. Marx uses a graphic image to describe this sort of alienation:

> Modern bourgeois society ... a society that has conjured up such gigantic means of production and of exchange, is like the sorcerer who is no longer able to control the powers of the nether world whom he has called up by his spells.[28]

In the *Grundrisse*, again, the connection of alienated forms of economic relation and alienated forms of labour is clearly spelled out.

> Activity, regardless of its individual manifestation, and the product of activity, regardless of its particular make-up, are always *exchange value*, and exchange value is a generality in which all individuality and peculiarity are negated and extinguished ... The social character of activity, as well as the social form of the product, and the share of individuals in production here appear as something alien and objective, confronting the individuals, not as their relation to one another, but as their subordination to relation which subsist independently of them and which arise out of collisions between mutually indifferent individuals.[29]

In *Capital*, Marx analyses alienated economic and social relations of this sort under the heading of the 'fetishism of commodities'. Exchange value achieves a quasi-objective existence, it appears to be a property of the object. Economic relations take on a seemingly objective and independent form as economic laws. In this way social relations take on the 'fetishized' form of relations between things.

Mainstream economics regards economic laws as objective and timeless, like laws of nature. According to Marx, however, they are created by the specific social and historical conditions of bourgeois society. With altered social conditions they can therefore be changed.

To maintain that these notions are historically specific is not to suggest that they are mere subjective social appearances or purely conceptual occurrences. On the contrary, economic relations are objective social and historical phenomenon. 'The categories of bourgeois economics consist precisely of forms ... of thought which are socially valid, and therefore objective, for the relations of production belonging to this historically determined mode of social production.'[30]

Thus, these categories are not universal. The economic relations that they describe came into being with the rise to predominance of commodity production;[31] and they will cease to operate in the future when bourgeois relations of production cease to be the predominant form of economic life.[32]

Alienation and the Critique of Capitalism

These ideas are at the basis of Marx's criticisms of capitalism. Although there is undoubtedly a moral dimension to Marx's critique of capitalism, this is not the main character of his critique even in his early work. And, in particular, this is not the main significance of the concept of alienation. Its main purpose rather is to analyse the nature of capitalist economic forms. Their impact is not entirely negative, as the moral interpretation tends to imply, it is more complex and contradictory. Marx understands the effects of capitalism in historical and dialectical terms and this leads towards a historical rather than a merely moral form of criticism.

Precapitalist forms of labour, such as craft work, are limited in content and scope. Such work is restricted to specific materials and techniques and it is individual and small in scale. Economic life before the growth of capitalist relations of production took place within the context of the household and of personal and local relationships. The development of capitalism means that people are detached from these relationships and subjected to new economic relations that involve abstract and alien forms of work and social life. However, the impact of these developments is not entirely negative. For in the process people are progressively freed from the confines of natural and immediate relations. They are subjected to economic relations through which their activities and connections become wider and more universal; and through these they acquire new capabilities and develop in individuality, self-consciousness and freedom.[33]

This not to say that alienation is a satisfactory condition to be welcomed. It is a condition of distress and suffering. However, these negative aspects themselves give rise to the forces to overcome them. Seen in this light, capitalism and its economic forms – alienation and abstract labour – are not purely negative phenomena. They play also a positive role in the process of human development. Marx's judgement on them is not one of mere moral condemnation, it is relative and historical.[34] Relative to earlier forms of social relation, alienation is a positive development in the way I have indicated; but as conditions for its overcoming are created it becomes something negative and a hindrance to development.

These dialectical and Hegelian themes are central to Marx's account of alienation and his critique of bourgeois society. However, they are ignored or even positively denied in much of the recent discussion of Marx's thought. For example, these Hegelian aspects of Marx's thought are rejected entirely by Althusser and his followers;[35] and they are usually overlooked by analytical Marxists as well.[36]

Overcoming alienation means regaining control of our productive activity and economic life. This cannot be achieved by a return to immediate production for use without the mediation of exchange relations. That is what sometimes appears to be implied by thinkers unduly influenced by Aristotle, or by various forms of Green romanticism.[37] Such regression is now out of the question and, in any case, it would be undesirable: it ignores the progress – both material and moral – that economic development has brought about. Rather what Marxism envisages is that the economic development will eventually create the conditions through which alienation can be overcome by the social appropriation of control over the economy by the 'associated producers'. Then, economic life will no longer take an alienated and hostile form.

This does not require the complete elimination of the role of exchange, or consideration of value, or of abstract labour, which would be possible only with a return to the simplest and most primitive form of economic and social life. Rather what is envisaged is the social organization and control of production and exchange. This will involve the overcoming of the subordination of use value to exchange value, of the domination of commodity production in economic life, and the re-appropriation of control over our social relations and economic life, and with that the end of fetishism.

The concept of alienation and its expression in the ideas of fetishism and abstract labour, embodies these wider – social, moral, political, economic – themes. It has a fundamental role in Marx's economic thought.

Notes

1 'Alienation' is one of the standard translations of both *Entfremdung* and *Entäußerung* in Marx's work. I am not aware of any clear evidence that Marx uses these terms to denote different concepts. Like most other authors in English I will not distinguish between these terms.
2 Esp Marx 1975a; Marx 1975b.
3 Marx 1976, 102–3.
4 Esp Marx 1975a; Marx 1975b.
5 Marx and Engels 1927.
6 Musto 2010, 89.
7 For example, Tucker 1961, Fromm 1963, Schaff 1963. See Kolakowski 1978, Vol. 3 ch. 13.
8 Althusser 1969.
9 Cohen 1978, Roemer 1986.
10 Althusser 2006, 211, 258; cf Roche 2005, McLellan 1973, Introduction.
11 Marx 1973. First published in 1953.
12 McLellan 1973.
13 Marx 1978, 53.
14 Marx 1976, 283.
15 For a fuller account of the relation of Marx's ideas to Hegel's, see Sayers 2011b, chapter 2.
16 'Through estranged labour man not only produces his relationship to the object and to the act of production as to alien and hostile powers; he also produces the relationship in which other men stand to his production and product, and the relationship in which he stands to these other men' (Marx 1975a, 331).
17 Marx 1975a, 330. Marx identifies four aspects of alienated labour in this passage (alienation from the product, the activity of labour, our species being, and of man from man). For a fuller account see Ollman 1971 and Sayers 2011b, chapter 6.

18 Esp. in Marx 1971, Marx 1973, Marx 1976.

19 Marx 1976, chapter 1.

20 Marx 1976, 134–5. There are significant theoretical problems with Marx's account of abstract labour, but these are not relevant to the continuities of Marx's thought to which I am pointing here (Kay 1999, Meikle 2007; Arthur 2013).

21 Marx 1971, 30, cf. Marx 1973, 103–6.

22 Marx 1973, 104.

23 Marx 1976, 153–4.

24 Plato 1987, Book I, Sayers 1999, 14–15.

25 Meikle 1995.

26 Aristotle 1981, 1257a1255, 1281–1252. Associated with this, Aristotle distinguishes a 'natural' from an 'unnatural' method of 'acquiring goods' (*chrēmatistikē*), Aristotle 1981, I.ix.

27 Marx 1973, 297.

28 Marx and Engels 1978, 478.

29 Marx 1973, 157.

30 Marx 1976, 169.

31 There is some apparent ambiguity in Marx about whether alienation is specific to capitalism, for at times he appears to imply that alienation is a feature of all class divided societies. However, the main account given in the *1844 Manuscripts*, and the later notions of fetishism and abstract labour, clearly imply that alienation is specific to capitalism. For a fuller discussion see Sayers 2011b, 87f.

32 There has been considerable controversy about whether the law of value will continue to operate in communist society (Bukharin and Preobrazhenskii 1969, Mandel 1968).

33 Sayers 2011a.

34 Sayers 2011b, chapter 6.

35 Cowling 1989, Cowling 2006, Cullenberg 1995, Resch 1992.

36 Exceptionally, however, G. A. Cohen gives an excellent account of them in places (Cohen 1988, Cohen 1978, Introduction). Otherwise, unfortunately, the anti-historical and anti-Hegelian assumptions of Cohen's analytical approach entirely eclipse his awareness of these themes.

37 MacIntyre 1998, Gorz 1989.

References

Althusser, L. 1969. *For Marx*. London: Allen Lane.

———. 2006. *Philosophy of the Encounter: Later Writings, 1978–1987*. London: Verso.

Aristotle. 1981. *The Politics*. Trans. by T.A. Sinclair and revised by T.J. Saunders. Revised ed. Harmondsworth: Penguin.

Arthur, C. J. 2013. "The Practical Truth of Abstract Labour." In *In Marx's Laboratory: Critical Interpretations of the Grundrisse*, R. Bellofiore, G. Starosta and P. Thomas, ed., 101–120. Leiden: Brill.

Bukharin, N. I., and E. A. Preobrazhenskii. 1969. *The ABC of Communism*. Harmondsworth: Penguin.

Cohen, G.A. 1978. *Karl Marx's Theory of History: A Defence*. Oxford: Clarendon Press.

———. 1988. "The Dialectic of Labour in Marx." In *History, Labour, and Freedom*, 183–208. Oxford: Clarendon Press.

Cowling, M. 1989. "The Case for Two Marxes, Restated." In *Approaches to Marx*, M. Cowling and L. Wilde, eds., 14–32. Milton Keynes: Open University Press.

———. 2006. "Alienation in the Older Marx." *Contemporary Political Theory* 5: 319–339.

Cullenberg, S. 1995. "Althusser and the Decentering of the Marxist Totality." In *Postmodern Materialism and the Future of Marxist Theory: Essays in the Althusserian Tradition*, A. Callari and D. F. Ruccio, eds., 120–149. Hannover, NH: Wesleyan University Press.

Fromm, E. 1963. *Marx's Concept of Man*. New York: Frederick Ungar.

Gorz, A. 1989. *Critique of Economic Reason*. London: Verso.

Kay, G. 1999. "Abstract Labour and Capital." *Historical Materialism* 5(1): 255–280.

Kolakowski, L. 1978. *Main Currents in Marxism*. Trans. by P.S. Falla. 3 vols. Oxford: Oxford University Press.

MacIntyre, A. 1998. "The Theses on Feuerbach: A Road Not Taken." In *The Macintyre Reader*, Kelvin Knight, ed., 223–234. Cambridge: Polity Press.

Mandel, E. 1968. *Marxist Economic Theory*. 2 vols. London: Merlin Press.

Marx, K. 1971. *A Contribution to a Critique of Political Economy*. Moscow: Progress.

———. 1973. *Grundrisse: Foundations of the Critique of Political Economy (Rough Draft)*. Trans. by M. Nicolaus. Harmondsworth: Penguin.

———. 1975a. "Economic and Philosophical Manuscripts of 1844." In *Early Writings*, 279–400. Harmondsworth: Penguin.

———. 1975b. "Excerpts from James Mill's Elements of Political Economy." In *Early Writings*, 259–278. Harmondsworth: Penguin.

———. 1976. *Capital*. Trans. by B. Fowkes, Volume 1. Harmondsworth: Penguin.

———. 1978. "Contribution to the Critique of Hegel's Philosophy of Right, Introduction." In *The Marx-Engels Reader*, R. C. Tucker, ed., 53–65. New York: W.W. Norton.

Marx, K. and F. Engels. 1927. *Marx-Engels Gesamtausgabe*. Berlin: Marx-Engels-Verlag.

———. 1978. "Manifesto of the Communist Party." In *The Marx-Engels Reader*, R. C. Tucker, ed., 473–500. New York: W.W. Norton.

McLellan, D. 1973. *Marx's Grundrisse*. St Albans: Paladin.

Meikle, S. 1995. *Aristotle's Economic Thought*. Oxford: Clarendon Press.

———. 2007. "Marx's Two Theories of Value." http://marxandphilosophy.org.uk/assets/files/society/word-docs/meikle2010.doc (accessed October 2, 2016).

Musto, M. 2010. "Revisiting Marx's Concept of Alienation." *Socialism and Democracy* 24(3): 79–101.

Ollman, B. 1971. *Alienation: Marx's Conception of Man in Capitalist Society*. Cambridge: Cambridge University Press.

Plato. 1987. *The Republic*. Trans. by H.D.P. Lee. 2nd revised edition. Harmondsworth: Penguin.

Resch, R. P. 1992. *Althusser and the Renewal of Marxist Social Theory*. Berkeley: University of California Press.

Roche, J. 2005. "Marx and Humanism." *Rethinking Marxism* 17(3): 335–348.

Roemer, J. E., ed. 1986. *Analytical Marxism*. Cambridge: Cambridge University Press.

Sayers, S. 1999. *Plato's Republic: An Introduction*. Edinburgh: Edinburgh University Press.

———. 2011a. "Macintyre and Modernity." In *Virtue and Politics: Alasdair Macintyre's Revolutionary Aristotelianism*, P. Blackledge and K. Knight, eds., 79–96. Notre Dame: University of Notre Dame Press.

———. 2011b. *Marx and Alienation: Essays on Hegelian Themes*. Basingstoke and New York: Palgrave Macmillan.

Schaff, A. 1963. *A Philosophy of Man*. New York: Monthly Review Press.

Tucker, R. C. 1961. *Philosophy and Myth in Karl Marx*. Cambridge: Cambridge University Press.

14

PRIMITIVE ACCUMULATION

Rajesh Bhattacharya and Ian J. Seda-Irizarry

Introduction

The concept of "primitive accumulation" has a checkered history within the Marxist tradition. In the writings of Karl Marx, the concept was used to uncover the origin of the capitalist mode of production through historical analysis. For a long while, its use was confined to transition studies—i.e. studies of transition to the capitalist mode of production, particularly in "backward" countries. However, in recent times, the concept has been used in the context of richer capitalist economies as well. The theoretical significance of the primitive accumulation, already visible in Marx's writings, was later elaborated upon and developed by a number of Marxists.

For the most part, Western Marxist discourse in the 20th century did not find any theoretical space for the concept of primitive accumulation in the analysis of advanced capitalist societies that were supposedly built on the firm foundations of constitutionality, property, and rights. It was presumed that primitive accumulation was unfolding in the "underdeveloped" world where the transition to the capitalist mode of production was tearing apart and uprooting communities, common properties, and non-market social institutions through blatant use of force and coercion by the state on behalf of emergent capitalists. While the predatory state was seen as running amok in the rest of the world, such extra-market coercive processes were assumed to be absent in the developed world, where the silent workings of the market system ensured the reproduction of capital and the legal and social institutions reined in the predatory impulses of capital and the state.

However, with the dismantlement of the welfare state and its regulatory instruments in the developed world and the increased global competition resulting from successful capitalist transition in other parts of the world in the last four decades, the veil over capital has been lifted, exposing its violent face as workers' rights and social security measures are curtailed, property in means of production are privatized on a large scale, and financialization of the economy leads to a systematic destruction of workers' pension funds and foreclosure of mortgaged houses. At the same time, faster accumulation in parts of the developing world in a reconfigured geography of production has meant dispossession on a scale never seen before. By way of intellectual response to these two developments, there is renewed interest in the concept of "primitive accumulation" among critics of contemporary capitalism.

Despite its enduring appeal, the theoretical significance of primitive accumulation in Marxian political economy is far from settled.

Karl Marx's Concept of "Primitive Accumulation"

In February of 1858, while working on the first draft (*Grundrisse*) of what would become his magnum opus, *Capital* (1990), Marx wrote a letter to his friend Ferdinand Lassalle where he expressed that the work he was "concerned with is a *Critique of Economic Categories* or, if you like, a critical exposé of the system of bourgeois economy" (Engels 1987: 270). For Marx, *kritik* did not imply engaging in an absolute rejection of something, but instead it meant an assimilation/appropriation and transcendence of that which was given. In the realm of theory this meant examining the system of categories deployed by bourgeois political economy, pointing to the nature of its abstractions (limits, biases, inconsistencies, etc.) and dialectically utilizing some of those same categories to produce new ones with meanings that diverged radically from the original ones. Understood in this sense, Marx's *critique of political economy*, is both inside and outside the tradition of classical political economy.

As Marx made clear in *Capital*, the necessity of accounting for a "previous accumulation" had been acknowledged by classical political economists for explaining capital, as well as for justifying profit.[1] Adam Smith (1937: 48) talked about "previous accumulation of stock" which sets in motion wage labor. Nassau Senior (1965) had provided a justification of profit based on his abstinence theory, which also explained the origin of capital. By investing primitive accumulation with a radically new meaning, Marx developed a powerful critique of these "bourgeois" accounts of the emergence of capital-wage labor relation which tried to argue that abstinence, hoarding, and saving were undertaken by the "diligent, intelligent and above all frugal elite," a decision that explained their accumulated wealth and property *vis a vis* the precarious condition of the "lazy rascals" who had "nothing to sell but themselves" (Marx 1990).[2] For Marx this "nursery tale" (Marx 1990, 874) was yet another example of how "bourgeois" history tended to naturalize, eternalize, and legitimize an emerging capitalist society while obscuring the history of class struggles. In this regard it is important to remember that since his early writings Marx had consistently confronted "bourgeois" theories and the nature of their theoretical abstractions. In the *Economic and Philosophical Manuscripts* of 1844 his critique was aimed at the ways in which the concepts of wages, rents, and profits were naturalized into ahistorical categories in an apologetic theoretical scaffold that celebrated the virtues of private property and markets while obscuring the state of dependency and powerlessness of those that had nothing but themselves to sell in the market.

In *Grundrisse*, Marx devoted considerable space to the analysis of various types of pre-capitalist property relations in relation to communal modes of production and appropriation to highlight its contrast with property relations necessary for capitalist production for profit and accumulation (Marx 1973: 471–9). In the passages on original accumulation, Marx writes eloquently of the condition of labor in capitalist social relations—a condition in which living labor is confronted by past, objectified labor as an instrument of domination.[3]

Marx's concept of primitive accumulation is developed more comprehensively in the eighth and final part of volume one of *Capital*, titled "So-Called Primitive Accumulation" where he provides the reader with a mass of material pertaining to the *historic* rise of capitalism as the hegemonic socio-economic system in Western Europe.[4] This section, consisting of eight chapters, comes after Marx has developed the concept of capital through the construction of abstract theoretical categories (e.g. abstract labor, labor power, surplus value etc.) earlier in the book. His turn to concrete history at this point reflects Marx's awareness of the inevitable challenge of a historical mode of analysis, i.e. one must account for the prehistory of the historicized object of analysis—in this case, capitalist mode of production.

In *Capital*, Marx sought to show how the "so-called primitive accumulation ... is nothing else than the historical process of divorcing the producer from the means of production" and how it created the market for labor power by producing a class of "bird-free" laborers—freed from both the bondage of feudal class relations as well as from all property in means of production (Marx 1990: 874, 896). Marx's focus on *dispossession/separation* of the direct producers required him to point to the complex interaction of multiple processes that led to expropriation and other forms of forced separation of direct producers—from English enclosures to colonization, slavery, overseas plunder and coercive national policies pertaining to wages, taxes, trade and credit.

This complex, prolonged, and tortuous history produced both wage-laborers and industrial capitalists. In contrast to the "freedom, equality, property and Bentham" (Marx 1990: 280) of the markets with rights-bearing and rights-respecting members of the bourgeois society, Marx de-naturalized the history of capital and emphasized the constitutive role of expropriative force—of negation and erasure of (other) rights and property (Marx 1990: 927)—that laid the foundations of a bourgeois society founded on capitalist industrial wealth. In his writings, primitive accumulation is an expansive concept that connects the theoretical concept of capital as a social relation—a relation between moneyed people and dispossessed laborers—to the concrete and convergent histories of enrichment of a class of people (capitalists) and the dispossession of another class of people (workers). However, it required a whole set of interventions to transform and consolidate the encounter between moneyed people and dispossessed laborers into an industrial capitalist relation.

The type-form of primitive accumulation was of course the enclosure of agricultural land and expropriation of peasantry from farmland in England, both through private initiatives and legislations, at different points of time between 15th and 18th centuries. Customary rights enjoyed by direct producers in the traditional economy were abrogated through multiple legislations (Tigar and Levy 1977). Perelman (2000) mentions "Game Laws" in Britain that prevented the common people from hunting in the woods and thus securing any means of independent subsistence.[5] Legislations were passed so that industrial by-products would not provide "economic resources outside the matrix of the wage-relation" (McNally 2012: 49).

While emphasizing the centrality of dispossession in the genesis of capitalist social relations, Marx connected it to a wide range of diverse events. For example, Marx pointed out how public debt and the fiscal system contributed to the "capitalization of wealth and the expropriation of the masses" (Marx, 1990: 919–21), and how protectionist trade policies were "artificial means of manufacturing manufacturers, or expropriating independent workers, of capitalizing the national means of production and subsistence ..." (Marx 1990: 921). Marx also recognized the crucial importance of how "[t]he discovery of gold and silver in America, the extirpation, enslavement and entombment in mines of the indigenous populations of that continent, the beginnings of the conquest and plunder of India, and the conversion of Africa into a preserve for the commercial hunting of blackskins, are all things which characterize the dawn of the era of capitalist production" and why "[t]hese idyllic proceedings are the chief moments of primitive accumulation" (Marx 1990: 915).[6]

Also important in the development of Marx's argument is his exploration of some of the political and cultural conditions of existence required to develop and sustain the labor market given the resistance of the dispossessed producers. In his examination of the "Bloody

Legislation against the Expropriated" he documents how, during the end of the 15th and the whole of the 16th century, legislation against vagabondage was passed and enforced in England. Similarly, intellectual as well as legislative attacks on the "sloth" and leisure (as evident in the eradication of national holidays) produced the discourse of industrious and deserving labor (Perelman 2000). E. P. Thompson (1967) chronicles the cultural interventions in the life of working people to orient them to the new work regime under capitalism—symbolized in the "clock" as the regulator and the measurer of a new concept of work measured in clock hours.

For Marx, these processes together contributed to the creation of a working class "which by education, tradition, and habit looks upon the requirements of [the capitalist] mode of production as self-evident natural laws" (Marx 1990, 899). In short, the separation of direct producers from independent access to means of production and subsistence is the theoretical core of the concept of primitive accumulation as deployed by Marx; however, concrete historical processes of such separation are varied and multiple. But Marx's reference to the extraordinary range of interventions as moments of primitive accumulation clearly shows that separation of direct producers from means of production may not necessarily give birth to the capitalist class relations. Hence the ultimate outcome of primitive accumulation will have to be historically investigated in concrete social contexts.

Contemporary Uses of Primitive Accumulation

After Marx, the use of primitive accumulation came to be confined to historical accounts of transition to capitalism in developing countries. It is interesting that the concept of primitive accumulation resurfaced in the context of rapid industrialization in Soviet Russia. Yevgeni Preobrazhensky coined the term *primitive socialist accumulation* to refer to the processes of financing socialist industrialization in a largely agrarian economy. In more recent times, Marxist writings on primitive accumulation have rescued the notion from its marginal position in the Marxian discourse, and placed it right at the heart of contemporary analyses of capitalism. The concept has been deployed in diverse contexts, such as present day land-grabs (Basu 2007; Hall 2013), gender and reproduction (Federici 2004; Werholf 2000), intellectual property rights (Harvey 2006, Basu 2008; Perelman 2002), and financialization and neoliberalism (Harvey 2003).[7] Further, the salience of primitive accumulation in contemporary political economy has also motivated a reconceptualization of the concept itself. Throughout *Capital*, Marx appears to move back and forth between a teleological view of historical change and a contextual understanding of social transformation that is informed by contingency. The former narrative employs a teleological understanding of historical materialism to posit primitive accumulation as the "becoming of capital," an initial stage in a historical journey through the various modes of production in which the capitalist mode of production supersedes pre-capitalist ones. The starting point is the encounter between the owners of money and the dispossessed workers where capital, once constituted, reproduces this relationship of dispossession on an expanded scale, driven by the forces of production (Engels 1987; Kautsky 1910).[8]

This particular historicist reading of the concept of primitive accumulation is an example of a Hegelian reading of Marx which builds on the "being-becoming" distinction to explain the emergence of a self-reproducing totality, in this case, capital.[9] Primitive accumulation is posited as the historical precondition for the capitalist class relation, and therefore "disappear [s] as real capital arises" (Marx 1973: 459) given that capital can now secure its own conditions of existence from within itself.[10] Thus capital, once arisen, creates new capital through exploitation and accumulation rather than through appropriation of wealth from outside. At the same time, it overcomes natural constraints on the labor supply through the dynamics of the industrial reserve army, which is inescapably tied to the dynamics of the business cycle. The conditions of (expanded) reproduction of capital can now be secured within the capitalist economy. It is otherwise during the "becoming" of capital when capital secured its conditions from outside, i.e. the non-capitalist space.

On the other hand, in an influential intervention, Louis Althusser, in his very last writings, argued that Marx's chapters on primitive accumulation in *Capital* are exemplary instances of anti-essentialist epistemology that Marx brought to the study of political economy—and that these chapters (along with similar chapters like those on the struggles over the length of the working day) stand outside the *formal* essentialist architecture i.e. outside the "fictitious unity," of *Capital*. Althusser advances a historical-aleatory reading of capital where the encounter between owners of money and dispossessed was not a fated event and neither is the stability of the encounter rationally ordained.

The elements of the capitalist mode of production were not fated to come together, since they "do not exist in history so that a mode of production may exist, they exist in history in a 'floating' state prior to their 'accumulation' and 'combination,' each being the product of its own history, and none being the teleological product of the others or their history" (Althusser 2006: 198). As opposed to the *necessity* or *inevitability* of the encounter, Althusser emphasized its contingency.

> 'It so happens' that this encounter took place, and 'took hold', which means that it did not come undone as soon as it came about, but *lasted*, and became an accomplished fact, the accomplished fact of this encounter, inducing stable relationships and a necessity the study of which yields 'laws'—tendential laws, of course…What matters about this conception is less the elaboration of laws, hence of an essence, than the *aleatory character of the 'taking-hold' of this encounter, which gives rise to an accomplished fact* whose laws it is possible to state.
>
> *(Althusser 2006: 197; emphasis in original)*

The "encounter" and its stability is contingent and provisional and thus vulnerable to dissolution or transformation. In this sense, primitive accumulation can be thought of as the process that continually reproduces the encounter constitutive of capitalist mode of production, but this reproduction is always contingent and uncertain. In Althusser's rendition, primitive accumulation points to the provisional stability and radical uncertainty that is internal to the capitalist mode.[11]

Both Rosa Luxemburg and Lenin had theoretically resurrected the idea of primitive accumulation in the context of a mature and expanding capitalist mode of production—the necessity of a non-capitalist space for capital to invade, and thereby destroy, in order to secure natural resources, cheap labor, markets for final products, and also for profitable investment of accumulated capital. Luxemburg and Lenin thus connected primitive accumulation to the internal contradictions of a capitalist economy, manifested in the problems of underconsumption or falling rate of profits among others. However, both Lenin and Luxemburg have a functional view of the non-capitalist "outside" grounded in arguments based on capital's needs.

David Harvey has taken the Luxemburg thesis and stripped it of its teleological implications. Harvey (2003) argues that capital, when faced with a crisis of overaccumulation, actively "creates" its outside at one point in time and space to destroy it at another, Harvey prefers the term "accumulation by dispossession" to primitive accumulation to emphasize the point that primitive accumulation is a continuous process and not one that ends with the rise of capitalist mode of production. In line with Harvey, various contemporary Marxist writings use a notion of "primitive accumulation" as an ongoing process that secures conditions of reproduction of the capitalist mode of production.[12] The moment one theorizes "primitive accumulation" as internal to the workings of a capitalist economy, the idea of self-reproducing, self-subsistent capitalist mode of production has to be jettisoned and with it must go the teleology inherent in the being-becoming distinction. We therefore, have a new theoretical problematic inaugurated by contemporary writings of Marxists on primitive accumulation.[13]

In these current approaches the process of *privatization* is seen as one of the most potent tools for primitive accumulation, especially the waves of privatization that have accompanied the last decades of capitalism. Andreasson (2006) points to an expanding sphere of dispossession based on an extension of private property regimes not only by traditional means, but also, and increasingly so, by more sophisticated and novel means like "intellectual property rights." Boyle (2002) refers to "the enclosure of the intangible commons of the mind" as the "new kind of enclosure movement".[14] This period is also characterized by the undermining of the "commons" created by welfare states of richer countries via privatization and commoditization under what is referred to as "neoliberal capitalism" (De Angelis 2001; Harvey 2003, 2006) and by the integration of state assets in China and the former Soviet Union into the metabolism of global capital accumulation (Harvey 2003: 149). Finance is also seen as an instrument of accumulation by dispossession, where financial markets facilitate large-scale redistributions of wealth in favor of global corporate capital.[15]

Further, the "neoliberal" state itself engages in redistributive policies—from lower income to upper income social classes as also from public to private domains—through privatization but also through tax incentives and subsidies to businesses coupled with a reduction in social expenditure. Internationally, carefully manipulated debt traps (Latin American countries in the 1980s and 1990s) and financial crises (Asian Crisis in 1997–8) have resulted in transfer of wealth from poorer to richer countries. Crises lead to devaluation of assets, which are subsequently seized by corporate capital. Nation-states and international organizations like World Bank, IMF etc. work in tandem to enable "accumulation of dispossession" through careful management of crises.

The centrality of primitive accumulation to reproduction of capitalism, as conceptualized variously in contemporary contributions, however, raises the issue of how to distinguish between capitalist accumulation and primitive accumulation. The distinction has traditionally often been drawn on the basis of the salience of economic versus extra-economic, market versus non-market, productive versus appropriative forces. Primitive accumulation has often been identified with the state as the monopoly owner of arbitrary power. Yet, nature, economy, culture and politics may all play a role in primitive accumulation understood as separation of direct producers from means of production. The distinction between capitalist accumulation and primitive accumulation becomes a theoretical problem in itself (Zarembka 2002; De Angelis 2001; Bhattacharya, 2010).

Primitive Accumulation and the "Outside" of Capital

Contemporary conceptualizations of primitive accumulation also point to another theoretical problematic—the logical necessity of an "outside" of capital if primitive accumulation is theorized as constitutive of capitalist mode of production. In the historical rise of industrial capitalism, entire pre-capitalist societies from which capitalism emerged were the "outside" of capital and capital historically grew *out* of it. To talk about primitive accumulation as a continuous process, we must theorize an *enduring* "outside" of capital—not merely that from which capital emerges and leaves behind—but that which marks the limits of capital.

In the Marxian literature we can identify three different notions of the "outside" of capital with slight variations within. First, there is an "outside" that is *historically given*—e.g. traditional, pre-capitalist societies where "attachment" to means of production still exists in the form of communal rights over means of production and subsistence, artisans and petty producers with their own means of production, peasants working on family farms and so on. Luxemburg's (2003) theory of underconsumption and Lenin's (1916) theory of imperialism are classic examples of this particular deployment of the concept of the pre-capitalist "outside" while Meillassoux's (1972) and Wolpe's (1972) contributions lay emphasis on the importance of this "outside" to cheapening the value of labor power when part of the reproduction costs of labor power are borne by the "outside."

Basu (2007, 2008) emphasizes how, through primitive accumulation, exclusive control over property rights in markets and over resources of production is achieved by global capital to extract "ground rent" for providing access to such monopolized items. Such extraction of ground rent, preceded by and made possible by primitive accumulation, can leave intact historically given non-capitalist modes of production—e.g. extraction of ground rent by multinational corporations for use of genetically modified seeds by peasants in developing countries.

The second notion of the "outside" explains it as the result of capital's own development. This follows the recognition that capital may not be able to secure its conditions of existence internally, especially conditions associated with its stabilization in moments of crisis.

> [C]apitalism necessarily and always creates its own 'other'. The idea that some sort of 'outside' is necessary therefore has relevance. But capitalism can either make use of some pre-existing outside.......or *it can actively manufacture it*.......capitalism always requires a fund of assets *outside of itself* if it is to confront and circumvent pressures of overaccumulation. If those assets, such as empty land or new raw material sources, do not lie to hand, *then capitalism must somehow produce them*.
>
> *(Harvey 2003:141–3, emphasis added)*

Sanyal (2007) argues that while capital may be economically self-subsistent, the political conditions of reproduction of capital—particularly in the postcolonial context—may require it to actively engage in the reproduction of a non-capitalist "outside"." While asserting that primitive accumulation is inescapable for expanded reproduction of capital, Sanyal argues that victims of primitive accumulation—the dispossessed producers—may not be absorbed in capitalist wage-labor relation. Sanyal contrasts the classical narrative of primitive accumulation ("enclosures" followed by "bloody legislations" forcing the dispossessed laborers into factory employment) with the postcolonial context where the dispossessed are turned away from the factory gates. This excluded labor force emerges as a "surplus labor" that has to be dealt with via welfarist policies of the state. The excluded labor force is often reunited with means of production in a petty production economy (creating much of the vast informal economy in developing economies). Thus reproduction of postcolonial capitalism involves two simultaneous and contradictory processes—primitive accumulation, which enables a flow of means of production form the non-capitalist space to the capitalist space, and welfarist governance that necessitates a flow of surplus in the reverse direction re-constituting a non-capitalist space by reuniting excluded labor with means of production. The reconstituted non-capitalist space becomes the target of fresh waves of primitive accumulation.

Finally, the "outside" can also be conceived as the product of *resistance* to capital. In the developed countries, examples of this resistance are welfare state institutions created under public pressure to directly provide use-values to the citizens, "commons" created by communities, sites of self-employed production, legal barriers to exploitation implemented because of militant worker's movements, etc.[16] In developing countries, commoning as a social process can be seen even in urban areas as collective encroachment on urban space by squatters and vendors, through rampant piracy of copyrighted products and through moral assertion of rights to livelihoods independent of the regime of private property rights and markets, that force the state to tolerate such demands on grounds of "exception" while upholding property and market as the "norm."

The theoretical recognition of an "outside" of capital is not unproblematic, given that "[a]nalyzing primitive accumulation requires some conception of where the 'boundaries' of capitalist social relations are: of what is 'inside' capitalism and what is 'outside' it" (Hall 2012: 1194).

Conclusion

Separation from the means of production and subsistence provides one of the conditions of existence of one important dimension of the capitalist mode of production: *generalized commodity production*, that is, a situation where the capacity to work itself has become a commodity (labor power) on a large scale and the worker's subsistence becomes to a great extent market-dependent.[17] This opens the door for understanding Marx's analysis of abstract labor as socially necessary labor time, where the operation of the market "translates concrete (individual) labor into abstract (social) labor, and it does so via the medium of money" and why "commodity producers experience the law of value—exchange governed by socially necessary labor time—as an external pressure" (McNally 1993:178–9). In other words, primitive accumulation gives new meaning to how institutions like markets, money, and the division of labor—all of them predating capitalism—work within capitalism, as parts of a system whose purpose is the self-expansion of value. These are the same institutions whose operations under the capitalist mode of production contribute to obscure the processes of surplus labor extraction that sustains capitalist profits. Primitive accumulation therefore can be conceived as serving historical and theoretical functions, functions united dialectically in Marx's discourse that seeks to understand "the origin of the intertwining between 'abstract concepts' and 'concrete reality'" (Mezzadra 2011: 305).

Notes

1 The expression Marx used in German was "*ursprüngliche Akkumulation*," where *ursprüngliche* is translated into English, sometimes as "original," and sometimes as "primitive." See Bonefeld (2002: 2–4) and Bautista (2012: 195) for discussions on the theoretical implications of the different translations.

2 Marx famously ridiculed such ahistorical recountings of the origin and distribution of property and wealth in modern society by comparing the "bourgeois" version of primitive accumulation with the role of the original sin in theology (Marx, 1990: 873).

3 See Marx (1973: 461–2, 471) for examples of his treatment of this topic.

4 In this respect there is a lot of literature on the studies Marx did during the last decade of his life on non-western and pre-capitalist societies, and how this endeavor altered significantly his

perspectives on history to the point that he abandoned the unilinear approach to historical change that had tainted many of his earlier works (see Dussel, 1990 and Anderson, 2010).

5 One of Marx's earliest newspaper articles, published in five parts in 1842 in the *Rheinische Zeitung*, was related to the "Debates on the Law on the Theft of Wood" that were taking place in the Rhineland.

6 For classic renditions of the roles that the Americas, Africa, and Asia had in explaining European development, see Galeano (1997), Rodney (1981), Hobson (2004), and Habib (1975).

7 Given the magnitude of this literature, we cannot review it here. See Bhattacharya (2010) and Hall (2012, 2013) for general reviews of the literature.

8 For a comprehensive discussion of the logic and development of the "modes of production" theory in the Marxian theoretical tradition, refer to Olsen (2009).

9 This reading finds support in some parts of Marx's writings, like Marx's chapter on "The Historical Tendency of Capitalist Accumulation" (Marx, 1990: 927–8) in volume 1 of Capital.

10 In *Grundrisse* Marx (1973: 459) mentions that "[o]nce developed historically, capital itself creates the conditions of its existence," a statement that can be plausibly interpreted to support this conclusion of the independence of capital once it has been fully constituted. Chakrabarti and Cullenberg (2003) refer to this type of logic as the "metaphysics of full presence," where capital does not require a "non-capitalist outside" to reproduce itself.

11 See Read (2002; 2003) for a further discussion of the role of the "aleatory" in capital's development.

12 Klein (2007) complements these theoretical issues with empirical examples that highlight how natural or man-made disasters (i.e. financial crisis) have been used to push forward capitalist reforms.

13 "The disadvantage of these assumptions [in the traditional understanding of primitive accumulation] is that they relegate accumulation based on predation, fraud, and violence to an 'original state' that is considered no longer relevant or, as with Luxemburg, as being somehow 'outside' of capitalism as a closed system" (Harvey, 2003: 144).

14 See also Harvey (2006), and Perelman (2002).

15 See Harvey (2006: 154).

16 See De Angelis (2001: 19).

17 Wood (2002) underlines how capitalism is about market dependence, and that such dependence might exist in situations where the laborers have direct control or access to means of production (i.e. land). For a contrasting view see Kozel (2006).

References

Althusser, L. 2006. *Philosophy of the Encounter: Later Writings, 1978–1987*. London and New York: Verso.

Anderson, K. 2010. *Marx at the Margins: On Nationalism, Ethnicity, and Non-Western Societies*. Chicago: University of Chicago Press.

Andreasson, S. 2006. "Stand and Deliver: Private Property and the Politics of Global Dispossession." *Political Studies* 54(1): 3–22.

Bautista, J. J. 2012. *Hacia la Descolonización de la Ciencia Social Latinoamericana: Cuatro Ensayos Metodológicos y Epistemológicos*. Bolivia: Rincón Ediciones.

Bhattacharya, R. 2010. *Capitalism in Post-Colonial India: Primative Accumulation Under Dirigiste and Laissez Faire Regimes*. Dissertations. Paper 252. http://scholarworks.umass.edu/open_access_dissertations/252

Basu, P. K. 2007. "Political Economy of Land Grab." *Economic and Political Weekly* 42(14): 1281–1287.

——. 2008. *Globalisation: An Anti Text; A Local View*. Delhi: Aakar Publications.

Bonefeld, W. 2002. "History and Social Constitution: Primitive Accumulation is not Primitive." *The Commoner*, March. Available at http://www.commoner.org.uk/debbonefeld01.pdf (accessed October 2, 2016).

Boyle, J. 2002. "Fencing off Ideas: Enclosure & the Disappearance of the Public Domain." *Daedalus* 131(2): 13–25.

Chakrabarti, A. and S. Cullenberg. (2003). *Transition and Development in India*. London: Routledge.

De Angelis, M. 2001. "Marx and Primitive Accumulation: The Continuous Character of Capital's Enclosures." *The Commoner* 2, September. Available at http://www.commoner.org.uk/02deangelis.pdf (accessed October 2, 2016).

Dobb, M. H. 1947. *Studies in the Development of Capitalism*. New York. International Publishers.

Dussel, E. 1990. *El último Marx (1863–1882) y la liberación latinoamericana*. México: Siglo XXI.

Engels, F. 1987. "Anti-Dühring." In *K. Marx and F. Engels, Collected Works,* volume 25. New York: International Publishers.

Federici, S. 2004. *Caliban and the Witch: Women, the Body, and Primitive Accumulation*. New York. Autonomedia.

Galeano, E. 1997. *Open Veins of Latin America: Five Centuries of the Pillage of a Continent*. New York: Monthly Review.

Habib, I. 1975. "Colonialization of the Indian Economy, 1757–1900." *Social Scientist* 3(8): 23–53.

Hall, D. 2012. "Rethinking Primitive Accumulation: Theoretical Tensions and Rural Southeast Asian Complexities." *Antipode* 44(4): 1188–1208.

———. 2013. "Primitive Accumulation, Accumulation by Dispossession and the Global Land Grab." *Third World Quarterly* 34(9): 1582–1604.

Harvey, D. 2003. *The New Imperialism*. New York: Oxford University Press.

———. 2006. "Neo-liberalism as Creative Destruction." *Geografiska Annaler* 88B(2): 145–158.

Hobson, J. M. 2004. *The Eastern Origins of Western Civilization*. Cambridge: Cambridge University Press.

Klein, N. 2007. *The Shock Doctrine: The Rise of Disaster Capitalism*. New York: Henry Holt.

Kozel, P. 2006. *Market Sense: Towards a New Economics of Markets and Society*. New York: Routledge.

Lenin, V. I. 1916. *Imperialism, the Highest Stage of Capitalism*. Chicago. Chicago International.

Luxemburg, R. 2003. *The Accumulation of Capital*, trans. by A. Schwarzschild. London and New York: Routledge.

Marx, K. 1973. *Grundrisse*. London: Penguin Books.

———. 1990. *Capital*, Volume 1. London: Penguin Classics.

Marx, K. and F. Engels. 1983. *Karl Marx/Frederick Engels Collected Works*, Volume 40. New York: International Publishers.

McNally, D. 1993. *Against the Market: Political Economy, Market Socialism and the Marxist Critique*. London: Verso.

———. 2012. *Monsters of the Market: Zombies, Vampires and Global Capitalism*. Chicago: Haymarket Books.

Meillassoux, C. 1972. "From Reproduction to Production: A Marxist Approach to Economic Anthropology." *Economy and Society* 1(1): 93–105.

Mezzadra, S. 2011. "The Topicality of Pre-history: A New Reading of Marx's Analysis of "So-called Primitive Accumulation." *Rethinking Marxism* 23(3): 302–321.

Olsen, E. 2009. "Social Ontology and the Origins of Mode of Production Theory." *Rethinking Marxism* 21(2): 177–195.

Perelman, M. 2000. *The Invention of Capitalism: Classical Political Economy and the Secret History of Primitive Accumulation*. Durham: Duke University Press.

———. 2002. *Steal this Idea: Intellectual Property Rights and Corporate Confiscation of Creativity*. New York: Palgrave Macmillan.

Read, J. 2002. "Primitive Accumulation: The Aleatory Foundation of Capitalism." *Rethinking Marxism* 14(2): 24–49.

———. 2003. *The Micro-Politics of Capital: Marx and the Pre-history of the Present*. Albany: State University of New York Press.

Rodney, W. 1981. *How Europe Underdeveloped Africa*. Washington, DC: Howard University Press.

Sanyal, K. 2007. *Rethinking Capitalist Development: Primitive Accumulation, Governmentality, and Post-Colonial Capitalism*. New Delhi: Routledge.

Senior, N. W. 1965. *An Outline of the Science of Political Economy.* New York : A. M. Kelley.

Smith, A. 1937. *The Wealth of Nations.* New York: The Modern Library.

Thompson, E. P. 1967. "Time, Work-Discipline and Industrial Capitalism." *Past and Present* 38(1): 56–97.

Tigar, M. E. and M. R. Levy. 1977. *Law and the Rise of Capitalism.* New York: Monthly Review Press.

Werholf, C. V. 2000. "'Globalization' and the 'Permanent Process of 'Primitive Accumulation': The Example of the MAI, the Multilateral Agreement on Investment." *Journal of World-Systems Research* 6(3): 728–747.

Wolpe, H. 1972. "Capitalism and Cheap Labour-Power in South Africa: From Segregation to Apartheid." *Economy & Society* 1(4): 425–456.

Wood, E. M. 2002. *The Origin of Capitalism: A Longer View.* New York: Verso.

Zarembka, P. 2002. "Primitive Accumulation in Marxism, Historical or Trans-historical Separation from Means of Production?" *The Commoner*, March.

15

DEMAND AND SOCIALLY
NECESSARY LABOR-TIME

David Kristjanson-Gural

The question of how to integrate demand goes to the heart of our understanding of value theory because it challenges us to decide what it means for a commodity to have value. Marxian theorists take one of three approaches to the question of how to deal with variations in demand—how a change in demand affects the value and exchange-value of a commodity.[1] The first approach, the traditional one, maintains that demand affects the determination of the value of commodities only indirectly by changing the decisions of producers concerning the labor requirements for production. The second approach, which I refer to as the monetary approach, interprets demand as fully determining the value of commodities. In the monetary approach, the market-price is identified with the exchange-value so that changes in demand directly affect the magnitude of value attributed to each commodity. The third approach, which I call the diachronic approach, argues that in Chapter 10 of Volume 3 of *Capital*, Marx provides a method of determining the value of a commodity under conditions of excess or deficient demand. According to this interpretation demand directly affects the magnitude of a commodity's value. It does so by affecting the magnitude of labor-time considered to be "socially necessary." The conditions of production, however, define a range within which the exchange-value can vary. Each of these approaches draws upon exegetical evidence and analytic reasoning to defend the interpretation and each comes to a different conclusion concerning what value means and how value and exchange-value are related.

Marx on Socially Necessary Labor and the Role of Demand

Theorists in the three approaches disagree over what Marx means by socially necessary labor-time and how demand affects the determination of value and exchange-value. Traditional theorists emphasize the first of two meanings that are attributed to the term: labor is socially necessary if it is expended with the average degree of skill and intensity prevalent at the time. Here, demand has no direct effect on the magnitude of a commodity's value since production conditions alone determine the magnitude of value. Marx, however, attributes a second meaning to this modifier and this second meaning suggests that demand plays a direct role in the determination of value.

(S)uppose that every piece of linen in the market contains no more labor-time than is socially necessary. In spite of this, all these pieces taken as a whole, may have had superfluous labor-time spent upon them. If the market cannot stomach the whole quantity at the normal price of 2 shillings a yard, this proves that too great a portion of the total labor of the community has been expended in the form of weaving. The effect is the same as if each individual weaver had expended more labor-time upon his particular product than is socially necessary.

(Marx 1954, 109)

In Volume III, Marx adds:

in general too much social labor has been expended in this particular line; in other words, a portion of this product is useless. It is therefore sold solely as if it had been produced in the necessary proportion. This quantitative limit to the quota of social labor-time available for the various spheres of production is but a more developed expression of the law of value in general, although the necessary labor-time assumes a different meaning here. Only just so much of it is required for the satisfaction of social needs.

(Marx 1959, 636)

These passages apparently contradict earlier statements where Marx argues that socially necessary labor-time value is determined solely by the average labor-time required in production. Indeed, it implies that labor expended with average skill and intensity but in excess of existing social need is both socially necessary in the first sense and not socially necessary in the second. Marxian theorists have thus encountered the problem of how to make sense of this apparent contradiction.

In Chapter 10 of Volume 3 of *Capital*, Marx develops three examples to illustrate how demand contributes to the determination of market value—the exchange-value of a commodity considered at the industry level with competing producers all operating with varying compositions and productivities to produce identical products. The interpretation of these three examples highlights the differences between the traditional, monetary and diachronic approaches to demand.

In the first case, the commodity is produced by a number of techniques each providing roughly equal proportions of the total supply. The numerical average of these techniques defines the labor-time socially necessary to produce the commodity and thus determines the market-value. In the second case, one technique provides the bulk of the output of the industry. Here, the individual value of this dominant technique may define the market-value even if it does not represent the numerical average of the total labor expended (Rubin 1973, 176). In both cases, Marx assumes demand is just sufficient to absorb the existing supply at a market-price equivalent to the market-value.

Marx's third case concerns the determination of market-value under conditions in which demand deviates from supply when the market-value is determined by one of the two above mentioned methods. Here, Marx argues that the market-value may be determined by one of the extreme techniques of production (the most or least efficient producer) and that it is the magnitude of demand which determines the extent to which the market-value deviates from the determination by the average or dominant technique (Marx 1959, 184–5).

While the magnitude of effective demand for the commodity has until this point in the analysis simply been assumed, it becomes "of essential importance as soon as the product of an entire branch of production is placed on one side, and the social need for it on the other. It then becomes necessary to consider the extent, i.e., the amount of this social want" (Marx 1959, 185). The introduction of this new contingency requires the reevaluation of what it means to say that a commodity represents a given amount of socially necessary abstract labor-time.

> Just as it is a condition for the sale of commodities at their value that they contain only the socially necessary labor-time, so it is for an entire sphere of production of capital, that only the necessary part of the total labor-time of society is used in the particular sphere, only the labor-time which is required for the satisfaction of social need (demand). If more is used, then, *even if each individual commodity only contains the necessary labor-time, the total contains more than the socially necessary labor-time*; in the same way, although the individual commodity has use-value, the total sum of commodities lose some of its use-value under the conditions as...*the rise or fall of market-value which is caused by this disproportion*, results in the withdrawal of capital from this branch of production and its transfer to another...
>
> *(Marx 1968, 521, emphasis added)*

While Marx introduces this contingency in his discussion of the determination of market-value, more than once he states that the analysis applies to the determination of the price of production with the appropriated modifications. Marx indicates this progression in the following passage in which he alludes to the development of a more developed category of exchange-value:

> Our analysis has revealed how the market value (and everything said concerning it applies with the appropriate modifications to the price of production) embraces a surplus-profit for those who produce in any particular sphere of production under the most favorable conditions. With the exception of crises, and of over-production in general, this applies to all market-prices, no matter how much they may deviate from market-values or *market-prices of production*.
>
> *(Marx 1959, 198; see also page 179)*

Theorists in the three approaches disagree over the interpretation of these key passages.

Seminal Contributions: Rubin and Rosdolsky

Rubin (1973) argues that Marx's third method for the determination of market-value is erroneous. According to Rubin, the correct method of determining the market value of a commodity in Marx's third case, when demand does not equal supply, is to define the market-value according to the individual value of the technique capable of responding to the necessary adjustment in the quantity produced. Rubin argues for this correction of Marx's argument with reference to the necessity of maintaining a state of equilibrium among industries—any other determination of market-value would destroy the condition of equilibrium which is assumed to exist between branches. For Rubin, the market-value thus serves to define the value which maintains a state of equilibrium between the various branches of production. If the market value were determined by the average technique, but the more efficient technique were capable of expanding production, this would lead to an expansion of the more efficient technique and a breakdown in the condition of equilibrium between industries.

According to Rubin, the term "socially necessary", in the second sense that Marx identifies, refers to an abnormal situation of deviations of market demand from market supply. It does not therefore refer to the determination of market value; rather, it refers to the deviation of market-price from market-value. For Rubin, a consistent interpretation of Marx's theory of value depends upon maintaining this distinction and traditional theorists have accepted this reasoning (Shaikh 1981, 278).

In contrast to Rubin, Rosdolsky (1954) offers an interpretation of the determination of market-value that accepts Marx's statements concerning the role of demand. He argues that when demand deviates from supply, the market-value *can* equal the individual value of one of the two extreme groups of producers as Marx claims. Rosdolsky considers the case in which the predominant group in the industry is using the less efficient technique of production. In order for the market-value to equal the individual value of the less efficient group of producers, the demand for the commodity at the average value need only slightly exceed supply. However, in order for the market-value to equal to the individual value of the most efficient producers, supply must significantly exceed demand.

> If demand is only slightly greater than supply, the individual value of the unfavor-ably produced commodities regulates the market-price... Should demand be weaker than supply, the favorably situated part, whatever its size, makes room for itself forcibly by paring its price down to its individual value. The market-value cannot ever coincide with this individual value of the commodities produced under the most favorable conditions, except when supply far exceeds demand.
>
> *(Marx 1959, 184–5)*

The existence of excess or insufficient demand creates a deviation of market-price from market-value. However, as Rosdolsky notes, Marx clearly states that there are *two* distinct deviations that occur:

> Should [the quantity produced] be smaller or greater, however, than the demand for them, there will be deviations of the market-price from the market-value. And the first deviation is that if the supply is too small, that market-value is always regulated by the commodities produced under the least favorable circumstances and, if the supply is too large, always by the commodities produced under the most favorable conditions; that therefore it is one of the extremes which determines the market-value, in spite of the fact that in accordance with the mere proportion of the commodity masses produced under different conditions, a different result should obtain. If the difference between demand and the available quantity of the product is more considerable, the market-price will likewise be considerably above or below the market-value.
>
> *(Marx 1959, 185–6)*

Rosdolsky thus rejects Rubin's "correction" of Marx: he concludes that the relative strength of demand affects the determination of the market-value directly by affecting the way that the labor expended on the production of the commodity is counted. Reference to the market-value does not imply determination by the industry average except in the special case in which demand and supply coincide at the average value. However, in the general case it cannot be assumed that markets clear and, as a result, profit rates across industries will differ. He argues that Marx's analysis in this chapter provides a way to analyze how the market-value is determined when the possibility of excess or insufficient demand is introduced and profit rate differ across industries. In this case, the market-value moves within the range determined by the conditions of production according to the strength of effective demand for the commodity in question, "provided the demand is large enough to absorb the mass of commodities at values so fixed" (Marx 1959, 185).

The traditional interpretation thus accepts Rubin's argument that Marx erred in suggesting that demand directly affects value. The monetary approach accepts the conclusion that demand affects value but ignores Marx's analysis in Chapter 10 in which he discusses the limits, determined by the conditions of production, within which the market-value can move. The diachronic approach extends Rosdolsky's interpretation, in which Marx's statements about the effect of demand on the determination of market-value are accepted, and applies this analysis to inter-industry competition to further develop the concept of the price of production to define the market-price of production along the lines that Rosdolsky, following Marx, suggests.

Traditional Approaches

Subsequent theorists have developed three distinct positions concerning the role of demand in the determination of value that accept Rubin's argument that demand does not directly affect the magnitude of value or exchange-value. Semmler (1984) and Lianos and Droucopoulos (1992) defend a "linear production theory" that defines the commodity's exchange-value with reference only to the average technique of production in each industry. This view does not integrate the second meaning of socially necessary labor-time—labor expended in accordance with existing social need. Changes in demand affect only market-prices which rise and fall above the prices of production determined by average labor requirement in each industry and the requirement that each industry achieves the general rate of profit. Market prices gravitate toward prices of production as a result of the profit rate differential that is created by excess or deficient demand.

Demand thus affects value only indirectly, by changing the relationship between market price and the exchange-value (price of production), altering the relative rates of profit among industries, eliciting movements of capital and changing the conditions of production in the industry. "The change in the relative market values—and later the prices of production— are determined by laws that are different from those of supply and demand, which regulate the *fluctuations* of the market prices" (Semmler 1984, 24). At the same time, conditions of exchange do play an indirect role in the regulation of value through changes in the relative rates of profit and the subsequent movements of capital that they cause. Dualist models, including the Sraffian models that use physical quantities to solve for prices of production, commonly adopt this approach.

Shaikh (1981) and Itoh (1988) develop a "regulating capital theory" in which exchange-value is determined not by the average technique, but by the technique that regulates the market-price in the industry. They define the regulating capital in slightly different ways. Shaikh reasons that since variations in demand provoke capital movements, it will be the techniques that dominate the industry that determine the center of gravity of the market-price since these will define the price of production once the perturbation of demand is resolved by capital flowing into or out of the industry. It is not necessary therefore to determine the average conditions of production; it is sufficient to identify the dominant or regulating capital.

Itoh (1988) defines the regulating capital as the most efficient generally available technique of production that is capable of responding to variations in demand. It is this technique that determines the price at which there is no incentive for producers to enter the industry. Since new production must be assumed to be undertaken by the most efficient generally available technique, if the rate of profit offered by this technique is higher than average, expansion of production in the industry will be expected to occur. A dynamic theory of price adjustments should therefore consider this "regulating" technique of production as defining the market price of production in order to theorize market processes. Sekine (1980) extends this approach and argues that it is necessary to consider the "marginal response ratios" of each technique of production in the industry - the proportion of the increase in demand that is met by each technique. The commodity's market-price of production is determined by weighting the individual values of the various techniques according to their response ratio.[2]

Itoh and Sekine also identify a further theoretic development of the exchange-value, in this case the "price of production," that Marx alludes to. The resulting price-form, the market-price of production, is used to show the effects of competition within and across industries once demand conditions are incorporated into the analysis. These authors conclude that the market-price of production is contingent on multiple factors and therefore can only be used to establish that a unique market-price of production is possible, not to theorize changes that may occur in markets due to competition.

None of these traditional theories of the role of demand adequately incorporate the second sense of socially necessary and they provide no direct role for demand in the determination of values. Value is determined by the labor-time socially necessary in the first sense, that required on average to produce the commodity, where the average is calculated according to the mean or the modal or regulating capital. Changes in demand act only to regulate the market-price, creating incentives for capital movement, but not directly affecting the determination of commodity values.

The strength of this approach lies in resolving questions that do not rest on the short-run adjustment process. These include the resolution of the question of the relationship between value and exchange-value and the way that changes in productivity affect the distribution of value in the long run. Working with the average or dominant technique of production in the industry allows theorists to utilize the input-output matrices to mathematically establish the effect of changes in technical conditions of production on the long-run value and exchange-value in competing industries. It also permits the careful specification of the determination of values and prices of production that is needed to resolve differences concerning the proper specification of value and exchange-value that lie at the root of the transformation problem.

The difficulty with the traditional theory is not that it gives a poor account of long-run changes in prices; rather it lies in what the theory ignores by directing its focus only to the long-run and abandoning attempts to theorize the adjustment of prices in the short-run. Long and significant deviations of market prices from these prices of production can be expected to occur even with capital mobility given the presence of long-lived capital and the uncertainty and variability of demand. By relegating these factors to the determination of market prices and labeling them contingent, the traditional theory ignores precisely those factors that have the most immediate effect on economic outcomes. Indeed, the extremely limited role for demand in this approach can be established by showing that the trajectory of price changes in the industry remains the same whether or not demand rises or falls even in the long run (Horverak 1988). The concepts of value and exchange-value, which are able to show the distribution of value among producers within and industry and among competing industries, are not used to show how demand redistributes value and instead are utilized only to determine long-run trajectories of market-prices. Since the short-run distribution of value is vital to an understanding of Marxian theories of crises as well as to the theory of money, this feature of the traditional interpretation represents a serious weakness.

Monetary Approaches

According to monetary theorists, demand directly determines the magnitude of a commodity's value, but this conclusion is justified in two different ways. An early approach, which came to be known as the Rubin School, argues, following Rubin, that the reduction of concrete, private labor to abstract, social labor can only occur through exchange. Value-form theorists, on the other hand, argue along Hegelian lines that the contradiction between the value and the exchange-value of the commodity necessarily implies the expression of value in the form of money.

The Rubin School takes issue with two elements of the traditional attempt to theorize the relationship between value and price. First, since traditional theorists assume that value exists prior to and independently of exchange, they leave no meaningful role for money. Second, the distinctions between private and social labor; concrete and abstract labor, do not have any meaningful content. Instead, the Rubin School theorists argue that the act of exchange articulates the private concrete labors of producers into a social division of labor. Consequently, it is exchange that validates private, concrete labor as socially necessary, abstract labor. Value is therefore determined not in production but through exchange.

In this approach, labor is not simply assumed to be simple homogenous labor at the outset; instead, the reduction of concrete labor to abstract labor is understood to result from the act exchange itself. Colletti (1973) justifies this conclusion on the basis of the characteristics of capitalist commodity production.

> Lacking any conscious assignment or distribution on the part of society, individual labor is not *immediately* an articulation of social labor; it acquires its character as a part or *aliquot* of aggregate labor only through the *mediation* of exchange relations or the market.
>
> *(Colletti 1973, 462, emphasis in original)*

Indeed, there appears to be no other way to effect the reduction from one to the other. As Gerstein notes: "… the process of commodity production is not *directly* social…[As a result]…there is no way to reduce observable concrete labor to social abstract labor in advance, outside of the market which actually effects the reduction" (Gerstein 1976, 52, emphasis in original).

One important implication of this view is that value can only be measured in units of money. Since "abstract labor can be *observed* in only one place—the market—…its palpable reality takes the form of money…abstract labor as such can be 'measured' only when it takes the independent form of money, a form that poses it against the bodily form of the commodity in which it is embodied" (Gerstein 1976, 53; see also DeVroey 1981, 189).

A second implication is that Marx's theory of value, according to the Rubin School, cannot provide the basis for a quantitative theory of price determination. Because the market itself determines the magnitudes of abstract labor and because the actual relations of exchange are subject to contingencies which lie outside the purview of theory, "…in principle, Marx's theory of value cannot be used to obtain prices" (Gerstein 1976, 53). Furthermore, the determination of value with reference to exchange ratios in the market implies that value cannot be the only determinant of prices, as Rubin himself argued. This approach thus rejects both Marx's theory of prices and his theory of exploitation (DeVroey 1981, 193).

A second monetary approach reaches similar conclusions from different premises. For value-form theorists, money must express values as a result of the dialectical development of the form of value in *Capital*. According to this Hegelian interpretation of Marx's methodology, the contradiction between the use-value and the exchange-value of the commodity results in the development of the money form as the expression of the essence of value. "Just as the value of a commodity is only expressed in exchange relation, so can the magnitude of value only be expressed in these relations" (Eldred and Hanlon 1981, 35). Value cannot therefore be considered to exist prior to the exchange of commodities.

Demand directly affects the determination of the value of commodities in this view, since exchange relations in the market determine the value of commodities. "The commodity's price expresses the extent to which the particular concrete dissociated labor embodied in the commodity are acknowledged as universal... For this reason, and in contrast to Marx, fluctuations in price are to be regarded as fluctuations in the commodity's magnitude of value" (Eldred and Hanlon 1981, 39).

A number of theorists have attempted to develop a monetary approach that can be used to quantitatively analyze value. These approaches incorporate a definition of the value of money to translated value magnitudes into quantities of abstract labor-time. Some argue that this conversion can only be applied at the macro level. These theorists thus interpret Marx's value theory as a macroeconomic theory and forgo any attempt to calculate individual prices or values (Bellofiore 1989; Foley 2000). Others argue that, contrary to Foley's position, the value of money can be applied at the level of individual prices (Mohun 1994; Moseley 1993; 2005; McGlone and Kliman 1996; Kliman 2006).

For Mohun, the conditions of production of a commodity prior to and independent of exchange determine the commodity's value as a distinct magnitude of socially necessary labor-time. Value is determined without reference to exchange and "measured in terms of socially necessary time (standardizing for different work intensities, productivity levels, skills and so forth" (Mohun 1994, 395).

Abstract labor, on the other hand, is a magnitude that *is* determined through the exchange of commodities against money. The role of money as the equivalent form of value serves to effect the reduction from concrete, private labor to abstract social labor in the way Rubin suggests. Exchange with money determines the magnitude of the *form of value*, which is denominated in money units. Expressed in money,

> use-value appears directly as value, concrete labor as abstract labor, and private labor as social labor... The value of a commodity is thereby expressed in units of the universal equivalent... and expresses the value of any commodity as a sum of money, or in (money) value-form.
>
> *(Mohun 1994, 395)*

The value of money thus "enables a translation between prices into labor-times" (Mohun 1994, 409). For Mohun, "[t]his is the fundamental meaning of 'price'; 'price' is a representation of a proportion of society's total labor-time allocated to a particular commodity. In this sense prices are forms of value, of abstract labor" (Mohun 1994, 403).

Both prices of production and market prices are thus conceived as forms of value. The former are defined under conditions of profit rate equalization among industries; the latter are "what is observed at any particular time in the market, determined by prevailing demand and supply conditions... [D]eterminations generating market prices differing from prices of production can be understood as a concretization of the analysis" (Mohun 1994, 399). So according to Mohun, the exchange of commodities merely redistributes labor-time among the industries according to the level of demand. Market prices are themselves forms of value and can be translated from money magnitudes into magnitudes of abstract labor by dividing them by the value of money. The abstract labor theory of value inspired by Rubin, combined with the definition of the value of money thus provides a strictly quantifiable theory of the relationship between value and price.

McGlone and Kliman (1996) and Kliman (2006) argue that the market-price of constant capital in the previous period determines its value in the current period. This temporary single-system solution thus adopts a monetary approach to demand that follows the Rubin School theorists. The value of the constant capital component of value entering and leaving a given production period is determined by its market-price. Kliman argues that this temporal approach is able to resolve difficulties in translating value and price magnitudes and provides a more consistent theory of crisis than the simultaneous approaches of linear production theory (Kliman 2006). However, there is no development in Kliman of the market-value or the idea that there are limits, determined by the techniques of production, to the movement of market-value as demand varies, so his approach, in spite of its attention to techniques of production, does not incorporate the second sense of socially necessary labor-time. Moseley (2005) also overlooks the determination of market-values. He argues that because Marx defines capital first with reference to money (money which begets money), the idea of value as a magnitude of money is conceptually prior in Marx to the idea of value as socially-necessary, abstract labor-time. Value magnitudes are therefore amounts of money that correspond to a magnitude of abstract labor. He does not introduce the idea of the second meaning Marx attributes to socially necessary labor-time and therefore follows the monetary approach in which demand fully determines the magnitude of value.

Monetary theories have the great merit of recognizing the important role that exchange plays in the determination of value and the integration of private, concrete labor into a social division of labor that is a key element of the way Marx distinguishes capitalist commodity exchange from other modes of production. Money, too, is given a central role: it is integrated into the way commodities function rather than simply assigned the role of measuring value. The factors affecting the function of money in capitalist economies, the form that money takes, the ways in which it is created and distributed, and the contradictions that ensue are all integrated into the analysis in a coherent manner.

By incorporating demand directly into the determination of the magnitude of value, however, the early monetary theorists encounter three difficulties. First, by collapsing the quantitative determination of value into one dimension—money units or price—these approaches forfeit the ability to conceptualize exploitation as unpaid labor. "It has no power to *explain* the determination of prices by values, since the latter are measurable only in units of the former" (Gleicher 1983, 105). Second, neither approach incorporates the second meaning of socially necessary labor. As a result the market value and market price are conflated and the determination of the former with reference to the conditions of production as suggested by Marx's third method is lost. Third, the value-form approach leads to the abandonment of the quantitative theory of price determination.

Later monetary theorists partially resolve some of these difficulties. It might be argued that by defining market price as value, Mohun in effect incorporates the second meaning of socially necessary. However, by defining value as the socially necessary labor-time required to produce a commodity, and the value form as the abstract labor attributed to it in exchange, the second meaning of socially necessary is only applied to value, not to exchange-value. Socially necessary must therefore be understood only with reference to the first meaning—labor of average intensity and duration—in order to maintain the proposition that production conditions alone determine the value of commodities. Furthermore, and contrary to Mohun's claim, the value of money cannot serve to translate the values of individual commodities into prices. By leaving the value of constant capital out of the determination of the value of money, the latter serves only to measure the value produced by the new labor expended. The analysis cannot therefore account for the transfer of value into and out of the period due to the use of constant capital. Foley (2000) acknowledges this implication, which is why he argues for the redefinition of the theory of value as a theory of aggregate value flows.

In each of these monetary approaches, however, socially necessary labor-time is defined solely with reference to the first meaning identified by Rubin. There is no mention of the second sense of the term—labor expended in accordance with existing social need. By defining value and exchange-value as the money price realized in exchange, these approaches lose the ability to distinguish value and exchange-value. They are therefore unable to theorize how demand affects the redistribution of value from those who have produced it, to those who receive it in exchange.

Diachronic Approaches

The final approach follows Rosdolsky's interpretation of Marx's analysis of demand. I refer to this approach as "diachronic" because a key insight common to these theorists is the idea that the order of exposition represents a diachronic progression in the meaning of value and its relationship to exchange-value. A recognition of this diachronic ordering helps to resolve the apparent contradictions and difficulties encountered by alternative explanations. Horverak (1988) and Indart (1990) provide early attempts to explain the relationship between value and exchange-value under conditions of excess or deficient demand. They both conclude that Marx did not err when he described the third possibility he considers in Chapter 10. When demand exceeds supply at the market-value, the market-value and market-price both rise in tandem. When demand exceeds supply at a market-value determined by the least efficient technique of production, the market-price will then deviate above the market-value of the commodity. The opposite occurs with excess supply. The conditions of production thus define a range within which the market-value can vary and the market-price moves with the market-value within this range.

Horverak and Indart argue that in the first two examples Marx develops in Chapter 10 he assumes that the effective demand for the commodity is just sufficient to absorb the supply at the market-value "no matter which of the three aforementioned cases regulates this market-value. This mass of commodities does not merely satisfy a need, but satisfies it to its full social extent" (Marx 1959, 185). Provided the market-value lies within the range defined by the techniques of production, the labor expended on the commodity satisfies "the full social extent" of the need for the commodity. The question of the distribution of demand arises only in the third case Marx considers—when the industry is considered in relation to competing industries. At that point the possibility of a divergence between demand and supply must be taken into account.

This explanation allows this approach to integrate both senses of socially necessary labor-time while recognizing that initially, in Volume I, the first sense of the term is dominant since the second sense is not yet relevant. Only with the introduction of competing industries in Volume III does Marx relax the assumption that demand is just sufficient to absorb the supply and the assumption that the labor required for its production is socially necessary in the second sense is no longer enforced. It must be established through successful competition in the market.

Market-value is thus not a fixed magnitude determined solely with reference to the conditions of production independent of exchange as in traditional, linear production theory. However, market-value is not simply equal to the market-price as in the monetary approach. Instead, the market-value varies with the market-price according to the strength of effective demand within the limits imposed by the conditions of production. Outside these limits there is a deviation of market-value from market-price. The conditions of production in the industry thus impose a strict limit to the range in which the market-value can move. "For according to Marx's conception, market-value can only move within the limits set by the condition of production (and consequently the individual value) of one of the three categories of producers" (Rosdolsky 1954, 92).

However, since inter-industry competition implies exchange at prices of production, not market-values, this diachronic interpretation must be applied to the formation of prices of production. These theorists argue that just as the introduction of competing industries implies the evolution of exchange-value from market value to price of production, the introduction of demand requires a further evolution in the exchange-value from price of production to market-price of production. Roberts (1997; 2004; 2005) extends the arguments of Wolff, Callari and Roberts (1984) to explain how exchange effects a conversion of private, concrete labor to socially necessary, abstract labor in the formation of prices of production. Here, the value of the means of production in the period are determined not by the concrete labor-time required on average to produce them, but by the socially necessary abstract labor those means of production represent in equivalent exchange. The exchange-value of the means of production thus denotes the value of that those means of production transfer to the commodity in the production process. This non-dualist approach both resolves the transformation problem and explains what the monetary theorist could not explain—how exchange could directly take part in the formation of value while maintaining a quantitative theory of value at the micro level.

Roberts, however, maintains the assumption that demand is just sufficient to absorb the supply: he thus only considers the prices of production, not how those prices of production are affected by variations in demand. Integrating demand into Roberts' approach to abstract labor implies defining the techniques of production in each industry and showing how changes in demand affect the determination of exchange-value when demand deviates from supply. The resulting market-price of production incorporates the effect of demand at the level of analysis that introduces competing industries and can thus be used to show how variations in demand redistribute socially necessary, abstract labor-time among competing producers in different industries (Kristjanson-Gural 2003; 2005).

This interpretation thus accomplishes two things that the traditional "centers of gravity" explanation attempted to do. It shows that the conditions of production determine the value and exchange-value by setting limits on the movement of the market-prices of production. It also consistently integrates the concept of the market-price of production that Marx alludes to but does not develop (Kristjanson-Gural 2009). The approach also achieves what the monetary theory argues is essential. It provides a meaningful role for exchange in the determination of value and incorporates money. The monetary expression of value, defined with reference to the total value in circulation, is used to convert the monetary expression of value and exchange-value from money units to units of socially necessary labor-time. Both value and exchange-value continue to be denominated in both labor-hours and money (Kristjanson-Gural 2008). The approach thus integrates the strengths of the monetary approach, while retaining the micro-economic analysis of how changes in conditions of production affect profitability and the distribution of value that the traditional, linear production theory develops.

Further applications of the analysis include the development of Marx's theory of both absolute and differential rent as special cases of the market-price of production under conditions of non-reproducible elements of constant capital (Balardini Chapter 11, this volume). Further applications to introduce monopoly pricing have yet to be explored. The question of demand is a crucial and largely overlooked aspect of Marx's theory of value. Further debate about and development of demand in Marx's value theory and the related concept of the market-price of production is clearly warranted.

Notes

1 For clarity, value is the socially necessary abstract labor-time required to produce a commodity; its exchange-value is the socially necessary labor-time the commodity represents in equivalent exchange. Both value and exchange-value manifest in money form and can be measured in both money and labor units. Prior to introducing competing producers, value and exchange-value have the same magnitude. With competing producers *within* an industry the exchange-value is its market-value; with competing industries it becomes the price of production; with competing industries and variations in demand it becomes the market-price of production. Market prices are distinct from exchange-values. They are the average money prices for all producers of a given commodity over a given period.
2 Sekine's and Itoh's interpretation of the market-price of production has a curious affinity to marginal cost analysis in neoclassical economics.

References

Bellofiore, R. 1989. "A Monetary Labor Theory of Value." *Review of Radical Political Economics* 21 (1–2): 1–25.

Colletti, L. 1973. "Some Comments on Marx's Theory of Value." In *From Rousseau to Lenin: Studies in Ideology and Society.* New York: Monthly Review Press.

DeVroey, M. 1981. "Value Production and Exchange." In *The Value Controversy*, I. Steedman and P. Sweezy, eds., 173–201. London: Verso.

Duménil, G. 1983. "Beyond the Transformation Riddle: A Labor Theory of Value." *Science and Society* 47(2): 427–450.

Eldred, M. and M. Hanlon. 1981. "Reconstructing Value-Form Analysis." *Capital and Class* 13: 24–60.

Foley, D. 1982. "The Value of Money, the Value of Labor Power and the Marxian Transformation Problem." *Review of Radical Political Economics* 14(2): 37–49.

———. 2000. "Recent Developments in the Labor Theory of Value." *Review of Radical Political Economics* 32(1): 1–39.

Gerstein, I. 1976. "Production, Circulation and Value: The Significance of the 'Transformation Problem' in Marx's *Critique of Political Economy.*" *Economy and Society* 5(3): 243–291.

Gleicher, D. 1983. "A Historical Approach to the Question of Abstract Labor." *Capital and Class* 21: 97–122.

Horverak, O. 1988. "Marx's View of Competition and Price Determination." *History of Political Economy* 20(2): 275–297.

Indart, G. 1990. "The Formation and Transformation of Market-value: A Note on Marx's Method." *History of Political Economy* 22(4): 721–743.

Itoh, M. 1988. *The Basic Theory of Capitalism.* Totowa, NJ: Barnes & Noble.

——. 2005. "The New Interpretation and the Value of Money." In *Marx's Theory of Money: Modern Appraisals*. New York: Palgrave Macmillan, 177–191.

Kliman, A. 2006. *Reclaiming Marx's Capital: A Refutation of the Myth of Inconsistency*. Lanham, MD: Rowan & Littlefield.

Kristjanson-Gural, D. 2003. "Demand and the (Re)distribution of Value: An Overdetermined Approach." *Rethinking Marxism* 15(1): 117–140.

——. 2005. "Exchange, Demand and the Market-price of Production: Reconciling Traditional and Monetary Approaches to Value and Price." *Research in Political Economy* 22: 171–202.

——. 2008. "Money is Time: The Monetary Expression of Value in Marx's Theory of Value." *Rethinking Marxism* 20(2): 257–272.

——. 2009. "Post-Structural Logic in Marx's Theory of Value." *Rethinking Marxism* 21(1): 14–33.

Lianos, T. and V. Droucopoulos. 1992. "Price determination in Chapter X of Volume II of Marx's Capital." *Review of Radical Political Economics* 24(1): 89–100.

Marx, K. 1954. *Capital: A Critique of Political Economy*, Volume 1. Moscow: Progress Publishers.

——. 1959. *Capital: A Critique of Political Economy*, Volume 3. Moscow: Progress Publishers.

——. 1968. *Theories of Surplus-Value*, Part 2. Moscow: Progress Publishers.

McGlone, T. and A. Kliman. 1996. "One System or Two? The Transformation of Values into Prices of Production Verses the Transformation Problem." In *Marx and Non-equilibrium Economics*, A. Freeman and G. Carchedi, eds. Cheltenham: Edward Elgar.

Mohun, S. 1994. "A Re(in)statement of the Labour Theory of Value." *Cambridge Journal of Economics* 18: 391–412.

Moseley, F. 1993. "Marx's Logical Method and the 'Transformation Problem'." In *Marx's Method in Capital: A Re-examination*, F. Moseley, ed. Atlantic Highlands, NJ: Humanities Press International.

——. 2005. "Money Has No Price: Marx's Theory of Money and the Transformation Problem." In *Marx's Theory of Money: Modern Appraisals*. New York: Palgrave Macmillan.

Roberts, B. 1997. "Embodied Labor and Competitive Prices: A Physical Quantities Approach." *Cambridge Journal of Economics* 21(4): 483–502.

——. 2004. "Value, Abstract Labor and Exchange Equivalence." In *The New Value Controversy and the Foundations of Economics*, A. Freeman, A. Kliman, J. Wells, eds. Cheltenham: Edward Elgar.

——. 2005. "Quantifying Abstract Labor: 'Aliquot Part' Reasoning in Marx's Value Theory." *Research in Political Economy* 22: 137–170.

Rosdolsky, R. 1977 [1954]. *The Making of Marx's Capital*. London: Pluto Press.

Rubin, I. I. 1973. *Essays on Marx's Labor Theory of Value*. Montreal: Black Rose Books.

Sekine, T. 1980. "The Law of Market Value." *Science and Society* 44: 420–444.

Semmler, W. 1984. *Competition, Monopoly, and Differential Profit Rates*. New York: Columbia University Press.

Shaikh, A. 1981. "The Poverty of Algebra." In *The Value Controversy*, I. Steedman and P. Sweezy, eds., 266–301 London: Verso.

Wolff, R. D., A. Callari, and B. Roberts. 1984. "A Marxian Alternative to the Traditional 'Transformation Problem'." *Review of Radical Political Economics* 16(2/3): 115–136.

PART III

Capitalist Production and Reproduction

16

THE CAPITALIST FIRM

David M. Brennan

Karl Marx unveiled his theory of the enterprise or firm over the entire three volumes of *Capital*. One reason for the extensive and evolving presentation of the enterprise in *Capital* is that "every site exhibits a changing configuration of class and nonclass processes. In Marxian theory nothing can be fixed in the notion of what an enterprise or state means" (Resnick and Wolff 1987a, 165). Marx addressed a variety of different types of enterprises but mostly focused on three types of capitalist enterprises, those being industrial or productive, merchant, and money lending enterprises. For Marx it was the varied class processes that constituted these enterprises that made them worth differentiating and were vital for his understanding of capitalism more generally.[1]

Resnick and Wolff (1987a; 1987b) have done some of the most extensive methodological and analytical work of representing Marx's original theory of the enterprise, and their writings substantially inform this presentation. It is important to provide an alternative to traditional Western Marxism's view of the firm, which has a history of being preoccupied with accumulation and crisis theory that led to a "bipolar understanding of class and a related essentialist conception of the capitalist firm" (Norton 2001, 24). Traditional, though non-original, Marxian theories resulted in an overly abridged theory of the firm, simply pitting capitalist against labor and privileging the role of accumulation in the firm. The presentation here not only seeks to contrast with the traditional Marxian view, but also provides an alternative conceptualization of the firm to Adam Smith's focus on labor specialization, Alfred Marshall's reliance on the profit maximizing representative firm, and "contractual" approaches produced by Ronald Coase and Eugene Fama.[2] Distinct from other theories of the capitalist firm, Marx's approach is able to reveal exploitation, expose conflict over the production and distribution of the surplus, uncover evolving and contradictory class dynamics, and ultimately aid in understanding and envisioning non-exploitative forms of production.

The first volume of *Capital* focuses on productive capitalist enterprises. Marx's attention to commodity production and the capitalist firm was in response to previous theories in political economy, such as Smith's, but Marx also wanted to reorient what he correctly viewed as the future direction of theories of the capitalist enterprise, which incorporated Jeremy Bentham's perspective on individualism and utility and the basic treatment of production as being just another application of exchange, say between employees and employers.

The first few chapters of *Capital* concerned commodities, exchange and money, which enabled Marx to differentiate simple exchange from something very different in production. He did not want to treat production as an extension of exchange. Near the end of the initial chapter on exchange, to indicate that he is moving away from the idea that exchange is the source of profit, he writes, "we shall at last force the secret of profit making" (Marx 1954, 172). But before getting into the substance of capitalist production, he makes one last assurance to the reader that what is to come is a very different type of analysis of the firm, one not based on a framework of freely and fairly exchanging commodities such as labor-power. Marx writes:

> This sphere that we are deserting, within whose boundaries the sale and purchase of labour-power goes on, is in fact a very Eden of the innate rights of man. There alone rule Freedom, Equality, Property and Bentham. Freedom, because both buyer and seller of a commodity, say of labour-power, are constrained only by their own free will. They contract as free agents, and the agreement they come to, is but the form in which they give legal expression to their common will. Equality, because each enters into relation to each other, as with a simple owner of commodities, and they exchange equivalent for equivalent. Property, because each disposes only of what is his own. And Bentham, because each looks only to himself. The only force that brings them together and puts them in relation with each other is the selfishness, the gain and the private interest of each. Each looks to himself only, and no one troubles about the rest, and just because they do so, do they all, in accordance with the pre-established harmony of things, or under the auspices of an all-shrewd providence, work together to their mutual advantage, for the common weal and in the interest of all. On leaving this sphere of simple circulation or of exchange of commodities, which furnishes the "Free-trader Vulgaris" with his views and ideas, and with the standard by which he judges society based on capital and wages, we think we perceive a change in the physiognomy of our *dramatis personae*.
>
> *(Marx 1954, 172)*

Instead of beginning with individuals and trade, Marx begins his theory of the enterprise with class and production. Class processes are defined in relation to the production, appropriation, distribution and receipt of surplus value (Resnick and Wolff 1987a, 109–63). While power and property may provide important conditions of existence for various class processes and participants, a definition of class based solely on surplus value provides a uniquely Marxian view of class. Productive laborers are the producers of surplus value. They are the people who contribute more to the value of a produced good or service than they receive in wages. Within capitalism, productive or industrial capitalists are the ones who appropriate or take initial ownership of this surplus value. The theorization of the fundamental class process, the production of surplus value and its appropriation, the existence of exploitation, and the struggles between productive labor and capitalists constitute a large portion of volume one of *Capital*.

With only the above notions of class coupled with a labor theory of value one can grasp the classic conflict between labor and capital at the site of production.[3] Here one appreciates struggles over wages, the length of the working day, working conditions and the intensity of labor. For many this is all they recognize from a Marxian analysis of the firm. However, to leave the analysis there is to ignore most of the richness of Marx's and Marxian contributions to a theory of the capitalist enterprise.

Fortunately, Marx provided a theory of the capitalist enterprise that, while published in 1887, went well beyond just capital versus labor and remains relevant for understanding modern capitalist firms. As did Marx, we can begin first with a theory of the productive capitalist enterprise and then describe merchant and money lending enterprises. A productive enterprise is the site of the production of surplus value. This site will contain productive workers who produce commodities or services. As they are paid less than the value that they contribute, they produce surplus value that is appropriated by the productive capitalists who are legally entitled to the surplus. In most modern corporations it is the boards of directors who occupy the position of capitalist (Resnick and Wolf 1987b, 211–13). However, once capitalists appropriate the surplus, they will have to distribute the surplus. These distributions can be divided into distributions made inside the firm and distributions made outside the firm. Distributions inside the firm may go to pay managers, in-house lawyers, marketing staff and information technology support staff, to name a few common subsumed class distributions today. These employees are the unproductive workers. The label unproductive indicates only that they do not directly produce surplus value yet receive an initial distribution of it. They receive a distribution because they provide essential conditions of existence of capitalist production today. These subsumed class participants are essential in providing cultural, administrative, legal, technical and other conditions of existence that allow the firm to function as a capitalist firm. For example, in-house lawyers produce the necessary legal documents to do business within a state that has laws which need to be followed. Marketers entice consumers to purchase items and hence help in the realization of the surplus produced by productive labor. Some of this surplus may go to managers who monitor and evaluate the work of productive labor.

Some distributions of the surplus will go outside the firm to provide other conditions of existence. Perhaps surplus distributions will go to banks to repay debt. Shareholders may get a cut of the surplus in the form of dividends. The state will get a distribution of the surplus in the form of taxes. As banks, shareholders and the state provide different conditions of existence from those provided internally to the firm, they nonetheless also occupy a subsumed class position. These distributions play a critical role in the continuation of the firm as a productive capitalist enterprise.

In the case of productive enterprises, what constitutes the optimal distributions of surplus will vary greatly from firm to firm, even in the same industry, as the *social* relations within each firm vary. For example, consider hypothetically two different capitalist furniture-manufacturing firms. One firm may have a very paternalistic relationship with employees, with good health insurance, company picnics and frequent donut-laden meetings with supervisors and shop floor carpenters. Such an enterprise will require many surplus distributions to sustain that environment. Yet another furniture manufacturer may have very impersonal and confrontational relationships with employees. Here too, the firm will spend its surpluses, but in other ways including subsumed class expenses to search for new laborers to replace those that leave, high legal expenses to fight employee complaints and high costs of surveillance technology to ensure high productivity. In either case, the issue of spending the surplus is not about the technical aspects of making furniture but rather about each firm functioning within a set of relations of production. In this example, each firm constitutes itself differently, with distinctive social conditions of production.

Concurrent with ever-present class conflicts between productive laborers and the capitalist over the size of the surplus, there are also subsumed class conflicts over the surplus distributions. It is likely that managers are looking for higher salaries and more money and human resources to manage, alongside all the other subsumed class demands. Marketing departments desire more compensation and control over more resources, as does the information technology support staff. Outside the firm, subsumed class conflicts will participate in the dynamics of interest rate variations. Corporate governance tussles with shareholders will affect dividend distributions. Political circumstances will alter tax rates. The outcome of these subsumed class struggles will feed back into the productive labor struggles, as capitalists may seek even higher levels of exploitation to pay for higher manager salaries, dividends, taxes, etc.

While a Marxian theory of the enterprise is class-focused, it is important to keep in mind that there are also a host of nonclass aspects to consider. Product market competition is one such example. Specifically, price competition between firms will cause a distribution of the surplus via the pricing mechanism which affects the size of the surplus realized by individual firms (Roberts 1988). Ultimately neither the size of the surplus nor the distributions are the result of a rational optimization of surplus, but rather they are overdetermined by the class and nonclass conflicts within and outside the firm. Such a perspective, with surplus flows moving in and out of the firm, understands the boundaries of the firm to be quite permeable. It is the concrete analyses of these surplus flows and the class relationships behind them that is the focus of many Marxian investigations of capitalist enterprises.

Of course, not all firms produce surplus value. However, by focusing on the flows of surplus value, one can theorize other firms' relationships to productive, surplus value producing firms. Merchant firms help in the realization of previously produced surplus value by advertising, displaying and making products readily available to final consumers. In return for this service, they receive a cut of the surplus produced by the productive enterprise. For example, Walmart is primarily a merchant firm, as it does not produce the goods it sells in its stores but displays them for sale to the final consumer (Mulder 2011). Walmart pays less than the full value for an item from the producer and then sells the commodity at the full value. The difference between the two values is the merchant's distribution of the surplus created by the productive enterprise. A productive capitalist may seek to sell goods in this fashion instead of employing its own internal sales force, opening retail stores, and/or maintaining a web site for sales to final consumers.

The identification of a merchant firm that is distinct from a productive capitalist firm is valuable in understanding modern capitalism. While merchants do not exploit labor, as no surplus is produced by the merchant enterprise, they may provide some important conditions for the existence of exploitation. Specifically, if merchants with market power demand a larger cut of the surplus than they were previously receiving, productive capitalists may then seek higher levels of exploitation from productive laborers, so that they can satisfy these higher demands on the surplus.

Employees of merchant enterprises are not producing surplus and hence cannot be exploited, in the sense of having surplus that they produce appropriated by someone else. Furthermore, as these employees are not receiving an initial distribution of the surplus—as that goes to the boards of directors of the merchant firms—but receive instead a subsequent distribution from the merchant enterprise, they are in a nonclass position. This does not mean that employees of merchants are necessarily adequately compensated or treated well. These employees may be subjugated in the workplace, may suffer wages below a living wage, and may be denied healthcare coverage by their employer. One question that arises is this: why should Marxism treat the workers of merchant enterprises in a theoretically different way from productive workers in productive capitalist firms? The answer speaks to what is unique about Marxism. Marxism is a class theoretic perspective with a notion of class defined in relation to surplus value. It is this focus on surplus value production, appropriation, distribution and receipt which provides Marxism with the theoretical space "to carefully distinguish class from nonclass processes in order to highlight the existence and unique effectivities of the former" (Resnick and Wolff 1987a, 165). One aspect of theorizing the nonclass position of merchant firm employees is to appreciate their role in relation to a fundamental class process. Today many merchant firms, by selling capitalist produced goods, support the capitalist fundamental class process. However, by accepting that the merchant firm is not a productive capitalist enterprise, one appreciates the fact the merchant enterprise can support noncapitalist production processes as well. Specifically, merchant firms can help the realization of surplus produced by any fundamental class process, such as ancient, communist, etc.

This ability to support any type of productive enterprise is true of money lending enterprises as well. Money lent to productive capitalist class enterprises provides important conditions of existence for that fundamental class process, and in return, interest payments become a distribution of the surplus created. In such a case, the money lending firm would be in a subsumed class position and subsequent distributions by the financial enterprise, such as payments to their employees, would be nonclass distributions. While lending to productive capitalist firms is substantial, there are also loans to support ancient class production by individuals and feudal class production in the home. The Laboral Kutxa, which is associated with the Mondragon Corporation, is an example of a bank financing a variety of cooperative, non-exploitative and productive enterprises. Hence, money lending is not exclusively a tool to support exploitative enterprises.

Many loans support nonclass processes such as home or auto buying. Clearly, the nonclass processes of personal debt may interact with fundamental class processes, as evidenced by the housing collapse beginning in 2007. A non-Marxian view of the crisis may see only the financial difficulties and not explore the class dimensions driving the personal debt explosion. A Marxian perspective on the Great Recession finds that the dynamics of increased exploitation in capitalist enterprises played a critical role in the rise in personal debt (Wolff 2012).

Overall, given the multiple forces on capitalist enterprises by productive labor and subsumed class participants, both internal and external to the firm, capitalists may respond by seeking to change who is employed in the firm and with whom they engage outside the firm. The firm may fire disgruntled productive workers or supervisors. The firm may seek to change relations with the state, shareholders, merchants and moneylenders via changes in the corporate funding of various political movements and specific candidates, attempts to buy back shares from shareholders, changes in who sells their products, and the refinancing of debt, which may change who holds the debt. Viewed in this light, the productive capitalist enterprise is the site of an ongoing jockeying for position regarding surplus value.

Merchant and moneylending enterprises too may seek to change which capitalist enterprise they seek to do business with or engage with various non-capitalist enterprises or participate in nonclass lending. By exposing these class and nonclass dynamics, one gains a distinctly Marxian theory of the capitalist firm, which includes the following three characteristics.

1

Capitalist productive enterprises cannot be reduced to profit-maximizing behavior. This is the case both with respect to the behavioral assumption that firms seek only to maximize profits—although they may do so at times—and with respect to the consequences of profit-maximizing behavior. With respect to the notion that firms always seek to maximize profits, Marxian theory makes clear that firms are provoked by multiple demands concerning how the surplus is produced, the amount of the surplus, and all distributions of it. Hence, there is no mechanism to guarantee maximum profits. Consider a commonplace notion of profit where, "[p]rofit is the surplus remaining after total costs are deducted from total revenue, and the basis on which tax is computed and dividend is paid. It is the best known measure of success of an enterprise."[4] Yet, as productive labor is successful in getting higher incomes with a given intensity of labor and length of the working day, profits fall. As unproductive labor, such as CEOs, managers and supervisors are successful in acquiring higher salaries, profits fall. As banks increase fees and landlords increase rents, profits fall. Therefore, it is quite possible that neither internal employees nor external institutions have an omnipresent and clear financial interest in the maximization of the firm's profits. But what about the capitalist boards of directors? Clearly, they seek to maximize profits, if for no other reason than that they are the legal agents of the shareholders, placed in office to maximize returns for them. While this is often assumed in some theories of the firm, legally, at least in the US, that is not the case. "Although elected by the shareholders and removable by them for cause and possibly without cause, the directors are not agents of the shareholders. Nor are directors, in the strict sense, trustees. Their position is *sui generis*" (Henn 1970, 415–16). Boards of directors are able to consider a firm's actions with respect to a host of constituents and a variety of effects beyond the firm.[5] Hence, there is no legal mandate to maximize profits.

Nor is there necessarily a functional reason to maximize profits, as the firm must constantly address its changing class conditions of existence if it wants to survive. From a Marxian perspective, profits are not a measure of the success or failure of the enterprise, because profits themselves do not reveal the class conditions which gave rise to them. The capitalist fundamental class process within an enterprise may be able to thrive with high levels of exploitation and very low levels of profits—due to large subsumed class payments—and likewise be in jeopardy with low levels of exploitation and high levels of profits—due to small subsumed class payments. It all depends on the specific conditions of existence confronting the firm. Therefore, "to conclude that a capitalist enterprise is in a period of crisis because of some calculated decline in the profit rate is to make a non-Marxian, nonclass explanation of the enterprise" (Resnick and Wolff 1987a, 183).

2

Related to point #1 above, as the conditions of existence constantly change, capitalist enterprises as a whole cannot privilege one class distribution over others. Yes, Marx wrote, "Accumulate, Accumulate! That is Moses and the prophets!" (Marx 1954, 558). However, this was written in the chapter where Marx extends the subsumed class distributions from that which went only towards capitalist consumption to then include both capitalist consumption and accumulation distributions. Marx's statements on accumulation were critical of the economic theories of his time, which viewed wealth as being due entirely to capitalists' abstinence from consumption, for not including the exploitative production processes which were the source of the surpluses. Later in *Capital* Marx allowed for many additional uses of the surplus that produced a richer view of the enterprise than one wherein the capitalist firm is a mere accumulator of capital.

Because the conditions of existence change constantly for each firm, the class and nonclass distributions must continually change for a firm to exist. This can lead to some interesting decisions for firms. For example, a capitalist firm at a certain period in time and given the peculiarities of the industry may actually benefit by offering higher wages to productive workers. Ford's famous $5 a day in 1914, which almost doubled wages for autoworkers at the time, is a case in point. The increased wages reduced worker turnover and provided incentives for increased productivity at Ford.[6] Perhaps the increased wage led to increased levels of exploitation. In any case, this example demonstrates that firms do not have a necessary desire to reduce wages for employees at all times. Certainly, many firms face a confluence of class conflicts that often result in decreased real wages for productive and many unproductive employees. Nevertheless, it is one thing to theorize that decreased wages happen via a concrete set of class and nonclass constellations, and another to see firms as necessarily always seeking to reduce wages. Hence, the Marxian view of the firm cannot be reduced to simple conflicts between capital and labor involving fixed positions on wages and working conditions. This view is at odds with many influential Marxists. An example of a contrarian view is found in Harry Braverman's *Labor and Monopoly Capital*. There he makes the argument for the "*progressive alienation of the process of production*" (Braverman 1974, 58; Braverman's italics). While alienation may have been and may still be a wide-spread result of capitalist practices, alienation, at least as understood here, would not be considered a timeless, universal and necessary aspect of capitalist enterprises.

3

The Marxian method presented here is also at odds with approaches to firm theory that rely on the notion of the representative firm or the typical firm. Neoclassical analyses of the firm have used that approach, and the technique exists in Marxism as well. Paul Baran and Paul Sweezy in *Monopoly Capital*, defending their analysis of "the typical unit of Big Business, the modern corporation," write:

> we are not interested in realism of a photographic kind.... The point is that the decisive units of the economy are mistakenly moving toward a definite, recogniz-able pattern, and this pattern itself is much more important than any of the concrete approximations to it.
>
> *(Baran and Sweezy 1966, 15)*

One result of this is that they overly privilege the role of accumulation in firms at the expense of other conditions of existence. The approach suggested here is more in keeping with the insights of Antonio Gramsci. When commenting on Fordism in American he writes:

> [s]ince there has never functioned and does not function any law of perfect parity of systems and production and work methods valid for all firms in a specific branch of industry, it follows that every firm is, to a greater or lesser degree, "unique" ....
>
> *(Gramsci 1971, 313)*

Examples of Marxian investigations of specific firms include Brennan (2003a and 2003b), who provides a class analysis of Enron, Mulder's (2011) class inquiry into Walmart, Mulder's (2015a) analysis of the Green Bay Packers professional American football team along with other firms, and Mulder's (2015b) Marxian examination into the British Broadcasting Corporation Symphony Orchestra and the London Symphony Orchestra.

Yet the power of a Marxian theory of the enterprise is not limited to investigations of single firms. The insights of that theory of the enterprise can inform investigations of industries such as liberal arts colleges (Curtis 2001), Major League Baseball (Weiner 2003), and unionization (Annunziato 1990). Additionally, the Marxian theory of the firm can advise theories of the relations between capitalism, socialism and other forms of production (Gibson-Graham 1993; McIntyre 1996).

To conclude, a Marxian theory of the enterprise or firm is distinctively about class. It seeks to specify exactly where exploitation exists and its concrete conditions of existence. With this knowledge comes a uniquely Marxian perspective on capitalism. But, at the same time, the Marxian theory of the enterprise also provides insights, examples and possibilities for non-exploitative enterprises. Therein lies the revolutionary potential of this perspective.

Notes

1 Olsen argues that, "in *Capital* Marx develops his theory of capitalism primarily through a close analysis of the capitalist enterprise" (forthcoming).
2 Hodgson (1998) forms a taxonomy of the main theories of the firm, both orthodox and heterodox, and places all theories of the firm into two, sometimes overlapping, categories, competency-based and contractarian. He places Marxian firm theory in a sub-category of competency-based theory referred to as evolutionary.
3 It is always important to remember that Marxism and neoclassical theory employ very different theories of value. This point and the specific differences in the theories of value are explicitly presented by Resnick and Wolff (1987b).
4 See the entry "profit" from businessdictionary.com.
5 See Brennan (2005) for a more detailed investigation of the legal framework in which boards of directors operate. While not from a Marxian class perspective, the work of Berle and Means (1932) is informative here as it argues for how ownership and control have become decoupled in modern corporate structures.
6 http://www.forbes.com/sites/timworstall/2012/03/04/the-story-of-henry-fords-5-a-day-wages-its-not-what-you-think/ (accessed June 1, 2016).

References

Annunziato, F. 1990. "Commodity Unionism." *Rethinking Marxism* 3(2): 8–33.
Baran, P. and P. Sweezy. 1966. *Monopoly Capital*. New York: Monthly Review Press.
Berle, A. and G. Means. 1932. *The Modern Corporation and Private Property*. New York: Macmillan.
Braverman, H. 1974. *Labor and Monopoly Capital*. New York: Monthly Review Press.
Brennan, D. 2003a. "Enron: Understanding Deregulated Markets, Accounting Scandals, and Lost Savings." *Rethinking Marxism* 15(4): 554–564.
——. 2003b. "Enron and Failed Futures: A Critical Appraisal of Policy and Corporate Governance in the Wake of Enron's Collapse." *Social Text* 21(4): 35–50.
——. 2005. "'Fiduciary Capitalism,' the 'Political Model of Corporate Governance,' and the Prospect of Stakeholder Capitalism in the United States." *Review of Radical Political Economics* 37(1): 39–62.
Curtis, F. 2001. "Ivy-Covered Exploitation: Class, Education and the Liberal Arts College." In *Re/Presenting Class: Essays in Postmodern Marxism*, J. K. Gibson-Graham, S. A. Resnick and R. Wolff, eds., 81–104. Durham: Duke University Press.
Gibson-Graham, J. K. 1993. "Waiting for the Revolution, or How to Smash Capitalism while Working at Home in Your Spare Time." *Rethinking Marxism* 6(2): 10–24.
Gramsci, A. 1971. *Selections from the Prison Notebooks*. New York: International Publishers.
Henn, H. 1970. *Handbook on the Law of Corporations and Other Business Enterprises*. St. Paul, MN: West.

Hodgson, G. 1998. "Evolutionary and competence-based theories of the firm." *Journal of Economic Studies* 25(1): 25–56.

Marx, K. 1954. *Capital*, Volume 1. Moscow: Progress Publishers.

McIntyre, R. 1996. "Mode of Production, Social Formation, and Uneven Development, or Is There Capitalism in America?" In *Postmodern Materialism and the Future of Marxian Theory*, A. Callari and D. Ruccio, eds., 231–256. Hanover, NH: Wesleyan University Press.

Mulder, C. 2011. "Wal-Mart's Role in Capitalism." *Rethinking Marxism* 23(2): 246–263.

——. 2015a. *Transcending Capitalism through Cooperative Practices*. New York: Palgrave Macmillan.

——. 2015b. "State Capitalism vis-à-vis Private Communism." *Rethinking Marxism* 27(2): 258–271.

Norton, B. 2001. "Reading Marx for Class." In *Re/Presenting Class: Essays in Postmodern Marxism*, J. K. Gibson-Graham, S. A. Resnick and R. Wolff, eds., 23–55. Durham: Duke University Press.

Olsen, E. Forthcoming. "Class Analytic Marxism and the Recovery of the Marxian Theory of the Enterprise." In *Marxism Without Guarantees: Economics, Knowledge, and Class*, T. Burczak, R. Garnett, and R. McIntyre, eds. London and New York: Routledge.

Resnick, S. A. and R. Wolff. 1987a. *Knowledge and Class: A Marxian Critique of Political Economy*. Chicago: University of Chicago Press.

——. 1987b. *Economics: Marxian versus Neoclassical*. Baltimore: Johns Hopkins University Press.

Roberts, B. 1988. "What Is Profit?" *Rethinking Marxism* 1(1): 136–151.

Weiner, R. 2003. "Power Hitters Strike Out: New Perspectives on Baseball and Slavery." *Rethinking Marxism* 15(1): 33–48.

Wolff, R. 2012. *Democracy at Work: A Cure for Capitalism*. Chicago: Haymarket Books.

17

MARXIAN THEORIES OF THE LABOR PROCESS

From Marx to Braverman

Richard McIntyre

The contemporary idea of "the labor process" is based on Marx's distinction between labor and labor power. The employer can buy people's ability to work, their labor power, but in general not their actual labor. Political-economic analysis of work, then, is the study of how the employer/capitalist induces and commands workers to perform "surplus labor," labor whose value is over and above that necessary to reproduce the workers and replace machinery, buildings and raw materials.

Adam Smith began *The Wealth of Nations* with three chapters on the division of labor. He saw this division as the primary cause of the wealth of nations, especially as the market expands so that this division can be deepened, extended and mechanized. Thus, work and the separation of work into its constituent elements is the starting point of modern political economy. Marx added many things to this analysis. For our purposes the key concepts are the labor/labor power distinction, his concept of the reserve armies of the unemployed and habituation of the worker to the capitalist rules of the workplace.

The analysis of the labor process is literally the centerpiece of Marx's *Capital* volume 1. The chapters on the labor process occupy the middle 400 pages of an 800-page book; Marx must have thought he was on to *some*thing. Oddly, the ideas in these chapters were hardly developed by his followers for over a century. Beginning with Harry Braverman's *Labor and Monopoly Capital* (1974) a small library of books and articles has appeared, building on and criticizing Braverman and Marx to analyze current labor process developments. In this essay I will summarize Marx's treatment, the context for Braverman's intervention and some of its consequences. In a second entry I will touch on some of the post-Braverman literature, especially insofar as it examines the change in capitalism dating from the 1970s, and especially globalization as it relates to the labor process.

Marx

In chapter 7 of volume 1 of *Capital*, Marx sets out to resolve the problem he has set up in the first six chapters: if all goods are sold at their value, including labor power, where do profits come from? To the individual putting his money in the bank or in a treasury bond, it appears that that money grows by its own nature. But this is absurd. Where does the increment come from? The short answer that Marx gives in chapters 5 and 6 is "not through exchange." While he recognizes the historical and contemporary role played by merchant and interest-bearing capital, they are, he argues, in a subordinate role in the industrial capitalism that became prevalent in nineteenth-century England. Merchant companies and banks can redistribute but not create value. Value is created in production, and the key condition for this is the generalized existence of wage labor. Here, Marx believed he had found the unique commodity that produces more value than it embodies.

The value of labor power is initially determined—as is the value of everything else—by the value of the commodities needed to (re)produce it. Workers must be housed, fed, clothed and trained, and another generation must be raised to replace the current one as it wears out. The value of the commodities needed to do this (over)determines the value of labor power. But the value of labor power also has a "historical and moral element" to it, as normal human needs vary given geography, the development of civilization, the state of the class struggle, etc. The labor time "necessary" to reproduce the working class is socially variable. So labor power is a different sort of commodity in its value creating potential *and* in the determination of its own value. The latter is assumed equal to the wage in the first volume of *Capital*, and Marx makes little attempt to analyze these historical and moral elements.

To examine the value creating power of labor we have to leave the world of the market—as Marx calls it the world of freedom, equality, property and Bentham—and enter the hidden abode of production, a realm of un-freedom. Here the worker produces more new value than she is paid for, or what Marx terms *surplus value*.

The diagram below represents Marx's analysis. During part of the day, A–B, the worker produces new value sufficient to reproduce herself and the means of production she uses. During the rest of the day, B–C, she produces new value that, under the conventional property rules of capitalism, goes to the capitalist as surplus.

A.................B.................C

The labor process involves the processes of producing commodities *and* surplus value. In the labor process human labor is purposively combined with raw materials and tools to create useful objects *and* surplus value. Marx calls the simplest form *absolute surplus value*. This is when the working day, week or year is extended beyond what is necessary to reproduce the worker and the means of production. Workers are paid the value of what they sell—the value of their labor power—so it is not in the labor market but in the labor process that they are exploited. In the diagram increasing absolute surplus value involves moving point C to the right.

Why would the worker agree to work longer than is necessary to reproduce herself? First, a group of wage laborers must exist, in other words a group that has no alternative but to sell their labor power in order to survive. Wage labor that has been stripped of ownership of the means of production is not a natural category, and Marx notes in passing that its existence is "clearly the result of a past historical development, the product of many economic revolutions, of the extinction of a whole series of older forms of social production." This is a violent process of legal expropriation, but he postpones the development of this point to the end of the book. Second, the worker's sale of her labor power for money involves another element of compulsion because of unemployment or what Marx describes as "the reserve army of labor." Since there are generally more sellers than buyers, capitalists are typically able to set the terms of employment, including working hours.

It is no accident that some of the earliest forms of labor organization had as their goal the reduction of the working day. The working day, week, year and life are also influenced by a whole series of cultural and legal factors, and Marx provides a rich analysis of some of these, both in England and elsewhere in his long chapter on the working day. This conjunctural analysis of class struggle is also an extended examination of some of the limits of and possibilities for reform within capitalism (McIntyre 2008, 134–61).

As it becomes more difficult to extend the working day, week and year capitalists turn to a second strategy of reducing necessary labor time through technological change and organizational innovation. In fact capitalists pursue such a strategy even before the potentials of absolute surplus value are exhausted: competition forces them to. This involves moving point B in the diagram to the left, and this move is the starting point for the contemporary labor process literature.

New ways of organizing the division of labor, new forms of cooperation in the workplace and new machines all can reduce the amount of time it takes to reproduce the worker, leaving more of the working day to produce surplus value for the capitalist. Some of these innovations, especially those involving new forms of workplace cooperation, prefigure the better society that Marx believes will emerge from capitalism, but under capitalist relations of production they tend to mainly benefit the capitalist and to degrade the worker. Marx describes the factory regime, the division of labor internal to the firm, as a planned despotism that is the reverse image of the anarchy of the market and the social division of labor outside the firm.

The Labor Process and Class Struggle

In the 1930s the Italian trade union and communist leader Antonio Gramsci examined *Fordism* as not just a new way of organizing the labor process but a new way of organizing society. For Gramsci (1971), Fordism meant machine-paced production of standardized goods, with workers being paid enough to purchase those goods while becoming standardized themselves, through moral coercion inside and outside the workplace. This was the product of a new "historic bloc" that could resolve some of capitalism's dilemmas through a peaceful revolution. Fordism appeared first in the USA because that country lacked the "vast army of parasites" that still prevailed in much of Europe. Gramsci was interested in whether such an alliance of class forces and hegemonic ideas was possible in Europe. His concepts were not influential in the English-speaking world until the 1970s when *The Prison Notebooks* were first translated. The concept "Fordism" remains influential if now primarily as something different from what has emerged in the rich countries since the 1970s (Harvey 1991). Marxists provided little else of value in the analysis of the labor process until the 1970s.

In the midst of the heightened worker militancy of the late 60s and 70s a number of books emerged on the labor process. The most influential was Harry Braverman's *Labor and Monopoly Capital*. Braverman investigated *Taylorism* as a hegemonic idea that rationalized and degraded work and the worker in the twentieth century.

Braverman characterizes Taylorism as the scientific management of work flow, or as Braverman puts it, the scientific process of removing skill from the shop floor. Braverman analyzed the general extension of the principles of Taylorism to all kinds of work. Labor engaged in circulation of commodities, money changing, information exchange, etc. is or will be deskilled, as is much administrative work.

Braverman related this transformation of work in "monopoly capitalism" to the makeover of all aspects of life in the twentieth century. Rather than deskilling, it seems to me that Braverman's book is about commodification of social life *and* the degradation of work. For instance, family life is transformed as production leaves the household in favor of consumption. The destruction of the old form of the family creates the possibility for transition to a higher form, but in capitalism these possibilities are underdeveloped, as are the possibilities for cooperation inside the workplace.

Braverman's critics were many and quick. It was claimed that he drew too much from American sources, treated workers as objects, class struggle in the labor process was of minor import, worker resistance to changing labor processes was totally neglected, the focus was on the male industrial worker, etc. Some argued that both Braverman and Marx miss the ways in which new technologies, by increasing interdependence, increase the capacity for sabotage and disruption. Others claimed that he overestimates the importance of control and underestimates the importance of ideology, which induces consent and encourages workers' willing cooperation with management.

Rick Edwards' alternative to Braverman was particularly influential (Edwards 1979). Since the working class is fragmented, and oligopoly allows paying off the top fraction, the only sensible strategy for the working class is defending the terrain of social democratic compromise—i.e., the New Deal—and extending it where possible. Unfortunately for Edwards and similar radical analyses, that compromise fell apart in the 1980s and 90s due to the capitalists' counteroffensive and the global expansion of the reserve army.

Marx and Braverman *do* seem to understand what workers are forced to cope with—speed-up, layoffs, deskilling, authoritarianism. And they show that capitalism is characterized by fetishisms that obscure—for everyone—the origin of surplus value in exploitation. It *seems* that the worker is being paid for the value of what she produces, but actually, according to Marx, she is paid for the value of what she sells, her labor power. Of course some labor power is worth more than others, as it takes more time to produce a skilled worker than an unskilled worker.

Marx did not fully theorize how the subjective, lived experience of the working class influenced the labor process, perhaps because of his hostility to the utopian socialists. Nor did he solve the problem of political consciousness, and Braverman sees it as wise to avoid this question. Historically, management strategy has fluctuated between repressing workers and seeking their consent by involving them in decision-making. In the end Marxists have generally understood the repressive side to be the more important.

The threat of capital mobility, plant closure, and direct and technological supervision in the workplace are all disciplining forces. These may provoke resistance, but Marx assumes that in the end worker resistance must give way so long as that resistance stays within the bounds of economistic trade unionism.

Marxists want to know "what is to be done?" So far there is no general answer from labor process analysis. But that analysis has illuminated the exploitation in capitalist relations of production as well as the reason for various management strategies to extract labor from labor power.

Labor and Monopoly Capital

Braverman thought he was writing a book on occupational shifts in the U.S. but came to realize that no one had really examined changes in the labor process *within* occupations alongside the co-evolution of management and the structure of the corporation. Although it was a commonplace among Marxists that the capitalist production process is incessantly transformed by the accumulation of capital, Braverman found little in the Marxian tradition to guide his study beyond volume 1 of *Capital*. Marx's writing in the middle sections of that book are certainly powerful and prophetic, but Braverman attributed that absence also to the seemingly more pressing concerns of imperialism, war and economic crisis in the twentieth century, and the tendency within the trade union movement to be more concerned with distribution than production. More important, perhaps, in the one state that openly declared itself Marxist there was more of an attempt to adopt the lessons of the capitalist labor process than to overthrow it. Soviet social scientists dismissed job satisfaction studies as meaningless in a workers' state. No appreciable difference in the organization of the labor process occurred in the Soviet Union, and some Western analysts took this to mean a convergence between the two systems; only one way to organize production was even possible. Braverman was critical of technological determinism. "The concrete and determinate forms of society are indeed 'determined' rather than accidental, but this is the determinacy of the thread by thread weaving of the fabric of history, not the imposition of external formulas" (Braverman 1998, 15). A better lesson might be that the Soviet system was not different from the capitalist system on this count because it was in fact just another form of capitalism, state capitalism in this case.[1]

Thus the analysis of the labor process, once a strong point of Marxism, became one of its weak points. This changed somewhat with the Cuban revolution, the Chinese Cultural Revolution, and the various radical movements of the 1960s. Braverman found the latter particularly important as the discontents of youth, women, blacks and other groups occurred against the background of capitalism functioning at its peak rather than during one of its periodic breakdowns. "Dissatisfaction centered not so much on capitalism's inability to provide work as on the work it provides" (Braverman 1998, 10). This was signified for Braverman and many others by the 1972 "Lordstown strike" at GM against the pace of the assembly line, but one can see this kind of dissatisfaction in any number of strikes and actions during the international wave of worker militancy in the late 1960s and early 1970s (Barkin 1983). That this dissatisfaction was bought off in some places by higher wages does not change the fact that its source was working conditions, not pay. Braverman quotes a job design consultant to the effect that "We may have created too many dumb jobs for the number of dumb people to fill them" (Braverman 1998, 24).

The "deskilling hypothesis" became central to the labor process debate, but in fact Braverman never uses the term. He was quite aware that it was labor costs not skill content that management was primarily concerned with. He did see "job enrichment" as applying mostly to office rather than line employees and as representing a change in management style rather than "a genuine change in the position of the worker" (Ibid., 26). Workers were given the illusion of making decisions rather than actual power to make them, and he uses the homely example of removing the powdered egg from baking mixes to reduce the guilt of the housewife.

Braverman went far beyond the question of skill at work. In his chapter titled "The Habituation of the Worker to the Capitalist Mode of Production" he notes that the working class is not made once and for all but must be adjusted to work in its capitalist form with each generation. This habituation, as he says, "becomes a permanent feature of capitalist society" (Ibid.,140). It had been known since the Hawthorne experiments of the 1920s that productivity had little relationship to ability—and in fact sometimes a negative relationship—and that collective resistance to the pace of work was a central problem for management. Two tendencies developed, with industrial engineers trying to minimize the role of the individual while personnel administrators celebrated it. Braverman develops the example of Ford, where high wages certainly played a role in habituating workers to soul-deadening employment but could not eliminate resistance. Worker hostility:

continues as a subterranean stream that makes its way to the surface when employment conditions permit, or when the capitalist drive for greater intensity of labor oversteps the bounds of physical and mental capacity. It renews itself in each new generation, expresses itself in the unbounded cynicism and revulsion which large numbers of workers feel about their work...

(Braverman 1998, 151).[2]

In the chapter on "the universal market" Braverman examines the subordination of individual, family and social needs to the market as these are reshaped to meet the needs of capital. All of society, he says, has been transformed into a gigantic marketplace, and this had been little investigated when he was writing. Of course it has been since, and it is peculiar that Braverman chooses the market rather than the factory as his preferred metaphor. Nonetheless Braverman anticipates arguments made subsequently by feminist scholars: the transformation of the family from production to consumption unit and urbanization as encouraging the commodity form. Home labor becomes costly relative to market purchase, but as Braverman notes, this is reinforced by social custom, the deterioration of homemaking skills, and the drive of housewives and teenagers for an income of their own. This is just the first step, as in time the satisfaction of physical but also emotional needs are outsourced from the household. Both social life and production are evacuated from the household, leaving only consumption. New commodities substitute for both household production and the human relations formerly provided by families. Entertainment and sport too are transformed from areas of self-production to production for profit. Of course there is resistance to this, but "underground" innovations are quickly incorporated into profit-making enterprise. Caring labor is increasingly commoditized, creating new occupations and industries. "... the inhabitant of capitalist society is enmeshed in a web made up of commodity goods and commodity services from which there is little possibility of escape.... This is reinforced ... [by] the atrophy of competence" (Braverman 1998, 281).

Increased dependence on the market is the other side of the coin of increased dependence on capital for employment. Most of the new "service sector" jobs are less susceptible to technological change and thus are low productivity and low wage. These jobs, along with clerical work, are what originally drew women out of the household and into paid employment. Braverman's treatment of the universal market was prescient, anticipating the work of Arlie Hochschild, David Harvey, Naomi Klein, and Juliet Schor.

Finally Braverman deals with "the structure of the working class and its reserve armies" focusing on the proletarianization of agricultural populations and women. Many of the former first entered industrial work, but these jobs began to shrink earlier on in the face of automation, sloughing off those workers into low-productivity service sector employment. He quotes Marx on this process of reserve army formation at length, closing with "The whole form of the movement of modern industry depends, therefore, upon the constant transformation of a part of the labouring population into unemployed or half-employed hands" (Braverman 1998, 383). Thus in the age of scientific-technological progress the most rapidly growing occupations are those not touched by that progress: retail sales, some clerical work, etc. The masses thrown off by imperialist penetration of the colonies and neo-colonies are also available as surplus populations so that the reserve armies become internationalized and the female population becomes "the prime supplementary reservoir of labor" (Ibid., 385).

Braverman uses Marx's categories of the latent, stagnant, and floating parts of the reserve armies: those not fully integrated into capitalist production, those with irregular employment, and those who once had good jobs but are now out of work. The latent part figures in a critical way in the debates over immigration, while in the U.S. the stagnant part (along with paupers and the "lumpenproletariat") is managed through prison policy. Portions of the white male working class had moved into the floating reserve army in the 1970s and this has accelerated since. Braverman was also prescient in noting that the most rapidly growing industries were those with the lowest wages, many below subsistence level. The rapid expansion of workers drawing welfare benefits of one kind or another—primarily food stamps in the U.S.—is not surprising on this account, nor is the polarization of income which in fact Braverman noted (Braverman 1998, 397). The multiple job holding that is necessary to support a family on jobs paying less than subsistence causes family tensions, as Braverman observes.

There *is* a good amount of material on the degradation of work in *Labor and Monopoly Capital*. Contemporary analysts have been less kind to this aspect of Braverman's book to the extent that it is interpreted to mean the deskilling of jobs. In his chapters on Taylorism and the scientific revolution he emphasizes the separation of conception and execution in the workplace as management breaks craft workers' monopoly of skills, concentrating skilled work in the management suite while production work is mechanized, simplified and dehumanized. While initially applied to production jobs, this process would, he argued, be extended to white-collar employment as well, so that the status and salary differentials attached to these jobs would be eroded over time.

The consensus in the literature now is that deskilling is at best a tendency, the desire on the part of management to control labor—as opposed to minimizing the cost—was overstated by Braverman, and the purely American focus occluded other possibilities. In the German model skill was retained in production through a different structure of class-state relations and system of education and training (Thelen 2004). Both Marx and Braverman seem overly focused on the Manchester (internal economies of scale) rather than the Birmingham (agglomeration economies) model, as Harvey has noted (Harvey 2010, 214–15, 289). But *Labor and Monopoly Capital* was also a useful corrective to the unrealistically optimistic theories of post-industrialism, knowledge economy, and informational society that became popular in the 1980s and 90s, as well as to the continuing claims for a "skills gap" in the American economy. Moreover, the separation of conception and execution *in space* is a key aspect of production in contemporary global supply chains, as is discussed in the second part of this entry.

Notes

1 For a contemporary discussion of determinism in labor process theory see Basole 2013.
2 Burawoy (1979) captures this succinctly in his formulation resistance-adaptation-habituation as the typical timeline of workplace struggles.

References

Barkin, S., ed. 1983. *Worker Militancy and Its Consequences*, 2nd edition. New York: Praeger.
Basole, A. 2013. "Class Biased Technological Change and Socialism." *Rethinking Marxism* 25(4): 592–601.
Braverman, H. 1998 [1974]. *Labor and Monopoly Capital: The Degradation of Work in the Twentieth Century.* New York: Monthly Review.
Burawoy, M. 1979. *Manufacturing Consent: Changes in the Labor Process under Monopoly Capitalism.* Chicago: University of Chicago Press.

Edwards, R. 1979. *Contested Terrain: The Transformation of the Workplace in the 20th Century.* New York: Basic Books.

Gramsci, A. 1971. *Selections from the Prison Notebooks.* Edited by Q. Hoare and G. Nowell Smith. New York: International Publishers.

Harvey, D. 1991. *The Condition of Postmodernity: An Enquiry into the Origins of Cultural Change.* Hoboken: Basil Blackwell.

———. 2010. *A Companion to Marx's Capital.* London: Verso.

Hochschild, A. and A. Machung. 2012. *The Second Shift: Working Families and the Revolution at Home.* London: Penguin.

Klein, N. 2009. *No Logo.* New York: Picador.

Marx, K. 1977 [1867]. *Capital: A Critique of Political Economy,* Volume 1. London: Penguin.

McIntyre, R. 2008. *Are Worker Rights Human Rights?* Ann Arbor: University of Michigan Press.

Schor, J. 1993. *The Overworked American: The Unexpected Decline of Leisure.* New York: Basic Books.

Thelen, K. 2004. *How Institutions Evolve: The Political Economy of Skills in Germany, Britain, the United States, and Japan.* Cambridge: Cambridge University Press.

18

MARXIAN LABOR PROCESS THEORY SINCE BRAVERMAN[1]

Richard McIntyre

Labor Process Theory since Braverman

Braverman's *Labor and Monopoly Capital* (1974) was clear and timely. Some commentators referred to the flood of articles and books that followed as "Bravermania."[2] In this essay I will focus on a selection of work associated with the International Labor Process Conference, which has been meeting in one form or another since 1982, and the work of Michael Burawoy, especially his book *The Politics of Production*.[3] These works remain rooted in Marxism without seeking to defend any particular orthodoxy. For Marx's and Braverman's analysis see the first part of this essay.

There is a voluminous management literature now that looks at the labor process instrumentally, in other words seeking to determine the best ways to organize work so as to maximize profits, maintain the enterprise as a going concern, etc. Some of this has been influenced by the post-Braverman international labor process debate discussed below, but I will touch on this work only in passing. My focus is on Marxian theories of the labor process.

The "Core" Theory of the Labor Process

Ongoing research on the labor process has been institutionalized through the annual international labor process conference and related book series. This project grew out of the debate over *Labor and Monopoly Capital* in the UK at the end of the 1970s and has produced a rich body of case studies exploring various techniques of management control and to some extent worker resistance/accommodation (Smith and Thompson 2016). It has also produced a theoretical framework linking labor process issues to a broader political economy.

The "core theory" (Thompson 2010) starts from the indeterminacy at the heart of the labor process, i.e., the difference between what the employer pays for (labor power) and what the employer wants (labor, or work done.) Four principles make up the core theory:

1   The labor process has a privileged position in political economy because it is where surplus value is produced and is a central part of human experience;
2   Competition impels capitalists to constantly revolutionize production;

3   Some system of managerial control is necessary because market mechanisms alone do not regulate the labor process;
4   Social relations between labor and capital in the workplace can be characterized as "structured antagonism."

In both the core theory and in Burawoy's work there is an initial move away from simplistic Marxist notions of this structured antagonism. Burawoy's influential participant-observer studies suggested strongly that capital-labor relations in the workplace do not dictate those in society, nor can they be derived from those in society. Core theory indicated the same.

Some of the initial debate over the labor process had attempted to reinsert worker resistance, often seeing class-consciousness as the norm and seeking to explain why it did not arise in particular cases. A dialectic of control and resistance became a principal feature of labor process writing in the work of Richard Edwards (1979), Andrew Friedman (1977), and Burawoy's earlier book, *Manufacturing Consent* (1979). Burawoy (1985) went beyond the simple presumption of resistance as the norm and, following Gramsci, focused on the production of consent in what he called *factory regimes*. Burawoy developed a *politics of production* through identification of different regimes, which he viewed as internal states with their own rules of citizenship.

The characteristic regime studied by Marx was market despotism, in which inter-firm competition was fierce, the state stood outside the wage labor relationship, labor was subordinate to capital and completely separated from the means of production, and the normal condition of the labor market was one of surplus labor. The relaxation of any of these assumptions produced a wide variety of factory regimes—paternalism, patriarchy, the company state, bureaucratic despotisms, collective self-management, hegemonic regimes, etc. (Burawoy 1985, 12, 91).

The contrast between market despotisms and hegemonic regimes is of most interest. Burawoy noted that with the advent of social insurance and labor law the worker was no longer completely dependent on the employer for his survival and no longer completely powerless in the workplace. This meant that employers needed to achieve worker consent to produce surplus labor, primarily by identifying the interests of the worker with those of the enterprise, and the interests of the capitalist class as those of society as a whole. In the American case this helps us make sense of the agency of the capitalist class in resisting those aspects of the New Deal that promoted social security and worker rights (McIntyre and Hillard 2013; McIntyre 2013).

The UK labor process group paralleled Burawoy to some extent in creating a control-resistance-consent model while reasserting the lack of necessary connection between workplace struggles and class struggles in society. Employers' need to control the labor process would give rise to various forms of resistance on the part of workers. Both groups would engage in bargaining and negotiation, eventually leading to some form of consent. Initially there was a lingering sense in some of this work that collective worker organization and action was the norm and the absence of it required explanation. Simultaneously, though, historically informed labor sociologists were discovering that all national cases are exceptional: there is no typical pattern of working class formation (Zolberg 1986).

The desire not to read off society-wide politics from workplace politics was historically accurate, but it left labor process theory with no way to theorize the normative basis for worker consent[4] and the primarily national context for the vast majority of case studies "largely failed to capture the complexities of relations between capital, labor, and the state within the international division of labor" (Thompson and Newsome 2004, 143). These remain active areas of research.

Lean Production and High Performance Work

On the other hand, labor process research did provide a position from which to criticize theories of flexible specialization and lean management. In the 1990s a "mutual gains enterprise" was thought to be emerging from new strategies of teamwork, flexibility and responsibility (Kochan and Osterman 1994). Labor process scholars produced many case studies showing that these new strategies actually created an "invisible iron cage" of control. Lean production does not do much to alleviate the "mind-numbing stress" of mass production; it simply removes obstacles to the extraction of effort. Power in the enterprise moves upward while accountability and increased effort moves down (Thompson and Newsome 2004, 147; Hillard and McIntyre 1998). Workers are expected to contribute to continuous improvement while accepting that they will be policed more closely. In lean production the ideological dimension of management expands so that management works more actively to align worker attitudes with corporate goals.

What this all means for worker resistance and collective action is not clear. Lean or high performance production exists alongside strategies of bureaucratic rationalization, work intensification and scientific management. Whereas Foucauldians and human resources scholars emphasized the hegemony of cultural control and electronic surveillance, writers in the labor process tradition began to examine worker resistance, misbehavior and disengagement outside of traditional trade union activity. This misbehavior is seen as flowing partly from identity politics but as yet remains unconnected to collective resistance or politics outside the workplace, although some authors see the existence of such behavior as a sign that labor's capacity to resist is not now as weak as low levels of strike activity appear to indicate (Barnes and Taksa 2012).

Lean and high performance work systems have not fulfilled the promise of their advocates. Stress at work has increased alongside growing contingency and insecurity. Effort has been collectivized while risk has been de-collectivized. Some recent work points to the dominance of finance capital and financial markets or merchant capital rather than anything cooked up in the HR department as the primary cause of these developments (Lazonick and Sullivan 2000; Lichtenstein 2013).

Marx argued that capitalists' insatiable quest to appropriate surplus value revolutionizes the productive forces, but these revolutions create conditions inconsistent with further accumulation and reproduction of class relations, making capitalism inherently unstable and crisis prone. Inside the enterprise the dilemma for the capitalist is to mobilize the positive powers of cooperation through mechanisms that may often in fact be coercive.[5] Job enrichment, labor management cooperation, worker-management integration, etc. seem specifically designed to mask the basic relation of domination and subordination that necessarily prevails in the labor process.

Routinization of tasks requires sophisticated managerial, technical and conceptual skills, and powers of adaptability, which counter the tendency to the degradation of labor. Thus, as Marx notes in section 9 of chapter 15 of *Capital* volume 1, destruction of individual trades also helps develop many-sided abilities, fluidity and adaptability. As Harvey puts it:

> Herein lies a deep contradiction: on the one hand, capital wants degraded labor, unintelligent labor, the equivalent of a trained gorilla to do capital's bidding without question, at the same time as it needs this other kind of flexible, adaptable and educated labor, too.

(Harvey 2010, 231)

One answer was the educational clauses of the factory acts. "Capital needs fluidity of labor and therefore has to educate the laborers while breaking down old paternalistic, patriarchal rigidities" (Harvey 2010, 233).

It is not skill that is abhorrent to Capital, just those skills that cannot be monopolized by employers. Capitalists individually and as a class seek to eliminate or find substitutes for such skills. Today this would include skills of the engineers, scientists, managers, designers, etc. Much hangs on whether such skills are totally incorporated as a power of capital "through the formation of a distinctive fraction of the bourgeoisie ... or whether they can be captured as part of the collective powers of labor" (Harvey 1982, 109).

Based largely on the European survey of working conditions, close observers argue that recently there has been an overall rise in skill requirements together with a general intensification of work effort (McGovern 2013). But certainly the degradation of work in many occupations continues. Whatever one thinks about the value of such surveys, a rise in the mean of a survey-based variable does not imply that capitalism has suddenly stopped chewing up (some) people's lives. And around this rising mean there is much variation. Recent analysis of the American labor market turns up little evidence of the popularly imagined mismatch between skills and available jobs (Cappelli 2015; Abraham 2015).

Work effort has increased partly due to advances in computerized monitoring, especially for mid- and low-level jobs. What this all means for job satisfaction is not clear, though making people work harder and reducing their independence is generally not popular. Labor process theory was and is a useful corrective to the more optimistic theories of post-industrialism, knowledge economy and informational society that became popular in the 1980s and 90s, as well as contemporary claims about skills shortages. The persistence of claims of a skills gap in manufacturing is belied by even casual analysis of the data. The reading, writing and math skills that American manufacturers demand are at the community college level or lower (Osterman and Weaver 2014). Employment problems in manufacturing in the U.S. are much more likely due to inadequate demand than to inadequate skills. This is as true today as it was 25 years ago when I was part of a research team examining skills mismatch at the end of the 80s boom. Why this myth persists is an interesting question but beyond my scope here. As Paul Krugman wrote in a recent column:

> the belief that America suffers from a severe "skills gap" is one of those things that everyone important knows must be true, because everyone they know says it's true. It's a prime example of a zombie idea—an idea that should have been killed by evidence, but refuses to die.
>
> *(Krugman 2014).*[6]

There are definitely places where both Marx and Braverman imply a one-way trend of degradation of the worker and work, however inconsistent this may be with their dialectical method. Core labor process theory and Burawoy have corrected this one-sidedness and recreated the possibility for a more dialectical treatment of skill.

The Post-Postwar Period

The end of the post-World War II boom in the 1970s led to increasing international competition, threatening both the social state and the internal rules governing the hegemonic factory regime. Burawoy's concept of *hegemonic despotism* is helpful here. Whereas workers could expect to share in productivity gains under the hegemonic regime, increasingly those gains were used to lower prices or pay stockholders and top executives. As communications and transportation technologies advanced, capitalists found it possible to relocate production to poor countries in which wages were significantly lower while productivity was not. Free trade agreements and laws created in those countries secured these new investments.

Employers continued to encourage the identification of the interests of workers with those of the enterprise but increasingly did so to push for concessions bargaining and de-unionization. Employment policy and labor economics shifted their focus from workforce development and labor demand to education, human capital theory and labor supply.

This response broke with the Fordist connection between productivity and wages but not the Taylorist tendency to decompose the labor process. The response by capital to slowing and unstable demand was a series of innovations all gathered under the sign of "flexibility"—subcontracting, outsourcing, use of temporary workers, casualization, segmentation, declining social and legal protection on the job, increase in work intensity, privatization of the costs of workforce preparation and maintenance, multitasking, etc. What this was NOT was a decline in the influence of large enterprises and enterprise groups, or in the separation of conception and execution.

The description of this shift as a return to the market is wrong. Boltanski and Chiapello (2007, 223) capture this shift nicely: "groups, composed of a large number of small units, resorting to sub-contractors who are not necessarily more numerous in each instance, but are more integrated into the running of the head firm…".[7] This has been accompanied by an increase in various automatic forms of workplace monitoring and monitoring from a distance, so it might be better to describe this as the recasting rather than the revolt against Taylorism: reduced unplanned break time, individualized work situations and remuneration, and a transference of the costs of activating the labor force from companies to individuals or, in those countries practicing active labor market policies, to the state. "… the costs of the change in strategy by firms have been paid for largely by the community—something which those in revolt against the rates of compulsory tax levies fail to mention" (Boltanski and Chiapello 2007, 254).

A necessary condition for this recasting of Taylorism was the end of even a rhetoric of full employment. Whereas Keynes and his allies struggled for a firm commitment to full employment at Bretton Woods and after, American negotiators and the dominant political coalition in the U.S. post-1938 saw free trade with a moderate commitment to domestic employment policies as sufficient, and this group won the day. Thus, although effective full employment was won between 1955 and 1965 in much of the developed world, institutions to maintain it were never created. The pushback against full employment during the crisis of the 1970s was against a weak institutional wall.

That pushback, in the form of class war from above and its ideological expression, neo-liberalism, was enormously effective. It has certainly produced a change in employment relations, but to the extent that labor process theory was grounded in a basically Marxist method of understanding those relations, it has not discredited that theory.

Globalization and the Labor Process

Braverman emphasized the separation of planning and labor process design from its execution. This separation affects the structure of the firm, as embodied in the production/nonproduction distinction, and also the location decisions of the firm (corporate headquarters vs. manufacturing plants). Certain developments central to globalization can be understood through this lens. The computing and electronics industries in particular can be understood as examples of a sort of "Bravermanian product cycle."[8]

It is well known that East Asia has become a center for cross-border activity by transnational corporations (Hart-Landsberg 2013). The ratio of exports to GDP in the region grew from 15% in 1982 to 45% in 2006, much faster than the ratio for low- or middle-income countries in general or for the world as a whole. The region's share of manufactured exports also rose dramatically with an increased focus on information and communications technology (ICT) and electrical components. ICT and electrical exports made up 75% of the region's exports by 2007. The growing importance of parts and components highlights the central role of cross-border production networks. More than half of all East Asian trade was intraregional in 2007, as against a third for NAFTA and a fifth for the EU15.

China plays a key role. Essentially the rest of East Asia exports to China and China exports to the U.S. and EU. While China's rise has been dramatic, it is generally misinterpreted as establishing China as a rival to American and European capitalisms and as the predominant player in East Asia. But in Braverman's conception-execution dyad China works but does not think. This can be illustrated by looking at the share of value-added that China captures in ICT.

In addition to Braverman this example draws on the "appropriability" framework developed by Berkeley Business School professor David Teece.[9] The classic example for Teece is the IBM PC, in which Intel and Microsoft rather than IBM increasingly captured profits. The latter lost control of key interfaces by the late 1980s. The focal point in the Teece model is who is able to "appropriate" profits by developing and retaining control of products that are complementary to an initial innovation. While IBM developed the personal computer, Intel controlled chip production and Microsoft controlled the operating system, and thus they were able to appropriate profits.

Power to appropriate can be almost anywhere in the value chain. In electronics there is fierce competition between Original Design Manufacturers (Foxconn, etc.). Brand-name vendors do conceptualization, branding and marketing, distribution is done by global wholesalers, and sales by specialized and general retailers, as well as own-store networks such as Apple.

Kraemer, Linder and Dedrick (2011) have shown that, with the iPod and iPad, Apple introduced a dominant design and thus had great latitude in introducing complementary products and controlling interfaces. Unlike IBM, Apple maintained competition among suppliers and secrecy and quality control in design.[10]

Apple continues to capture the largest share of value from these innovations. While most of the components are manufactured in China, the primary benefits go to Apple, as it continues to keep most of its product design, software development, product management, marketing and other high-wage functions in the U.S. China's role is different from what most casual observers would think. With its control over the supply chain, Apple has the power to make and break the fortunes of many of its suppliers. There is little surplus value appropriated in electronics assembly. This has consequences for understanding China's rise as well as arguments in the U.S. that bringing high-volume electronics assembly back to the U.S. is the path to "good jobs" or economic growth.

We can think about this in terms of Braverman's concept of the decoupling of conception and execution and Marx's idea in *Capital* volume 3 that in the process of capitalist development the functions of the capitalist are broken up and performed by a variety of social actors. The popularly imagined figure of the capitalist as Mister Moneybags disappears in favor of an array of people in different social and geographical locations all seeking to occupy the most desirable and protectable place in the (surplus) value chain.

This means that labor processes are increasingly unlikely to exist in close proximity to processes of the receipt and distribution of surplus value. Production, receipt, and distribution of surplus value happen in different locations and are often unconnected in social analysis because of that. If workers are enraged by workplace conditions they can be told that their direct employer has nothing to do with it, as the rules of the game are set in Cupertino, Portland or Seattle (McIntyre 2008.)

What does this mean for resistance and working class formation? There is no consensus in contemporary working class studies. There is no justifiable belief that any general process of class formation flows from capitalist development itself. The optimistic perspective is that capitalist industrialization in China and elsewhere is re-creating the kinds of conditions that spawned radical working class organizing in nineteenth-century Western Europe and the USA. For instance, Beverly Silver demonstrates that the movement of the auto industry to greenfield sites in Europe, Europe's periphery and then to South Africa, South America and Korea, led to a typical cycle of unrest, class formation and resistance (Silver 2003). Even more optimistically, Hardt and Negri see the growth of a "multitude," something like the old picture of the unified working class, now produced by changes in the labor process breaking down differences between industrial worker, service worker and peasant, and globalization creating a kind of unity against empire (Hardt and Negri 2000). Yet one of the originators of modern labor process theory, Michael Burawoy, is pessimistic that this all adds up to very much (Burawoy 2010).

The labor process *has* changed in certain definite ways, both in its material conditions and its geography. Much of the observable resistance is overdetermined by local conditions and by the different kinds of capitalisms prevailing across the industrial, post-industrial, and industrializing nation-scape.[11] Labor process theory continues to help us to understand the shifting international division of labor that provokes these resistances.

Notes

1 I thank participants at the 32nd annual International Labor Process Conference in London, April 2014 for their critical and helpful comments. This is the second of two parts.

2 Surveys of this literature at different points and from various perspectives include Littler and Salaman (1982), Spencer (2000), Baldoz, Koeber and Kraft (2001) and O'Doherty and Wilmott (2009).

3 Another key work is Bowles (1985). Bowles presents a precise model of the importance of command in the workplace for the extraction of labor from labor power. He relates this to technological change, the functioning of the reserve army of labor, and management strategies such as divide and rule. He does not address forms of resistance.

4 One way to theorize the normative basis of consent is through the work of Michel Foucault. Some labor process theorists turned to Foucault to explain how corporate values and surveillance and a culture of self-discipline combined to transform worker identities. Capitalist work and employment relations tend to individualize workers and undermine their search for a stable and secure identity. Surveillance replaced resistance as the central theoretical category and collective resistance, both formal and informal, came to be seen as impossible. There is a similarity with mainstream management arguments that control and bureaucracy have been displaced by a culture of commitment. This tendency seems less popular in labor process theory circles today, perhaps because it has moved more thoroughly into management theory (see for instance O'Doherty and Wilmott 2009). For an attempt to bring Foucault and Marx together in labor process analysis see Sakolsky (1992). An interesting attempt to build a theory of worker consent on the work of Spinoza is Lordon (2014).

5 This fellow "the capitalist" is an elusive figure. In *Capital* volume 3 Marx demonstrates that the capitalist disappears in the course of the development of capitalism even as the capitalist class process of the appropriation of surplus value continues. Capitalism literally becomes a process without a subject. This is a problem for socialist strategy, which very definitely requires a target, and perhaps partly explains the failure of the labor process literature to develop a robust theory of collective action.

6 See also Head (2014).

7 Although they are generalizing from the French experience, this pattern seems close to being a general development.

8 Thanks to Erik Olsen for this formulation.

9 Core labor process theory has begun to include geography and comparative work (McGrath-Clamp, Herod and Rainnie 2010; Hauptmeier and Vidal 2014) as have American labor sociologists, who concentrate on how globalization affects the structure of antagonism in the workplace (Baldoz et al. 2001). Still, the Teece approach (Teece 1986) stands out for its link between the restructuring of the capitalist enterprise along "volume 3" lines and the location of surplus value appropriation. In Marxian terms "appropriability" is actually the ability to receive rather than appropriate surplus value. Disentangling these terms is beyond our scope here. Smith (2016) provides a good starting point for addressing how surplus flows have changed with globalized capitalism.

10 This would not have been possible without access to the vast reserves of army in China. The creation of these reserves, a fundamentally political process, is beyond our scope here but see Cantin and Taylor (2008).

11 Examining these different resistances and struggles is beyond my scope. For the important case of China see Friedman (2014).

References

Abraham, K. 2015. "Is Skill Mismatch Impeding U.S. Economic Recovery?" *ILR Review* 68: 291–313.

Baldoz, R. C. Koeber, and P. Kraft. 2001. "Introduction: Making Sense of Work in the Twenty-First Century." In *The Critical Study of Work: Labor, Technology and Global Production*, R. Baldoz, C. Koeber, and P. Kraft, eds., 3–20. Philadelphia: Temple University Press.

Barnes, A. and L. Taksa. 2012. *Rethinking Misbehavior and Resistance in Organizations.* Bingley: Emerald Group.

Boltanski, L. and E. Chiapello. 2007. *The New Spirit of Capitalism.* London: Verso.

Bowles, S. 1985. "The Production Process in a Competitive Economy: Walrasian, Neo-Hobbesian, and Marxian Models." *American Economic Review* 85(1): 16–35.

Burawoy, M. 1979. *Manufacturing Consent: Changes in the Labor Process under Monopoly Capitalism*. Chicago: University of Chicago Press.

——. 1985. *The Politics of Production: Factory Regimes under Capitalism and Socialism.* London: Verso.

——. 2010. "From Polanyi to Pollyanna: The False Optimism of Global Labor Studies." *Global Labour Journal* 1(2): 301–313.

Cantin, É. and M. Taylor. 2008. "Making the Workshop of the World: China and the Transformation of the International Division of Labor." In *Global Economy Contested: Power and Conflict across the International Division of Labor*, M. Taylor, ed., 51–76. London: Routledge.

Cappelli, P. 2015. "Skill Gaps, Skill Shortages, and Skill Mismatches: Evidence and Arguments for the United States." *ILR Review* 68: 251–290.

Edwards, R. 1979. *Contested Terrain: The Transformation of the Workplace in the 20th Century.* New York: Basic Books.

Friedman, A. 1977. *Industry and Labour: Class Struggle at Work and Monopoly Capitalism.* London: Macmillan.

Friedman, E. 2014. *Insurgency Trap: Labor Politics in Postsocialist China.* Ithaca, NY: ILR Press.

Hardt, M. and A. Negri. 2000. *Empire.* Cambridge, MA: Harvard University Press.

Hart-Landsberg, M. 2013. *Capitalist Globalization: Consequences, Resistance, and Alternatives.* New York: Monthly Review Press.

Harvey, D. 1982. *The Limits to Capital.* Oxford: Basil Blackwell.

——. 2010. *A Companion to Marx's Capital.* London: Verso.

Hauptmeier, M. and M. Vidal, eds. 2014. *Comparative Political Economy of Work.* London: Palgrave MacMillan.

Head, S. 2014. *Mindless: Why Smarter Machines Are Making Dumber Humans.* New York: Basic Books.

Hillard, M. and R. McIntyre. 1998. "The Ambiguous Promise of High Performance Work Organization." *Review of Radical Political Economics* 30(3): 25–33.

Kochan, T. and P. Osterman. 1994. *The Mutual Gains Enterprise: Forging a Winning Partnership among Labor, Management, and Government.* Boston: Harvard Business School Press.

Kraemer, K. G. Linder, and J. Dedrick. 2011. "Capturing Value in Global Networks: Apple's iPad and iPhone." http://pcic.merage.uci.edu/papers/2011/value_ipad_iphone.pdf (accessed August 6, 2016).

Krugman, P. 2014. "Jobs and Skills and Zombies." *New York Times*, March 31: A21.

Lazonick, W. and M. Sullivan. 2000. "Maximizing Shareholder Value: A New Ideology for Corporate Governance." *Economy and Society* 29(1): 13–35.

Lichtenstein, N. 2013. "The Return of Merchant Capitalism." *International Labor and Working Class History* 81: 8–27.

Littler, C. and G. Salaman. 1982. "Bravermania and Beyond: Recent Theories of the Labour Process." *Sociology* 16(2): 251–269.

Lordon, F. 2014. *Willing Slaves of Capital: Spinoza and Marx on Desire.* Trans. by G. Ash. London: Verso.

Marx, K. 1977 [1867]. *Capital: A Critique of Political Economy*, Volume 1. London: Penguin.

——. 1993 [1894]. *Capital: A Critique of Political Economy*, Volume 3. London: Penguin.

McGovern, P. 2013. "The Experience of Work in Comparative Perspective." In *Comparative Employment Relations in the Global Economy*, C. Frege and J. Kelly, eds., 71–88. London: Routledge.

McGrath-Champ, S. A. Herod, and A. Rainnie, eds. 2010. *Handbook of Employment and Society: Working Space.* Northampton, MA: Edward Elgar.

McIntyre, R. 2008. *Are Worker Rights Human Rights?* Ann Arbor: University of Michigan Press.

——. 2013. "Labor Militance and the New Deal: Some Lessons for Today." In *When Government Helped: Learning from the Successes and Failures of the New Deal*, S. D. Collins and G. Schaffner Goldberg, eds., 120–145. Oxford: Oxford University Press.

McIntyre, R. and M. Hillard. 2013. "Capitalist Class Agency and the New Deal Order: Against the Notion of a Limited Capital-Labor Accord." *Review of Radical Political Economics* 45(2): 129–148.

O'Doherty, D. and H. Wilmott. 2009. "The Decline of Labour Process Analysis and the Future Sociology of Work." *Sociology* 43(5): 931–951.

Osterman, P. and A. Weaver. 2014. "Why Claims of Skills Shortages in Manufacturing are Overblown." Economic Policy Institute. http://www.epi.org/publication/claims-skills-shortages-manufacturing-overblown/ (accessed August 6, 2016).

Sakolsky, R. 1992. "Disciplinary Power, the Labor Process, and the Constitution of the Laboring Subject." *Rethinking Marxism* 5(4): 114–126.

Silver, B.. 2003. *Forces of Labor: Workers' Movements and Globalization since 1870.* Cambridge: Cambridge University Press.

Smith, C. and P. Thompson. 2016. "Background of the International Labour Process Conference." http://www.ilpc.org.uk/Background.aspx (accessed August 6, 2016).

Smith, J. 2016. *Imperialism in the Twenty-First Century: The Globalization of Production, Super-Exploitation, and the Crisis of Capitalism.* New York: Monthly Review.

Spencer, D. 2000. "Braverman and the Contribution of Labour Process Analysis to the Critique of Capitalist Production—Twenty-Five Years On." *Work, Employment & Society* 14(2): 223–243.

Teece, D. 1986. "Profiting from Technological Innovation: Implications for Integration, Collaboration, Licensing, and Policy." *Research Policy* 15: 285–305.

Thompson, P. 2010. "The Capitalist Labour Process: Concepts and Connections." *Capital & Class* 34(1): 7–14.

Thompson, P. and K. Newsome. 2004. "Labour Process Theory, Work and the Employment Relation." In *Theoretical Perspectives on Work and the Employment Relationship*, Bruce E. Kaufman, ed., 133–162. Ithaca, NY: ILR.

Zolberg, A. R. 1986. "How Many Exceptionalisms?" In *Working-Class Formation: Nineteenth-Century Patterns in Western Europe and the United States*, I. Katznelson and A. R. Zolberg, eds., 397–456. Princeton: Princeton University Press.

19

ACCUMULATION

Bruce Norton

A capitalist firm accumulates capital when it uses a portion of its received surplus value to purchase additional means of production and labor power, then using the latter to produce capitalist commodities (Marx 1976, 709). The term thus designates a simple and readily understandable process. Firms use a portion of their net income to purchase two things needed if they are to continue and perhaps grow.

The word, however, also points to larger theoretical constructions. When Marx introduces accumulation in the last quarter of *Capital* volume 1, he sets in motion not only capitalist firms but also the interacting system they together form. Capitalists, as Marx shows, need to reinvest and expand in order to survive and prosper; they tend to accumulate capital in order to continue their existence. In turn that expansion may produce forces that react back upon continued capitalist functioning. Consideration of accumulation, then, offers an expanded arena for critical evaluation and analysis. Not simply founded on class exploitation, as is argued, capitalism can be shown to tend to develop in destructive ways as it shapes and reshapes itself over time.

The destruction Marx focused upon in volume 1 concerned the lives of working people. His accumulation, unlike Adam Smith's, is "antagonistic": the accumulation of wealth is also accumulation of excess population, labor market distress and renewed entrapment of workers in an unfair and unreliable position of dependence. What might be progress under different conditions is not just that in capitalism. The technological improvement characteristic of the system "undergoes a complete inversion," as "the higher the productivity of labour, the greater is the pressure of the workers on the means of employment, the more precarious therefore becomes the condition for their existence, namely the sale of their own labour-power..." (Marx 1976, 798). A many-layered pool of underemployed and unemployed people—a "relative surplus population"—accumulates along with capital. Periodically replenished by the system's characteristic crises, the numbers of sidelined, devalued, or discarded workers are also bolstered via more particular channels as employment opportunities in agricultural and older industries decline over time, working conditions render some workers' health too damaged for continued employment and so on. Marx throws into the mix "a self-reproducing and self-perpetuating element of the working class" (Marx 1976, 796).

> Accumulation of wealth at one pole is therefore, at the same time, accumulation of misery, the torment of labor, slavery, ignorance, brutalization and moral degradation

at the opposite pole, i.e. on the side of the class that produces its own product as capital.

(Marx 1976, 799)

Uncharacteristically turning to italics, Marx presents these dynamics as "*the absolute general law of capitalist accumulation.*"[1]

If accumulation theory is particularly concerned with capitalism's destructive effects upon those who depend on it for employment,[2] some traditions add a second focus: theorization of capitalism's *self*-destructive trajectory. A prominent aspect of the classical Marxism popularized by Friedrich Engels and Karl Kautsky (1870s–1915), influentially restressed in the early twentieth century by figures including Rosa Luxemburg (1972, originally in German 1915) and Henryk Grossman (1992, originally in German 1929), this more particular understanding was taken up anew in English-speaking countries in the 1960s and 70s.[3] Theorists ranging from Paul Baran and Paul Sweezy to Paul Mattick, Sr. and Ernest Mandel in effect took their bearings from a conception which first appears in *The Communist Manifesto*: capitalism is marked by a fateful contradiction between its forces and relations of production. It is a mode of production which incessantly expands the productive forces in ways that overflow and undermine its own capacities. Marxian accumulation theory's task is, then, to show the precise way in which this essential contradiction develops and the inevitability with which its system-limiting effects will bind.

As Paul Baran and Paul Sweezy had it in 1966, capitalism undermines itself once accumulation generates market concentration in a wide array of industries. Following Josef Steindl (1976), they take as their starting point the principle that capitalist firms inherently seek to expand, a principle the tradition understands as implying that firms seek to save and then reinvest profit—accumulate capital—at fixed rates. In the late nineteenth-century U.S., larger firms cleared the way for expansion by lowering prices so as to drive smaller competitors out of business. With the continued growth of concentration this channel is eventually blocked. Firms earn high profit margins per unit of sales and hence tend to accrue retained earnings, but their ability to carry out the corresponding investment spending lags. The result is an economy in which, absent occasional effects of counteracting demand-stimulating influences like war or innovation, economic growth must slow.[4]

In effect the posited urge to accumulate has produced a barrier preventing its own unrestricted expression. The normal workings of the economy produce stagnation. As *Monopoly Capital* concluded, the result is an overall society pervaded by waste, irrationality and inability to ascribe meaning and purpose to social life, a society calling out for radical transformation.[5]

More often the internally determinate stresses and limits Marxian theorists have seen structuring the accumulation process have been rooted not in its creation of market concentration but in what are seen as constitutive features of the capitalist production process. Since the late 1960s influential and creative schools of several varieties have argued that well-defined imperatives molding accumulation's trajectory stem from capitalists' continuing struggle to extract surplus value from productive workers and to compete with other capitalists for profit.

Mattick Sr.'s *Marx and Keynes* (1969) offered an influential interpretation along these lines. Capitalists are forced by competition with other firms in their industry to continually increase the productivity of labor, cut costs of production below industry average and seek extra-normal profit and the protection from elimination by lower-cost firms it allows. The result is a continual increase in productivity and fall in the exchange value of commodities.

Like other falling rate of profit theorists, Mattick saw these developments as inextricably tied to a fateful further component: mechanization that is increasingly reliant on constant capital (fixed and circulating constant capital) in proportion to labor power. Ordinarily the productivity of labor grows via labor-saving technical change, they argue, citing Marx in section 3 of *Capital* volume 3 as well as passages in volume 1 and the *Grundrisse*.

The result is that at a given rate of surplus value (the ratio of surplus value to variable capital) the average rate of profit the entire system affords is pushed down, as constant capital expenditures rise relative to the surplus-creating variable capital (labor power). Rising rates of surplus value and other "countertendencies," some of which are outlined by Marx in *Capital* volume 3, may well offset the rise in any particular period—they are also predicted effects of accumulation's basic dynamic. Government policies or other temporarily stimulative forces may also come into play. But the profit-dampening change in the composition of capital is expected to be sufficiently relentless as to resist being offset forever.

Deeply influenced by Henryk Grossman's reading of *Capital*, Mattick saw the resulting tendency of the rate of profit to fall as the centerpiece of specifically Marxian economic theory. For him the tendency is indeed "a theoretical conclusion derived by applying the labor theory of value to the capital formation process" (Mattick 1969, 63). And an explanation of capitalist crises is Marxian, as Mattick, David Yaffe, Mario Cogoy Anwar Shaikh and others argued in the 1970s, only insofar as it starts from these basic dynamics.[6] The claim has held some sway; the tradition became, as Simon Clarke notes, "the orthodox Marxist theory of crisis" to the present day (Clarke 2012, 93).

The approach understands the overall rate of profit as the crucial determinant of the rate of accumulation, and the rate of profit as coming under periodic attack from accumulation's own continued progress. Mattick Sr. quotes *Capital* volume 3 to the effect that capitalists are pushed to periodic "overproduction" and "overaccumulation," bursts of accelerated expansions of capital stock even in the face of declining profit opportunities. Then crises erupt. Capitalism depends upon them. By destroying the exchange value of existing fixed capital stocks as firms are forced into bankruptcy, the crises restore overall rates of profit and pave the way for a new period of expansion (Mattick 1969, 71).

The show won't go on forever, as he suggested, though the timing of the end is admittedly difficult to predict. Although the analysis

> points to the historical limits of capitalism, there is no way of telling when these limits will be reached…. But since capitalism is beset by crises of always greater destructiveness, the social convulsions released by any crisis could—with luck—lead to social actions that could end the capitalist system.
>
> *(Mattick 1969, 99–100)*

Ernest Mandel's influential interpretation of Marxian economics both reinforced this sort of accumulation theory and gave it new shape. His long wave theory envisioned binding "laws of motion" of capitalist development pushing the system toward falling profit and increasing dysfunction, on the one hand, offset by recurring periods of relative buoyancy (also explicable as results of capitalism's inner laws of motion) pushed by waves of technological innovation, on the other (Mandel 1975). Mandel thus sought a more fully determinate analysis of capitalism's ability to sustain expansions like the postwar boom in Europe and the U.S. Despite the expansive episodes, an ultimately constrictive set of forces remained operative. Mandel's 1976 introduction to a new translation of *Capital* volume 1 presented Marx's "fundamental aim" as to "lay bare the laws of motion which govern the origin, the rise, the development, the decline, and the disappearance of a given social form of economic organization: the capitalist mode of production" (Marx 1976, 12). The product of the "rock-like foundation of scientific truth" Marx's analysis created for the proletarian movement (Marx 1976, 17) (and again presented as only productive of revolutionary change insofar as complemented by related but not entirely predictable subjective and organizational factors) Marxian economic theory as Mandel understood it envisioned a system entirely structured by a few abstractly depictable laws of motion.

By the late 1970s falling rate of profit frameworks began to be applied to empirical analyses of the U.S. economy as it traversed the long postwar boom and entered its aftermath. Advocates including Fred Moseley and Andrew Kliman have since extended their studies into the first decade of the twenty-first century.

Meanwhile an important alternative interpretation, also "productionist" in orientation, moved away from direct concern with secular changes in the rate of profit. Ben Fine and Laurence Harris (1979) also started from the principle that to be conceived in Marxian terms the accumulation process must be seen as fundamentally shaped by capitalists' struggles to extract unpaid labor from labor power in the sphere of production as these struggles fuel constant mechanization. But they viewed prior theorists as erring by confining their analysis of the resulting forces to the sphere of production, rather than looking to where they say Marx himself situated them: a complex capitalist whole constituted by contradictory interactions between the sphere of production and the sphere of exchange.

In such an analysis one centerpiece of falling rate of profit theory is sustained. There is indeed a tendency for the "organic composition of capital" to increase as competition fuels mechanization. But Fine and Harris emphasize that that is merely to say that the ratio of constant to variable capital measured at original valuations, the values reigning *before* the technical change occurred (or "in the sphere of production" considered in isolation), rises. What then comes to center stage is the disruption produced when the system must adjust to falling values as the changes ripple through the sphere of exchange, a sphere loosely identified with counter-tendencies to the falling profit tendency. "How the actual process of adjustment happens…" as Alfredo Saad-Filho writes, "is crucial to the process of accumulation, because the sudden devaluation of large masses of capital can lead to financial upheaval and crises" (Saad-Filho 2002, 80). The Law of the Tendency of the Rate of Profit to Fall (LTRPF), still a central finding, now points analysts' attention to this contradictory inner structure of the capital accumulation process, highlighting both ongoing day-to-day pressures to cut costs and restructure and recurrently erupting outbreaks of acute stress.

Notably, in this framework the rate of profit might fall without provoking crisis; or it may fall as a result rather than a cause, the product of a disruption in exchange which imperils realization of commodity values.[7] Theorists such as Simon Clarke (2012, 93) and Fine and Saad-Filho criticize traditional falling rate of profit frameworks for failing to explain exactly how a fall in the rate of profit, were it to occur, would necessarily lead to crisis. "In contrast," as the latter write, "if the LTRPF is understood as the combination of contradictory tendencies operating across production and exchange, crises can be analyzed on the basis of the process of *accumulation*" (Fine and Saad-Filho 2010, 102; see also 101).

In any case, broadly speaking, the two versions of productionist accumulation theory reach similar conclusions about what to expect in the short term. The accumulation process periodically creates its own disruptions; the distress firms experience during the disruptions leads to destruction of capital values, nourishes continued centralization of capital, and (unless prevented from doing so by policy-makers, as traditionalists including Kliman [2012] and Mattick Jr. [2011] argue happened in recent decades with slowed growth the result [cf. Weeks 2010, 139]) restores conditions for continued accumulation. Capitalism is thus "not only the most productive, but also the most *systematically destructive* mode of production in history" (Saad-Filho 2002, 108; Saad-Filho's italics).

With David Harvey's adoption of a similar reading of Marx (1982), and prolific and creative promulgation of the framework by Harvey, Fine, Saad-Filho, Weeks, and others, this analysis of accumulation has risen to particular prominence among English-speaking interpretations of Marxian economics in recent decades.

Other traditions have also grown. A 1970s turn arose from developments within the world of academic economics. "Profit-squeeze" theorists like Andrew Glyn and Bob Sutcliffe (1972) and Raford Boddy and James Crotty (1974) found neither monopoly capital nor falling rate of profit analysis adequate for interpreting the end of the long postwar boom. What they did find useful was a conclusion Marx stressed in part 7 of *Capital* volume 1: capitalism will not sustain wage-increasing high employment levels over time, since a rise in wages sufficiently high would dampen profits and stop the boom. Marx originally made the point as part of his indictment of the fate of working people at the hands of accumulation in chapter 25 of volume 1. Kalecki (1971, first published 1943) had re-emphasized it in the context of Keynesian policy ideas. At the tail end of the 1960s expansion profit-squeeze theorists took the analysis up anew. Full employment in European and U.S. labor markets had shifted power to workers, as they argued, and national income accounts showed the results: rising wages, reduced productivity growth, falling profit shares and profit rates and reduced rates of capital accumulation.

In explaining the downfall of the long postwar boom and its aftermath these authors thus offered an approach to accumulation theory which emphasized class conflict and indicted capitalism as a system but did not attempt to link the argument to capitalism's tendency toward inevitable dysfunction of a sort attributable to unruly productive forces. The approach was in principle open to expansion,[8] including incorporation of demand factors, financial dynamics, and shifting domestic policy and international trade and investment tides; it has been expanded in these various dimensions in subsequent decades.[9] Andrew Glyn's remarkably useful *Capitalism Unleashed* (2006), in particular, documents a multifaceted deterioration of working people's options, resources, and experiences during the first three decades after the mid-1970s.

From the 1960s on new currents in Marxian philosophy also stimulated new kinds of analysis. Louis Althusser sought to distance Marxian thought from "Hegelian" conceptions of society as a totality whose various parts express a structuring essence or essential contradiction.[10] Althusser's Marxian appropriation of overdeterminist causal reasoning envisioned an alternative kind of whole, one whose aspects constitutively and complexly give shape to one another. From this perspective economic determinist reasoning was suspect. Future trajectories were not safely predictable.

Althusser's criticisms of traditional Marxian uses of Hegel were joined by others. In his own words, Gilles Deleuze "could not stand ... Hegel, the triad and the operation of the negation" (Interview in Deleuze and Parnet 2007, 14). Influenced early in his career by Althusser,[11] Deleuze spent a prolific life's work (often writing with Felix Guattari) trying to conceptualize capitalism and life on Spinozan, Nietzschean, and Bergsonian—in any case non-Hegelian—terrain. Neither Althusser's nor Deleuze and Guattari's writing supported the expectation that an "accumulation process" unfolds as the predictable expression—self-destructive or not—of its own internal and abstractly definable determinations.

Thus for post-Althusserian economic analysts like Stephen Resnick and Richard Wolff, the implications of capitalists' various and changing strategies for surviving and growing are not readily calculable in advance (see, e.g., Resnick 2001). Firms make a variety of expenditures in addition to accumulation in order to promote their survival, and each expenditure type (not solely purchase of constant capital and additional labor power) has complex and ever-changing social and economic effects. All firm strategies and expenditures merit analysis; Resnick and Wolff's firms "exist in contradiction," teeming with diverse attempts to gain revenue, on one side, and ever-changing needs for expenditures (replete with actively competing class positions and interests inside and outside the firm), on the other (see Resnick and Wolff 1987, 164–230). As they write,

> It seems to us that much of the Marxian literature has often reduced the behavior of the industrial enterprise to a small number of economic processes within it. These processes are understood to be the ultimate determinants of an industrial enterprise's development. Typically they include such ... economic processes as the purchase of additional constant and variable capital (accumulation of capital), the determination of market prices, and the physical/technical labor process of producing commodities.
>
> *(Resnick and Wolff 1987, 319 n. 1)*

Rejecting such narrowly delineated conceptions of the enterprise, they also reject the "structuralist" logics of accumulation some Marxian economic traditions build upon them (Wolff and Resnick 2012, 32).[12]

This new approach to the firm informs important interventions by various former students of Resnick and Wolff. Stephen Cullenberg's analysis of falling rate of profit theory controversies (1994) finds participants on contending sides of 1970s debates deploying different but in both cases reductionist conceptions of firms. Falling rate of profit theorists envisioned an accumulating enterprise driven by its role within a Hegelian-style unfolding capitalist totality. Critics in the Okishio theorem debates countered with a "Cartesian" firm, an engine indifferent to the whole, which, however, propels and shapes the larger economy through its carefully rational profit-maximizing decisions. "Each approach," as Cullenberg writes,

> reduces the capitalist firm to a single goal whose realization is the essence of capitalist development.... It is assumed that the nature of the capitalist enterprise is a given, and it is only the economic environment which changes in the various analyses, and that environment never reacts back on the nature of the capitalist enterprise.
>
> *(Cullenberg 1994, 104)*

David Ruccio and Jack Amariglio develop a related critique in the context of their critical evaluation of modernist tendencies in modern economics. Like Cullenberg they stress parallels between Marxian accumulation arguments and neoclassical economics.[13] In modernist fashion, both traditions search for an order underlying apparent disorder, though on the Marxist side the order in question is one which ultimately creates disorder. To find their respective orders both require a particular kind of agent—a centered representative firm thought to relentlessly pursue a singular intention. (For their part, as we have seen, modernist Marxian firms of at least some varieties pursue super-profit or market share by cutting costs through technological change.) The competition they engage in is then a "fundamentally predictable, unified, and orderly process" and its results are accordingly unified and foreseeable (Ruccio and Amariglio 2003, 229). Like Resnick and Wolff, Ruccio and Amariglio read passages in volume 3 of *Capital* to recuperate conflict, disorder and continual transformation within and on the boundaries of enterprises—a starting point from which intra-industry competition looks like a much less reliable fulcrum for the construction of abstract accumulation trajectories (Ruccio and Amariglio 2003, 216–51).[14] The reading also recuperates class, bringing to the fore and highlighting the complex distributions of surplus value which this view stresses as central (along with production of surplus value and various non-class processes) to capitalist enterprise's sustenance.

In Resnick and Wolff's overdeterminist approach, in any case, the two-stage process of theory construction pursued by Baran and Sweezy and Paul Mattick, Sr.—wherein one first identifies a destructive abstract logic of accumulation and then brings in more concrete historically transient modifying factors, whose existence does not, however, change the logic itself—is not suggested.[15] While the process of capitalist economic growth Resnick and Wolff envision is destructive, the proof is in the historical (relatively concrete) analysis, rather than a self-destructive logic of accumulation established and fixed at a more abstract level.

In line with their view that class is a crucial concern in Marxian theory, Resnick and Wolff focused on rising rates of exploitation, deteriorating wage and employment trends and rising consumer indebtedness as defining features of material life in the U.S. after the mid-1970s (Resnick and Wolff 2006, 341–53). In recent years Richard Wolff has used the perspective to fuel a critical discussion of both contemporary capitalism's crisis susceptibility and its longer-term contours. Wolff presents capitalism as a system that no longer works in higher-income countries to provide the basic payoffs which had formerly enabled it to avoid popular criticism. In his longer-term analysis Wolff points particularly to the greatly increased ease with which firms became able to move production abroad after 1970 (e.g., Wolff 2014). He thus focuses attention directly on the class structure of capitalist enterprises—non-employee boards of directors and their ability to redirect surplus income toward production abroad in the interests of shareholders—as a place where those seeking change need to look.

Resnick and Wolff also break from prior accumulation theorists in how they understand theory. Denying the viability of truth claims supported by rationalist or empiricist epistemologies, they situate thinking as a process among other processes, shaping and shaped in return (Wolff and Resnick 2012, 151). Theoretical frameworks are, then, ideally evaluated in part on the basis of their likely effects. Resnick and Wolff's view is that class-focused Marxian theory can offer people useful insights for transformation—including on the enterprise level, here and now—which other frameworks do not see.

In contrast productionist frameworks are generally presented as the results of a unique process of conceptual elaboration (often referred to simply as "Marx's theory") thought to identify and correspond with a singular logic of capitalist development. In some cases Marx's debt to and continuity with Hegel's *Logic* is stressed as a factor fueling this achievement— precisely (as the influential Roman Rosdolsky put it) by enabling Marx to link his "general concept of capital" (as developed in the *Grundrisse* and *Capital* volumes 1 and 2) to determinate implications for capitalist competition (*Capital* volume 3) and the contours of capitalist development as a whole (Rosdolsky 1977, 42–4). Other contributors to the tradition reject the notion that Marx's reasoning is Hegelian, but nevertheless point to Marx's more openly interactive "materialist dialectic," as the source of a special conceptual grasp on forces structuring capitalist history (e.g., Mattick, Jr. 1993; Saad-Filho 2002).

An important dimension of that truth is its political implication. These theories explain how particular problems of economic and social life are inextricably rooted in a pervasive, integrated and inherently intractable economic system. A revolution, a general overthrow of that totality once and for all, is then the scale at which efforts to change must aim (see Cullenberg 1994, 106–7).

After the breakup of classical Marxism, however, these traditions have had difficulty envisioning exactly *how* the political transformation they looked to would actually occur, and *what* it would produce.[16] Monopoly capital and traditional falling rate of profit theorists (though notably not Fine and Saad-Filho[17]) in effect present an evolutionary vision in which (1) accumulation proceeds along its (primarily) internally-structured growth process, (2) accumulation's inner contradictions produce economic distress, (3) people are moved to mobilize against capitalism, (4) political revolution occurs and (5) a new system is created. But how revolution might occur at stage (4), if it did, and what would come after a political revolution against capitalism, when it did, are only vaguely indicated. Moreover the economic determinist expectations concerning worker political mobilization at stage (3) have also come under attack.[18] The political defeats which followed the capitalist crises of the 1970s underlined the problem.

A more general question posed by some who reject rationalist epistemologies is whether the entire construct, built by people seeking to end capitalist exploitation, actually facilitates that goal. J.K. Gibson-Graham (1996) vividly develops the case that it does not. The vision is immobilizing and self-defeating for leftists, she argues, rather than empowering and enlightening. By wrongly construing capitalism (at links [1] and [2]) as an all-powerful, self-structuring expansive and invasive system, the traditional approach undermines people's ability to see the variety of class processes already existent in all societies, and invest confidently in building alternative forms of enterprise and activity. Conceptualized as inferior to the aggressive, dominating and self-producing "capitalist system" Marxists have constructed as their target, any such possibilities for change now are dampened—put off to the future—and even future possibilities rendered less likely, because very difficult to visualize. Asking readers to nourish and enact more than simply oppositional desires, Gibson-Graham (1996; 2006) poses a direct challenge to the political precepts at work in traditional Marxian accumulation frameworks.[19]

For similar reasons some theorists now set about their work analyzing the history of capitalist enterprises and societies along pathways which deliberately avoid invoking conceptions of an internally determinate accumulation logic. In *Carbon Democracy* (2011; see 7 n. 15, for example*)* Timothy Mitchell's capitalism is constitutively molded by shifting kinds of energy extraction and use. William Connolly's *Capitalism and Christianity, American Style* (2008) uses Deleuze and Guattari's concepts of machinic assemblages to analyze ways in which projective dimensions of certain kinds of evangelical Christianity provide a "resonance machine" supporting and informed by the harsh dimensions of contemporary U.S. capitalism.[20] Andriana Vlachou (e.g., 2005a, 2005b) breaks with assumptions that either the capitalist or the communal form of surplus appropriation is necessarily linked to a determinate ecological trajectory, then reassembles links more conditionally. In an activist vein, the popularly-aimed *Democracy at Work* (Wolff 2012) and *Take Back the Economy* (Gibson-Graham et al. 2013a) both argue that changes in the parts (including the class structure of commodity-producing enterprises) significantly change the whole—even before general political change might occur. Adaman and Madra (2002) and Conill et al. (2012) respectively provide theoretical and empirical elaborations for such an approach, the latter focused upon crisis-period Spain.

More generally Callari and Ruccio (2010; see also 1996) build on Amariglio and Callari (1993), Resnick and Wolff, Gibson-Graham and others to attack the "unidimensional view of society, social agents, and social change" which conceptions of "the economy as a disembedded and self-regulating structure" have nourished,[21] particularly insofar as they have left their mark on understandings of socialism (Callari and Ruccio 2010, 407).

Michael Hardt and Antonio Negri's *Empire* (2000), on the other hand, uses similar ingredients—Spinoza, Deleuze and Guattari, and Michel Foucault (along with much else)—to situate capitalism once again as a totality unfolding along its own lines to produce communism, this time on a global scale. Though theirs is a world of singularities interacting in a plane of immanence (Deleuzian terminology pointing to the positivity and irreducible difference of all things given), in their interpretation contemporary immanence is a place in which "the truth of the new humanity is determined historically, technically, and politically. For this very fact, because there cannot be any external mediation, the singular is presented as the multitude" (Hardt and Negri 2000, 73).

And the multitude ("the plural multitude of productive, creative subjectivities of globalization that have learned to sail on this enormous sea"), in turn, is an antagonistic revolutionary subject pushing ever more against the boundaries of current structures (Hardt and Negri 2000, 60).[22]

The argument draws upon and extends Italian *operaist* traditions, which since 1961 have scrutinized capitalist factories and workplaces (and later by extension "capitalist societies") for the kinds of proletarian subjects they were thought to nourish and rely upon (these "class compositions" including in turn the "professional" [skill-protecting] worker, the "mass" worker, and the "social" worker).[23] *Operaists* tend to conceive these subjects, once produced, as agents who in turn ultimately move capitalism through its successive crises, stages and death-throes.[24] As Ernesto Laclau notes, citing an assessment by Jacque Ranciere, there is a certain familiarity to the vision:

> Disruptive forces operating through a purely immanent movement are what Marxist theory called 'productive forces' and there would be, according to Ranciere, a strict homology between the place of productive forces and that in which multitudes, as described in *Empire*, act.
>
> *(Laclau 2004, 22).*

Perhaps *operaismo*, which began as an oppositional and militant alternative to the dominant Italian left's self-defined historic role furthering the development of the productive forces, parallels in this general respect the framework from which it sought to break.

Meanwhile actual "productive forces," variously interpreted, continue to erode and slow the accumulation process in innovative and impressive analyses offered by other twenty-first-century theorists. Both Robert Brenner (e.g., 2006) and co-authors Gérard Duménil and Dominique Lévy (e.g., 2004, 2011) understand Marxian theory as a forces of production/relation of production approach, and present their work in that light. Both use the general framework to offer empirically elaborated accounts of the overall contours of recent capitalist dynamics, Brenner focusing upon global production in the decades since World War II, Duménil and Lévy extending their analysis of the U.S. and other countries back to the late nineteenth century. Prominent participants in a larger recent resurgence of Marxian economic thought, both provide compelling explanations for the persistence of hard times for working people in the high-income countries from the 1970s on.

Brenner starts from a familiar premise. Capitalism's competitive structure consistently pushes firms to invest in fixed capital embodying cost-cutting new technologies. Citing the *"unplanned, uncoordinated, and competitive* nature of capitalist production" (Brenner 2006, 7; Brenner's italics), he sees manufacturing firms as tending to do this without full regard for competitors' capacity. As potential output increases and prices fall, earlier-generation competitors find their fixed capital investments no longer realizing expected revenues. Rather than exiting, however, these higher-cost producers now tend to hang on, reluctant to abandon very large fixed capital commitments and to some extent enabled to indulge that reluctance by supportive state policies. As a result major world industries face lingering overcapacity and average rates of profit fall. Brenner's forces of production expand in ways that dampen profit rates and clog accumulation's forward path, but now by producing chronic excess capacity (as in monopoly capital theory), rather than mechanized capital composition. From this starting point Brenner has developed an accomplished analysis of events of recent decades, including high-income country currency and policy dilemmas and the great growth of speculative financial activities (Brenner 2002; 2006).

The interpretation offered by Duménil and Lévy tacks closer to orthodox mid- to late twentieth-century Western economists' readings of Marx in one way: as they have it the progress of accumulation may well push the organic composition of capital up and profit rates down. This dynamic remains "Marx's analysis" and a "crucial component of the dynamics of capitalism."

At the same time, as Duménil and Lévy continue, "capitalism must not be understood as a passive victim of the tendency of the profit rate to fall, sliding to the tomb." Rather the "continuous and active process of the reaction of capitalism to its inner tendencies" can in some circumstances entirely dominate the tendency itself (Duménil and Lévy 2014, 48). Indeed, during the decades since 1980 it is the reaction rather than the "law" which has prevailed.

Duménil and Lévy argue that a neoliberal period of capitalist accumulation that began in 1980 is one of a succession of "phases" of the longer-lived "modern capitalism." Modern capitalism began in the U.S. as a result of changes in the relations of production around the turn of the twentieth century. These changes included a move to corporate legal forms beginning in 1900, related growth of enterprise-serving banks, and a managerial revolution separating ownership from management and producing growing numbers of managers and clerical workers (Duménil and Lévy 2011, 12, 90–8). Periodizing capitalist development in this way, Duménil and Lévy set the system's relations of production in motion, their changes shaping capitalist development alongside changes in the more traditional agent, the "forces of production."

In doing so, they introduce a more open and complex role for class concepts than is available in most traditional approaches to accumulation theory. Falling rate of profit analysts build for the most part[25] on a static foundational conceptualization of one capitalist class process, the capitalist's struggle to pump surplus value from productive workers, particularly as it is thought to express itself via mechanization. In contrast Duménil and Lévy contend that understanding the dynamics of modern capitalism requires a "tri-polar" approach distinguishing between capitalists (whom they define as owners), workers (or "popular classes"), and modern capitalism's newly emerging managers. Further, understanding accumulation dynamics requires continuing openness to the possibility that shifting political alliances within and between subsets of the three groups—secularly changing class alliances—might periodically reshape how the whole they help form works.

In turn, several sorts of destabilizing dynamics might shake the system as growth proceeds. Periods when upper capitalists are able to bring managers under their leadership without substantial countervailing powers—periods of "financial hegemony"[26] in the authors' term— have led to troubles unrelated to falling profit rates. As Duménil and Lévy remind us, Marx himself sometimes stressed these general sorts of issues. "In the *Manifesto* Marx caricatured capitalist classes as apprentice 'sorcerers' initiating processes that they, later, become unable to control; the ample developments of Volume III of *Capital* concerning fictitious capital prolong this early analysis…" (Duménil and Lévy 2014, 46).

Thus an initial phase of U.S. modern capitalism (the "first financial hegemony," extending roughly from 1900 to the New Deal, marked by top capitalist dominance of decision-making in league with compliant managers) culminated in the Depression, which a falling rate of profit dynamic played no particular role in fomenting, as they argue.

The "postwar compromise" social order or phase which then ensued was structured in part by a very different leading class alliance, now between managers and popular classes under managerial leadership. Accumulation under these conditions emphasized reinvestment of industrial enterprise profit along with maintenance of workers' standards of living.[27] As Duménil and Lévy contend, this phase of modern capitalism did indeed eventually encounter the traditionally expected falling profit rate between 1965 and 1980. The crises associated with the fall underlined the old coalition's inability to lead, and culminated in formation of modern capitalism's most recent phase.

The neoliberal social order which followed, modern capitalism's second period of financial hegemony, was then first of all marked by top capitalists' recharged abilities to act as they will. Securely allied with obedient managerial ranks, top capitalists sought shareholder value, unfettered globalization, continued financialization and ever-higher top incomes. The crisis that began in 2007, unrelated to any sustained fall in aggregate profit rates as they argue, again demonstrated the destructive powers that capitalism's apprentice sorcerers can unleash under such conditions (Duménil and Lévy 2014, 47–8).

Like Resnick and Wolff, Glyn, and others, Duménil and Lévy have moved Marxian accumulation theory toward acceptance of indeterminacy (while retaining the general expectation of recurrent dysfunction).[28] Hence the sort of abstractly set logic of accumulation needed to lock down a long-term fate—the kind of accumulation theory that Rosa Luxemburg had proclaimed Marxism's reason for existing and that leading mid-twentieth-century theorists all pursued—is not needed or endorsed. The shift has enabled the growth of more historically attuned varieties of Marxian economic analysis. And it has helped to renew and continue a quest Marx himself pursued in part 7 of *Capital* volume 1—the quest to uncover and highlight the damage to working people's lives that contemporary capital accumulation processes entail.

Notes

1 "Like other laws," Marx continues, "it is modified in its working by many circumstances, the analysis of which does not concern us here" (Marx 1976, 798). Note that one thing that Marx does not assert in this section is the view often attributed to him that the progress of capitalist development will lead to lower average absolute living standards for workers. Instead, Chapters 23 through 25 of *Capital* volume 1 trace a complex variety of dependencies and misfortunes suffered by those reliant on the sale of labor power for their livelihood. Marx explicitly includes relative impoverishment as well as increasingly precarious employment conditions among the maladies. "In proportion as capital accumulates," he writes, "the situation of the worker, be his payment high or low, must grow worse" (Marx 1976, 799). Ernest Mandel discusses in illuminating detail the discrepancy between Marx's own presentation in *Capital* and commonly accepted "absolute immiseration" interpretations (Marx 1976, 69–72). See also Michael Heinrich (2012, 123–9).

2 Michael Heinrich stresses this aspect of Marxian accumulation theory, writing that "Marx's intent" in *Capital* as a whole was indeed "to point out the human and social costs connected with capitalist development" (Heinrich 2012, 35).

3 Luxemburg's commitment on the issue echoed through subsequent decades with particular clarity. Rebutting Eduard Bernstein's attack on "breakdown" theory, she refused any concession, writing that "[i]f we assume, with the 'experts', the economic infinity of capitalist accumulation, then the vital foundation on which socialism rests will disappear. We then take refuge in the mist of pre-Marxist systems..." (Luxemburg 1972, 76). Both Henryk Grossman (1992, 71) and Paul Sweezy (1970, 207 [first edition 1942]) quote these sentences as inspirational motivation for the choices they make in developing their otherwise very different later frameworks.

4 Skillfully developing and applying the framework in subsequent decades, the *Monthly Review* school has among other things been a leading early source of analysis of the "financialization" of accumulation. Paul Sweezy and Harry Magdoff lucidly stressed the U.S. economy's explosively growing finance sector early on (see, e.g., Sweezy and Magdoff 1987), placing the phenomenon within the context of the system's growing surplus and stagnationist tendencies. Contemporary monopoly capital theorists Foster and McChesney (2012, 28) argue that "global monopoly-finance capital" is producing "a process of monopolistic capital accumulation so extreme and distorted" as to fuel monstrously growing income inequality in the higher-income countries, and financial instability and ecological crisis worldwide. For a lucid review and criticism of the tradition's approach to financialization see Lapavitsas (2013).

5 Baran and Sweezy put their critique of U.S. culture in the context of a whole structured by a "contradiction between the increasing rationality of society's methods of production and the organizations which embody them on the one hand and the undiminished elementality and irrationality in the functioning and perception of the whole..." (Baran and Sweezy 1966, 341).

6 Stephen Cullenberg (1994) offers a lucid analysis of debates among these and other falling rate of profit theorists and their critics. Simon Clarke emphasizes that this sort of argument was actually not espoused by many Marxists before the 1970s, as crisis theorists at different times emphasized the anarchy of capitalist production, underconsumption sources of cyclical or secular slowdown, and sectoral disproportionalities instead. Dominant views changed over time, Clarke notes, often without much note being taken of the fact (Clarke 1994).

7 In rendering Marx's treatment of crises, Fine and Saad-Filho also stress that other crisis-generating factors—disproportionality, underconsumption, periodic wage pressures and so on—may also come into play (Fine and Saad-Filho 2010, 81).

8 Some early arguments related to the framework did deploy a power-theoretic essentialism, as argued in Norton (1988).

9 See e.g. Marglin (1990). In the U.S. especially, some analysts sympathetic to profit squeeze interpretations went on to endorse and contribute to social structures of accumulation theory. (See the essay by McDonough in this volume.)

10 The very useful presentation in Cullenberg (1994, 19–50) traces the particular Hegelian arguments that have influenced falling rate of profit traditions.

11 "... this liberation of Marx from Hegel, this reappropriation of Marx, this uncovering of differential and affirmative mechanisms in Marx, isn't this what Althusser is accomplishing so admirably?... [U]nder the false opinions, the false oppositions, you discover much more explosive systems, unsymmetrical wholes in disequilibrium..." (Deleuze 2004, 145; an interview that occurred in 1969).

12 For examples of Resnick and Wolff's criticisms of traditional accumulation theories, see Resnick and Wolff (2006, 293–96).

13 Garnett (1995a) also probes modernist parallels between neoclassical and some Marxian traditions and suggests (1995b) a way to read *Capital* volume 1 chapter 1 as a work containing both modernist and postmodern "voices."

14 For more see the section entitled "Contradictions in and Competition Among Enterprises," in Resnick and Wolff (1987, 192–200).

15 Nor does Marx himself construct such an abstractly fixed scaffolding in volume 1 part 7, as argued in Norton (1994) and (2001), who reread widely quoted passages to find Marx incorporating historical changes into capitalists' reinvestment rates, rather than construing accumulation as the

preset product of an abstract logic. Casting a wider net, Amariglio (2010) finds in Marx's definition of the primitive communal class process a cultural/political component, ruling out even class process identification in abstract, strictly economic, terms, while Kayatekin and Charusheela (2004) develop a similar angle on feudal class processes.

16 See Diskin (1996) for an illuminating discussion of classical Marxism's conception of socialism's creation within the development of capitalism.

17 Fine and Saad-Filho (2010) attach a much-reduced political dimension to their accumulation analysis. As they write, crises do not in themselves tend to precipitate worker revolt. Indeed,

> a recession is a time when the working class tends to be weakened. In addition, changes within a mode of production, let alone the transition from one to another, cannot be read off from economic conditions alone, because they are highly dependent on political and ideological conditions. These, together with the labour movement's economic position, tend to be at their strongest when conditions are prosperous. So the relationship between economic analysis and revolution is not only complex, but is dependent upon other influences as well…
>
> *(Fine and Saad-Filho 2010, 85–6).*

18 See for example James O'Connor (1987), Ernesto Laclau and Chantal Mouffe (1985), Lauren Berlant (2011) and Frederic Lordon (2014) for differing efforts, all fruitful. Lordon in particular offers an extraordinarily stimulating interweaving of Spinozan affect theory and Marxian class analysis.

19 Bergeron puts Gibson-Graham and other thinkers to powerful use in advocating a global-level "politics of location." She calls for an "alternative feminist discourse of global capitalism through which contradictory and heterogeneous subjectivities are recognized and produced not only in the processes of global capitalism but also in the gaps and margins of these processes…"—a view she contrasts with a capital-centric "politics of abstraction" she finds in much left thinking on the subject (Bergeron 2006, 160–3).

20 An assemblage may be viewed as an ongoing linkage of various parts of life and the world in a way which avoids conceiving any part as expressive of essential determinations emanating from another part, in the manner Hegelian reasoning is charged with doing.

21 From slightly different angles, Madra and Özselçuk (2010) produce an innovative weaving of psychoanalytic and accumulation-theoretic concepts which contests the "reproductionism" or internally self-constituted accumulation dynamic they see at work in some Lacanian conceptions of capitalism, and Gibson-Graham et al. (2013b) challenge accumulation theorists to recognize fluidity and possibility rather than the closed circuitry of posited self-defining circuits of capital.

22 As the passage continues: "(the multitude) are in perpetual motion and they form constellations of singularities and events that impose continual global reconfigurations on the system" (Hardt and Negri 2000, 60). Hardt and Negri further invest the multitude with a sort of constitutive "antagonism to every form of domination" (Hardt and Negri 2000, 90), which Ernesto Laclau finds unpalatable: "The ability and the will to resist are not a gift from heaven but require a set of subjective transformations that are only the product of the struggles themselves *and that can fail to take place*. What is missing in *Empire* is any coherent theory of political subjectivity…" (Laclau 2004, 28; Laclau's italics).

23 Maurizio Lazzarato's (2012) stimulating work on "the indebted man" of neoliberal capitalism might also be situated at least partially in this light.

24 Maria Turchetto (2009) offers an informative critical account of *operaismo* from its founding through the publication of *Empire*, upon which I draw here.

25 Moseley (e.g., 2003) prominently incorporates growing unproductive claims on surplus value into his empirical analyses of U.S. profit-rate trends. For their part Baran and Sweezy (1966) also emphasized the growth of unproductive claims on surplus, but positioned these strictly as secondary "counteracting" forces growing in response to the system's already established surplus-expanding and demand-dampening inner logic.

26 Financial hegemony "refers to the fact that capitalist classes—actually Finance, the upper fraction of capitalist classes and financial institutions—benefit from a rather unchecked capability to lead the economy and society in general in accordance with their own interests or what they perceive as such" (Duménil and Lévy 2011, 15).

27 For a contrary view of U.S. capitalism in this period see McIntyre and Hillard (2013).

28 Insofar as crisis theory is concerned, Simon Clarke has also contributed notably to this shift. He continues to regard the "overproduction" tendency spurred by capitalist firms' competitive drive for super-profits as "the essential characteristic of capitalist production," in this way centering his analysis of capitalism, as orthodox tradition would have it, on the inherently destructive power of the system's productive forces. But he denies the existence of any necessary connection between such an overproduction tendency and the generation of particular capitalist crises. "While the tendency to crisis might be inherent in capitalism," he writes, "the determinants and characteristics of any particular crisis are always singular, embedded in the concrete characteristics of capital accumulation at a particular time and place, not reducible to a single abstract determinant, and so the analysis of crisis presupposes a concrete analysis of the contemporary configurations of capital" (Clarke 2012, 91, 95).

References

Adaman, F. and Y. Madra. 2002. "Theorizing the Third Sphere: A Critique of the Persistence of the 'Economistic Fallacy'." *Journal of Economic Issues* 36: 1045–1078.

Amariglio, J. 2010. "Subjectivity, Class, and Marx's 'Forms of the Commune'." *Rethinking Marxism* 22: 329–344.

Amariglio, J. and A. Callari. 1993. "Marxian Value Theory and the Problem of the Subject: The Role of Commodity Fetishism." In *Fetishism as Cultural Discourse*, E. Apter and W. Pietz, eds., 186–216. Ithaca, NY: Cornell University Press.

Baran, P. and P. Sweezy. 1966. *Monopoly Capital: An Essay on the American Economic and Social Order.* New York: Monthly Review Press.

Bergeron, S. 2006. *Fragments of Development: Nation, Gender, and the Space of Modernity.* Ann Arbor: University of Michigan Press.

Berlant, L. 2011. *Cruel Optimism.* Durham, NC: Duke University Press.

Boddy, R. and J. Crotty. 1974. "Class Conflict, Keynesian Policies, and the Business Cycle." *Monthly Review* (October): 1–17.

Bowles, S., D. Gordon, and T. Weisskopf. 1983. *Beyond the Wasteland.* New York: Anchor Press/ Doubleday.

Brenner, R. 2002. *The Boom and the Bubble: The U.S. in the World Economy.* London and New York: Verso.

——. 2006. *The Economics of Global Turbulence: The Advanced Capitalist Economies from Long Boom to Long Downturn, 1945–2005.* London and New York: Verso.

Callari, A. and D. F. Ruccio. 2010. "Rethinking Socialism: Community, Democracy, and Social Agency." *Rethinking Marxism* 22: 403–419.

——. 1996. "Introduction: Postmodern Materialism and the Future of Marxist Theory." In *Postmodern Materialism and the Future of Marxist Theory: Essays in the Althusserian Tradition*, A. Callari and D. F. Ruccio, eds., 1–48. Hanover, NH: Wesleyan University Press.

Clarke, S. 1994. *Marx's Theory of Crisis.* New York: St. Martin's Press.

——. 2012. "Crisis Theory." In *The Elgar Companion to Marxist Economics*, B. Fine and A. Saad-Filho, eds., 90–95. Cheltenham: Edward Elgar.

Conill, J., M. Castells, A. Cardenas, and L. Servon. 2012. "Beyond the Crisis: The Emergence of Alternative Economic Practices." In *Aftermath: The Cultures of the Economic Crisis*, M. Castells, J. M. G. Caraça, and G. Cardoso, eds., 210–250. Oxford: Oxford University Press

Connolly, W. E. 2008. *Capitalism and Christianity, American Style.* Durham, NC: Duke University Press.

Cullenberg, S. 1994. *The Falling Rate of Profit: Recasting the Marxian Debate*. London: Pluto Press.

Deleuze, G. 2004. *Desert Islands and Other Texts, 1953–1974*. Edited by D. Lapoujade; trans. by M. Taormina. Los Angeles: Semiotext(e).

Deleuze, G. and F. Guattari. 1983. *Anti-Oedipus: Capitalism and Schizophrenia*. Trans. by R. Hurley, M. Seem, and H. R. Lane. Minneapolis: University of Minnesota Press.

——. 1987. *A Thousand Plateaus: Capitalism and Schizophrenia*. Trans. and with a foreword by B. Massumi. Minneapolis: University of Minnesota Press.

Deleuze, G. and C. Parnet. 2007. *Dialogues II*. Trans. by H. Tomlinson and B. Habberjam. New York: Columbia University Press.

Diskin, J. 1996. "Rethinking Socialism: What's in a Name?" In *Postmodern Materialism and the Future of Marxist Theory: Essays in the Althusserian Tradition,* A. Callari and D. F. Ruccio, eds., 278–299. Hanover, NH: Wesleyan University Press.

Duménil, G. and D. Lévy. 2004. *Capital Resurgent: Roots of the Neoliberal Revolution*. Cambridge, MA: Harvard University Press.

——. 2011. *The Crisis of Neoliberalism*. Cambridge, MA: Harvard University Press.

——. 2014. "The Crisis of the Early 21st Century: Marxian Perspectives." In *The Great Recession and the Contradictions of Contemporary Capitalism*, R. Bellofiore and G. Vertova, eds., 26–49. Cheltenham: Edward Elgar.

Fine, B. and L. Harris. 1979. *Rereading Capital*. New York: Columbia University Press.

Fine, B. and A. Saad-Filho. 2010. *Marx's Capital*. 5th edition. London: Pluto Press.

Foster, J. B. and R. W. McChesney. 2012. *The Endless Crisis: How Monopoly-Finance Capital Produces Stagnation and Upheaval from the U.S.A. to China*. New York: Monthly Review Press.

Garnett, R. F., Jr. 1995a. "Markets, Modernism, and Marx: Some Thoughts on Economics after the Cold War." *Rethinking Marxism* 8(3): 26–37.

——. 1995b. "Marx's Value Theory: Modern or Postmodern?" *Rethinking Marxism* 8(4): 40–60.

Gibson-Graham, J.K. 1996. *The End of Capitalism (As We Knew It): A Feminist Critique of Political Economy*. Malden, MA: Blackwell Publishers.

——. 2006. *A Postcapitalist Politics*. Minneapolis: University of Minnesota Press.

Gibson-Graham, J.K., J. Cameron, and S. Healy. 2013a. *Take Back the Economy: An Ethical Guide for Transforming Our Communities*. Minneapolis: University of Minnesota Press.

Gibson-Graham, J.K., E. Erdem, and C. Özselçuk. 2013b. "Thinking with Marx for a Feminist Postcapitalist Politics." In *Marx' Kritik der Gesellschaft*, R. Jaeggi and D. Loick, eds. Berlin: Akademie Verlag. http://www.communityeconomies.org/site/assets/media/Esra_Erdem/Gibson Graham_Erdem_Ozselcuk-.pdf (accessed August 1, 2016).

Glyn, A. 2006. *Capitalism Unleashed: Finance, Globalization, and Welfare*. Oxford: Oxford University Press.

Glyn, A. and R. B. Sutcliffe. 1972. *Capitalism in Crisis*. New York: Pantheon Books.

Grossman, H. 1992. *The Law of Accumulation and Breakdown of the Capitalist System: Being Also a Theory of Crises*. Trans. and abridged by J. Banaji. London: Pluto Press.

Hardt, M. and A. Negri. 2000. *Empire*. Cambridge, MA: Harvard University Press.

Harvey, D. 1982. *The Limits to Capital*. Chicago: University of Chicago Press.

Heinrich, M. 2012. *An Introduction to the Three Volumes of Karl Marx's Capital*. Trans. by A. Locascio. New York: Monthly Review Press.

Kalecki, M. 1971 [1943]. "Political Aspects of Full Employment." In *Selected Essays on the Dynamics of the Capitalist Economy, 1933–70*, 138–145. Cambridge: Cambridge University Press.

Kayatekin, S. and S. Charusheela. 2004. "Recovering Feudal Subjectivities." *Rethinking Marxism* 16: 377–396.

Kliman, A. 2012. *The Failure of Capitalist Production: Underlying Causes of the Great Recession*. London: Pluto Press.

Laclau, E. 2004. "Can Immanence Explain Social Struggles?" In *Empire's New Clothes: Reading Hardt and Negri,* P. A.Passavant and J. Dean, eds., 21–30. London and New York: Routledge.

Laclau, E. and C. Mouffe. 1985. *Hegemony and Socialist Strategy: Towards a Radical Democratic Politics*. London: Verso.

Lapavitsas, C. 2013. *Profiting Without Producing: How Finance Exploits Us All*. London and New York: Verso.

Lazzarato, M. 2012. *The Making of the Indebted Man: An Essay on the Neoliberal Condition*. Cambridge, MA: Semiotext(e)/MIT Press.

Lordon, F. 2014. *Willing Slaves of Capital: Spinoza and Marx on Desire*. Trans. by G. Ash. London and New York: Verso.

Luxemburg, R. 1972. *The Accumulation of Capital: An Anti-Critique*. Edited by K. J. Tarbuck; trans. by R. Wichmann. New York: Monthly Review Press.

Madra, Y. and C. Özselçuk. 2010. "Enjoyment as an Economic Factor: Reading Marx with Lacan." *Subjectivity* 3: 323–347. http://www.communityeconomies.org/site/assets/media/yahyamadra/Subjectivityv2b.pdf (accessed August 1, 2016).

Mandel, E. 1975. *Late Capitalism*. Trans. by J. De Bres. London: Verso.

Marglin, S. A. 1990. "Lessons of the Golden Age: An Overview." In *The Golden Age of Capitalism: Reinterpreting the Postwar Experience*, S. A. Marglin and J. Schor, eds., 1–38. Oxford: Oxford University Press.

Marx, K. 1976. *Capital: A Critique of Political Economy*, Volume 1. Trans. by B. Fowkes. Introduction by E. Mandel. London: Penguin Books.

——. 1981. *Capital: A Critique of Political Economy*, Volume 3. Trans. by D. Fernbach. Introduction by E. Mandel. London: Penguin Books.

Marx, K. and F. Engels. 1982. *The Communist Manifesto*. New York: International Publishers.

Mattick, P., Sr. 1969. *Marx and Keynes: The Limits of the Mixed Economy*. Boston: Porter Sargent.

Mattick, P., Jr. 1993. "Marx's Dialectic." In *Marx's Method in Capital: A Reexamination*, F. Moseley, ed., 115–133. Atlantic Highlands, NJ: Humanities Press.

——. 2011. *Business as Usual: The Economic Crisis and the Failure of Capitalism*. London: Reaktion Books.

McDonough, T., M. Reich, and D. M. Kotz, eds. 2010. *Contemporary Capitalism and its Crises: Social Structure of Accumulation Theory for the 21st Century*. Cambridge: Cambridge University Press.

McIntyre, R. and M. Hilliard. 2013. "Capitalist Class Agency and the New Deal Order: Against the Notion of a Limited Capital-Labor Accord." *Review of Radical Political Economics* 45: 129–148.

Mitchell, T. 2011. *Carbon Democracy: Political Power in the Age of Oil*. London and New York: Verso.

Moseley, F. 2003. "Marxian Crisis Theory and the Postwar U.S. Economy." In *Anti-Capitalism: A Marxist Introduction,* A. Saad-Filho, ed., 211–223. London: Pluto Press.

Norton, B. 1988. "The Power Axis: Bowles, Gordon, and Weisskopf's Theory of Postwar U.S. Accumulation." *Rethinking Marxism* 1: 6–43.

——. 1994. "Moses and the Prophets! Radical Economics and the Search for a Foundation (in Marx's Analysis of Accumulation in Volume 1 of *Capital*)." *Review of Radical Political Economics* 26: 111–118.

——. 2001. "Reading Marx for Class." In *Re/presenting Class: Essays in Postmodern Marxism*, J.K. Gibson-Graham, S. A. Resnick, and R. Wolff, eds. Durham, NC: Duke University Press.

O'Connor, J. 1987. *The Meaning of Crisis: A Theoretical Introduction*. New York: Blackwell.

Resnick, S. A. 2001. "Class, Contradiction, and the Capitalist Economy." In *Phases of Capitalist Development: Booms, Crises and Globalizations*, R. Albritton, M. Itoh, R. Westra, and A. Zuege, eds., 179–194. Basingstoke and New York: Palgrave.

Resnick, S. A. and R. D. Wolff. 1987. *Knowledge and Class: A Marxian Critique of Political Economy*. Chicago: University of Chicago Press.

——. eds. 2006. *New Departures in Marxian Theory*. New York: Routledge.

Rosdolsky, R. 1977. *The Making of Marx's Capital*. Trans. by P. Burgess. London: Pluto Press.

Ruccio, D. F. and J. Amariglio. 2003. *Postmodern Moments in Modern Economics*. Princeton: Princeton University Press.

Saad-Filho, A. 2002. *The Value of Marx: Political Economy for Contemporary Capitalism*. London and New York: Routledge.

Steindl, J. 1976. *Maturity and Stagnation in American Capitalism*. 2nd edition. New York: Monthly Review Press.

Sweezy, P. M. 1970 [1942]. *The Theory of Capitalist Development*. New York: Monthly Review Press.

Sweezy, P. and H. Magdoff. 1987. *Stagnation and the Financial Explosion*. New York: Monthly Review Press.

Turchetto, M. 2008. "From 'Mass Worker' to 'Empire': The Disconcerting Trajectory of Italian *Operaismo*." In *Critical Companion to Contemporary Marxism*, J. Bidet and S. Kouvelakis, eds., 285–308. Chicago: Haymarket Books.

Vlachou, A. 2005a. "Environmental Regulation: A Value-Theoretic and Class-Based Approach." *Cambridge Journal of Economics* 29: 577–599.

——. 2005b. "Debating Sustainable Development." *Rethinking Marxism* 17: 627–638.

Weeks, J. 2010. *Capital, Exploitation and Economic Crisis*. London and New York: Routledge.

Wolff, R. D. 2012. *Democracy at Work: A Cure for Capitalism*. Chicago: Haymarket Books.

——. 2014. "Capitalism's Deeper Problem." Video at http://billmoyers.com/2014/07/15/capitalism%E2%80%99s-deeper-problem/ (accessed August 1, 2016).

Wolff, R. D. and S. A. Resnick. 2012. *Contending Economic Theories: Neoclassical, Keynesian, and Marxian*. Cambridge, MA: MIT Press.

20

MARXIAN REPRODUCTION SCHEMES

Andrew B. Trigg

Introduction

Marx's reproduction schemes are thought to represent one of the first-ever two-sector macroeconomic models, and the first-ever model of balanced economic growth. Marx models the interaction between two great departments of production—each specialized in making capital and consumption goods—showing the conditions required for reproduction and balanced growth. The fundamentals of how a capitalist system functions are captured in this simple but sophisticated framework.

The problem, however, is that Marx's reproduction schemes are contained in notes that after Marx's death formed the basis for the second volume of *Capital*, as assembled and published by Engels. These notes were far from being finished, comprising disparate tables and models, with no summary available from Marx of the purpose of the reproduction schemes. And this has left the field wide open for scholars to make their own interpretations. As commented by Joan Robinson, "The waters are dark and it may be that whoever peers in them sees their own face" (Robinson 1968, 111).

This openness also has some advantages. The reproduction schemes can be seen as providing a framework in which different ideas and theories can be organized. This chapter will show how ideas from the pantheon of political economy—Leontief, Keynes, Kalecki, Luxemburg, Graziani, Minsky—can be integrated into the reproduction schemes. The chapter will start by using Marx's schemes of simple and reproduction to piece together different strands of political economy—not, that is, in a crude attempt at tight synthesis, but in a spirit of critical appraisal. In the last part, the monetary theories of Graziani and Minsky will be shown to overestimate the amount of borrowing required for reproduction, which has implications for how we might theorize financial fragility.

The Reproduction Schemes

The starting point for understanding the reproduction schemes is to set them in the context of Marx's method of abstraction. Although economists tend to be drawn towards concrete phenomena, in the *Grundrisse* Marx proposes a method of empirical enquiry that seeks through abstraction to capture the most important elements.

The economists of the seventeenth century, e.g., always begin with the living whole, with population, nation, state, several states, etc.; but they always conclude by discovering through analysis a small number of determinant, abstract, general relations such as division of labor, money, value, etc.

(Marx 1973, 100)

A method of successive approximations is required that starts as an abstraction of the most important relations, before moving towards concrete reality. Levels of analysis "approach step by step the form in which they appear on the surface of society" (Marx 1981, 117).

The first most abstract stage of Marx's method of abstraction is to start with simple circulation, where commodities circulate for commodities—as formulated by Marx in the opening chapters of *Capital*, volume 1. This abstract starting point allows Marx to introduce the division of labor between simple commodity producers. A baker, for example, may exchange bread that is exchanged for shoes produced by the shoemaker. Ratios of exchange are determined by the labor embodied in these commodities, a starting point for Marx's labor theory of value. A rudimentary role for money as a means of circulation and unit of account is also established in this approach. But, sophisticated as this is, there is no macroeconomic surplus produced by the system as a whole. Individual producers may produce more than they consume, for exchange with other producers, but for the system as a whole there is no surplus.

Enter simple reproduction: stage 2 in Marx's successive approximations, moving with great speed from the start of volume 1 to its later chapters and through to volume 2 of *Capital*. Here we abandon simple circulation, with its independent producers working hard to exchange their wares. Production is transformed into two great industrial agglomerations: the first produces capital goods, such as machinery and raw materials; the second produces consumption goods. Any pretence of connection between producers and their outputs is abandoned in this production structure. The producers in these departments are a pool of wage labor, employed by capitalists who control their outputs and harness the use value of these outputs for mass production. Workers in the capital goods department produce outputs that are used in the consumption goods sector. They do not have any control over these outputs. Similarly, workers in the consumption goods department, though producing goods for their own subsistence consumption, also produce goods that are appropriated by capitalists for their own luxurious consumption (see Olsen 2015 for an empirical treatment of unproductive expenditures in the reproduction schemes)

The elements of these two departments are organized according to Marx's value categories. For each department $i = 1,2$; means of production (produced by department 1) are used up as constant capital, C_i; consumption goods are used up as variable capital, V_i. The remaining surplus value (S_i) is all used up as capitalist consumption. Hence for each department the total value produced (W_i) is:

$$W_i = C_i + V_i + S_i \tag{1}$$

For the reproduction schemes it is assumed throughout that commodities are exchanged at these values; labor values are assumed equal to money prices. I also assume here that all capital inputs are used up during the period of production (see Carchedi and de Haahn 1995 for an attempt to consider fixed capital). On this basis the simple reproduction scheme takes the form of Table 1 (see Marx 1978, 473).

A key additional assumption is that the rate of surplus value (S_i/V_i) is uniform between the two sectors at 100 per cent. For department 1, we can see that at this rate of exploitation 1,000

Table 1 Marx's Scheme of Simple Reproduction

	C_i	V_i	S_i	W_i
Dept. 1	4,000	1,000	1,000	6,000
Dept. 2	2,000	500	500	3,000
Total	6,000	1,500	1,500	9,000

units of variable capital generate 1,000 units of surplus value. Combined with 4,000 units of constant capital, a total value of 6,000 is produced by department 1.

Under the social division of labor, the two departments exchange capital goods for consumption goods. Department 1 sells 2,000 units of capital goods, which are used up as C_2 for department 2. These are exchanged for 2,000 units of consumption goods produced by department 2. For these outputs to be sold, they have to be required by the capitalists in the other sectors. Like two drunken men holding each other up, the capitalists in the two departments, sodden with surplus value, are mutually dependent.

The total surplus value of 1,500 is realized in the expenditure of capitalists in both departments on 1,500 units of surplus consumption goods. This means that the system is static, with none of the surplus directed to expansion: a situation that is somewhat unrealistic but not irrelevant to the study of capitalism. This is an abstract starting point for unravelling the complexities of capitalism. For Marx even under capital accumulation "simple reproduction still remains a part of this" (Marx 1978, 471).

To capture the expansion of capital out of surplus value we have to move to a third more concrete level of abstraction: the scheme of expanded reproduction (Marx 1978, 586–89). As shown in Table 2, an examination of department 1 shows how this differs from the simple reproduction scheme of Table 1. Department 1 still produces 6,000 units of value, but only requires 5,500 to be used up to replace constant capital. There is a surplus of 500 units of constant capital that can be used to expand the stock of capital in the next production period. This represents both a solution and a problem for the capitalist juggernaut. It shows how it can expand, but it also requires a solution as to how the surplus capital goods are demanded. Whereas simple reproduction is directed to a basic goal, the satisfaction of capitalist consumption, under expanded reproduction the goal is one of expansion of capital and the successful intertwining of outputs with consumption.

The Structure of Demand

Showing how outputs and consumption can be intertwined under expanded reproduction requires a focus on the structure of demand. This requires a synthesis between three key strands of modern economics. The first of these is classical input-output analysis, as

Table 2 Marx's Scheme of Expanded Reproduction

	C_i	V_i	S_i	W_i
Dept. 1	4,000	1,000	1,000	6,000
Dept. 2	1,500	750	750	3,000
Total	5,500	1,750	1,750	9,000

Table 3 Expanded Reproduction in an Input-Output Table

	Dept. 1	Dept. 2	dC	dV	u	W_i
Dept. 1	4,000	1,500	500			6,000
Dept. 2	1,000	750		150	1,100	3,000
S_i	1,000	750				
Total	6,000	3,000				9,000

developed by Wassily Leontief, which has its roots in the Marxian reproduction schemes (see Gilibert 1998).

The expanded scheme of Table 2 can easily be transformed into input-output form, as shown in Table 3. In this format, the rows represent outputs and the columns inputs. Department 1, for example, produces 4,000 units for itself, 1,500 units for consumption by department 2 and 500 units for additional constant capital, *dC*. Reading down the first column, department 1 uses up 4,000 inputs from itself and 1,000 inputs from department 2, together with a surplus value element of 1,000 units viewed as value added. The surplus produced by department 2 is directed to new variable capital (*dV*) and capitalist consumption (*u*).

Following the procedure developed in Trigg (2006, 17–19), this input-output scheme can be formalized using matrix algebra. This involves specifying the underlying physical structure of the scheme using the Leontief equation

$$\mathbf{X} = \mathbf{AX} + \mathbf{h}[\mathbf{lX}] + \mathbf{F} \tag{1}$$

where $\mathbf{X}$ is a vector of gross physical outputs, $\mathbf{A}$ is a square matrix of interindustry coefficients, $\mathbf{h}$ is a column vector of worker consumption coefficients, $\mathbf{l}$ is a row vector of labor coefficients and $\mathbf{F}$ is a column vector of final demands. By specifying a net output vector $\mathbf{Q} = (\mathbf{I} - \mathbf{A})\mathbf{X}$ in which $\mathbf{I}$ is the identity matrix

$$\mathbf{Q} = \mathbf{h}[\mathbf{vQ}] + \mathbf{F} \tag{2}$$

where $\mathbf{v} = \mathbf{l}(\mathbf{I} - \mathbf{A})^{-1}$ is a row vector of labor values, i.e., the vertically integrated labor coefficients defined by Pasinetti (1981). Pre-multiplying (2) by $\mathbf{v}$, we have

$$\mathbf{vQ} = \mathbf{vh}[\mathbf{vQ}] + \mathbf{vF} \tag{3}$$

which rearranges to

$$\mathbf{vQ} = \frac{1}{1 - \mathbf{vh}} \mathbf{vF} \tag{4}$$

This equation relates a second strand of modern economics to the Marxian reproduction schemes: the multiplier analysis of Keynesian economics. From this demand-side perspective, final demand ($\mathbf{vF} = dC + dV + u$) consists of additions to constant and variable capital together with capitalist consumption—as represented in Table 3 by *dC* of 500, *dV* of 150 and *u* of 1,100, a total final demand of 1,750. This final demand generates a total value ($\mathbf{vQ}$) of output, as represented by the 9,000 units of value produced in Table 3. The term $1/1 - \mathbf{vh}$ is a scalar Keynesian multiplier that in Marx's example takes a value of $5\frac{1}{7}$. Locating the

Keynesian multiplier in Marx's reproduction schemes can be traced back to the work of Lianos (1979).

Following an insight originally made by Olgin (1992), a term representing surplus value can also be identified in the Keynesian multiplier. Marx's category, the value of labor power, is represented in the denominator of the multiplier by the term $\mathbf{vh}$, the labor embodied ($\mathbf{v}$) in worker consumption per unit of labor ($\mathbf{h}$). Hence the denominator of the multiplier represents the share of surplus value produced per unit of labor, $e = 1 - \mathbf{vh}$.

Under Marx's assumption throughout the first two volumes of *Capital* that money prices ($\mathbf{p}$) are equal to values ($\mathbf{v}$), we can specify net money output as $y = \mathbf{v}Q = \mathbf{p}Q$ and final demand as $f = \mathbf{vF} = \mathbf{pF}$. The Keynesian multiplier therefore takes the form

$$y = \frac{1}{e} f \tag{5}$$

The final stage in our synthesis is to consider the insights of Michal Kalecki, who engaged directly with the reproduction schemes. Kalecki identified the key role of capitalist spending in determining the level of profits: according to the *Kalecki principle*, capitalists earn what they spend. If we denote capital accumulation by the term $I = dC + dV$, then by rearranging (5), total surplus value ($S = ey$) is determined by the relationship

$$S = u + I \tag{6}$$

Total surplus value is determined by the expenditure of capitalists either on their own consumption or on investment. And, under the assumption that prices are equal to values, this total surplus value is also equal to total profits (P):

$$P = u + I \tag{7}$$

Furthermore, Kalecki breaks down capitalist consumption into a constant component (B_0) and a part dependent on profits according to the proportion λ, such that

$$u = B_0 + \lambda P \tag{8}$$

Substituting (8) into (7)

$$P = B_0 + \lambda P + I \tag{9}$$

and hence

$$P = \frac{B_0 + I}{1 - \lambda} \tag{10}$$

Here the Kalecki multiplier ($1/1 - \lambda$) captures the determination of profits by investment. Since profits are identical to final demand (f), equation (10) can be substituted into (5) to give

$$y = \frac{1}{e(1 - \lambda)} (B_0 + I) \tag{11}$$

This multiplier relationship demonstrates the synthetic potential of the reproduction schemes. It combines Keynesian and Kalecki multipliers with a structure based on Marx's category of surplus value, all derived from a representation of the reproduction schema using Leontief's input-output analysis. This provides a genuinely *post*-Keynesian contribution, in the sense that it moves the project beyond the limited one-good world inhabited by the Samuelson textbook Keynesians of the neoclassical synthesis. By drawing on Marx, Leontief and Kalecki, our adaptation of the reproduction schemes pulls Keynes's legacy towards a classical tradition, based on industrial interdependence and structure. It also helps develop Kalecki's legacy in response to the critique of Steedman (1992) that Kalecki failed to take into account input-output relations. A limitation of this interpretation, however, as shown by Brennan (2014), is that even Kalecki himself struggled in his empirical analysis to maintain Marxian class-based categories when transferring the reproduction schemes to a national accounting context.

This location of the multiplier in the reproduction schemes also relates Marx's system to the model of economic growth developed by Domar (Trigg 2006, 53–7). It does not prove that balanced growth must take place, only that certain conditions are required for this growth, however unlikely they are to be established. The key demand requirement is that investment must grow at the required rate, and its impact must be provided by the correct multiplier mechanism. Furthermore, this opens up a problem of how the money can be found for growth to be financed. A hoard of gold money, which would be sufficient under simple reproduction to finance capital outlays, will soon become exhausted under expanded reproduction.

This opens up two questions raised by Rosa Luxemburg: "Where does the demand come from?" and "Where does the money come from?" Her *Accumulation of Capital*, published in 1913, is considered to be the first major work on political economy to explore the reproduction schemes. In it she seems to adopt something close to the Kalecki principle: "If the capitalists themselves have set in motion all the money which circulates in society, they must also advance the money needed for the realization of their own surplus value" (Luxemburg 1951, 71). As shown by Bellofiore (2014), Rosa Luxemburg was not an underconsumptionist. The problem of demand relates to the demand of capitalists realizing their surplus value, not the consumption of the masses.

But Luxemburg also views money as something of a distraction. "It is not the source of money that constitutes the problem of accumulation, but the source of the demand for the additional goods produced by the capitalized surplus value" (Luxemburg 1951, 147). Following Kotz (1991, 73), however, in a contribution to *Rethinking Marxism*, it can be argued that questions of money and demand are related issues "since the monetary problem seems to be an aspect of the demand problem." In the analysis that follows we shall see that the Kalecki principle can also be invoked to look at money related issues.

The Circuit of Money

The Kalecki principle allows a sharp focus on the circulation of money in the reproduction schemes. As shown by Sardoni (1989), in the second volume of *Capital* Marx is explicit about how capitalists cast money into circulation: "The capitalist class itself casts into circulation the money that serves towards the realization of the surplus value contained in its commodities" (Marx 1978, 409). In expanded reproduction, the money cast into circulation consists of both unproductive capitalist consumption and expenditure on investment. For Sardoni (1989, 214): "Capitalists' profits therefore now depend on their consumption and investment expenditure, just as in Kalecki's analysis."

The field of Marxian economics, as taught in universities, has been so influenced by orthodox economic techniques that it has tended to ignore Marx's writings on money. It was only in the 1970s that something of a revival of Marx-based monetary theory took place, as exemplified by de Brunhoff's *Marx on Money* (1973). Subsequently, the theory of monetary circuits, pioneered by Graziani (1989), has been used to model Marx in a modern setting, moving away from metallic money to a focus on the issuing of loans by banks. This has been regarded as a significant contribution to Marxian economics (Bellofiore and Realfonzo 1997), with its incorporation of Marx's distinction in the reproduction schemes between investment and consumption goods.

For Nell (1998), however, the structure of reproduction is regarded as incomplete in Graziani's circuit. The failure to identify a multiplier relationship overestimates the amount of money that is required for reproduction to take place. A multiplier such as that defined in (11), derived from a fully interconnected reproduction scheme, offers a precise specification of the monetary requirements of reproduction. Under the Kalecki principle, the outlay on capitalist consumption and investment ($B_0 + I$) creates a greater volume of income (y), depending on the size of the multiplier. The initial outlay can be viewed as money that is borrowed from banks by the capitalists, which is then injected into the departments of production. The multiplier then becomes the velocity of circulation, the amount of time in which each unit of money injected turns over in the economy. In Marx's example of expanded reproduction (Table 3), the size of the velocity of circulation (multiplier) is $5\frac{1}{7}$; hence the initial outlay of 1,750 circulates $5\frac{1}{7}$ times around the economy to create a total value of 9,000.

Since the 2008 global financial crisis, issues relating to money and finance have become prominent, in particular the prophetic insights of Hyman Minsky. It is not so well known that Minsky based his financial instability hypothesis on the Kalecki principle (Minsky 1978). With aggregate profits driven by capitalist expenditure, financed by loans, any faltering of this expenditure can have disastrous consequences, leading to a constraint on profits, making capitalists unable to pay off their debts.

There is, however, a problem raised by Toporowski (2008) concerning the ability of capitalists to pay off loans out of profits. He argues that Minsky fails to take into account the difference between debts of individual capitalists and those of the capitalist class as a whole. Minsky overestimates the debts incurred by capitalists—towards those producing capital goods there is an immediate flow of money that allows them to incur no further financial or business liabilities (Toporowski 2008, 734). These capitalists may gain assets while others carrying out the capital investment may incur liabilities—with assets and liabilities cancelling out at the aggregate level.

This critique is extended by Trigg (2014), using Marx's empirical example (Table 3) of an expanded reproduction scheme. As shown in Table 4, more detail can be specified about the destination of new capital and capitalist consumption. Part of the new constant capital is earmarked for use in department 1 in the next period ($dC_1 = 400$); the other part ($dC_2 = 100$) is earmarked for use in department 2. Similarly, new variable capital is earmarked for use in department 1, as specified by $dV_1 = 100$, with $dV_2 = 50$ sent to department 2. Capitalist consumption is split into two parts, u_1 and u_2, expenditure by capitalists in each department.

Now assuming that there is no borrowing within departments, we can examine the reproduction scheme to see if liabilities arise between departments. To do this the outlays and receipts of each department are put in a balance sheet (Table 5). The outcome is that no liabilities are incurred by either department; all outlays are balanced by receipts. Department 2, for example, has outlays of 3,000 balanced by receipts of 3,000. The Kalecki principle, that

Table 4 Expanded Reproduction and the Destination of Surplus Outputs

	Dept. 1	Dept. 2	dC_1	dC_2	dV_1	dV_2	u_1	u_2	Receipts
Dept. 1	4,000	1,500	400	100					6,000
Dept. 2	1,000	750			100	50	500	600	3,000
Outlays	5,000	2,250	400	100	100	50	500	600	9,000

Table 5 Outlays and Receipts under Expanded Reproduction

Department 1		Department 2	
Outlays	Receipts	Outlays	Receipts
4,000 (C_1)	4,000 (C_1)	1,500 (C_2)	1,000 (V_1)
1,000 (V_1)	1,500 (C_2)	750 (V_2)	750 (V_2)
400 (dC_1)	400 (dC_1)	100 (dC_2)	100 (dV_1)
100 (dV_1)	100 (dC_2)	50 (dV_2)	50 (dV_2)
500 (u_1)		600 (u_2)	500 (u_1)
			600 (u_2)
6,000	6,000	3,000	3,000

capitalists earn what they spend, applies in this case to both departments, and not just to the economy as a whole. This further extends the critique of Minsky, by casting doubt on how debts and financial fragility can originate in the structure of production. This is of course a specific two-sector numerical example, but it provides just a hint that Marx's reproduction schemes provide a starting point for exploring the conditions under which Minsky's hypothesis might hold.

Conclusions

Marxian reproduction schemes have been shown to provide an organizing framework for different components of political economy: from the multiplier to the Kalecki principle, money circuits and Minsky's financial instability hypothesis. The reproduction schemes formalize the precise conditions in which money circuits and finance can function in a sustainable capitalist system. And they offer a basis for critical engagement with theories that are at times not defined with the degree of rigor offered by the reproduction schemes.

These analytical tools are available to Marxists and post-Keynesians at a time when political economy is starting to recover some of its roots in the early part of the twentieth century. The bright flame of Marxism was almost cut off at birth by the age of extremes under Hitler and Stalin. And many of those socialists that survived, such as Kalecki, were subject to much repression. But as shown in the recent first translation into English of the book *Rosa Luxemburg: Theory of Accumulation and Imperialism* (2014) authored by Kalecki's Polish colleague, Tadeusz Kowalik, the reproduction schemes are central to the history of Marxism. Kowalik "found the roots of twentieth-century political economy in the discussions of Marx's schemes of capitalist reproduction . . . ." (Toporowski 2014, xi). Moreover, Kowalik's important book opens up the importance of a socialist critique of political economy. For him, followers of Kalecki should not scramble to prove that he was a precursor of Keynes; instead, they should highlight the advantages of Kalecki's grounding in the reproduction schemes. Furthermore, following Luxemburg and the subsequent Marxist tradition, the reproduction schemes can be interpreted as a tool for socialist planning, beyond the confines of our analysis of capitalist reproduction.

References

Bellofiore, R. 2014. "Luxemburg and Kalecki: The Actuality of Tadeusz Kowalik's Reading of *Accumulation of Capital*." In *The Legacy of Rosa Luxemburg, Oskar Lange and Michal Kalecki*, vol. 1, R. Bellofiore, E. Karwowski, and J. Toporowski, eds., 78–103. Basingstoke: Palgrave Macmillan.

Bellofiore, R. and R. Realfonzo. 1997. "Finance and the Labor Theory of Value." *International Journal of Political Economy* 27(2): 97–118.

Brennan, D. 2014. "'Too Bright for Comfort': A Kaleckian View of Profit Realization in the USA, 1964–2009." *Cambridge Journal of Economics* 38: 239–255.

Carchedi, G. and W. de Haan. 1995. "On the Replacement of Fixed Capital in Marx's Simple Reproduction." *History of Political Economy* 27(3): 599–604.

de Brunhoff, S. 1973. *Marx on Money*. New York: Urizen Books.

Gilibert, B. 1998. "Wassily Leontief." In *The Elgar Companion to Classical Economics*, H.D. Kurz and N. Salvadori, eds., 40–45. Cheltenham: Edward Elgar.

Graziani, A. 1989. "The Theory of the Monetary Circuit." *Thames Papers in Political Economy*. London: Thames Polytechnic.

Kotz, D. M. 1991. "Accumulation, Money and Credit in the Circuit of Capital." *Rethinking Marxism* 4: 119–133.

Kowalik, T. 2014. *Rosa Luxemburg: Theory of Accumulation and Imperialism*. Trans. and edited by J. Toporowski and H. Szymborska. Basingstoke: Palgrave Macmillan.

Lianos, T. P. 1979. "Domar's Growth Model and Marx's Reproduction Scheme." *Journal of Macroeconomics* 1(4): 405–412.

Luxemburg, R. 1951 [1913]. *The Accumulation of Capital*. London: Routledge & Kegan Paul.

Marx, K. 1973. *Grundrisse*. Harmondsworth: Penguin.

——. 1976. *Capital*, Volume 1. Harmondsworth: Penguin.

——. 1978. *Capital*, Volume 2. Harmondsworth: Penguin.

——. 1981. *Capital*, Volume 3. Harmondsworth: Penguin.

Minsky, H. 1978. "The Financial Instability Hypothesis: A Restatement." *Thames Papers in Political Economy*. London: Thames Polytechnic.

Nell, E. J. 1998. *The General Theory of Transformational Growth*. Cambridge: Cambridge University Press.

Olgin, D. S. 1992. "On an Accidental Proof to the 'Fundamental Marxian Theorem.'" *History of Political Economy* 24(2): 471–475.

Olsen, E. 2015. "Unproductive and Endogenous Technological Change in a Marxian Model of Economic Reproduction and Growth." *Review of Radical Political Economics* 47(1): 34–55.

Pasinetti, L. L. 1981. *Structural Change and Economic Growth*. Cambridge: Cambridge University Press.

Robinson, J. 1968. "Marx and Keynes." In *Marx and Modern Economics*, D. Horowitz, ed., 103–116. London: MacGibbon and Kee.

Sardoni, C. 1989. "Some Aspects of Kalecki's Theory of Profits: Its Relationship to Marx's Schemes of Reproduction." In *Kalecki's Relevance Today*, M. Sebastiani, ed., 206–219. Basingstoke: Macmillan.

Steedman, I. 1992. "Questions for Kaleckians." *Review of Political Economy* 4: 125–151.

Toporowski, J. 2008. "Minsky's Induced Investment and Business Cycles." *Cambridge Journal of Economics* 32: 725–737.

——. 2014. "Preface." In T. Kowalik, *Rosa Luxemburg: Theory of Accumulation and Imperialism*, J. Toporowski and H. Szymborska, trans. and eds., vii–xiii. Basingstoke: Palgrave Macmillan.

Trigg, A. B. 2006. *Marxian Reproduction Schema: Money and Aggregate Demand in a Capitalist Economy*. London: Routledge.

——. 2014. "Financial Fragility and the Kalecki Principle under Expanded Reproduction". In *The Legacy of Rosa Luxemburg, Oskar Lange and Michal Kalecki*, Volume 1, R. Bellofiore, E. Karwoski, and J. Toporowski, eds., 205–214. Basingstoke: Palgrave Macmillan.

21

TENDENCY OF THE RATE OF PROFIT TO FALL

Long-term Dynamics

Andrew Kliman

Adam Smith, David Ricardo and other classical political economists held that the rate of profit—profit as a percentage of the amount of money invested in production—tends to fall in the long run. The fall in the rate of profit was inferred from evidence that interest rates had fallen. Smith justified this inference by arguing that the two rates will tend to move in the same direction.

Karl Marx accepted these economists' claim that the rate of profit tends to fall over time, but not the theories that they had put forward to account for the fall. He held that their attempts to explain it were "contradictory" and that the fall in the rate of profit had remained an unsolved "mystery" until he offered his own "law of the tendential fall in the rate of profit" (Marx 1991a, 319). Thus, although he was not the first to argue that the rate of profit tends to fall, Marx did take credit for being the first to offer a "law," or explanatory theoretical principle, that successfully accounts for the falling tendency. He repeatedly stressed that it is "the most important law" of political economy, the solution of the central puzzle around which "the whole of political economy since Adam Smith revolves" (Marx 1973, 748; 1991b, 104; 1991a, 319).

Nevertheless, the law has always been and remains extremely controversial, even among those who identify themselves as Marxists. The same is true of the empirical claim that the rate of profit tends to fall.

The law, which Marx put forward in Part 3 of the third volume of his book *Capital*, is that "[t]he progressive tendency for the rate of profit to fall is thus simply *the expression, peculiar to the capitalist mode of production*, of the progressive development of the social productivity of labour" (Marx 1991a, 319, emphasis in original). In other words, rising productivity tends to depress the rate of profit. This conclusion follows in a fairly straightforward manner from the following three points developed earlier in the book:

1 To remain competitive, capitalists must reduce costs of production, and they do so largely by boosting labor productivity (the amount of product per unit of labor performed). The productivity increases are achieved mainly by adopting new technologies that replace workers with machines. Thus, what Marx called the technical composition of capital, the ratio of machines and other means of production to the number of workers employed, tends to rise over time.

2 The amount of new value—and, all else being equal, also the surplus-value—generated by each dollar of capital investment tends to fall as a result. This follows from Marx's theory that workers' labor is the exclusive source of new value. When workers are replaced by machines, more of each dollar invested in production is spent on means of production that do not generate new value, and less is spent to hire the workers whose labor does generate it. Thus, the ratio between these two sums of money, which Marx called the value composition of capital, tends to rise along with the rise in the technical composition. (This is a tendency rather than a guaranteed outcome since other factors also affect the value composition.)

3 In the economy as a whole, what is true of value and surplus-value is also true of price and profit. Individual businesses and industries may obtain prices that exceed the amounts of value they produce and thereby obtain more profit than the surplus-value they produce, but Marx's theory holds that such gains come at the expense of other capitalists. For example, monopoly power allows some businesses to raise their prices and thereby bring in more profit, but this is fully offset by lower prices and profits for the remaining capitalists. The sum of all prices equals the sum of all values, and the sum of all profits equals the sum of all surplus-values. Marx's law, which pertains to the rate of profit of the economy as a whole, is therefore not affected by discrepancies between surplus-value and profit.

The basic idea behind Marx's law can thus be expressed in terms of price and profit, without explicit reference to the terminology of his value theory, as follows: when productivity increases, less labor is needed to produce a product, so it can be produced more cheaply. As a result, its price tends to fall. And when prices tend to fall, so do profits and the rate of profit. (Strictly speaking, the price level need not fall; it is sufficient that the rate of inflation falls.)

Marx (1991a, 339) recognized that various "[c]ounteracting influences must be at work, checking and cancelling [*durchkreuzen und aufheben*] the effect of the general law and giving it simply the character of a tendency." For example, the value composition of capital can rise more slowly than the technical composition because means of production become cheaper as productivity increases. Or the rate of surplus-value (roughly speaking, the ratio of profit to wages) may rise, and this implies that profit may increase more rapidly than the new value generated in production. When rising productivity leads to lower prices, workers need less money than before to attain the same standard of living. Consequently, as shares of the new value, wages tend to fall and profit tends to rise.

However, Marx argued that this latter counteracting factor can have only a limited effect. The amount of value workers create does not depend on the physical productivity of their labor. The length of the workday thus sets a strict maximum limit to the amount of surplus-value created. If the workforce originally consists of one hundred people, and half of their labor-time—say, four hours—consists of surplus labor (labor for which no equivalent is paid and which therefore creates surplus-value), then the amount of surplus-value created is (the monetary expression of) $4 \times 100 = 400$ labor-hours. Now, if labor-saving technological change causes the workforce to shrink to forty-nine or fewer workers, the amount of surplus-value created must fall, even if the full eight-hour workday now consists of surplus labor because the workers have been forced to "live on air." "[T]herefore, the compensation for the reduced number of workers[,] provided by a rise in the level of exploitation of labour[,] has certain limits that cannot be overstepped" (Marx 1991a, 356).

Smith, Ricardo and other classical political economists believed that the falling tendency of the rate of profit would eventually result in a stationary state, or no-growth economy. As opportunities to obtain greater profit diminished, so would capitalists' willingness to undertake additional productive investment. In contrast, Marx argued that the tendency of the rate of profit to fall produces boom-and-bust cycles. (There seems to be no textual evidence that supports the legend that he claimed that this tendency would cause capitalism to collapse in an automatic or quasi-automatic manner.)

"Permanent crises do not exist," according to Marx (1989, 128, starred note), because the financial crises and downturns (recessions, depressions) that result indirectly from the fall in the rate of profit cause a portion of the capital-value invested in production to be destroyed by means of bankruptcies, write-offs of bad debt, falling prices of means of production, idled plant and equipment and so on. New owners can therefore acquire businesses cheaply and without assuming all of the previous owners' debts, which implies that their rate of profit—profit as a percentage of the *reduced* amount of capital-value *they* have invested—is greater than the pre-existing rate. Thus, the destruction of capital-value eventually leads to a restoration of the rate of profit and a new phase of capitalist expansion.

In Marx's view, the fall in the rate of profit is only an indirect cause of financial crises and downturns. He acknowledged that it reduces capitalists' willingness to invest in production, but argued that the immediate cause of the downturn is a financial crisis, and he attributed these crises to a combination of debts that cannot be repaid and an increase in speculative and fraudulent behavior that occurs when the rate of profit falls. Capitalists take excessive risks or engage in fraud in order to obtain a higher rate of profit than the now-reduced average rate, in part because they need additional profit to repay their debts.

The cycle described above should not be confused with short-term business cycles. Marx accounted for the latter primarily by arguing that wages rise in relation to profit in the expansionary phase of the cycle, which leads to a decline in productive investment, a contraction of economic activity and a fall in wages relative to profits that sets the stage for renewed expansion.

Marx thought that capitalism was once justified, from a long-term historical perspective, because it contributed to human development by greatly increasing our scientific and productive powers. Yet the increases in productivity produce a tendency for the rate of profit to fall, which in turn leads to "bitter contradictions, crises, spasms[—the] violent destruction of capital not by relations external to it, but rather as a condition of its self-preservation" (Marx 1973, 751). He argued that this self-destructive aspect of capitalism is "the most striking form in which advice is given it to be gone and to give room to a higher state of social production" (Ibid.).

Other theories attribute economic downturns and crises to low productivity, sluggish demand, the anarchy of the market, state intervention, high wages, low wages and so forth. Such theories suggest that capitalism's crisis tendencies can in principle be substantially lessened or eliminated by fixing the specific problem that is making the system perform poorly. Marx's law is unique in that it suggests that economic crises are inevitable under capitalism, because they are not caused by "relations external to it," that is, by factors that can be eliminated while keeping the system intact. To do away with these crises, a different socioeconomic system is needed.

One of the main reasons that Marx's law has always been controversial is this revolutionary implication of his theory of crisis based on the law. In recent years, especially, much of the left chooses to stress the economic successes of capitalism and to argue that the fruits of its success are distributed inequitably. The idea that capitalism is inherently self-limiting and crisis-ridden does not fit together easily with such arguments.

The other main reason that the law is controversial is that it seems counterintuitive to many commentators. It relies heavily on his value theory, but that theory is frequently dismissed, partly because it is supposedly inconsistent or otherwise incorrect and partly because it is supposedly "metaphysical." The latter objection seems to mean that, because values and surplus-values are not directly observable, arguments based on them are unsafe. Robert Brenner (1998, 11–12, n.1), a Marxist historian, has also famously argued that the law "flies in the face of common-sense" since "it seems intuitively obvious" that the new technologies which individual capitalists adopt in order to raise their own rates of profit must end up raising the economy-wide rate of profit as well. (Marx had argued that the capitalists who innovate produce the fall in the economy-wide rate but shift the consequences onto other capitalists while enhancing the profitability of their own businesses because their costs of production are now lower.) And the so-called Okishio theorem, which will be discussed below, formalizes what seems to be a widespread intuition that increases in productivity must lead to a higher, not lower, rate of profit.

As Stephen Cullenberg (1994) usefully points out, there have been two main types of technical objections to Marx's law (apart from empirical objections), one pertaining to whether technological progress *must* cause the rate of profit to fall, the other pertaining to whether it *can* do so. He further notes that the first type of objection predominated until about the mid-1970s while the second has predominated ever since.

The first type of objection, put forward by Joan Robinson (1941, 243–5), Paul Sweezy (1970, 102–4) and others (see, e.g., Heinrich 2013), is that the counteracting factors to the tendency of the rate of profit to fall can always offset, or more than offset, the tendency. For this reason, and because two of these counteracting factors—the cheapening of means of production and reduced wages—are wholly or partly the consequences of the *same* techno-logical progress that produces the tendency, Marx was not entitled to privilege one effect of technological progress as the "law" and relegate the others to secondary status.

It is important to understand the special sense in which these critics use terms like "can always." What they mean is that there are hypothetical cases, which do not violate laws of logic or nature or the premises of Marx's argument, in which the tendency fails to dominate over the counteracting factors. This does not imply that such cases are likely or even plausible. No responsible defender of Marx's law disputes the idea that the counteracting factors "can always" be stronger in this special sense, but the likelihood and plausibility of such cases are indeed contested. Consider, for example, the argument that, even if the value composition of capital continually rises, the rate of profit can always increase because the rate of surplus-value can always increase more rapidly than the value composition. This is not impossible, strictly speaking, not even in light of Marx's point that the length of the workday sets a rigid maximum limit to the amount of surplus-value a worker can create. As this maximum limit is approached, however, the extra surplus-value that a worker can create becomes smaller and smaller, which means that the rate of profit can continue to rise only if the increases in the value composition become infinitesimally small.

Defenders of Marx's law (see Kliman, Freeman, Potts, Gusev and Cooney 2013) also contend that the critics' argument attacks a strawman, or perhaps some falling-rate-of-profit theory other than Marx's. His law does not say, much less attempt to prove, that the rate of profit must inevitably fall in the long run. Its purpose is *explanatory*; it accounts for what Marx and the classical economists regarded as the confirmed fact that the rate of profit does tend to fall. Although he clearly believed that the tendency is stronger than the counteracting factors—the contrary belief is inconsistent with the evidence available to him—his claim to have proven the law is not an assertion that it must inevitably remain stronger. It is an assertion that his value theory, in conjunction with his theory of capitalist accumulation, is able to explain what he regarded as a confirmed fact.

The claim that the rate of profit must inevitably fall in the long run has nevertheless garnered a good deal of support as well as much criticism. Cullenberg's (1988, 1994) work challenging the falling-rate-of-profit thesis is directed principally against this claim and its supporters, rather than against Marx's law understood as an explanation of the rate of profit's tendency to fall. Inspired by Stephen Resnick and Richard Wolff's overdeterminist perspective, Cullenberg (1988, 41) is suspicious of economic laws (i.e., of statements of supposedly invariant outcomes) and of "modernist" theorists' typical lack of "attention to the historical specificity and heterogeneity of capitalist enterprises." He argues against the assumption that all firms share the same basic motivation and calls attention to the fact that technological changes, as well as changes in the efficiency and intensity of labor, affect different firms in different ways. They will thus act differently from one another, and the effects of their actions on the aggregate economy will also differ. As a result, there is no inevitable trend, downward or upward, in the economy-wide rate of profit. Writing from a similar perspective, Norton (2001) has more recently argued against the prevailing belief that Marx argued that capitalist firms are primarily concerned to re-invest their profits rather than to distribute the profits to shareholders or use them in other ways.

The second type of technical objection challenges Marx's claim that new technologies which replace workers with machines can cause the economy-wide rate of profit to fall even though they increase the rates of profit obtained by firms that introduce these technologies. Arguments of this sort first appeared in 1899, only five years after volume 3 of *Capital* was published. However, they did not command widespread attention until the latter part of the 1970s, when a paper by Nobuo Okishio (1961), a Japanese Marxist economist, became widely known and extensively discussed in the West. Okishio attempted to provide a formal proof that Marx's law does not hold true; technologies that raise the innovating firm's rate of profit *cannot* cause the economy-wide rate to fall (although it can fall for other reasons). Since the attempted proof was initially regarded as successful, this conclusion became known as "Okishio's theorem." Okishio restricted his attention to cases without fixed capital (means of production that last more than one period), but John Roemer (1981, 108–9) later deduced the same conclusion from a model in which fixed capital is employed.

Once it became widely known, discussion of Okishio's theorem largely eclipsed the debate over whether the counteracting factors offset the tendency of the rate of profit to fall. This probably occurred because arguments that the rate of profit *might not* fall do not discredit Marx's theory as effectively as the argument that it *cannot* fall for the reasons he stated.

Initially, a wide variety of counterarguments were offered in attempts to circumvent Okishio's theorem. For example, it was shown that the rate of profit can fall if an increase in real (i.e., physical) wages accompanies the technological innovation (ironically, this was one of the main things that Okishio himself wished to show); and if cutthroat competition compels firms to adopt new technologies that are suboptimal when considered in the abstract; and if there are joint products, two or more products produced by a single production process; and if new techniques become prematurely obsolete. However, none of these contributions vindicated Marx's claim that the rate of profit can fall *because* productivity increases. Nor did they disprove the alleged theorem; they obtained results that differed from Okishio's only because they altered one or another of his assumptions.

More recently, however, the main criticism of the alleged theorem has come from proponents of the temporal single-system interpretation (TSSI) of Marx's value theory. They stress that Okishio and Roemer failed to prove that "the" rate of profit cannot fall for the reasons Marx claimed; the rate of profit that cannot fall is conceptually different from the rate to which his law refers. They also claim to have proven that Marx's rate can fall under conditions in which the alleged theorem says it cannot, and that it falls *because* productivity increases.

Specifically, TSSI authors argue that Marx's rate of profit is profit as a percentage of the amount of money that has actually been invested in production (net of depreciation). This is very close, if not identical, to the standard meaning of the term *rate of profit*. However, the proponents of Okishio's theorem mean something quite different by the term: profit as a percentage of the replacement cost (or current cost) of a business's means of production, the amount of money that would currently be needed to replace them. If prices of means of production fall—because, for instance, productivity increases—the amount of money that is currently needed to replace the means of production now in use falls in relation to the amount of money that was actually invested to acquire them in the past. The denominator of Okishio's rate of profit therefore falls in relation to the denominator of Marx's rate, and this causes Okishio's rate to rise in relation to Marx's rate. Consequently, technological innovations that must result in an increase in Okishio's rate can indeed cause Marx's rate of profit to fall and, proponents of the TSSI claim, they can do so *because* productivity increases.

At first, the TSSI critique was basically ignored or dismissed. Somewhat later, Duncan Foley (1999), David Laibman (2000) and others challenged it by offering algebraic examples in which Marx's rate of profit does not fall. Proponents of the TSSI countered that the point of these examples is unclear, since Okishio's theorem "asserts that *no* viable technical change lowers the profit rate. Even one counterexample is sufficient to refute the theorem. We have provided not one, but many, such counterexamples" (Freeman and Kliman 2000, 247).

Foley (2000) and Laibman (2000) ultimately acknowledged, even if only implicitly, that Marx's rate of profit can fall under conditions in which the alleged theorem says that "the" rate of profit cannot fall. However, they continued to argue that the theorem is true, on the grounds that it was always meant to be a theorem on the replacement-cost rate of profit rather than Marx's rate. Kliman and Freeman (2000, 290) responded by quoting from Okishio's paper: "[our] conclusions are negative to [the] Marxian *Gesetz des tendenziellen Falls der Profitrate* [law of the tendential fall in the profit rate]."

Critics of Marx's law and the TSSI defense have also argued that Okishio's theorem is true, even if the rate of profit employed in the proof of the theorem is not Marx's, because it is "a mathematical theorem and does not contain any logical flaws. One can object to its assumptions as being inappropriate or not the same as Marx's assumptions. ... But the theorem is logically sound" (Robin Hahnel, quoted in Kliman 2012a, 106–7). Kliman (2014, 658, n.21) has replied that the theorem is logically invalid because it is guilty of equivocation, using the same term in different senses within the same argument. (For example, the following argument is logically invalid because the term "man" is used in two different senses: "Man is the only rational animal. No woman is a man. Therefore, no woman is rational.") The "rate of profit" employed in the mathematics is the replacement-cost rate, while Okishio's conclusions refer to the rate of profit to which the "Marxian *Gesetz*" pertains. Thus, "the theorem cannot possibly do damage to Marx's law. As a theorem on Marx's law, it does no damage because it is false. As a disinterested exercise in applied mathematics, it does no damage because it is not a theorem on Marx's law" (Ibid.).

Laibman (1999, 223), Gérard Duménil and Dominique Lévy (2011a, 37), Deok-Min Kim (2012, 255, 260) and others have argued that the trend in Marx's rate of profit is of little importance. What really matters is the trend in Okishio's replacement-cost rate of profit, since the latter, they contend, is the expected rate of profit that governs investment decisions.

This claim has been challenged by proponents of the TSSI (see Kliman and Freeman 2000, 287–8) and by Christian Lager (1998). As Okishio (2001, 497) himself noted, the replacement-cost rate will coincide with the expected rate of profit only "if prices and wages at [time] $t + 1$ are expected to be the same as at [time] t." The replacement-cost and expected rates of profit are both based on current investment costs, but the replacement-cost rate compares these costs to profits based on *current* prices while the expected rate of profit compares them to profits based on expected *future* prices. The two rates will differ whenever prices are expected to change. (Although Marx's law pertains to the actually realized rate of profit, not the expected rate, it too compares investment costs based on one set of prices to profits based on prices of a later time.)

In the wake of the recent Great Recession, there has been a substantial increase in research that estimates trends in rates of profit. These investigations neither confirm nor refute Marx's law. Since the law is a particular explanation of *why* the rate of profit supposedly tends to fall, a falling rate does not, by itself, tend to confirm the law. Conversely, the law is consistent with a rising rate of profit in some countries and during some spans of time, at least, so a rising rate does not, by itself, tend to disconfirm the law. Another difficulty is that some data that would be needed to conduct an appropriate and direct test of the law, particularly data for the world economy as a whole, are unavailable.

Some empirical studies have decomposed movements in rates of profit into those associated with changes in the rate of surplus-value and those associated with changes in the value composition of capital, but since these variables themselves have multiple potential causes, this does not provide a satisfactory *causal* explanation of movements in the rate of profit. Very few studies have attempted to isolate the actual causes of changes in rates of profit. (See, however, Kliman 2012a, 133–8 where causes of U.S. corporations' rate of profit between 1947 and 2007 are investigated and the argument is made that Marx's law "fits the facts.")

Measurement of movements in rates of profit is nonetheless potentially important in order to understand why the Great Recession and its prolonged aftermath occurred. Some authors argue that there was a "slight upward trend" (Duménil and Lévy 2011b, 60) to U.S. corporations' rate of profit from the early 1980s onward, as a result of neoliberalism and financialization. They thus reject the idea that falling profitability is among the causes of the recession. Other authors (e.g. Kliman 2012a, Freeman 2012) argue that the rate of profit either failed to recover in a sustained manner from the recessions of the mid-1970s and early 1980s, or continued to trend downward, and suggest that the fall in the rate of profit is one of the indirect causes of the recession and its aftermath. (No one argues that it was a direct cause, since no one contends that the rate of profit fell during the bubble that preceded the recession.)

This is actually a *conceptual* controversy rather than an *empirical* one. The facts are not seriously in dispute. Instead, the key issue involved in the debate between the TSSI's supporters and opponents over the logical validity of Okishio's theorem has resurfaced here in a different context. Once again, what one group calls "the rate of profit" is the replacement-cost rate. It rose. The other group uses the term "rate of profit" to refer to profit as a percentage of the actual amount of money that was invested in production (the capital stock's historical cost). It either continued to fall or failed to recover in a sustained manner (depending on the measure of profit considered). The trajectories of "hybrid" rates of profit, which value capital investment at historical cost but use replacement-cost depreciation data to compute profit (see Basu and Vasudevan 2013), lie in between these extremes.

What would be needed to resolve the dispute over the trend in "the" rate of profit during the last several decades is sustained discussion of the meaning and significance of the quite different measures that are called "the rate of profit." Does a certain measure actually help to answer a particular question? If so, how? Such discussion has not (yet) taken place. Duménil and Lévy (2011a, 37, 37 n.36) have dismissed TSSI authors' concept of the rate of profit as "[f]iddling with definitions." Kliman (2012b, 294) has responded that Duménil, Lévy and others have "fail[ed] to disclose the full meaning, and meaninglessness, of what they define as 'the rate of profit.'"

This controversy has spilled over into the political realm. Most trade unions and electoral and non-electoral groups on the left have a redistributionist orientation and/or regard neoliberalism and financialization as a new phase of capitalism and are hostile to explanations of the Great Recession that appeal to a fall in the rate of profit or Marx's law. Their websites frequently carry writings by and highlight the research conducted by those who argue that the rate of profit rebounded under neoliberalism. Parties belonging to the Committee for a Workers International, a Trotskyist organization, recently suspended two members who contend that a falling rate of profit is among the causes of the recession.

References

Basu, D. and R. Vasudevan. 2013. "Technology, Distribution and the Rate of Profit in the US Economy: Understanding the Current Crisis." *Cambridge Journal of Economics* 3(1): 57–89.

Brenner, R. 1998. "The Economics of Global Turbulence." *New Left Review* 229: 1–265.

Cullenberg, Stephen. 1988. "The Capitalist Enterprise and the Contradictory Movement in the Rate of Profit." *Review of Radical Political Economics* 20(2–3): 41–47.

———. 1994. *The Falling Rate of Profit: Recasting the Marxian Debate*. London: Pluto Books.

Duménil, G. and D. Lévy. 1999. "Response to David Laibman." *Research in Political Economy* 17: 229–233.

———. 2011a. "The Crisis of the Early 21st Century: A Critical Review of Alternative Interpretations." www.jourdan.ens.fr/levy/dle2011h.pdf (accessed August 14, 2016).

———. 2011b. *The Crisis of Neoliberalism*. Cambridge, MA: Harvard University Press.

Foley, D. K. 2000. "Response to Freeman and Kliman." *Research in Political Economy* 18: 279–283.

Freeman, A. 2012. "The Profit Rate in the Presence of Financial Markets: A Necessary Correction." *Journal of Australian Political Economy* 70: 167–192.

Freeman, A. and A. Kliman. 2000. "Two Concepts of Value, Two Rates of Profit, Two Laws of Motion." *Research in Political Economy* 18: 243–267.

Heinrich, M. 2013. "Crisis Theory, the Law of the Tendency of the Profit Rate to Fall, and Marx's Studies in the 1870s." *Monthly Review* 64(11). monthlyreview.org/2013/04/01/crisis-theory-the-law-of-the-tendency-of-the-profit-rate-to-fall-and-marxs-studies-in-the-1870s (accessed August 14, 2016).

Kim, D.-M. 2012. "Profit Rates: Current Cost vs. Historical Cost." *Marxism 21* 9(4): 248–262.

Kliman, A. 2012a. *The Failure of Capitalist Production: Underlying Causes of the Great Recession*. London: Pluto Books.

———. 2012b. "Response to Critiques of *the Failure of Capitalist Production*." *Marxism 21* 9(4): 263–315.

———. 2014. "The Whiggish Foundations of Marxian and Sraffian Economics." *Cambridge Journal of Economics* 38(3): 643–661.

Kliman, A. A. Freeman, N. Potts, A. Gusev, and B. Cooney. 2013. The Unmaking of Marx's *Capital*: Heinrich's Attempt to Eliminate Marx's Crisis Theory. http://papers.ssrn.com/sol3/papers.cfm?abstract_id=2294134 (accessed August 14, 2016).

Kliman, A. and A. Freeman. 2000. "Rejoinder to Duncan Foley and David Laibman." *Research in Political Economy* 18: 285–293.

Lager, C. 1998. "On the Notion of the Rate of Profit." *Review of Political Economy* 10(4): 447–458.

Laibman, D. 1999. "Okishio and His Critics: Historical Cost versus Replacement Cost." *Research in Political Economy* 17: 207–227.

———. 2000. "Two of Everything: A Response." *Research in Political Economy* 18: 269–278.

Marx, K. 1973. *Grundrisse: Foundations of the Critique of Political Economy.* London: Penguin Books.

———. 1989. *Karl Marx, Frederick Engels: Collected Works*, Volume 32. New York: International Publishers.

———. 1991a. *Capital: A Critique of Political Economy*, Volume 3. London: Penguin Books.

———. 1991b. *Karl Marx, Frederick Engels: Collected Works*, Volume 33. New York: International Publishers.

Norton, B. 2001. "Reading Marx for Class." In *Re/Presenting Class: Essays in Postmodern Marxism*, J.-K. Gibson-Graham, S. A. Resnick, and R. Wolff, eds., 23–55. Durham, NC: Duke University Press.

Okishio, N. 1961. "Technical Changes and the Rate of Profit." *Kobe University Economic Review* 7: 85–99.

———. 2001. "Competition and Production Prices." *Cambridge Journal of Economics* 25(4): 493–501.

Robinson, J. 1941. "Marx on Unemployment." *Economic Journal* 51: 234–248.

Roemer, J. 1981. *Analytical Foundations of Marxian Economic Theory.* Cambridge: Cambridge University Press.

Sweezy, P. M. 1970. *The Theory of Capitalist Development: Principles of Marxian Political Economy.* New York: Modern Reader Paperbacks.

22

BUSINESS CYCLES

Short-term Dynamics

Erdogan Bakir and Al Campbell

Introduction

Since at least the middle of the 1800s, since long before modern national accounting was developed, it has been universally recognized that a characteristic of developed capitalist economies is that periods of output growth alternate with periods of contraction. Originally called "trade cycles," these repeating expansions and contractions came to be known as "business cycles" by the second half of the 20th century. The term is somewhat unfortunate in the sense that there is neither theoretical nor empirical support for these expansions/contractions having the regularity of repetition suggested by the word "cycle," but it is nevertheless the term that has come to be universally used for this characteristic of capitalism.

Marxist economics understands capitalism to be driven by the self-expansive nature of capital, effected through its pursuit of profits.[1] This makes both the theoretical and empirical study of the rate of profit central to Marxism's understanding of the functioning of the capitalist system and, of particular importance for this article, to the behavior of its business cycles.

The connection of the rate of profit to business cycle fluctuations in the growth of output occurs primarily through several influences on investment, both as a "push" and a "pull." On the one hand, given that the driving force of capitalism is the pursuit of profits, higher rates of profit constitute greater motivation to invest. This causes an increased rate of growth of output in two ways. First, investment is the most variable of the three standard components of total demand: consumption, government spending and investment. Any increases in demand usually, excepting a rigid supply constraint, increases output and does so beyond its own magnitude through the well-known multiplier effect. Second, real investment occurs through new capital equipment (or sometimes directly through improving the process of production) with increased labor productivity, again increasing output. On the other hand, increased profits provide an increased amount of capital available to be invested, to be thrown back into the circuits of capital. However, the post-2009 weak expansion in the U.S. is a striking current reminder that this push-effect of increased available capital to invest has a complex relation to the profit rate. Despite large amounts of capital available for reinvestment because of the high rates of profits on existing productive capital, real investment and hence growth has remained low because capital does not perceive opportunities for high profits on new productive investment. Hence capital is simply "sitting on" large reserves of potentially investable capital or investing them only in financial assets, waiting for conditions to change to where it can get higher rates of return on real investment, thus yielding the current weak output growth.

While Marx and Engels and subsequent Marxists for almost a century certainly noted that business cycles existed, their discussions of them were almost always only in relation to their central concern of capitalist crises.[2] Two positions were dominant in the popular Marxist discourse. In the one, each business cycle was a crisis, and as capitalism continued to develop and in particular as capital continued to accumulate, each business cycle would have a tendency to be a more and more severe crisis. Eventually this would generate a crisis severe enough so that the working class, given its particular state of organization and level of consciousness, would act in response to the crisis and overturn capitalism. In the other common Marxist argument, business cycles were not considered to be crises. Rather, they were understood to be the way capitalism (temporarily) resolves its crises, by liquidating enough capital to create the conditions for the resumption of the accumulation of capital. The point here is not that these two positions are irreconcilable, which they aren't. The point is rather that in the late 1970s when the dominant modern frame for Marxist empirical/ theoretical considerations of business cycles that this article will discuss was first developed, the basic nature of the relation between business cycles and crisis theory was a contested issue. From this the frame that was developed then was consciously intended to address both business cycles and crisis theory, and almost all Marxist works on business cycles continue to today to have their implications for capitalist crises as an important concern. While the business cycles and crises must not be misunderstood as being a single issue, it remains true today that an article about "Marxist business cycle theories" cannot be written without reference to Marxist crisis theories.

Marxist Business Cycle Theories

As noted in the introduction, almost all the early work that was to later become the basis for Marxist business cycle theories was done as crisis theories. As such, the focus was on the fall in the rate of profit in each cycle. To have a cycle, one of course needs to also explain what can cause a falling profit rate to reverse and start rising. Basically each theory of the cause for a falling rate of profit when extended to business cycles just went on to add that the cyclical upturns were caused by a reversal of the conditions that caused the cyclical downturns, as will be further discussed below. Hence the starting point for the modern Marxist discussion of business cycles was the then-current Marxist theories of crises, theories of a falling rate of profit.

Early Marxist crisis theories developed three different causal explanations for the falling rate of profit:[3] rising organic composition of capital, overproduction/underconsumption, and a wage squeeze. In his seminal papers for modern Marxist business cycle research, Weisskopf (1978, 1979)[4] introduced the following simple formula as useful for empirically/theoretically considering the dominant crisis theories and then discussed at length what it indicated about those theories.

$$r = \frac{P}{K} = \frac{P}{Y} \times \frac{Y}{Y^*} \times \frac{Y^*}{K} \tag{1}$$

where r is the rate of profit, P is total profits, Y is net output, K is the capital stock and Y* is the potential output that could be created with the existing K. We will call the terms P/Y the profit share, Y/Y* the capacity utilization and Y*/K the potential output-capital ratio.

The basic concept of the rising organic composition of capital argument is that over time capitalism keeps increasing the amount of capital it uses for a given amount of labor and therefore for a given potential output. Equation 1 shows that if the direct effect of such an increase in K on the potential output-capital term (Y*/K) is greater than any secondary effects the change in K causes in the terms P/Y and Y/Y*, the profit rate will fall. Similarly, overproduction/underconsumption[5] implies that there is not enough demand for producers to supply the output that they could create, and that therefore they will lower production below potential production causing a fall in the rate of profit from a decline in the actual capacity utilization (Y/Y*). Finally, if we consider profits broadly so they are everything not paid to workers as wages (so taxes, rents, interest payments and so on are all just considered transfers of profits from where they are produced to someone else), then by definition net output is just the sum of wages and profits, $Y = W + P$. With this we see that if total wages (W) increase[6] the rate of profit falls from a decrease in the profit share (P/Y).

As Weisskopf pointed out in his original paper, all the various concepts (or any combinations of them) were logically consistent with driving business cycles. What actually drove the various cycles (or their secular trend) "can therefore only be made with reference to specific historical circumstances, and by means of an analysis of the empirical evidence." (Weisskopf 1978, 256) As with any scientific theory about the real world, once one has eliminated logically inconsistent alternatives, further theoretical understanding of what is being considered is linked to empirical observation (but not reducible to it—"facts" do not "speak for themselves").

Empirical Research and Further Development of Marxist Business Cycle Theories

The basic approach presented by Weisskopf in his seminal papers has been followed, and significantly further developed, by the majority of Marxists who have subsequently done empirical/theoretical work on the profit rate.[7] It has become the most common (though not universal) approach to Marxist empirical studies of the rate of profit. The largest and best known part of such work remains concerned with the secular behavior of the profit rate.[8] Among the works in this tradition investigating the U.S. economy[9] are Duménil, Glick and Rangel (1984, 1987); Michl (1988); Wolff (2001, 2003); Duménil and Lévy (2002a, 2002b, 2004a, 2011); Brenner (2002); Harvey (2005); and Glyn (2006). A very few studies used this framework for its other purpose of considering the behavior of capitalist business cycles themselves, including Hahnel and Sherman (1982); Henley (1987); a series of works by Goldstein in the late 1990s (1996, 1999, 2002); Bakir (2006, 2015); Bakir and Campbell (2006); and Cámara Izquierdo (2013).

Two issues are always key in determining the nature of empirical results that one gets when investigating theoretical issues: what particular combinations of categories of real-world data one uses to represent the theoretical categories involved, and what particular data sets one uses for the categories of real-world data that one has chosen to use. The many variations on these issues in the works of the researchers just referred to generally leave most results qualitatively the same, and hence support similar theoretical conclusions. A few procedures adopted by small minorities of empirical researchers yield qualitatively different results, and from those some qualitatively different theoretical conclusions. Given both the intention of this article and its space limitation, we will present our own empirical results as "broadly representative" of the majority of the empirical work on U.S. business cycles, and use it to indicate theoretical conclusions that can be made about the nature of U.S. business cycles. The technical details of our specific treatment are presented in Bakir (2015). We end this section by discussing some of the treatments of concepts that yield qualitatively different results from the "generalized majority" position.

The quality of U.S. government economic data involved in computing a national private rate of profit[10] dramatically improved after WWII, and hence all the work referred to above considers a time frame from then until the time of the study. Considering a business cycle to be from trough to trough, the first postwar cycle started in 1949. When Weisskopf published his work he was able to study five cycles up to 1975. Using quarterly data, figure 1 summarizes profit rate behaviors of the U.S. economy through the beginning of the 11th cycle that we are in presently. The vertically striated background sections indicate the B phases in each cycle (explained below), with the recessions as defined by the National Bureau of Economic Research's Business Cycle Dating Committee being the periods following them to the end of the cycle.

Figure 1 immediately presents visually the most important broad result of Marxist empirical studies of business cycles (the dark vertical lines separate the cycles), strong support for the Marxist understanding of them as profit rate driven. Almost without exception,[11] each cycle consists of three phases. In the first phase called A, the profit rate is rising and output is expanding. The rising profit rate serves as both "push" and "pull" for increased investment that increases growth, as explained in the introduction. In phase B (indicated by background light vertical lines) the profit rate stops rising and starts to fall (which will be discussed further below) while output continues to grow. The extended nature

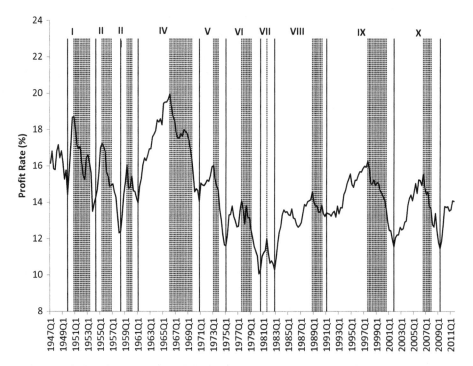

Figure 1　Profit Rate in the Nonfinancial Corporate Sector in the Post-war Business Cycles

of the process of reducing investment because of the fall in the rate of profit and the lag of the effects of reduced investment on growth together yield the continued though slowing growth in this phase. Eventually the effects of the falling rate of profit cause growth to first stop and then reverse, initiating phase C characterized by a continued fall in the rate of profit and an output contraction (recession). A phase A of a new cycle is initiated when the fall in the rate of profit and its effects on the economy have proceeded far enough to create the conditions for the rate of profit to once again begin to rise.

The empirical support for the Marxist explanation of the business cycle output downturn in phase C of each cycle as caused by the preceding fall in the rate of profit in phase B immediately posed the question: what causes the rate of profit to begin to fall in phase B of each cycle? As discussed in the introduction, three explanations for a falling rate of profit (be it a secular fall, or our concern in this article, the business cycle downturns) were dominant in the Marxist discourse in the 1970s. Weisskopf's empirical work found that for the five pre-neoliberal business cycles which he could study, a rise in the organic composition of capital proxied by the potential output/capital ratio (Y*/K) contributed very little to the phase B profit rate downturn, the realization failure proxied by the capacity utilization (Y/Y*) contributed only moderately, and a wage squeeze (which he referred to as the rising strength of labor, unfortunately, as indicated above) proxied by the wage share (W/Y) was by far the major contribution.

Since a "stylized fact" of neoliberalism is that labor lost power to capital (everywhere, but particularly in the U.S.), would one expect that a wage squeeze could no longer cause business cycle downturns after the full onset of neoliberalism? In fact the dominance of the rise of the wage share (W/Y) as the cause of the business cycle downturns remained true going into the neoliberal period, but what caused this continued dominance changed economically in a fundamental way in accord with the new neoliberal economy.

Bakir and Campbell (2006) and Bakir (2015) evince in a detailed empirical presentation the important continuity and the important change in the operation of the business cycle in the U.S. under neoliberalism. What remained the same as in the earlier post-WWII period was that of the three factors discussed above, the phase B fall in the rate of profit that leads to the later cyclical downturn in output was dominated by the fall in the profit share (P/Y), or equivalently (as indicated above), by the rise in the wage share (W/Y).

To understand the change in the business cycle dynamics, it is necessary to separate the price indices from the real quantitates.

$$\frac{W}{Y} = \frac{\omega L}{Y} = \frac{p_w}{p_y} \times \frac{w}{y/L} \tag{2}$$

where W, Y, ω, and L are as defined above, p_w and p_y are the wage and output price indices, y is the real output, and w is the average hourly real wage.

Weisskopf had already noted that both the ability of workers to gain significantly greater real wage gains than real productivity gains and the price effects contributed to phase B profit downturns. What he did not stress was that the real effects were consistently more important than the price effects, notwithstanding that the latter were not negligible. And of course what he could not have noted then was that exactly this was to reverse under neoliberalism, with price effects becoming more important than real effects. Hence under neoliberalism, despite the cyclical downturn continuing to come from an increased wage share, this now involved a very different economic content in that it no longer represented important real wage gains for

Table 1 Growth Rates of Wage Share and Its Component Variables in Phase B of Each Cycle (%)

					Cycles				
	I	*II*	*III*	*IV*	*V*	*VI*	*VIII*	*IX*	*X*
W/Y	2.5	2.4	2.0	1.7	2.6	2.4	0.9	2.1	2.6
p_w/p_y	1.1	−1.3	0.7	0.6	0.8	1.2	1.4	1.6	1.5
w/(y/L)	1.4	3.7	1.3	1.1	1.7	1.2	−0.4	0.5	1.2
w	3.0	4.1	3.1	2.5	−0.6	0.7	−1.2	3.5	1.8
y/L	1.6	0.4	1.8	1.4	−2.3	−0.5	−0.8	3.0	0.6

workers. This change is consistent with the general stylized fact of a weakened labor movement under neoliberalism.

Table 1 indicates how the phase B increase in the real wage to productivity ratio w/(y/L) dominated the price effect p_w/p_y for cycles I-V during the post-WWII compromise period, and how that was subsequently reversed. The well-known attack on real-wage growth that began in the early 1970s is already apparent in Table 1, but the domination of the real effects over the price effects continued in the first of the two 1970s transitional cycles, cycle V, because of the collapse in productivity and the continued slow growth of the price effects. By cycle VI at the end of the 1970s the continued restrained real wage growth and the staunched real productivity decline combined with the significantly increased price effects to give equal contributions from the price and real effects. After that price effects came to be more important than real effects in the subsequent three periods of fully consolidated neoliberalism, cycles VIII, IX and X.

We will end this section by discussing three conceptual issues involved in calculations of the rate of profit that cause minor to major changes in the empirical results.

i

Pre-tax vs post-tax profits. There is an important economic issue connected to this difference: what rate of profit are we interested in? That must depend on what question we are interested in answering. For example, if we are interested in determining what part of total output is captured by capital and what goes to workers, then because the state is part of capital's infrastructure for the operation of capitalism we would use pre-tax profits. If instead we are interested in what incentives and resources private capital have to throw capital back into the circuits of accumulation, then we would consider the post-tax profits.

Empirically these differ. For a graphical presentation of the persistent difference, see Basu and Vasudevan (2013, Figure 1). To a first approximation these look like the same graph simply offset by a constant. A more careful examination reveals a slight narrowing of the gap over the whole period due to the well-known reduction in corporate tax rates. This narrowing is presented more clearly in a graph by Bakir (2015, Figure 5) where the axes for the two graphs are shifted so the graphs roughly coincide from the mid-1980s onward, thus displaying a gap before that due to the higher corporate tax rates. As most work with the rate of profit concerns how it changes over time, the relatively constant gap means that for most purposes one will get the same qualitative economic results using either series. To the extent that most work with the profit rate is concerned with private capital's behavior and accumulation, after-tax profits are used somewhat more often.

ii

Including interest payments in profits vs excluding them. Nonfinancial businesses treat net interest payments as operating expenses, and so the after-tax profits given in the BEA's NIPA tables are the sum of dividend payments plus retained earnings. We and a number of other authors argue that the net interest payments are analogous to dividend payments and should be treated as a distribution of profits (to the capital they took loans from as opposed to the capital that owns the enterprise). Bakir and Campbell (2010, 336, 340) detail this treatment, including an indication of data sources for all these components and a graph of the relative contributions of these three components of profits over the years.

Empirically including or excluding interest payments makes much less difference in the level of profits than the issue of before vs after taxes. (See again Basu and Vasudevan, 2013, Figure 1). From WWII until the late 1960s the two series were practically identical. They then diverged some in the 1970s and 1980s due first to the high interest rates and subsequently to the increased indebtedness of nonfinancial corporate business. The gap was then narrowed with the reduction of interest rates in the 1990s and their further extreme reduction in the 2000s, and with non-financial corporate business reversing its debt problem by 2000 to become a net creditor (Bakir and Campbell, 2010, 332), though the gap was not entirely eliminated as it had been prior to the 1970s.

iii

Historical cost vs replacement cost of capital. Economically, we and the large majority (but not all) of Marxists doing empirical research on the profit rate now and over the last four decades (for example, all the ones mentioned in the introduction) would argue it does not make sense to use the historical cost of capital data. The capitalist decision-makers whose choices determine the dynamics of capital and from that (and the class struggle) the rate of profit make their choices based on the replacement cost of capital, so that is the relevant variable for considerations of the dynamics of the profit rate. Empirically using the historical cost gives a "falling rate of profit bias" (a clockwise rotation) in the presence of inflation of capital prices, which is significant for strong inflation and negligible for minimal inflation. For a detailed discussion of all the technical issues involved in this difference and their effects on the resulting profit rates, see Basu (2013).

Conclusion

Marxist theories' attention to the profit rate as centrally important for understanding the dynamics of capitalism is empirically supported as also being centrally explanatory for capitalist business cycles. Empirical work since the late 1970s has determined that it is the wage share (a "wage squeeze") more than the organic composition of capital (accumulation of capital relative to labor) or the capacity utilization (realization) that causes the cyclical downturns in the rate of profit that in turn cause the business cycles. But even when the wage squeeze was predominantly the result of real wages rising faster than real productivity in the long post-1966 decline in the profit rate that led to the neoliberal restructuring, this cannot be simply blamed on "greedy workers" as argued by conservatives. The 1971 to 1975 and 1975 to 1981 cycles that cover most of the fall were characterized by sharp reductions in wage gains compared to the preceding period, and in the former case an actual decline. To the contrary, the cause of the "wage squeeze" was a sharp decline in the growth of real productivity relative to the preceding period, negative in both cycles and dramatically so in the first. While the rise in the wage share continued to be the dominant cause of the cyclical downturn during the neoliberal period, it came to represent very different economics. The shift in the relative price indices of output and wages came to be the more important factor as opposed to the earlier domination of the gains in the real wage to productivity ratio. That this change occurred reflects the increased role of financial mechanisms in neoliberalism, and above all the decreased relative power of the working class.

Notes

1 While the majority of Marxists would endorse this terse statement, we consider it valuable to consider the critique of it by the Marxist school of thought associated with the Association for Economic and Social Analysis (AESA). We consider it a fact that not every action of every firm is always motivated by profit maximizing and seeking to accumulate their profits, and the AESA correctly argues against such "profit rate reductionism" which has appeared in some Marxist literature. We do consider that "on average," "over the long run," and "aggregated over firms and time" the pursuit of profit and accumulation does emerge from the other important factors as central. Hence while we accept "overdetermination" and "decentering" in the sense of a necessary rejection of "profit rate reduction-ism," we do not agree with the extension of that to what we consider to be a general position of this school of thought, that all factors need to be treated symmetrically, none prioritized for understanding the general behavior of capitalism. Resnick and Wolff (1987) comprehensively lays out the broad theoretical basis for this AESA position, Cullenberg (1994) applies it directly to the issue of the (falling) rate of profit, and Norton (1994) presents the arguments for this position in a particularly well-written and accessible short article. This disagreement on the degree of importance of the profit rate to capitalism's performance is largely irrelevant for the focused topic of this paper, where we show empirically that without exception the downturn in business cycles since WWII involves first a downturn in profits and soon thereafter a downturn in output, and then discuss what factors are most important in those business cycle profit rate downturns.
2 This followed from the fact that early Marxists, including Marx, while they were careful to theoretically stress that a quantitative time frame for a crisis of capitalism linked to its transcendence could not be specified, all believed such a crisis was coming "soon" and hence focused their attention on understanding what such a crisis would involve.
3 The exact chronology of when each suggested explanation first appeared in the Marxists discussions is not important for this article and will not be addressed here for reasons of space. For works on Marxist crisis theories including disproportionality, which later disappeared as a generalized crisis theory, see Shaikh (1978), Perelman (1987) and Clarke (1994). On the emergence of these three strands as central by the 1970s, see among others Weisskopf (1979), Reuten (2002) and Bakir (2006). Of concern here is only that at the end of the 1970s when the approach to business cycle research described here arose, all three of the positions were supported by significant numbers of Marxists and as a result were then the object of an important ongoing debate.
4 Reading these papers underlines the intimate interconnection of the beginning of modern Marxist business cycle research and the existing crisis theories.
5 In a sense overproduction and underconsumption denote the same problem looked at from opposing sides; there is not enough demand to buy all the goods produced if production is at capacity. This is also often referred to in Marxist literature as a realization problem. However, they often carry slightly different connotations. Overproduction tends to focus on the growth of capital and from that productive capacity (why potential supply is greater than demand), while underconsumption tends to focus on things that reduce demand and hence why demand falls short of potential supply.
6 If we write $P/K = Y/K - W/K$, we can state this more carefully to say that if increases in wages cause any increase in output, the profit rate still falls as long as (which is almost always the case) the

increase in Y/K is less than the increase in W/K. This "wage squeeze" is also often expressed in both mainstream and Marxist literature in terms of the growth of the hourly wage rate (ω) and labor productivity (Y/L) (or the corresponding real terms to be discussed below), where L is the total labor hours: the profit share $P/Y = 1 - W/Y = 1 - \omega L/Y = 1 - \omega/(Y/L)$, so the profit share (and hence the profit rate as long as wage-induced changes in Y/Y* and Y*/K from the new wages are secondary) falls if the growth of the hourly wage rate is more than the growth of labor productivity. This adds a note of caution to calling something like the fall in the rate of profit at the end of the 1960s and early 1970s a "wage squeeze" with its implication of "greedy workers." This fall could as well result from a fall in the growth of labor productivity as from an increase in the growth of hourly wages. There was in fact a strong such fall at that time. This fall in the growth of labor productivity itself could result from either changed relations of production or simply a slowed increase from technological advances in capital.

7 Two fundamentally different Marxist approaches to business cycles and crises involving empirical work are much less broadly used and for reasons of space can only be indicated and not discussed here. Although Sherman (1991; Sherman and Kolk 1996) specifically presents his model as Marxist, numerous other commentators have argued it is actually essentially Keynesian. (e.g., Glombowski [1982]). Anwar Shaikh has argued for decades that capitalists determine the dynamics of the system on the basis of marginal profit rates as opposed to the profit rate, and has just released a comprehensive statement of his approach and his related empirical work (Shaikh 2016).

8 Cycles are sometimes considered in this literature in order to study the changes in the secular trend over time. Our purpose in discussing cycles is to investigate the cyclic behavior itself, as an aid to understanding the dynamics of capitalism.

9 Very similar procedures applied to other developed or underdeveloped countries generally yield qualitatively very different results. This is an area of comparative research that has hardly been started, determining if the differing results come from the differently defined operational variables (often due to different national accounting procedures) or if these truly represent significantly different business cycle dynamics for different capitalist countries, and if so what that means theoretically about the nature of world capitalism.

10 Weisskopf and many of the works in that tradition cited used the nonfinancial corporate sector as a proxy for the private capital sector, because the data was most complete for that sector and because it constituted roughly 70% of the total. Some of the later works cited above extended that to include the non-financial non-corporate sector. The data for the financial sector presents particular problems, and as far as we are aware there are only three works on this in this tradition in the literature; Duménil and Lévy (2004b), Bakir and Campbell (2013) and Bakir (2015).

11 Cycle VII was exceptionally short due to economic policies that caused the rate of profit to return to falling before the expansion would have led to its fall without those policies, and as a result the economy went right from phase A to phase C in that business cycle.

References

Bakir, E. 2006. "The Post-World War II Nonfinancial Corporate Business Rate of Profit in the United States: Cycles, Trends, and the Effects of Financialization." Ph.D. dissertation, University of Utah.

——. 2015. "Capital Accumulation, Profitability, and Crisis: Neoliberalism in the United States." *Review of Radical Political Economy* 47(3): 389–411.

Bakir, E. and A. Campbell. 2006. "The Effect of Neoliberalism on the Fall in the Rate of Profit in Business Cycles." *Review of Radical Political Economics* 38(3): 365–373.

——. 2010. "Neoliberalism, the Rate of Profit and the Rate of Accumulation." *Science & Society* 74(3): 323–342.

——. 2013. "The Financial Rate of Profit: What Is It, and How Has It Behaved in the United States?" *Review of Radical Political Economy* 45(3): 295–304.

Basu, D. 2013. "Replacement versus Historical Cost Profit Rates: What Is the Difference? Does It Matter?" *Metroeconomica* 64(2): 293–318.

Basu, D. and R. Vasudevan. 2013. "Technology, Distribution and the Rate of Profit in the US Economy: Understanding the Current Crisis." *Cambridge Journal of Economics* 37(1): 57–89.

Brenner, R. 2002. *The Boom and the Bubble*. London: Verso.

Cámara Izquierdo, S. 2013. "The Cyclical Decline of the Profit Rate as the Cause of the Crisis in the United States (1947–2011)." *Review of Radical Political Economics* 45(4): 463–471.

Clarke, S. 1994. *Marx's Theory of Crisis*. New York: St. Martin's Press.

Cullenberg, S. 1994. *The Falling Rate of Profit*. London: Pluto.

Duménil, G, M. Glick, and J. Rangel. 1984. "The Tendency of the Rate of Profit to Fall in the United States." *Contemporary Marxism* 9: 148–164.

——. 1987. "The Rate of Profit in the United States." *Cambridge Journal of Economics* 11(4): 331–359.

Duménil, G. and D. Lévy. 2002a. "The Field of Capital Mobility and the Gravitation of Profit Rates (USA 1948–2000)." *Review of Radical Political Economics* 34(4): 417–436.

——. 2002b. "The Profit Rate: Where and How Much Did It Fall? Did It Recover? (USA 1948-2000)." *Review of Radical Political Economics* 34(4): 437–461.

——. 2004a. *Capital Resurgent*. Cambridge, MA: Harvard University Press.

——. 2004b. "The Real and Financial Components of Profitability (United States, 1952–2000)." *Review of Radical Political Economics* 36(1): 82–110.

——. 2011. *The Crisis of Neoliberalism*. Cambridge, MA: Harvard University Press.

Glombowski, J. 1982. "A Comment on Sherman's Marxist Cycle Model." *Review of Radical Political Economy* 14(1): 42–49.

Glyn, A. 2006. *Capitalism Unleashed*. Oxford: Oxford University Press.

Goldstein, J. 1996. "The Empirical Relevance of the Cyclical Profit Squeeze: A Reassertion." *Review of Radical Political Economics* 28(4): 55–92.

——. 1999. "The Simple Analytics and Empirics of the Cyclical Profit Squeeze and Cyclical Underconsumption Theories: Clearing the Air." *Review of Radical Political Economics* 31(2): 74–88.

——. 2002. "The Profit Squeeze Is Supported by the PW Cycle Indicator." *Review of Radical Political Economics* 34(1): 75–77.

Hahnel, R. and H. Sherman. 1982. "The Rate of Profit over the Business Cycle." *Cambridge Journal of Economics* 6: 185–194.

Harvey, D. 2005. *A Brief History of Neoliberalism*. Oxford: Oxford University Press.

Henley, A. 1987. "Labour's Shares and Profitability Crisis in the U.S.: Recent Experiences and Post-war Trends." *Cambridge Journal of Economics* 11: 315–330.

Michl, T. 1988. "The Two-Stage Decline in U.S. Nonfinancial Corporate Profitability, 1948–1986." *Review of Radical Political Economics* 20(4): 1–22.

Norton, B. 1994. "Moses and the Prophets! Radical Economics and the Search for a Foundation." *Review of Radical Political Economics* 26(3): 111–118.

Perelman, M. 1987. *Marx's Crises Theory: Scarcity, Labor, and Finance*. New York: Praeger.

Resnick, S. A. and R. D. Wolff. 1987. *Knowledge and Class: A Marxian Critique of Political Economy*. Chicago: University of Chicago Press.

Reuten, G. 2002. "Business Cycles: Marxian Approach." In *Encyclopedia of Macroeconomics*, B. Snowdon and H. Vane, eds., 73–80. Cheltenham: Edward Elgar.

Shaikh, A. 1978. "An Introduction to the History of Crisis Theories." In *U.S. Capitalism in Crisis*, Union for Radical Political Economics, ed., 219–241. New York: Economics Education Project of the Union for Radical Political Economics.

——. 2016. *Capitalism: Real Competition, Turbulent Dynamics, and Global Crises*. Oxford: Oxford University Press.

Sherman, H. 1991. *The Business Cycle*. Princeton: Princeton University Press.

Sherman, H. and D. Kolk. 1996. *Business Cycles and Forecasting*. New York: Harper Collins College Publishers.

Union for Radical Political Economics (URPE), ed. 1978. *U.S. Capitalism in Crisis*. New York: Economics Education Project of the Union for Radical Political Economics.

Weisskopf, T. 1978. "Marxist Perspectives on Cyclical Crises." In *U.S. Capitalism in Crisis*, Union for Radical Political Economics, ed., 241–260. New York: Economics Education Project of the Union for Radical Political Economics.

——. 1979. "Marxian Crisis Theory and the Rate of Profit in the Postwar U.S. Economy." *Cambridge Journal of Economics* 3(4): 341–378.

Wolff, E. 2001. "The Recent Rise of Profits in the United States." *Radical Review of Political Economics* 33: 315–324.

——. 2003. "What's Behind the Rise in Profitability in the US in the 1980s and 1990s?" *Cambridge Journal of Economics* 27(4): 479–499.

23

NEOLIBERALISM

Alfredo Saad-Filho

Neoliberalism (also spelled neo-liberalism) defies simple definition. In the Marxian literature, it has been understood in four closely related ways: as a set of *ideas* inspired by the
Austrian and Chicago schools of economics and German Ordoliberalism and elaborated
under the umbrella of the Mont Pelerin Society; as a set of *policies, institutions and practices*
inspired and/or validated by those ideas; as a *class offensive against the workers and the
poor*, led by the state on behalf of the bourgeoisie in general or finance in particular; and as a
material structure of social, economic and political reproduction, in which case neoliberalism
is the mode of existence of contemporary capitalism or a system of accumulation.

The differences between these understandings of neoliberalism are symptomatic of the
distinct methodologies and viewpoints within contemporary Marxism, their relationship with
influential non-Marxist approaches in the social sciences, and the complexity of neoliberalism itself. From a Marxian perspective, these analytical tensions can be felt at three
interlocking levels.

First, all neoliberal experiences share significant commonalities; some are relatively
abstract and universal, for example the growing power of finance and the curtailment of
political democracy, while others are relatively concrete and (country-)specific, such as
privatization and the spread of non-governmental organizations into areas that, previously,
were the domain of state institutions. While these commonalities imply that neoliberalism
cannot be adequately described in purely contextual terms, they are also insufficiently
general or historically distinctive to define a new mode of production. Inevitably, then,
analyses of neoliberalism straddle across levels of abstraction within capitalism, including
(some understanding of) such basic concepts in Marxist theory as the commodity, value and
labor power all the way to conjunctural description, by way of specific understandings of
exploitation, class, competition, price formation, finance, the state and international trade.

Second, Marxist analyses are by definition systemic, and seek to encompass the economic, sociological, institutional, political, legal, cultural, ideological and other aspects of
neoliberalism. This necessarily includes how, why and to what extent the neoliberal
"reforms" have transformed economic and social reproduction after the disarticulation of
the Keynesian-social democratic compact in the leading capitalist economies, the paralysis
of developmentalism, the implosion of the Soviet bloc, the dramatic transformations in China
and the crises in the European periphery. This historically grounded and interdisciplinary

approach is both superior to and incompatible with the narrow focus provided by most traditional disciplines in the social sciences. Among its many advantages, it allows Marxist explanations to offer more comprehensive and logically coherent explanations of the origins of neoliberalism and its recurrent crises than rival interpretations can provide. Nevertheless, the contributions of those social science disciplines inevitably remain influential in the background. This helps to explain the distinct conceptualizations of the key features of neoliberalism observed in the Marxist literature and the diverse understandings of their articulation and relations of determination. It follows that Marxist analyses can more or less legitimately reach very different conclusions about the vitality of contemporary capitalism, its vulnerability to crisis, the scope for electoral politics, the feasibility of radical alternatives, and so on.

Third, while the schematic depiction of the key ideas underpinning neoliberalism can plausibly eschew the domain of the "international" by focusing, instead, on the realm of ideas or the description of stylized institutions, actually existing neoliberal experiences are completely inseparable from highly complex global processes, especially imperialism and globalization. From this angle, too, neoliberalism cannot be encapsulated into a soundbite: it can neither be defined purely conceptually, nor captured inductively through the description of historical experiences.

Identification of these analytical difficulties can help to contextualize the four Marxist understandings of neoliberalism identified above; it can also support claims for the potential superiority of Marxist views over rival explanations of neoliberalism. For example, while Marxist analyses are necessarily systemic, class-based and nested on a grand theory (in the sense of Mills 1959), competing interpretations tend to be either middle-range or descriptive, unsystematic and (sometimes despite appearances to the contrary, as in many varieties of Keynesianism) methodologically individualist.

Neoliberal Ideas

As a system of ideas, neoliberalism draws upon the contributions of a wide spectrum of variously talented, frequently inconsistent and sometimes spectacularly cantankerous writers, including Friedrich von Hayek, Ludwig von Mises, Wilhelm Röpke, Ludwig Erhard, Milton Friedman, James Buchanan, Gary Becker and Ayn Rand (Burgin 2012; Cahill 2014; Dardot and Laval 2013; Mirowski and Plehwe 2009; Stedman Jones 2012).

They argue, in profoundly dissimilar ways, that differently endowed property-owning individuals exchanging goods, services and (in certain cases) information in minimally regulated markets can allocate resources more efficiently than either democratic processes or state guidance. Their arguments seek to legitimize extreme versions of free-market capitalism, and they have frequently promoted US geopolitical interests either directly or indirectly. Unsurprisingly, they were welcomed by powerful interests. Many contributors to the neoliberal literature benefitted from substantial economic, political and institutional support received from private as well as public sources, which unquestionably enhanced the public visibility and political impact of their interventions (Birch and Mykhnenko 2010).

This propitious milieu nurtured several lines of criticism of Soviet-style socialism, Keynesianism, developmentalism and "excessive" democracy since the mid-twentieth century. They were loosely co-ordinated through the Mont Pelerin Society and the extensive networks of academic institutions, think tanks and *faux* "grassroots" associations established by the neoliberal lobby (Mirowski 2009). Some of those views were precariously articulated with a rapidly expanding body of neoclassical economic theory in the 1950s–60s through monetarism. After the disintegration of monetarism in the 1980s, in the wake of the failure of Friedmanite ideas to inspire effective policy-making in several advanced economies and the inability of monetarist writers to address the criticisms addressed to them, neoliberal ideas were strapped more or less awkwardly to different versions of "supply-side" and new classical economics, new Keynesianism and new institutionalism (Fine, Lapavitsas and Pincus 2001; Fine and Milonakis 2009; Milonakis and Fine 2009). In the late 1990s similar ideas were recycled in social democratic garb through the so-called Third Way, which was described in the Marxist literature as a position akin to "neoliberalism with a human face."

Closer examination reveals considerable tensions between the theories underpinning neoliberalism. For example, while the Austrian school emphasizes the inventive and trans-formative subjectivity of the individual and the spontaneous emergence of an increasingly efficient order beyond individual reason through market processes, neoclassical economics focuses on the efficiency properties of a static equilibrium achieved entirely in the logical domain on the basis of unchanging individuals, resources and technologies. Neither captures the political economy and moral philosophy associated with Adam Smith, despite an obsessive recourse to (different interpretations of) the "invisible hand" (Fine and Saad-Filho 2014). In turn, the inconsistencies of monetarism had been exposed in merciless detail by Marxist and other heterodox economists even before "early" neoliberal policymakers admitted their inability to identify or control the money supply and deliver macroeconomic stability and growth in the 1980s. Finally, the Third Way was analytically vacuous, and its fleeting renown was predicated on political opportunism and the willful abandonment of intellectual integrity. It dissolved into irrelevance faster than one could spell "triangulation" (a badge of political expediency rendered temporarily famous by US President Bill Clinton and UK Prime Minister Tony Blair) (Callinicos 2001).

The inconsistencies and policy failures associated with neoliberalism would swiftly have condemned rival heterodoxies to oblivion. In sharp contrast, the institutional sources of support available to the neoliberal literature ensured that it would expand relentlessly from its strongest base in economics to claim hegemony across a whole spectrum of neighboring social sciences. This literature has also promoted a populist understanding of "competitiveness" and "democracy" that has been deployed repeatedly, if incoherently, in order to validate selected policy reforms and repression against the opposition. In this discourse, competition is presented in the short-termist (Chicagoan) sense associated with the operation of financial markets (the closest real-world equivalent to "perfect competition"), while democracy is circumscribed to the (Hayekian) view of competition between shades of neoliberalism in the political markets. The significance of these ideas in the legitimation of the status quo and the neoliberal policy reforms has reinforced an idealist conception of neoliberalism both within and outside Marxism, in which social organization essentially derives from pre-existing ideologies. It incorrectly follows (see below) that social and economic transformation must be driven by ideational change (Cahill 2013).

Policy Shifts and Institutional Changes

Marxist studies have shown that the neoliberal policies implemented through Reaganism, Thatcherism and the (post-)Washington Consensus are largely inspired by the Chicago School, and they are supported by five ontological planks (Saad-Filho and Johnston 2005). First, the dichotomy between markets and the state, implying that these are rival and mutually exclusive institutions (significantly, this dichotomy is rejected by the Ordoliberals). Second, the assumption that markets are efficient while state intervention is by definition wasteful because it distorts prices and misallocates resources (in comparison with what an ideal market would have done), induces rent-seeking behavior and fosters technological backwardness. Third, the belief that technological progress, the liberalization of finance and capital movements, the systematic pursuit of "shareholder value" and successive transitions to neoliberalism around the world have created a global economy characterized by rapid capital mobility within and between countries and (an ill-defined process of) "globalization." Where they are embraced, rapid growth ensues through the prosperity of local enterprise and the attraction of foreign capital; in contrast, reluctance or "excessive" state intervention (however it may be determined) drives capital, employment and economic growth elsewhere (Kiely 2005). Fourth, the presumption that allocative efficiency, macroeconomic stability and output growth are conditional upon low inflation, which is best secured by monetary policy at the expense of fiscal, exchange rate and industrial policy tools. Fifth, the realization that the operation of key neoliberal macroeconomic policies, including "liberalized" trade, financial and labor markets, inflation targeting, central bank independence, floating exchange rates and tight fiscal rules is conditional upon the provision of potentially unlimited state guarantees to the financial system, since the latter remains structurally unable to support itself despite its escalating control of social resources under neoliberalism.

Marxist analyses have also shown that the neoliberal policy reforms are usually implemented through a two-stage process (Fine and Saad-Filho 2014). The first (transition or shock) phase of neoliberalism requires forceful state intervention to contain labor, disorganize the left, promote the transnational integration of domestic capital and put in place the new institutional framework. The second (mature) phase focuses on the stabilization of the social relations imposed in the earlier period, the consolidation of financial sector control of resource allocation, state management of the new modality of international integration of production, and the introduction of specifically neoliberal social policies both to manage the deprivation created by neoliberalism and to reconstitute society along neoliberal lines (see below). All of them require extensive regulation, despite the rhetorical insistence of all manner of neoliberals on the need to "roll back" the state.

Marxist critiques of these policies and their institutional framework have offered rich insights about the features and repercussions of the neoliberal transition in various countries. However, neoliberalism cannot be reduced to a collection of policies, which would suggest that a multiplicity of discrete policy initiatives may be sufficient to reverse or even transcend neoliberalism. Policy changes are certainly essential, but the scope for such changes can be questioned in the light of the political means available to the left, the strength of the coalitions potentially committed to them, and the scope to drive the required distributional, regulatory and policy reforms given the neoliberal transformation of the state in recent decades. None of these can be adequately assessed without a prior understanding of the systemic features of neoliberalism and the transformations that it has wrought on class relations and institutions and the processes of economic and social reproduction.

Classes and Class Struggle

Marxism is intimately wedded to class analysis through its logical structure, historical development and unique commitment to the abolition of capitalism by means of communist revolutions led by the working class. Class analysis has informed Marxian interpretations of neoliberalism in two ways.

On the one hand, Marxian studies of neoliberalism are overtly informed by a class perspective. This explains their focus on the modalities of exploitation emerging through financialization, globalization and the neoliberal reforms, including the "flexibilization" and intensification of labor, the limitation of wage growth, the rollback of collective bargaining and the changes in the welfare regime and how they have affected the workers, women, minorities, immigrants, and so on. Marxian and closely related analyses have also examined the effects of privatization and the appropriation of the "commons" (i.e., areas where property rights were either absent or vested upon the state) (Harvey 2005), and the destructive consequences of the financialization of social reproduction for the working class (Krippner 2011; Montgomerie 2009). And Marxian analyses have illuminated the destabilizing implications of neoliberalism and its propensity to generate macroeconomic crises that penalize disproportionately the working class and the poor (Duménil and Lévy 2011; McNally 2014).

On the other hand, Marxist political economy directly informs political activism by shedding light on the limitations and contradictions of neoliberalism and suggesting how mass action can disrupt the reproduction of neoliberal societies. In doing this, Marxism supports the search for an alternative future in which the vast majority can realize their potential beyond the systemic constraints imposed by the contemporary form of capitalism.

In both cases, Marxian approaches rightly show that analyses of neoliberalism and the conditions for transcendence must take into account the power relations embodied in the structure of society, the state, production, technology, trade and finance. However, taken to the extreme this approach might suggest that neoliberalism is a "capitalist conspiracy" against the workers, in which case there would be nothing systemic or historically specific about it (since capitalists and the state have always conspired against the workers). Alternatively, they could also be read as implying that "things were much better" under previous systems of accumulation (Keynesian, developmentalist, and so on), in which case they should, in principle, be restored.

These conclusions would be illegitimate. First, the Marxist literature demonstrates that the key features of neoliberalism are articulated systemically; they were not designed arbitrarily by right-wing political parties, libertarian think tanks or more or less secretive debating societies (Mont Pelerin, Bilderberg and Davos, among others) and they cannot be unpicked or reversed at will. Second, even if the superiority of previous systems of accumulation in terms of growth, employment or distribution could be demonstrated, this does not imply that they could be revived. After all, there were material reasons behind their decline; moreover, if they were so obviously superior from the point of view of capital the capitalists themselves—currently enjoying much greater power than before—would already have prompted the reversal of history. This implies that neoliberalism offers distinctive advantages to capital beyond reformist demands for growth, full employment or distributional improvements. Finally, and more interesting from a Marxist perspective, there is no reason why the aspirations of the working class should be circumscribed by those earlier systems of accumulation, as if they represented the best of all possible worlds.

Neoliberalism, Financialization and Globalization

Most Marxist analyses insist that financialization is the defining feature of accumulation under neoliberalism and that it has driven the restructuring of the global economy since the 1970s. Financialization has been described in different ways, but in essence it expresses the control of interest-bearing capital (IBC) upon the allocation of social resources and social reproduction more generally, through distinct forms of fictitious capital (Fine 2013–14). These processes have been buttressed by extensive institutional transformations expanding and intensifying the influence of finance over the economy, ideology, politics and the state (Duménil and Lévy 2004; Panitch and Gindin 2012).

The prominence of finance under neoliberalism cannot be attributed to a "distortion" of pre-existing competitive or industrial capitalism or to a financial sector "coup" against productive capital, as if finance were an independent sector that, in the late 1970s, managed to wriggle itself into a lording position over capitals which it must, ultimately, also be parasitical upon. For finance is not merely the pool of liquid capital held by the financial institutions, standing in opposition to the "real" (productive) capital metaphorically stuck to the ground.

In neoliberal economies, transnationally integrated finance controls the allocation of resources, including the volume and composition of output and investment, the structure of demand, the level and structure of employment, the financing of the state, the exchange rate and the pattern of international specialization, and it restructures capital, labor, society and the state accordingly. As such, *finance has become the mode of existence of capital in general*, and its prominence expresses the subsumption of sectoral capitals by (the interests of) capital as a whole. These are both expressed and imposed through the regular operation of the financial markets, and through the institutions, rules and ideas attached to them. In policy terms, the prominence of finance implies that accumulation is not regulated by contingent sectoral coalitions but by the capitalist *class*. It also follows that there is no "antagonism" between production and finance under neoliberalism, and there should be no expectation that industrial capital might "rebel" against finance and push for the restoration of old systems of accumulation. Quite the opposite: industrial capital has become structurally embedded into IBC, and it reproduces itself according to the financial logic of the system of accumulation (Rude 2005; Panitch and Konings 2008; Saad-Filho 2008; 2011).

The structurally dominant position of finance under neoliberalism has supported the development of a whole array of instruments of fictitious capital, the expansion of purely speculative activities and the explosive growth of rewards to high-ranking capitalists and managers in every sector, especially finance itself, funded by a rising rate of exploitation. Financialization has also driven the restructuring of production through the transnationalization of circuits of accumulation, which is commonly described as "globalization."

These developments have recomposed the previous "national" systems of provision at a higher level of productivity at firm level, created new global(ized) production chains connected through transnational patterns of ownership, finance and circulation of the output, reshaped the country-level integration of the world economy, and facilitated the introduction of new technologies and labor processes while compressing real wages. Finally, financialization has also supported the reconstitution of US imperialism in the wake of the collapse of the Bretton Woods System, US defeat in the Vietnam War and the Iranian revolution (Gowan 1999, Kotz 2015). As a result, corporate power has increased almost everywhere, a globalized and US-led financial system has acquired unmatched policy influence, the political spectrum has shifted to the right, social democracy has imploded, left parties and mass organizations have shriveled, and the trade unions have been largely muzzled or disabled by legal and behavioral changes and shifting patterns of employment. Neoliberalism has also created an income-concentrating dynamics of accumulation that can be limited, but not reversed, by marginal (Keynesian) interventions.

In summary, while financialization expresses IBC control of the main sources of capital and the levers of economic policy in most countries, globalization reflects the centralization of those levers in US-led financial institutions and their regulation by US-controlled international organizations. These relations of mutual determination have established the material basis of neoliberalism (Albo 2008; Saad-Filho and Johnston 2005).

The structures of accumulation outlined above imply that neoliberalism cannot be adequately described simply through libertarian ideas or fanciful notions concerning the "withdrawal" of the state or the "expansion" of markets in general or finance specifically. Neoliberalism draws upon the power of the state to impose, under the ideological veil of non-intervention, the hegemony of globalized finance in each area of social life, not least in production itself, and it requires the state to drive, underwrite and manage the internationalization of production and finance in each territory. The ensuing—typically *neoliberal*—modality of social reproduction is the historically specific mode of existence of contemporary capitalism, or the dominant system of accumulation. It encompasses the currently dominant forms of production and employment, international exchanges, the state, ideology and the mode of reproduction of the working class.

At a further remove, neoliberalism has redefined the relationship between the economy, the state, society and the individuals. It has constrained the latter to give their lives an entrepreneurial form, subordinating social intercourse to economic criteria, and has nullified the previous structures of political representation. The ideology of self-responsibility has been especially significant since it is antagonic with any form of working class agency or culture: it deprives the citizens of their collective capacities, values consumption above all else, places the merit of success and the burden of failure on isolated individuals, and suggests that the resolution of every social problem requires the further individualization and financialization of social intercourse.

Contradictions and Limitations

Neoliberal ideology is too fragmented to provide a coherent representation of society. It offers, instead, a populist discourse drawing upon poorly defined notions of "individual freedom," "competition" and "democracy" that justify a set of loosely articulated finance-(i.e., capital in general-)friendly state policies and practices giving neoliberalism a semblance of purpose in the realm of ideas and considerable resilience in practice. Those policies cannot be contested easily, since the neoliberal restructuring of the economy and society drastically narrows the scope for debates about economic policy.

Despite these strengths, neoliberalism remains limited by five contradictions identified in different strands of the Marxist literature.

First, the neoliberal restructuring of production introduces mutually reinforcing policies that dismantle the systems of provision established previously (which are defined, often *ex post*, as being "inefficient"), reduce the degree of coordination of economic activity, create socially undesirable employment patterns, feed the concentration of income and wealth, preclude the use of industrial policy instruments for the implementation of socially determined priorities, and make the balance of payments structurally dependent on international flows of capital. In doing this, neoliberalism fuels unsustainable patterns of production, employment, distribution, consumption, state finance and global integration, and it increases economic uncertainty, volatility and vulnerability to (financial) crisis.

Second, financial sector control of economic resources and the main sources of capital allows it to drain resources away from production; at the same time, neoliberalism systematically favors large capital at the expense of small capital and the workers, belying its claims to foster competition and "level the playing field." As a result, accumulation in neoliberal economies tends to take the form of bubbles which eventually collapse with destructive implications and require extraordinarily expensive state-sponsored bailouts. These cycles include the international debt crisis of the early 1980s, the US savings and loan crisis of the

1980s, the stock market crashes of the 1980s and 1990s, the Japanese crisis dragging on since the late 1980s, the crises in several middle income countries at the end of the twentieth century, and the dotcom, financial and housing bubbles of the 2000s, culminating with the global meltdown that started in 2007.

Third, neoliberal policies are justified ideologically through the imperatives of "business confidence" and "competitivity." This is misleading, because confidence is elusive, ungrounded in reality, self-referential and volatile, and it systematically leads to the over-estimation of the levels of investment that will ensue from the pursuit of finance-friendly policies. In turn, the pursuit of competitivity amounts to the self-infliction of capital's imperatives ("flexibility," conformity, low wages, and so on), usually for someone else's profit.

Fourth, neoliberal policies are not self-correcting. Instead of leading to a change of course, failure to achieve their stated aims normally leads to the deepening and extension of the "reforms" with the excuse of ensuring implementation and the promise of imminent success this time around.

Fifth, neoliberalism is inimical to economic democracy and it hollows out political democracy. The neoliberal discourse and practice of TINA (There Is No Alternative) blocks the political expression of dissent and feeds apathy, populism and the far right. This is the outcome of a neoliberal political project including a modality of democracy that isolates the political from the socioeconomic sphere, restricts democracy to the former, and limits democracy to voting in elections while, simultaneously, imposing a strongly illiberal agenda towards civil liberties and collective action. The crisis of this modality of democracy has become evident through increasing global instability and the proliferation of "pseudo-" or "illiberal" democracies and "electoral authoritarian" regimes, "failed states," civil wars and "terrorism," especially in the postcolonial world. The limitations of conventional democracy have also raised concerns in the "advanced" West, where large numbers of people now reject ritualistic elections leading to power scarcely distinguishable political parties as a means of addressing their economic and political concerns. Despite their limitations, the "Arab Spring" and the emerging popular movements in crisis-hit Western economies have reiterated their aspiration for a substantive form of democracy, encompassing the "economic" domain that has been insulated by neoliberalism—that is, including substantive choices about the nature of social provision, the structure of employment, and the distribution of income (Ayers and Saad-Filho 2015).

The economic contradictions of neoliberalism, the incremental sclerosis of the political institutions regulating its metabolism and the inevitable corrosion of its ideological foundations make this system of accumulation vulnerable to *political* challenges. This does not imply that electoral strategies are sufficient (after all, the electoral system has been thoroughly contaminated by neoliberal capitalism), or that changes in social, industrial, financial or monetary policies can fulfill radical expectations. Quite the contrary: neoliberalism has repeatedly demonstrated its resilience both in practice and in the realm of ideas. But the demand for *the expansion and radicalization of political and economic democracy* can integrate widely different struggles, delegitimize neoliberalism and support the emergence of alternatives.

References

Albo, G. 2008. "Neoliberalism and the Discontented." In *Socialist Register* 44, L. Panitch and C. Leys, eds. London: Merlin Press.

Ayers, A. and A. Saad-Filho. 2015. "Democracy against Neoliberalism: Paradoxes, Limitations, Transcendence." *Critical Sociology* 41(4–5): 597–618.

Birch, K. and V. Mykhnenko, eds. 2010. "Introduction: A World Turned Right-Way Up." In *The Rise and Fall of Neoliberalism: The Collapse of an Economic Order?*, K. Birch and V. Mykhnenko, eds., 1–20. London: Zed Books.

Burgin, A. 2012. *The Great Persuasion: Reinventing Free Markets since the Depression*. Cambridge, MA: Harvard University Press.

Cahill, D. 2013. "Ideas-Centred Explanations of the Rise of Neoliberalism: A Critique." *Australian Journal of Political Science* 48(1): 71–84.

———. 2014. *The End of Laissez-Faire? On the Durability of Embedded Neoliberalism*. Cheltenham: Edward Elgar.

Callinicos, A. 2001. *Against the Third Way*. London: Polity Press.

Dardot, P. and C. Laval. 2013. *The New Way of the World: On Neoliberal Society*. London: Verso.

Duménil, G. and D. Lévy. 2004. *Capital Resurgent: Roots of the Neoliberal Revolution*. Cambridge, MA: Harvard University Press.

———. 2011. *The Crisis of Neoliberalism*. Cambridge, MA: Harvard University Press.

Fine, B. 2013–14. "Financialization from a Marxist Perspective." *International Journal of Political Economy* 42(4): 47–66.

Fine, B. and A. Saad-Filho. 2014. "Politics of Neoliberal Development: Washington Consensus and Post-Washington Consensus." In *Politics of Neoliberalism*, H. Weber, ed., 154–166. London: Routledge.

Fine, B. and D. Milonakis. 2009. *From Economics Imperialism to Freakonomics: The Shifting Boundaries between Economics and Other Social Sciences*. London: Routledge.

Fine, B., C. Lapavitsas, and J. Pincus, eds. 2001. *Development Policy in the Twenty-First Century: Beyond the Post-Washington Consensus*. London: Routledge.

Gowan, P. 1999. *The Global Gamble: America's Faustian Bid for World Dominance*. London: Verso.

Harvey, D. 2005. *A Brief History of Neoliberalism*. Oxford: Oxford University Press.

Kiely, R. 2005. *The Clash of Globalisations: Neo-Liberalism, the Third Way and Anti-Globalisation*. Leiden: Brill.

Kotz, D. 2015. *The Rise and Fall of Neoliberal Capitalism*. Cambridge, MA: Harvard University Press.

Krippner, G. 2011. *Capitalizing on Crisis: The Political Origins of the Rise of Finance*. Cambridge, MA: Harvard University Press.

McNally, D. 2014. *Global Slump: The Economics and Politics of Crisis and Resistance*. Oakland: PM Press.

Mills, C. W. 1959. *The Sociological Imagination*. Oxford: Oxford University Press.

Milonakis, D. and B. Fine. 2009. *From Political Economy to Economics: Method, the Social and the Historical in the Evolution of Economic Theory*. London: Routledge.

Mirowski, P. 2009. "Postface: Defining Neoliberalism." In *The Road from Mont Pèlerin: The Making of the Neoliberal Thought Collective*, P. Mirowski and D. Plehwe, eds., 417–456. Cambridge, MA: Harvard University Press.

Mirowski, P. and D. Plehwe, eds. 2009. *The Road from Mont Pèlerin: The Making of the Neoliberal Thought Collective*. Cambridge, MA: Harvard University Press.

Montgomerie, J. 2009. "The Pursuit of (Past) Happiness? Middle-Class Indebtedness and American Financialisation." *New Political Economy* 14 (1): 1–24.

Panitch, L. and S. Gindin. 2012. *The Making of Global Capitalism: The Political Economy of American Empire*. London: Verso.

Panitch, L. and M. Konings, eds. 2008. *American Empire and the Political Economy of Global Finance*. London: Palgrave.

Rude, C. 2005. "The Role of Financial Discipline in Imperial Strategy." In *Socialist Register* 41, L. Panitch and C. Leys, eds. London: Merlin Press.

Saad-Filho, A. 2008. "Marxian and Keynesian Critiques of Neoliberalism." In *Socialist Register* 44, L. Panitch, C. Leys, G. Albo, and V. Chibber, eds. London: Merlin Press.

———. 2011. "Crisis in Neoliberalism or Crisis of Neoliberalism?" In *Socialist Register* 47, L. Panitch, G. Albo, and V. Chibber, eds. London: Merlin Press.

Saad-Filho, A. and D. Johnston. 2005. "Introduction." In *Neoliberalism: A Critical Reader*, A. Saad-Filho and D. Johnston, eds., 1–6. London: Pluto Press.

Stedman Jones, D. 2012. *Masters of the Universe: Hayek, Friedman, and the Birth of Neoliberal Politics*. Princeton: Princeton University Press.

24

FINANCIALIZATION

Dick Bryan and Michael Rafferty

Financialization is one of those terms that came in the 1990s with a rush of popularity. Like its precursor, globalization, it describes something palpable in the world about the nature of economic and social change and the spread of financial practices, but it is a term without an agreed general meaning.

In Marxism, analysis of the social impact of finance has a much longer tradition. This entry looks first at those antecedents before focusing on the current meaning of "financialization," which is now prominent in describing the way the advanced capitalist economies have reorganized in response to crises, and especially the 2007–8 global financial crisis.

Theoretical Antecedents

Marx's writing is rich in its engagement with money and finance, and they are integral to his examination of the contradictions of capitalism and crisis. Money itself first appears in Marx as the fetishized form of alienated social relations between people and production and between classes, before it later becomes central to his exposition of value and capital accumulation. Accordingly, the money substance (gold, dollars, etc.) is always ambiguous, for it is treated as an objective unit of measure (things are equivalent in terms of money), but it can never exist outside the contradictory social relations it is used to describe (and measure).

When Marx framed money as the universal equivalent form of value, he vacillated between treating money as just another commodity (like gold) with its own value defined in terms of its costs of production, and a highly abstracted unit of measure, which could not be tied to the specifics of its own production costs. To explain trade, the former sufficed, for money merely converted the value of one good into another, and the money commodity is really a proxy for a unit of socially necessary labor time. But to explain accumulation in all its dimensions, money had also to cover paper documents (financial contracts) and bank deposits, none of which could adequately be thought about in terms of gold: finance had to be an abstraction from the domain of labor values. We can think of this as the difference between medium and mediator of exchange.

Reconciling these perspectives (money as cash in simple exchange and finance as credit over time) has always been a challenge for Marxism (and indeed for all theories of money).

Rosa Luxemburg (1913) notably sought to address this problem by making money a discrete "department" of the economy, distinct from the departments of producer goods and consumer goods. Others, invoking Marx's early writings on money, point to the irreducibility of these two dimensions of money, and focus on the tensions between the two as an expression of class contradictions (Žižek 2005).

Finance (or money over time, with a rate of interest) not only carries the ambiguities of money, but itself is integral to the circuit of capitalist reproduction, and hence to breaks in that circuit. In the first chapter of *Capital*, Marx talks of the problem for capitalist accumulation when there are breaks in the circuit because money is not converted into commodities (e.g. hoarding).

As Marx built his analysis of accumulation in Volumes 2 and 3 of *Capital*, these insights on breaks in the circuit became elaborated, by considering the role of money as a form of capital, alongside productive and commodity capital. Here, a central question is the role finance plays in capital accumulation: is it used to purchase extant "output" in the form of commodities for consumption (or existing financial and physical assets), or channeled specifically to the acquisition of assets for the future production of surplus value (interest-bearing capital, which lays claim to a share of the produced surplus)? The former is circulating titles to ownership, and hence producing nothing new; the latter produces new value (and surplus value). Further, interest-bearing capital itself can be bought and sold, creating the analytical problem that finance initially acquired to advance the production of new value may be transformed back into "mere" credit.

From the perspective of capital accumulation, credit not directed to promote new production of value was deemed "fictitious capital": fictitious in the sense that it would be double counting to measure both interest-bearing capital for accumulation and credit for the acquisition of existing assets (Fine 2013).

This distinction became critical to 20th-century Marxism. In the late 19th century Rudolf Hilferding was observing the institutional unification of industrial, mercantile and banking interests in Europe, and their capacity to use the state to build or protect monopolistic practices. In 1910 Hilferding published *Finance Capital*, focusing on the power of these combines to accumulate fictitious capital. Hilferding's work on finance directly influenced not only Lenin's writing on Imperialism, but also the "neo-Marxist" school of Monopoly Capitalism, which focusses on the combined capacity of big banks and big industry to create market control in capital accumulation and acquire wealth via monopoly rents, disconnected from the production of new value. More broadly, Hilferding's work opened up the question of how we think about connections within the capitalist class between industrialists who over-see the production of surplus value and financiers who fund investment, trade capital assets, and appropriate a share of that surplus. For Hilferding, this problem arose because of the institutional blurring of finance and industry, but it also raises conceptual questions about the relationship of different temporal (and spatial) moments of money and finance in the circuit of capital. Herein lies the basis of a distinction between "productive" (of surplus value) and "unproductive" (or "fictitious") capital, which features prominently in current debates about financialization.

Historical Antecedents

Following the end of the post-war Bretton Woods Agreement and the associated floating of currencies and increasing international financial mobility, many measures of financial activity, both by market value and by turnover, started increasing rapidly. The 1970s and especially the

1980s saw increasing international investment, both direct and portfolio. This period also saw the growth of "offshore" lending for such investment, known initially by its location as Eurofinance, where hard currency reserves of the Soviet Union and the surpluses of the oil-rich Middle Eastern countries were part of a growing global market for debt. Wholesale money market traders (then referred to as merchant banks, but now called investment banks and hedge funds) were borrowing at exchange rates and interest rates different from those available in the formal, national markets, creating both large volumes of lending and expanding opportunities for arbitrage (profiting between multiple prices for the same type of commodity or financial asset). These markets were also largely beyond the capacities of nation-state regulation, and any possible forms of regulation were being opposed by financial institutions that wanted to be part of this newly emerging frontier.

So just as the initial debates about globalization were about how capital mobility was breaking down nation-state capacities, so there was a variant of the financialization debate, concerning the way in which the increasing mobility of finance was a challenge to nation state capacities and whether financial mobility was contributing to the creation of a single, global market. This debate sits inside wider debates about the nature of neo-liberalism, and whether we are seeing a declining role and capacity of nation states, or states themselves, implementing policies to facilitate the development and global expansion of financial markets and institutions.

With the growth of off-shore financial markets and increasing capital mobility came the growth of awareness of interest rate and currency risks, and that awareness saw the initial growth of financial derivative markets and products. Arbitrage and risk trading were the catalyst of a process of financialization beyond the domain of borrowing and lending. Eurofinance markets may have offered lower interest rates, but borrowers carried foreign exchange risks on those loans. There was also the issue of borrowing at variable interest rates offshore, compared with fixed rates at home. The variable rates may have been lower, but they could change, and in the environment of the mid-1970s and 80s, those changes could be dramatic. Hedging these currency and interest rate risks was the domain of interest rate and foreign exchange futures, options, and swaps markets, and the development of these derivative markets from the 1970s proved critical to "financialization." Derivative markets could be framed as providing means to insure against currency and exchange risks (linking the present to the future) by means of diversifying risk exposures (via swaps) or locking in some or all of the risks of future exchange rate or interest rate movements. In the process, they provided opportunities to speculate on future price movements.

Concurrently, in the late 1970s there were two critical developments. One was the publication of the Black Scholes formula for pricing financial options, framed exactly in terms of how much an option should cost to hedge the value of a portfolio (or in this case, loan). The other was release by Texas Instruments of the first hand-held computer into which the Black Scholes formula could be loaded, giving the possibility of instant calculation of the cost of a hedge. Derivative trading expanded rapidly. But wherever there is a platform to hedge, there is also a platform to take speculative positions on the future. So people on the "other side" of a hedge could be an organization with the opposite risk, or it could be someone merely placing a bet on what the future holds. We will return shortly to issues of "speculation."

These derivative market transactions grew far more rapidly than the growth in the under-lying international loans, for to hedge any position requires active trading whenever circumstances change (and that became an ongoing threat for many internationally oriented firms). Moreover, because financial derivatives trade exposure to change in the value of an underlying asset but without necessarily trading the asset itself (the change in interest rates or exchange rates, but not the loan itself), derivatives offered a cheap and effective way to take financial positions: to move out of one position (for example a bet that the Euro would fall) meant simply placing a bet in the opposite direction (a bet that the Euro would rise), all of it escalating trading volumes.

This trading activity was also related to the growth of specialist sorts of banks (or branches of banks) and other financial institutions. Organizations like investment banks and hedge funds came into being precisely to trade risks for hedgers and speculators alike. These institutions also started trading on their own behalf (proprietary trading, which is now banned), using what they thought was their close knowledge of movements to take financial positions on trends in a range of financial and "real world" indicators.

The effect, from the 1980s, was a rapid growth in financial market activity. In this context a range of other factors also warrants mention, like the rise of private pension schemes, the privatization of publicly-owned assets and the dot-com boom (and bust). They all pointed to financial market activity growing much more quickly than the production of goods and services, investment in new plant and equipment, or the level of global trade.

These sorts of developments were associated with an interpretation of financialization as a "pattern of accumulation in which profit making occurs increasingly through financial channels rather than through trade and commodity production" (Krippner 2005).

With technology (software and hardware) changing rapidly, these volumes of trade continue to grow, with the current driver being algorithmic high frequency trading. Toscano (2013, 68) contends that "in 1945, US stock was held on average for four years; this dropped to eight months in 2000, two months in 2008, and 22 seconds in 2011." In a similar vein, the Bank for International Settlements (2013, 9) triennial survey of global foreign exchange markets estimates that daily turnover (in 2013 dollars) has increased from $1.5 trillion in 2001 to $5.3 trillion in 2013. For many Marxists this is evidence of financialization as the growth of fictitious capital.

Qualitative Change in Finance

Discrete from, but compatible with, the identification of the growth of finance-as-industry is an emphasis on finance-as-calculative-logic, and the way in which financial practices are coming to pervade the way in which decisions are made, in business, governments and wider society. This emphasis is at the core of the oft-cited definition of financialization provided by Gerard Epstein (2005) as . . . "the increasing importance of financial markets, financial motives, financial institutions, and financial elites in the operation of the economy and its governing institutions, both at the national and international levels."

There is a number of strands in the emphasis on finance as a calculative logic.

Shareholder Value

Shareholder value refers to the influence placed by shareholders (or the institutions that represent them) on corporate managers, pressing them to cut corners and invest shorter-term in order to get high profits and declare higher dividends for shareholders. In effect, shareholder value is an agenda both to intensify the rate of surplus value extraction and to bring forward profits based on yet-to-be-produced surplus.

Whilst companies owned by shareholders (called joint stock companies) started in the 1850s, shareholder value recognizes the shift from large personal family shareholdings to financial institutions as the primary nominal shareholders. (This has been a challenge for Marxian notions of a capitalist "class," for it de-personalizes the notion of capital ownership.) Shareholding institutions now have significant voting rights and their agendas are often short-term, looking for immediate share value appreciation rather than long-term growth. So the proposition is that pressure comes onto corporations to deliver short-term yield, and this flows through to pressures in the workplace, with demands for higher surplus value and more flexibility. With the rise of pension funds (sometimes called superannuation) there is the irony that it is increasingly workers' savings in the form of ownership stakes in corporate equities that become the source of pressure for the delivery of shareholder value. So it could be said that in "pension fund capitalism" workers have contradictory interests: as owners they seek to intensify their own exploitation in the workplace! For Resnick and Wolff (1987) this contradictory position can be understood as workers being involved in both a fundamental class process as producers and also in a subsumed class capacity as receivers of surplus value: the "worker" is variously constituted.

The shareholder value approach to financialization remains centered on the workplace, whilst other approaches extend beyond the workplace. Resnick and Wolff were significant in creating the conceptual space to theorize these multiple modes in which workers' engage capital accumulation.

Debt

Credit and debt have a long history. Marx wrote about "the credit system" as integral to the funding of investment in large-scale production. But credit and debt have changed markedly in the era of "financialization," and it could be argued that the category of "interest-bearing capital" used by Marx to explain a circuit of industrial capital, is now too general a category to permit precise explanatory capacity. The period since the 1990s has seen significant growth in debt-like instruments. In the corporate world these instruments have become quite complex, where the distinctions between debt and equity has been blurred, so they do not show up so much as bank debt on corporate balance sheets, but rather as a range of leveraged positions. Preference shares, for example, are part share (exposure to share price movements) and part debt (guaranteed "dividend"; no voting rights). These sorts of blended assets signal the importance of a more general term like "capital," for it signals that ownership in all its variations involves a command over the path of accumulation. Nonetheless, there are familiar versions of explaining the 2007–8 global financial crisis in terms of mounting debt and leverage.

It is more in relation to households that debt has acquired greater focus in the analysis of financialization. Whilst Marx had focused on households as the site of the reproduction of labor power, the focus in financialization is on growing mortgage, auto loan, student loan and credit card debt. Central to the rise of financialization from the 1980s has been the way in which debt has funded consumption in a period of stagnant or falling real wages (Resnick and Wolff 2010).

This recognition opens a number of dimensions of financialization. One is the notion of debt as a "second round" of increasing appropriation of surplus value—the first round in the workplace via falling wages in the context of increasing productivity; the second in the home, via the increasing amount of household income that is required to service debt (Lapavitsas 2013). Another dimension of financialization relates to predatory lending practices in which individuals and households are encouraged or pressed to undertake loans that they cannot afford to repay. Subprime lending, made infamous in the mortgage-backed securities defaults that triggered the global financial crisis, is the most conspicuous case here, but education debt, leaving university graduates with debts that will prevent them saving to acquire other assets, is a looming expression of this problem. For many, this is a form of life-long austerity, or expropriation.

Following the work of Graeber (2011), this new focus on debt as a generalized form of social subordination has fostered a politics of debt resistance, found in the "occupy" movement, leading to organizations like "Strike Debt" (2012).

Inside Finance

A newer frontier addressing the social and economic meaning of financial change involves going "inside" financial markets, institutions and the design of financial products. This has become the analytical domain of anthropologists, social theorists, geographers and "radical" accountants, who approach financialization and Marxian economics via micro-foundations, somewhat akin to Marx's interest in social and technological change in factories. In finance, this research involves ethnographies of trading rooms and markets, studies of the discourses of money, finance and financial data, and of the design of financial products like subprime loans, credit default swaps (CDSs) and collateralized debt obligations (CDOs). Collectively, the message of this body of analysis is that the details of finance need to be taken seriously in Marxian economics. It is insufficient to treat financial innovation by taxonomic judgments about the difference between credit and interest-bearing capital or ethical judgments about its social worth.

In the context of the global financial crisis, this body of work has sought to identify how products and financial practices operated so as to generate a crisis that no-one had predicted; at least not in terms of the details of the cascading crashes of mortgage-backed securities, CDOs and CDSs bringing down leading investment banks, creating a crisis of liquidity. In this context, some Marxists draw on Hyman Minsky's propositions about corporate propensities to increase their leveraging either by borrowing too much or carrying levels of debt that are only sustainable in boom times, and the financial instability that inevitably follows as boom conditions wain. Minsky's "financial instability hypothesis" is framed within a post-Keynesian framework, but its emphasis on financially-generated instability clearly resonates with some Marxist interpretations of the crisis-propensity of capitalism. It remains a point of contention whether Minsky and Marx provide (or could provide) a unified theory of crisis in relation to finance (e.g. Crotty 1986; Bellofiore and Halevi 2011) or whether Minsky's Keynesian roots constitute his and Marx's as competing theories (e.g. Ivanova 2012; Magdoff and Bellamy Foster 2009; Palley 2010).

Inside Financial Calculus: Issues for Marxism

Aside from specifics of the recent financial crisis, there is a number of strands to this "inside finance" analysis of financialization that resonate with Marxian economics.

One is the relation of financialization to households. There was mention above, in relation to debt, that households taking on more debt generally means an increasing proportion of wages going to debt repayments. The formal economic question here is about how this process relates to the value of labor power and to the measurement of surplus value. It leads to the question of how we think about accumulation and surplus value in relation to finance as well as production.

The wider social question is about how households (or individuals), in the context of an increasing array of risks that they now have to manage, are being incorporated into capital and accumulation in new ways, not just as borrowers but as financial subjects (what Resnick and Wolff would characterize as workers' subordinate class roles). Household contracts for credit, and also contracts for insurance and other services are locking households into financial processes and ways of calculating, generating new political pressures to be "financially compliant."

Framed this way, the global financial crisis was built on a failure of the financialized subject (working-class borrowers). Subprime loans leading up to the financial crisis revealed that households not complying with their contracts could crash the financial system. The response in the US, dating from before the actual crisis, was financial reforms that emphasized contractual compliance. Changes to bankruptcy laws in 2005, making it harder for individuals to default on loans, complemented President George Bush's aspiration of an "ownership society" built on notions of "individual responsibility." (Following the literature on governmentality [Foucault] the term "responsibilization" is applied to the expectation of households in relation to finance.) Whilst the agenda placed households in the calculative logic of capital and the vision of capital ownership for all, the effect was to place financial demands on workers that corporations, with limited liability, are not required to face.

For Marxists, this all points to a repositioning of households in relation to finance that resonates with the expectations of workers in the workplace in the 19th century in response to technological change and the need to deliver efficiency for capital. There Marx referred to the "real subsumption" of labor to capital. The recent reforms around households and finance could be thought of as an emergent shift toward the "real subsumption" of households to finance (Cowen 1976; Bellofiore and Halevi 2011).

There are direct consequences here for the understanding of gender relations within households, and caring roles within markets, as a direct consequence of financialization (Folbre 2012; Fukuda-Parr, Heintz and Seguino 2013; Adkins 2015).

Another strand of "inside finance" analysis addresses the social meaning of financial derivatives. This body of research is located in social theory and especially cultural studies, where a new body of scholars are entering debates about Marxian value theory via the analysis of money and finance (e.g. Grossberg, Hardin and Palm 2014). Randy Martin (2015) coined the term "the derivative form" or a "derivative logic" (in parallel with Marx's value form and logic of capital). Martin has explored how the heuristic of derivatives can be used to understand many aspects of social organization, from cultural processes, to university governance, to military strategy in the "war against terror." The essence of this analysis is the identification that the derivative involves two things: leverage (purchasing a large risk exposure on a small outlay) and decomposing things we have generally thought of as whole into a range of attributes. (In financial markets, the objective is to break down an equity or a loan or a portfolio into its elemental and different risks, so that each of these risks might be priced and traded discretely.) In relation to households, for example, we see that risks once borne by the state are now transferred to the household, and households are required to make decisions about what aspects of life and household assets should be insured, and how to leverage household positions for gain.

It will be apparent here that this framing of financialization leads to a quite distinctive version of class politics. This politics is not centered on class relations in the workplace, but class relations that engage no less consumer and financial relations: a politics that resonates strongly with the "occupy" movement and "Strike Debt," perhaps with a conception of finance broader than both of those movements, at least as they are popularly understood.

Debating Financialization

The social theory issues just identified suggest an opening up of Marxist categories to bring them into engagement with these new sorts of developments. Issues of class, production, money, labor and value all need to be re-evaluated in the light of financialization (although not just financialization). Marxism framed in the interpretation of Resnick and Wolff, focusing on the relationship between fundamental and subsumed class processes, in which people engage in multiple class and non-class relations, is designed to meet precisely these sorts of needs.

Conversely, there is a more formal Marxian economics which holds to the integrity of the conventional categories, and claims that "financialization" is best understood in terms of its impact on long-term trends in capital accumulation and trends in the rate of profit.

It is appropriate to start with the latter. For much of Marxian economics the critical theoretical issue is the distinction between economic processes that produce new (surplus) value and processes that circulate extant value. For processes that circulate value, profitability is derived from surpluses generated in productive activities. Hence the issue of financialization is the rise of a sector which has been highly profitable, yet deemed unproductive. Some suggest that there is something unsustainable about a shrinking proportion of economic activities carrying the mantle of producing the whole of surplus value. Onto this proposition are built analyses that contend that financial sector growth was a systematic policy of central banks to reflate the global capitalist economy in the aftermath of the end of the long boom in the 1970s: it was a speculative bubble that burst in the crisis of 2007 and 2008 (Brenner 2006; 2009).

When the focus is on aggregated trends in productive and fictitious or speculative capital, the issues addressed by those going "inside finance" are of at best second-order concern. The political focus for the conventional Marxist economists is instead on the in-built crisis propensities of an economy over-burdened by speculative finance (Duménil and Levy 2011). For some, especially in the context of financial crisis, this points to a necessary post-capitalist politics. For others there arises the politics of regulation, the need to "contain" finance, and turn banking into a servant of real investment as a sort of financial public utility. This latter proposal articulates with broader critiques of "neo-liberalism."

For those going inside finance, the technical processes of markets and institutions open up a challenge to a number of the popular propositions of contemporary Marxism, including challenging the dichotomy between production and speculation, and hence opening debate about the sources of surplus value production.

There are a number of themes here. One, broadly associated with autonomist Marxists Hardt and Negri (2004), challenges narrow conceptions of "production" in the factory and labor. Work inside finance could, in general, be depicted as "immaterial labor," whose contribution to accumulation is clear, but often indirect and invariably unmeasurable. This approach thereby challenges that Marxian economics which wants to clearly delineate productive from unproductive labor (conceptually and spatially) and capital involved in production as distinct from that in the circulation of value.

Another aspect of financialization, and one with echoes of Hilferding's concept of finance capital, is the growth of financial activities inside "industrial" firms. For many years auto and other durable goods manufacturers had credit divisions for their dealerships and to provide consumer credit. But we have seen most large industrial firms also develop specialist treasury functions to help them manage surplus cash and secure finance. These functions, akin to an investment banking role, have often gown into significant operations (see Froud, Sukhdev, Leaver and Williams 2006 for a significant study of General Electric). This development invokes the question of whether industrial firms have become speculative and risky. It also points to a need to grasp the increasing fluidity and fungibility of all capital.

A further theme points to the case that, since the end of Bretton Woods there has not been a socially agreed, stable invariant monetary unit of measure. Whilst the US dollar may have assumed the mantle, with the Federal Reserve cast as a central bank with a global agenda (Panitch and Gindin 2013), the dollar has been far from stable: it is no longer within the capacity of nation states to give stability to "their" currency or "their" interest rates. With the unit of measure itself determined within a market calculus, it is apparent that there are only relative measures of value. States seek to present relative values as absolute ones (Bretton Woods, the US dollar, LIBOR), but they can only carry the appearance of absolute measures for a finite time.

Risk trading in financial markets is the individual path available to simulate inter-temporal and cross-currency stability. Framed this way, perhaps financial trading is an (ultimately unsuccessful) attempt to *produce* individual stability, and here depicting it as an act of production is to challenge the dichotomy between production and speculation. Moreover, perhaps we need to think of risk itself as a commodity being produced and traded: this is, in effect, the nature of insurance (Bryan and Rafferty 2006).

These sorts of questions re-open how we think about value creation and measurement within Marxian theory, for they directly challenge a juxtaposition of production and speculation. They also point to a different class politics.

The conventional Marxist analysis of financialization points to agendas of confronting the capacities of banks (and states) to generate an environment in which returns to "speculation" exceed those of returns to "real production." There are then well-recognized debates between those who would reform finance and banking, and those who foretell the likelihood of further and deeper crises as credit-driven bubbles burst, which points to the need to transcend capitalist property relations.

For those who challenge the distinction between production and circulation, there is no such propensity as a long-term trend. The focus is instead on a politics of resistance to the subordination of individuals to the calculative agenda of capital articulated as financialization. In this agenda there is no strong reason to privilege a class politics centered solely on struggles in the workplace, for capital's domination of workers (now framed as households) can be seen as extending into more and more facets of life: work, consumption and finance. "Households" then stands as an inadequate term, for it does not innately define a class position, for all classes live in households. So is it a problem of language or of politics? Therein lies a political debate.

References

Adkins, L. 2015. "What Can Money Do? Feminist Theory in Austere Times." *Feminist Review* 109: 31–48.

Bank for International Settlements. 2013. "Triennial Central Bank Survey Foreign Exchange Turnover in April 2013." www.bis.org/publ/rpfx13fx.pdf (accessed August 14, 2016).

Bellofiore, R. and J. Halevi. 2011. "A Minsky Moment? The Subprime Crisis and the 'New' Capitalism." In *Credit, Money and Macroeconomic Policy: A Post-Keynesian Approach*, C. Gnos and L.-P. Rochon, eds., 13–32. Cheltenham: Edward Elgar Publishing.

Brenner, R. 2009. "What Is Good for Goldman Sachs Is Good for America: The Origins of the Present Crisis." https://escholarship.org/uc/item/0sg0782h#page-1 (accessed August 16, 2016).

——. 2006. *The Economics of Global Turbulence: The Advanced Capitalist Economies from Long Boom to Long Downturn, 1945–2005*. New York: Verso.

Bryan, D. and M. Rafferty. 2006. *Capitalism with Derivatives: A Political Economy of Financial Derivatives, Capital and Class*. Basingstoke: Palgrave Macmillan.

Cowen, M. P. 1976. "Capital and Peasant Households." Department of Economics, University of Nairobi.

Crotty, J. 1986. "Marx, Keynes, and Minsky on the Instability of the Capitalist Growth Process and the Nature of Government Economic Policy." In *Marx Keynes, and Schumpeter: A Centenary Celebration of Dissent*, D. Bramhall and S. Helburn, eds., 297–326. Armonk, NY: M.E. Sharpe.

Duménil, G. and D. Lévy. 2011. *The Crisis of Neoliberalism*. Cambridge, MA: Harvard University Press.

Epstein, G. 2005. "Introduction." In *Financialization and the World Economy*, G. Epstein, ed., 3–16. London: Edward Elgar.

Fine, B. 2013. "Financialization from a Marxist Perspective." *International Journal of Political Economy* 42(4): 47–66.

Folbre, N. 2012. *For Love and Money. Care Provision in the United States*. New York: Russell Sage Foundation.

Froud, J., J. Sukhdev, A. Leaver, and K. Williams. 2006. *Financialization and Strategy: Narrative and Numbers*. London: Routledge.

Fukuda-Parr, S. J. Heintz, and S. Seguino. 2013. "Critical Perspectives on Financial and Economic Crises: Heterodox Macroeconomics Meets Feminist Economics." *Feminist Economics* 19(3): 4–31.

Graeber, D. 2011. *Debt: The First 5000 Years*. Brooklyn, NY: Melville House.

Grossberg, L., C. Hardin, and M. Palm. 2014. "Contributions to a Conjunctural Theory of Valuation." *Rethinking Marxism* 26(3): 3006–3035.

Hardt, M. and A. Negri. 2004. *Multitude: War and Democracy in the Age of Empire*. New York: Penguin.

Hilferding, R. 1981 [1910]. *Finance Capital. A Study of the Latest Phase of Capitalist Development*. T. Bottomore, ed. London: Routledge & Kegan Paul.

Ivanova, M. 2012. "Marx, Minsky, and the Great Recession." *Review of Radical Political Economics* 45(1): 59–75.

Krippner, G. 2005. "The Financialization of the American Economy." *Socio-Economic Review* 3(2): 173–208.

Lapavitsas, C. 2013. *Profiting Without Producing: How Finance Exploits Us All*. London: Verso.

Luxemburg, R. 1951 [1913]. *The Accumulation of Capital: A Contribution to an Economic Explanation of Imperialism*. Edited by Dr. W. Stark. London: Routledge & Kegan Paul.

Magdoff, F. and J. B. Foster. 2009. *The Great Financial Crisis: Causes and Consequences*. New York: Monthly Review Press.

Martin, R. 2015. *Knowledge LTD: Toward a Social Logic of the Derivative*. Philadelphia: Temple University Press.

Palley, T. 2010. "The Limits of Minsky's Financial Instability Hypothesis as an Explanation of the Crisis." *Monthly Review* 61(11): 28–43. http://monthlyreview.org/archives/2010/volume-61-issue-11-april-2010/ (accessed August 14, 2016).

Panitch, L. and S. Gindin. 2013. *The Making of Global Capitalism: The Political Economy of American Empire*. London: Verso.

Resnick, S. A. and R. D. Wolff. 1987. *Knowledge and Class*. Chicago: University of Chicago Press.

——. 2010. "The Economic Crisis: A Marxian Interpretation." *Rethinking Marxism* 22(2): 170–186.

Strike Debt. 2012. *The Debt Resistors' Operations Manual.* http://strikedebt.org/The-Debt-Resistors-Operations-Manual.pdf (accessed August 14, 2016).

Toscano, A. 2013. "Gaming the Plumbing." *Mute* 3(4): 74–85.

Žižek, S. 2005. "The Parallax View." *New Left Review* 25: 125–135.

PART IV

Capitalism, Non-Capitalism and Transitions

25

PRODUCTIVE
SELF-EMPLOYMENT
IN MARXISM

Satyananda Gabriel

Introduction

The ancient class process is another name for productive self-employment, where the adjective productive refers to the production and self-appropriation of a surplus (in kind or in value form). Self-employment has held an almost mythic status in the history of the US and many other parts of the world. However, discussions of productive self-employment are largely absent from the neoclassical orthodoxy, various Keynesian and institutionalist insurgencies and Marxism, although it is in the Marxian literature where we find the largest body of theoretical work on ancients and self-exploitation (Gabriel 1989; 1990). Many in the Marxian world, however, frown at the use of Marx's adjective "ancient," as in "the ancient mode of production" and prefer other, "less provocative" terms, such as independent commodity production or peasant mode of production.

Most past conceptions of the ancient mode of production and of ancient direct producers have assumed that this unique mode of appropriating and distributing value was of only minor consequence in any given social formation and that ancient direct producers (whatever appellation is used to describe them) are relatively insignificant in shaping the economy. Why even mention the productively self-employed, much less the ancient mode of production or self-exploitation, given this widespread presumption of insignificance? After all, when ancients are mentioned, it is typically assumed, implicitly or explicitly, that self-exploiting direct producers are teleologically inferior to capitalists, just as "primitive" communism was always assumed to be teleologically inferior to the ancient mode of production and most other modes of production, including the as yet unrealized communism of Marx's imagination. Unlike the proletariat, ancients are assumed to be only background players on the stage of history. But are ancients really just "residual elements" in the chemistry of the past, present and future? To answer we must examine the ancient mode of production.

The Ancient Mode of Production

This unique class process, where the producer of surplus is simultaneously the appropriator *and* first distributor of surplus on an *individualized basis* (creating a network of relationships where the agents are dependent for all or a portion of the ancient surplus to cover at least a portion of their livelihood) has a special place within many cultures. It is often represented in literature, where it is quite clear that self-employment is significant, at least locally. Charles Dickens, in his classic *Great Expectations* (1861), featured the character of Joe Gargery, an ancient blacksmith, depicted as a heroically honest, hardworking and good-hearted human being, a character constructed to evoke sympathy from the reader. The contemporary author Donna Tartt created a similarly heroic ancient direct producer in her recent Pulitzer Prize winning best-seller *The Goldfinch* (2013), which was an homage to *Great Expectations*. She created a parallel character to Joe Gargery in the guise of James "Hobie" Hobart. Hobart was an ancient furniture restorer and replica antique furniture maker whose well-deserved reputation as an honest artisan is put at risk by a self-deluded, romanticist central character, a character not unlike Dickens' Pip. Ancients have played a key role in many other works, including some that have reproduced the meme of the ancient road to wealth, the idea of the self-exploiting direct producer pulling himself up by his bootstraps to become successful (which usually means having transitioned to a capitalist exploiting others). Chinua Achebe's short story, "A Civil Peace" (1971), where the character Jonathan Iwegbu digs up his buried bicycle at the end of the Biafran Civil War and starts a taxi service from which he uses the proceeds to later open a bar, is one such example of this.

In the media, especially in the US, we are often bombarded with stories of the self-made man or woman, who starts as ancient direct producer/entrepreneur, risking money and expended labor-time to make a go at business. The meme ends with the formerly self-exploiting direct producer employing the labor of others and becoming fabulously famous and wealthy. This tale of ascendance is often based, albeit loosely, on some actual person. For example, there is the tale of Bill Whyte, who founded the personal products company W. S. Badger Company. Because he started as a carpenter, he suffered from cracked skin during the winter months. He decided to find a safe but effective solution to the cracked skin and developed a nontoxic natural ingredient skin balm in his kitchen one winter that soothed and eventually eliminated the cracked skin problem. Later, he sold the balm to other carpenters and craftspeople, producing the concoction late at night and delivering it in tins on weekends (Lourie and Smith, 2013). This version of the Horatio Alger story has become an important implicit (and sometimes explicit) meme in discussions of capitalism. Most of the time this occurs because no distinction is made between self-exploitation (where the ancient direct producer pushes herself to perform surplus labor in order to pay landlords, lenders or the tax man) and capitalist exploitation. In other cases, the distinction is deemed irrelevant on the assumption that successful ancients necessarily become capitalists or are permanently relegated to an insignificant place in a capitalist society.

Anyone seeking to analyze productively self-employed producers must confront this mythic status of the ancient. The decision in Gabriel (1989; 1990) to label them as participating in the ancient class process was to an extent an attempt to state at least two principles:

1   This is a much older economic process than capitalism and it is not capitalism. The ancient class process or mode of production is the basis of much of the mythology stolen to service capitalism in an attempt to try to make a cultural case for capitalism, even though they are as distinct from each other as any two other class processes. Capitalism is not slavery, feudalism, or self-employment. In fact, as Marx elaborated in the first volume of *Capital*, the ancient mode of production was, in part, an obstacle to the rise of capitalism and had to be weakened for capitalism to prevail (Marx 1977[1], 931).

Absorbing the ancient mythology of "working for oneself" as a meme supportive of capitalism was a bonus for those working for capitalism's rise.

2   Another reason for choosing the terminology of the ancient class process is to make more transparent the class aspects of "ancient" Greece and the interactions of these class aspects with Greek class-based democracy and markets (Gabriel 1989: 135–142). There are numerous methods for demonstrating the contradictions between this mythology of ancient Greece and democratic political processes with the reality of nineteenth century capitalism, where individual producers were hardly "free" but sold their laboring potential in "free" markets. It is important not to conflate democracy and markets with capitalism. Democracy and markets exist and shape other class processes, including the ancient class process. Thus, while the ancient mode of production blocked the expansion of capitalism into certain social sites, free markets provided conditions for the existence of both capitalist exploitation and ancient appropriation. While there are numerous instances where ancient societies had to give way to capitalism, ancient direct producers have continued to survive in the interstices of capitalist society.

Marx wrote that the struggle against social injustice could not be successful without an understanding of exploitation, and in particular of the capitalist exploitation that was dominant in England and other industrialized European nations at the time of his writings. Marx examined the conditions under which alternative forms of surplus appropriation might block or displace capitalist exploitation. Conditions of existence of the alternative forms are the unelaborated *anti-conditions* of existence for capitalist exploitation. They are unelaborated precisely because they serve as counterweights to elaborated concepts that together form conditions of existence of capitalist exploitation. Among these anti-conditions are to be found the conditions of existence for the theoretical construct of the ancient form of surplus appropriation and of social formations within which this ancient form of surplus appropriation prevails. Marx's writings contain distinct references to ancient society or related concepts, such as "small producers," "artisans," "independendent prorietors," "petty producers," "individual producers," "simple commodity producers" and "independent craftsmen." However, Marx did not elaborate the conditions of existence of an ancient social formation, and for many years there has been much debate over the definition and significance of these producers in Marxian theory.

Using the scattered references to ancient society in Marx, Barry Hindess and Paul Q. Hirst created their conceptualization of the "ancient mode of production" (Hindess and Hirst 1975). Hindess and Hirst interpreted Marx as championing economic processes as an essential determinant of the mode of production. In addition, their theoretical construct of the "ancient mode of appropriation of surplus labor" defined as "appropriation by *right of citizenship*" (Hindess and Hirst 1975, 82) is based on an essentialist reading of Marx, which posits that political processes should "occupy the place of dominance in the social formation" (Hindess and Hirst 1975, 14). Hindess and Hirst conflate fundamental and distributive class processes, as well as a variety of other nonclass economic processes within their essentialized ancient mode of production. This is unfortunate, as it eliminates the potential contradictions among and between these various economic processes and other social processes, thereby obscuring the definition and significance of their essentialized "ancient mode of production" which rests at the ontological center of the ancient social formation.

The *ancient fundamental class process* conceptualized in this article contrasts with Hindess and Hirst's "ancient mode of production." The uniqueness of the ancient fundamental class process exists by virtue of the concepts of *ancient necessary and surplus labor.*

Ancient necessary labor is that portion of the total product of the ancient producer that goes to meet his/her subsistence needs. The ancient producer will not labor if she does not retain some bundle of use-values embodying this necessary portion of her total labor for personal consumption. Her labor in excess of this is defined as *ancient surplus labor* (Marx 1977, vol. 1, 324–25). What makes the ancient fundamental class process so distinctive from other processes is the type of private appropriation of surplus labor that unites the production and appropriation of surplus labor on an individualized basis. This unified production and appropriation of surplus labor in a single human being constitutes *self-exploitation*. This coalescence of the production and appropriation of surplus labor within the ego of the individual human being exists in no other class process.

The existence of self-exploitation presumes certain social and natural conditions. The need to secure these conditions of existence presents the ancient producer/appropriator with a problem of allocating her labor-time in order to produce enough surplus to secure the conditions of existence of the ancient fundamental class process. This may necessitate a distribution of the ancient surplus to a variety of social agents who will provide these conditions of existence. This distribution of ancient surplus is called the *ancient distributive class process*. The term "distributive class process" is synonymous with the term "subsumed class process." The adjective "distributive" is more descriptive of the relationship whereby surplus value is apportioned to various social agents (See Gibson-Graham and O'Neill 2001 and Gabriel 2006 for examples of the distributive class process). The ancient distributive class process is composed of two positions: the position of the first distributor of ancient surplus labor and the position of receiver of this distributed ancient surplus labor. The latter position may be held by a variety of social agents, including the individual holding the ancient fundamental class position. On the other hand, the ancient producer/appropriator may serve only as distributor of already appropriated surplus labor. In any case, the ancient producer/appropriator must hold at least this one position in the distributive class process. Since she is the first receiver of her ancient surplus labor, it follows that she must be the first distributor of that appropriated surplus labor.

The ancient, as first distributor of her appropriated surplus labor, must then apportion this surplus labor among the potential distributive class recipients in order to secure the conditions for continuation of self-exploitation. On this point the demands upon the ancient as distributor of the surplus may directly conflict with the impulses of the ancient as performer or the ancient as appropriator of surplus labor. For instance, the ancient may wish to allocate her appropriated surplus labor in ways that conflict with the demands of the distributive class agents receiving the surplus. Nevertheless, the demands of the distributive class agents must be satisfied if the conditions for further self-exploitation are to be met. These contradictory impulses must be resolved within the ancient class process in order for the process to continue.

This conceptualization of the ancient class process represents an *anti-essentialist* interpretation of the ancient mode of surplus labor appropriation and formation of ancient society, based on the concepts and critical reading of Marx forged into a unified theoretical framework by Stephen A. Resnick, Richard D. Wolff, and other members of the school of Marxian thought they founded (Resnick and Wolff 1987a; 1987b).[1] This school of Marxian thought, distinguished in part by a theoretical vocabulary borrowed and modified from the French philosopher Louis Althusser, is influenced by the concept of *overdetermination*.

Freud used the concept "overdetermination" in his analysis of dreams to refer to the way in which the content of dreams was not simplistically determined by a finite set of life-events but was instead the product of the totality or gestalt of life experiences, including the state of mind of the dreamer at the moment of revealing the dream. Thus, in the interpretation (or reading) of an individual's dreams, the meaning is always partially understood and necessarily open to further interpretation (Freud 1950). Louis Althusser borrowed and then transformed this term in order to construct an understanding of his reading of Marx, in particular as a means of producing an understanding of Marx's radical epistemological and ontological break from essentialist discourse (Althusser 1970, 87–128).[2]

Overdetermination implies that no aspect of reality is insignificant in the shaping of any other aspect of reality. The dialectic of overdetermination is the dialectic of ceaseless change, of the constant pushes and pulls of the unique influences that come together to constitute each and every aspect of reality.[3] These unique influences create contradictions. The significance of this to the ancient class process is the way in which it can be combined with other class processes, both exploitative and non-exploitative. An ancient who also hires workers and appropriates a surplus from those wage laborers participates simultaneously in the ancient and capitalist class processes. The ancient may also within the same enterprise engage in self-exploitation and receive distributive class payments from a capitalist enterprise. In both of these cases, the ancient has a complex position within more than one class process, resulting in what Levin (2014) calls *class structural hybridity*. Levin understands the need to theorize complexity in the various class processes (slave, feudal, ancient, capitalist and communist) and the way in which these distinct class processes shape each other, the larger society and the path forward, including transition from one type of society to another. A failure to recognize this complex role of the ancient in capitalist and other societies makes it less likely that we can understand transition.

Thus, the presence of the ancient fundamental class process within any given social formation implies the existence of unique contradictions associated with the interaction of this fundamental class process and other social and natural processes. The contradictions bred in this interaction propel the social formation in question down a uniquely overdetermined path of change.

Ancients and the Transition Debate

Marx often used teleological language to describe the presence of anti-conditions of the existence of capitalist exploitation, often referring to such conditions as "pre-capitalist."[4] This is both unfortunate and misleading in Marx's analysis of the conditions of existence and anti-conditions of existence of capitalist exploitation. Marx and Marxist theorists have expressed in their theoretical work an interest in the diachronic relationship between social formations (or class societies), otherwise known as the temporal/historical relationship of these social formations one to the other. This has led to Hegelian conceptions of history as a coherent and orderly progression of distinct class societies with a beginning point and an endpoint. In other words, by referring to the process of self-appropriation and distribution of surplus as "pre-capitalist," not only is the process seen as something belonging to a past, a past devoid of capitalism, but also a process not co-existing with capitalism.

The costs of such a conception of human history are great. It severely restricts the kinds of questions asked about the constitution and path of change of determinant social formations, whether in the temporal past, present or future. Rather, it is much more useful to reconceptualize the periodization of history along class lines as an overdetermined product wherein no *necessary* path of transition from one type of social formation to another is posited. The complexity of the social formation, as understood in the term overdetermination, implies that every constituent process must have its own effects upon the historical movement of the social formation. No social or natural processes are conceived of as insignificant. History is in part influenced by struggles over class, but it cannot be reduced to an underdetermined outcome of such struggles.[5]

Possibly the greatest amount of theoretical labor expended on making sense of the diachronic relationship between social formations is the long-running debate over the transition from feudalism to capitalism. This debate is influenced by a desire of Marxist theorists to understand how a transition out of capitalism might be possible. Two of the key figures in this debate, and indeed major influences upon Marxian theory in general, have been Maurice Dobb (1978) and Paul Sweezy (1970).

Dobb and Sweezy both suggest the presence of self-exploitation during the period of transition from feudalism to capitalism as they refer to "independent handicraft production," [Dobb 1978, 7] "pre-capitalist petty mode of production," [ibid., 19] and "pre-capitalist commodity production." [Sweezy, in Sweezy et al 1978, 50 n. 22] Each of these appellations suggests that the direct producer engages in the private individualized appropriation of his own surplus labor, i.e. self-exploitation. However, each of these terms is beset by the underlying epistemological and ontological restrictions of both Dobb's and Sweezy's theoretical framework. For example, while Marx's use of the term "pre-capitalist" within the context of constructing an understanding of the transition into capitalism represents a sort of Hegelian hiccup, it did not represent any underlying and consistent teleological view of human history. The case with Dobb and Sweezy is quite different. For them, the term "pre-capitalist" implies an empiricist[6] and teleological[7] conception of those societies upon which the adjective "pre-capitalist" is appended. These societies are conceptualized as having occurred prior to the historical development of capitalism. Significantly, this conception also contains a notion of such societies as historically backwards from the standpoint of human development (i.e. closer to some vision of human primitive origins and further from some vision of advanced communism) vis-à-vis capitalism.[8]

In other words, Dobb and Sweezy, as well as other Marxist theorists, conceive of a general path of historical development (which need not be unilinear) in which capitalism is placed towards the more "progressive" pole and societies labeled "pre-capitalist" are situated in the rear of historical evolution. Furthermore, the transition from one determinate class society to another is viewed as the *underdetermined* product of certain specified conditions wherein the seeds of the new society were sown in the ground of its antecedent society.[9] Dobb and Sweezy share an economic determinist understanding of the principal forces governing this transition, although they vigorously disagree about which essential economic aspect is the key or central determinant.

The consequences of Sweezy's and Dobb's teleological and essentialist conceptions of self-exploitation go beyond the way they conceive of the transition. In particular, it imposes additional limitations upon the analysis of capitalist social formations. Even if it is accepted that self-exploitation occurs within capitalist society, it is viewed as hardly of any consequence in social analysis. However, many analyses contest this proposition. Steinmetz and Wright (1989) argue that self-employment has been prevalent and critical in the social formation of the US. In particular, they cite that in a 1980s US survey of adults in the workforce nearly 32% came from families in which the head of the household was self-employed most of the time and that 46% came from households in which the head of household had been self-employed at least part of the time. In an analysis of the modern trucking industry in the US, Fried and Wolff (1994) show that the ancient class process was prevalent in the 1930s, but through political, social and economic processes, it was undermined and curtailed by the transition to capitalism in that industry, only to be dominated by ancients again beginning in the 1970s when political, social and economic processes once again changed in favor of the ancient class process in the trucking transport industry. Rio (2005) similarly shows a class transition in the US household domestic service sector that was dominated by feudal and slave class processes in the early history of this country and gradually changed to be primarily dominated by ancients during the post WWII period.

In research on developing countries and those that have gone through "post-Communist" transition, there is a growing consensus that self-employment has been a critical component in the maintenance of the modern economy by actually *enhancing* capitalist accumulation through linkages with capitalist firms. Self-employed producers have provided these firms with the capacity to reduce labor costs, avoid government regulations, and respond quickly to shifts in the demand for goods and services. At the same time, ancient direct producers have been able to accumulate a sizable surplus in many of these economies allowing them to thrive and not be swept away by the capitalist class structure (Hanley 2000).

Conclusion

Self-employment or the ancient fundamental and distributive class process has often been conceived, in teleological fashion, as simply a precursor to the growth of capitalist exploitation or as a sort of "residual" class phenomenon existing in the interstices of societies dominated by other "more fundamental" methods of appropriating the fruit of surplus labor. This article explains why such teleological and essentialist conceptions of ancient producers obscure and ignore the social consequences of self-appropriation including the dynamic influence the ancient fundamental class process has upon all other aspects of society, as well as the similarly dynamic influence of these other aspects upon the existence and reproduction or non-existence of self-exploitation.

Notes

1 The earlier of these two works, *Economics: Marxian versus Neoclassical*, contrasts this particular version of Marxian theory to neoclassical theory.
2 Resnick and Wolff further transformed the Althusserian concept of overdetermination as part of their reading of Marx and their production of new knowledge about the effect of class upon other social and natural processes and vice versa.
3 Marx referred to the constitution of a social formation as the culmination of the unique interaction of more social and natural conditions than could ever be named or identified. This means that any given social formation is overdetermined by all the conditions that have influenced it up to the present moment:

> ... these different forms of the commune ... depend partly on the natural inclination of the tribe, and partly on the economic conditions in which it relates as proprietor to the land and soil in reality, i.e. in which it appropriates its fruits through labour, and the latter will itself depend on climate, physical make-up of the land and soil, the physical determined mode of its exploitation, the relation with hostile tribes or neighbor tribes, and the modifications which migrations, historic experiences, etc. introduce.
>
> *(Marx 1973, 486)*

4 See Marx, *Grundisse*, as reprinted in David McLellan (1977, 371), where Marx refers to "the obstacles created by the relationships and means of pre-capitalist production."
5 For a further discussion along these lines, see Resnick and Wolff 1987b, pp. 122–4.

6 Sweezy outlines an empiricist methodology in the following manner: "to formulate hypotheses about what is essential, to work these hypotheses through, and to check the conclusions against the data of experience" (Sweezy 1970, 13). Dobb delineates his empiricist ontological position (in which a dichotomy between the thinking process and "actuality" is explicitly stated) when he proposes a simple test of the utility of a theory. According to Dobb, this utility depends upon "whether a given structure of assumptions and definitions affords an abstract model which is sufficiently representative of actuality to be serviceable...." (Dobb 1978, vii). Thus, both Sweezy and Dobb defend their theoretical arguments by an appeal to a set of given, autonomous facts.

7 This teleology is both intersystemic, as well as intrasystemic, in the sense that it refers to the positing of a predictable internal process of evolution within any given society, as well as a predictable process of transition from one form of society to another. As Sweezy writes:

> Social systems, like individuals, go through a life cycle and pass from the scene when 'from forms of development of the forces of production' they 'turn into their fetters.' The process of social change, however, is not purely mechanical; it is rather the product of human action, but action which is definitely limited by the kind of society in which it has its roots.
>
> *(Sweezy 1970, 20)*

8 In a sense, they are conceived of as ways of life that history has passed by on the road to advanced communism, and are consequently considered to be of lesser importance to social analysis. Their usefulness being restricted primarily to historical analysis of past transitions that have led to the emergence of capitalist society.

9 As Dobb writes: "Important elements of each new society, although not necessarily the complete embryo of it, are contained within the womb of the old ..." (Dobb 1978, 11). And in a more detailed elaboration of the necessary movement of social change and transition: "If it be right to maintain that the conception of socio-economic systems, marking distinct stages in historical development, is not merely a matter of convenience but an obligation ... then this must be because there is a quality in historical situations which both makes for homogeneity of pattern at any given time and renders periods of transition, when there is an even balance of discrete elements, inherently unstable. It must be because society is so constituted that conflict and interaction of its *leading elements*, rather than the simple growth of some single element, form the principal agency of movement and change, at least so far as major transformations are concerned. If such be the case, once development has reached a certain level and the various elements which constitute that society are poised in a certain way, events are likely to move with unusual rapidity, not merely in the sense of quantitative growth, but in the sense of a change of balance of the constituent elements, resulting in the appearance of novel compositions and more or less abrupt changes in the texture of society. To use a topical analogy: it is as though at certain levels of development something like a chain-reaction is set in motion." (Dobb 1978, 12–13). Emphasis added.

References

Achebe, C. 1971. "Civil Peace." In *The Story and Its Writer: An Introduction to Short Fiction*, 4th ed., A. Charters, ed. Boston, MA: Bedford Books of St. Martin's Press.

Althusser, L. 1970. *For Marx*. Trans. by Ben Brewster. New York: Random House.

Dickens, C. 1861. *Great Expectations*. London: Chapman and Hall.

Dobb, M. 1978. *Studies in the Development of Capitalism*. New York: International Publishers.

Freud, S. 1950. *The Interpretation of Dreams*. Trans. A. A. Brill. New York: Modern Library.

Fried, G. F. and R. D. Wolff. 1994. Modern Ancients: Self-Employed Truckers." *Rethinking Marxism* 7(4): 103–115.

Gabriel, S. 2006. *Chinese Capitalism and the Modernist Vision*. London and New York: Routledge.

——. 1989. "Ancients: A Marxian Theory of Self-Exploitation." Ph.D. dissertation. Amherst, MA: University of Massachusetts-Amherst.

——. 1990. "Ancients: A Marxian Theory of Self-Exploitation." *Rethinking Marxism* 3(1): 85–106.

Gibson-Graham, J.K. and P. O'Neill. 2001. "Exploring a New Class Politics of the Enterprise." In *Re/Presenting Class: Essays in Postmodern Marxism*, J.K. Gibson-Graham, S. A. Resnick, and R. D. Wolff, eds. Durham: Duke University Press.

Hanley, E. 2000. "Self-employment in Post-communist Eastern Europe: A Refuge From Poverty or Road to Riches?" *Communist and Post-Communist Studies* 33: 379–402.

Hindess, B. and P. Q. Hirst. 1975. *Pre-Capitalist Modes of Production*. London: Routledge & Kegan Paul.

——. 1977. *Mode of Production and Social Formation*. New Jersey: Humanities Press.

Levin, K. M. 2014. "Class Hybrids: From Medieval Europe to Silicon Valley." *Rethinking Marxism* 26(1): 95–112.

Lourie, B. and R. Smith. 2013. *Toxin Toxout*. New York: St. Martin's Press.

McLelland, D. 1977. *Karl Marx: Selected Writings*. Oxford: Oxford University Press.

Marx, K. 1973. *Grundisse*. Trans. by M. Nicolaus. New York: Vintage.

——. 1977. *Capital*, 3 volumes. New York: Vintage.

Resnick, S. A. and R. D. Wolff. 1987a. *Economics: Marxian Versus Neoclassical*. Baltimore: John Hopkins Press.

——. 1987b. *Knowledge and Class: A Marxian Critique of Political Economy*. Chicago: University of Chicago Press.

——. 2006. *New Departures in Marxian Theory*. New York: Routledge.

Rio, C.. 2005. "'On the Move': African-American Women's Paid Domestic Labor and the Class Transition to Independent Commodity Production." *Rethinking Marxism* 17(4): 489–510.

Steinmetz, G. and E. O. Wright. 1989. "The Fall and Rise of the Petty Bourgeoisie: Changing Patterns of Self-Employment in the Postwar United States." *American Journal of Sociology* 94(5): 973–1018.

Sweezy, P. M. 1970. *The Theory of Capitalist Development*. New York: Monthly Review Press.

Sweezy, P., M. Dobb, C. Hill, G. Lefebvre, K. Takahashi, G. Procacci, J. Merrington and E. Hobsbawm, eds. 1978. *The Transition from Feudalism to Capitalism*. London: Verso.

Tartt, D. 2013. *The Goldfinch*. New York: Little, Brown and Company.

26

SOCIALISM AND COMMUNISM

Theodore Burczak

Classical socialism was a movement to replace the unplanned and exploitative institutions of capitalism with national planning, public ownership and distribution according to human need rather than by the arbitrary capriciousness of the market. Its goals were to distribute economic resources broadly among the people in order to create the conditions for widespread, substantive freedom and to end alienating, exploitative labor processes. Socialism promised all people the resources to live a flourishing life, not just the market freedom to exchange, which offered no guarantee of a decent standard of living. This traditional socialist project was derived from Marx and Engels' dream of a future that would transcend the allocative and distributional anarchy of the market through the abolition of private property and the establishment of social ownership of the means of production and central planning. For instance, in the *Manifesto of the Communist Party*, Marx and Engels explicitly called for "abolition of property in land" and the "extension of factories and instruments of production owned by the State" (Marx and Engels 1978, 490). In *Socialism: Utopian and Scientific*, Engels lamented the anarchy of the market while describing socialism as a state in which "[s]ocialized production upon a predetermined plan becomes henceforth possible" (Engels 1978, 717). Socialism, or perhaps the more advanced form of communism, would realize the human potential to harness productive forces to achieve a rational economic order, social justice and real freedom for all.

Traditional notions of socialism and communism are often defined in terms of ownership rights in the means of production, which are sometimes understood to be the product of an evolutionary process driven by technological development. From a property oriented perspective, socialism involves state ownership of the means of production, perhaps by the state taking over what Lenin called the commanding heights of production. Communism represents a higher form of development in which productive property becomes the common property of the working class, as the state withers away. One implication of these conceptions of socialism and communism is that social coordination would have to take place through some sort of planning process, since the abolition of private ownership of land, natural resources and productive capital effectively eliminates the possibility of moving means of production from one set of hands to another through a market exchange process. The inability to exchange property rights in the means of production liberates society to coordinate the use of those means through central direction, as in a firm, to achieve production that satisfies human needs rather than expands private profit.

Friedrich Hayek famously argued against these conceptions, calling the attempt to create social order and economic justice through rational planning a "fatal conceit" (Hayek 1988). He criticized socialist theory for its failure to recognize that knowledge of resource scarcities, consumer preferences, cost effective technologies, management techniques and other relevant details of economic life were not scientific data that could be articulated into an all-encompassing plan. Rather, this knowledge, such as it is, exists as the subjective, ever-shifting and possibly erroneous ideas of diverse individuals. Subjective knowledge required a constant testing ground to prove its worth, which Hayek argued was best provided by a private property, competitive market economy that was subject to the accounting conventions of profit and loss.

To be sure, Marx also recognized the dispersion of human knowledge in a market economy. However, as Chris Sciabarra argues in his fascinating *Marx, Hayek, and Utopia* (1995), Marx viewed the dispersal of knowledge as a result of workers' alienation from the means of production, a transitory side effect of the property relations of capitalism. This stands in contrast to Hayek, who viewed the strictures on human knowledge as "existentially limiting," that is, as natural and transhistorical properties of human existence (Sciabarra 1995, 119). Sciabarra understands Marx to accept epistemic fragmentation as only a temporary feature of social development, to be overcome in a socialist or communist society. For Marx, development of the forces of production and cooperative work relations would allow tacit and dispersed knowledge to be articulated and integrated in consciously directed economic activity, thereby solving Hayek's supposedly permanent knowledge problems. Sciabarra calls this Marx's "synoptic delusion": the idea that one can consciously design a new society to achieve social justice. Many interpreters of Marx have embraced and extended this premise to argue that a Marxian vision of communism or socialism could be realized *only* by a centrally planned economy.

Yet empirical events at the end of the twentieth century (e.g., the collapse of the Soviet Union, the adoption of a market model in China, the poverty of North Korea) appear to have eliminated national economic planning as an attractive or viable option. The teleology in Marx's theory of historical materialism, where development of the forces of production inevitably creates the conditions for social advance towards social and communal ownership is also widely rejected. What then happens to socialist and communist ideas in the twenty-first century? Is there any meaningful notion of socialism that can accommodate Hayek's epistemological critique of state ownership, central planning and social justice? Can socialist goals be achieved without central planning and the abolition of private property?

Jack Amariglio and David Ruccio argue that non-teleological, anti-essentialist versions of what might be called a postmodern Marxian theory resist the capitalism-as-irrational/socialism-as-rational dualism that characterizes a significant portion of modern radical social theory. They criticize the delusions of rational planning, claiming to find "no evidence that planning means stability and order, nor … that it implies a 'better' method to get at the 'true' needs of individuals and/or enterprises" (Amariglio and Ruccio 1998, 250). They even take the quasi-Hayekian stance that "the disorderliness [disequilibrium] of markets can (at certain times, in particular circumstances) lead to the satisfaction of social needs" (Amariglio and Ruccio 1998, 251). From their perspective, disorder, decentering and uncertainty are ubiquitous "facts" of social existence. The aspiration of rational economic planning to achieve social justice is thus directly called into question by postmodern Marxism.

The most influential strand of postmodern Marxism derives from the path-breaking work of Stephen Resnick and Richard Wolff, who initiated what some have called the "Amherst school" of postmodern Marxism (Resnick and Wolff 1987). Resnick and Wolff advocate an epistemology that understands all human knowledge to be the product of a unique, complex and open-ended socialization rather than as a mirror of nature, and an ontology that understands the constitution and causation of social events to be the overdetermined product of various—perhaps an infinity of—natural and social forces. Since it is impossible for human knowledge to capture all possible lines of causation of social events, Resnick and Wolff reason that every social theory must inevitably specialize, adopting a favored conceptual entry point into social analysis and seeking to trace, albeit partially and provisionally, its causal connections to the rest of the social totality.

The entry point for postmodern Marxism is the concept of class. Resnick and Wolff define class as the process of producing, appropriating and distributing surplus labor. This idea of class is distinct from other more commonly held notions of class that focus on the distribution of income, wealth and power or the cultural habits of different groups of people. It also gives rise to somewhat non-traditional definitions of capitalism and socialism. Classical Marxism understands capitalism as a form of economy that combines widespread private property and more or less free markets to produce exploitation. Classical Socialism, then, aims to abolish exploitation by replacing private property with social property and markets with central planning. For the postmodern Marxists, however, there is no one-to-one relationship between the presence or absence of private property, markets, and central planning and the existence of exploitative class processes in which the producers of surplus labor do not participate in its appropriation. Class exploitation can persist in the presence of central planning and socialized property. Resnick and Wolff argue, for example, that the Soviet Union did not eliminate exploitation. They regard the Soviet experience as an example of state capitalism, rather than socialism or communism, in which state officials hired workers and appropriated surplus labor and its product (Resnick and Wolff 2002). Thus, rather than focusing on forms of ownership or exercises of power, the positive goal of postmodern Marxism is to envision and enact non-exploitative alternatives, where exploitation is understood to exist when performers of surplus labor do not participate in the appropriation of that surplus, and where non-exploitation is understood to exist when surplus producers share in the appropriation process (more on appropriation below). Because it rejects essentialist and teleological modes of analysis, it is a Marxian theory "without guarantees." Another way to say this is that it is a Marxian theory that focuses on the organization of production processes in society, rather than on the particular results of those processes. One could call this Marxism "libertarian," paralleling Robert Nozick's idea that a libertarian order is one in which society recognizes rules of just transfer (whenever individual property owners consent to trade justly held property, justice is achieved), regardless of the resulting distribution of those transfers. Postmodern Marxism is similarly process oriented in that it aims to achieve a type of shared appropriation, in which the producers of surplus labor participate in the process of appropriating the product of their efforts.

In an important contribution, Stephen Cullenberg (1992) argues that confining our attention to forms of shared appropriation results in a "thin" theory of socialism, which Cullenberg views as an advantage. He contends that an important reason why people view socialism as a failure is because socialists have often promised too much. Socialism has been understood as a utopia that would end the exploitation and alienation of labor; eliminate business cycles and poverty; abolish racial, sexual and gender oppression; and establish more harmonious relations between people and the environment. If we instead see the primary goal of a Marxian socialism or communism to be the abolition of exploitative forms of appropriation, instead of socializing the means of production and implementing central planning, this reduces the political, cultural and economic burden on socialism, perhaps making it more feasible as an institutional alternative. A thin socialist perspective focuses attention on a Marxian notion of procedural fairness in which those who work should also appropriate the product of their labor, without the need to embrace central planning and state ownership of the means of production. Nevertheless, embracing only a notion of procedural fairness leaves thin socialism unable to address distributive injustices of unmet basic needs and dramatically unequal allocations of wealth, income and opportunity. A thinly socialist or communist economy in which appropriation is not exploitative can still yield gender and ethnic inequality, wasteful consumption and production, and environmental degradation, possibilities that have long been concerns in the diverse strands of the Marxian tradition. Thus, defining socialism and communism exclusively in terms of alternative forms of non-exploitative appropriation may be too limiting.

In part to address this problem, George DeMartino (2003) uses Resnick and Wolff's tripartite definition of the class process as the production, appropriation and distribution of surplus labor to make an important contribution to thinking about economic justice and post-capitalist social forms. DeMartino argues that class justice has three dimensions: productive justice, appropriative justice and distributive justice. This nifty reframing allows DeMartino to reconcile Marx's famous expression of productive and distributive justice—"From each according to ability, to each according to his needs"—to his separate concern with appropriative justice, by seeking an end to the exploitative appropriation by non-producers. It also enables us to see how the three components of the class process and corresponding notions of class justice might interact, sometimes contradict and sometimes enable each other in socialist and communist societies. Thinking of the three dimensions of class processes enables "thicker" notions of socialism and communism.

DeMartino argues that productive class justice is related to the first part of the Marxian ethic, "From each according to ability." For DeMartino "[p]roductive class justice refers to the fairness in the allocation of the work of producing the social surplus" (DeMartino 2003, 8). We can interpret such fairness in at least three distinct ways. First, productive class justice could mean that workers have the incentive to contribute with maximum effort and productivity, a goal which might conceivably be achieved in an economy of capitalist firms. Van der Veen and Van Parijs (1986), for instance, adopt this perspective when they argue that retaining free market capitalism might be the most effective way to achieve the abundance of surplus that would enable maximum satisfaction of needs (a form of distributive class justice). Towards that end, van der Veen and Van Parijs propose the institution of a high universal basic income in an otherwise capitalist economy, an arrangement they call "a capitalist road to communism." For them, communism is defined by a system in which labor becomes life's prime want and in which distribution takes place according to need. A basic income large enough to achieve universal need satisfaction, funded by the highest possible marginal tax rate consistent with this distributive goal, would balance a potentially unavoidable tradeoff. That is, there might be a tension between producing for maximum need satisfaction and providing the incentive for capitalist employers to create work environments attractive enough to retain workers to produce a surplus that could be subsequently distributed through the tax and transfer system. In that case, a democratic society inspired by socialist and communist ideas might choose to sacrifice shared appropriation for maximum surplus production (a potential type of productive class justice) via capitalist processes, *if* some mechanism existed to distribute the increased surplus to universal need satisfaction.

A second and slightly different way to interpret the goal of productive class justice is as minimizing work roles not involved in the production of surplus. Bowles and Jayadev (2007, 1), for instance, point to the massive amount of unproductive guard labor ("the police, private security guards, military personnel and others who make up the disciplinary apparatus of a society") employed in US capitalism as a consequence of class conflict engendered by capitalist production and inequality. Roberts (2014) discusses the large rise in employment in the financial sector in terms of the expansion of unproductive activities that siphon surplus away from rewarding productive workers and growing productive activities. Seen in this light, productive class justice leads to an investigation of how we might reduce forms of labor parasitic on the creation of goods and services that more directly increase the well-being of the typical member of capitalist, socialist or communist society.

A third way to see the possibility of productive class justice is in terms of sharing productive and unproductive work roles. This notion of productive class justice might apply to Marx and Engels' vision of de-specialized labor patterns articulated in *The German Ideology*:

> [I]n communist society, where nobody has one exclusive sphere of activity but each can become accomplished in any branch he wishes, society regulates the general production and thus make it possible for me to do one thing today and another tomorrow, to hunt in the morning, fish in the afternoon, rear cattle in the evening, criticize after dinner, just as I have a mind, without ever becoming hunter, fisherman, shepherd, or critic.
>
> *(Marx and Engels 1970, 53)*

It is an open question, though, whether a complex society could ever successfully "regulate general production," which would probably require some kind of central planning to achieve this level of freedom and equity in the work of producing the social surplus. However, applying this conception of productive class justice to household production may be more fruitful. For example, in their important application of class theory to understand different forms of household production, Fraad, Resnick, and Wolff suggest that "a policy of regular, systemic rotation of persons across all the [work roles] in the household might well be deemed a condition of existence of household communism" (Fraad et al. 1989, 58). In this case, a kind of productive justice in the household might also contribute to a form of appropriative justice, if rotation of domestic work roles facilitates the equal participation of household members in determining how necessary and surplus household labor is performed.

Distributive class justice is related to the second half of the Marxian ethic, "to each according to need": how might society's surplus product be best distributed to meet human needs? DeMartino (2003, 2000) and Burczak (2006) see Martha Nussbaum's (2011) and Amartya Sen's (1999) capabilities theory of justice as developing a complex, non-essentialist theory of distribution according to need that is compatible, to a large degree, with post-modern Marxism and thereby quite useful in thinking about what it means to work towards distributive class justice, whether or not the other dimensions of class justice have been achieved. We might imagine, for instance, capitalist, cooperative or independently contracting firms that pay taxes out of the surplus to a democratically organized government body, which in turn distributes the surplus to promote the attainment of universal need satisfaction or equal attainment of the capability to live well.

In the capability framework developed by Nussbaum and Sen, one of the primary goals of governmental and non-governmental organizations should be to ensure that all people have the means or resources to develop their capacity to lead choiceworthy lives. A choiceworthy life is one that a person has reason to value, because the available options allow her to achieve vital, or essential, human functions. Social institutions should ensure, to the extent that natural, technical and social constraints permit, that all individuals have the necessary means enabling choice of a complete, flourishing human life. Flourishing is defined in terms of the attainment of essential functionings. For Nussbaum, in order to lead a flourishing life, a person must be well nourished and educated, have access to adequate health care and shelter, have property that allows exploration of one's subjective appraisal of beneficial opportunities, and possess the ability to participate in social institutions and interactions with dignity.

While specifying a universally valid definition of the essential human functions is surely controversial, since it might seem to depend upon an objective account of good human living, Nussbaum proposes that the capability approach reaches its account of flourishingly *inter-subjectively*, through a cross-cultural conversation oriented towards answering the question: what makes us recognize others as human? As a result of this conversational approach, a list of essential human functions is always a social product, not fixed in stone, thereby remaining subject to revision through ongoing dialogue and interrogation. Nevertheless, a provisional list permits us to examine the extent to which social institutions allow individuals the opportunity to lead lives that enable them to achieve the characteristic human functions. The list provides a benchmark to judge whether the prevailing set of social structures and distribution of resources enable all people to lead flourishing lives, if they so choose. If not, then from the capability perspective, government has an obligation, in the interest of moving towards distributive (class) justice, to design and implement policies that enhance the capability of people to achieve the essential human functions, or the opportunity to lead flourishing lives.

Van der Veen and Van Parijs capitalist road to communism via establishment of a sizeable universal basic income is one concrete form in which socialist or communist government might distribute the surplus to attain human needs. But while attractive for its simplicity and appeal to equal treatment, a basic income can lead to differentially abled individuals achieving quite different degrees of need fulfillment. A blind person, for instance, requires greater resources to achieve the same degree of flourishing as someone with sight. Ernesto Screpanti (2004) thus argues for a different type of social income funded out of tax revenues in the form of various social goods—e.g., education, health care, social spaces—that meet needs more directly, making it congruent with Nussbaum's and Sen's capabilities approach. Screpanti also notes that free time away from work to enjoy consumption possibilities can be conceived of as a type of social good that can be increased through government policies reducing the length of the working day. While Screpanti interprets "the historical tendency toward expansion of social goods … as constituent of a process of construction of communism and extension of freedom" (Screpanti 2004, 187), in a framework that places alternative forms of appropriating surplus at the center of analysis, we might instead see the expansion of social goods, including labor legislation to reduce work hours, as a movement towards distributive class justice.

John Roemer (1996) proposes another model to achieve a type of socialist distributive justice, reasoning that corporate profit income should be distributed equally to all adult citizens. To achieve such a distribution, he advocates eliminating the capitalist, corporate stock market and replacing it with a socialist, coupon stock market. In Roemer's model, all citizens would be given an equal endowment of coupons that could only be used to buy shares of corporate stock. Corporations would issue the shares and exchange the coupon revenue for cash at the state treasury in order to raise funds to buy capital equipment. The government would tax citizens to fill this investment fund in the treasury. The amount of tax revenue in the fund, in conjunction with the volume of shares issued during any time period, would determine the cash price of a coupon. Citizens who purchased shares would receive a portion of the firm's profit resulting from the use of capital equipment, but they would have no right to determine the composition of firm management.

While citizens could not exchange coupons for cash, they would be permitted to sell their shares for coupons at any time, and they would do so if they thought they could turn around and purchase shares in other companies that promised a higher profit flow. In this way, the coupon price of shares would reflect citizens' expectations about the future profitability of firms, thus providing information about the effectiveness of firm management. A citizen's stock holdings would be sold at death, and the coupon revenue would return to the state, preventing concentration of coupon and stock wealth through inheritance.

One advantage of a coupon stock market is that all people would receive an annual sum of money independent of their wage and salary income. For instance, in 2014, an egalitarian distribution of US corporate profits to all adult (over 18) US citizens would have yielded about $8,500 per person, a sum large enough to make a substantial dent in US poverty. The second substantial benefit of this plan is that it would reduce the political power that a few wealthy elites enjoy under capitalism. Roemer reasons that the concentration of stockholding in capitalism means that a few shareholders have the incentive to influence the political process in order to increase their profit incomes. Such influence is used to minimize anti-pollution laws, labor regulations and other legislation that threatens to reduce profits as well as to increase the probability that governments will undertake profit-enhancing foreign aggression, perhaps, for instance, to ensure the flow of cheap oil. An equitable distribution of profit income would reduce the concentrated benefit of lobbying against policies that increase the public good at the expense of profits. Because it is costly to engage in political lobbying and because the benefits of lobbying would be diffused with the dispersed distribution of profit income, Roemer expects that his coupon stock market would lead to a government that was more interested in policies to enhance the common good. An egalitarian distribution of corporate profits—a type of socialist class justice—would thus help to achieve what others have called an effective property-owning democracy.[1]

Interrogating the contours of appropriative class justice deserves special attention in a postmodern Marxism that is principally concerned with ending exploitative class processes, since the understanding of exploitation and its absence in production is inextricably tied with the concept of appropriation. Resnick and Wolff define appropriation to mean to "receive ... directly into his or her hands" (Resnick and Wolff 1987, 146). Their definition might be restated as "becoming the first title holder of an asset." In this definition, appropriation does not occur as the result of an exchange, because during exchange already-defined property rights are transferred between two parties.[2] Thus, where the notion of distributive class justice is concerned with the characteristics of *results*, appropriative class justice focuses on how the production *process* is organized.

In his classic presentation of the labor theory of property, John Locke (1980) confined the issue of appropriation to the first ownership of previously unowned (or commonly owned) natural goods. In his important book, *Property and Contract in Economics* (1992), David Ellerman argues that the question of appropriation can also refer to the assignment of property rights to newly manufactured commodities that are produced using inputs with clearly defined property titles. In the process of production, new goods are created that were not previously owned by anyone, and thus they cannot be acquired through exchange. For example, an automobile that emerges at the end of an assembly line has no obvious, pre-existing property right attached to it. This automobile must be appropriated; someone must become its first owner.

Ellerman points out that appropriation can also be seen to have another aspect. In the process of fabricating a commodity like an automobile, some property titles are extinguished. For example, the electric power that is used to manufacture a car in a capitalist enterprise no longer exists as a legal entity that can again be bought and sold after the car has been produced. The firm is the last owner of the electric power that is embodied in the newly produced car. Perhaps more significantly, in a typical capitalist production process, the capitalist is the last owner of workers' labor time. As Marx noted, in a capitalist enterprise, "the worker works under the control of the capitalist to whom his labor belongs" (Marx 1976, 291). To be the last owner of a property right is sometimes referred to as expropriation. Ellerman asks us to think of this expropriation as the "appropriation of the liabilities" involved in manufacturing the automobile. When we are alert to this additional dimension of appropriation, it focuses our attention on the appropriation of the *entire product* of the firm—output assets and input liabilities—rather than to just the surplus product.

To speak of the appropriation of the entire product in Ellerman's sense refers to being the first owner of all outputs or assets created in the production process, as well as to be the last owner of all the input liabilities, especially labor time, consumed in the production process. While Marx apparently nowhere offers a clear definition of the concept of appropriation, Ellerman's notion does capture two characteristics of the capitalist labor process that Marx noted to be particularly important: that workers do not own any of the product their labor jointly creates and that capitalists are the last owners of workers' labor time (Marx 1976, 291–2). Although the Resnick-Wolff concept of class asks us to focus our attention on the appropriation of surplus labor and its product, it is very hard to imagine an institutional arrangement that would permit worker involvement in the appropriation of surplus labor and its product without also facilitating worker participation in the appropriation of necessary labor and its product. Thus, in what follows we will employ the Ellerman notion of appropriation to imagine post-capitalist, non-exploitative futures.

Thinking about appropriation in terms of first ownership of all produced outputs as well as last ownership of all input liabilities allows us to sidestep some aspects of a thorny debate, explained clearly by Roberts (2014), regarding the question of which workers should be regarded as productive of surplus in considering notions of socialism and communism. Abolishing exploitation involves ending the appropriation of surplus labor exclusively by non-producers, and Marx believed this could be accomplished through "the ultimate abolition of the wages system" for all workers (Marx 1965, 79). Interestingly, Marx's conclusion dovetails nicely with Ellerman's advocacy of what he calls universal self-employment—independent contracting or working in a democratic, worker-directed, cooperative enterprise—through a prohibition of the wage-for-labor-time contract, on the grounds that wage-labor is incompatible with a purported inalienable right to self-governance (a right which, to be sure, might be rejected by many Marxists). But clearly abolition of the wages system would do more than end the appropriation of surplus labor by non-producers; it would also prohibit the wage-for-labor-time exchange more generally, which would end the appropriation of the liability for workers' time by a non-producing hiring party. The issue in ending exploitation becomes more than reassigning first ownership of the produced commodities embodying surplus; it also leads to thinking about how appropriation occurs when any labor is hired. Who *is* and who *should be* the last owner of workers' time: some non-working (potentially exploiting) hiring party, as in private and state capitalism, the workers themselves, or perhaps a co-determined enterprise where community members and labor (or labor and capital owners) cooperatively manage and share appropriation?

With this conception of appropriation in mind, one way to conceptualize socialism is as a system in which workers appropriate their own product, in terms of owning any commodities they might generate from their efforts and in terms of being the last owners of their used-up labor time. Understood in this way, socialism would be compatible with a mixed system of independent contractors and cooperatively organized worker-managed enterprises, where all workers (and only workers) in the firm participate in the appropriation process. A socialism that included only independent contracting and self-managed enterprises could possibly be implemented in a private property, market system, where the wage-for-labor-time exchange (i.e., labor rentals) was legally abolished. Jaroslav Vanek, an influential proponent of worker self-management, proposed a constitutional amendment to prohibit human rentals as one method to achieve this goal. He offered the following language:

> Whenever people work together in a common enterprise (whatever their number), it is they and they only who appropriate the results of their labors, whether positive (products) or negative (costs and liabilities), and who control and manage democratically on the basis of equality of vote or weight the activities of their enterprise. These workers may or may not be owners of the capital assets with which they work, but in any event such ownership does not impart any rights of control over the firm.
>
> *(Vanek 1996, 29)*

Communism would impose additional restrictions on production methods, requiring the end of any form of individual appropriation and mandating collective appropriation in all cases, thereby restricting both the capitalist firm and the independent contractor. Resnick and Wolff (1988) introduce a distinction between two possible types of communism. Type I communism would involve an institutional arrangement in which "all adult individuals in society participate collectively … as appropriators of surplus labor, but only some individuals (a smaller number) perform surplus labor" (Resnick and Wolff 1988, 142). One possible institutional form in which workers share, presumably democratically, in the process of appropriation with non-producers would require the board of directors of each enterprise to be composed of workers and elected members of the relevant community, however specified, perhaps as regional or national representatives. Such a communist board of directors, with both workers and delegates of citizens from the surrounding area, would manage the production process (i.e., appropriate the liabilities) and appropriate the output of the enterprise. Ownership of the means of production could take many conceivable forms, whether individually, worker, or community owned.

Resnick and Wolff's type II communism exists when only performers of surplus labor participate in appropriation; non-producers are excluded. Wolff develops a version of this idea in his book *Democracy at Work* (2012), in which he advocates replacing the capitalist firm with what he calls "workers' self-directed enterprises." In a workers' self-directed enterprise, each productive worker serves as an equal member of the firm's directing board. Wolff indicates that productive workers could hire unproductive workers into an employment relationship, rather than inviting them to join a firm as co-members, since they are not engaged in generating a surplus. As he puts it, in a workers' self-directed enterprise, productive workers would use a "portion of the surplus to hire and provide operating budgets as needed to managers, clerks, security guards, lawyers, and other workers not directly engaged in producing surpluses" (Wolff 2012, 124). A workers' self-directed enterprise thus contrasts with a cooperative, self-employment firm in which no person is employed by another since all self-employed workers, whether classified as productive or unproductive, collectively appropriate the whole product.[3] Self-employment firms do not fall neatly into either Resnick and Wolff's type I or type II form of communism, which is why they might be thought of as socialist rather than communist. But just as self-employment firms can exist with multiple types of ownership rights in the means of production, a system of workers' self-directed enterprises could also permit private property rights in land and capital goods, the production for profit, and commodity markets. But whatever the form of property ownership, in a socialist or communist system, property rights would convey no appropriation rights.

Appropriative class justice clearly requires some form of workplace democracy and worker appropriation, and since it is possible for a democratic workplace to rent privately owned, community-owned or state-owned capital goods, appropriative class justice could be achieved without the traditional socialist method of "socializing the means of production."[4] Herbert Gintis (2010), however, argues that workplace democracy and worker appropriation require worker ownership of capital goods, since non-working owners will be reluctant to lend or rent capital equipment without some degree of control over the production process and the corresponding use and maintenance of the capital that they own or that serves as loan collateral. Consequently, Gintis maintains that worker appropriation also requires worker ownership of productive property. Such an arrangement is feasible in production processes with a low capital-labor ratio, but in many large-scale enterprises (i.e. precisely those most likely to take advantage of the corporate form to raise the necessarily great amounts of capital), worker ownership is not attractive to ordinary workers. To see why, consider that in 2012, 53,500,000 people were employed by US corporations that had a total market capitalization of $18,668,333,210,000.[5] Capital per worker in the corporate sector was thus about $350,000, an amount much greater than the average net worth of a typical member of the working class. Even if we can imagine an economic or political mechanism that would transfer firm ownership directly to its workers, it would be too risky for most of those workers to hold the bulk of their assets in their workplaces, thereby deriving both their labor incomes and capital incomes from their jobs. If worker appropriation were legally mandated, per the Vanek amendment, and if worker ownership were required to make this successful, workers would likely exercise undue caution in the conduct of their enterprises.

Since feasible types of appropriation are often not independent of the ownership and distribution of productive assets, for the foreseeable future it is difficult to conceptualize socialist and communist forms of appropriation without also considering how ownership rights to productive assets are distributed. There are many alternatives. David Schweickart (2012) advocates a post-capitalist model that he calls "economic democracy." He imagines a future in which small firms "operate pretty much as they do now", while large firms— perhaps those that currently are organized as corporations—are "'owned' by society as a whole" (Schweickart 2012, 206–7). Socialized firms would be controlled by their workers, not state officials, who would elect representatives to the firms' boards of directors, thus achieving a type of socialist appropriative justice. Schweickart proposes that public banks finance investment in these enterprises with funds raised through a capital assets tax levied on all firms. While this model avoids the difficulties of full worker ownership, rules and institutions would have to be carefully designed to ensure that democratic firms perform adequate maintenance of the capital stock and to guard against capture of the investment financing process by special interests.

To help facilitate worker appropriation without socializing ownership of the "commanding heights," Theodore Burczak (2006) suggests implementing a socialist "stakeholding" grant, drawing upon Bruce Ackerman and Anne Alstott's (1999) model of a stakeholding society. Ackerman and Alstott argue for implementing a sizable cash payment—an $80,000 basic capital grant—to adult citizens at the age of maturity to enable the achievement of real equality of opportunity. Their stakeholding proposal is "based on the community's obligation to give each person equal respect by providing her with equal resources to develop her unique talents" (Ackerman and Alstott 1999, 194). With adjustments, Ackerman and Alstott's stakeholding proposal offers an attractive institutional structure to achieve a type of socialist distributive justice with the ability to enable democratic workplaces. While Ackerman and Alstott use possession of the means to attend college as the standard proxy for equality of opportunity—thus an $80,000 capital grant—a socialist or communist system that retained private property might use possession of the means to purchase the average capital stock per worker as the standard measure of equal opportunity. This first revision of the Ackerman-Alstott proposal is based upon a view of the stakeholder grant as a share of the accumulated capital stock of the society into which a person is born. A second modification to the Ackerman and Alstott plan is necessary so that the grant is directed towards uses enabling non-exploitative work environments. Ackerman and Alstott argue for no limit on how people could use their capital grant because they accept the liberal belief that there are plural conceptions of the good life. They insist that once the government provides individuals with the means to achieve opportunity, it is up to those individuals to decide the best use of their grant, even if that includes a yearlong party on the beach. From a Marxian perspective, a wealth grant is not valuable for its own sake but for its ability to enhance non-exploitative work opportunities, either through self-employment or by providing a funding source to finance worker-owned and self-managed enterprises. A grant could perform this function if it were limited to investments in human and physical capital: post-secondary education, vocational training, equipment to become an independent contractor, and potential membership fees to join a worker-owned and self-directed firm.

Instead of basic capital grants, Joseph Blasi, Richard Freeman, and Douglas Kruse (2013) advocate a type of shared capitalism, which has the promise to evolve towards socialist and communist forms of appropriation, through various changes in tax policy to encourage capitalist firms to share profits with their workers and to distribute stock ownership widely to all employees. For example, they suggest that income tax law might favor interest income earned by lending to firms partly or wholly owned by workers, that lower estate taxation be levied on small business enterprises sold to workers upon the owner's death, and that deductibility of stock options and stock grants from corporate taxation be allowed only if these options are available to all corporate employees. While they argue that profit sharing and the expansion of worker ownership is a way to reduce inequality (and to enhance socialist distributive justice), these proposals are also intended to enable the evolution of what we have called socialist appropriative justice.[6]

A final type of shared appropriation and another evolutionary form between capitalism and socialism—achievable when the ownership of productive assets is distributed unequally—is to mandate that the board of directors of the enterprise be composed partly of representatives elected by workers and partly of representatives elected by capital owners. Such a system of co-determined enterprises is widely practiced in contemporary Germany, where the law mandates that large firms reserve at least one third of board seats for representatives of the firm's workers.

Socialists and communists have ample reason to reject Hayek's diagnosis of being afflicted with a fatal conceit, as long as the search for more egalitarian forms of productive, appropriative and distributive class justice does not rely on the presumption that abolition of capital markets, state ownership and national economic planning are the means and the end of post-capitalist development. A vast network of law, culture, property rights, exchange mechanisms and public policy sustains the microeconomics of the exploitative capitalist firm and "free market" production and distribution. Non-exploitative firms and egalitarian types of production and distribution likewise have the capacity to develop through socialist and communist interventions in this same network, without the need for an imagined singular rupture with the "capitalist system" (Gibson-Graham 2006).

Notes

1 Roemer (2013) has subsequently rejected this model, anticipating difficulties with implementing and sustaining the coupon stock market. In its place, he now argues for a more traditional social democratic model that retains capitalist work relations but implements a highly progressive tax system to fund an extensive set of welfare-expanding institutions. Social democracy (like the coupon stock market) might achieve a form of socialist distributive class justice, but it makes no attempt at productive or appropriative class justice.
2 In a provocative essay, the subjectivist Austrian economist Israel Kirzner (1979) suggests that the economic meaning of a commodity is never a settled issue in that buyers of commodities might see very different uses and values in those commodities than do sellers, giving rise to the possibility that new value arises, and is appropriated by the entrepreneurial purchaser, in the act of exchange itself. The difficulties such a concept of appropriation in exchange poses to thinking through non-exploitative forms of economy will be left aside in this essay.
3 The joint notions of division of labor and comparative advantage (i.e., that someone who is absolutely more productive might have a comparative advantage at an unproductive activity) seem to make the distinction between productive and unproductive labor inside the firm difficult to operationalize.
4 Related discussions of producer cooperatives where workers assume the role of appropriator can be found in Jossa (2014) and Kristjanson-Gural (2011).
5 US Census, http://www.census.gov/library/publications/2015/econ/g12-susb.html; World Bank, http://data.worldbank.org/indicator/CM.MKT.LCAP.CD (accessed April 28, 2016).
6 Bowles and Gintis (1998) suggest an alternative set of public policies that might favor the gradual evolution of democratically self-managed workplaces in a market economy.

References

Ackerman, B. and A. Alstott. 1999. *The Stakeholder Society.* New Haven, CT: Yale University Press.
Amariglio, J. and D. Ruccio. 1998. "Postmodernism, Marxism, and the Critique of Modern Economic Thought." In *Why Economists Disagree*, D. Prychitko, ed., 237–273. Albany: State University of New York Press.
Blasi J., R. Freeman, and D. Kruse. 2013. *The Citizen's Share.* New Haven, CT: Yale University Press.
Bowles, S. and H. Gintis. 1998. *Recasting* Egalitarianism. London and New York: Verso.
Bowles, S. and A. Jayadev. 2007. "Garrison America." *The Economists' Voice* 4(2): 1–7.
Burczak, T. 2006. *Socialism after Hayek.* Ann Arbor: University of Michigan Press.
Cullenberg, S. 1992. "Socialism's Burden: Toward a 'Thin' Definition of Socialism." *Rethinking Marxism* 5 (Summer): 64–83.
DeMartino, G. 2000. *Global Economy, Global Justice: Theoretical Objections and Policy Alternatives to Neoliberalism.* London and New York: Routledge.
——. 2003. "Realizing Class Justice." *Rethinking Marxism* 15 (January): 1–31.
Ellerman, D. 1992. *Property and Contract in Economics.* Oxford: Basil Blackwell.
Engels, F. 1978. *Socialism: Utopian and Scientific.* In *The Marx-Engels Reader*, 2nd edition, R. Tucker, ed., 683–717. New York and London: W. W. Norton.

Fraad, H., S. A. Resnick, and R. D. Wolff. 1989. "For Every Knight in Shining Armor, There's a Castle Waiting to Be Cleaned." *Rethinking Marxism* 2 (Winter): 9–69.

Gibson-Graham, J. K. 2006. *A Postcapitalist Politics*. Minneapolis: University of Minnesota Press.

Gintis, G. 2010. "Hayek Plus Sen Rings a Bell." Amazon review, September 9, http://www.amazon. com/review/R353KJO6WNGME0/ref=cm_cr_dp_title/186-1918575-8051514?ie=UTF8&ASIN= 0472069519&channel=detail-glance&nodeID=283155&store=books (accessed October 8, 2016).

Hayek, F. 1988. *The Fatal Conceit*. Chicago: University of Chicago Press.

Jossa, B. 2014. *Producer Cooperatives as a New Mode of Production*. London and New York: Routledge.

Kirzner, I. 1979. *Perception, Opportunity, and Profit*. Chicago: University of Chicago Press.

Kristjanson-Gural, D. 2011. "Value, Cooperatives and Class Justice." *Rethinking Marxism* 23 (July): 352–363.

Locke, J. 1980. *Second Treatise on Government*. Edited by C. B. Macpherson. Indianapolis, IN: Hackett.

Marx, K. 1965. *Wages, Price, and Profit*. Peking: Foreign Language Press.

——. 1976. *Capital*, Volume 1. Trans. by B. Fowkes. New York: Vintage.

Marx, K. and F. Engels. 1970. *The German Ideology*. New York: International Publishers.

——. 1978. *Manifesto of the Communist Party*. In *The Marx-Engels Reader*, 2nd edition, R. Tucker, ed., 683–717. New York and London: W. W. Norton.

Nussbaum, M. 2011. *Creating Capabilities: The Human Development Approach*. Cambridge, MA: Belknap Press.

Resnick, S. A. and R. D. Wolff. 1987. *Knowledge and Class*. Chicago: University of Chicago Press.

——. 1988. "Communism: Between Class and Classlessness." *Rethinking Marxism* 1(1): 14–42.

——. 2002. *Class Theory and History: Capitalism and Communism in the USSR*. London and New York: Routledge.

Roberts, B. 2014. "Productive/ Unproductive: Conceptual Topology." *Rethinking Marxism* 26(3): 336–359.

Roemer, J. 1996. *Equal Shares: Making Market Socialism Work,* ed. E. O. Wright. London and New York: Verso.

——. 2013. "Thoughts on Arrangement of Rights in Productive Assets." *Analyse and Kritik* 1: 55–63.

Schweickart, D. 2012. "Property-Owning Democracy or Economic Democracy?" In *Property-Owning Democracy: Rawls and Beyond*, M. O'Neill and T. Williamson, ed., 201–222. Malden, MA: Wiley-Blackwell.

Sciabarra, C. 1995. *Marx, Hayek, and Utopia*. Albany: State University of New York Press.

Screpanti, E. 2004. "Freedom and Social Goods." *Rethinking Marxism* 16(1): 185–206.

Sen, A. 1999. *Development as Freedom*. New York: Anchor Books.

Van der Veen, P. and P. Van Parijs. 1986. "A Capitalist Road to Communism." *Theory and Society* 15(5): 635–655.

Vanek, J. 1996. "The Austrians and Self-Management: A Positive Essay." In *Advances in Austrian Economics*, volume 3, P. Boettke and D. Prychitko, ed., 27–40. Greenwich, CT: JAI Press.

Wolff, R. D. 2012. *Democracy at Work: A Cure for Capitalism*. Chicago: Haymarket Books.

27

INTERNATIONAL MIGRATION

Esra Erdem and Maliha Safri

Introduction

This essay presents a critical overview of Marxian scholarship addressing the interrelation between class and migration. Certainly, how migration affects the logic of exploitation is a central theme, as is the history of labor, xenophobia, strike-breaking and striking that involves migrants. We cannot do full justice to the rich variation of migration patterns across the globe and readily admit that our geographical situatedness (in the U.S. and Europe) heavily affects the material we select. Ultimately, though, we argue that the conceptualization of migration contributes to Marxian theory as it crystallizes tensions in and issues concerning the conceptualization of unemployment, the reserve army, exploitation and the capitalist/postcapitalist divide.

Inserting the Migrant into Modes of Production

In pre-capitalist economies, as well as in the transition to capitalism, migration assumed central importance in articulating social relations and the mode of production. To begin with, transatlantic slavery was thoroughly organized by forced migration, which structured the production of cash crops such as tobacco, cotton and sugar in the Americas. The brutal exploitation of enslaved migrant labor power did not only render the slave mode of production viable, however. The profits generated from slavery were to prove crucial in financing the Second Industrial Revolution and spurring capitalist expansion in England (Williams 1944; Grelet 2001; Beckert 2014; Baptist 2014). The thread of migration weaves not only through the ways that slavery was deeply embedded in capitalism, but also in the transition from feudalism to capitalism.[1]

In the transition from feudalism to capitalism in Europe, human mobility drove the growth of cities that also occurred with a larger shift in the locus of production from farm to factory. Driven off the land in the process of primitive accumulation, displaced peasants played a key part in the consolidation of the capitalist mode of production (Marx 1976). Accompanying these processes, repressive measures such as the Poor Laws in England were instrumental in molding mobile populations, considered as vagabonds, into a docile work force (Polanyi 1944). In short, rural-to-urban migration significantly increased the supply of cheap labor power at the disposal of industrial capital, while dramatically transforming the socio-cultural fabric underlying relations of production.

Marx was among the first to show the implications of the bourgeois conception of liberty for capitalism and labor mobility. In discussing how the dynamics of capital accumulation brought with it a constant relocation of workers away from declining sectors of the economy towards expanding industries, he pointed out that civic liberties such as the freedom of movement and contract were crucial for these shifts to take place. On the other hand, if workers had not also been "free" in the sense of being dispossessed of the means of production to secure their livelihood, they would not have had to move in search of employment.

Building on these insights, migrants have typically been conceptualized in Marxian theory as part of the "reserve army of labor," i.e., a geographically flexible pool of unemployed workers that capital can call upon as needed.[2] The availability, size and composition of such a reserve army, however, depend (among other things) on how sovereign states regulate the mobility across their borders. Today, labor migration programs serve as an instrument to both facilitate and control capital's access to the international labor market.[3] Nevertheless, the constitution of a reserve army is far from straightforward, as it involves negotiating the interests of migrants, capital and the nation state (both sending and receiving).

The complexities pertaining to this encounter between capital and labor power in the context of migration regimes have been studied in considerable detail by scholars associated with the "autonomy of migration" approach. Inspired by the *operaismo* tradition within Italian Marxism (see Virno and Hardt 1996 and Wright 2002 for overviews), autonomist accounts of migration have argued that the process of migration under capitalism is characterized by a fundamental tension between the logic of mobility and the logic of exploitation. While labor migration constitutes a productive force that helps capital retain its dynamism, the mobility of labor power must simultaneously be controlled and harnessed towards the extraction of surplus value.[4] Migration management policies devised by nation states play a crucial role in the mediation of this tension.[5] At the same time, it would be a serious misperception to assume that the movement of people across borders can be fully calibrated through recruitment programs and border controls. The authorities oftentimes try to channel clandestine patterns of mobility devised by migrants through reactive measures such as the closing of legislative loopholes, the introduction of additional routes and technologies of border patrol, etc.[6] But, as recent refugee movements demonstrate, an "excess" of irregular migration will always remain, proving metaphors of total control such as "Fortress Europe" illusory (Mezzadra and Neilson 2013; Bojadžijev and Karakayalı 2010; Papadopoulos, Stephenson and Tsianos 2008).[7]

The autonomist accounts of migration thus resist totalizing mechanics that pitch migrants as objects "pushed and pulled" by markets, narratives that have come to dominate mainstream economic models of migration. They still conceptualize migration as central to the encounter between labor and capital, but dismiss the often-used hydraulic metaphor of migration flows and a resulting (illusory) sense of control over the supply of labor in conjunction with the business cycle (Mezzadra and Neilson 2013).

Value of Migrant Labor Power, Exploitation and Resistance

We return to how migrant labor power is implicated in the logic of exploitation but is marked by specificity as well. Migrant workers share with all productive workers in capitalist firms a relation to exploitation and the extraction of surplus labor. But the migrant also constitutes a particularity to the extent that he/she experiences a different rate of exploitation. Thus, the universality of migrants' human and worker rights have to be considered in conjunction with the reality of super-exploitation. To assert migrant human and worker rights underlines a universal equality, and yet, to see their super-exploitation, we have to be sensitive to the fact that there are structural differences, too.

Three prominent lines of argument have been developed to explain how capitalists can pay migrants below the value of domestic labor power. First, it has been argued that migrants' value of labor power is lower (at least in the initial stages after arrival), since the reference point is still the lower costs associated with the reproduction of labor power in the country of origin. Secondly, the precarious legal and economic status of many migrant workers results in a weaker bargaining position vis-à-vis employers.[8] Consequently, they cannot afford to turn down a poorly paid job even though they know it is unjust. This is particularly true for undocumented migrants who routinely experience wage theft, or are not paid legally mandated overtime or are paid less than they were promised. As migrants revise upwards their value of labor power the longer they stay in the destination country, the problem of wage discrimination deepens into unequal exchange. In the first case the wage gap between migrant and native workers results from their different values of labor power, and in the second case, the wage gap results from pure discrimination as immigrants settle into receiving countries.[9]

Thirdly, in what came to be known as the segmented labor market (SLM) approach, scholars described how capitalists create a smokescreen to divide immigrant and non-immigrant workers into separate, segregated labor markets for the express purpose of maximum surplus-extraction (Reich 1981; Gordon, Edwards and Reich 1982; Drago 1995). Drawing together institutionalists and Marxists, the SLM approach has been highly influential in theorizing racialized and gendered discrimination in the labor market by shifting away slightly from the question of unequal exchange, and towards the segregation of occupations. While unequal wages for the same job (i.e., pure and illegal discrimination) is still a problem, it pales in comparison to why some groups are absent altogether from certain occupations and labor markets. Contrary to Becker's neoclassical economic model, which posited the eventual erosion of discriminatory barriers through market competition (Bohmer 1999), SLM theorists like Reich (1981) have shown that wage gaps could be maintained in the long run, resulting in lower average earnings for all workers and higher profit rates for capitalists.

Obviously, this raises the question of why capital has been so successful in pitting immigrant and non-immigrant workers against each other. While the history of Marxism abounds in declarations of international class solidarity, the fact is that the class antagonism between capital and labor has been overdetermined by intraclass ethnic and racial divisions.[10] Writing on the Irish question, Marx diagnosed with characteristic fire:

> England now possesses a working class divided into two hostile camps, English proletarians and Irish proletarians. The ordinary English worker hates the Irish worker as a competitor who forces down the standard of life. He cherishes religious, social, and national prejudices against the Irish worker. His attitude towards him is much the same as that of the poor whites to the Negroes in the former slave states of the U.S.A. The Irishman pays him back with interest in his own money.... This antagonism is the secret of the impotence of the English working class, despite its organization. It is the secret by which the capitalist class maintains its power. And that class is fully aware of it.
>
> *(Marx 1977 [1870], 169)*

Numerous accounts in labor history demonstrate how wage competition, job segregation, and color bars in trade union organization have marred the relationship between im/migrant and non-immigrant workers. However, it would be too crude to argue that it was the "divide and conquer" strategy of capital that implanted racism in the minds of an unassuming working class. Race and class are distinct yet overdetermined social relations; neither is reducible to the other. Nor do capitalists or the proletariat form homogeneous interest groups that neatly align themselves on a particular side of the racial divide.[11] The "capitalist class" (the same knowing English capitalist class Marx alludes to in the passage above) who maneuvered behind the curtain to foment racism, sexism and xenophobia does not exist as a homogenous class with homogenous interests, and neither for that matter do the workers.

The extent to which equal citizenship rights constitute not just a necessary but also a sufficient condition for overcoming discrimination against immigrants continues to be intensely debated within the Left. Balibar (2004) has argued that the reification of that division between the deserving citizenry and the rightless *"sans-papiers"* (the undocumented) created a new apartheid structure in Europe. Echoing the enthusiasm of the "new labor" activists and organizers, Balibar sees the *sans-papiers* as exemplary of insurgent citizenship, i.e., pushing Western democracy to be more inclusive and to live up to its full democratic ideals.

Neither did immigrant workers simply allow themselves to be instrumentalized as pawns in the class struggle waged in factories. There are numerous accounts of immigrant strikes in the nineteenth and early twentieth century, which were to usher in major changes in the relation between capital and labor. The famous 1912 strike in Lowell, Massachusetts, for example, brought together Italian, Polish, Hungarian, Portuguese, French-Canadian, Slavic and Syrian immigrants in what would be a massively well-known and successful worker strike organized by the Industrial Workers of the World. Women strikers held aloft signs saying "We want bread, but roses too!"—signifying that immigrant workers were both raising economic demands around wages and also forcing recognition of their basic humanity and dignity. In the 1960s and early 1970s, South European migrants staged several wildcat strikes against wage discrimination, poor working and housing conditions, and the complacency of white-dominated trade unions in West Germany (Bojadžijev 2008). More recently, a new wave of immigrant labor organizing in the U.S. has energized both theoretical work and the labor movement. Among the catalysts was a major 1990 strike by mostly Latino and undocumented janitors in Los Angeles (Milkman 2006). Out of this emerged a "new labor" movement, made up mostly of immigrants in domestic work, taxi and livery, construction, grocery retail and other low-wage industries in the service sector that were well outside the conventional manufacturing-based organizing models of trade unions. The permanent "precarity" characterizing many of the occupations with heavy immigrant concentrations, job insecurity (which sometimes could mean employment-by-the-day) and the potential status as undocumented immigrants, required different models of organizing, such as cooperation with immigrant community organizations and the staging of highly visible publicity campaigns against poor working conditions in renowned companies. The unorthodox and courageous examples of labor organization and resistance that have taken place in recent decades have inspired many to look to the new immigrant class struggles as a harbinger, and perhaps even the base, of a nation-wide renewal of the labor movement (Ness 2005; Davis and Chacon 2006).

Postcapitalism and Migration

In this closing section, we would like to point out that the interrelation between class and migration is not limited to capitalism or pre-capitalist modes of production. Rather, it extends to myriad postcapitalist[12] practices in which migrants' economic subjectivities are currently articulated. The Marxian tradition in which we place ourselves sees noncapitalist economic forms, organizations and class processes as already existing, rather than deferred to a post-revolutionary conjuncture (Resnick and Wolff 1987; Gibson-Graham 1996). In our examination of postcapitalism, we focus on one particular pathway of migrants and cooperativism and readily admit that this is only one of many directions to take in examining postcapitalism. Worker cooperatives offer workers one alternative means of securing their livelihood in a democratic workplace, where surplus labor is produced, appropriated and distributed collectively (Resnick and Wolff 1987; Wolff 2012). For this reason, we describe not only how migrants are participating in cooperatives today, but how in the U.S. they are in fact the dominant urban constituency that is forming, running and incubating other worker cooperatives.

In the United States, some of the most prominent worker cooperatives are run by immigrant women: WAGES (Women's Action to Gain Economic Security) in San Francisco, UNITY Housecleaners in Long Island, and *Si Se Puede* in Brooklyn, New York. In the largest worker cooperative in the U.S., Cooperative Home Care Associates in the Bronx, 70% of the member-owners are Latina first- and second-generation immigrant women. Not only are immigrants themselves participating in these noncapitalist enterprises, they are enthusiastically trying to spread the model and sharing their own learning experiences by incubating other worker cooperatives (Bransburg 2011). However, cooperative structures vary widely, even when all members are immigrants, as demonstrated in at least one comparative case study of two Latina domestic worker cooperatives in which class dynamics varied by factors such as the organizational structure of the cooperative, the target consumer market (high-end or low-end) and by the immigration and social status of worker-members (Salzinger 1991).

Another point of intersection between migration and postcapitalism is through remittances. By sending money home to family members in the country of origin, migrant remittances are financing different economic practices, some capitalist and others not. One concrete project in the Philippines, the NGO Unlad Kabayan, established a "Migrant Savings for Alternative Investment" program, which pools funds from Filipina migrant domestic workers in Hong Kong in order to help build community enterprises in the migrants' regions of origin (Gibson-Graham 2006). A portion of the remittance-financed projects are assuming noncapitalist organizational forms. Another case is of a Mexican worker cooperative (Mujeres Embasadoras de Nopales de Ayoquezco) supported by migrant remittances that has now extended beyond growing nopal (prickly pear) to starting the first industrial processing plant in Ayoquezco (Safri and Graham 2015). The workers (who are all female relatives of migrants and recipients of remittances sent home by migrant workers) grow, process, package, market and export nopal among other foods.

Ultimately, though, worker cooperatives may be one step towards a postcapitalist politics of migration, but only one of many steps required and certainly not without internal contradictions.

Such tensions and contradictions are at work in one of the most celebrated areas and examples of worker cooperatives in the Italian Emilia Romagna region of Italy, famous for the high concentration of worker cooperatives. A high-profile series of strikes from 2011–13 inside these cooperatives brought into sharp relief the different working conditions of immigrant and native Italian workers (Sacchetto and Semenzin 2016). A major point of contention turned out to be rooted in the practice of hiring immigrants as non-member workers, thus putting them in a disadvantageous position in terms of lower wage levels, higher work intensity and job insecurity—in effect replicating the segmented labor market described above as characteristic of capitalist relations of production. The now-hybrid cooperative composed of native member-workers and immigrant non-members transforms from being a non-exploitative enterprise to an exploitative two-tiered one. Native workers "deserve" to participate in economic decision-making over surplus, but immigrant workers are the excluded party bearing the brunt, proving that xenophobia and racism are not exclusive to any singular mode of production.

Conclusion: The Figure of the Migrant

So often in political economy, the migrant is positioned as an object that is either pushed or pulled by labor markets, as super-exploited, deployed as a tool against native workers, and so on. These accounts, even perhaps with the good intentions of encircling the issue of exploitation, are characterized by problems. New Labor scholarship brings to our attention one of these problems when it describes how migrant-led labor movements and campaigns have proved historical turning points and may just be a backbone of the contemporary one as well. *Operaismo* has turned the full sophistication of its approach to the particular process of migration, showing that it is not reducible to a symptom of capitalism. The figure of the migrant exceeds the capacity of capitalism to control; it is an eruption of excess that cannot in fact be controlled in the last instance by capital and is daily seen in the global clandestine migration escaping borders everywhere. Migration is the unruly evidence of capitalism's inability to totalize and tame, even as it is unmistakeably marked and cut by it.

We conclude by exceeding the capitalist frame itself, by pointing to the research area that we daresay is crucial but under-researched: how does migration interact with postcapitalism or anticapitalism? Even such a question requires further exploration—what is the difference between anticapitalist and postcapitalist? What political implications follow? We have pursued only one path, the cooperative connection, showing some of the potential contradictions that may emerge. Such issues require our most trenchant and insightful scholarship and contribute to answering to one of the most pressing political questions for Marxism: What is to be done?

Notes

1 Many researchers from the post-Althusserian tradition have argued that different modes of production (feudalism, slavery and even communism) are class processes that are current and exist simultaneously with capitalism. In using the term "pre-capitalist," then, we describe points in history in which migration majorly impacted the course of slavery and feudalism. However, we also think that migration intersects with contemporary slave and feudal class processes, especially since undocumented migrants are often most vulnerable to these forms of exploitative conditions.

2 Historically, the function of a reserve army has also been occupied by women and racialized groups of domestic labor. Despite this functional similitude, however, it should be noted that racism, nationalism and sexism each construct distinct processes of othering. Hence, the capitalist instrumentalization of each category of reserve army involves different social and cultural antagonisms.

3 For a classic example see Castles and Kosack (1973) on worker recruitment in post-World War II Europe.

4 In *Capital* Marx gives a pertinent example of how the mobility of labor power constitutes a condition of existence for the production and capitalist appropriation of surplus value. Reminding his readers that "capital is not a thing, but a social relation between persons" he recounts the situation of a Mr. Peel who:

> took with him from England to Swan River, West Australia, means of subsistence and of production to the amount of £50,000. Mr. Peel had the foresight to bring with him, besides, 300 persons of the working class, men, women, and children. Once arrived at his

destination, 'Mr. Peel was left without a servant to make his bed or fetch him water from the river.' Unhappy Mr. Peel who provided for everything except the export of English modes of production to Swan River!

(Marx 1990, 932–33)

5 While the economic conjuncture doubtless plays a significant role, the scope of such programs and the eligibility criteria attached are always overdetermined by socio-political considerations. In the case of imagined communities based on the principle of ethnic homogeneity (jus sanguinis) such as Germany, it has proven politically impossible to pass pro-immigration legislation despite intense pressure from employers facing labor shortages.

6 The argumentation here echoes the *operaist* position that industrial capital introduces new technologies of production in an effort to regain control over the labor process. A similar argument about the failure of migration policies can be found in Castles (2004).

7 Similarly, De Genova (2005) refers to the militarization of the U.S.-Mexico border as a spectacle that is characterized by illusory control.

8 De Genova (2005) has studied the deportability of irregular migrants as a powerful threat strengthening the position of employers in the United States. In contemporary China, the residential permit system (*hukou*) in effect strips internal migrants of their citizenship rights if they leave their birthplace without the requisite passes. Their precarious situation (lower than legal minimum wages, no access to social services, dangerous working conditions, being subject to arrest and detention) in many ways parallels that of undocumented immigrants in other countries.

9 In both cases, the employer of migrants experiences relative expansion of value, by shrinking the portion of the day devoted to necessary labor and expanding the portion of the day devoted to the production of surplus. This is not to say, however, that employers of migrants do not also undertake strategies aimed at absolute expansion of surplus, as when they extend the working day by employing immigrants, especially undocumented ones. Migrants go from experiencing equal exchange because they first arrive with a value of labor power closer to the one in the country of origin, even if it is a lower one than the receiving country. As they revise their standard of living the longer they stay, but still continue to receive lower wages due to wage discrimination, then the migrants experience unequal exchange, since their value of labor power increases but the wages received do not.

10 From the Chinese immigrant workforces used to break railroad strikes in the U.S. (Briggs 2001) to Moroccan workers being hired by French coal mines after strikes in the 1960s, the examples are too numerous to list here. Using im/migrant workforces as strike-breakers, capitalists have deployed and continue to employ immigrant workers strategically to erode the bargaining power of non-immigrant workers over wages and working conditions all over the world (Bacon 2014). Employers are also not above scapegoating immigrant workers for problems that the employers themselves have helped generate (Davis and Chacon 2006).

11 In the apartheid era in South Africa, for example, the interests of capitalists facing an international embargo differed starkly from the interests of white trade unions. Under the fascist regime in Germany, Jewish capitalists themselves became the target of anti-Semitism.

12 A postcapitalist vision should not be understood as coming after capitalism, or denying its existence, but instead as enacting political and economic forms that are not capitalist (Gibson-Graham 1996, 2006; Mance 2007). The prefix of "post" stands more for a different way of perceiving the economy and economic development that does not focus on capitalist growth as the exclusive means by which well-being is improved (Safri 2015).

References

Bacon, D. 2014. "Why Is This Farm Using Guest Workers as Strike Breakers?" *The Nation*, May 2.

Balibar, E. 2004. *We the People of Europe? Reflections on Transnational Citizenship*. Princeton: Princeton University Press.

Baptist, E. E. 2014. *The Half Has Never Been Told: Slavery and the Making of American Capitalism.* New York: Basic Books.

Beckert, S. 2014. *Empire of Cotton: A Global History.* New York: Alfred A. Knopf.

Bohmer, P. 1999. "Marxist Theory of Racism and Racial Inequality." In *Readings in Black Political Economy*, J. Whitehead and C. K. Harris, eds. Dubuque, IA: Kendall/Hunt.

Bojadžijev, M. 2008. *Die windige Internationale: Rassismus und Kämpfe der Migration.* Münster: Westfälisches Dampfboot.

Bojadžijev, M. and S. Karakayalı. 2010. "Recuperating the Sideshows of Capitalism: The Autonomy of Migration Today." *e-flux* 17 (June). http://www.e-flux.com/journal/recuperating-the-sideshows-of-capitalism-the-autonomy-of-migration-today/ (accessed August 6, 2016).

Bransburg, V. 2011. "The Center for Family Life: Tackling Poverty and Social Isolation in Brooklyn with Worker Cooperatives." *Grassroots Economic Organizing Newsletter* 2(8). http://geo.coop/node/636 (accessed August 6, 2016).

Briggs, V. M., Jr. 2001. *Immigration and American Unionism.* Ithaca, NY: Cornell University Press.

Castles, S. 2004. "Why Migration Policies Fail." *Ethnic and Racial Studies* 27(2): 205–227.

Castles, S. and G. Kosack. 1973. *Immigrant Workers and Class Structure in Western Europe.* London: Institute of Race Relations.

Davis, M. and J. Akers Chacon. 2006. *No One is Illegal.* Chicago: Haymarket Press.

De Genova, N. 2005. *Working the Boundaries.* Durham, NC: Duke University Press.

Drago, R. 1995. "Divide and Conquer in Australia: A Study of Labor Segmentation." *Review of Radical Political Economics* 27(1): 25–70.

Gibson-Graham, J. K. 1996. *The End of Capitalism (As We Knew It): A Feminist Critique of Political Economy.* Oxford: Blackwell Publishers.

——. 2006. *A Postcapitalist Politics.* Minneapolis: University of Minnesota Press.

Gibson-Graham, J. K., S. A. Resnick, and R. D. Wolff, eds. 2000. *Class and Its Others.* Minneapolis: University of Minnesota Press.

Gordon, D., R. Edwards, and M. Reich. 1982. *Segmented Work, Divided Workers.* New York: Cambridge University Press.

Grelet, S. 2001. "The Art of Flight: An Interview with Yann Moulier-Boutang." *Rethinking Marxism* 13(3/4): 227–235.

Mance, E. 2007. "Solidarity Economics." In *What Would It Mean to Win?*, Turbulence Collective, ed., 66–73. Oakland, CA: PM Press.

Marx, K. 1976. *Capital*, Volume 1. London: Penguin Books.

——. 1977 [1870]. "Letter to Meyer and Voght." In *Writings*, Volume 3, 169. New York: Vintage.

Mezzadra, S. and B. Neilson. 2013. *Border as Method.* Durham, NC: Duke University Press.

Milkman, R. 2006. *L.A. Story: Immigrant Workers and the Future of the U.S. Labor Movement.* New York: Russell Sage Foundation.

Ness, I. 2005. *Immigrants, Unions and the New U.S. Labor Market.* Philadelphia: Temple University Press.

Papadopoulos, D., N. Stephenson, and V. Tsianos. 2008. *Escape Routes: Control and Subversion in the 21st Century.* London: Pluto Press.

Polanyi, K. 1944. *The Great Transformation.* Boston: Beacon Press.

Reich, M. 1981. *Racial Inequality.* Princeton: Princeton University.

Resnick, S. A. and R. D. Wolff. 1987. *Knowledge and Class.* Chicago: University of Chicago Press.

Roberts, B. 2011. "Exploitation, Appropriation, and Subsumption." *Rethinking Marxism* 23(3): 341–351.

Ruccio, D. 2011. "Cooperatives, Surplus, and the Social." *Rethinking Marxism* 23(3): 334–340.

Sacchetto, D. and M. Semenzin. 2016. "Workers' Cooperatives in Italy: Between Solidarity and Autocratic Centralism." In *Social Economy in China and the World*, N. Pun, B. Hok-bun Ku, H. Yan, and A. Koo, eds., 135–155. New York: Routledge.

Safri, M. 2011. "Worker Cooperatives: A Class Analysis." *Rethinking Marxism* 23(3): 329–333.

——. 2015. "Mapping Noncapitalist Supply Chains: Toward an Alternate Conception of Value Creation and Distribution." *Organization* 22(6): 924–941.

Safri, M. and J. Graham. 2015. "International Migration and the Global Household: Performing Diverse Economies on the World Stage." In *Making Other Worlds Possible*, G. Roelvink, K. St. Martin, and J. K. Gibson-Graham, eds., 244–268. Minneapolis: University of Minnesota Press.

Salzinger, L. 1991. "A Maid by Any Other Name." In *Ethnography Unbound*, M. Burawoy, ed., 139–160. Berkeley: University of California Press.

Virno, P. and M. Hardt, eds. 1996. *Radical Thought in Italy: A Potential Politics*. Minneapolis: University of Minnesota Press.

Williams, E. 1944. *Capitalism and Slavery*. Chapel Hill: University of North Carolina Press.

Wolff, R. D. 2012. *Democracy at Work: A Cure for Capitalism*. Chicago: Haymarket Books.

Wright, S. 2002. *Storming Heaven: Class Composition and Struggle in Italian Autonomist Marxism*. London: Pluto Press.

28

AGRICULTURE AND THE AGRARIAN QUESTION

Elizabeth A. Ramey

Introduction

Marxian political economists have grappled with the "agrarian question" since the late nineteenth century, when European Marxists confronted the vitally important question of making sense of the agrarian peasantry's role in the rapidly emerging European capitalist economies. Framed in this way, the agrarian question presented urgent theoretical and practical political challenges as Marxian revolutionaries considered what class alliances might best serve to push forward the communist project. The question of the relationship between agriculture and capitalist development has continued to fuel debate since Marx and his followers first confronted what was then called "the peasant question." Over 125 years later, the agrarian question remains a puzzle.

Three critical areas of interest have emerged within the literature since the agrarian question was first formulated (Byres 1986; Bernstein 1996). These three areas can be traced to their origins in the works of the Classical Marxists. The first area is represented by Engels' investigation of the politics of the European peasantry, with a focus on the French and German socialist party platforms and possibilities for political alliances. The second evolved from the first and involves the examination of the possibilities for capitalist transformation in agricultural production. The third engages the matter of agriculture and its role in the economic development of the broader economy. Each of these themes will be explored in turn, as well as major works associated with them, in hopes of providing a balanced overview of a somewhat neglected but provocative strand of thought within the Marxian tradition.

The First Agrarian Question: Engels and the Peasantry

By the late nineteenth century, it was evident that Marxist theorists needed to come to terms with the continued political and economic importance of the peasantry across Europe. Capitalist industrial development in European societies had failed to displace what Marxists commonly viewed as a backward, anachronistic vestige of a pre-capitalist society. The agrarian question was thus motivated by the dilemma of incomplete or blocked capitalist (or later socialist) development. The existence of a peasantry was viewed as an undesirable indicator of this dilemma. The expectation that successful development requires (and is an indicator of) the marginalization or extinction of peasants and vice versa has been embedded in the agrarian question discussion since its inception.

Since the peasant had not yet faded from the scene in the course of economic development, it was necessary to examine his politics. Where would he stand in relation to the socialists' aspirations to capture political power? Would he be reactionary or revolutionary? Thus, the agrarian question began as the "peasant question."

In his extensive work on the agrarian question, T. J. Byres (1986) identifies politics as the first of three broad themes, or "problematics" established in the works of the European Marxists of the late nineteenth century. For him, Engels' 1894 work, *The Peasant Question in France and Germany*, most clearly exemplifies the political problematic from which the other two themes, production and accumulation, emerged.

Surveying the European economic landscape, Engels noted that the dominance of peasant agriculture in most regions of Europe at the time meant that peasants were "a very essential factor of the population, production and political power" (Engels 1894, 2). Peasants, who owned or rented the land they worked with their families, occupied a middle class, a "survival of a past mode of production" (Ibid., 4) that was neither fully capitalist exploiter nor dispossessed proletarian. This ambiguous middle ground rendered the peasants' political allegiances vulnerable to manipulation and false promises from "the wolf in sheep's clothing of the big landowner" or the bourgeoisie, for whom "it has not been particularly difficult to render the socialist workers suspicious and odious in the minds of the peasants..., as lazy, greedy, city dwellers who have an eye on the property of the peasants" (Ibid., 2–3). Thus, Engels argued the socialist party could no longer afford to ignore the countryside in the political struggle, lest the sleeping giant be mobilized on behalf of their enemies. "[M]ay this party calmly leave the doomed peasant in the hands of his false protectors until he has been transformed from a passive into an active opponent of the industrial workers?" (Ibid.).

For Engels, it was the lower strata—the "small" and "middle" peasants—of the economically differentiated European peasantries whose material interests would most closely align with those of the industrial working class, and hence the socialist party. Indeed, Engels argued, in many ways the economic circumstances of the small peasant were even more precarious than those of the proletariat, trapped as he was under an onerous burden of debt and ever-intensifying global competition, and locked in a losing battle to save his land. It was his "deep-rooted sense of property" (Engels 1894, 5) that not only distorted his political allegiances, but hastened his economic ruin, as well. "It is precisely the individual farming conditioned by individual ownership that drives the peasants to their doom. If they insist on individual operation, they will inevitably be driven from house and home and their antiquated mode of production superseded by capitalist large-scale production" (Ibid., 14). For Engels, there was no doubt that the small peasant, "like every other survival of a past mode of production, is hopelessly doomed. He is a future proletarian" (Ibid., 5).

Hence, Engels concluded that the resolution of the "peasant question" was really no resolution at all. The socialist party would take the side of the small peasants, but could not promise to protect their property unless they were prepared to "make them a promise which we ourselves know we shall not be able to keep" (Engels 1894, 13). The only tenable position for the party was "to make clear to the peasants again and again that... it is absolutely impossible to preserve their small holdings for them as such, that capitalist large-scale production is absolutely sure to run over their impotent antiquated system of small production as a train runs over a pushcart" (Ibid., 15).

The Second Agrarian Question: Kautsky, Lenin, and Capitalist Agriculture

Engels' analysis of the "peasant question" was driven by practical political concerns and lacked a systematic theoretical analysis. It was Karl Kautsky, arguably the most influential Marxist theoretician of the time, who did the work of applying and extending Marx's theory to the countryside. The results of that project, based on his empirical study of German agriculture, were published in his 1899 work, *The Agrarian Question*. Upon its publication, Lenin wrote, "Kautsky's book is the most important event in present-day economic literature since the third volume of *Capital*. Until now, Marxism has lacked a systematic study of capitalism and agriculture. Kautsky has filled this gap" (Lenin 1899a, 94). Lenin himself had just completed the manuscript of his own work on Russian agriculture, *The Development of Capitalism in Russia*, published a few months later. Kautsky's and Lenin's works constitute the principal expositions of the "production problematic" of the agrarian question.

Like Engels, Kautsky was motivated by concern for the politics of the German peasantry, but in addressing that concern, he shifted his focus from the political to the economic. This shift reflects a materialist conception that political actions and interests would follow from economic actions and interests. Kautsky, like Engels, assumed that the basis for socialism in the countryside was the proletarianization of the peasantry. Kautsky wrote, "Two souls inhabit the breast of the dwarf-holder: a peasant and a proletarian" (1899, 324). The proletarian soul could only be strengthened, and the revolutionary potential of the peasantry realized, if the mass of small peasants became dispossessed wage laborers. Hence, the key to the political analysis lay in understanding how capitalist development would unfold in the countryside. As Kautsky explained, his purpose was to consider "*whether, and how, capital is seizing hold of agriculture, revolutionizing it, making old forms of production and property untenable and creating the necessity for new ones*" (12, emphasis in original).

Like Engels, Kautsky recognized that the processes of economic differentiation among the peasants were important and so examined these processes in detail. Kautsky began with the presumption that theoretically, peasant agriculture was destined to suffer the same fate as petty commodity production in manufacturing. Capital accumulation and competition would favor the concentration and consolidation of peasant farms into larger production units, their owners transformed into members of the rural bourgeoisie. Smaller farms would be competed away, their inhabitants transformed into rural wage laborers working for the remaining large capitalist farms. Hence, as in industry, the process of capitalist development in agriculture would generate the opposing classes of capitalist farmer and rural proletarian.

Empirical evidence, however, did not support the predicted demise of small peasant farmers. On the contrary, the 1895 German census indicated "the small farm has not lost ground to the large since the 1850s," and in fact, "small farms seem to be growing in some areas" (Kautsky 1899, 11). Kautsky argued, therefore, that Marx's theory of capitalist development could not simply be applied to agriculture. "Agriculture does not develop according to the pattern traced by industry: it follows its own laws" (Ibid.). Kautsky identified several obstacles to capitalist transition in agriculture. While large farms were still technically superior and more efficient, small farms could nevertheless survive, perhaps indefinitely, due to a variety of factors, including the "over-exploitation" of peasant labor-power through self-exploitation and exploitation of family labor. This ability of peasants to reduce their own consumption or to expand their work in response to competition would lower their average cost of labor power relative to hired farm labor. In addition, small peasants would be functional to capitalist development in the countryside by providing a part-time labor force to the larger capitalist farms. Hence, Kautsky's empirical analysis indicated that peasant agriculture could be integrated into capitalist agriculture without dissolution.

In spite of his complex and nuanced economic analysis, Kautsky's political conclusions reflected the stereotype of peasants as a conservative, largely passive base for the traditional social order and collapsed back into a more simplistic view of historical necessity. For him, the very tendency for peasants to over-exploit themselves that was the source of their competitive advantage would keep them forever backward and impoverished. "We have to confess that as far as we are concerned the sub-human diet of the small peasant is no more an advantage than its superhuman industriousness. Both testify to economic backwardness" (Kautsky 1899, 116). This, along with their isolation and ignorance of their true interests, "often harnessing the same vigour used by other classes for their emancipation in the cause of their own exploiters," trumped any revolutionary potential. He recommended that the socialists neutralize rather than mobilize the peasantry (Ibid., 10).

The Agrarian Question was not translated into English until 1988, in part because of Kautsky's break with the Russian Marxists over the Russian Revolution. Unlike "Renegade Kautsky," Lenin remained in the good graces of what became "Official Marxism" after 1917. Hence, while Kautsky's work was extremely influential in the pre-World War I period in Europe, Lenin's work was much more widely translated and read. *The Development of Capitalism in Russia* was his effort to extend Marx's theory to the analysis of Russia. He began work on the book in 1896 while in prison, and completed it three years later while in exile in Siberia. In spite of these limitations, Lenin was able to base his analysis on a detailed and extensive census of peasant households in Russia known as the *Zemstvo* statistics, which he painstakingly analyzed in this work.

Like Kautsky, Lenin emphasized processes of peasant differentiation as the key to understanding the rise of capitalist agriculture. He identified two different paths of transition. These were the Prussian Path, or capitalism from above, and the American Path, or capitalism from below.[1] Lenin argued that the Russian peasantry was already in a state of disintegration, or "depeasantisation," and that the formation of the rural bourgeoisie and proletariat was in progress. Among the factors shaping this process of capitalist transformation in agriculture were technological change, intensified global competition and increased use of debt to maintain peasants' consumption.

For Lenin, unlike for Kautsky, the peasantry held great revolutionary potential. The harsh conditions of self-exploitation, or what he called "plunder of labour," made the small peasants more amenable to political alliance with the workers. The large numbers of small peasants, rural proletarians and semi-proletarians meant that such an alliance was necessary in order for the revolution to succeed (Lenin, 1899b).

The Third Agrarian Question: Preobrazhensky

The second agrarian question highlighted by Kautsky's and Lenin's work on the character of farm production was extremely influential in the pre-WWI period in Europe. The center of Marxian influence and scholarship on the agrarian question shifted, however, with the Russian Revolution in October 1917. After the Revolution, the practical concerns of managing economic development and agrarian change in the Soviet Union came to dominate work on the agrarian question. The overriding concern for Russian Marxists became how to transform and industrialize the ruined Russian economy and avoid political unrest. Hence, Russian Marxists turned their attention to the accumulation question, or how peasant agriculture in the largely rural and agrarian economy could be used to finance capital accumulation and transformation in the rest of society.

The economy of the newly formed Soviet Union, crippled by World War I and civil war, had reached a crisis point by 1921. Economic output remained far below pre-war levels. Growing unrest between and among both workers and peasants threatened to unravel the worker-peasant alliance upon which the revolution was based. Lenin enacted the New Economic Policy (NEP) in 1921 in an attempt to ameliorate the crisis. The NEP formed the context for the bitter inter-party struggle known during the 1920s as the "industrialization debates" ignited by Lenin's death in 1924. The chief intellectual architect of the right-wing strategy behind the NEP, which remained official policy until 1928, was Nikolai Bukharin. Opposite him was Evgenii Preobrazhensky, the principle theoretician of the left opposition led by Leon Trotsky. Preobrazhensky's detailed intervention in the debate was *The New Economics*, published in 1926.

While both sides of the debate agreed that industrialization was necessary in order to preserve socialism, at issue was the appropriate pattern and pace to achieve that goal. The success or failure of any plan hinged on the peasantry. Economically, the NEP appeared to be a success—both industrial and agricultural output recovered pre-war levels by 1927—but it came with its own set of ideological and political contradictions. It allowed the growth of private markets in agriculture, albeit tightly controlled and managed, alongside the state-controlled sectors. As such, it represented a partial retreat from the state planning that was identified with socialism.[2] Bukharin argued that this type of retreat was necessary to placate the peasantry, who could easily "veto" industrialization policy by refusing to purchase industrial goods or by consuming and hoarding their produce. Because of this veto power, Bukharin argued that the Soviet Union should allow rural conditions to dictate the pace of industrialization. He advocated a policy of "snail's pace" industrialization and "balanced growth" between agriculture and industry (Preobrazhensky 1921, n.p.).

Preobrazhensky, on the other hand, worried that allowing capitalism to develop in the countryside would produce a powerful class of rich peasants and merchants with an interest in overturning the revolutionary aims of socialism and the means to do so.[3] Thus, the political dangers of the NEP would ultimately overwhelm any economic gains. Preobrazhensky argued that the Soviet Union must accomplish self-consciously and within a few decades what had occurred spontaneously over several centuries for countries such as England and Germany. He developed the concept of "primitive socialist accumulation," analogous to Marx's primitive capitalist accumulation, to capture this idea.

Primitive socialist accumulation was "a period of the creation of the material prerequisites for socialist production" (Preobrazhensky 1926, 81). Isolated as it was, the Soviet Union had to rely on internal surpluses to generate primitive accumulation, or on the raw materials, food and workers, freed from non-industrial production and required to foster the growth of the industrial sector. As Preobrazhensky explained, "petty production serves as the nutrient base both for capitalist and for socialist accumulation" (Ibid., 78). He favored a strategy of manipulating the "price scissors" or terms of trade between agriculture and industry, rather than direct taxation, in order to avoid political backlash. By raising the price of industrial relative to agricultural goods, the state could siphon surplus from the peasants and transfer it to industry. For Preobrazhensky, the period of primitive socialist accumulation must be relatively brief due to the unstable political situation. As he explained, "How to pass as quickly as possible through this period, how to reach as quickly as possible the moment when the socialist system will develop its natural advantages over capitalism, is a question of life and death for the socialist state" (Ibid., 89).

Agrarian Questions Today: The United States

Underlying the primary contributions to these agrarian questions is an implicit vision of capitalism (or socialism) and its relation to the peasant. As Gibson-Graham discusses, the capitalism that appears in most Marxian accounts, including those discussed above, has certain essential properties: unity, singularity and totality. Capitalism is unified in the sense that it is a self-contained, self-regulating whole. Internal laws of motion propel it almost inexorably along a universal, prescribed path of development. It is singular in the sense that is has no peer or rival. It tends not to exist with non-capitalist economic forms, and when it does, it is dominant. Others forms are marginal, residual and contingent—a sign of underdevelopment. Capitalism is total in the sense that it contains and subsumes all else within it. There is no "outside" of capitalism (Gibson-Graham 2006, 253–9).

This vision of capitalism bears on the agrarian question literature as well. In producing its knowledge of the peasant, it therefore produces its knowledge of capitalism and vice versa. As we have seen, "peasant" and "capitalist" are assumed to be mutually exclusive categories. Peasants are therefore engaged primarily in non-capitalist forms of economic activity. Of the two, "capitalist" is a more developed, more efficient and desirable economic form. Such non-capitalist or pre-capitalist forms precede and must ultimately give way to capitalism. (Likewise, capitalism is an essential prerequisite for socialism.) The existence of peasants is a sign of backwardness and incomplete development. If peasants do continue to exist within (not alongside) capitalism, their presence is something that needs to be explained (or explained away)—to be fixed on the Marxian theoretical landscape in a way that both acknowledges their existence but effectively denies them autonomy or efficacy. As we will see, this continues to be relevant for agrarian questions today.

As we have seen, the classical agrarian question had three layers of meaning, politics, production and accumulation. Each layer emerged from the one before as Marxists sought to respond to urgent concerns of the time. These questions, in various forms, remain just as urgent today. Peasant farms are still the dominant forms of agricultural production world-wide. The classical agrarian questions concerning issues of economic development and agrarian transition most clearly still pertain in the case of poor, developing countries. Indeed, most contemporary literature focuses on this aspect of agrarian questions. (See Bernstein 1996; Akram-Lodhi and Kay 2010a; Akram-Lodhi and Kay 2010b for detailed reviews.)

Agrarian questions, however, remain just as pertinent in industrialized countries such as the United States, where capitalist development has gone farthest in transforming the food and agriculture system. Even in such highly developed capitalist economies, peasants remain the dominant agents of agricultural production. There, peasant farms are known as family farms.[4] The family farm remains politically influential, culturally iconic and numerically ubiquitous. According to the United States Department of Agriculture, 97 percent of the 2 million farms in the United States in 2014 were family farms (MacDonald 2014).[5]

Family farms are embedded in what is known as an "industrial agriculture complex," sandwiched between sprawling capitalist behemoths known collectively as "agribusiness." Across the twentieth century, farmers were encouraged to transform their farms into "factories in the field" by applying industrial logic to farm production. The result was the rise of large-scale, specialized farms that mass-produce standardized products and with less need for skilled labor (or labor of any kind) thanks to mechanization and the adoption of other new technologies embodied in purchased inputs. Farmers now purchase the chemical, biological and mechanical inputs they previously produced themselves. As a result, the modern industrial farmer is surrounded by an array of massive capitalist enterprises supplying inputs, as well as transporting, processing, packaging and marketing the outputs of farm production. While farming itself accounts for a vanishingly small share of economic output in the United States, the industrial agriculture complex is populated by some of the world's largest corporations—economic and political powerhouses.

Family farms have been transformed within capitalism, but not necessarily to capitalist farms themselves, although this question, along with the definition of family farm, is by no means settled. Indeed, much of the agrarian question literature that does pertain to industrialized countries tends to focus on explaining the conundrum of the family farm. (See Reinhardt and Barlett 1989; McLaughlin 1998 for reviews of this literature.) For those who subscribe to the particular view of capitalism discussed above, a family farm – or noncapitalist entity – is something that does not belong in a capitalist economy. As such, its continued presence is dealt with in various ways. One strategy is to continue to argue that the family farm is already, or is in the process of becoming, capitalist. A second strategy is to attribute the conundrum to certain obstacles to capitalist development in agriculture, without which the family farm is unable to fend off the forces leading to its demise. The two strategies often go together. Richard Lewontin, for example, employs both strategies in arguing that the "maturing of capitalism" in agriculture has been forestalled until very recently due to farmers' decision-making authority over agricultural production processes. The rise of agribusiness has been accompanied by a loss of this authority, and is a harbinger of farmers' proletarianization (Lewontin 2000).

Other theorists have dissented from this predominant view, contributing to an alternative literature in which family farms are not cast as passive, anachronistic economic forms, paradoxically existing in the crevices of a capitalist economy, but as dynamic, robust, adaptable, complex and stable non-capitalist forms, existing alongside and participating in a capitalist economy. Notable among these dissenters is the Russian economist A. V. Chayanov, whose work *The Theory of Peasant Economy* was published in 1925. Using the same data that Lenin used for his study, supplemented with his own and his students' fieldwork, Chayanov argued that peasant or family farming was an efficient and viable mode of production that could compete successfully with capitalism in agriculture. This is because farm families, lacking the imperative to turn a profit while paying market wages, could rely on the flexibility of unpaid family labor in order to reduce costs (Chayanov 1925).

Chayanov's work inspired renewed debate about family farms when the English translation was published in 1966. Since then, others have contributed to this dissenting perspective in examining the multiple survival strategies and adaptations that family farms have employed to survive in the United States. In one recent example, E. A. Ramey (2014) identifies various survival strategies employed by Midwestern family farms across the twentieth century, including the adoption of new farming technologies and intense rates of exploitation of unpaid family labor. Participation in off-farm wage labor, she argues, has increasingly become a strategy facilitating the survival of non-capitalist family farms, not their transition into capitalist forms. (For a review of further literature on the resilience of family farms see Brookfield 2008.)

Conclusion: Agrarian Questions for the Twenty-First Century

Thanks to industrial agriculture and the strategies family farmers have employed in order to adapt to a changing environment, family farmers in the U.S. rank among the most productive humans in history. Yet in the twenty-first century, industrial agriculture is fraught with controversy. This same system has been implicated in a growing array of serious human health, environmental, social and ethical concerns. Michael Pollan's *The Omnivore's Dilemma* (2006) provided a popular account of some of these issues, and along with a virtual cascade of other scholars and journalists writing for a popular audience, has helped inspire a burgeoning alternative foods movement.

Marxian theorists have engaged with various topics in this literature, including corporate power, democracy and inequality; environmental sustainability and climate change; hunger and obesity; issues with applying machine logic to natural systems; and alienation, deskilling and loss of farmer autonomy. Robert Albritton's *Let Them Eat Junk* (2009) provides an overview of the numerous problems associated with industrial agriculture from a Marxian perspective. For him, "the entire spirit of capitalist production, which is oriented towards the most immediate profit, stands in contradiction to agriculture, which has to concern itself with the whole gamut of permanent conditions of life required by the chain of human generations" (Marx in Albritton 2009, 2). Like other Marxian theorists, his purpose is to demonstrate that capitalism is fundamentally inconsistent with a rational food provisioning system.

Increasing numbers of people are coming to recognize that the food and agricultural system is broken. Indeed, it is a compelling example of what is wrong with a capitalist economy. They are rebelling against the system and establishing alternative food chains and practices. Perhaps no other issue has inspired such broad-based, popular support for *systemic change* and acceptance of the critique of capitalism. Food and agriculture issues present a unique opportunity for Marxian theorists, as experts on systemic critique with a large body of work on agrarian transition, to support this movement.

Clearly then, a new set of agrarian questions is relevant. What role does the family farm play in producing the contradictions associated with industrial agriculture? What role might it play in the transition to a non-capitalist, non-exploitative alternative agriculture? How might transformation in the food and agriculture sector ramify throughout the economy in capitalist and non-capitalist spaces? Fully engaging this new set of agrarian questions to interrogate the potential role of family farms in social change requires adopting an alternative underlying discourse of capitalism, however.

The view of capitalism as unified, singular and total, with all of its predictions about the prognosis for peasants and family farms has not been borne out historically or in contemporary societies. The result has been to marginalize Marxian scholarship in this area as the existing scholarship on agrarian questions in industrialized countries has largely been focused on whether and how family farms persist within industrialized economies. Caught in the narrow confines of a particular vision, much of the agrarian question literature has therefore lost its relevance and political urgency. Indeed, it seems unclear how it offers a distinct alternative to neoclassical considerations of agriculture, which share a similar disdain for family farms. The implication is that Marxian theoretical work on family farms and their role in any future agricultural transition is underdeveloped. What is needed are complex, nuanced and systematic analyses of the role of non-capitalist entities like family farms in capitalist societies. The dissenting analyses discussed above represent steps toward this alternative perspective.

Rescuing the family farm from the margins of Marxian scholarship requires building on this work by developing an alternative discourse of capitalism and exploring agrarian questions along these lines. Gibson-Graham argues for a vision of capitalism that is "uncentered, dispersed, plural, and partial in relation to the economy and society as a whole" (Gibson-Graham 2006, 259). In this way, space is opened to imagine, expect, and identify the presence of non-capitalist entities, including non-exploitative ones, in society today, and to ask new questions about their role in social change. No longer is capitalism an all-encompassing monolith that must be changed all at once or not at all. With non-capitalist spaces opened up, the possibilities for effective political and economic interventions are thereby multiplied. With such a perspective, alternative forms of agricultural production—including family farms—become viable and visible on their own terms, rather than in relation to capitalism. This allows for recognition that such forms can succeed and have already taken hold—not just in some distant past or future, but today. Imagining capitalism and the family farm in this way opens up the possibility for revitalizing work on agrarian questions, and for Marxian scholars to fully engage these crucial contemporary issues.

Notes

1 In the Prussian Path, capitalist farmers emerge from the class of former feudal lords. In the American Path, capitalist farmers emerge from an increasingly differentiated peasantry (Byres 2012).
2 For a detailed discussion of how the Soviet "socialism" was actually state capitalism, see Resnick and Wolff 2002.
3 Indeed, the NEP did just that. Faced with internal upheaval and the threat of foreign intervention, Stalin was forced to end the NEP and adopt a brutal industrialization program, the first of the Five Year Plans, in 1928.
4 Perhaps reflecting the belief in peasant backwardness shared by Marxist and non-Marxist alike, great pains have been taken in the United States to differentiate the "peasant" from the "family farmer." A notable exception among Marxists is Rosa Luxemburg who refers to U.S. family farmers as peasants in *The Accumulation of Capital* (1913). Byres's definition of peasant farming as "production by petty producers using their own means of production and their own labor (although not necessarily exclusively so)" fits family farming as well (Byres 2012, 11). Hence, the difference between "peasant" and "family farmer" seems to be nothing more than semantics (Brookfield 2008, 111). It should be noted, however that the definition of "family farm" is a widely debated subject complicating the agrarian question literature.
5 No existing "official" definition of family farms includes any explicit mention of class. For example, the definition of a family farm developed by the USDA distinguishes family farms on the basis of property and power. That is, a family farm is one whose "principal operator and people related to him or her by blood or marriage own most of the farm business" (MacDonald 2014). The principal operator is defined as "the person who is responsible for the on-site, day-to-day decisions of the farm or ranch business." Clearly, this definition subsumes a wide variety of farms under the single category of family farm, including ancient and feudal enterprises run primarily with family labor to large capitalist enterprises run primarily with hired labor. The United Nations Food and Agriculture Organization definition adds a further criterion: participation in farm labor processes. In this definition, the farm family must not only own and manage the farm business, but also provide most of the farm labor. By this more restrictive definition, family farms account for 87 percent of farms and 57.6 percent of agricultural production in the United States (MacDonald 2014).

References

Akram-Lodhi, A. H. and C. Kay. 2010a. "Surveying the Agrarian Question (part 1): Unearthing Foundations, Exploring Diversity." *The Journal of Peasant Studies* 37(1): 177–202.
——. 2010b. "Surveying the Agrarian Question (part 2): Current Debates and beyond." *The Journal of Peasant Studies* 37(2): 255–284.
Albritton, R. 2009. *Let Them Eat Junk: How Capitalism Creates Hunger and Obesity.* London and New York: Pluto Press.

Bernstein, H. 1996. "Agrarian Questions Then and Now." *The Journal of Peasant Studies* 24(1-2): 22–59.

Brookfield, H. 2008. "Family Farms Are Still Around: Time to Invert the Old Agrarian Question." *Geography Compass* 2(1): 108–126.

Byres, T. J. 1986. "The Agrarian Question, Forms of Capitalist Agrarian Transition and the State: An Essay with Reference to Asia." *Social Scientist* 14(11/12): 3–67.

——. 2012. "The Agrarian Question and the Peasantry." In *The Elgar Companion to Marxist Economics*, B. Fine and A. Saad-Filho, eds., 10–15. Cheltenham: Edward Elgar.

Chayanov, A. V. 1925. *The Theory of Peasant Economy.* Manchester: Manchester University Press.

Engels, F. 1894. "The Peasant Question in France and Germany." https://www.marxists.org/archive/marx/works/download/Engles_The_Peasant_Question_in_France_and_Germany.pdf (accessed June 1, 2016).

Gibson-Graham, J. K. 2006. *The End of Capitalism (As We Knew It): A Feminist Critique of Political Economy.* Minneapolis: University of Minnesota Press.

Kautsky, K. 1899. *The Agrarian Question.* Trans. by P. Burgess. London and Winchester, MA: Zwan Publications.

Lenin, V. I. 1899a. "Book Review: Karl Katusky. Die Agrarfrage." In *Lenin Collected Works*, 4:94–99. Moscow: Progress Publishers. https://www.marxists.org/archive/lenin/works/1899/mar/kautsky.htm (accessed June 1, 2016).

——. 1899b. *The Development of Capitalism in Russia.* https://www.marxists.org/archive/lenin/works/1899/devel/index.htm (accessed June 1, 2016).

Lewontin, R. 2000. "The Maturing of Capitalist Agriculture." In *Hungry for Profit: The Agribusiness Threat to Farmers, Food, and the Environment*, F. Buttel, F. Magdoff, and J. B. Foster, eds., 93–106. New York: Monthly Review Press.

Luxemburg, R. 1913. *The Accumulation of Capital.* https://www.marxists.org/archive/luxemburg/1913/accumulation-capital/ (accessed July 1, 2016).

MacDonald, J. 2014. "Family Farming in the United States." USDA, Economic Research Service. http://www.ers.usda.gov/amber-waves/2014-march/family-farming-in-the-united-states.aspx#.VYhFq6bvjOo (accessed June 1, 2016).

McLaughlin, P. 1998. "Rethinking the Agrarian Question: The Limits of Essentialism and the Promise of Evolutionism." *Human Ecology Review* 5(2): 25–39.

Pollan, M. 2006. *The Omnivore's Dilemma: A Natural History of Four Meals.* New York: Penguin Press.

Preobrazhensky, E. 1921. "Biographical Note." In *From N.E.P. to Socialism*. Trans. by B. Pearce. https://www.marxists.org/archive/preobrazhensky/1921/fromnep/index.html (accessed June 1, 2016).

——. 1926. *The New Economics.* Trans. by Brian Pearce (1965). Oxford: Clarendon Press.

Ramey, E. A. 2014. *Class, Gender, and the American Family Farm in the 20th Century.* London: Routledge.

Reinhardt, N. and P. Barlett. 1989. "The Persistence of Family Farms in United States Agriculture." *Sociologia Ruralis* 29(3/4): 203–225.

Resnick, S. A. and R. D. Wolff. 2002. *Class Theory and History: Capitalism and Communism in the U.S.S.R.* New York and London: Routledge.

29

ECONOMIC DEVELOPMENT

Anjan Chakrabarti and Anup Dhar

The post-war Marxian and neo-Marxian approaches to "development" have stretched from critiques of "underdevelopment" under national and global capitalist systems to that of viewing imperialism as a pioneer of development. After the collapse of "planned socialism" and the post-globalization adjustment by remaining "socialist" nations, which increasingly veered towards capitalist development, we are now confronted with the problem of distinguishing the Marxian understanding of development from other versions, especially the mainstream ones. In this context, one wonders about the very existence of the critical relation between Marxism and development, between class and social needs. Responding to this crisis, we present below some theoretical advances expounded from a newly developed Marxian theory of development that has tried to critically engage with the question of "economic development" by taking into consideration this historical backdrop and theoretical literature.

Debates and Counter-Debates on the Underdevelopment Thesis

The linkage between Western countries and the "backward nations" became important in early twentieth-century Marxian literature.[1] Nikolai Bukharin and Vladimir Lenin expressed doubts on imperialism's progressive impetus in the stage of monopoly capitalism, which they contended had become a barrier to the development of the forces of production. Instead, imperialism should be seen as an instrument for capturing markets and plundering the resources of backward nations for the benefit of monopoly capital and imperial powers, and in the process may have become a cause of the underdevelopment of imperialized/colonized nations. The only way to break the shackles of underdevelopment was to overthrow or bypass capitalism by initiating a socialist revolution in the world and particularly the underdeveloped countries. The *underdevelopment thesis* was developed and popularized during the 1950s–1970s by scholars like Paul Baran, Paul Sweezy, A.G. Frank and others. Through various approaches such as "center-periphery," "unequal exchange" or "world systems" they made a case for the "development of underdevelopment" theses by tracing the cause of underdevelopment in the so-called periphery countries/regions to be that of development of the core developed countries/regions. Instead of facilitating development of forces of production, it was argued that capitalism paradoxically shored up underdevelopment in the periphery.

This thesis drew sharp responses. Criticizing Lenin's position, Bill Warren (1980) provocatively declared imperialism and its modern version in neocolonialism (i.e. the post-independent status of the peripheral countries) to be the pioneers of capitalism. Justifying the capitalist penetration of third world countries through imperialism, Warren argued that imperialism helps to break feudal/pre-capitalist fetters and unleash the forces of production and creates an advanced capitalist society in these countries. Even if one accepts the argument of under-development theorists about international bondage, the satellites are still better off as compared to the counterfactual situation of the absence of foreign investment and international exchange relations, a protectionist agenda that was favored by underdevelopment theorists. The eco-nomic rise of least developed countries such as in East Asia was showcased as empirical evidence of Warren's position.

Intervening in the debates on transition from feudalism to capitalism in Western Europe and particularly England, Robert Brenner (1977) argued that the motor of change within the heart of historical materialism was not any economic element such as forces of production but the political aspect of class struggle. He turned his criticism against the economic essentialism in Dobb (development of forces of production as the prime mover) and non-class emphasis in Sweezy (external trade as the prime mover) into a full-fledged attack on the underdevelopment theories (Hilton 1978). The latter were criticized for ignoring or demoting class relations, class exploitation and class struggle and focusing on non-Marxian ways of explaining underdeve-lopment. Brenner averred that advanced countries were not dependent on the underdeveloped countries for growth or luxury consumption and that the economic plight of the underdeve-loped countries should be identified in its *internal* class structure and the politics of class struggle and not in their externalized relationship with the developed countries.

Finally, the Althusserian articulation approach critiqued underdevelopment theories for the demotion of questions of class structure and mode(s) of production. Modifying the classical version of historical materialism through concepts like traditional mode of produc-tion and colonial mode of production, Rey (1978) claimed that capitalism is innately dynamic and cannot be blamed for underdevelopment. Underdevelopment in the peripheries arises because of the pre-capitalist relations of production that arrest or slow down the development of capitalism. So the cause of underdevelopment resides in the existing social formation in the peripheral countries. Capitalism will be justified in its elimination of such feudal modes of production through violence; it will hence have to dispossess peasants of land. However, this violence will in the end be counterproductive and will stir up the conditions for deeper and expansive forms of class struggle and a socialist revolution.

All these responses in turn were roundly criticized and found to be wanting for being methodologically deterministic (economic or political) and teleological, for considering vio-lence as necessary for capitalism and for social change/transition, for their inadequate theoriza-tion of categories of class and modes of production and for their inherent capitalocentrism. Faced with internal criticisms within Marxism, the influence of these approaches waned by the 1980s. Moreover, in the post-globalization world, with the production of social life in the so-called peripheries being increasingly hooked to the circuits of global capital and with global capitalism now appearing from within the erstwhile underdeveloped countries (for example, note the shift of capitalism to BRICS), periphery as a pure, unadulterated space of local capital/non-capital or as a satellite to industrial capitalism in the West became incongruous.

Marxian Critique of Mainstream Development

In the class-focused Marxian approach pioneered by Resnick and Wolff, the "economy" is seen as decentered and disaggregated, consisting in turn of a variety of capitalist and non-capitalist class processes overdetermined by other non-class, including non-economic, processes. The epistemological roots of mainstream development can be discerned through a class-focused scrambling of economic dualism. Economic dualism presumes a "hegemonic self" and a "lacking other" (for example, capital and pre-capital) as a starting point, examples being Arthur Lewis's agriculture-industry divide or formal-informal economy divide. It takes as *a priori* two constitutive centrisms (from within the decentered and disaggregated economic reality, however): "capital as center" or capitalocentrism and "Europe or West as center" producing Euro-centrism or Orientalism. In the mainstream developmental paradigm, capitalocentrism and Orientalism emerge as mutually constitutive, as a stapled logic reinforcing one another, forming in turn the stable deterministic core of economic dualism. What the class-focused approach shows is why and how the capitalocentric-Orientalist picture ingrained in economic dualism that supposedly mirrors the economy is in fact a political construct that perpetuates a deterministic and teleological imagination of development to emerge (Chakrabarti and Dhar 2010).

To begin with, the *making* of economic dualism helps occult the question of class (processes) and indeed the class-focused language of the economy. The foreclosure of class process erases possibilities associated with the category "class process" and makes impossible the conception of a decentered and disaggregated economic reality. Thus any meaningful presence of the differentiated "what are not capitalist" class processes is disabled; rather, the diverse existence of a multitude of "what are not capitalist class processes" are grouped into the homogenous whole "non-capitalism"; furthermore, non-capitalism in the global South becomes the undifferentiated *lacking other* of modern European-style industrial capitalism through Orientalism.

The Orientalist gaze works in tandem to displace the non-capitalist into *pre*-capitalist, where pre-capitalist is not merely a homogenous space in relation to the capitalist space, but also reflective of, and in turn reflecting, the abnormality of what is known as *third world*. The heterogeneous "what are not capitalist" class space is re-presented into a lacking, redundant, underdeveloped other—a *pre*-capitalist *other* of the capitalist class process—rendered, depending upon convenience, the "victim other," "the evil other" and "the redundant other." In this way, "traditional pre-capitalist third world" comes to symbolize a signpost of economic backwardness; the household, agriculture and informal sector emerge as traditional sites of such backwardness; peasant families, indigenous populace, tribal groups, informal sector workers, the poor, poor and hapless women and poor children appear as harbingers of pathology, as victims of the so-called traditional structures of decrepitude, as "third worldliness" as a whole and as legitimate subjects (actually *objects*) of the "uplifting mission" and of external/outside (inter)national interventions. The multitude of non-capitalist class processes, now re-presented as pre-capitalist, are thus left with only two possible futures—mutation into capitalist class process or mutilation through primitive accumulation.

But the third worldish other, the pre-capitalist other, the lacking other, is not tout court the *outside* vis-à-vis modern capitalism, but rather what is perceived as *lacking* in relation to the latter. It is not defined by "what it is" but by what is lacking or is absent in modern capitalism; it is thus not the Other qua Other; it is capital's internal other, albeit lacking. Clearly, the "lived experience" of the outside of capital or the Other qua Other of capital is more than that imagined through the re-presentation of the outside/Other as lacking or third worldish.

There is thus an occulting of the Other qua Other in the dualistic model. We have provisionally called this Other qua Other *world of the third* (as distinguished from third world). Therefore, from a class-focused perspective, the developmental paradigm, even in its hegemonic existence, is not structured on two, but, instead, on three axes: (i) modernism/ capitalism as "p," (ii) the lacking other/third world as "~p," which is however *foregrounded* and (iii) the foreclosed Other/world of the third. If third world is the *constitutive inside*, or the "appropriate(d) other" of development, then world of the third is the *constitutive outside*, the "inappropriate(d) Other."

Because of foreclosures of class and world of the third (Chakrabarti, Dhar and Cullenberg 2012), "capital" and "modern" emerge as nodal points anchoring the capitalocentric-Orientalist epistemology of what comes to be defined as the dual economy and development. It becomes the basis of organizing our thought-world and associated practices and experiences, achieved by displacing and reducing the otherwise decentered and disaggregated economic reality into the structure of the two, "p" and "~p," where the former (p) is valued and the *other* (~p) is seen as "lacking p" and hence devalued. When such dualistic imaginations of the economy and transition find sufficiently deep roots through processes of interpellation and subjectification in and through concrete situations, institutions and practices, they tend to define without doubt—especially in the global South—our everyday and commonsense understanding of economy, culture, politics and progress. "West is now everywhere, within the West and outside: in structures and minds" (Nandy 1983, xii).

Tragically, even adherents of the post-developmentalist school who are critical of capitalism or are sympathetic to a possible outside to capitalism often fail to distinguish between the logic and register of the *lacking*, yet appropriated other and the *different*, hence non-appropriated Other. The consequences are far reaching.

Interrogating Post-Development and Empire

Post-developmentalist approaches criticize mainstream development by focusing on (i) the Orientalist construction-denigration of Southern economies as "third world," (ii) the essentialism driving the received notion of Southern or third world economies and (iii) the destructive power and the havoc wreaked upon non-Western and non-modern economies by the modern Western idea(l)s of progress grounded on capitalist development with its teleological moorings (Escobar 1995). They seek freedom and revitalization of "third world" from this universal project of capitalist development. Two criticisms of post-developmentalist approaches readily follow.

Gibson-Graham and Ruccio (2001) point to post-developmentalism's realist epistemology, i.e. "the presumption that economic knowledge reflects the true state of a real entity called the 'economy' (generally understood as a locus of capitalist dominance)" (Ibid., 162) and the reduction of the economy to capitalism which in turn is taken as "somehow extra-discursive and beyond the forces of deconstruction...[appearing] as an ontological given, disproportionately powerful by virtue of its indisputable reality in a world of multivalent concepts, shifting discursive practices and unstable meanings" (Ibid., 165). The result is that "rather than representing the economy as a radically heterogeneous social space, post-developmentalist critics reinforce the discursive hegemony of capitalism and thereby tend to marginalize the very alternative economic practices they seek to promote" (Ibid., 166).

Post-developmentalism's acceptance of the received economic representation (with its inherent realism and capitalocentrism) excludes the possibility of viewing the economy as decentered and disaggregated. From another angle, it implies that post-developmentalist scholars would not be in a position to appreciate the emergence of the dual(istic) model of the economy or its centrist logic from within a decentered and disaggregated economic space. Instead, as the true reality of the economy, what would get accepted is the given dual economic structure, divided between modern capitalist economy (p) and traditional pre-capitalist economy(~p), thereby leaving little scope for escape from the boundaries imposed by it.

The second criticism follows from our conceptualization of world of the third as distinct from third world. The underlying epistemology of capitalocentric-Orientalism motoring economic development makes invisible this distinction, and post-developmentalists fail to detect it (Chakrabarti and Dhar 2010). Therefore, Escobar notes that "the development discourse...has created an extremely efficient apparatus for producing *knowledge about, and the exercise of power over, the Third World*" (Escobar 1995, 9; italics added). He deposits faith in rescuing the "third world" by arguing that "the Third World is contested reality whose current status is up for scrutiny and negotiation" (Ibid., 214–15). In general, the post-developmentalists end up with the same dual model of (p, ~p) and fret over the devalued representation of (~p). Their opposition to economic dualism problematizes and defends the same "x." The point is missed that the "making-unmaking" of third world is not just an empirical affair, but also, and primarily so, a matter related to how the *outside* is conceptualized in relation to the center (stapled capital-modern) from within a decentered and disaggregated economy. There is an urge to resist the negative representation of third world without quite realizing that, as the "lacking and constitutive inside" of capitalist development, there can be no conceptualization of third world except in its denigrated form.

Had the *outside* been theorized, it would have become clear that *development's object of control, regulation and penetration is not third world, but instead world of the third*. World of the third harbors the possibility of a non-capitalist language-logic-lived experience-ethic outside of and beyond the circuits of (global) capitalist modernity; and that puts under erasure capitalist ethic and language. However, in developmental logic, world of the third is displaced into "third world"—third world as *pre*-capitalist—as a lower step in the ladder of capital-logic and linear time. World of the third as also the critique of the capitalist present and future is thus reduced to a third worldish *past*. To be stuck in the dual frame not only (fore)closes the imagination/articulation of non-capitalist alternatives—alternatives to capitalist development—but additionally leaves the examination of the hegemonic *Inside* (i.e. global capitalism) inadequate.

The inability to theorize the outside is by no means restricted to post-developmentalists. Renditions of globalization in which the "local" is assumed to be subsumed within the global become problematical as well. For example, absence of an *outside* to the global marks the rendition of "Empire" in Hardt and Negri (2000). They aver that globalization has relocated entire nations into the logic of global capital, thereby rendering redundant the idea of an outside. Third world as the resisting outside thus becomes historically obsolete. Resultantly, world of the third is doubly forgotten in Hardt and Negri's Empire by the denial of the existence of even the third world.

Unpacking Formal-Informal Dualism

The unpacking of the formal-informal economic dualism and the counter-cartograph of the economy through the class-focused decentering takes off by identifying three broad types of labor in the everyday: (i) individual labor (A), (ii) non-labor (B), and (iii) collective labor (C). To this we add two other criteria: distribution and remuneration. In the case of distribution, we simply take two forms of output distribution—commodity and non-commodity—and for workers' remuneration too two forms—wage and non-wage. This way we end up with twenty-four different *class sets* (Cullenberg 1992).

Even at this elementary level the economy appears as the institutional configuration of innumerable forms of these twenty-four class sets. Considering further overdetermining conditions of existence (processes of distribution and receipt of surplus, social needs, race,

Table 1

Sl. No.	Performance of Surplus Labor	Workers' Access to Appropriated Surplus	Output Distribution	Workers' Remuneration
1	A	A	Com	Wage
2	A	A	Non-Com	Wage
3	A	A	Com	Non-Wage
4	A	A	Non-Com	Non-Wage
5	A	B	Com	Wage
6	A	B	Non-Com	Wage
7	A	B	Com	Non-Wage
8	A	B	Non-Com	Non-Wage
9	C	A	Com	Wage
10	C	A	Non-Com	Wage
11	C	A	Com	Non-Wage
12	C	A	Non-Com	Non-Wage
13	A	C	Com	Wage
14	A	C	Non-Com	Wage
15	A	C	Com	Non-Wage
16	A	C	Non-Com	Non-Wage
17	C	B	Com	Wage
18	C	B	Non-Com	Wage
19	C	B	Com	Non-Wage
20	C	B	Non-Com	Non-Wage
21	C	C	Com	Wage
22	C	C	Non-Com	Wage
23	C	C	Com	Non-Wage
24	C	C	Non-Com	Non-Wage

Com: commodity; Non-Com: non-commodity

caste, gender, property structures, power relations, etc.) for these class sets would only deepen the level of heterogeneity in the economy. Because no one class process can be reduced to another, the class-focused economy is constitutionally disaggregated. Insofar as the economy cannot be reduced to one or a set of class sets (say, capitalist or feudal), the class-focused economy is also decentered.

Economic dualism is untenable once the class-focused perspective to the economy and the economic is inaugurated. The international symposium on the informal sector organized by International Labour Organsation/International Confederation of Free Trade Unionsin 1999 classifies the informal sector workforce into three major groups: (i) owner-employers of micro enterprises using a few paid workers, with or without apprentices; (ii) own-account workers owning and operating one-person businesses, who work alone or with the help of unpaid workers, generally family members and apprentices; and (iii) dependent workers, paid or unpaid, including wage workers in micro enterprises, unpaid family workers, apprentices, contract labor, home workers and paid domestic workers. These three settings could potentially map out into the twenty-four class sets, dispersed into exploitative class sets of capitalist, feudal, slave and CA communitic types (5–12, 17–20), independent class sets (1–4) and non-exploitative class sets of AC communitic and communist types (13–16, 21–24).[2] Once the capitalocentric-Orientalist picture of the economy is abandoned in favor of a class-focused decentered economy, there no longer exists any logical basis for hailing a specific economic organization, say, the capitalist one, or even a group of class sets, as the privileged formal sector. Similarly, no basis exists for assigning "informal" to a particular class set. The received terms "formal sector" and "informal sector" and the dualism formal/informal dissolve into the heterogeneous and overdetermined infinity of the class processes in an economy.

Moreover, various kinds of class sets may encompass the formal sector. Let us rule out the possibilities of (i) unpaid labor or payment in kind and (ii) non-commodity from the definition of formal sector; then, the formal sector could comprise class sets (5, 9, 13, 17, and 21), wherein capitalist class set is only one type, namely (5, 17). By contrast, class set 21 would be a communist class set in which collective performance and appropriation of surplus appears in relation with the market form of labor power and output. It is equally possible that many of these class sets could be within the informal sector, which in turn makes the division between formal and informal at best hazy and at worst impossible. Reduction of the formal sector to capitalism and the informal sector to non/pre-capitalism becomes untenable in our rendition of development.

Finally, as the class sets are in continuous flux and change from within and from one type to another, it also renders the question of transition open-ended and non-teleological (Chakrabarti and Cullenberg 2003); which is in contrast to the deterministic route of *formalization* of the economy forwarded by the mainstream approaches such as ILO (International Labour Organization 2002).

What does economic dualism mean in the backdrop of such a decentered and disaggregated economy? The dualistic structure suggests a further reconfiguration of this economy by *fixing and hence privileging* a particular class process, say, capitalist or (5, 17), as symbolizing the formal sector and the other class processes, now homogenized into non-or pre-capitalist, as the informal. Further, recall that mainstream literature attributes a positive sign to the characteristics of the "formal" which, by default, is the capitalist class process here (for example, see Porta and Shleifer 2014). At the same time, defined as lacking those attributes, the non-capitalist class processes are consequently positioned as devalued in relation to capitalist class processes, and the non-capitalist class processes consequently get clubbed into the homogeneous figure: *pre*-capitalist. The formal-informal dual is typically mapped into the capitalist-precapitalist duality posited in terms of the privileged center of the formal sector à la the capitalist sector. Any subsequent endeavor to smuggle in heterogeneity remains incarcerated within this pre-constituted dual structure.

While the ILO discourse brings into contention the lack of formal centric aspects of rights and laws, recognition, decency, security and so on in its characterization of the category of informal, in economic terms, the most important distinction is made with respect to productivity (value added) and competitiveness. Once this capitalocentric-Orientalist view is accepted, transitional logic under the formal-informal dual model is laid bare as a (political) attempt to govern the re-location and re-construction of the socio-economic contours of informality through the lens of and in favor of privileged entities of capitalist and modern. Porta and Shleifer (2014) argue that informal enterprises are unproductive and stagnant. For a medium sample country, informal enterprises add fifteen per cent of value per employee of formal enterprises. This means that the informal sector is overwhelmingly clogged by simple reproduction enterprises unable to generate substantial surplus value for reinvestment in capital accumulation, which makes them incapable of growing and competing. This difference in productivity is reflected in differences in income, quality of product and competition, making them conclude the following for informal sector enterprises: "Far from being reservoirs of entrepreneurial energy, they are swamps of backwardness. They allow their owners and employees to survive, but not much more" (118). Attempts to valorize informal sector or to rethink long-run development by building on it are futile and counterproductive, a position that is widely shared by policy-makers across the world (see, for example, India Ministry of Finance 2013 in the case of India). In addition to being seen as a *victim* of its own backward structural deficiencies (as ILO and the World Bank claim), the recalcitrant presence of informality also emerges as a *threat* to the transition of underdeveloped economies to modern capitalist ones. The transition logic stemming from the development frame entails that the informal sector must (be made to) wither away.

Development Crisis as Transitional Crisis

An analogous and in fact the original classical development narrative informs the Lewisian dual model of small *industrial* capitalist economy and predominantly *agricultural* pre-capitalist economy such that, via the capitalocentric-Orientalist logic of transition, the latter gets truncated and the former expands rapidly (Escobar 1995, Chakrabarti 2014). East Asia in the 1960s–1980s and post-Mao China (ongoing) are often held as successful examples of such a transition. However, it is also widely recognized that the Lewisian transitional logic has run into problems in many parts of the world. Take the case of India. The fact that people are leaving the rural economy *en masse* is an "opportunity" even as the fact that, despite high economic growth for the last two decades, those same people are not able to find jobs in the labor-absorbing formal sector (resulting in the rapidly burgeoning informal sector) signals a transition crisis (India Ministry of Finance 2013). In this context, the strategy of the formalization of the informal sector is indispensable for completing the development utopia. Resultantly, the two logics of transition, from agricultural to industrial and from informal to formal, have been telescoped into a united rationale in the contemporary development paradigm.

Development as Growth: Global Capitalism and Primitive Accumulation

Following liberalization policies in the post-globalization period, global capital was privileged as the "center" with the intent to remap economies in relation to this new centrism. Since mass poverty is seen as emanating from the "traditional," "pre-capitalist" socioeconomic structure, the "magic medicine" supposed to eradicate poverty is structural transformation (the basis of structural adjustment), which would eliminate or transform these backward qua third world structures in favor of modern infrastructures and institutions, attitudes/habits (including laws), education for generating human capital and modes of governance to facilitate capitalism-induced growth. Growth to reduce mass poverty can thus be achieved only through a structural transition of the third world in the image of modern capitalism. Notwithstanding the many hiccups and turns (inequality, re-distribution, human development, etc.), this remains the number one objective and strategy of development (see any World Bank Report to verify this point). Marxism, on the other hand, argues that this lengthy process involves the disruption and separation from means of production and means of subsistence of the world of the third subjects, which among other things, brings about the mass commodification of labor power. This process of "separation" can transpire through piecemeal disruption or large-scale displacement through primitive accumulation. As the strategy of growth-induced development changed in the course of history, so did the form and pattern of primitive accumulation as a continual process of capitalism-induced growth. Take the case of India.

The post-1991 reforms in India implanted the centricity of global private capital as against self-reliant state capital during the planning period and began the long-drawn-out process of creating a competitive market economy. Through outsourcing, sub-contracting, offshoring and body shopping, the global capitalist enterprises forged relations with local enterprises procreating and circumscribed within a nation's border (the local market) and with enterprises outside the nation's border (the global market). Specifically, via the local-global market, global capital was linked to the ancillary local enterprises (big and small scale, local capitalist and non-capitalist) and other institutions (banking enterprise, trading enterprise, transport enterprise, etc.) and together they formed the *circuits of global capital*. Induced by the expansion of the circuits of global capital (inclusive mainly of manufacturing and services), rapid growth of the Indian economy is feeding into an explosive process of urbanization and producing along the way a culture of individualization, consumerism, new ideas of success, entrepreneurship and human capital, new ways of judging performance and conduct, changing labor/gender/caste-related customs and mores, etc. Resultantly, a social cluster of practices, activities and relationships transpires that literally captures the production of an encampment; we named it the "camp of global capital." Circuits-camp of global capital is provisionally named "global capitalism."

World of the third, on the other hand, constitutes the overdetermined space of capitalist and non-capitalist class enterprises that procreate *outside* the exchanges within the local-global market and hence circuits of global capital. The social cluster of practices, activities and relationships connected to the language-logic-ethos-lived experience of this space constitute the "camp of world of the third." The spatial associate of the logical *Other* of development in the era of neo-liberal globalization and global capitalism is the circuits-camp of world of the third. We can make no *a priori* value judgment regarding world of the third; that, in concrete manifestation, could be in "agriculture" or the "informal" sector; in rural or urban, in India or in Paris; solely or a mixture of good, bad or ugly, rich or poor, liberal or totalitarian, exploitative or non-exploitative, etc. This does not mean that the border between the two camps are rigid and compartmentalized; rather, flows of all kinds (economic, political, cultural and natural) spill over from one to the other thereby constituting and transforming one another, even to the extent that what is in world of the third presently can become part of the circuits of global capital in the future and vice versa (Chakrabarti et al. 2012, ch. 7–9).

It may be recalled that what for us is circuits-camp of world of the third is for modernist discourses like development "third world": this is the Orientalist moment through which capital and modern concomitantly emerge as the privileged center. It is what turns the disaggregated non-capitalist space into a pre-capitalist one. As a figure of lack, third world epitomizes mass poverty, arising in no small part due to *inefficient* and *non-competitive* practices, activities and "backward" institutions; third world as nurturing excess labor, as harboring a large army of the unemployed/underemployed. Rather than appreciating the possibility of an *outside* to the circuits of global capital, one loses sight of the world of the third through its foreclosure. Instead, what awaits us is a devalued space, a lacking underside—third world—that needs to be transgressed-transformed-mutilated-assimilated. This foreclosure of world of the third through the foregrounding of third world (or, by substitute signifiers such as social capital, community, etc.) helps secure and facilitate the hegemony of (global) capital and modernism over world of the third.

This changing map of the Indian economy was/is driven by, among other things, the primacy accorded to global capitalist sites of performance, appropriation and distribution of surplus value which, via the central policy objective of high growth rate, resulted in the expansion of the circuits-camp of global capital producing in turn a new wave of primitive accumulation with reference to world of the third. Global capital has been expansive, but not necessarily inclusive. It structurally excludes. The hitherto (en)closed bastion of agriculture and forest economy is fast crumbling under the relentless barrage of global capital and global market producing in turn (i) continual internal crisis and migration of its younger population and (ii) an enduring process of alienation and expropriation of land, forest, rivers, etc. However, what appears as progressive from a modernist perspective comes to be seen as wrongful wounding and violence (including what Jonathan Lear (2007) calls "loss of concepts," a "loss of events," a "loss of mental states" and at least a "threatened loss of identity") from the perspective of world of the third. This in turn allows us to make sense of the countrywide resistance against this process without reducing the content of the resistance to capitalocentric-Orientalist logic or its mechanics of cost-benefit calculation. In post-colonial conditions, we not only have a materially divided society (structurally, income-wise, socially), but also a nation with divided perspectives and understanding of what is "progress" and "just." This makes it imperative for Marxism to take a position vis-à-vis primitive accumulation, not to extol it as "historically inevitable" but critically analyze it by deconstructing historical inevitability and its underlying deterministic teleology towards capitalism and modernism (Chakrabarti and Dhar 2010).

Development as Social Needs: Class and Redistribution

Like the classical development approach that emphasizes growth, classical Marxian approaches with their emphasis on modes of production have emphasized the centrality of production in theorizing (stages of) development; distribution has been traced to the point of production. However, without accounting for redistribution there is simply no way to make Marxian theory relevant in contemporary development analysis that combines economic growth with redistribution programs (such as under the human development approach or inclusive growth/development). As it stands, there is no Marxian theory (or, for that matter any theory) that integrates production, distribution and redistribution in one frame, and specifically class with social needs.

The class-focused approach does not per se account for the "marginal" existence of the poor, the old and so on who provide no necessary conditions of existence to any class process. If we are to follow the class distributions that tie payments to conditions of existence the agents provide, then these people, incapable of being such condition providers, do not qualify as justifiable recipients of the fragments of subsumed class payments, which is why surplus cannot be exhausted in the payment of subsumed class processes; there must be a remainder after subsumed class payments. There must conceptually be two forms of distribution: one directed as subsumed payments (towards the point of production) named as *production surplus* and the other over and above the production surplus named as *social surplus*. Social surplus targets the various socially determined needs of the people (such as relating to poverty, environment, children, unemployed, old, etc.) who provide no conditions of existence to the fundamental class processes of performance and appropriation of surplus.

Distribution of surplus aimed at providing conditions of existence to class processes is conceptually distinct from those surplus distributions directed at reproducing social needs. Himself aware of this division, Marx in "Critique of the Gotha Programme" not only referred to the distribution of surplus related to production but also distributions mentioning, in his own words, "the general costs of administration not belonging to production," "that which is intended for the common satisfaction of needs, such as schools, health services, etc." and "funds for those unable to work, etc., in short for what is included under the so-called poor relief today" (Marx 1977, 13–30).

Moreover, our understanding of need is not referring to a natural space, consisting of some pre-defined objective ends. "Need" as such is an empty category that manifests in concrete/specific form in a historical context, through conflicts over interpretations and social struggles.

Therefore, the emergence of need as specific social need and its character is socially determined and remains open to interpretation, change and even to dissolution. Need-related development struggles are over the meanings of needs and of their character and also over the manners, mechanisms and forms of appropriating and distributing social surplus and who should be considered as the rightful recipient of social surplus. Players engaging in the need space include central governments, regional governments, local bodies, NGOs, international agencies such as the World Bank, class structures, political parties and social movements.

Having defined and defended social surplus, let us summarize our surplus scheme in accounting terms (Chakrabarti, Cullenberg and Dhar 2008). Denote the total surplus (surplus value plus surplus product) of a nation as TS, decomposed into production surplus and social surplus. Define SV^1 as the sum total of surplus value directed towards production surplus (subsumed payments, SC) and SV^2 as the remaining surplus value directed towards social surplus (SS). Moreover, many goods may be directly consumed. Let SUV be the surplus appropriated in use value form and let the distribution SSE be divided between production surplus and social surplus.[3] Summing these, our analytical terrain encompassing production, distribution (to the point of production) and redistribution (away from production) becomes:

$$\text{Surplus} = \left\langle \underbrace{\left\{ SV^1 = \sum_{i=1}^{n} SC_i \right\} + \left\{ SUV' = \sum_{r=1}^{s} SSE \right\}}_{\text{Production Surplus}} \right\rangle$$

$$+ \left\{ \underbrace{\left\{ SV^2 = SS = \sum_{k=1}^{m} SS_k \right\} + \left\{ SUV'' = \sum_{z=1}^{g} SSE \right\}}_{\text{Social Surplus}} \right\}$$

If the struggles over production surplus are over class-related processes and hence are class struggles, then the struggles over social surplus pertaining to struggles for or against various needs are need-related development struggles. Class and need struggles (which in turn are impacted by all kinds of non-class and non-need struggles) are locked in over-determined and contradictory relations.

While this open-ended development space is sensitive to alternative interpretations and invocations of social needs that may have counter-hegemonic potential (call it radical needs), there is always a robust attempt, especially by state and international agencies, to promote those social needs that will ensure the control and regulation of world of the third subjects (by giving it a victim/marginalized/evil status). Call the latter hegemonic needs. Open to radical and hegemonic needs, our theory of development opens the need space to the possibility of intense and unpredictable development struggle.

The Development State: Compassionate and Violent

Marxian literature on the state had paid particular attention to the place and function of state in a scenario of development centralized on modernization and capitalism. The problem has been that thus far Marxian theories have been drawn to a critique of the "capitalist" state (as, say, in many underdeveloped and developing countries), but at the same time have considered state as essential to its political project to achieve "socialism" (ironically, often the name for state capitalism as in the USSR and private capitalism as in China). This paradox stems from the inability to separate the category of socialism/capitalism from the state, thereby confusing socialism/capitalism with which political force has state power and with their dubious identification with planning or market. The source of confusion in turn stems from the inability to realize that socialism from a Marxian perspective requires at the minimum certain justice conditions connected to its evaluative space—productive justice, appropriative justice, economic democracy/justice and development justice. Bringing into play these justice conditions (as well as multiple other considerations) in the overdetermined and contradictory reality, including within the open-ended site of the state, is bound to have distinct and differentiated patterns of impact on the place and function of state as against the ruling dispensation's attempt to hoist the development state over the post-colonial economies through modernization and capitalism. Take the case of India.

By invoking and activating hegemonic social needs via the redistribution of social surplus, capitalist development focuses on the compassionate face of the state, on how it engages in the act of handholding with respect to world of the third, albeit in the name of uplifting third world from its so-called decrepitude. Propelled by capitalism-induced, growth-obsessed policies of the state, the other dimension of development releases the violent logic of creation and expansion of the circuits-camp of global capital through primitive accumulation, a process encouraged and facilitated by the state. In the name of uplifting the third world, the developmental state in one turn intervenes in world of the third via various inclusion-based social programs targeting social needs even as it comes down hard on world of the third to facilitate the process of primitive accumulation. Resistance to capitalist development must thereby encompass both axes: through challenges to primitive accumulation it must force the state to abandon its support for it, and by foregrounding radical needs it must compel the state to address these. Connecting these oppositional imperatives to class exploitation and to the proposition of post-capitalist imaginations and projects, actual and potential, will challenge in turn the hegemony of capitalist development. It is only then that the horizon of post-development gets actualized.

Notes

1 See Larrain (1989), Chakrabarti and Cullenberg (2003) and Ruccio (2011) for an extensive review and analysis.
2 Communitic class process (CA and AC) refers to two possible scenarios where (i) even as direct producers may collectively (C) produce surplus, only one of these producers (A) appropriates the surplus (say, the male head of family in family agricultural unit) and the rest are excluded, and (ii) even as direct producers perform surplus labor individually (A), the appropriation is done collectively (C) such that nobody is excluded from participation in it (say, all members of independent farm units come together to appropriate the surplus even as the produce is individually created in their respective farms) (Chakrabarti and Dhar 2010).
3 For simplicity's sake, we presume that SUV is measured in socially necessary abstract labor time too.

References

Brenner, R. 1977. "The Origins of Capitalist Development: A Critique of Neo-Smithian Marxism." *New Left Review* 104: 25–93.

Chakrabarti, A. 2014. "A Post-Colonial Critique of Economic Dualism and Its Politics." *Journal of Contemporary Thought* 40 (Winter): 158–165.

Chakrabarti, A. and S. Cullenberg. 2003. *Transition and Development in India*. New York: Routledge.

Chakrabarti, A., S. Cullenberg, and A. Dhar. 2008. "Rethinking Poverty beyond Non-Surplus Theories: Class and Ethical Dimensions of Poverty Eradication." *Rethinking Marxism* 20(4): 673–687.

Chakrabarti, A. and A. Dhar. 2010. *Dislocation and Resettlement in Development: From Third World to World of the Third*. London: Routledge.

Chakrabarti A., A. Dhar, and S. Cullenberg. 2012. *World of the Third and Global Capitalism*. New Delhi: World View Press.

Chakrabarti, A., A. Dhar, and B. Dasgupta. 2015. *The Indian Economy in Transition: Globalization, Capitalism and Development*. New Delhi: Cambridge University Press.

Cullenberg, S. 1992. "Socialism's Burden: Toward a 'Thin' Definition of Socialism." *Rethinking Marxism* 5(2): 64–83.

Escobar, A. 1995. *Encountering Development: The Making and Unmaking of the Third World*. Princeton: Princeton University Press.

Gibson-Graham, J. K. and D. Ruccio. 2001. "After Development: Negotiating the Place of Class." In *Re/presenting Class: Essays in Postmodern Political Economy*, K. Gibson, J. Graham, Stephen R. and R. Wolff, eds., 158–181. Durham, NC: Duke University Press.

Hardt, M. and A. Negri. 2000. *Empire*. Cambridge, MA: Harvard University Press.

Hilton, R., ed. 1978. *The Transition from Feudalism to Capitalism*. London: Verso.

India Ministry of Finance, Economic Division. 2013. *Economic Survey 2012–13*. New Delhi: Oxford University Press.

International Labour Office. 2002. *Decent Work and the Informal Economy: Sixth Item on the Agenda*. Report (International Labour Conference), 90th Session, 6. Geneva: ILO.

Kanth, R. K., ed. 1994. *Paradigms in Economic Development: Classic Perspectives, Critiques and Reflections*. New York: Routledge.

Larrain, J. 1989. *Theories of Development*. Cambridge: Polity Press.

Lear, J. 2007. "Working through the end of civilization." *International Journal of Psychoanalysis* 88: 291–308.

Marx, K. 1977. "The Critique of the Gotha Programme." In *Karl Marx: Selected Writings*, 2nd edition, D. McLennan, ed., 13–30. New York: Oxford University Press.

Nandy, A. 1983. *The Intimate Enemy: Loss and Recovery of Self under Colonialism*. New Delhi: Oxford University Press.

Porta, R. L. and A. Shleifer. 2014. "Informality and Development." *Journal of Economic Perspectives* 28(3): 3–24.

Rahnema, M. and V. Bawtree. 1997. *The Post-Development Reader*. London: Zed Books.

Rey, P. P. 1978. *Les alliances de classes*. Paris: Maspero.

Ruccio, D. 2011. *Development and Globalization: Marxian Class Analysis*. New York: Routledge.

Warren, B. 1980. *Imperialism: Pioneer of Capitalism*. London: Verso.

30

TRANSITION

Anjan Chakrabarti and Anup Dhar

The starting point of a coherent deterministic theory of transition can be traced to Fredrick Engels (Olsen 2009). Taking inspiration from Engels, the rise of deterministic theories of transition was, as Olsen showed, coterminous with the evolution of the Mode of Production and Social Formation (MPSF) approach that in turn developed the philosophy of dialectical materialism and laid down the foundation of classical historical materialism (CHM). CHM was in turn deployed to explain the societal components and their connections, and more importantly for us, they helped chart the logic of transition of society that was teleological in character. While Stalinism helped popularize this approach globally, post-Stalinist trends (despite denunciations of Stalin and of orthodoxy) continued to flourish under the spell of variants of CHM.

Challenges to this approach appeared from within Marxism: Lenin, Luxemburg, Gramsci, Mao Tse Tung, the Frankfurt School, Althusser and Hindess and Hirst were some of the detractors who dissented variedly and questioned the dominance of determinism in general and of economic/class determinism in particular. In what turned out to be a futile endeavor, Althusser and his disciples attempted to reform CHM by modifying the philosophy of dialectical materialism through the category of overdetermination even as the determination of society in the last instance by the economic was maintained. Challenges to CHM were also forthcoming from the Southern context, especially in connection with the issue of development (see the entry "Economic Development" in this volume).

Given the welter of competing theories of/in CHM, we focus here on depth at the cost of width. Rather than presenting the much-discussed couple of historical materialism and dialectical materialism, we unpack briefly G. A. Cohen's (1978; 1988) defense of CHM, where he dismissed the idea of dialectical materialism as a viable conceptual frame for explaining transition from one stage to another. Instead, he crowned functional explanation (FE) with that privilege. Moreover, Cohen's rendition of transition brings to the forefront basic features and criticisms that we believe can be commonly directed at CHM in general. Some of the criticisms give way to rethinking the relation of transition with Marxism in new directions, two of which we will cover subsequently.

Model I: Deterministic Theory of Transition

Using Marx's 1959 "Preface to A Critique of the Contribution to Political Economy" as containing a series of defendable truth claims, Cohen defines *society* or *social totality* as a holistic articulation of independent and compartmentalized levels related to one another in a hierarchical way: forces of production/FOP (consisting of material means of production and labor power), class relations of production/ROP (defined in terms of economic power[1] with respect to means of production and labor power), superstructure (political [including state], law and cultural [education, etc.] aspects of society) and social consciousness (the site of subject formation). In his version of CHM, the ***Primacy Thesis*** is that the exogenously given FOP indexed by technological development determine the ROP and by default ultimately everything that appears subsequently. This is technological determinism. While class ROP could be multiple, society or the social formation is ultimately reduced to "dominant" production relations that will be historically selected to develop the FOP. Superstructure that appears depends on and is caused/explained by the class ROP. This is what we call class determinism, the fact that institutions, politics (particularly, class politics) and subjectivity get ultimately reduced to class ROP; and, since class ROP embody economic structure, economic determinism and class determinism coincide. Finally, because the structure (consisting of FOP, ROP and superstructure) also determines the subject/consciousness, we have structural determinism. It is deterministic epistemology that runs through the sinews of CHM.

Not only is there a primacy of FOP in the conceptualization of society, but FOP also enjoy privileged status in the transition of society. This is captured by the ***Development Thesis***, the axiom that FOP develop progressively over time. But before proceeding to Marx's theory of history, we need to discuss an issue of central importance.

Recall Marx's observation in the Preface that "men enter into definite, necessary relations that are indispensable and independent of their will, ROP which *correspond* to a definite stage of development of their material productive forces." For Cohen, the term *correspondence* harbors a fundamental puzzle. On the one hand, it is claimed that FOP exist independently and are causally prior to ROP; they explain the existence of ROP. On the other hand, it is also claimed that ROP influence and control the FOP. How can both be true?

Making a decisive contribution to CHM, Cohen argues that this type of correspondence between the different structures recognized by Marx can only be consistently understood by *functional explanation* (FE), whereby the existence of the cause is explained in terms of its effect. Following FE, the following appears:

1) The level of development of productive power explains why certain relations and not others would advance productive power.
2) Relations which advance productive power obtain because they advance productive power.
   It follows that
3) The level of development of productive power explains the nature of the productive relations.

Proposition 1 asserts which ROP, say of k type, *would* be appropriate to develop the FOP. Proposition 2 affirms that the fact that relations of type k facilitate the development of FOP explains why that type of relations *obtain*. Combining 1 and 2 gives proposition 3, which guarantees the primacy of the FOP over ROP even as ROP facilitate the development of the FOP. The puzzle is resolved.

The logic of FE likewise rationalizes correspondence among the other levels of society, culminating in the following propositions:

4) The economic structure explains the nature of the superstructure.

5) Economic structure and superstructure explain the social being and embedded consciousness (subject).

Finally, these propositions combine with the Development Thesis, declaring that

6) The productive forces tend to develop throughout history.

(3), (4), (5) and (6) would deliver a coherent and consistent explanation of CHM and its theory of history. Particularly, the roles of Primacy Thesis (3) and Development Thesis (6) are central to establish the underlying logic of transition in CHM.

Given this Development Thesis, the basic idea of transition in historical materialism is that the FOP "select" particular ROP that in turn will promote the development of the FOP as consistently explained through FE. Similarly, political and other cultural institutions/ practices correspond to the ROP, and forms of social consciousness take shape around the received superstructure. If, at any point, ROP fetter the free development of the FOP, a condition of social crisis of historic proportion arises that can be resolved only with the advent of new ROP that will provide maximum scope for the productive use and development of the FOP. Evidently, the embedded rationality of people trying to overcome the state of material scarcity (always choosing superior ways of creating wealth at the expense of other options) will ensure that such an optimal relation of production obtains. Anything else (that is, choice of any other ROP) will be suboptimal, entailing irrational behavior of people. Inter alia, such suboptimal historical choices will be rejected and never adopted. The optimal change in economic structure in turn brings about a change in the superstructure, and the latter in turn brings about a change in forms of consciousness.

Does history follow a certain pattern that ties together the optimal change from one epoch to another? Here, Cohen (1978, 1–27, 175–215) draws upon a detailed correspondence between the images of history in Hegel and Marx. It is however the case, Cohen contends, that Marx's materialism triumphs over Hegel's idealism because, unlike Hegel's, his is not just a philosophy of history but a theory of history that is able to contribute to a rigorous explanation of the inner dynamics of society and its transition. He also warns that what is valuable in Hegel's concept of dialectics is its "descriptive residue" (not its explanatory feature), which, when one starts to explain Marx's theory of history, emerges as good imagery to capture the ascent in the stages that Marx denotes.

The sequence can be discerned from the Hegelian triad of undifferentiated unity/affirmation, differentiated disunity/negation and differentiated unity/negation of negation. It transits in rank order. Adapting this imagery in CHM, history moves from undifferentiated unity (primitive communism) to differentiated disunity (slave, feudal and capitalist society, that is, societies divided by optimality crisis and class division/conflict), arriving finally at differentiated unity (communism or a materially abundant society with no optimality crisis and consequently no classes and no class conflict). This transition follows a series of sequential shifts in the ROP that, following FE, are historically selected by the level of FOP at each transition point.

Clearly, this stage-based way of looking at history embraces a predetermined underlying purpose guiding the movement of society in a definite direction. This inexorable logic of transition is historicist: a rational, ordered, progressive movement of society from a preordained origin to a predestined end. The rational element is the essence—here, the FOP; its development signals progress which is coterminous with a higher order of society. This progressive movement starts from a given point—primitive communism—and moves in a law-like and ordered fashion to end where history is destined to reach, finally: communism.[2]

"Progress" is judged by the proximity of a stage to communism. Each optimal choice in this direction is thus progressive. The class who makes it happen is revolutionary, and those vying to retain the old ROP and other suboptimal ROPs are reactionary or irrelevant. Can one skip stages? No way, answers Cohen. Till the time there is further room for the existing ROP to develop the FOP, the former will not perish. Attempts to bring about socialism before the time of capitalism is complete (as in erstwhile Soviet Union or Maoist China) are doomed to fail.

The medium of transitional change is class struggle. Class struggle is secondary in the sense that it appears at the level of "main events of that course [of history] and the surface relief of society" and is not the "fundamental explanation of the course of history and the structure of society" (Cohen 1988, 14). Unlike locating continuous class battle through strategic behavior (say, in a game theoretic situation as some argued), Cohen attributes the meaning of class struggle in Marx to class wars to settle transitional questions and also credits Marx for his thesis that the resolution of class wars depends on the "character of the FOP." This explains the importance of class struggle qua class war in the transition of society, but its secondary presence to that of the fettering of the FOP by the extant ROP under the condition of the assumed inevitability of the development of FOP must not be forgotten.

We surmise that that if determinism is the undisputed logic of the social in CHM then historicism is the undisputed logic of transition; the two logics supplement one another. The essence (FOP) serves as the rational element whose inexorable growth also serves as the engine to explain the transition of society.

Dialectical Materialism as an Explanatory Mechanism of Transition

Dialectical Materialism tends to embrace Hegelian dialectics (which it merges with some purported laws of natural science) as an explanatory device (Olsen 2009). Through a law-like shift from the quantitative to the qualitative (signifying the point of contradiction between FOP and ROP being burst asunder to usher in new ROP) that moves through the schema of negation of negation, the inexorable development of FOP in each stage in history is guaranteed through a change in property/power relations of class and consequently the superstructure. As Althusser (1969) argued, in its popular version, dialectical materialism following Hegel reduces the complex society into a simple essence (say, FOP) and its transition into an auto journey of the same essence; through this expressive causality, its explanation of society and history simplifies what is otherwise complex, straightens in a somewhat Euclidean fashion what is otherwise full of curves, breaks and new articulations, renders transparent and certain what is otherwise uncertain, murky and contingent.

While dialectical materialism shares some of the main features of Cohen's frame (such as determinism and historicism), Cohen rejects it as an inadequate logic for explaining transition. He debunks the idea of process, interpenetrability and laws of motion as asserted by dialectical materialism. Instead, he theorizes the components (FOP, ROP, superstructure and consciousness) as levels that must be defined as independent and autonomous of one another and whose relations are explained by FE. Interpenetration will only make the definitions murky and their roles/relations unclear; he faults Marxists for undertaking such sloppy theorization. Moreover, Cohen would dismiss the theory of dialectical materialism for delivering a philosophy of history and not a *theory* of history. "Negation of Negation" has no explanatory import as dialectical materialism often tends to convey. A theory of transition must explain the mechanism through which certain components rise and then fall, and in the process help locate and differentiate one stage from another; and on this issue dialectical materialism has a sloppy answer (with its somewhat vague inflexion point from quantitative to qualitative) and FE a very good one.

Interestingly, the importance of a non-Hegelian explanatory device that would resolve the above mentioned fundamental puzzle in CHM is also acknowledged at the level of mode of production and superstructure by Althusser (1969). He tries to resolve the primacy of the former and the important role of the latter through concepts such as "determination in the last instance" of the economic, "effectivity," "relative autonomy" and "reciprocal action." Cohen, of course, remains unfazed by this theorization, which, for him, is inadequate and inconsistent insofar as resolving the fundamental puzzle of CHM is concerned. If one adds to this the criticisms that structuralism now takes over the mantle of essence (Hindess and Hirst 1977) and that "determinism in the last instance" is still determinism, then the very purpose of Althusser's critique of Hegelian dialectics and the creation of a reformed CHM is undermined (Resnick and Wolff 1987, ch. 2).

Criticisms

Determinisms and Teleology

Criticisms against CHM's various determinisms (technologist, class, economic and structuralist, etc.) and teleology (historicism) were particularly fierce and well documented (Laclau and Mouffe 1985; Resnick and Wolff 1987; Gibson-Graham 1996; Chakrabarti and Cullenberg 2003; Ruccio 2011); so were charges of definitional and logical inconsistencies in mode of production and class analysis (Hindess and Hirst 1977; Hindess 1987).

Economism

Arguing against the Smithian explanation of growth-driven economic development to be pioneered by the individual economic actors trying to achieve greater productivity and hence efficiency, which he claimed is an approach shared by Dobb, Sweezy and Cohen's CHM, Brenner (1986) emphasizes the political qua class struggle and the contingent nature of its outcome as against the economic/technologist imperative. Brenner's attack is not directed at CHM per se, which he accepts with some modifications (such as defining class ROP in terms of property), but his bone of contention seems to be over the main causal factor of transitional change. Specifically, Brenner replaces the primacy of FOP with property relations such that the essential motor of transition of society is now class struggle over property relations rather than the FOP and their presumed development. But then, a question remains: is Brenner lapsing into political qua class essentialism as the major driver of transition? Moreover, given CHM, it may be argued that, in the long run, the development of society and the specific form of class struggle and, subsequently, its outcome will depend on the level of development of the FOP. If agreed, then, in the last instance, Brenner's political emphasis of class struggle depends ultimately on the economic, thereby undercutting his critique of economic determinism.

Historical Inevitability in Transition

An *other* Marx, Late Marx, when faced with the "Russian Road/Question" (as revealed in a correspondence with Russian Marxists regarding the route of the country's transition that began in the 1870s and continued till his death), ended up challenging the very idea of "historical inevitability" and with it the stagist theory of history (Marx 1983; Bailey and Llobera 1981; Shanin 1983; Chakrabarti and Dhar 2010, ch. 6 and 7).

To begin with, it is worth recalling the exuberance of the triumph of global capitalism that Marx and Engels had forwarded earlier in *The Communist Manifesto*:

> The bourgeoisie ... compels all nations, on pain of extinction, to adopt the bourgeois mode of production; it compels them to introduce what it calls civilisation into their midst, i.e., to become bourgeois themselves. In one word, it creates a world after its own image.
>
> *(Marx and Engels 2005, 34)*

Looking back at history, while Marx's description of capitalism going global is truly of the contemporary, there is enough reason to cast doubt on the ability of the bourgeoisie to impose its stamp over the entire world, in all relationships and in all spaces as described in the *Manifesto*; one can even have doubts regarding whether the bourgeoisie wants to do it at all so long as the capitalist organization of exploitation is secured from challenges. There is certainly also a triumphant inevitability attributed to this imagery in Marx, in which the (White Western) bourgeoisie personifying this historicist logic plays a "revolutionary" role. This seems to substantiate the claim of historical inevitability in the stage-based sequence in Cohen's rendition and in fact generally in CHM.

When quizzed over the question of whether or not backward Russia should inevitably take the path of capitalist development as it had unfolded in England and other Western European countries, Marx became skeptical. Reacting against Mikhailovskii, who emphasized the aspect of teleology in his work, Marx hit back that he certainly did not propose "to metamorphose our historical sketch of the genesis of capitalism in Western Europe into a *historico-philosophical theory of general development, imposed by fate on all peoples, whatever the historical circumstances in which they are placed*, in order to eventually attain this economic formation which, with a tremendous leap of the productive forces of social labour, assures the most integral development of every industrial producer." (Marx in Shanin 1983, 59) Taking up the specific case of historical inevitability for "backward" Russia, he harped on the possibility of many alternative paths, including to post-capitalist directions. His argument opens the space for contingency in history, thereby casting doubt on the idea of teleology, as highlighted by Cohen. Again, taking up the case for the Russian land commune and pointing to the astronomical costs of following blindly a supra-historical logic, Marx writes in the following remarkable passage:

> At the same time as the commune is being bled and tortured and its land made barren and poor, the literary lackeys of the "new pillars of society" refer ironically to the wounds which have been inflicted on the commune as symptoms of its spontaneous decrepitude. They claim that it is dying a natural death and the kindest thing would be to put an end to its agony. Here we are no longer dealing with a problem to be solved, but quite simply with an enemy who must be defeated. In order to save the Russian commune there must be a Russian revolution. And the Russian government and the "new pillars of society" are doing their best to prepare the masses for such a catastrophe. If the revolution takes place at the right time, if it concentrates all its forces to ensure the free development of the village commune, the latter will soon

emerge as the regenerative force in Russian society and as something superior to those countries which are still enslaved by the capitalist regime.

(Marx in Marx and Engels 1970, 161; originally written by Marx in late February and early March 1881)

Marx turns the historicist logic and its claimed scientific inevitability tied to the origin and so-called progressive evolution of capitalism and industrial society upside down. He also unveils in the process the "masked political character" of capitalism and the "hidden hostility" of the modern West to Other Worlds and possibilities (no longer seen as passé or regressive) that can be derived from it. The aspect of being "torn asunder" deemed as revolutionary in the *Manifesto* is here projected as violent, retrograde and catastrophic. Late Marx thus overturns Cohen's Marx and indeed the whole history of CHM.

The implication is far reaching. Once we break away from the teleological theory of transition there is no need to be enslaved to capitalism in thinking the transitional paths. Rather, the *path* itself becomes open to multiple possibilities. In the process, it opens up the very question of transition and the concept of "progress" as theoretical categories. We must again ask the question: what then *is* transition in a Marxian frame?

Model II: Non-Deterministic Theory of Transition

Persuaded by a substantial body of arguments against CHM and a big-bang approach to transition it proposes, the second account of transition takes off from a class-focused Marxian approach to advocate a non-deterministic displacement of the disaggregated class structures of a society (Chakrabarti and Cullenberg 2003). The fundamental difference between the two approaches is based on a methodological departure imposed by the commitment to non-determinism and non-teleology in the class-focused approach.

Depicting the class-focused reality as the combined effects of an infinite number of mutually constituting class and non-class processes (where change in each affects and changes the others), transition of this overdetermined and contradictory reality cannot be reduced to any deeper-level essence with predetermined rationale (such as FOP) and hence with no underlying purpose (say, as in Development Thesis in CHM) in driving the movement of society. Instead, the contradictory pulls and pushes guarantee that change is multi-directional, uneven and unpredictable. Being in a state of such flux, societal transition cannot be rationally ordered and tied to any predestined end.

In order to unpack the potentially multifaceted class nature of society and the simultaneity in its movement, we take recourse to the idea of class sets as laid down in the entry on economic development in this volume. We identify class sets in terms of the performance and appropriation of surplus labor (FCP), which is of three types, namely, self-appropriation, exploitative appropriation and collective appropriation. Distribution takes the form of commodity and non-commodity, while workers' remuneration appears in two forms, wage and nonwage. The combination of these three elements help create 24 class sets, which represent the multifaceted institutional settings in which any class structure may exist in an economy. As decentered and disaggregated, the economy cannot be reduced to a capitalist sector, which itself is now disaggregated into various class set types (including state and private forms). Furthermore, non-capitalist forms are, by definition, differentiated into various types (slave, feudal, communist, communitic and independent). Considering further conditions of existence of these class sets such as the subsumed class conditions referring to distribution and receipt of surplus, property structure, power structure, income distribution, etc. will only reveal the deepened state of heterogeneity of the class structures and hence of the decentered class-focused economy.[3]

By focusing on these class sets, a picture of the class differentiation within an economy can be gleaned and transition theorized in terms of an uneven, disaggregated and interconnected series of distinctive changes in the types and forms of class structures (Chakrabarti and Cullenberg 2003). Transition may transpire when there would a direct change in the type (say, from capitalist to communist) or form (say, from state capitalist to private capitalist) of class sets or when any of the conditions of existence of the class sets affect the class sets. Class and non-class processes affect one another, continually producing in turn their heterogeneous, fluid and simultaneous movement and thereby placing social reality in a state of flux and indeterminacy.

The ceaseless process of transition due to overdetermination[4] and contradiction of social processes produces not a chaotic theory of history, as is often mistakenly understood, but rather a theory of history (held together by the discursive focus point of class and the class-focused economy) that is able to describe societal movement in all its chaotic dimensions. What is lost, however, in this approach to transition is the eschatological, teleological ordering of societies according to some linear notion of "progress."

The decentered and disaggregated economy opens the door to rethinking transition that need not be capitalist or seen through the lens of capitalism. The class-focused Marxian approach to transition is not agnostic or indifferent to the direction of societal change it favors. In other words, it recognizes that the trajectory of transition is not just a struggle over what one means by transition (say, big bang versus micro-multilayered), but also over the desirable and actual trajectory of transition from within a decentered and disaggregated economy. In this context, Marxian justice criteria criticize all exploitative types (feudal, slave, capitalist, CA communitic) and would defend the adoption of communist and AC communitic class structures for their non-exploitative features.[5] It would also defend distributive justice and development justice. These just criteria would constitute the Marxian standpoint.

What the above discussion means is that the synchronic simultaneity of class sets movement (pointing to the way the class-focused economy changes) is supplemented by a somewhat weakened diachronic nature of class sets movement as well (pointing to the *kind of change* that actually does or could transpire at the micro level). In CHM, the former is reduced to the latter and that too in a deterministic way. Here, transition proceeds through the combined effects of the two and in which neither of the arms can be taken as a priori, predictable or definitive in any way. Rather than to be seen as a sign of weakness, this in turn opens the alternative door to enact actual and possible socio-political transformation through intervention at the micro level plateau of the class-differentiated economy on grounds of Marxian justice. From a Marxian standpoint, transition is not "anything goes" but a transition whose character of change (progressive or regressive) can be identified and actively intervened upon to give it direction.

The important point to note is that the meaning of progress and development has no originary, teleological or evolutionary bias in this theory of transition. It rejects the argument that says that the evolution of society follows some pre-given pattern, implying a definitive movement towards a non-exploitative and relatively "fair" society. What it says, in contrast, is that it is a desirable solution and one should advocate and struggle for it when the situation demands and possibilities arise. But struggling for it, of course, does not guarantee that it is going to materialize. Furthermore, even if we assume that such a social state of affairs is achieved, the combined effects of the overdetermined and contradictory processes prevent that scenario from being taken as permanent. Some class structures might move back to exploitative forms and the social distribution of wealth may again become extremely "unfair." In other words, a permanent state of a society without any exploitation and with a relatively "fair" distribution of income as the definite end of history is not guaranteed (however desirable it may seem) in this theory. Rather, the class and non-class struggle for transition from the standpoint of Marxian justice considerations is a permanent struggle. This is in contrast to the CHM idea of class struggle to maintain concept(s) of progress that is linked to the driving forces (say, FOP) underlying the linear evolution of society and whose resolution is a foregone conclusion in the last instance. This ideal of progress acts both as the essence of societal development and the telos of the transition process, something that is rejected in the class-focused theory of transition.

Model III: Transition as Political

The third model sees transition as an out-and-out political question (and not a historical or a technological question). In a somewhat autocritical vein, transition is theorized as a question of the "politics of time" and the "politics of space"—as also a question of the politics of interpretation and the politics of transformation (Chakrabarti, Dhar and Dasgupta 2015).

Politics of Time

Because Model I reduces heterogeneous experiential temporalities in both the West and the non-West—temporalities tied to *non*-capitalist (not *pre*-capitalist) class processes and class sets—into either capital-centric or modernity-centric imaginations of time, time is in the process (s)tilted; time is also rendered linear and step-ladder. Gibson-Graham (1996) through her critique of capitalocentrism (which reduces the Other's temporalities and experiences—especially the non-capitalist ones—to the time-language-logic of capital) cracks the inviolability of the delusion of capital as essence and telos of all transition. The delusion also helps silence, render "unutterable" and "unknown," "shroud," and "hide" class *exploitation*, the *violence* of primitive accumulation, and world of the third as the non-capitalist *outside* to the circuits of global capital (see the previous chapter on economic development in this volume).

Politics of Space

Because Model I drags heterogeneous orderings of space in both West and non-West in terms of class processes into the advanced/developed/modern first world and the backward/lacking/lagging/pre-modern third world, it is an Orientalist representation. Late Marx resists—as we have seen above—both capitalocentrism and Orientalism. This theory, premised on a critique of the politics of time and politics of space in Model I—and a critique of capitalocentrism and Orientalism in CHM and in developmental thinking and practice, as also building on Model II, works its way through a Model III of transition, a model that sees transition as not simply change (whether as diachronic or as synchronic simultaneity described earlier) but as a dialectic of the *changed* and the *unchanged*, as also a dialectic of the *expressed* and the *secret* (Derrida calls it *crypted* [1986]), where it is the unchanged in transition that is kept secret and it is the changed that is rendered expressed.

Transition, then, is about the "unchanged *face* of change" and the "changing *phases* of the unchanged." Do the phases *hide* the face? Do the phases work as a *mask*? We would like to mark the distinction between face and phase rather sharply; face is character-logical, which tells us what or who one is—what capitalism cannot be without: exploitation and primitive accumulation—while phase is temporal, something that is in passing or could pass. One could move from the "welfare state" or "developmental state" to "neoliberal globalization"; one can move from a strong foregrounding in-charge in-control kind of state to a state that is slowly backgrounding itself and handing over power and authority to the competitive market economy. The overdetermination of the changing phase (say, within and between capitalism[s]) and of the unchanged face (say, exploitation and primitive accumulation) is how we are setting up the "transition question" vis-à-vis capitalism.

Integrating this insight into our proposed theoretical perspective, Marx is seen as interested in the connection of class process and class struggle with the *transition* of economy/society, which in our case would mean an alteration from one form of exploitation to another. The organization of exploitation as it appears across history (from slavery to feudalism to capitalism) marks transitional phases, which, among other things, are different variations of an embodied system of class exploitation; one need not draw any other inference regarding chronology or valuation of time and space in this representation, something that—as we explained earlier—Late Marx seemed to move away from. The phases of transition span the changing forms of exploitation even as the aspect of exploitation per se remains intact. It is as if the forms of exploitation are changing even as the content of exploitation is static. The static in movement is the secret of transition, whose crypting is what keeps the transition (of phases) going and alive. Transition thus encapsulates both change and no change, a redefinition that changes the political contour. Class struggle to preserve class organization of exploitation (even when changing its form) and class struggle with the objective to dissolve class organization of exploitation became fundamentally dissimilar. Transition through class struggle is transition in class exploitation. Transition of class-divided society is to cross the horizon of class exploitation. It also means that, for Marx, the struggle against capitalism for a post-capitalist future of non-exploitation (and for making primitive accumulation nonexistent) is simultaneously a struggle to transcend transition. Class struggle for a post-capitalist future must be a struggle for a post-transition future (Chakrabarti et al. 2015, ch. 5).

The question of transition thus becomes a political question between the delusional hope around expressed changes on the one hand and the inertia or the staticity of the crypted on the other. The crypt (Abraham and Torok 1986) is our theoretico-political shorthand for the experience and phenomenon of the "secret" in transition; it signifies the *unchanged* in the changing phases; it is the *secret static* under the condition of apparent and incessant movement. We would like to argue, for example, that the crypt of current global capitalist transition is:

1 class as processes pertaining to surplus labor,
2 world of the third (and *not* third world) as the *outside* to the circuits of global capital and
3 primitive accumulation.

The political question in transition thus resides in whether the change is brought about *by* protecting the crypt, or whether it is change *to* protect the crypt (for example, change from national capitalism to global capitalism protects the crypt of capital-in-transition), or is the change unfolding following incessant struggles *over* the crypt (for example, where the *given* of capitalist transition itself is put to question, as Late Marx did in the context of the Russian commune). We would like to ask: are current transitions then about changes *in* capitalism and not *of* capitalism, changes in capitalism, that in turn keep the crypt protected? Therefore, while much of the economic, political, cultural, even natural landscape changes, what does not change is the crypt. Some questions like the question of class as process, some perspectives like the perspective of world of the third as the *outside* and not the third worldish *underside* of the circuits of global capital, some experiences like the experience of class exploitation, the experience of outsided-ness, and the experience of violence-violation in the context of primitive accumulation remain buried, forgotten, crypted, even as the world goes into frenzy regarding transition. Some signifiers, like class, world of the third and primitive accumulation remain tabooed in the varied new and old discourses that circulate. Some other signifiers like competition, profit, growth, third world, etc. are instead foregrounded, and "incitement to discourse" around transition is organized around such foregrounded signifiers. Transition is, then, marked by both movement, i.e., movement in foregrounded signifiers, and invariance, i.e., invariance of tabooed signifiers. The Marxian politics of transition hence lies in questioning and transforming that which is *invariant*.

This theorization seeks a move from an obsession with *transition* in much of Marxism and progressivist and developmental thinking to *transformation*. Would that mean a conceptual transition from *what is* to *what it is to be*? In other words, would it be a conceptual transition from mere description to the *ought*, to the *ethic* of transition? Marxism is not mere description of the delusional veil called transition of surfaces; Marxism is also transformative praxis in just and desirable directions. Hence one needs to engage with what is discursively buried, hidden, in the transparent script of transition. The loss of the elements of the crypt in the language of transition and the non-mourning for such loss—as if the elements are stashed away in a secret vault, only to be forgotten—is a political condition that needs to be undone. What is at stake (in politics) is *what takes places secretly* (i.e., that which deludes) or *takes a secret place* (i.e., that which is foreclosed), in order to keep the crypt safe (Derrida 1986, xv).

The imagination of the political has hitherto been colonized by the concept of "transition." In classical Marxism, it is not called transition, however. It is called "historical materialism." Much of the Marxian imagination has been unnecessarily colonized by the concept, language and framework of transition qua historical materialism. Historical materialism is a sophisticated theory of transition, but it is a ridiculously naive and banal theory of transformation. For example, Soviet society did transit from private capitalism to state capitalism (Resnick and Wolff 2002), but it hardly underwent Marxian transformation in terms of transformation in the logic-language-ethos of surplus exploitation as also new subject-formation. In other words, there were changes in foregrounded signifiers, but there was no fundamental change in the crypted signifiers. The question of transition hence must turn into a movement where the crypt itself becomes the object of political inquiry, and not where political change is circumscribed, wittingly or unwittingly, by the preservation of the crypt. This is a subtle but profound difference that this theorization of transition unpacks. Thus, even "radical" politics—Marxian and non-Marxian—may ultimately never get to the point of reorienting themselves to the objective of transformation, notwithstanding previous and ongoing attempts to the contrary. In other words, while the crypt even if secret is very much alive/real, politics addressing it is absent or muted. On the other hand, Marx's idea of the political is envisioned in terms of *transformation* of the crypt. Transformation could then perhaps be the logic-language-ethos of a post-transition imagination of transition; a transition imagination not reduced to historical materialism or liberal gradualism.

The conjecture is the following: let us not be *slaves* of transition. Let us be *sculptors* of transformation. Let us not just look for *alternative transitions*. Let us look for *alternatives to transition*.

Notes

1 Others define class ROP fundamentally in terms of property rather than power. Notably, since the basic structure of CHM remains intact, the transition logic hardly changes when such internal adjustments happen.
2 There is a controversy within Marxism regarding the validity of Asiatic as a mode of production, but we must shelve that issue for the moment.
3 Each class set pertains to a specific class structure that is a conceptual site of the combined effects of class and non-class processes, including the aspects included in the definition of class set.
4 In this case, the aspect of "determination in the last instance by the economic" (which we saw being retained in Althusser 1969) in the definition of overdetermination is given up (Resnick and Wolff 1987, ch. 2). Overdetermination is the mutual constitutivity of ceaselessly changing processes, none more important than the other.
5 For definitions of AC and CA communitic class process, see the previous chapter on economic development in this volume.

References

Abraham, N. and M. Torok. 1986. *The Wolf Man's Magic Word: A Cryptonymy*. Trans. by N. Rand. Minneapolis: University of Minnesota Press.
Althusser, L. 1969. *For Marx*. Trans. by B. Brewster. London: Allen Lane, The Penguin Press.
Bailey, A. M. and J. P. Llobera. 1981. *The Asiatic Mode of Production: Science and Politics*. London: Routledge & Kegan Paul.
Brenner, R. 1986. "The Social Basis of Economic Development." In *Analytical Marxism*, J. E. Roemer, ed., 23–53. Cambridge: Cambridge University Press.
Chakrabarti, A. and S. Cullenberg. 2003. *Transition and Development in India*. New York: Routledge.
Chakrabarti, A. and A. Dhar. 2010. *Dislocation and Resettlement in Development: From Third World to World of the Third*. London and New York: Routledge.
Chakrabarti, A., A. Dhar, and B. Dasgupta. 2015. *The Indian Economy in Transition: Globalization, Capitalism and Development*. New Delhi: Cambridge University Press.
Cohen, G. A. 1978. *Karl Marx's Theory of History: A Defence*. Oxford: Oxford University Press.
———. 1988. *History, Labor and Freedom*. Oxford: Oxford University Press.
Derrida, J. 1986. "Foreword." In *The Wolf Man's Magic Word: A Cryptonymy*, N. Abraham and M. Torok, eds., Nicholas Rand, trans., xl–xlviii. Minneapolis: University of Minnesota Press.
Gibson-Graham, J. K. 1996. *The End of Capitalism (As We Knew It): A Feminist Critique of Political Economy*. Oxford: Blackwell.
Hindess, B. 1987. *Politics and Class Analysis*. Oxford: Blackwell.
Hindess, B. and P. Hirst. 1977. *Mode of Production and Social Formation: An Auto-Critique of "Pre-Capitalist Modes of Production."* London: Macmillan.
Laclau, E. C. and Mouffe. 1985. *Hegemony and Socialist Strategy: Towards a Radical Democratic Politics*. Trans. by W. Moore and P. Cammack. London: Verso Press.
Marx, K. 1983. "Marx-Zasulich Correspondence: Letters and Drafts." In *Late Marx and the Russian Road: Marx and "The Peripheries of Capitalism"*. Edited by T. Shanin, 97–126. New York: Monthly Review Press.
Marx, K. and F. Engels. 1970. "First Draft of the Reply to V. I. Zasulich's Letter." In *Karl Marx and Fredrick Engels, Selected Works*, Volume 3. Moscow: Progress Publishers.
———. 2005. "The Communist Manifesto: In *Manifesto: Three Classic Essays on How to Change the World*, 27–68. Melbourne and New York: Ocean Press.
Olsen, E. K. 2009. "Social Ontology and the Origins of Mode of Production Theory." *Rethinking Marxism* 21(2): 177–195.
Resnick, S. A. and R. D. Wolff. 1987. *Knowledge and Class: A Marxian Critique of Political Economy*. Chicago: University of Chicago Press.

——. 2002. *Class Theory and History: Capitalism and Communism in the USSR*. New York: Routledge.

Ruccio, D. 2011. *Development and Globalization: Marxian Class Analysis*. New York: Routledge.

Shanin, T., ed. 1983. *Late Marx and the Russian Road: Marx and "The Peripheries of Capitalism"*. New York: Monthly Review Press.

PART V

Marxian Traditions

31

POSTMODERNISM

Jack Amariglio and David F. Ruccio

In the latter part of the twentieth and the early part of the twenty-first century, the intellectual movement generally referred to as postmodernism has fundamentally transformed the Marxian critique of political economy. Postmodernism (and, with it, poststructuralism and deconstruction) has been utilized to engage in a fundamental rethinking of key concepts and conceptual strategies of Marxian economic theory. It has also helped to identify and extend aspects of the Marxian tradition that had been forgotten or suppressed by modernist approaches, and to explore overlaps with other disciplines (such as anthropology, philosophy, and literary criticism) and other theoretical traditions within economics (especially institutionalism, feminism, postcolonialism, and Austrian economics). The result has been the emergence of distinctly postmodern interpretations of Marxian economic theory.

Traditional interpretations of Marxian economics have mostly been based on a modernist approach. Modernist Marxist economists tend to invoke a "mirror of nature" epistemology and a deterministic notion of causality. For these scholars, Marx's *Capital* presents a science of law-driven capitalism based on an objective labor theory of value (as against, for example, the preference-based subjective theory of value of neoclassical economics). The problem of Marxist economics, on this interpretation, is to identify the order underlying the apparent disorder of capitalism—and to point in the direction of a transition from capitalist disorder to the planned order of socialism.

One illustrative example of modernist Marxian economics concerns the relationship between production and exchange. According to the modernist reading, the value and surplus-value (the extra value created by laborers and appropriated by capitalists) created in the orderly process of capitalist production determine, and thus explain, the prices and profits that obtain in the chaotic and uncertain realm of capitalist exchange. Since the anarchy of a capitalist economy leads to crises, modernist Marxists argue that the disorder and irrationality of private property and markets can and should be replaced by the order and rationality of state property and planning within socialism.

Postmodern interpretations are quite different. In them, the theory of knowledge most often is relativist (Marx's and Marxian approaches, like all economic theories, can be distinguished by particular entry points, logics, discursive structures, and sets of social consequences) and causality is nondeterministic (in the sense that everything is conceived to be both cause and effect). The aim of Marxist economics, according to such approaches, is to produce a particular class-analytical story about capitalism and non-capitalism and to point toward nonexploitative or communal ways of organizing the economy and social life.

Again, the relationship between the processes of production and exchange can be used to illustrate the approach. On a postmodern interpretation, production and exchange—each comprising a particular and changing combination of order and disorder—exist on the same discursive level. Thus, for example, capitalists need to purchase commodity inputs, at their exchange-value, which are then used to produce new commodities, which in turn need to be sold to realize the embodied value and surplus-value. So, each commodity has two numbers attached to it—production value and exchange-value—each of which simultaneously determines the other. Capitalism faces problems, related to class exploitation, that occur in both production and exchange (and the interaction between them). For postmodern Marxian economists, socialism is a constantly changing way of eliminating capitalist exploitation (and its conditions and consequences) and enabling situations in which workers collectively appropriate and distribute the surpluses they create.

Postmodernisms

Since its inception, postmodernism has had at least four different meanings in relation to Marxian theory. Some have taken it to identify, following the work of Fredric Jameson (1991) and David Harvey (1989), a particular world-historical *phase*—the cultural logic of the contemporary stage of capitalism (which is often referred to as "late capitalism," due to the work of Belgian Marxist Ernest Mandel [1975]). The idea is that mass commodification (along with changes in global production and the rise of new information technologies) has reached a point where it has created the conditions for a distinct postmodern culture, characterized by fragmentation, depthlessness, generalized alienation, and a lack of historical perspective. A second approach, which is mostly associated with Jean-François Lyotard (1984), focuses on changes in discourse itself, especially those that pertain to knowledge, technology, and science. This notion of postmodernism as a *condition* of contemporary life involves an incredulity toward post-Enlightenment metanarratives (including Marxism) and the emergence of new scientific "games" in which meaning and consequence are always in play. Postmodernism has also acquired a third meaning, more connected to a new *style* of theorizing, which can be traced to the work of Michel Foucault (1972 and 1973) and Jacques Derrida (1976). While Foucault's "archaeology" emphasized the radically changed conditions of different forms of knowledge over time (thereby challenging the idea of the "progress" of science), Derrida focused on the "undecideable" moments created by the play of words and signs within a text, including for some followers the "text" of the world.

There has been a great deal of debate about the extent to which these different interpretations of postmodernism are compatible with Marxism and other forms of critical social theory. (Good overviews of the debate include Best and Kellner 1991, Sarup 1993, and Drolet 2003. Major criticisms of postmodernism include Hutcheon 1989, Callinicos 1990, and Eagleton 1996.) But the approach that has exercised the most influence over recent Marxian economic theory is actually a fourth one, the idea of postmodernism as *critique*. While it is informed by the other three approaches, postmodernism as critique tends to eschew stage, condition, and style in favor of challenging and posing alternatives to modernist ways of interpreting and deploying Marxian economic categories and forms of analysis.

The general relationship of postmodernism as critique to Marxian economics has been elaborated in different but related ways in three texts: *Knowledge and Class*, by Stephen Resnick and Richard Wolff (1987); *The End of Capitalism (As We Knew It)*, by

J. K. Gibson-Graham (1996); and *Postmodern Moments in Modern Economics* (2003) by David F. Ruccio and Jack Amariglio.

The authors of *Knowledge and Class*, perhaps ironically, were inspired by the work of Louis Althusser (and Balibar 1970) and set out to criticize the modernist determinisms or essentialisms that had characterized much of existing Marxian economic theory (ironic in the sense that Althusser has often been characterized as a modernist "structuralist"). While Resnick and Wolff do not explicitly refer to postmodernism, they do utilize many of the concepts and conceptual strategies that had, in the work of Richard Rorty (1979) and others, become associated with postmodernism. Thus, for example, they criticize both major forms of post-Enlightenment epistemology (empiricism and rationalism) that rely on the modernist dichotomy between theory and reality as well as the various types of determinism (of an economic "base," a human essence, and so on) that are based on cause-and-effect notions of causality. Resnick and Wolff then elaborate a nondeterministic or postmodern interpretation of both epistemology (the discursive world comprises a variety of theories that produce different and incommensurable "realities" within theory, which shape and are shaped by the world outside of discourse) and causality (everything is conceived to be both cause and effect simultaneously, constituted in a contradictory fashion by everything else in the social totality). They refer to this alternative approach (via a radical extension of Althusser's original borrowing of Freud's term) as "overdetermination."

Gibson-Graham (the pseudonym for Julie Graham and Katherine Gibson) follow a somewhat different approach, under the influence, in addition to many of the same sources as Resnick and Wolff, of feminist and queer theory. For them, one of the key problems of modernist Marxian economics has been the language—the depiction and analysis—of capitalism as a unified, totalizing system, governed by a singular logic, often referred to as capitalism's "laws of motion," which they refer to as "capitalocentrism." They set out to "decenter" what we mean by capitalism, both by discursively constituting capitalism as smaller and less unified than has been the case in modernist Marxism and by creating discursive space, within the contemporary economic and social landscape, of many different forms of non-capitalism. The result is a conception of the economic space as a field of difference, constituted by various instances of capitalist and noncapitalist kinds of transactions, types of labor, and enterprises (including ways of producing, appropriating, and distributing surplus), and the complex and contradictory interactions among them.

Ruccio and Amariglio developed still another way of understanding and using postmodernism in Marxian economic theory: in terms of "moments." Their idea is that the predominant modernism—the scientism, determinism, humanism, and much else—of much existing economic theory (including but certainly not limited to Marxism) has also given rise to a series of postmodern moments—instances in which apparent anomalies, such as uncertainty, the instability of subjectivity, the possibility of various rationalities, and so on, have threatened to overrun and overturn the limits of modernism. Such disruptions, in Marx's texts and across the history of Marxian economics, if appropriately identified and developed, can serve both to deconstruct modernist Marxian theory (including dichotomies such as science/ideology, order/disorder, and much else) and to point in the direction of different, postmodern formulations of key notions within Marxian economics (such as decentered notions of the enterprise, uncertainty about profits, and the disorder of capitalist competition).

Over the course of the past thirty years, these three texts (and their original sources and influences as well as other work in postmodernism, poststructuralism, and deconstruction) have generated a large and still-growing body of work with a postmodern orientation within

Marxian economic theory. Its authors have made contributions in a wide variety of specific areas, including philosophy, value theory, subjectivity, class, and socialism and communism.

Marxian Economics

The philosophy of Marxian economics—both epistemology and methodology—has often been interpreted through the lens of modernism. Postmodern Marxists have sought to challenge that framing and to reinterpret, in a more postmodern vein, the philosophical orientation of the Marxian critique of political economy. In terms of epistemology, they have eschewed "scientism" (the idea that there is or can be a singular truth based on a privileged language or method) in favor of different scientific or discursive frameworks (the idea that there are or can be multiple truths based on different, incommensurable languages and methods). Thus, for example, from a postmodern perspective, Marxian economics differs from both neoclassical and Keynesian economics (Resnick and Wolff 2012) not on the basis of one being more scientific than the others or their having a better grasp on reality, but because they have different entry points (class, human nature, and structures) and logics (determinism and overdetermination). What this means is that, in terms of assessing the differences among the truths produced in and through these theories, the emphasis is not on their correspondence or not with a supposedly extra-theoretical reality, but on their different economic and social consequences. In addition, postmodern Marxists have focused on the role of the body and power in modernist conceptions of knowledge (Amariglio 1988), criticized the privileged role of mathematics in economic discourse (Ruccio 1988), identified the significant overlaps with the non-modernist tendencies in other philosophical positions (e.g., Deweyan pragmatism [Wilson 1996 and Aoki 2005], feminism [Gibson-Graham 1996 and Bergeron 2006], institutionalism [Cullenberg 2000], and postcolonialism [Charusheela 2000]), and analyzed the "performativity" of economic discourses (the extent to which Marxian and other economic theorists create, in part, the realities they seek to analyze [cf. Gibson-Graham 1996 and Madra and Adaman 2014]).

Deterministic notions of causality in modernist interpretations of Marxian economic theory have been challenged in a similar manner. Determinism is based on the idea that causality runs in one direction, from causes to effects. Thus, for example, economic determinism presumes that the economy (mode of production or one part thereof, such as relations or forces of production) determines, in the first or last instance, all other aspects (such as culture and politics) of social totalities. The other major form of determinism in Marxian economics, theoretical humanism, presumes that human nature, itself usually reduced to one of its components, such as rationality or needs or class interests, is the "essence" that can be used to explain economic and social practices and institutions. Postmodernism rejects determinism in favor of alternative notions of causality, which focus on the randomness of causation and the effectivity of chance, the indeterminacy of events, the multiplicity of possible causes, the fluidity of the relationship between seeming causes and possible effects, and the reversibility of positions between causes and effects. Postmodernists, of course, have had to confront the charge of "everythingism" (Carling 1990, and the response by Resnick and Wolff 1992), in other words, that giving up determinism means surrendering to the claim that "everything goes"—that both theory and concrete analyses are rendered impossible. A postmodern answer has been to suggest both alternative notions of causation (overdetermination, juxtaposition, synchronic simultaneity, and ceaseless change) and the importance of conjunctural analyses (that are always specific, partial, and incomplete). Postmodern criticisms of determinism affect a wide variety of specific topics within Marxian economics, including the "law" of capitalist accumulation (Norton 1986), the necessity/contingency dualism in Marxian crisis theory (DeMartino 1993), notions of totality in theories of the falling rate of profit (Cullenberg 1994), and the subservient or secondary role of consumption (McIntyre 1992, Diskin and Sandler 1994, Pietrykowski 1994, and MacNeill 1997).

Given its key role in the Marxian critique of political economy, it is not surprising that value theory has been one of the major sites of tension between modernist and postmodern interpretations of Marxian economic theory. The examples above highlight the relationship between production and exchange—whether, as modernists interpret it, production determines exchange (in an essentialist manner), or, as postmodernists see it, production and exchange are mutually constitutive (by relinquishing the usual depth metaphors). On the latter view, the discussion of production and exchange across the three volumes of *Capital* is not a matter of hierarchical causal significance (production being "more important" than exchange), but a discursive presentation, in steps—from production in volume 1 to exchange in volume 2, and then, in volume 3, both realms together—of a decentered totality. But postmodernism has influenced many other aspects of Marxian value theory as well. At the most general level, postmodernists have read *Capital* as representing a radical break (in both object and analytical method) from classical political economy (Wolff, Callari, and Roberts 1984 and Roberts 1987), combining both modern and postmodern moments or strands (Garnett 1995), making it possible to see and count the class content of the quantitative relations of capitalism (Roberts 1996), containing a socially contingent (as opposed to a unchanging, embodied labor) conception of value (Biewener 1998), and being based on different levels of abstraction each of which contains new contingencies (Kristjanson-Gural 2008b). The result is an approach that focuses on both the production/appropriation and distribution/receipt of surplus-value (Resnick and Wolff 1987), the simultaneity of the realization of value and the redistributions of surplus-value as a result of capital mobility, monopoly power, and much else (Roberts 1988), the non-inevitable tendency of the rate of profit to fall (Cullenberg 1998), how demand and supply act together to determine both value and exchange-value (Kristjanson-Gural 2003), and the role of money as a central component of a commodity-producing economy in the sense that it represents the means by which private expenditures of labor are articulated in a social division of labor (Kristjanson-Gural 2008a).

One of the features of modernist Marxian economics is an essentialist conception of the subject. Thus, for example, when commodity fetishism (as presented by Marx in chapter 1 of volume 1 of *Capital*) is interpreted as a theory of the subject within capitalist societies, the subject of such fetishism is often taken to be to be the effect of an underlying economic reality: such subjects are thought to then possess a "false consciousness." However, when commodity fetishism is developed in a more postmodern vein, subjects and their forms of consciousness are seen as both shifting products and producers of history and society; they are as much a cause or condition of the "fetishizing" economic processes of commodity exchange, constituted in and through politics and culture, as they are a result of this commodity exchange (as Amariglio and Callari 1989 argue). The implications for Marxian economic theory of such a postmodern approach to subjectivity, together with Althusser's (1971) notion of a "process without a subject" (that is, the idea that history is not the work of a subject, whether absolute or human) and his theory of the ideological interpellation of the subject (Althusser 2001), have been enormous (Özselçuk 2013). Thus, for example, it has become possible to argue that a society in which the products of human labor take the form of commodities can be and often is accompanied by a variety of individual and collective subjectivities (Ruccio 1992); that Lacanian psychoanalytic theory (Özselçuk and Madra

2010) can be a useful complement to Marxism in theorizing both the emptiness of the subject (the extent to which it is never entirely determined or subjected by social reality) and the performativity of resubjectification (both the obstacles to and the possibilities of the formation of new, noncapitalist subjectivities, as discussed by Graham and Amariglio 2006, Madra 2006, Özselçuk 2006, Byrne and Healy 2006, Rebello 2006, and Sato 2006); that the rethinking of noncapitalist subjectivities such as those of feudalism can help us identify both the acceptance of subordination and forms of resistance (Kayatekin and Charusheela 2004); and, finally, that communal subjectivities are constitutive both of the various types of historical communal societies (Amariglio 2010) and of a way of "traversing the fantasy" beyond capitalism today (Madra and Özselçuk 2010).

Class analysis is arguably the central component of Marxian economic theory. And it, too, has been revised and rethought through the lens of postmodernism. In the most general terms, the idea of class as being the essential determinant of economic and social reality has been discarded in favor of its discursive importance (as one of the defining features of a particularly Marxian analysis, a point of entry into social reality, without according class any more causal significance than the other processes that make up a specific society or social situation). In addition, class analysis has been decentered—in terms of both society as a whole (there can be and often are different class structures within a social formation) and any individual within a society (who may and often does occupy multiple class positions within space and over time). The result is that, from a postmodern perspective, class is seen more as an adjective than a noun (attached to a subset of the processes that make up society, instead of as the designator of specific groups within society), while class struggle becomes the object of conflicts and tensions (defined in terms of the particular aspects of the society individuals and groups struggle over, quantitatively and qualitatively, as against the subjects of such struggles).

Two entire volumes—*Class and Its Others* (Gibson-Graham, Resnick, and Wolff 2001a) and *Re/Presenting Class: Essays in Postmodern Marxism* (Gibson-Graham, Resnick, and Wolff 2001b)—have been devoted to developing and deploying the new lines of inquiry created by postmodern interpretations of Marxian class analysis. The specific topics of this novel form of class analysis include the following: the noncapitalist nature of the independent commodity production of African-American women involved in domestic labor (Rio 2001); the existence of significant differences among various groups of self-employed, "contingent" workers (Hotch 2001); the importance of identity formation in determining the class nature of household production (Cameron 2001); the significance of the articulated mix of class processes for determining the "class mapping" of a space such as Los Angeles (Arvidson 2001); the problematic nature of the blue-collar/white-collar binary that has long held sway in left-wing and union politics (Southern 2001); the tensions among different distributions of the surplus (rather than a singular drive to accumulate capital) for capitalists (Norton 2001); the role of community development practices in creating notions of collectivity that look beyond capitalist exploitation (Biewener 2001); how struggles over distributions of the surplus can reconfigure capitalist enterprises and their effects on the wider society (Gibson-Graham and O'Neill 2001 and Vlachou 2001); the consequences for historical communal societies of unequal distributions of the surplus (Saitta 2001); the role of culture (in southern U.S. sharecropping) and politics (in Iran) in constituting the conditions of existence of feudal, ancient, and capitalist class processes (Kayatekin 2001 and Gabriel (2001); and the class structure of liberal arts colleges, where credit-hour commodities are produced by wage-worker professors (Curtis 2001). Other examples include the changing class structure of U.S. households (Fraad, Resnick, and Wolff 2009), the class consequences and contradictions generated by remittances within immigrant households (Safri 2009), the capitalist structure of the production of Broadway musicals (Mulder 2009), and the hybrid (communist, capitalist, and so on) class structures of enterprises (Levin 2014). These postmodern interpretations of Marxian class analysis serve to challenge the persistence of capitalism at the heart of postdevelopment discourses (Gibson-Graham and Ruccio 2001), to cultivate a desire for class justice (DeMartino 2003), to confront and deconstruct the hegemony of power essentialism within radical politics (Wolff and Resnick 2005), and to create new possibilities of political transformation by identifying and cultivating fields of class difference (Gibson-Graham 2005).

Finally, postmodernism has served to challenge and move beyond modernist Marxian conceptions of socialism and communism (cf. Burczak 2006). Of particular concern to postmodern thinkers has been the "fullness" attached to ideas like socialism and communism, that is, their role in describing entire economies and societies that either have been or can be created "after" capitalism, which are often characterized by an orderliness associated with forms of property ownership, planning, and much else that are said to overcome the disorder created by capitalist markets. The role of postmodernism within Marxian economic theory has been, on one hand, to narrow the focus of what we mean by socialism and communism and, on the other hand, to broaden their reach by identifying socialist and communist impulses in and around contemporary capitalism. The narrowing has occurred as a result of identifying the specifically class dimensions of Marxian conceptions of socialism and communism (Resnick and Wolff 1988 and Diskin 1996), which in turn leads to a "thin" conception based only on the social predominance of the collective appropriation of the surplus (Cullenberg 1992). At the same time, socialism and communism have been broadened to include antiessentialist notions of subjectivity—of both collective social agency (Ruccio 1992) and communal class positions (Amariglio 2010)—and, following on the debates concerning subjectivity, an axiom of justice that does not describe an ideal social order, but rather an axiom whereby no one is excluded from the appropriation and distribution of the surplus (Madra 2006).

Much, of course, remains to be done to continue to develop the insights and implications of a postmodern approach (Bergeron 2012 and Kayatekin 2012). Many concepts that are central to Marxian economic theory—from alienation to utopia—continue to be interpreted and utilized according to modernist protocols. If they are rethought and redeployed in postmodern directions, we can expect to see a continued loosening of the orthodoxies associated with Marxian economic theory and the remaining constraints imposed on the Marxian critique of political economy.

Acknowledgements

We want to thank the editors for inviting us to contribute and their patience in awaiting this entry, and Dwight Billings for his comments and suggestions on the initial draft.

References

Althusser, L. 1971. "Lenin before Hegel." In *Lenin and Philosophy and Other Essays*, 71–84. New York: Monthly Review Press.

——. 2001. "Ideology and Ideological State Apparatuses (Notes Towards an Investigation)." In *Lenin and Philosophy and Other Essays*. Trans. by B. Brewster, 85–126. New York: Monthly Review Press.

Althusser, L. and E. Balibar. 1970. *Reading Capital*. Trans. by Ben Brewster. London: New Left Books.

Amariglio, J. 1988. "The Body, Economic Discourse, and Power: An Economist's Introduction to Foucault." *History of Political Economy* 20(4): 583–613.

——. 2010. "Subjectivity, Class, and Marx's 'Forms of the Commune'." *Rethinking Marxism* 22(3): 329–344.

Amariglio, J. and A. Callari. 1989. "Marxian Value Theory and the Problem of the Subject: The Role of Commodity Fetishism." *Rethinking Marxism* 2(3): 31–60.

Aoki, M. 2005. "Whipping Boy or Ally? Rethinking Dewey on Education and Capitalism." *Rethinking Marxism* 17(1): 119–137.

Arvidson, E. 2001. "Los Angeles: A Postmodern Class Mapping." In *Class and Its Others*, J. K. Gibson-Graham, S. A. Resnick, and R. D. Wolff, eds., 163–189. Minneapolis: University of Minnesota Press.

Bergeron, S. 2006. *Fragments of Development: Nation, Gender, and the Space of Modernity*. Ann Arbor: University of Michigan Press.

——. 2012. "Postmodern Subjects and the Power of Economics." *Rethinking Marxism* 24(3): 338–343.

Best, S. and D. Kellner. 1991. *Postmodern Theory*. New York: Guilford Press.

Biewener, C. 1998. "Socially Contingent Value." In *Marxian Economics: A Reappraisal*, vol. 2, *Price, Profits, and Dynamics*, R. Belllofiore, ed., 57–69: New York: St. Martin's Press.

——. 2001. "The Promise of Finance: Banks and Community Development." In *Re/Presenting Class: Essays in Postmodern Marxism*, ed. J. K. Gibson-Graham, S. A. Resnick, and R. D. Wolff, 131–158. Durham, N.C.: Duke University Press.

Burczak, T. 2006. *Socialism after Hayek*. Ann Arbor: University of Michigan Press.

Byrne, K. and S. Healy. 2006. "Cooperative Subjects: Toward a Post-Fantasmatic Enjoyment of the Economy." *Rethinking Marxism* 18(2): 241–258.

Callinicos, A. 1990. *Against Postmodernism: A Marxist Critique*. New York: St. Martin's Press.

Cameron, J. 2001. "Domesticating Class: Femininity, Heterosexuality, and Household Politics." In *Class and Its Others*, ed. J.K. Gibson-Graham, S. A. Resnick, and R. D. Wolff, eds. 47–68. Minneapolis: University of Minnesota Press.

Carling, A. 1990. "In Defence of Rational Choice: A Reply to Ellen Meiksins Wood." *New Left Review* 184 (November/December): 97–109.

Charusheela, S. 2000. "On History, Love, and Politics." *Rethinking Marxism* 12(4): 45–61.

Cullenberg, S. 1992. "Socialism's Burden: Toward a 'Thin' Definition of Socialism." *Rethinking Marxism* 5(2): 64–83.

——. 1994. *The Falling Rate of Profit: Recasting the Marxian Debate*. London: Pluto Press.

——. 1998. "Decentering the Marxian Debate over the Falling Rate of Profit: A New Approach." In *Marxian Economics: A Reappraisal. Essays on Volume II of Capital*, Volume 2: *Price, Profits, and Dynamics*, ed. R. Bellofiore, 163–176. New York: St. Martin's Press.

——. 2000. "Old Institutionalism, New Marxism." In *Capitalism, Socialism and Radical Political Economy: Essays in Honour of Howard Sherman*, R. Pollin, ed., 81–102. Cheltenham: Edward Elgar.

Curtis, F. 2001. "Ivy-Covered Exploitation: Class, Education and the Liberal Arts College." In *Re/Presenting Class: Essays in Postmodern Marxism,* ed. J. K. Gibson-Graham, S. A. Resnick, and R. D. Wolff, eds., 81–104. Durham, NC: Duke University Press.

DeMartino, G. 1993. "The Necessity/Contingency Dualism in Marxian Crisis Theory: The Case of Long Wave Theory." *Review of Radical Political Economics* 25(3): 68–74.

——. 2003. "Realizing Class Justice." *Rethinking Marxism* 15(1): 1–31.

Derrida, J. 1976. *Of Grammatology*. Trans. by G. C. Spivak. Baltimore: Johns Hopkins University Press.

Diskin, J. 1996. "Rethinking Socialism: What's In a Name?" In *Postmodern Materialism and the Future of Marxist Theory: Essays in the Althusserian Tradition*, ed. A. Callari and D. F. Ruccio, eds., 278–299. Hanover: Wesleyan University Press.

Diskin, J. and B. Sandler. 1994. "Essentialism and the Economy in the Post-Marxist Imaginary: Reopening the Sutures." *Rethinking Marxism* 6(3): 28–48.

Drolet, M., ed. 2003. *The Postmodernism Reader: Foundational Texts*. New York: Routledge.

Eagleton, T. 1996. *The Illusions of Postmodernism*. Malden, MA: Blackwell.

Foucault, M. 1972. *The Archaeology of Knowledge and the Discourse on Language*. Trans. by A. M. S. Smith. New York: Harper and Row.

———. 1973. *The Order of Things: An Archaeology of the Human Sciences*. Trans. by A. Sheridan. New York: Vintage.

Fraad, H., S. A. Resnick, and R. D. Wolff. 2009. "For Every Knight in Shining Armor, There's A Castle Waiting To Be Cleaned: A Marxist-Feminist Analysis Of The Household." In *Class Struggle on the Home Front: Work, Conflict and Exploitation in The Household*, G. Cassano, ed., 19–70. New York: Palgrave Macmillan.

Gabriel, S. J. 2001. "A Class Analysis of the Iranian revolution of 1979." In *Re/Presenting Class: Essays in Postmodern Marxism*, J. K. Gibson-Graham, S. A. Resnick, and R. D. Wolff, 206–226. Durham, NC: Duke University Press.

Garnett, R. F., Jr. 1995. "Marx's Value Theory: Modern or Postmodern?" *Rethinking Marxism* 8(4): 40–60.

Gibson-Graham, J. K. 1996. *The End of Capitalism (As We Knew It): A Feminist Critique of Political Economy*. Cambridge, MA: Blackwell.

———. 2005. "Dilemmas of Theorizing Class." *Rethinking Marxism* 17(1): 39–44.

Gibson-Graham, J. K. and P. O'Neill. 2001. "Exploring a New Class Politics of the Enterprise." In *Re/Presenting Class: Essays in Postmodern Marxism*, J. K. Gibson-Graham, S. A. Resnick, and R. D. Wolff, eds., 56–80. Durham, NC: Duke University Press.

Gibson-Graham, J. K., S. A. Resnick, and R. D. Wolff, eds. 2001a. *Class and Its Others*. Minneapolis: University of Minnesota Press.

———. eds. 2001b. *Re/Presenting Class: Essays in Postmodern Marxism*. Durham, NC: Duke University Press.

Gibson-Graham, J. K. and D. F. Ruccio. 2001. "'After' Development: Re-imagining Economy and Class." In *Re/Presenting Class: Essays in Postmodern Marxism*, J. K. Gibson-Graham, S. A. Resnick, and R. D. Wolff, 158–181. Durham, NC: Duke University Press.

Graham, J. and J. Amariglio. 2006. "Subjects of Economy: Introduction." *Rethinking Marxism* 18(2): 199–203.

Harvey, D. *The Condition of Postmodernity*. Oxford: Blackwell.

Hotch, J. 2001. "Classing the Self-Employed: New Possibilities of Power and Collectivity." In *Class and Its Others*, ed. J. K. Gibson-Graham, S. A. Resnick, and R. D. Wolff, 143–162. Minneapolis: University of Minnesota Press.

Hutcheon, L. 1989. *The Politics of Postmodernism*. New York: Routledge.

Jameson, F. 1991. *Postmodernism or, the Cultural Logic of Late Capitalism*. Durham, NC: Duke University Press.

Kayatekin, S. A. 2001. "Sharecropping and Feudal Class Processes in the Postbellum Mississippi Delta." In *Re/Presenting Class: Essays in Postmodern Marxism*, J. K. Gibson-Graham, S. A. Resnick, and R. D. Wolff, eds., 227–246. Durham, NC: Duke University Press.

———. 2012. "Walking in the Graveyard that Is Economics: Comments on *Postmodern Moments in Modern Economics*." *Rethinking Marxism* 24(3): 344–354.

Kayatekin, S. A. and S. Charusheela. 2004. "Recovering Feudal Subjectivities." *Rethinking Marxism* 16(4): 377–396.

Kristjanson-Gural, D. 2003. "Demand and the (Re)distribution of Value: An Overdetermined Approach." *Rethinking Marxism* 15(1): 117–140.

———. 2008a. "Money Is Time: The Monetary Expression of Value in Marx's Theory of Value." *Rethinking Marxism* 20(2): 257–272.

———. 2008b. "Poststructural Logic in Marx's Theory of Value." *Rethinking Marxism* 21(1): 14–33.

Levin, K. M. 2014. "A Class Theory of Hybrid-Directed Enterprises." *Rethinking Marxism* 26(4): 507–525.

Lyotard, J. F. 1984. *The Postmodern Condition: A Report on Knowledge*. Trans. by G. Bennington and B. Massumi. Foreword by F. Jameson. Minneapolis: University of Minnesota Press.

MacNeill, A. 1997. *New Directions in the Political Economy of Consumption*. Ph.D. dissertation, University of Massachusetts, Amherst.

Madra, Y. M. 2006. "Questions of Communism: Ethics, Ontology, Subjectivity." *Rethinking Marxism* 18(2): 205–224.

Madra, Y. M. and F. Adaman. 2014. "Neoliberal Reason and Its Forms: De-Politicisation Through Economisation." *Antipode* 46: 691–716.

Madra, Y. M. and C. Özselçuk. 2010. "Jouissance and Antagonism in the Forms of the Commune: A Critique of Biopolitical Subjectivity." *Rethinking Marxism* 22(3): 481–497.

Mandel, E. 1975. *Late Capitalism*. London: Verso.

McIntyre, R. 1992. "Consumption in Contemporary Capitalism: Beyond Marx and Veblen." *Review of Social Economy* 50(1): 40–60.

Mulder, C. 2009. *Unions and Class Transformation: The Case of the Broadway Musicians*. New York: Routledge.

Norton, B. 1986. "Steindl, Levine, and the Inner Logic of Accumulation: A Marxian Critique." *Social Concept* 3 (December): 43–66.

——. 2001. "Reading Marx for Class." In *Re/Presenting Class: Essays in Postmodern Marxism*, J. K. Gibson-Graham, S. A. Resnick, and R. D. Wolff, 23–55. Durham, NC: Duke University Press.

Özselçuk, C. 2006. "Mourning, Melancholy, and the Politics of Class Transformation." *Rethinking Marxism* 18(2): 225–240.

——. 2013. "Louis Althusser and the Concept of Economy." In *Encountering Althusser: Politics and Materialism in Contemporary Radical Thought*, K. Diefenbach, S. R. Farris, G. Kim, and P. Thomas, eds. London: Bloomsbury Publishing.

Özselçuk. C. and Y. M. Madra. 2010. "Enjoyment as an Economic Factor: Reading Marx with Lacan." *Subjectivity* 3: 323–347.

Pietrykowski. B. 1994. "Consuming Culture: Postmodernism, Post-Fordism, and Economics." *Rethinking Marxism* 7(3): 62–80.

Rebello, J. T. 2006. "The Economy of Joyful Passions: A Political Economic Ethics of the Virtual." *Rethinking Marxism* 18(2): 259–272.

Resnick, S. A. and R. D. Wolff. 1987. *Knowledge and Class: A Marxian Critique of Political Economy*. Chicago: University of Chicago Press.

——. 1988. "Communism: Between Class and Classless." *Rethinking Marxism* 1(1): 14–42.

——. 1992. "Everythingism, or Better Still, Overdetermination." *New Left Review* 195 (September–October): 124–126.

——. 2005. "The Point and Purpose of Marx's Notion of Class." *Rethinking Marxism* 17(1): 33–37.

——. 2012. *Contending Economic Theories: Neoclassical, Keynesian, and Marxian*. Cambridge, MA: MIT Press.

Rio, C. M. 2001. "'This Job Has No End': African American Domestic Workers and Class Becoming." In *Class and Its Others*, ed. J. K. Gibson-Graham, S. A. Resnick, and R. D. Wolff, 23–46. Minneapolis: University of Minnesota Press.

Roberts, B. 1987. "Marx after Steedman: Separating Marxism from 'Surplus Theory'." *Capital & Class* 11(2): 84–103.

——. 1996. "The Visible and the Measurable: Althusser and the Marxian Theory of Value." In *Postmodern Materialism and the Future of Marxian Theory*, A. Callari and D. F. Ruccio, eds., 193–211. Hanover, NH: Wesleyan University Press.

Rorty, R. 1979. *Philosophy and the Mirror of Nature*. Princeton: Princeton University Press.

Ruccio, D. F. 1988. "The Merchant of Venice, or Marxism in the Mathematical Mode." *Rethinking Marxism* 1(4): 37–68.

——. 1992. "Failure of Socialism, Future of Socialists?" *Rethinking Marxism* 5(2): 7–22.

Ruccio, D. F. and J. Amariglio. 2003. *Postmodern Moments in Modern Economics*. Princeton: Princeton University Press.

Safri, M. 2009. "Economic Effects of Remittances on Immigrant and Non-Immigrant Households." In *Class Struggle on the Home Front: Work, Conflict and Exploitation in the Household*, G. Cassano, ed., 176–196. New York: Palgrave Macmillan.

Saitta, D. 2001. "Communal Class Processes and Pre-Columbian Social Dynamics." In *Re/Presenting Class: Essays in Postmodern Marxism*, J. K. Gibson-Graham, S. A. Resnick, and R. D. Wolff, eds., 247–263. Durham, NC: Duke University Press.

Sarup, M. 1993. *An Introductory Guide to Post-Structuralism and Postmodernism.* 2nd ed. Athens: University of Georgia Press.

Sato, C. 2006. "Subjectivity, Enjoyment, and Development: Preliminary Thoughts on a New Approach to Postdevelopment." *Rethinking Marxism* 18(2): 273–288.

Southern, J. 2001. "Blue Collar, White Collar: Deconstructing Classification." In *Class and Its Others*, J. K. Gibson-Graham, S. A. Resnick, and R. D. Wolff, eds., 191–224. Minneapolis: University of Minnesota Press.

Vlachou, A. 2001. "Nature and Class: A Marxian Value Analysis." In *Re/Presenting Class: Essays in Postmodern Marxism*, J. K. Gibson-Graham, S. A. Resnick, and R. D. Wolff, eds., 105–130. Durham, NC: Duke University Press.

Wilson, L. 1996. *John Dewey's Pragmatism and Economic Method: Modernism and Postmodernism in Economics*. Ph.D. dissertation, University of Massachusetts, Amherst.

Wolff, R. D., A. Callari, and B. Roberts. 1984. "A Marxian Alternative to the Traditional 'Transformation Problem'." *Review of Radical Political Economics* 16(2/3): 115–135.

32

ANALYTICAL MARXISM

Roberto Veneziani

Introduction

What is Analytical Marxism? And, what is its contribution to Marxist thought? There is no consensus on the appropriate answer to either question. There is substantive confusion concerning the very definition of Analytical Marxism and, perhaps as a logical consequence, significant controversy surrounds its contribution and legacy.

While various predecessors have been identified,[1] the birth of Analytical Marxism (henceforth, AM) as a self-conscious school of thought dates back to the end of the 1970s, during the decline of structuralist Marxism, the renaissance of liberal egalitarianism, and the rebirth of interest in Marxism in analytical philosophy (Miller, 1983; Levine, 2003). In 1978, *Karl Marx's Theory of History: A Defence* appears in which Canadian philosopher Jerry Cohen provides a reconstruction of historical materialism (henceforth, HM) guided only by "two constraints: on the one hand, what Marx wrote, and, on the other, those standards of clarity and rigour which distinguish twentieth-century analytical philosophy" (Cohen, 1978, p. ix). In 1979, the most prominent members of AM start to meet, forming the core of the so-called "No-Bullshit Marxism September Group," or in short (and in somewhat more academically neutral terms) "September Group."

In the following decades, AM has provided some of the most controversial, analytically sophisticated, and thorough interpretations of Marx's theory, including some classic analyses in economic theory (Roemer, 1981, 1982); political philosophy (Elster, 1985; Cohen, 1988, 1995); history (Brenner, 1977); class theory (Wright, 1985, 1997); and political science (Przeworski, 1985a). AM has provided important insights on crucial topics in social theory, such as the theory of history, the class structure of advanced capitalist economies, and exploitation theory. AM analyses, however, have led to the rejection, or radical revision, of many concepts and propositions, such that the viability of a distinctively Marxist, or indeed analytical Marxist, perspective in social theory is put into question.

Thus, it should not come as a surprise that AM's contribution to Marxism (and social theory in general) and legacy have been at the centre of a heated debate. Many critics simply dismiss AM. At worst, AM is considered but a "particularly virulent" part of the anti-Marxist tradition and a "fundamentally dishonest" (Hunt, 1992, p.105) theoretical enterprise. At best, AM analyses are deemed, "as A.E. Housman once wrote in a review, 'little better than interruptions to our studies'" (Suchting, 1993, p.158).

Interestingly, a negative view on the legacy and future of AM is one of the few things that (some) analytical Marxists and their critics seemingly agree upon. As eloquently put by Levine, if the aim of AM was to discover the rational kernel of Marxist theory, and then reconstruct Marxism on that basis, it is tempting to conclude that "the operation succeeded (more or less), but the patient died" (Levine, 2003, p.132).

This paper aims to clarify the legacy and contribution of AM to social theory in general and Marxism in particular. As a first step in the investigation, the next section tries to define the object of analysis.

Analytical Marxism

Given the theoretical, methodological, and even political heterogeneity of analytical Marxists, it is difficult to define the boundaries of AM, either theoretically or in terms of membership (Ware, 1989; Wright, 1989; Nielsen, 1993). Contrary to a popular view, for example, AM and the September Group do not coincide: several analytical Marxists have never been members of the Group and, conversely, various members have never defined themselves as Marxists (analytical or otherwise).[2]

Similarly, attempts to identify a set of substantive propositions that constitute the core of AM (e.g., Tarrit, 2006 and Goldstein, 2006) are unconvincing. For such attempts usually conflate methodological statements (e.g. the rejection of dialectics) and substantive propositions (e.g. the rejection of the labour theory of value) and, given their inevitable vagueness, they are often inaccurate. For example, it is incorrect, or at least misleading, to claim that *all* analytical Marxists attribute a lack of clarity and rigour to Marx himself (Tarrit, 2006, p.598). Moreover, and perhaps more importantly, in order to identify a minimum common denominator for such a diverse group of theorists, these lists simply do not help to identify the differences between AM and alternative approaches, as well as within AM itself. It is true that "no analytical Marxist ...accepts the law of the tendency of the rate of profit to fall ... and ... only one, Brenner, ... still holds the labour theory of value expounded in volume I to be true" (Callinicos, 1987, p. 68). But this hardly identifies them as a group.[3]

According to Ware, indeed, there is "no one theory of [AM], not even a way of doing [AM]" (Ware, 1989, p. 5). Some authors actually emphasise the "alarming lack of unity" of AM (Bertram, 1998, p. 236) and prefer to call it an "affinity group" (Gintis, 1987, p. 983), with some critics moving from the acknowledgement of such heterogeneity to the unpersuasive claim that the attempt to define AM is self-defeating for its deep theoretical flaws and inconsistencies (Suchting, 1993).

Some common traits do exist that define "a style of theorizing" (Wright, Levine, and Sober, 1994, p. 56) if not a "fully fledged paradigm" (Carling, 1986, p.55). One of the main tenets of AM, and its main departure from classical Marxism, is the denial of a specific Marxist methodology. The classical view has been famously expressed by Lukacs:

> Orthodox Marxism ... does not imply the uncritical acceptance of the results of Marx's investigations. It is not the "belief" in this or that thesis, nor the exegesis of a "sacred" book. On the contrary, orthodoxy refers exclusively to method.
>
> *(Lukacs, 1971, p.1)*

According to AM, there exists no such different methodology:

> Too often, obscurantism protects itself behind a yoga of special terms and privileged logic. The yoga of Marxism is "dialectics". Dialectical logic is based on several propositions which may have a certain inductive appeal, but are far from being rules of inference ... In Marxian social science, dialectics is often used to justify a lazy kind of teleological reasoning.
>
> *(Roemer, 1986a, p. 191)*

Instead, Marxism should "subject itself to the conventional standards of social science and analytical philosophy" (Wright, Levine, and Sober, 1992, pp. 5–6). More precisely, Erik Olin Wright identifies four commitments that characterise AM.

Definition 1 (Wright, 1989, pp. 38–9)

AM is defined by an analysis of Marxist concerns that is focused through:

C1 "A commitment to conventional scientific norms in the elaboration of theory and the conduct of research."

C2 "An emphasis on the importance of systematic conceptualisation [...]. This involves careful attention to both definitions of concepts and the logical coherence of inter-connected concepts."

C3 "A concern with a relatively fine-grained specification of the steps in the theoretical arguments linking concepts."

C4 "The importance accorded to the intentional action of individuals within both expla-natory and normative theories."

Definition 1 forcefully suggests that the boundaries of AM are much wider and fuzzier than is commonly assumed. It encompasses all self-defined analytical Marxists; but it is sufficiently general to allow for a wide range of methodological and substantive positions, such that the school of British Marxist historians, and various analytically-oriented Marxist philosophers and social scientists may also be included, even if they do not explicitly associate themselves with AM. Indeed, "it would be arrogant to suggest that Marxism lacked these elements prior to the emergence of [AM] as a self-conscious school" (Wright, 1989, p. 39). Conversely, "Clarity and rigour are the virtues of *good* philosophy, of *good* thought in all fields. Analytical philosophy has no special monopoly on them" (Sayers, 1989, p. 81).

Nonetheless, C1–C4 are neither trivial nor uncontroversial. Two broad sets of objections can be identified in the literature. One focuses on AM's emphasis on formal logic and mathematical models; another disputes more generally the appeal to the analytical method. The next sections analyse the two objections in turn.

On the Use of Formal Models

Many critics question the very role of formal models in the social sciences, and the relevance of the results drawn from them. According to some, mathematical models are inherently associated with bourgeois science and politics. In the struggle for socialism "any means-ends or cost-benefit calculation would tend to produce reformist solutions" (Kieve, 1986, p. 574): the real issue is "not a question of quantitative, individualistic means-ends or petty cost-benefit calculations, but a question of life and death" (Ibid., p. 574). Somewhat less radically, Kirkpatrick claims that "The pursuit of mathematical clarity abolishes time, purges historical and social theory of their temporal dimension" (Kirkpatrick, 1994, p. 485; see also Bronner, 1990; Kennedy, 2005). As Bronner puts it:

> all political phenomena in general, and movements in particular, become equalized through the mathematical or game-theoretical laws in which they gain their defini-tion as social actors. At best, the question of qualitative change is circumvented ... Usually, however, all classes and movements are identified with specific units of analysis which are treated in the same way. Their unique character, as well as the constitutive role of the qualitatively different ideologies informing them, is subse-quently eradicated.
>
> *(Bronner, 1990, p. 250)*

The idea that formal models are inherently incompatible with Marxism is not wholly convincing: as Smolinski (1973) and Matthews (2002) have forcefully shown, Marx studied pure mathematics and was convinced about the opportunity to apply it to the social sciences. Further, the objection relies on the rather arbitrary claim that there is no mathematical object (in a potentially infinite set) that can be used to analyse any parts of Marx's theory. Finally, there is simply no reason to believe that mathematical models necessarily lead to static or ahistoric theories, let alone to the liquidation of "the normative purpose of the entire theoretical and practical enterprise" (Bronner, 1990, p. 248). This position seems as one-sided as the "mathematical fetishism" often attributed to AM.

Some objections reflect a post-modern epistemological stance that reduces mathematics, and indeed all scientific languages, to mere "discourses." Post-modern critics (Resnick and Wolff, 1987; Ruccio, 1988; Amariglio, Callari, and Cullenberg, 1989) deflate the explanatory power of formal models to the vanishing point, by interpreting mathematics as a "form of 'illustration.' For Marxists, mathematical concepts and models can be understood as meta-phors or heuristic devices" (Ruccio, 1988, p. 36). Yet it is unclear that this methodological stance can be supported by Marx's writings: Ruccio (1988) provides no textual evidence, whereas—as already noted—Smolinski (1973) and Matthews (2002) suggest a very different view. Another, well-known problem with this approach is that it is unclear how competing hypotheses can be rationally evaluated, let alone tested. Finally, this conception of mathe-matics reflects the post-modern denial of the explanatory power of theoretical abstractions.[4] Yet the emphasis on rather elusive "historically concrete social processes" does not lead beyond the formulation of rather vague general statements, such as the claim that Marxian classes "can be analysed as the determinate result of the entire constellation of social processes that can be said to make up a society or social formation at any point in time; in turn, it will be only one of the myriad determinants of those nonclass social processes" (Ruccio, 1988, p. 38).

Other critics argue that the emphasis on formalism leads AM to neglect important theoretical and political issues that resist mathematical formulation, whereas some critical facts about capitalist societies "can be established without mathematical proof" (Wood, 1989, p. 466). An emphasis on formalism can obscure important theoretical and political issues and "enervate Marxist theory in the name of rigor" (Anderson and Thompson, 1988, p. 228). Moreover, beyond its limited scope of application, the abstraction "loses in social and historical relevance what it gains in logical and analytical rigor" (Dymski and Elliott, 1989, p. 367). More generally, AM's formalism can obscure issues of empirical relevance since "'Does it make sense?' has priority over the question of its empirical truth" (Kirkpatrick, 1994, p. 43).

As acknowledged by analytical Marxists themselves (e.g. Roemer, 1981, pp. 2–4), these objections raise relevant issues and cannot be dismissed a priori. Yet, although they may provide robust support for methodological pluralism, they do not justify the rejection of AM *because* of its use of formal models. For AM is consistent with a methodological approach that acknowledges the usefulness of mathematics, but at the same time assigns no exclusive role to formal models and advocates a rigorous interpretation of assumptions and results, of their scope and limitations.

Indeed, these objections do not support the view that formal modelling should be rejected. Theoretical abstraction is essential to isolate the core features of a problem and the fundamental causal links. Formal modelling is *one* rigorous way of deriving causal explanations from a clearly stated set of assumptions. Besides, "lurking behind every informal causal explanation is a tacit formal model. All explanatory theories contain assumptions, claims about the conditions under which the explanations hold, claims about how the various mechanisms fit together" (Wright, 1989, p. 45). By making the assumptions explicit, proper formal modelling helps to subject them to critical scrutiny.

> "Mathematics," or models, cannot capture all that is contained in a theory. A model is necessarily one schematic image of a theory, and one must not be so myopic as to believe other schematic images cannot exist. Nevertheless ... the production of different and contradicting models of the same theory can be the very process that directs our focus to the gray areas of the theory.
>
> *(Roemer, 1981, p. 3)*

Formal models can also play a role in empirical social analysis: "since in real-life social situations it is generally hard to construct real experimental conditions for revealing the operation of causal mechanisms (or even, through comparative methods, quasi-experimental designs), thought experiments are essential to give plausibility to the causal claim we actually make about any concrete problem" (Wright, 1989, p. 45).

In summary, formal models cannot capture all that is relevant in Marxist theory, and the AM emphasis on the "contemporary tools of logic, mathematics, and model building ... [and the] unabashed commitment to the necessity for abstraction" (Roemer, 1986b, p. 3) are neither trivial nor innocuous. Nor does the adoption of formal models make AM superior to alternative Marxist approaches. Nonetheless, no argument is provided that conclusively establishes the inherent inadequacy of formal approaches in social theory, or that warrants the rejection of AM on a priori methodological grounds. From this perspective, the choice of the appropriate analytical framework is more important than abstract discussions on mathematics. And it is important to stress that AM does not entail the endorsement of a specific model, as discussed in the next section.

The Analytical Method

One of the most fundamental objections to AM on philosophical and methodological grounds focuses on the emphasis on analytical philosophy. According to some critics, the analytical method is based on "a framework of rigid and exclusive dichotomies" (Sayers, 1989, p. 83) and so produces "not clarity and rigour, but systematic misunderstanding and misinterpretation" (Sayers, 1989, p. 82). Others argue that the appeal to the clarity (potentially) gained in applying the analytical method is not neutral, "[C]larity was never a virtue of praxis theory, critical theory or ...Althusserian Marxism. Nor is clarity particularly a virtue of neofunctionalism, postmodernism, or structuration theory" (Porpora, 1995, p. 169). Furthermore:

> There may be disagreement over what it means to make an argument clear ... We may want to reflect on why we value clarity as much as we do, and on whether the same standards of clarity hold for any theoretical discourse, regardless of the nature of its object or objects.
>
> *(Kirkpatrick, 1994, p. 36)*

According to these authors, the adoption of analytical philosophy fundamentally and inevitably distorts Marxist theory, which should be analysed using a specific Marxist methodology, based on dialectics and/or methodological holism.

These sweeping criticisms are not entirely convincing, as they rest on an unproven impossibility claim and, most often, on a conceptual misunderstanding concerning the exact definition of AM.

First, there exists no convincing general proof, or robust argument, that no part of Marx's theory can be fruitfully analysed using analytical philosophy. Sayers (1989) argues that the debate on Marx and morality within AM is an example of the inability of analytical philosophy to capture the historical nature of Marx's theory. However Levine (1982) provides a reconstruction of Marx's approach that is broadly consonant to Sayers' own. According to Kirkpatrick (1994, p. 39), Cohen's "theory of history is subject to limitations of scope that would have been alien to Marx, who frequently makes use of the idea of history as an all-encompassing 'totality'." Yet, Cohen (1978) provides an exegetically rigorous, if not orthodox, analysis of HM, as acknowledged also by critics: "*Karl Marx's Theory of History*, whatever one thinks of the interpretation of [HM] offered there, is one of the classics of twentieth-century Marxist philosophy" (Callinicos, 2001, p. 171).

Second, an appeal to *the* appropriate Marxist methodology against the analytical emphasis of AM is rather misleading as there are several definitions of dialectics, and even methodological holism can be articulated in many different ways. Indeed, it is unclear that a dialectic approach is inherently incompatible with formal logic and there have been several recent formulation of dialectics in analytical terms (see, for example, the discussion of the concept of totality in Wright, Levine, and Sober, 1994, and the analytical approach to dialectics in Arnsperger, 2003, and Wood, 2004).

Besides, even assuming that there is a unique correct definition of dialectics, critics of AM acknowledge that an analytical approach provides a possibly partial, but not necessarily false picture of social reality (Devine, 1993, p. 51). For example, Sayers (1984, p. 3) argues that, albeit one-sided, analysis is "an indispensable feature of any scientific account." In the analysis of collective action, Bronner (1990, p. 252) argues that "rational choice can prove enormously useful within a broader theory with respect to showing the barriers to class consciousness." McCarney (1989, pp. 154ff) suggests that in Elster's account of dialectics—which he deems unsatisfactory—there are "elements ... that will serve as building blocks for a more adequate account of Marx." Finally, and perhaps more importantly, it is unclear how "dialectical logic" would per se be able to revert the negative conclusions reached by AM, especially in economics. The idea that the standard labour theory of value can be defended from AM criticisms based on "dialectics" (Moggach, 1991), for example, is rather unconvincing.[5]

Third, it may indeed be difficult to transpose Marxist theory within the positivist-empiricist tradition in analytical philosophy. And one may argue that the mainly negative conclusions of

AM prove that "the dangers of using philosophical tools especially designed to bury Marxism have been realised" (Kennedy, 2005, p. 341), including not only the analytical method but also methodological individualism and rational choice theory. Yet, these arguments conflate AM as identified in Definition 1 with a sub-school within AM, also known as Rational Choice Marxism (henceforth, RCM), whose main exponents are Jon Elster, Adam Przeworski, and John Roemer. RCM adopts C2 and C3 of Definition 1, but endorses more restrictive principles than those stated in C1 and C4, namely:[6]

C1'   The use of "state of the arts methods of analytical philosophy and 'positivist' social science" (Roemer, 1986b, pp. 3–4).
C4'   Methodological individualism (henceforth, MI) and rational choice explanations.

AM and RCM should be clearly distinguished. C1' and C4' are much stronger than C1 and C4, and RCM endorses a strongly reductionist stance that is not shared by all analytical Marxists. In Cohen's interpretation of HM, "Marxism is *fundamentally* concerned not with behaviour but with the forces and relations constraining and directing it" (Cohen, 1982, p. 489). Wright (1989) endorses a realist view of science and a pluralist methodological position. He (Wright, 1985, 1997, 2005) proposes a theory of class whose pivotal concepts are class relations and class structure, and "the rights and powers people have over productive resources are important for the structured interactive quality of human action" (Wright, 2005, p. 9). This:

> leaves open the best way to theorize choosing and acting ... There is ... no implication, as methodological individualists would like to argue, that the explanation of social processes can be reduced to the attributes of the individuals choosing and acting. The [social, or class] relations themselves can be explanatory.
>
> *(Wright, 2005, fn.11)*

The difference between AM and RCM is often overlooked, or considered secondary, however, both by analytical Marxists and by their critics. Carling (1986) claims C4' to apply to AM due to a very weak, if loose interpretation of rational choice and MI, which collapses C4' into C4.[7] Tarrit (2006) incorrectly ascribes logical positivism to AM. Philp and Young (2002) state that AM "involves the use of rational actor models" (2002, p. 314) and that reductionism is a "further hallmark of AM" (2002, p. 316).[8]

This leads to some confusion in the evaluation of AM. For the distinction between AM and RCM is theoretically important and has relevant consequences. It is inappropriate to argue that AM is inherently wrong because it subscribes to logical positivism. Although much of AM is indeed "grounded philosophically in an empiricist, and more specifically positivist, commitment to an instrumentalist theory of meaning" (Weldes, 1989, p. 360ff), contrary to a popular view (e.g., Kirkpatrick, 1994; Tarrit, 2006), AM does not necessarily endorse a positivist and empiricist stance. Marxist philosophers working within the analytical tradition argue that the latter is not defined by a set of common doctrines, but by common standards of successful practice (Ware, 1989; Nielsen, 1993; Wood, 2004), and have proposed interesting post-positivist analytical approaches to Marx where "the style of analytic philosophy is divorced from positivist substance" (Miller, 1984, p. 4). From this perspective, C1 only requires that Marxist propositions be subjected to rigorous empirical and theoretical scrutiny.

Even the negative conclusions reached by AM can be seen in a different light if AM and RCM are properly distinguished. The key point here is that C1' and C4' have much more stringent methodological and substantive implications than C1 and C4. After trying to analyse key parts of Marx's writings within the straightjacket of C4', RCM concludes that much (if not most) of Marxist theory has to be discarded, including the whole of Marxian economics, scientific socialism, dialectical materialism, and the theory of productive forces and relations of production (Elster, 1985), and the Marxist theory of class struggle and revolution (Elster, 1985; Przeworski, 1985a); or it has to be so substantially revised as to end up carrying only a distant similarity to the original theory, as in the case of Roemer's (1982) theory of exploitation. As Przeworski puts it:

> [I]f one accepts the methodological validity of individualistic postulates, most if not all traditional concerns of Marxist theory must be radically reformulated. Whether the eventual results will confirm any of the substantive propositions of Marxist theory of history and whether the ensuing theory will be in any distinct sense "Marxist", I do not know.
>
> *(Przeworski, 1985b, p. 400)*

The contribution of AM is quite different. For AM has reconstructed a set of core propositions that aim to provide the foundations of a distinctive Marxist approach in social theory.

The Core of (Analytical) Marxism[9]

According to AM, Marxism remains distinctive "in organizing its agenda around a set of fundamental questions or problems which other theoretical traditions either ignore or marginalize, and identifying a distinctive set of interconnected causal processes relevant to those questions" (Wright, 2009, p. 102). Levine (2003) argues that the rational kernel of Marxism reconstructed by AM comprises at least four components.

First is the Marxist theory of history, or HM, which aims to provide a theoretical explanation of long term historical trajectories. Unlike most currents of Western Marxism, AM considers HM as the most important distinctive theoretical component of Marxism. The AM interpretation of HM is articulated into two main theses. The first states that the level of development of productive forces (functionally) explains the nature of the economic structure. The second states that the nature of the economic structure (functionally) explains legal, political, and ideological superstructures.

According to AM, given the inherent tendency for the forces of production to develop, HM detects an endogenous process that supplies history with a determinate trajectory from one mode of production to another (Cohen, 1978; Wright et al., 1992). In recent contributions, analytical Marxists interpret HM as "a theory of historical possibilities opened up by the development of 'productive forces'" (Levine, 2003, p. 164). From this perspective, HM provides an account of socialism as a possible product of the materialist dynamics and contradictions of capitalism, which can "unify what would otherwise be a motley of well-meaning, but mainly reactive, causes into a movement with a serious prospect of changing life for the better" (Levine, 2003, p. 171). HM is thus the foundational theory of scientific socialism and a fundamental part of Marxist emancipatory social theory.

Second is a Marxist theory of classes, according to which the class structure of a society is central in the explanation of individual economic outcomes and life opportunities, class conflicts, and a range of key social phenomena (Wright, 1997, 2005). The main contribution of AM in class theory consists in the development of a rigorous conceptual apparatus for analysing complex class structures in advanced capitalist economies. Distinctive of Marxist class theory is the conception of classes "as being structured by mechanisms of domination and exploitation, in which economic positions accord some people power over the lives and activities of others" (Wright, 2009, p. 102). The standard Marxist analysis focuses on the exploitation resulting from differential ownership of capital. Whereas this explains the main class cleavage in capitalism, and the core difference with previous social formations, at a lower level of abstraction it is insufficient to analyse the complexities of class structure and class behaviour in advanced capitalism. Building on Roemer's (1982) theory of exploitation,[10] Wright identifies other types of productive assets—such as skills and organisational assets— that are unequally distributed among agents and give rise to specific relations of domination and exploitation. Then the class structure of an economy is multidimensionally defined by the ownership and control of the three types of productive assets.

Theoretically, this provides a unified framework to understand complex class structures in which "middle classes" are not seen as an exception or a transitory phenomenon in increasingly polarised societies, but arise from "contradictory class locations", whereby they may be exploited in one dimension (e.g., because they own little or no physical capital), but exploiters in others (e.g., thanks to their ownership of skills or organisational assets). Hence, this framework allows for a sophisticated analysis of class behaviour: for example, it clarifies the (complex) structure of material interests underlying the possibility of class alliances. Empirically, this theory has provided a fruitful framework for the construction of precise maps of class structures in advanced economies based on the ownership and control of productive assets, which can be consistently used to analyse classes over time and across countries (Wright, 1997; 2005).

Third is a Marxist theory of the state, which views states as expressing the rule of the economically dominant class: to each economic structure, there corresponds a different form of state. According to AM, the proletarian state is the only state whose historical aim is to eliminate the need for states, and socialists should aim to establish institutions that are progressively self-effacing, a view that is incompatible with the exclusive emphasis on the state common to all strains of modern political philosophy (see Levine, 2008).

Fourth is a set of socialist—albeit not specifically Marxist—normative commitments. The systematic discussion, and defence, of the normative dimension of Marxism is one of the most relevant contributions of AM. For "All classical Marxists believed in some kind of equality, even if many would have refused to acknowledge that they believed in it and none, perhaps, could have stated precisely what principle of equality he believed in" (Cohen, 1995, p. 5). According to AM, Marx was "a steadfast opponent of applications of moral theory in class-divided societies" (Levine, 2003, p. 137), but he did not oppose moral theory as such and was not shy "in condemning economic, social and political arrangements in normative and even moralistic terms" (Levine, 2003, p. 139). Marx's normative commitments include self-realisation, community, autonomy, and equality in a classless society (see Cohen, 1995).

The rigorous reconstruction of these propositions is arguably a significant, positive contribution of AM, which may play an important role for a revival of socialist theory.

Notes

1 For example, Nowak (1998) identifies a Polish school of Analytical Marxism in the 1950s and 1960s.
2 For example, other members of the "September Group" include Sam Bowles, Robert van der Veen, Pranhab Bardhan, and Hillel Steiner. However, it is not clear whether they should also be considered as analytical Marxists, according to Definition 1 above and therefore their work is not considered here.

3 Somewhat puzzlingly, after having listed a set of propositions that define AM, later in his analysis Tarrit (2006, p. 607) claims that the rejection of the falling rate of profit "is the only theoretical element on which all analytical Marxists agree."

4 See, for example, the concept of overdetermination developed by Resnick and Wolff (1987), which is a direct critique of the idea that it is possible to identify causes of social outcomes that are not themselves effects. I am grateful to an anonymous reviewer for this suggestion.

5 Some authors have offered a logically coherent explanation of the relationship between value and exchange-value based on a postmodern approach (see Wolff, Callari and Roberts, 1982). Yet, this involves a radical reconceptualisation of the labour theory of value and it is unclear what role "dialectics" plays, if any, in their formalism. For a more thorough discussion, see Mohun and Veneziani (2016).

6 For a thorough discussion of RCM, see Veneziani (2012).

7 Carling (1994) has later acknowledged the difference between AM and RCM.

8 Indeed, it is misleading to say that "[AM] cannot claim that their endeavours are within an analytical or positivist tradition and simultaneously subscribe to a critical realist view of science" (Philp and Young, 2002, p. 316). The alleged tension disappears provided one properly distinguishes AM and RCM.

9 The discussion in this section draws on Veneziani (2012).

10 For a thorough discussion, see Veneziani (2007; 2012; 2013).

References

Amariglio, J., A. Callari, and S. Cullenberg. 1989. "Analytical Marxism: A Critical Overview." *Review of Social Economy* 47: 415–432.

Anderson, W. H. L. and F. W. Thompson. 1988. "Neoclassical Marxism." *Science and Society* 52: 215–228.

Arnsperger, C. (2003). "Cohen, Rawls and the Advent of an Analytical Dialectics." Mimeo, Louvain-la-Neuve.

Bertram, C. 1998. "Review of 'Analytical Marxism: A Critique'." *Historical Materialism* 3: 235–241.

Brenner, R. 1977. "The Origins of Capitalist Development: A Critique of Neo-Smithian Marxism." *New Left Review* 104: 25–92.

Bronner, S. E. 1990. "Politics and Judgment: A Critique of Rational-Choice Marxism." *Review of Politics* 52: 242–264.

Callinicos, A. 1987. *Making History*. London: Polity.

——. 2001. "Having Your Cake and Eating It." *Historical Materialism* 9: 169–195.

Carling, A. H. 1986. "Rational Choice Marxism." *New Left Review* 160: 24–62.

——. 1994. "The Strength of Historical Materialism: A Comment." *Science and Society* 58: 60–72.

Cohen, G. A. 1978. *Karl Marx's Theory of History: A Defence*. Princeton: Princeton University Press.

——. 1982. "Reply to Elster on 'Marxism, Functionalism, and Game Theory." *Theory and Society* 11: 483–495.

——. 1988. *History, Labour, and Freedom*. Oxford: Oxford University Press.

——. 1995. *Self-ownership, Freedom and Equality*. Cambridge: Cambridge University Press.

Devine, J. 1993. "Micro-foundations and Methodology in Modeling Capitalism." *Review of Radical Political Economics* 25: 51–59.

Dymski, G. and J. E. Elliott. 1989. "Should Anyone Be Interested in Exploitation?" *Canadian Journal of Philosophy* Suppl. 15: 333–374.

Elster, J. 1985. *Making Sense of Marx*. Cambridge: Cambridge University Press.

Gintis, H. 1987. "Review of 'Analytical Marxism'." *American Political Science Review* 81: 983–984.

Goldstein, J. 2006. "Marxian Microfoundations: Contribution or Detour?" *Review of Radical Political Economics* 38: 569–594.

Hunt, E. K. 1992. "Analytical Marxism," In *Radical Economics*, B. Roberts and S. Feiner, eds., Boston: Kluwer.

Kennedy, S. 2005. "G.A. Cohen and the End of Traditional Historical Materialism." *Historical Materialism* 13: 331–344.

Kieve, R. A. 1986. "From Necessary Illusion to Rational Choice? A critique of Neo-Marxist Rational-Choice Theory." *Theory and Society* 15: 557–582.

Kirkpatrick, G. 1994. "Philosophical Foundations of Analytical Marxism." *Science and Society* 58: 34–52.

Levine, A. 1982. "Toward a Marxian Theory of Justice." *Politics and Society* 11: 343–362.

——. 2003. *A Future for Marxism?* London: Pluto Press.

——. 2008. *The General Will: Rousseau, Marx, Communism* (2nd Edition). Cambridge: Cambridge University Press.

Lukacs, G. 1971. *History and Class Consciousness*. Cambridge, MA: MIT press.

Matthews, P. H. 2002. "The Dialectics of Differentiation: Marx's Mathematical Manuscripts and Their Relation to His Economics." Working Paper 0203, Middlebury College.

McCarney, J. 1989. "Elster, Marx and Methodology." *Canadian Journal of Philosophy* Suppl. 15: 135–161.

Miller, R. W. 1983. "Marx in Analytic Philosophy: The Story of a Rebirth." *Social Science Quarterly* 64: 846–861.

——. 1984. *Analyzing Marx: Morality Power and History*. Princeton: Princeton University Press.

Moggach, D. 1991. "Monadic Marxism. A Critique of Elster's Methodological Individualism." *Philosophy of the Social Sciences* 21: 38–63.

Mohun, S. and R. Veneziani. 2016. "Value, Prices and Exploitation: The Logic of the Transformation Problem." Mimeo, Queen Mary University of London.

Nielsen, K. 1993. "Analytical Marxism: A Form of Critical Theory." *Erkenntnis* 39: 1–21.

Nowak, L. 1998. "The Adaptive Interpretation of Historical Materialism: A Survey. On a Contribution to Polish Analytical Marxism." *Poznan Studies in the Philosophy of the Sciences and the Humanities* 60: 201–236.

Philp, B. and D. Young. 2002. "Preferences, Reductionism and the Microfoundations of Analytical Marxism." *Cambridge Journal of Economics* 26: 313–329.

Porpora, D. V. 1995. "Review of 'Analytical Marxism'." *Contemporary Sociology* 24: 166–169.

Przeworski, A. 1985a. *Capitalism and Social Democracy*. Cambridge: Cambridge University Press.

——. 1985b. "Marxism and Rational Choice." *Politics and Society* 14: 379–409.

Resnick, S. A. and R. D. Wolff. 1987. *Knowledge and Class*. Chicago: University of Chicago Press.

Roemer, J. E. 1981. *Analytical Foundations of Marxian Economic Theory*. Cambridge, MA: Harvard University Press.

——. 1982. *A General Theory of Exploitation and Class*. Cambridge, MA: Harvard University Press.

——. 1986a. "'Rational Choice' Marxism: Some Issues of Method and Substance." In *Analytical Marxism*, J. E. Roemer, ed. Cambridge: Cambridge University Press.

——. 1986b. "Introduction." In *Analytical Marxism*, J. E. Roemer, ed. Cambridge: Cambridge University Press.

Ruccio, D. F. 1988. "The Merchant of Venice, or Marxism in the Mathematical Mode." *Rethinking Marxism* 1: 36–68. [Reprinted in 1991 in *The Social Scientist* 212–213: 18–46.]

Sayers, S. 1984. "Marxism and the Dialectical Method: A Critique of G.A. Cohen." *Radical Philosophy* 36: 4–13.

——. 1989. "Analytical Marxism and Morality." *Canadian Journal of Philosophy*, Suppl. 15: 81–104.

Smolinski, L. 1973. "Karl Marx and Mathematical Economics." *Journal of Political Economy* 81: 1189–1204.

Suchting, W. 1993. "Reconstructing Marxism." *Science and Society* 57: 133–159.

Tarrit, F. 2006. "A Brief History, Scope and Peculiarities of 'Analytical Marxism'." *Review of Radical Political Economics* 38: 595–618.

Veneziani, R. 2007. "Exploitation and Time." *Journal of Economic Theory* 132: 189–207.

——. 2012. "Analytical Marxism." *Journal of Economic Surveys* 26: 649–673.

——. 2013. "Exploitation, Inequality, and Power." *Journal of Theoretical Politics* 25: 526–545.

Ware, R. 1989. "Introduction." *Canadian Journal of Philosophy* Suppl. 15: 1–26.

Weldes, J. 1989. "Marxism and Methodological Individualism: A Critique." *Theory and Society* 18: 353–386.

Wolff, R. D., A. Callari, and B. Roberts. 1982. "Marx's—not Ricardo's—'Transformation Problem': A Radical Reconceptualisation." *History of Political Economy* 14: 564–582.

Wood, A. 2004. *Karl Marx*. London: Routledge.

Wood, E. M. 1989. "Rational Choice Marxism. Is the Game Worth the Candle?" *New Left Review* 177: 41–88.

Wright, E. O. 1985. *Classes*. London: Verso.

——. 1989. "What is Analytical Marxism?" *Socialist Review* 19: 35–56.

——. 1997. *Class Counts: Comparative Studies in Class Analysis*. Cambridge: Cambridge University Press.

——. 2005. "Foundations of a Neo-Marxist Class Analysis." In *Approaches to Class Analysis*, E. O. Wright, ed. Cambridge: Cambridge University Press.

——. 2009. "Understanding Class." *New Left Review* 60: 101–116.

Wright, E. O., A. Levine, and E. Sober. 1992. *Reconstructing Marxism*. London: Verso.

——. 1994. "Historical Materialism: Theory and Methodology." *Science and Society* 58: 53–60.

33

MARXISM AND KEYNESIANISM

Claudio Sardoni

Introduction

If one looks at Marxism and Keynesianism from an ideological and political perspective, the difficulty in finding a relationship between them is evident. At first glance, Marxist and Keynesian economics appear to be far apart, but there exist important points of contact between the two approaches to economic problems.

Keynes knew little of Marx. His knowledge of Marx's economics was mainly based on secondary literature,[1] but this did not prevent him from issuing trenchant judgments on Marx's economics in *The General Theory* as well as before and after its publication (see, e.g., Sardoni, 1997).

However, despite Keynes's opinion, there has always been a certain interest in the relation between Marxist and Keynesian economics.[2] Joan Robinson, one of the most prominent Keynesian economists, has showed a constant interest in Marx's economics and its relationship to the Keynesian approach. Moreover, Keynes himself, at some point in the evolution of his ideas toward *The General Theory*, came to consider Marx's ideas in a positive way, particularly with respect to the critique of Say's Law.

Here, we concentrate on Marx and Keynes on Say's Law and on Joan Robinson's idea that Keynesian economics would benefit from considering Marx's economics more thoroughly and seriously.

If Marx's critique of Say's Law is compared with Keynes's critique in *The General Theory*, they undoubtedly appear different. However, before the publication of *The General Theory* in 1936, Keynes carried out the critique of Say's Law along lines that are quite similar to those followed by Marx, in spite of the fact that their criticisms were addressed to two different versions of the law.[3] We look at this aspect of the relationship between the Marx's and Keynes's economics in the following section.

Joan Robinson considered Marx's schemes of reproduction as an important analytical device, starting from which a fruitful relation between Marxist and Keynesian economics could be established. In this perspective, she regarded Kalecki's approach to economic analysis as epitomic. Kalecki arrived at analytical results close to Keynes's by following an approach inspired by Marx rather than by the neoclassical Marshallian tradition. We deal with these aspects in the third section.

Marx's and Keynes's Critique of Say's Law

Marx

Marx expressed the essential characteristic of the capitalist process of production and circulation with the formula

$$M - C - M'$$

M is the amount of money capital advanced by capitalists to produce the amount C of commodities which, once sold, yield an amount of money M' larger than M; $M' - M$ is the money profit.

The objective of capitalist entrepreneurs is to produce and sell goods in order to obtain more money than they advanced to buy means of production and hire workers. They produce in order to make money profits. Two relevant analytical issues stem from this.

On the one hand, Marx set out to analyze how the capitalist drive for profits can lead to crises, characterized by a general overproduction of commodities; on the other hand Marx also analyzed the conditions under which the capitalist thrust to produce for profits can give rise to an orderly process of production, circulation and growth.[4] In both cases, at the core of Marx's analysis there is the role of money.

This section is concerned with Marx's theory of crises based on his rejection of Say's Law, but we limit our attention to the problem of the possibility of crises rather than the explanation of their actual occurring. The reason of this is that we can find analogies between Marx and Keynes only with respect to this aspect; their explanations of actual crises are significantly different.

Marx dealt with the problem of crises by starting from criticizing Ricardo, who held that general overproduction crises are impossible, that is to say that Say's Law holds. In Marx's analysis a general overproduction crisis is caused by an increase in the capitalists' propensity to hoard that amounts to a shift of aggregate demand from commodities to money (Marx, 1968, p. 505). Aggregate demand for goods falls short of their aggregate supply.

The reason why the capitalist class can increase its propensity to hoard is that capitalist entrepreneurs produce commodities in order to make profits. Marx criticized Ricardo for abstracting from this essential aspect (Marx, 1968, p. 529). According to Ricardo, the production and sale of commodities generates an income which is either spent on consumption or saved. What is saved is, however, spent: it is invested to employ additional workers. In this context, money is merely a device to make the exchange of commodities simpler. Money income is never kept idle; people do not draw any utility from holding money idle.[5]

By allowing for the possibility that money is kept idle, Marx pointed out that a capitalist economy is essentially different from a barter economy. Say's Law ceases to be valid and general overproduction crises become possible. Further, by pointing out that capitalist production is carried out in order to make profits, Marx explained why the capitalist class may wish to keep money idle. Whenever capitalist producers expect that production and investment are not profitable, they keep money idle and this causes overproduction of commodities.

Keynes

In 1933, Keynes drafted several chapters of *The General Theory* where the critique of the classical doctrine and Say's Law is based on the distinction between a co-operative economy and an entrepreneur (or monetary) economy, that is, the capitalist economy in which "we actually live". In this context, Keynes explicitly referred to Marx and recognized that, starting from the formula $M - C - M'$, he had pointed out an essential characteristic of capitalist economies.

A co-operative economy, even though money is used for exchanges, is basically equivalent to a barter economy where money is only a "transitory convenience" used to buy a predetermined share of the output. If some factors do not use all their rewards to buy a share of current output but employ part of them to buy a share of pre-existing wealth, the equality between aggregate demand and supply is still attained, provided that the sellers of pre-existing wealth use their proceeds to buy current output (Keynes, 1979, pp. 76–7). In other words, income may be spent on goods or saved but, nevertheless, what is saved is spent, i.e. it is invested.

For Keynes, classical economists could hold that Say's Law applies and that full employment is ensured by assuming that capitalist economies behave as if they were co-operative economies. But capitalist economies are essentially different (Keynes, 1979, pp. 78–9). Capitalist entrepreneurs start productive processes to earn a monetary profit and not to produce more goods and employ more labor. If production is expected to be unprofitable, money is kept idle (Keynes, 1979, p. 82).

Money is not current output, so that if the demand for it increases, while the demand for current output declines, there will be a decrease in production and employment. The characteristics of money are such that buyers are not pressed to convert money into goods and entrepreneurs find it convenient to keep money instead of producing goods when they expect that demand will not be sufficient to make their production profitable.

It is in the description of how an entrepreneur economy functions that Keynes referred to Marx's formula $M - C - M'$. Marx

> pointed out that the nature of production in the actual world is not, as economists seem often to suppose, a case of $C - M - C'$, i.e., of exchanging commodity (or effort). That may be the standpoint of the private consumer. But it is not the attitude of business, which is the case of $M - C - M'$, i.e., of parting with money for commodity (or effort) in order to obtain more money.
>
> *(Keynes, 1979, p. 81)*

Thus, both Marx and Keynes criticized their respective predecessors for having treated capitalist economies as if they were essentially the same as barter (or co-operative) economies. Say's Law applies in an economy in which money is only a medium of exchange, a "transitory convenience". But in a capitalist economy money is also used as a store of value. The profitability of production and investment is the essential factor determining how money is used. If capitalists' expectations concerning profitability are pessimistic, the demand for idle money rises while the demand for goods and labor decreases.

However, although Marx and Keynes started from similar criticisms of their predecessors, for a number of reasons they developed their analyses of the actual behavior of capitalist economies along different lines. The main difference between Marx and Keynes is that, for Marx, an imbalance between aggregate demand and supply inevitably gives rise to a general overproduction crisis whereas, for Keynes, it can also yield "underemployment equilibria."[6]

From Marx's Schemes of Reproduction to Kalecki and Post-Keynesian Economics

Marx's schemes of reproduction are one of the high points of his contribution to economic theory. They have attracted the attention of Marxist economists or with a strong interest in Marx and Classical economists.[7]

Marx's schemes provide a relevant contribution in two main respects. First, though only through numerical examples, Marx determined the conditions under which a multisector economy can reproduce itself and grow without experiencing excess supply or demand of any produced good. Second, through his analysis of the role of money in the process of reproduction, Marx pointed out the importance of capitalists' decisions concerning liquidity, which are crucial for the generation of the level of aggregate demand required to absorb the whole output and make the realization of monetary profits possible. Here, we do not deal with the determination of the conditions for the equality between supply and demand in each sector to concentrate on the macroeconomic aspects of reproduction and the role of money.[8]

At the aggregate level, an orderly capitalist process of simple or expanded reproduction must ensure that the capitalist class is able to realize the profits created in the process of production.[9] In order to realize profits, the sale of the produced aggregate output must yield an amount of money M' larger than the amount M that capitalists anticipated to start the production process. This requires that an additional quantity of money $(M' - M)$ is injected into the system.

Marx, in considering the possible sources of $(M' - M)$, concentrated on the necessity of a decrease in the liquidity preference of capitalists, who transform part of their money hoards into circulating money. Only the capitalist class owns the necessary additional quantity of money and the reason why it decides to dishoard part of its money is the necessity to finance its consumption and investment expenditures (Marx, 1956, pp. 338–9 and p. 425).[10] This additional quantity of money flows back to the capitalist class at the end of the process of circulation, so that money hoards will be restored.

Thus, for Marx, the possibility for the economy to grow is contingent on the capitalists' liquidity preference, which in turn depends on expected profits. If, because of pessimistic expectations about future profits, the capitalists' liquidity preference is high and they decide to advance an additional quantity of money $(M'' - M) < (M' - M)$, the level of aggregate profits would be negatively affected: aggregate monetary demand $(M + M'')$ would fall short of aggregate supply $(C' = M')$ and aggregate profits would decrease as their monetary value is $(M'' - M) < (M' - M)$.

It is this aspect of Marx's analysis of the process of growth that relates most directly to the Keynesian/Post-Keynesian approach. In particular, it relates to Kalecki's analysis of reproduction and growth. Kalecki can be regarded as the natural *trait d'union* between the Marxian and Keynesian traditions of thought.[11]

Kalecki (1968) considers a three-sectors closed economy. The three sectors are vertically integrated, i.e. they produce final goods as well as all the intermediate goods and raw materials required for their production. The total value of the output of Sector 1, I, is equal to the value of gross investment plus the respective intermediate goods and raw materials. The total value of the output of Sector 2, C_K, is equal to the value of consumer-goods for capitalists plus the respective raw materials and intermediate goods. The total value of the output of Sector 3, C_W, is equal to the value of consumer-goods for workers plus the value of the respective raw materials and intermediate goods. The wage bill in the three sectors is denoted by W_1, W_2 and W_3 respectively.

In the first two sectors, gross profits are given by

$$\Pi_1 = I - W_1$$
$$\Pi_2 = C_K - W_2$$

respectively. The third sector, after having paid wages to its workers, is left with $(C_W - W_3)$, which is bought by workers of the other two sectors. Equality between demand and supply of the consumption good for workers requires that

$$\Pi_3 = C_W - W_3 = W_1 + W_2$$

Therefore, total profits are

$$\Pi = \Pi_1 + \Pi_2 + \Pi_3 = I + C_K$$

Realized aggregate profits are determined by the capitalists' expenditure decisions (investment and consumption). Were the capitalists to decide to spend less than $(I + C_K)$, the economy as a whole would experience a lower level of profits as well as a lower level of production and employment.[12]

If the economy has to grow from one period to the next, from where do capitalists take the funds to finance their increased investment and/or consumption?[13] A problem of financing arises. The financing can be provided by the banking system. The increase in investment (and/or consumption) at the aggregate level is financed by banks, which become less liquid. At the end of the period, the loans are paid back and banks return to their initial liquidity position.

Banks play a crucial role in the process of growth of the economy. If banks have a high "liquidity preference" and do not lend to industrial capitalists, or if they lend less than it is needed to sustain a certain rate of growth, the process is necessarily stopped or slackened. Banks are capitalist firms as well; they may have a high "liquidity preference" if they expect that lending is not profitable enough or too risky.[14]

If we combine the industrial capitalists and financial capitalists into a "capitalist class", we have that this class determines the level of its own income through its degree of liquidity preference and its decisions to invest and consume. The capitalist class as a whole finances its own income by accepting a decrease in liquidity, even though at the end of the process its initial liquidity position is restored and it will earn a higher level of profits. In other words, it is the capitalist class which must throw into circulation the amount of money required to make it possible to realize the higher level of profits, that is to say, the higher level of produced surplus. Kalecki's analytical conclusions are very close to Marx's.

Joan Robinson is the Keynesian economist who perceived most clearly the importance of Marx's schemes and Kalecki's developments for the Keynesian approach to macroeconomics and the theory of effective demand (see, for example, Robinson, 1951; 1965; 1966). She believed that had Keynes started from Marx, rather than orthodox economics, he would have avoided "a lot of trouble" (Robinson, 1965, p. 96) and obtained more general and robust analytical results, like Kalecki did.[15] More recently, also other economists have dealt with the relationship between the Marxian/Kaleckian approach to growth and Keynesian economics.[16]

Notes

1 Joan Robinson (1973, p. ix) was convinced that Keynes "never managed to read Marx" and that, in any case, he "could never make head or tail of Marx" (Robinson, 1965, p. 96). More recently, Thweatt (1983) and Behrens (1985) have argued that Keynes's acquaintance with Marx's work was better than usually acknowledged.

2 In the years immediately following the publication of *The General Theory*, some attempts to compare Marx's and Keynes's economics in a systematic way were made; see, e. g., Fan-Hung (1939) and Alexander (1940). For more recent contributions, see Dasgupta (1983), Crotty (1985; 1986), Dillard (1984), Hein (2006) and Wolff and Resnick (2012).

3 Marx criticized Say's Law in its classical version, whereas Keynes attacked the neoclassical version of the law. On the differences between the two versions of Say's Law, see Sowell (1972) and also Sardoni (2011, pp. 47–50).

4 The problem of crises was analyzed by Marx, above all, in the second volume of *Theories of Surplus-Value* (Marx, 1968), where he criticized Ricardo's theory. The study of the conditions for an orderly capitalist process of growth is carried out by Marx especially in the second volume of *Capital* (Marx, 1956) by using his well known schemes of reproduction.

5 For Ricardo, exchange through money is not conceptually different from barter (Ricardo, 1951, pp. 291–2).

6 See Sardoni (1987; 2011) for a detailed treatment of this aspect.

7 Among the more recent works on Marx's schemes, Tsuru's contribution in the 1940s (Tsuru, 1942) may be considered a classic, but see Olsen (2013) for a criticism of Tsuru's views. Other works on Marx's schemes are Brody (1970); Harris (1972; 1978); Okishio (1988) .

8 For a detailed treatment of the determination of equilibrium conditions see, e.g., Sardoni (2009).

9 Marx, as well known, analyzed the origin of the surplus value and profits from workers' exploitation in the first volume of *Capital* (Marx, 1954).

10 In the case of simple reproduction, capitalists must advance only the amount of money required to finance their consumption.

11 For a more detailed examination of the relationship between Kalecki and Marx's schemes, see Sardoni (1989).

12 On the determination of aggregate profits, see also Kalecki (1965).

13 In an economy that does not grow, past realized profits are used to finance capitalists' consumption and current gross investment (equal, of course, to replacement investment), i.e. $\Pi_{t-1} = I_{t-1} + C_{k,t-1}$, with $I_t = I_{t-1}$ and $C_{k,t} = C_{k,t-1}$. The capitalist class as a whole owns the required funds to finance its desired expenditure.

14 The crucial role of banks in the process of growth was emphasized also by Keynes, who wrote:

> in general, the banks hold the key position in the transition from a lower to a higher scale of activity. If they refuse to relax, the growing congestion of the short-term loan market or the new issue market, as the case may be, will inhibit the improvement, no matter how thrifty the public purpose to be out of their future incomes.
>
> *(Keynes, 1973, p. 222)*

15 Kahn, at the 'circus' where we discussed the *Treatise* in 1931, explained the problem of saving and investment by imagining a cordon round the capital-good industries and then studying the trade between them and the consumption-good industries: he was struggling to rediscover Marx's schema. Kalecki began at that point.

> *(Robinson, 1965, pp. 95–6)*

16 Trigg (2002; 2006) concentrates on the analytical relationship between Marx's schemes, Keynes's multiplier and Domar's growth model. On the relation between Marx's and Domar's models, see

also Lianos (1979). Bhaduri (1986) has written an introductory macroeconomics textbook based on Marx's schemes and Kalecki's analysis.

References

Alexander, S. S. 1940. "Mr. Keynes and Mr. Marx." *Review of Economic Studies* 7(2): 123–135.

Behrens, R. 1985. "What Keynes knew about Marx." *Studi Economici* 26: 3–14.

Bhaduri, A. 1986. *Macroeconomics: The Dynamics of Commodity Production*. London: Macmillan.

Brody, A. 1970. *Proportions, Prices and Planning; A Mathematical Restatement of the Labor Theory of Value*. Amsterdam: North-Holland Publishing Company.

Crotty, J. 1985. "The Centrality of Money, Credit, and Financial Intermediation in Marx's Crisis Theory: An Interpretation of Marx's Methodology." In *Rethinking Marxism: Struggles in Marxist Theory. Essays for Harry Magdoff and Paul Sweezy*, S. A. Resnick and R. D. Wolff, eds., 45–81. Brooklyn, NY: Autonomedia.

——. 1986. "Marx, Keynes, and Minsky on the Instability of the Capitalist Growth Process and the Nature of Government Economic Policy." In *Marx, Schumpeter, Keynes: A Centenary Celebration of Dissent*, S. W. Helburn, and D. F. Bramhall, eds., 297–324. Armonk, NY: Sharpe.

Dasgupta, A. K. 1983. *Phases of Capitalism and Economic Theory*. Oxford: Oxford University Press.

Dillard, D. 1984. "Keynes and Marx: A Centennial Appraisal." *Journal of Post Keynesian Economics* 6 (3): 421–432.

Fan-Hung. 1939. "Keynes and Marx on the Theory of Capital Accumulation, Money and Interest." *Review of Economic Studies* 7(1): 28–41.

Harris, D. J. 1972. "On Marx's Scheme of Reproduction and Accumulation." *Journal of Political Economy* 80(3): 505–522.

——. 1978. *Capital Accumulation and Income Distribution*. Stanford: Stanford University Press.

Hein, E. 2006. "Money, Interest and Capital Accumulation in Karl Marx's Economics: A Monetary Interpretation and Some Similarities to Post-Keynesian Approaches." *European Journal of the History of Economic Thought* 13(1): 113–140.

Kalecki, M. 1965. *Theory of Economic Dynamics*, 2nd edition. London: Allen & Unwin.

——. 1968. "The Marxian Equation of Reproduction and Modern Economics." *Social Science Information* 7(6): 73–79.

Keynes, J. M. 1973. *The General Theory and After. Part II, Defence and Development*, Volume 14 of *The Collected Writings of John Maynard Keynes*. London: Macmillan.

——. 1979. *The General Theory and After. A Supplement*, Volume 29 of *The Collected Writings of John Maynard Keynes*. London: Macmillan.

Lianos, T. P. 1979. "Domar's Growth Model and Marx's Reproduction Scheme." *Journal of Macroeconomics* 1(4): 405–412.

Marx, K. 1954. *Capital*, Volume 1. Moscow: Progress Publishers.

——. 1956. *Capital*, Volume 2. Moscow: Progress Publishers.

——. 1968. *Theories of Surplus-Value*, Part 2. Moscow: Progress Publishers.

Okishio, N. 1988. "On Marx's Reproduction Scheme." *Kobe University Economic Review* 34: 1–24.

Olsen, E. K. 2013. "The Comparability of the Aggregates Revisited." *European Journal of the History of Economic Thought* 20(3): 489–512.

Ricardo, D. 1951. *On the Principles of Political Economy and Taxation*, Volume 1 of *Works and Correspondence of David Ricardo*. Cambridge: Cambridge University Press.

Robinson, J. V. 1951. "Marx and Keynes." In *Collected Economic Papers, Vol. I*, 133–145. Oxford: Basil Blackwell.

——. 1965. "Kalecki and Keynes." In *Collected Economic Papers, Vol. III*, 92–99. Oxford: Basil Blackwell.

——. 1966. *An Essay on Marxian Economics*. London: Macmillan, 2nd edition.

Robinson, J. V., ed. 1973. *After Keynes*. Oxford: Basil Blackwell.

Sardoni, C. 1987. *Marx and Keynes on Economic Recession*. New York: New York University Press.

——. 1989. "Some Aspects of Kalecki's Theory of Profits: Its Relationship to Marx's Schemes of Reproduction." In *Kalecki's Relevance Today*, M. Sebastiani, ed., 206–219. Basingstoke: Macmillan.

——. 1997. "Keynes and Marx." In *A 'Second Edition' of The General Theory*, Volume 2, G. C. Harcourt, and P. Riach, eds., 261–283. London and New York: Routledge.

——. 2009. "The Marxian Schemes of Reproduction and the Theory of Effective Demand." *Cambridge Journal of Economics* 33(1): 161–173.

——. 2011. *Unemployment, Recession and Effective Demand*. Cheltenham: Edward Elgar.

Sowell, T. 1972. *Say's Law: An Historical Analysis*. Princeton: Princeton University Press.

Sweezy, P. M. 1942. *The Theory of Capitalist Development*. New York: Monthly Review Press.

Thweatt, W. O. 1983. "Keynes on Marx's *Das Kapital*." *History of Political Economy* 15(4): 617–620.

Trigg, A. B. 2002. "Marx's Reproduction Schema and the Multisectoral Foundations of the Domar Growth Model." *History of Economic Ideas* 10(2): 83–98.

——. 2006. *Marxian Reproduction Schema*. London and New York: Routledge.

Tsuru, S. 1942. "Appendix A: On Reproduction Schemes." In *The Theory of Capitalist Development*, P. M. Sweezy, 365–374. New York: Monthly Review Press.

Wolff, R. D. and S. A. Resnick. 2012. *Contending Economic Theories*. Cambridge, MA.: MIT Press.

34

SOCIAL STRUCTURE OF ACCUMULATION

Terrence McDonough

Social Structure of Accumulation (SSA) theory is a theory of stages of capitalism. Capitalist stage theory focuses on periods intermediate in length between a short-run business cycle and overall capitalist history. These periods consist of a long period of relatively stable capitalist accumulation followed by a relatively long period of crisis and breakdown. Each of the periods of accumulation is underpinned by a set of institutions designated as an SSA. Examples from the United States include the competitive capitalist SSA in the latter half of the nineteenth century followed by the long depression, the monopoly capitalist SSA established at the beginning of the twentieth century and ending in the Great Depression and the postwar SSA, which ended with the Great Stagflation of the 1970s.

In a capitalist system, class divisions and capitalist competition combined with the central role of profit-making lead to periodic institutional instabilities and the interruption of accumulation. For stable accumulation to resume, these sources of instability must be countered through the construction of a new set of enduring economic, political and ideological institutions. The construction of such a social structure underpins the profit rate and creates secure expectations that stimulate long-term investment. This is the basis of a new period of accumulation and the new stage of capitalism. The ensemble of these institutions is the Social Structure of Accumulation (SSA).

As accumulation proceeds the institutions of an SSA are undermined by class conflict, capitalist competition and the process of accumulation itself. These forces and the inter-dependence of the institutions eventually lead to a breakdown in the set of institutions, a fall in the profit rate and the collapse of accumulation, initiating a period of crisis that is only overcome with the construction of a new set of institutions. Thus capitalist stages are constituted by the sets of interdependent economic, political and ideological institutions that underpin relatively successful periods of accumulation. The period of growth then ends with a succeeding period of crisis in which accumulation is slower and unstable. (For useful collections of articles explaining, reviewing and applying the SSA approach see Kotz, McDonough and Reich [1994]; McDonough, Reich and Kotz 2010; McDonough, Kotz and Reich 2014].)

The Social Structure of Accumulation (SSA) framework arose in the United States in the wake of the collapse of what many have termed the "Golden Age" of post-World War II capitalism. The mid-1970s was a period of capitalist crisis characterized by simultaneously high levels of unemployment and high levels of inflation. This "Great Stagflation" appeared to run counter to Keynesian orthodoxy, which held that the two macroeconomic problems should not increase simultaneously. This contradiction prompted a theoretical shift that developed alongside the period of economic distress. Monetarism and a variety of new free-market economic theories (e.g., supply-side economics, rational expectations and real business cycles) increasingly came to dominate establishment economics. These had in common a different role for government—lower taxes, deregulation and shifting income away from labor— policies that have been termed neo liberalism. The more radical Post-Keynesian school sought to resolve the problems by returning to the importance of uncertainty in Keynes' theory of investment and leavened this by explaining inflation as the result of distributional conflict. Some Marxian thinkers saw this new crisis as another crisis of capitalism similar to the two "Great Depressions"—the long depression at the end of the nineteenth century and the more familiar Great Depression of the 1930s. This observation would lead to the promulgation of general theories of capitalist stages and their subsequent crises.

Marxist theories of capitalist crisis had tended to locate crisis in fundamental tendencies of the capitalist economy which were always potentially present. These tendencies included the tendency of the rate of profit to fall, disproportionalities among economic sectors and a tendency for either overproduction or underconsumption. Thus the emergence of crisis would be the present expression these long-run secular tendencies. The new theories that arose in the 1970s and early 1980s in the wake of the stagflationary crisis did not share the same emphasis on these tendencies. Crises could arise due to the breakdown of the institutional framework which conditioned the previous period of capitalist expansion. Some of the previously identified secular crisis tendencies could play a role in the breakdown of a particular SSA, but they would not all necessarily be present in every crisis. This argument defined recurring crisis periods as more serious than downward fluctuations of the ordinary business cycle, but not as the expression of an ultimate crisis of capitalism.

In defining crisis in this way, these theories drew on another tradition within the Marxian literature. This was a stage theoretic tradition that began with Hilferding's (1910) seminal work on finance capital. Hilferding's work sought to explain the recovery of capitalism after the long depression at the end of the nineteenth century. While emphasizing the emergence of the dominance of finance capital, Hilferding developed a multi-institutional analysis which identified a number of important transformations in capitalism that served to resolve the long depression and inaugurate an era of renewed capitalist expansion. Nicolai Bukharin (1915) recapitulated Hilferding's multifactoral argument while placing the emphasis on the globalization of economic activity. The possibility of this shift of emphasis highlights the holistic character of this kind of analysis. In *Imperialism, the Highest Stage of Capitalism*, Lenin (1917) summarized Hilferding's argument but laid emphasis instead on the emergence of the monopoly stage. It was possible in these arguments for the emergence of finance capital or imperialism to temporarily resolve a crisis and set the foundations of a new stage of capitalism. This tradition was to be carried forward in the work of Ernest Mandel (1970; 1978; 1980), Paul Sweezy (1968) and Paul Baran (Baran and Sweezy 1966)

The new theories emphasized not only the recurring periods of crisis but also the periods of capitalist stability and expansion that preceded the crises. Crises arose after long periods (averaging twenty-five to thirty years) of relatively unproblematic capitalist reproduction and accumulation. In this way attempts to understand the serious character of the stagflationist crisis of the 1970s led to the formulation of theories of long periods of capitalist growth as well as long periods of capitalist crisis. These were variously characterized as theories of long waves in capitalist history and theories of capitalist stages. The new theories thus proposed an intermediate level of capitalist crisis, a new theory of long waves in capitalist history and a theory of capitalist stages.

Two strands of this approach arose in Europe. Ernest Mandel contributed his monumental work *Late Capitalism* (1978). Mandel's work on long waves was not, however, extensively developed by subsequent authors. The French Regulation School has been much more influential. Michel Aglietta's *A Theory of Capitalist Regulation* (1979) became the founding document of this school. The Regulation School contended that the dynamic tendencies of capitalism had to be institutionally "regulated" if they were not to prompt instability and crisis. The school identified different "regimes of accumulation" that united varieties of production regimes with the social consumption norms needed to realize profits. They also theorized "modes of regulation," which brought in other institutions such as money and the state. The regime of accumulation and an associated mode of regulation could create a period of capitalist stability like the post-World War II "Fordist" era. The potential of these institutional arrangements to underpin growth would, however, eventually become exhausted, leading to a period of crisis.

At roughly the same time as these European developments, the SSA framework emerged in the United States. Its founding document was *Segmented Work, Divided Workers: The Historical Transformations of Labor in the United States*, written by David M. Gordon, Richard Edwards and Michael Reich. David Gordon (1978; 1980) had previously published two articles that developed an approach to long cycle theory and stages of capitalist development. Gordon's innovations were undertaken against the background of the American Monopoly Capital School founded earlier by Paul Baran and Paul Sweezy. The Monopoly Capital School saw the Great Depression years as the expression of the long-run stagnationist tendency of monopoly capital (as first described by Lenin), which was only temporarily interrupted by the post-World War II expansion. In Baran and Sweezy's view, this expansion was consequent on a unique set of historical circumstances that were unlikely to be repeated, so that the stagnationist tendencies of monopoly capitalism were bound to reassert themselves.

The question that Gordon's long wave reformulation posed to the monopoly stage of capitalism tradition was whether the postwar expansion was not simply a confluence of circumstances but rather a powerful institutional reorganization of American capitalism, historically analogous to the earlier organization of monopoly capitalism. Gordon proposed a set of newly arrived institutions that accounted for the long period of American postwar prosperity. These included multinational corporations, dual labor markets, American international hegemony, a conservative version of Keynesianism and bureaucratic systems of workplace control. The crisis of the 1970s was consequent on the breakdown of the ability of these institutions to underpin further successful accumulation.

The addition of a new period of profound institutional transformation to the previously analyzed transition to monopoly capitalism raised the question: Could these successive institutional transformations be generalized in a comprehensive theory of the inauguration of stages of capitalism? In *Segmented Work, Divided Workers*, Gordon, Edwards and Reich firmly answered this question by proposing that both the monopoly capital transition and the post-World War II transition rested on the construction of Social Structures of Accumulation. The construction of an SSA formed the institutional basis for a new stage of capitalism. The disintegration of this SSA marked the termination of this stage.

In *Segmented Work* the framework was refined and perhaps more importantly applied to explain the history of capital-labor relations in the United States. The three authors had earlier brought segmented labor market theory together with the theorization of the transition to monopoly capital. Yoking the SSA approach to the history of capital-labor relations provided a clarifying framework for this history and at the same time provided a powerful illustration of the potential utility of the theory of SSAs. Gordon, Edwards and Reich had constructed a theory of long waves of growth and stagnation, a theory of capitalist stages, an intermediate theory of capitalist crisis and a framework for the understanding of major transitions in the history of capitalist institutions.

All the theories of capitalist stages have undergone changes and developments over the last few decades. More orthodox Marxists have generally rejected theories of capitalist stages, perhaps because Marxists in the value theoretic tradition that emphasizes the law of the tendency of the rate of profit to fall have been concerned to develop a secular theory of crisis. This approach has denied that the global neoliberal era that succeeded the Great Stagflation represented a resolution, however temporary, of that crisis. These analysts have seen the entire period since the mid-1970s as one of uninterrupted crisis. Thus Mandel's hypothesis of the possibility of capitalist recovery despite his affirmation of the falling rate of profit has lost contemporary relevance for these theorists.

Many Regulation School concepts have by contrast been widely diffused in the radical academy. The postwar regime of accumulation, which combined mass production with a linking of wages and productivity and then mass consumption, was labelled as "Fordism." This conception was widely discussed in conjunction with "the crisis of Fordism" and speculation on the nature of the "Post-Fordism" that was succeeding the earlier regime. In the face of this success, however, the Francophone Regulation School shifted its theoretical moorings. Renouncing Marxian theory, the French Regulation School has searched for an alternative theoretical framework in institutionalism and a microeconomics of "conventions."

The SSA framework has attracted more subsequent work than Mandel's theory of long waves but has not been as widely utilized as the Regulation School's characterization of Fordism and Post-Fordism. At the same time, it has largely retained its theoretical coherence. Writing in the late 1990s, Michael Reich (1997) identified the SSA perspective as rooted in "Marxian insights concerning class conflict over production and distribution at the workplace and in the political arena, and by Marxian and Keynesian macroeconomic analyses." This characterization is still basically accurate, although the American institutionalist tradition should also be acknowledged.

Initially the SSA framework was closely associated with the macro-modelling work of Samuel Bowles, David M. Gordon and Thomas Weisskopf in examining the "rise and demise" of the postwar SSA. In *Beyond the Wasteland: A Democratic Alternative to Economic Decline*, Bowles, Gordon and Weisskopf (1983) argued that the postwar SSA rests on three buttresses, Pax Americana, the limited capital-labor accord and the capitalist-citizen accord. These institutions originally raised the profit rate and their disintegration brought lower profit rates and the onset of crisis. This argument was further developed in a series of academic articles (Weisskopf, Bowles and Gordon 1983; Bowles, Gordon and Weisskopf 1986; 1989). In these articles, Weisskopf et al. (1983) find econometric support for the hypothesis that variations in profitability can be explained by variations in quantitative indicators of capitalist power in the postwar SSA. This modelling has been extended to Greece and South Korea (Mihail 1983; Jeong 1997), but has not been a major focus of the SSA literature in recent years. Nevertheless there has been further progress in the statistical identification of long waves of accumulation in a number of countries (Goldstein 1999; Li, Xiao and Zhu 2007).

The framework has been extended to countries outside of its initial application to the United States. India has proven to be an interesting arena for SSA studies. In *India Working*,

Barbara Harriss-White (2003) applies an SSA approach which emphasizes the social institutions that condition accumulation at a given point in time. She concentrates on a tight analysis of the informal economy outside the major urban areas. Gender, religion, space, classes and the state are all central to the analysis.

Shilpa Ranganathan and Harland Prechel (2007) develop a more historical analysis of SSAs in India. They identify a transition from colonial capitalism to national capitalism in the immediate post-colonial era. Significantly, another transition occurs to a more transnational form of capitalism following a debt crisis in 1991. William I. Robinson (2003; 2004; 2008) has developed comprehensive accounts of the history of SSAs in Latin America, addressing both Central and South America. He has located these developments in the context of his broader work, which argues that globalization is a qualitatively new epoch in world capitalism, characterized by the emergence of a transnational capitalist class and the re-articulation of most countries into a global production and financial system. The SSA framework has also been controversially applied to understanding apartheid in South Africa (Heintz 2002).

The SSA framework has been used to analyze the history of specific institutions. Prominently, a "spatialization" school has sought to directly extend Gordon, Edwards and Reich's history of labor control strategies into the modern era. Gordon, Edwards and Reich identified successive labor control strategies in proletarianization, homogenization and segmentation. Michael Wallace and David Brady (2010) identify a spatialization strategy based on controlling labor through capital mobility and the threat of capital flight. Following the original argument in *Segmented Work*, they argue this strategy forms the basis of the current SSA.

In addition to labor control, another strand of the literature has taken up the broader issue of social control in general. David E. Barlow, Melissa H. Barlow and Theodore G. Chiricos (1993, 146) observe that

> the criminal justice system is a vital component of the social structure of accumulation in capitalist societies. As the capitalist state's most openly coercive form of social control, criminal justice plays a critical role in maintaining social order, and thereby, establishing a favourable business climate.

They then conduct a careful long-wave/SSA history of criminal justice policy in the U.S. from 1789 to the present day. Raymond J. Michalowski and Susan M. Carlson (2000) examine the relationship between unemployment, crime and imprisonment. They accord great importance to distinct phases *within* SSAs.

Phillip Anthony O'Hara (1995) adds the family to the set of institutions that are crucial to conditioning accumulation in the U.S. in the postwar period. He also emphasizes the importance of household labor in general in capitalist economies. Racial questions are addressed by Francisco Valdes and Sumi Cho (2011). They use the SSA perspective as one source for the development of a critical race materialism. This critical race materialism then allows a reframing of the SSA analysis that includes racial dynamics.

Martin H. Wolfson (2013) has used the SSA framework as a backdrop to understand the history of finance in the United States. On a more microeconomic level, Harland Prechel (2000) has developed an SSA analysis of transitions in corporate form and strategy.

Kent A. Klitgaard and co-authors (Hall and Klitgaard 2012; Klitgaard and Krall 2012) have argued that ecological economics has made progress in understanding how the human economy is necessarily embedded in the larger biophysical ecosystem, drawing sustenance from that system and impacting on it. They contend, on the other hand, that ecological economics has an insufficiently sophisticated theory of the internal dynamics of the capitalist economy and its limits expressed in recurrent crises. They have proposed that SSA theory is well poised to fill this gap.

Finally, SSA theory has been brought up to date through a discussion of the emergence of a new SSA after the stagflationary crisis. This is found in institutional changes such as neoliberalism, globalization and financialization. This recent period has been characterized in a number of different ways. In parallel with the first writing on capitalist stages at the turn of the twentieth century, the analysis is multi-factoral, but with different writers placing particular emphasis on different institutions. Kotz and McDonough (2010) characterize the current SSA as global neoliberalism. Asimakopoulos (2009) describes a world SSA based on global segmentation of labor. Brady and Wallace, as discussed earlier, base the new SSA on the spatialization of labor control. William K. Tabb (2012) argues that financialization is the most important element of the current SSA. William I. Robinson (2012) contends, in line with his earlier work, that globalization is a qualitatively new epoch in world capitalism, characterized by the emergence of a transnational capitalist class and the re-articulation of most countries into a global production and financial system.

Both David M. Kotz (2010) and Duncan K. Foley (2012) use an analysis of the recent SSA and its crisis to categorize different kinds of structural crises. Kotz distinguishes between the crises that end a regulated form of SSA and those that end a liberal SSA. The latter are more severe, less easily resolved and more system-threatening. He contends that this is the kind of crisis we are facing today. Foley draws a distinction between crises caused by falling profitability and those caused by rising exploitation. The current crisis is of the latter type, and solving a severe shortfall in demand is the precondition for emerging from the crisis.

While a solid body of theory and applications has been established within the SSA framework, there are a number of tasks which remain pressing. There has been relatively little discussion of the philosophy of social science underlying SSA theory. Other Marxian approaches to capitalist stage theory have implicitly assumed a traditional dialectical materialism or an Althusserian approach (Lipietz 1993). Since the SSA approach proposes an intermediate level of structure between the conjuncture and the totality of capitalist history, this suggests an underlying depth ontology with layered social structures operating at multiple levels. One direction in which to pursue this would be within the critical realist philosophy founded by British philosopher Roy Bhaskar. The establishment of a depth ontology for stages of capitalism will involve the examination of actual determinative structures at play on several levels of abstraction and at the temporalities of capitalist history in total, the capitalist stage and the conjuncture. Such an analysis must ask whether a realist depth ontology actually functions to clarify the multileveled expression of social structures in a periodized capitalist history, thus serving as an underlaborer for stage theory.

The current conception of institutions within the SSA framework is borrowed from the Veblenian tradition of institutional economics. As such it is a rough and ready, partially empirical notion of institution revolving around custom, habits, rules and laws. These institutions are then regarded within the SSA framework as the crystallization of the balance of class forces at a particular point in time. The SSA framework would benefit from integrating sociological discussions of structure into its conception of institutions. The sociological tradition has a rich discussion of the origin of structural relations within society. While this discussion is more centered on the concept of agency than a Marxist approach would warrant, further consideration of this tradition could deepen the SSA theory's approach to institutions.

The framework could also extend its historical consideration of crises back to the first half of the nineteenth century in Europe, applying the SSA framework more thoroughly to earlier European history in order to expand the number of crisis periods under study. The investigation of earlier European crises will involve historical description and the construction of a narrative account of the genesis, development and emerging crises of sets of interdependent institutional structures and the comparison of these dynamics with subsequent stages of capitalism. The periods ending with depression of the 1820s and the revolutions of 1848 are prominent candidates for this kind of consideration.

Beyond these historical and theoretical tasks, the main concern of SSA theory in the immediate future will undoubtedly be to analyze the unfolding economic turmoil that began in 2007–8. At the time of writing the elite response to the crisis consists primarily of attempted intensifications of neoliberalism. SSA theory indicates that an intensification of the institutional structure that led to the crisis in the first place is highly unlikely to constitute a successful response. As this becomes clear, other possible resolutions will come to the fore. These resolutions are likely to be either major restructurings of institutions within capitalism or initiatives designed to take human society beyond the capitalist pattern of alternating periods of long-run growth and crisis. In either case, a deeper understanding and analysis will be urgent.

References

Aglietta, M. 1979. *A Theory of Capitalist Regulation*. London: Verso.

Asimakopoulos, J. 2009. "Globally Segmented Labor Markets: The Coming of the Greatest Boom and Bust, Without the Boom." *Critical Sociology* 35(2): 175–198.

Baran, P. A. and P. M. Sweezy. 1966. *Monopoly Capital*. New York: Monthly Review Press.

Barlow, D. E., M. H. Barlow, and T. G. Chiricos. 1993. "Long Economic Cycles and the Criminal Justice System in the U.S." *Crime, Law and Social Change* 19(2): 143–169.

Bowles, S., D. M. Gordon, and T. E. Weisskopf. 1983. *Beyond the Wasteland: A Democratic Alternative to Economic Decline*. Garden City, NY: Anchor Press/Doubleday.

——. 1986. "Power and Profits: The Social Structure of Accumulation and the Profitability of the Postwar US Economy." *Review of Radical Political Economics* 18(1–2): 132–167.

——. 1989. "Business Ascendancy and Economic Impasse: A Structural Retrospective on Conservative Economics, 1979–87." *Journal of Economic Perspectives* 3(1): 107–134.

Bukharin, N. 1973 [1915]. *Imperialism and World Economy*. New York: Monthly Review Press.

Foley, D. K. 2012. "The Political Economy of Postcrisis Global Capitalism." *South Atlantic Quarterly* 111(2): 251–263.

Goldstein, J. P. 1999. "The Existence, Endogeneity, and Synchronization of Long Waves: Structural Time Series Model Estimates." *Review of Radical Political Economics* 31(4): 61–101.

Gordon, D. M. 1978. "Up and Down the Long Roller Coaster." In *U.S. Capitalism in Crisis*, Crisis Reader Editorial Collective, ed., 22–35. New York: Union for Radical Political Economics.

——. 1980. "Stages of Accumulation and Long Economic Cycles." In *Processes of the World-System*, T. K. Hopkins and I. Wallerstein, eds., 9–45. Beverly Hills, CA: Sage Publications.

Gordon, D. M., R. Edwards, and M. Reich. 1982. "Long Swings and Stages of Capitalism." In *Segmented Work, Divided Workers: The Historical Transformation of Labor in the United States*, D. M. Gordon, R. Edwards, and M. Reich, eds., 18–47. Cambridge: Cambridge University Press.

Hall, C. A. S. and K. A. Klitgaard. 2012. *Energy and the Wealth of Nations: Understanding the Biophysical Economy*. New York: Springer.

Harriss-White, B. 2003. *India Working: Essays on Society and Economy*. Cambridge: Cambridge University Press.

Heintz, J. 2002. "Political Conflict and the Social Structure of Accumulation: The Case of South African Apartheid." *Review of Radical Political Economics* 34(3): 319–326.

Hilferding, R. 1980 [1910]. *Finance Capital*. London: Routledge & Kegan Paul.

Jeong, S. 1997. "The Social Structure of Accumulation in South Korea: Upgrading or Crumbling?" *Review of Radical Political Economics* 29(4): 92–112.

Klitgaard, K. A. and L. Krall. 2012. "Ecological Economics, Degrowth, and Institutional Change." *Ecological Economics* 84: 247–253.

Kotz, D. M. 2010. "The Final Conflict: What Can Cause a System-Threatening Crisis of Capitalism?" *Science and Society* 74(3): 362–379.

Kotz, D. M. and T. McDonough. 2010. "Global Neoliberalism and the Contemporary Social Structure of Accumulation." In *Contemporary Capitalism and Its Crises*, T. McDonough, M. Reich, and D. M. Kotz, eds., 93–120. Cambridge: Cambridge University Press.

Kotz, D. M., T. McDonough, and M. Reich. 1994. *Social Structures of Accumulation: The Political Economy of Growth and Crisis*. Cambridge: Cambridge University Press.

Lenin, V.I. 1969 [1917]. *Imperialism, the Highest Stage of Capitalism*. New York: International Publishers.

Li, M., F. Xiao, and A. Zhu. 2007. "Long Waves, Institutional Changes, and Historical Trends: A Study of the Long-Term Movement of the Profit Rate in the Capitalist World-Economy." *Journal of World-Systems Research* 13(1): 33–54.

Lipietz, A. 1993. "From Althusserianism to 'Regulation Theory.'" In *The Althusserian Legacy*, E. A. Kaplan and M. Spinker, eds., 99–138. London: Verso.

Mandel, E. 1970. *Marxist Economic Theory*. New York: Monthly Review Press.

——. 1978. *Late Capitalism*. London: Verso.

——. 1980. *Long Waves of Capitalist Development*. Cambridge: Cambridge University Press.

McDonough, T., D. M. Kotz, and M. Reich. 2014. *Social Structure of Accumulation Theory*, Volumes 1 and 2. Northampton, MA: Edward Elgar.

McDonough, T., M. Reich, and D. M. Kotz. 2010. *Contemporary Capitalism and Its Crises*. Cambridge: Cambridge University Press.

Michalowski, R. J. and S. M. Carlson. 2000. "Crime, Punishment, and Social Structures of Accumulation: Toward a New and Much Needed Political-Economy of Justice." *Journal of Contemporary Criminal Justice* 16(3): 272–292.

Mihail, D. M. 1993. "Modelling Profits and Industrial Investment in Postwar Greece." *International Review of Applied Economics* 7(3): 290–310.

O'Hara, P. A. 1995. "Household Labor, the Family, and Macroeconomic Instability in the United States: 1940s–1990s." *Review of Social Economy* 53(1): 89–120.

Prechel, H. 2000. *Big Business and the State: Historical Transitions and Corporate Transformation, 1880s–1990s*. Albany: State University of New York Press.

Ranganathan, S. and H. Prechel. 2007. "Political Capitalism, Neoliberalism, and Globalization in India: Redefining Foreign Property Rights and Facilitating Corporate Ownership, 1991–2005." In *Politics and Neoliberalism: Structure, Process and Outcome*, Harland Prechel, ed., 201–243. Amsterdam: JAI Press/Elsevier Ltd.

Reich, M. 1997. "Social Structure of Accumulation Theory: Retrospect and Prospect." *Review of Radical Political Economics* 29(3): 1–10.

Robinson, W. I. 2003. *Transnational Conflicts: Central America, Social Change, and Globalization*. London: Verso.

——. 2004. *A Theory of Global Capitalism: Production, Class, and State in a Transnational World*. Baltimore: Johns Hopkins University Press.

——. 2008. *Latin America and Global Capitalism: A Critical Globalization Perspective*. Baltimore: Johns Hopkins University Press.

——. 2012. "Global Capitalism Theory and the Emergence of Transnational Elites." *Critical Sociology* 38(3): 349–363.

Sweezy, P. 1968. *The Theory of Capitalist Development*. New York: Monthly Review Press.

Tabb, W. K. 2012. *The Restructuring of Capitalism in Our Time*. New York: Columbia University Press.

Valdes, F. and S. Cho. 2011. "Critical Race Materialism: Theorizing Justice in the Wake of Global Neoliberalism." *Connecticut Law Review* 43(5): 1513–1572.

Wallace, M. and D. Brady. 2010. "Globalization or Spatialization? The Worldwide Spatial Restructuring of the Labor Process." In *Contemporary Capitalism and Its Crises: Social Structure of Accumulation Theory for the 21ˢᵗ Century*, T. McDonough, M. Reich, and D. M. Kotz, eds., 121–144. Cambridge: Cambridge University Press.

Weisskopf, T. E., S. Bowles, and D. M. Gordon. 1983. "Hearts and Minds: A Social Model of US Productivity Growth." *Brookings Papers on Economic Activity* 2: 381–441.

Wolfson, M. H. 2013. "An Institutional Theory of Financial Crisis." In *The Handbook of the Political Economy of Financial Crises*, M. H. Wolfson and G. A. Epstein, eds., 172–190. New York: Oxford University Press.

35

MONOPOLY CAPITAL THEORY

Hans G. Despain

Monopoly capital most specifically refers to the theoretical "sketch" provided by Paul Sweezy and Paul Baran of the monopoly stage of capitalism, or "monopoly capitalism." The theory has developed to comprehend and explain financialization as a quintessential historical development within capitalism (Foster and Magdoff 2009; Foster and McChesney 2012; Despain 2009; 2013).

Monopoly capitalism denotes the stage of capitalism that began to emerge in the late nineteenth century or "the railway age" (Dobb 1946, 296) and is fully matured by the mid-twentieth century. Maurice Dobb referred to it as "a new age of monopoly" (Dobb 1937, 186; 1925, 97–112) and "the monopolistic age" (Dobb 1946, 321–5; also Sweezy 2004 and Despain 2016a).

By the 1920s a new wave of research and theory began to draw attention to forms of *imperfect* competition and market power. The voices leading this charge were numerous (Samuelson 1967). Nonetheless, it was a "new generation" of young Cambridge economists who especially cultivated the new theoretical understanding of the historical institutional development of capitalism (Marcuzzo 2007). It was especially this strand of "imperfect competition" theorists who would most influence the development of monopoly capital theory.

Maurice Dobb (1925) expounded a theory of monopoly capitalism in its historical development. Piero Sraffa (1926) developed a penetrating and influential critique of the hypothesis of perfect competition.

The Cambridge tradition of imperfect competition culminates in Robinson (1933), in which she demonstrates imperfect competition has significant social welfare implications. The Cambridge tradition can be differentiated from a separate strand of imperfect competition, or what Edward Chamberlin (1933) dubbed "monopolistic competition." Samuelson (1967, 20–1) contends, "Indeed the time has come when we may permit ourselves to use the terms monopolistic competition and imperfect competition interchangeably." This is misleading. Robinson underscores the welfare reducing effects of imperfect competition, while Chamberlin contends that the product differentiation of imperfect competition was welfare enhancing. Monopoly capital theory as it developed from the Cambridge tradition underscores the social welfare outcome of imperfect competition as both harmful and contradictory for the economic system. Early, Sweezy (1939) was able to demonstrate that oligopoly firms were likely to increase prices, but very capable to resist any forces to reduce prices. The welfare reducing implications were radically extended to implicate: 1) stagnation as the normal state of monopoly capitalism, 2) macroeconomic instability, 3) the importance of "waste," and 4) financialization as the quintessential form of waste of late monopoly capitalism.

The emphasis on the implication of monopolization on the macro dynamic differentiates the theory of monopoly capitalism from Robinson's and Chamberlin's theories. The theory of monopoly capitalism is the synthesis of the new world of imperfect competition and the implications of it for the structural dynamic of the macroeconomy.

The Historical Development and Macro Dynamics of Monopoly Capital Economy

It was first Michal Kalecki who "brought imperfect competition in touch with the theory of employment" (Robinson 1969, viii), and then developed a macroeconomic theory based on imperfect competition, or the "degree of monopoly." Kalecki rooted his analysis in the Marxian class composition conception of output and the monopolization tendencies of capitalism. Inspired by Marx, the Kaleckian view emphasizes that the forces of free competition generate a tendency toward the increasing concentration and centralization of capital.

Maurice Dobb (1925; 1946) demonstrates that the genesis of capitalism is a function of monopoly power and privilege of merchants and landlords. The historical evolution of capitalism necessarily generates an extension of giant firms as a logical and ontological consequence of *laissez-faire* capitalism as suggested by Marx's conceptions of concentration and centralization of capital.

Kalecki's notion of the "degree of monopoly" picks-up from these historical and ontological insights. Kalecki (1971, 43–61) argues that there is a strong link between the 'degree of monopoly' and the distribution of income. The degree of monopoly determines significantly the "mark-up" price of goods and services from average prime costs (comprising of wages and costs of material). At the level of the macroeconomy, Kalecki (2009, 30) argues the "average degree of monopoly" of the private sector is the primary determinant of "the relative share of wages in the gross income of the private sector." In agreement with the Keynesian perspective, the level of income is determined by aggregate demand and "the factors determining the distribution of income" or "distribution factors" (Kalecki 1971, 80–1), are primarily determined by the "long-run trends in the degree of monopoly" (Kalecki 1971, 65; Kalecki 2009, 47).

The long-run trends in the degree of monopoly tend to increase, because a high degree of monopoly provides a firm four main characteristics to survive, and *thrive*, in capitalistic competition (Dobb 1925, 157–75). First, size and scale allows a firm to bear various uncertainties. Second, it provides a firm the ability to effect changes. Third, the larger firm acts as a magnet for economic resources; investors, banks, financial houses prefer the stability and power of firms with size and scale. Fourth, the large firm that "already commands large capital will generally find it easier to raise additional capital and credit" (Dobb 1925, 167).

Following Dobb's lead, Kalecki argues that "Monopoly seems to be deeply rooted in the nature of the capitalist system: free competition, as an assumption, may be useful in the first stage of certain investigations, but as a description of the normal state of capitalist economy it is merely a myth (Kalecki quoted in Dobb 1973, 223). The implication is a shift from the notion of marginal productivity determining distribution of income to a focus on the degree of monopoly and the conflict between capitalists and workers.

Kalecki (1971) recognizes the importance of the facts that large firms controlled significant portions of a nation's capital stock (Ibid., 179–81) and investment activity (Ibid., 105–9). Through a multiplier process, fluctuations in investment spending cause corresponding fluctuations in economic activity as a whole (Ibid., 78–88). The main mechanism of adjustment for large firms is the degree of capital utilization. Thus, excess capacity becomes a lever of adjustment to a strong or weak economy (Ibid., 135–7). In turn, the degree of excess capacity is itself a function of the "degree of monopoly" (Ibid., 182).

In addition to the ability of large firms to command capital, accumulate, concentrate and centralize an industry (Kalecki 1971, 105–9), Kalecki underscores that in an environment where a few giant firms dominant an industry and compete alongside medium and small firms, i.e. monopolistic capitalism, there is a tendency for an *intensified* degree of exploitation (Ibid., 93–9). Kalecki maintains that monopolistic capitalism manifests tendencies toward both over-savings and under-investment generating instability and business cycle fluctuations (Ibid., 124–37).

Kalecki points out investment tends to expand productive capacity, therefore there will only be sufficient effective demand to keep this capacity occupied if investment continually expands (1971, 146–56). Without a special technological boost factor, there is according to Kalecki a chronic endogenous tendency for new investment to slacken toward zero (Dobb 1973, 232). This is the basis for a tendency toward secular stagnation.

Mature Monopoly Capital Development and Stagnation

Josef Steindl more fully develops the secular stagnation implications of the Kaleckian general theory in his *Maturity and Stagnation in American Capitalism* (1952). In the Steindlian view of secular stagnation there are "endogenous factors inherent in the development of capitalism–primarily the development of imperfect competition, monopoly and oligopoly" (Hansen 1955) whereby stagnation becomes the general tendency of modern capital accumulation. The essence of Steindl's theory is that the capital accumulation process under the ubiquitous presence of the strategies of giant firms gave rise to an increase in profits and a decline in the rate of utilization of capital stock, or an increase in "excess capacity."

According to Steindl, the rate of surplus value and the gross profit margin increase, while net realized profit rates may stagnate or fall due to excess capacity. For example, if a large firm experiences a decrease in demand, they have the power to resist price reductions, and instead decrease capacity utilization. It is the decrease in capacity utilization that tends to put a damper on investment demand and the likelihood of secular stagnation emerges.

Steindl's endogenous theory of capitalist development as the basis of secular stagnation was a massive step forward for understanding the macrodynamics and processes of capitalist accumulation under the regime of oligopolization of key industries. Steindl is able to place the emphasis squarely on development of imperfect competition, monopoly and oligopoly, and their ability to resist price competition, while simultaneously germinating the new nemesis of *excess capacity* and the tendencies toward secular stagnation.

Both Paul Sweezy (1954) and Alvin Hansen (1954) quickly pointed out that Steindl's theory fails to take account of important exogenous factors such as innovation and new industries that could forestall decline and crisis. Steindl embraced the criticism that he had "been wrong, however, to disregard the economic function of innovation in capitalism" (Steindl 1984, 176).

Steindl also believed he had underestimated the ability of oligopolies to move their investment activity into other industrial branches (Steindl 1984, 174), that is toward *corporate conglomeration*. Conglomerates became popular forms of company growth throughout the 1960s and after.

Nonetheless, Steindl contended that there is massive evidence that big firms prioritize safe investments above a mere profit motive. Thus, in concert with Kalecki, Steindl demonstrates the primary problems of mature capitalism are intensified exploitation, underemployment, high gross profits, over-savings, excess capacity, under-investment, and secular stagnation.

Development, Underdevelopment, and Stagnation in Monopoly Capitalism

Paul Baran's *The Political Economy of Growth* (1957) is the next major work in the direct line of Marx, Dobb, Kalecki, Sweezy, and Steindl. "Surplus" becomes paramount for Baran (1957, 22–43). It can be simply defined as the difference between a society's output and consumption (Ibid., 22). Although the concept of "surplus" is "undoubtedly somewhat tricky" (Ibid.) and imprecise, the conception of surplus is crucial for grasping the macroeconomic dynamic of monopoly capitalism (see Szlajfer 1984; Foster 2014, 24–50). Baran (1957) underscores oligopolistic firms form "privileged sanctuaries" by curtailing entry into the industry (Baran (1957, 77). Excess capacity of giant firms expands to endure fluctuations *and* to employ as a strategic weapon to curtail competitive entry. Thus, excess capacity expands, while inducements to investment weaken (Ibid., 123) and the economic surplus increases. The rate of profits is uneven, but high, and the mass of profits large. However, investment outlets become more difficult to find. Thus, consequently unemployment, under-employment and stagnation become the order of the age (Ibid., 85).

Baran's work was most influential in its theoretical grounding of Maurice Dobb's (1951) provocative notion that the underdeveloped countries of the world were highly unlikely to emulate the development of the advanced capitalist nations such as UK, France and the US. To be sure colonialism prohibited development. Baran's claim is that this tendency toward underdevelopment would continue post-decolonization. His argument for perpetual under-development decolonization centers on the fact that the global economy, as argued by Paul Sweezy (1942), is dominated by giant transnational private firms. Government support of giant corporations maintains and extends the oligopolization of the global economy (Baran 1957, 113–16).

The neo-imperialism that Baran was able to identify is that governments enabled global competition of "Titan" oligopoly giants.

> As Mr. Vogt put it at the conclusion of his book, "the human race is caught in a situation as concrete as a pair of shoes two sizes too small." The image is exact. But the pair of shoes are monopoly capitalism and imperialism.
>
> *(Baran 1957, 248)*

Wedged between the vice of the competition of transnational oligopolized Titan firms and the political aspiration of national governments "the capitalist system, once the mighty engine of economic development, has turned into a no less formidable hurdle to human advancement" (Baran 1957, 249). In concert with the global political economy of Maurice Dobb (1951), Baran argues "The establishment of a socialist planned economy is an essential, indeed indispensable, condition for the attainment of economic and social progress in underdeveloped countries" (Baran 1957, 261).

Economic Disorder and Social Disorders

Baran's innovative book was followed by the joint effort of Paul Baran and Paul Sweezy in their seminal book *Monopoly Capital: An Essay on the American Economic and Social Order* (1966). Baran and Sweezy provide a more complete theory of investment of giant firms. They theoretically confront the political and historical reactions to the strong and systematic tendency for the surplus to rise and the problems of excess capacity and *surplus absorption*. In this sense Baran and Sweezy represent further theoretical advancements in understanding the contradictions of monopoly capital.

The root of the contradictions is not the failures of the system, but its successes. The giant firms of monopoly capitalism increase productivity and profits. The abundant productive capacity and the high savings potential tends to cut off investment before full employment is achieved.

The motor force of any expansion is the creation of new productive capacity. Monopoly capital accomplishes new productive capacity brilliantly. The problem is that the rapid rise in the surplus during an expansion generates an investment-seeking portion. Monopoly capitalism has a self-contradictory dynamic. Put simply, the system has a "chronic inability to absorb as much surplus as it is capable of producing" (Baran and Sweezy 1966, 109).

The impressive productive capacity increase steadily *both* the surplus itself *and* the "supply of investment-seeking surplus," but simultaneously fail to "generate a corresponding rise in the magnitude of investment outlets" (Baran and Sweezy 1966, 88).

In terms of Marxian reproduction schemes, for the investment-seeking surplus to successfully be reinvested requires that the means of production (Department I) precipitously outpace the expansion of consumption goods and services (Department II). Eventually, the means of production become so built up that a social disproportionality manifests between productive capacity and corresponding consumer demand (Foster 1987, 61). "Twist and turn as one will, there is no way to avoid the conclusion that monopoly capitalism is a self-contradictory system" (Baran and Sweezy 1966, 108). Under the conditions of overexploitation and underemployment of the working class, excess capacity continually tends to cut off potential net investment because it is not profitable. The system fails to generate *both* the consumption and investment outlets for the rapid rise in surplus produced by giant firms.

Kalecki (Kalecki 1939, 149) calls this "the tragedy of investment." The tragedy underscores the fact that surplus that cannot be absorbed will not be produced. Thus, "it follows that the *normal* state of the monopoly capitalist economy is stagnation" (Baran and Sweezy 1966, 108).

Baran and Sweezy contend that consumption and investment are not the only two outlets for the absorption of surplus, it can also be *wasted* (Baran and Sweezy 1966, 79). Since the absorption by means of consumption and investment are endogenously circumvented, the issue of economic waste forms "the pivotal element around which Baran and Sweezy's *Monopoly Capital* was organized" (Foster 2014, 74) and constitutes the bulk of their theoretical consideration for understanding the macroeconomic dynamic of contemporary monopoly capitalism (Foster 2014, 89).

Baran and Sweezy argue the capitalist system increasingly relies on "waste" (Foster 2014, 12). Forms of waste include: 1) the sales effort, consisting of advertising, market research, sales outlets, various sales personnel expenses, public relations, lobbying, conspicuous or "showy" business space, product appearance, packaging, planned obsolescence, model changes, etc. (Baran and Sweezy 1966, 115–41); 2) war, militarism, imperialism, and other non-defense public spending (Baran and Sweezy 1966, 151–217); and 3) "diversion of potential surplus into the financial sector (listed as 'finance, insurance, and real estate' in the national account)" (Baran and Sweezy 1966, pp. 139–41).

With the system's increasing reliance on economic waste it appears as though secular stagnation is an illusion. Baran and Sweezy's argument is the contradictions of monopoly remain and analysis of circumstance reveals deep economic disorder and social disorders. High profit margin of Titan firms are prioritized and real human needs become more and more remote within the logic and macroeconomic dynamic of the monopoly capitalistic system.

The theory of monopoly capitalism became highly influential. It generated great debate and received deep criticism. The best source for the early debates and an impressive defense is found in John Bellamy Foster's (2014 [1986]) *The Theory of Monopoly Capitalism* (Despain 2014).

As insightful and revolutionary as *Monopoly Capital* is, the book is merely an "essay-sketch" and is far from being a comprehensive study of monopoly capitalism. Its most glaring shortcomings include: (1) absence of a thoroughgoing inquiry in to the labor process itself; (2) inadequate sketch of monopoly capitalism and the global order; and (3) inadequate account of the financial sector absorbing potential surplus. Each of these shortcomings would be well addressed as the theory monopoly capitalism developed.

The Degradation of Work in the Labor Process of Monopoly Capitalism

Harry Braverman's *Labor and Monopoly Capital: The Degradation of Work in the Twentieth Century* (1974) was a landmark accomplishment. Not since Marx's *Capital* had there been such through analysis of the labor process as a whole in the context of capital accumulation. Following Baran and Sweezy's *Monopoly Capital*, Braverman believed that historical development of monopoly capital and mega-corporations required a new analysis to complement that of Marx.

Braverman sets out to address a glaring contradiction in twentieth century labor process. On the one hand it is argued that technological innovation and automation require higher levels of education, intelligence and skills, on the other hand it is widely acknowledged that labor processes had been increasingly subdivided into petty operations. These "petty operations demand ever less skill and training; and that the modern trend of work by its 'mindlessness' and 'bureaucratization' is 'alienating' ever larger sections of the working population" (Braverman 1974, 3).

Braverman points out that the subdivision of labor accomplished two things: 1) greater productivity and lower costs; 2) increased control of the labor process by management and capital ownership (Braverman 1974, 78). The "control mechanisms" can be described in a double sense. First, the subdivision of work necessitates a 'conductor' or good management of worker activity. Second the mortal injuries of subdivided work increases worker alienation and worker dependence on the labor process of the system in place (Ibid., 197–206).

Monopoly capitalism thus constitutes the subdivision of labor and intensifies the mechanisms of control that management practices and the system itself imposes. This allows ever greater extraction of surplus labor from workers in monopoly capitalism.

Braverman predicts that the so-called "new middle class" of the "middling layers" of monopoly capital would also experience the "degradation" of work and pay structures to merge with conditions of "control" endured by blue-collar workers (Braverman 1974, 403–9). Recent work demonstrates just how prophetic Braverman's insights were (see Jonna and Foster

2014 and 2016). There is strong evidence that Braverman's basic insight that the accumulation process of monopoly capital necessarily manifests a tendency of progression of skill requirement, improvement of working conditions, and increased pay for the relative *few*. For the *vast majority* of workers there is a widening of the subdivision of work, a degradation of skill requirement, increased control from supervisors and managers, and stagnation and decline in pay.

The Global Order and Monopoly Capitalism

Baran and Sweezy (1966) contribute to regeneration in the exploration and critique of the new forms of imperialism in oligopolized global capitalism (Magdoff 1968, Magdoff 1978, Magdoff and Foster 2003). Baran (1957) and Sweezy (1942) both addressed imperialism in earlier work. Baran (1957, 177) had made the argument that the underdeveloped world had failed to develop under a free-market ideology and had merely "became an appendage of the 'internal markets' of Western Capitalism." Samir Amin (1976, 233–40) extends this analysis and demonstrates that the underdeveloped economies that opened global markets do not receive a "multiplier effect" from investment spending because the investment spending from international trade and the corresponding profits tend to be siphoned from the underdeveloped nations back to the developed world. Heavily influenced by Baran, Andre Gunder Frank (1967, 6–7)) argues that the "non-realization and unavailability for investment of 'potential' economic surplus is due essentially to the monopoly structure of capitalism." This generates a tendency toward uneven development, development of Western monopolized capitalist nations, and perpetual "underdevelopment" of the so-called "third world" (Frank 1967, 8).

Samir Amin (1977, 229–35) argues that this perpetual underdevelopment depends on two primary phenomena, the "superexploitation" of the working class of the underdeveloped world by the capitalist class of the developed world, and the rise of global transnational "monopolies" with easy capital mobility. Capital mobility allows for "imperial rents" for transnational giant firms via a process of "labour arbitrage," whereby large firms move their production operations to areas of the world with lower wages and a lack of laws that protect workers.

In *Capital*, Marx analyzes two ways in which capitalists increase the rate of surplus value. First, by lengthening the working day, or increasing absolute surplus value; second, reducing necessary labor time by means of increasing the productivity of workers producing consumption goods, or increasing relative surplus value. Marx further alluded to the possibility of pushing the wage of the worker below the value of labor-power, but he did not consider this option in depth because he assumed labor-power to bought and sold at its full value. Labor arbitrage constitutes a third way to increase surplus value. Today, labor arbitrage allows for transnational Titan firms to routinely buy and sell labor-power below its value (Smith 2016, 236–40). Smith well argues that transnational Titan firms extract surplus-value from workers in low-wage countries without having to "export their capital" (Ibid., 233). Smith contends that "what is urgently needed" is a conception that unites the economic essence of monopoly capitalism with the political essence that divides the global order "into oppressed and oppressor nations" (Ibid., 233). That theory is global labor arbitrage monopoly-finance capitalism (Ibid., 187–96, 297–301).

Joseph Halevi and Yanis Varoufakis also have innovated and extended the arguments of imperialism to incorporate the process of financialization and the flow money and wealth from the less-wealthy countries to the wealthiest countries (Halevi and Varoufakis 2003).

Monopoly-Finance Capital Theory

Costas Lapavitsas (2013, 15–20) correctly identifies monopoly capital theorists as among the first to appreciate the importance of the developments within the financial sector. Early on it was monopoly capital theorists who understood the importance of the process of financialization. They must be praised for both anticipating the collapse of 2007–8 and explaining the crisis and the durability of stagnation into the future. Lapavitsas further points out too many political economists fail to "realize their affinities with [and we could add, their theoretical debt to] the tradition of *Monthly Review*" (Lapavitsas 2013, 23).

Monopoly capital theory contends that it is all but impossible to understand the political economy of the twentieth (Sweezy and Magdoff 1972, 7–29) and twenty-first centuries (Foster and McChesney 2012, 29–64) without appreciating how the "financial explosion" reconfigured contemporary capitalism. For Baran and Sweezy (1966, 14–51), the development of monopoly capital was not the bastardization of pure capitalism, but the "legitimate" or evolutionary outcome of capitalist "laws" of development. Similarly, for Magdoff and Sweezy (1983), financialization is not merely parasitic upon 'functioning capitalists' but the logical and necessary development from the laws of capitalist development. In 1966 Baran and Sweezy contended that the private sales effort and public spending where the most important forms of waste. Today the excess surplus is primarily absorbed through the financial sector as argued by Foster and Magdoff (2009) and Foster and McChesney (2012). They underscore the importance of finance with their notion of monopoly-finance capital. It places the proper emphasis on the structural necessity of finance within monopoly capital.

This terminology is consistent with Sweezy's insistence that the full "triumph of financial capital" had become the axis of power both economically and politically. The triumph of financial capital would temporarily stabilize the macroeconomic variables and generate economic growth. But above all else the triumph of financial capital is itself a resplendent expression of stagnation (Sweezy 1994, 1–11).

The basic stagnation problem of monopoly capitalism has never subsided, but in fact worsened (Foster and Magdoff 2009, 5–7). Stagnation itself is a function of the fact that the surplus generated by monopoly capital becomes increasingly difficult for the system to absorb. It is in this sense that the financial explosion and triumph of financial capital was a most dazzling illustration of the "fundamental contradiction of capitalist society." Namely, the "contradiction between the ends of production regarded as a natural-technical process of creating use values, and the ends of capitalism regarded as a historical system of expanding exchange value" (Sweezy 1942, 172).

In other words, the financial activity of monopoly-finance capital is significantly a process of systemic *waste*. The fact does *not* make the waste unnecessary. Surplus absorption is necessary for the systemic reproduction. The point is that a substantial volume of financial activity does not lead to an increase in production. As captured in the title of Lapavitsas's recent book, capitalists today are *Profiting Without Producing* (2013).

The basic results of monopoly-finance capital are: the high productive capacity of monopoly-finance capital generates an enormous surplus, excess savings and excess capacity. Any fluctuation in demand has Titan firms attempt to maintain profit margins by decreasing output and employment, undesirable excess capacity emerges. Quantity adjustment often trumps price adjustment. There are not adequate profitable investment opportunities for the system to fully absorb the excess surplus in productive investment activity; thus, systemic reproduction requires *waste* to avoid the normal state of stagnation. Monopoly capital organization gives political advantage to capital over labor in the class struggle, increasing the rate of exploitation, and establishing superexploitation of the most vulnerable workers. Additional struggles exist between firms, where the control over price decisions by Titan corporations generates a hierarchy of profits rates, roughly ordered based on size of firm and relative 'degree of monopoly' and political power. The excess capacity significantly increases the potential rate of capital accumulation. In turn this generates a gap (or fundamental contradiction) between potential output (exchange value) and surplus absorption (use value); this fundamental contradiction manifests stagnation. "Waste" is the primary mechanism to overcome the fundamental contradiction. The sale effort, redistribution toward non-producing classes, government spending, and above all finance are the primary forms of waste, each manifesting new contradictions and problems for the system.

Conclusion: The Double Revolution of Monopoly Capital Theory

The first epigraph of *Monopoly Capital* is from Hegel who proclaimed: "*The truth is the whole.*" Baran and Sweezy sketch an essay that provides a theory and analysis of oligopolized capitalism capable of explaining the multifaceted social and ecology elements of the American economic system and global order.

The publication of *Monopoly Capital* by Baran and Sweezy was a pioneering and revolutionary advance in understanding twentieth century United States and global order. It placed the mega-corporations at the center of the social order and oligopolization as the essential feature of the social physiology. This aspect was an elaboration of Marxian political economy as initiated by Dobb, Kalecki, Sweezy, Steindl, and Baran. The real revolutionary thrust of Baran and Sweezy, albeit more tentative and exploratory than the monopoly capital elaboration on Marxian political economy, was their analysis on the quality of social being in an oligopolized order of social life. Baran and Sweezy were deeply concerned by the *degradations* of mental health, family life, race relations, democratic ideals and political participation, and human rights more generally. They were equally wary of the tendencies of increasing inequality, persistent poverty, impoverished schooling and the lack of learning and the fragmentation of knowledge. They argued media, cultural and leisure activities, along with teaching and knowledge production had come to reflect the dehumanized goals and profit driven aspirations of undemocratic totalitarian-designed oligopolized capitalism.

Monopoly capitalism economically tends towards stagnation, undesired excess capacity, inequality, instability, underemployment, and degradation of the work and the workplace. More sociologically, monopoly capitalism "for all the productivity and wealth which it has generated, has utterly failed to provide the foundations of a society capable of promoting the healthy and happy development of its members" (Baran and Sweezy 1966, 285). The Baran and Sweezy-inspired themes of political economy, culture, ecology, and human rights in the context of oligopolized capitalism have been further explicated and developed by thousands of theorists in thousands of articles and hundreds of books as well documented in the pages of *Monthly Review* and in book catalogues of Monthly Review Press.

References

Amin, S. 1976. *Unequal Development: An Essay on the Social Formations of Peripheral Capitalism.* New York: Monthly Review Press.

——. 1977. *Imperialism and Unequal Development.* New York: Monthly Review Press.

Baran, P. 1957. *The Political Economy of Growth.* New York: Monthly Review Press.

Baran, P. and P. Sweezy. 1966. *Monopoly Capital: An Essay on the American Economic and Social Order*. New York: Monthly Review Press.

Braverman, H. 1974. *Labor and Monopoly Capitalism: The Degradation of Work in the Twentieth Century*. New York: Monthly Review Press.

Chamberlin, E. 1933. *Theory of Monopolistic Competition*. Cambridge, MA: Harvard University Press.

Despain, H. G. 2009. "Review: *The Great Financial Crisis: Causes and Consequences*, by John Bellamy Foster and Fred Magdoff." *Journal of Economic Issues* 43(4): 1075–1077.

——. 2013. "Review Article: *The Endless Crisis: How Monopoly-Finance Capital Produces Stagnation and Upheaval from USA to China*, by John Bellamy Foster and Robert W. McChesney." *Marx and Philosophy Review of Books*, January 30th: http://marxandphilosophy.org.uk/reviewofbooks/reviews/2013/694 (accessed October 12, 2016).

——. 2014. "Review Article: *The Theory of Monopoly Capitalism: An Elaboration of Marxian Political Economy*, by John Bellamy Foster." *Marx and Philosophy Review of Books*, July 14th: http://marxandphilosophy.org.uk/reviewofbooks/reviews/2014/1076 (accessed October 12, 2016).

——. 2015. "Secular Stagnation: Mainstream versus Marxian Traditions." *Monthly Review* 67(4): 39–55.

——. 2016a. "Maurice Herbert Dobb (1900–1976)." In *The Palgrave Companion to Cambridge Economics*, R. Cord, ed., 623–648. New York: Palgrave Macmillan.

——. Forthcoming. "Why Secular Stagnation?: Larry Summers and Monopoly Power." *Monthly Review*.

Dobb, M. 1925. *Capitalist Enterprise and Social Progress*. London: Routledge & Kegan Paul.

——. 1937. *Political Economy and Capitalism*. London: Routledge & Kegan Paul.

——. 1946. *Studies in the Development of Capitalism*. London: Routledge & Kegan Paul.

——. 1951. *Some Aspects of Economic Development: Three Lectures*. London: Routledge & Kegan Paul.

——. 1973. *Theories of Value and Distribution since Adam Smith*. Cambridge: Cambridge University Press.

Foster, J. B. 1987. "What is Stagnation?" In *The Imperiled Economy: Macroeconomics from a Left Perspective*, R. Cherry, et. al. eds. New York: Union for Radical Political Economics.

——. 2014. *The Theory of Monopoly Capitalism: An Elaboration of Marxian Political Economy*. New York: Monthly Review Press.

Foster, J. B. and F. Magdoff. 2009. *The Great Financial Crisis*. New York: Monthly Review Press.

Foster, J. B. and R. W. McChesney. 2012. *The Endless Crisis: How Monopoly-Finance Capital Produces Stagnation and Upheaval from the USA to China*. New York: Monthly Review Press.

Frank, A. G. 1967. *Capitalism and Underdevelopment in Latin America*. New York: Monthly Review Press.

Halevi, J. and Y. Varoufakis. 2003. "The Global Minotaur." *Monthly Review* 55(3): 56–74.

Hansen, A. 1954. "Growth or Stagnation in the American Economy." *Review of Economics and Statistics* 36(4): 409–414.

——. 1955. "The Stagnation Thesis." In *Readings in Fiscal Policy*, A. Smithies and J. K. Butters, eds., 540–557. Homewood, IL: Richard D. Irwin.

Jonna, R. J. and J. B. Foster. 2014. "Beyond the Degradation of Labor: Braverman and the Structure of the U.S. Working Class." *Monthly Review* 66(5): 1–23.

——. 2016. "Marx's Theory of Working-Class Precariousness: Its Relevance Today." *Monthly Review* 67(11): 1–21.

Kalecki, M. 1939. *Essays in the Theory of Economic Fluctuations*. New York: Russell and Russell.

——. 1971. *Selected Essays on the Dynamics of the Capitalist Economy*. Cambridge: Cambridge University Press.

——. 2009. *Theory of Economic Dynamics: An Essay on Cyclical and Long-Run Changes in Capitalist Economy*. New York: Monthly Review Press.

Lapavitsas, C. 2013. *Profiting without Producing: How Finance Exploits Us All*. London: Verso.

Magdoff, H. 1968. *The Age of Imperialism: The Economics of U.S. Foreign Policy*. New York: Monthly Review Press.

——. 1978. *Imperialism: From Colonial Age to the Present*. New York: Monthly Review Press.

Magdoff, H. and J. B. Foster. 2003. *Imperialism without Colonies*. New York: Monthly Review Press.

Magdoff, H. and P. M. Sweezy. 1983. "Production and Finance." *Monthly Review* 35(1): 1–13.

Marcuzzo, M. C. 2007. "The 'First' Imperfect Competition Revolution." In *A Companion to the History of Economic Thought*, W. J. Samuels, J. E. Biddle, and J. B. Davis, eds. Malden, MA: Blackwell Publishing.

Robinson, J. 1933. T*he Economics of Imperfect Competition*. London: Macmillian.

——. 1969. *The Economics of Imperfect Competition*, 2nd edition. London: Macmillan

Samuelson, P. 1967. "The Monopolistic Competition Revolution." In *Monopolistic Competition Theory: Studies in Impact*, R. E. Kuenne, ed. New York: John Wiley & Sons.

Smith, J. 2016. *Imperialism in the Twenty-First Century: Globalization, Super-Exploitation, and Capitalism's Final Crisis*. New York: Monthly Review Press.

Sraffa, P. 1926. "The Laws of Returns under Competitive Conditions." *Economic Journal* 36(144): 535–550.

Steindl, J. 1952. *Maturity and Stagnation in American Capitalism*. Oxford: Oxford University Institute of Statistics Monographs.

——. 1984. "On Maturity in Capitalist Economics." In *The Faltering Economy: The Problem of Accumulation Under Monopoly Capitalism*, J. B. Foster and H. Szlajfer eds. New York: Monthly Review Press.

Sweezy, P. 1939. "Demand under Conditions of Oligopoly." *Journal of Political Economy* 47(4): 68–73.

——. 1942. *The Theory of Capitalist Development: Principles of Marxian Political Economy*. New York: Monthly Review Press.

——. 1954. "Maturity and Stagnation in American Capitalism." *Econometrica* 22(4): 531–533.

——. 1994. "The Triumph of Financial Capital." *Monthly Review* 46(2): 1–11.

——. 2004. "Monopoly Capitalism." *Monthly Review* 56(5): 1–10.

Sweezy, P. M. and H. Magdoff. 1972. *The Dynamics of U.S. Capitalism*. New York: Monthly Review Press.

Szlajfer, H. 1984. "Economic Surplus and Surplus Value Under Monopoly Capitalism." In *The Faltering Economy: The Problem of Accumulation Under Monopoly Capitalism*, J. B. Foster and H. Szlajfer eds. New York: Monthly Review Press.

36

MARXISM, FEMINISM AND THE HOUSEHOLD

Drucilla K. Barker and Suzanne Bergeron

At the intersection of Marxism and feminism lies a rich and diverse set of perspectives on the question of women, class and the household. Over the past fifty years, there have been significant debates within this literature about issues such as the conceptualization of work, the value of non-market production, the role of the household in the economy, the nature of instability and change in society, and the role of social reproduction in our vision of an equitable future. In this chapter, we provide a broad overview of these debates.

We begin by noting that Marx did not focus much on this issue in his published theories of capitalism and class. However, he did offer some discussion on the topic, for instance when discussing the tensions that working class women face in the household in *Capital Vol. 1* (Marx [1876] 1976) and critiquing the bourgeois family as oppressive to women in the *Communist Manifesto* (Marx and Engels, [1848] 1998). Engels' *Origin of the Family, Private Property and the State* more directly addresses the location of women in/and households in capitalist societies (Engels [1884] 2010). It is often viewed by Marxist-feminists as a foundational text (Benston 1969; Leacock 1974). In *Origins*, Engels challenges the commonly held idea that eternal and universal patriarchal power dynamics are the cause of gender inequity, replacing it with a historical view. Prior to the emergence of private property, he contends, societies were largely egalitarian when it came to gender. But with the emergence of private property and capitalism, this changed for a number of reasons. First, with the rise of private property, production for exchange replaced the production of use values that characterized primitive communism. With this shift production also increasingly occurred outside of the household and became intensified. This excluded women because they were no longer able to combine productive and reproductive work in use-value production as they had in the past. Second, private property ushered in a nuclear family form aimed at controlling women's sexuality and thus ensuring the legitimacy of heirs. While initially instituted among the propertied classes, the patriarchal family ideal eventually spread through society. While these shifts were uneven and contested, the household eventually became a place to which most women were relegated to a life of relative drudgery.

In the 1960s and 1970s, an emerging Marxist-feminist scholarship drew upon Engels' analysis to explain women's oppression, but with an important twist. It identified the household not only as a site of reproductive labor but as a site of production itself, where women's unpaid labor made an essential yet neglected contribution to the economy (Oakley 1974).

Feminists working in this vein coined the term "domestic labor" to describe unpaid house-work and care work, labor that was both devalued and necessary for the support and maintenance of productive labor within capitalism. Their strategies focused on making this work visible and valuable. The "Wages for Housework" movement, for instance, argued that because domestic labor contributed to production and surplus value by reproducing labor power, it should be compensated within the capitalist system (Dalla Costa and James 1972; Federici 1975). One conclusion that seemed to follow was that women getting wages for housework would have the bargaining power of waged workers and thus be able to wrest some surplus back from the capitalist class. Not all feminists working on these topics called for wages for housework, but many argued in a similar manner that the exploitation of women's work in the household was analogous to the exploitation of the proletariat and contributed to surplus value. Others, however, challenged this analogy between the proletariat and housewives on various grounds related to the calculability of women's household labor and the method by which surplus was extracted in the household. For instance, some argued that the household sphere, because it fosters relationships and emotional attachment, is not analogous to detached, commodified market labor (Himmelweit and Mohun 1977; Himmelweit 1995). These differences have been dubbed the "domestic labor debates" and generated a significant literature on whether Marxian measures of value and surplus value extraction could be extended to women's work in the household (see Delphy and Leonard 1980; Gardiner 1975; Himmelweit 1995; Molyneux 1979; Seccombe 1974).

By the late 1970s another strand of analysis emerged to challenge what was seen as the class-determinist frame of the earlier Marxist-feminist approach. These writers, often referred to as "socialist feminists," argued that reference to capitalist logic alone fails to identify why women are oppressed specifically as women. As the anthropologist Gayle Rubin put it,

> to explain women's usefulness to capitalism is one thing. To argue that this useful-ness explains the genesis of the oppression of women is quite another…Women are oppressed in societies which can by no stretch of the imagination be described as capitalist.
>
> *(Rubin 1975, 163)*

In a similar vein, Heidi Hartmann (1979) notes that is not only capitalists who benefit from women's household labor in contemporary society, but that men as a group also benefit from the gender division of labor in which women's devalued efforts produce goods and services in the home.

Lourdes Benería (1979) points out the basic contradiction facing women arises from the fact of their shared interests with men and their subordinate status to them. Thus it is not only the capitalist system that is at the source of women's oppression, but a dual system of capitalism and patriarchy at work (see also Eisenstein 1978). By positing the relationship between gender and class in two separate spheres, Hartmann and others working in this "dual systems" tradition have been able to theorize about the complex and contested relationship between capitalism and patriarchal household divisions of labor. For instance, as Nancy Folbre (1994) points out, the gender division of labor that relegates women to unpaid care work also makes a link between the masculinity and individual self-reliance, which masks capitalist exploitation. At the same time, this privileges paid labor as the source of wealth and human well-being. These processes also render invisible and devalue women's unpaid domestic labor, and further, even when this caring labor is performed by paid workers it is feminized, thus retaining its undervalued status.

Fraad, Resnick and Wolff (1994) build upon earlier Marxist-feminist and socialist-feminist insights regarding points of contact, complexity and contradiction between the spheres of capitalism and the household, but offer another way to make sense of how this might structure and/or undermine women's oppression. Taking an anti-essentialist class analytic approach, Fraad, Resnick and Wolff posit a landscape of economic difference in which there can exist multiple class processes within a complexly constituted economic and social system that it not entirely determined by capitalism. They then use that framework to analyze the ways in which surplus labor is produced, appropriated and distributed in households in the United States. Unlike many other theorists working on these topics, they do not posit any essential relationship between the class formation of the household, patriarchal power relations, and the needs of capitalist profitability. Rather they highlight the ways that the articulation of different economic spheres—as well as the power dynamics that underlie women's subordination—are changing, contextual and contradictory.

Further, unlike dual systems approaches, Fraad, Resnick and Wolff write about economic processes as distinct—although by no means determinant—from the political (such as patriarchal power dynamics) and social. While they identify the feudal class process in which dependent wives have their housework appropriated by husbands as the dominant form of household class system in the United States, they also discuss the existence of communal households, single adults who self-appropriate their surplus labor, and so forth. This focus on a variety of possible class processes, which are themselves relatively autonomous from capitalist class processes and for which capitalism is not determinant, challenges both singular-logic and dual-logic explanations for the exploitation of women's labor. It also creates space for examining interactions and contradictions among the mix of class processes and non-class processes—such as gender ideologies—that structure women's oppression.

The development of Fraad, Resnick and Wolff's anti-essentialist notion of class in the 1980s occurred at the same time that feminist theorists were questioning essentialist framings of gender itself, and positing new models that stressed the diversity of women's experiences (Spelman 1988). Increasingly, feminists examining the impact of class and gender on women's lives recognized that women are not a unified class, but face intersecting oppressions based on gender, race, sexuality and class differences (e.g. Joseph 1981; Molyneux 1979). bell hooks (1984), for instance, noted famously that the dominant feminist idea of women's liberation through equality in the labor force ignored the questions of which particular women had always engaged in paid labor and which had not, which had access to the "good jobs," and which would take care of the children and do the housework that those (white, middle class) women left behind. As Angela Davis (1983) argued, too often it was turning out that black women in the United States had to do their own housework and other women's as well. Attention to racial and class differences in relation to household labor is therefore crucial to both understanding and transforming conditions of class exploitation and gender oppression at the nexus of the household and the capitalist firm.

By the late 1980s, there was waning interest in the terms of the domestic labor debate around the role of women's unpaid labor in the capitalist economy and the household, and new ways of integrating Marxism and feminism emerged. In part, the abstractions involved in analyzing necessary and surplus labor were at odds with the complexities of concrete historical analysis and issues of agency and subjectivity that were increasingly being centered in studies of exploitation by both gender and class (Vogel 2000). In addition, by the 1970s and 1980s in the global North there was a decline in industry and a corresponding expansion of the service sector, including paid care work, that increasingly blurred the binaries of market/household, capitalism/ reproduction upon which domestic labor theories rest (Weeks 2007). Further, global restructuring transformed the nature of domestic labor and social reproduction. The declining dominance of the male bread-winner household and nuclear family form, rising global women's labor force participation, increased labor migration and global householding contributed to the emergence of other ways of thinking through the relationship between gender, household labor and capitalism.

This shift led to a number of different strands of analysis at the intersection of Marxism and feminism. The concept of social reproduction emerged to capture what had previously been termed domestic labor and to more broadly conceptualize the unpaid and paid reproduction of the labor force, such as meeting the care needs for children, adults, appropriately socializing children, and even necessary care of the self (Bakker and Gill 2003; March and Runyan 2000; Nakano Glenn 1992; Peterson 2003). Some work in this area focused on the ways that capitalism was depleting social reproductive labor by placing more and more burdens on women. For instance, neoliberal restructuring policies in the 1980s and 1990s cut government supports for care work and put the burden onto women's unpaid labor in households to pick up the slack (Elson and Cagatay 2000), creating a depletion of care on the global stage (Hoskyns and Rai 2007). At the same time, women were increasingly drawn into low-paid service jobs as this work was shifted to the market. This rearranging of boundaries between household/market and reproductive/productive work thus resulted in both a privatization of reproductive work formerly provided socially, and a commodification of care work (Barker and Feiner 2004).

In the wake of these crises of care and new forms of gender and class exploitation related to women's role in social reproduction, the issues initially raised in the domestic labor debates have recently seen a resurgence (Weeks 2011; Federici 2012; Vogel 2000; Vrasti 2016). These scholars contend that the quotidian tasks of cooking, cleaning, raising children, caring for the elderly, and caring for one's self are central not only to the workings of capitalism but also to the functioning of any society regardless of its economic organization. Confining them to the boundaries of the patriarchal family, however veils their importance. In the current conjuncture, this justifies the neoliberal indifference of capital and the state to the costs of social reproduction.

For example, in the introduction to her book *Revolution at Point Zero*, Silvia Federici (2012) revisits her involvement in the Wages for Housework (WfH) movement in the 1970s. In her telling of the story, proponents WfH viewed housework as the foundation for capitalism and saw class struggle not only among the male proletariat but also among the "enslaved, the colonized, the world of wageless workers...and the proletarian housewife" (Federici 2012, 7). WfH was informed by the Italian concept of the "social factory," a stage in capitalism wherein "every social relation is subsumed under capital and the distinction between society and factory collapses" (Ibid.). That is, exploitation is not confined to the work-place but in the constitution of everyday life. The social factory began and was centered in the kitchen, the bedroom, and the home. In Federici's telling, WfH was not a demand for actual wages as it was a call for revolution. In her 1975 essay, "Wages Against Housework," she argued,

> Many times the difficulties and ambiguities which women express in discussing wages for housework stem from the fact that they reduce wages for housework to a thing, a lump of money, instead of viewing it as a political perspective...
>
> *(Federici 1975, 75)*

The movement, then, was about the dual goals of demystifying women's subordination and revealing the mechanisms through which capitalism maintains its power and keeps the working class divided. Understanding the movement as a revolutionary gesture aimed at undermining capitalism is quite different from thinking about it in terms of paying wages to housewives. The demand for wages for housework was, then, a demand for the ability to refuse housework and to refuse the privatized form of the family as the sole guarantor of reproductive labor.

Kathi Weeks has a similar reading of the WfH literature informed by Hardt and Negri's autonomous Marxism and stated in terms of the demand for basic income (Weeks 2011). In the structural shifts that have characterized the past fifty years, the relationship between production and reproduction has become far more complex than the one mapped by the WfH movement in the 1970s. As discussed above, the line between production and reproduction has become blurred as the goods formally provided by the family are replaced by commodities and services such as eldercare and childcare are now forms of waged employment. Just as reproduction has come to more closely resemble production, production has come to resemble reproduction in the sense that not only are physical goods produced but also immaterial affects, "social landscapes, communicative contexts and cultural forms" (Weeks 2011, 141). Affective labor is one type of immaterial labor, the labor of human contact and interaction. It is both corporeal and affective in the sense that its products are intangible feelings of well-being, satisfaction, and so forth, producing social networks and forms of community. Thus reproductive labor, the production of producers and consumers with the attitude, affective capacities, and communication skills required by a post-industrial economy is no longer confined to the family or household, but rather is the result of larger social processes (Hardt and Negri 2000).

This point about production is crucial to Week's call for a basic income as it is has become more and more difficult to identify precisely who the workers are who have created the tangible and intangible products of immaterial labor. Just as the demand for wages for housework revealed the dependence of waged labor on reproductive labor, the demand for basic income reveals the ways that all people contribute to society in various ways regardless of whether they have monetary value or even measurable (McKay and Vanevery 2000, cited in Weeks 2011). The demand for basic income breaks the link between wages and income and reveals the arbitrariness of which activities are waged and which are not. This move has the potential to reveal the workings of gender, class, race and colonial power that have resulted in an ever increasing disparity between the rich and poor.

The post-industrial, informational economy described by Weeks is also a global economy. Globalization, guided by neoliberal policy agendas, has led to dramatic changes in the ways that social reproduction is structured. Although the processes through which labor power is reproduced are undergoing dramatic changes, domestic labor remains at the center (Federici 2012; Vogel 2000; Vrasti 2016). Globalization has resulted in an increase in the participation of women all over the world in waged labor, but on a highly unequal basis. The women who hold good jobs—whether as knowledge workers in the information economy, as executives and managers in traditional industries, or as professionals in the service sector—are well compensated for their labor, while other, feminized workers—male as well as female—assemble products or provide services necessary for the daily functioning of highly paid workers (Peterson 2003). These services are provided by women and men on the bottom of the ladder of privilege, many of whom are migrant workers from the global South. While partially alleviating the crises of social reproduction in the global North, their own lives are marked by poverty and precarity. These workers are what have been termed "disposable populations"—dangerous, disenfranchised and undeserving of the rights and privileges of human dignity (Chang 2000). As Gutiérrez-Rodríguez notes, waged domestic work is linked to the "dehumanization of those who work to ensure that others have agreeable surroundings for living and recreating life" (Gutiérrez-Rodríguez 2007, 72).

A different approach is taken by J.K. Gibson-Graham, who holds that much of the feminist literature on social reproduction, while highly imaginative and politically powerful, also troublingly represents the economy as a singular space of capitalist logic. For example, the social reproduction and globalization literature described above typically adds reproductive labor to the equation in order get a more complete picture of the "logic" of capitalism, rather than taking the opening to challenge the idea of a singular logic itself (Gibson-Graham 2008). In contrast, Gibson-Graham, drawing upon the anti-essentialist class theoretic approach of Resnick and Wolff (1987) and Fraad, Resnick and Wolff (1994) explicitly emphasizes economic difference to signify the possibility for enacting post-capitalist alternatives. For example, rather than presenting the super-exploitation of women as an inevitability of crises of capitalism, Gibson-Graham highlights the unevenness of these processes and the diversity of responses. While it is true that women in some households may be squeezed in terms of increased reproductive labor burdens, other households may also be transformed to more egalitarian structures, while still others may turn away from capitalist and/or patriarchal relations to create alternative paid and unpaid ways of meeting care needs such as through cooperatives and gift economies in ways that challenge capitalist subjectivities and goals. Jenny Cameron's (1996) research on households in Australia, for instance, highlights a diversity of class forms that include some divisions of labor in which women assume the care role, others in which men and women head independent households, and partner households that have a more cooperative structure. Maliha Safri and Julie Graham's (2010) research on global households highlights the emergence of communal householding and post-capitalist subjectivities among Mexican men who have migrated to the United States. Stephen Healy (2008) has examined how informal caregiving for the elderly has introduced a new division of labor in households that is not limited to a privatized care squeeze, but includes community-based mutual aid practices. McKay (2004) finds that structural changes have taken place in Filipino transnational families with men taking up traditionally female tasks such as child care and laundry, while returned women enter the traditionally masculine sphere of government. This suggests that the contours of household production may, in a range of different contexts, be shifting away from a gender division of labor, organized under a patriarchal mode of production, toward a collective or communal mode of production in which men and women share decision making and production responsibilities.

Looking at the relationship between the market and household in this way allows for the household itself to register as a site of class struggle and possibility for reducing care burdens, rather than a ready-made site for capitalist exploitation. Using this diverse economy lens also moves us away from essentialist gendered framings of women as always already careers in presumably heterosexual households (Bedford 2009; Bergeron 2011). Further de-essentializing both gender and class, this recognition that many households represent alternative forms of economy outside of the patriarchal and heterosexual norm such as individually-headed, cooperative, care among friends, etc., makes it becomes impossible to assume a particular division of labor from which a feminized caring subjectivity springs.

Rethinking the class system and the gender division of labor is also the project of Wanda Vrasti (2016). She begins by noting that today's economic crises are simultaneously a crisis of social reproduction and a crisis of imagination. Social reproduction is no longer the exclusive concern of women, and really it never was. It is more than just domestic labor; it includes the provision of housing, education, health care, municipal services including transportation, sanitation and utilities, and old age security. One of the consequences of neoliberal policy making is that the costs of social reproduction previously assumed by governments and employers are shifted onto individuals and families, making it increasingly difficult to meet their basic needs (Roberts 2013). The crisis of imagination identified by Vrasti is that neoliberal dogma about the naturalness of capitalist market relations as best way to organize society still holds despite all evidence to the contrary. The two crises are complementary; an answer to the crisis of imagination lies in conceiving of a politics of resistance that is also a politics of reconstruction and reproduction. Anti-capitalist strategies must work toward a form life that is opposed to "the individualizing morality of debt and work" (Vrasti 2016, 249). She proposes that the feminist perspectives and practices engendered by the materialist feminism of the 1970s, especially the WfH contributions, are tools for combating the isolation and fractures imposed by capitalism. Contesting the gender division of labor, by making reproductive work a central, equally shared, and valued activity is necessary to creating sustainable cultures of resistance, or what Federici (2008) calls, self-reproducing movements. In this vision reproductive labor contains the resources and relations necessary to build solidarity among people and connect them to the world. A guiding principle of a self-reproducing movement would not be to do away with the quotidian tasks of reproduction, but to reorganize them along more participatory and egalitarian lines. It is also to do away with the distinction between production and reproduction. Examples of self-reproducing movements can be found in prefigurative communities ranging from the Black Panthers with their free breakfasts for children, to intentional communities like The Farm in Tennessee, the Zapatista movement in Mexico, the *buen vivir* movement in Latin America, and most recently the Occupy Movement. Self-reproducing movements place care and reproduction at the center of life, value and thus have the power to bring people together and promote a dimension of collective living that is fast disappearing under capitalism. Although some of these movements have been more successful than others, Vastri argues that the principles and values associated with feminism, gender equality, the provision of basic needs, socialization and care of children, and attention to emotion, have to be part of a radical politics.

In conclusion, the critical engagements of those working at the intersection of Marxism and feminism over the past fifty years has identified and challenged multiple forms of injustice in contemporary societies. By bringing together a class analysis of surplus labor production and exploitation with a feminist analysis of how power operates at the intersection of gender, class, race, nationality and sexuality, scholarship in this tradition has been able to transform the way that work and its value has been conceptualized. Further, Marxist-feminists have not simply added domestic labor to the equation, although that in itself is an important contribution. They have also transformed our vision of the entire economic landscape. Work in this tradition has, for instance, highlighted the diversity of class forms in society, including previously neglected feudal and patriarchal as well as communal and egalitarian class relationships in households. In addition, by foregrounding the relationship between social reproduction and production, Marxist-feminism has offered powerful insights into the connections and slippages between capitalism and household economic forms. In doing this it has also created space for identifying instabilities and fractures within our current gender and class systems from which we can create effective movements for social change. Finally, by centering reproductive activities in our future visions, Marxist-feminism has contributed to the emergence of just, sustainable, post-capitalist alternatives.

References

Bakker, I. and S. Gill. 2003. "Power, Production and Social Reproduction." In *Power, Production and Social Reproduction: Human In/security in the Global Political Economy*, I. Bakker and S. Gill, eds., 3–16. Basingstoke: Palgrave Macmillan.

Barker, D. K. and S. Feiner. 2004. *Liberating Economics: Feminist Perspectives on Families, Work, and Globalization*. Ann Arbor: University of Michigan Press.

Bedford, K. 2009. *Developing partnerships: Gender, Sexuality, and the Reformed World Bank*. Minneapolis: University of Minnesota Press.

Benería, L. 1979. "Reproduction, Production and the Sexual Division of Labour." *Cambridge Journal of Economics* 3(3): 203–225.

Benston, M. 1969. "The Political Economy of Women's Liberation." *Monthly Review* 21: 13–27.

Bergeron, S. 2011. "Economics, Performativity and Social Reproduction in Global Development." *Globalizations* 8(2): 15–25.

Cameron, J. 1996. "Throwing a Dishcloth into the Works: Troubling Theories of Domestic Labor." *Rethinking Marxism* 9(2): 24–44.

Chang, G. 2000. *Disposable domestics: Immigrant Women Workers in the Global Economy*. Cambridge, MA: South End Press.

Dalla Costa, M. D. and S. James. 1972. *The Power of Women and the Subversion of the Community*. Bristol: Falling Wall Press.

Davis, A. Y. 1983. *Women, Race & Class*. New York: Vintage Books.

Delphy, C. and D. Leonard. 1980. "A Materialist Feminism Is Possible." *Feminist Review* 4: 79–105.

Eisenstein, I. 1978. *Capitalist Patriarchy and the Case for Socialist Feminism*. New York: Monthly Review Press.

Elson, D. and N. Cagatay. 2000. "The Social Content of Macroeconomic Policies." *World Development* 28(7): 1347–1364.

Engels, F. 2010. *The Origin of the Family, Private Property and the State*. London: Penguin Classics.

Federici, S. 1975. *Wages against Housework*. London: Power of Women Collective.

———. 2008. "Precarious Labour: A Feminist Perspective." *The Journal of Aesthetics and Protest* 1(9): 21–35.

———. 2012. *Revolution at Point Zero: Housework, Reproduction, and Feminist Struggle*. Oakland, CA: PM Press.

Folbre, N. 1994. *Who Pays for the Kids?: Gender and the Structures of Constraint*. London: Routledge.

Fraad, H., S. A. Resnick, and R. D. Wolff. 1994. *Bringing It All Back Home: Class, Gender, and Power in the Modern Household*. London: Pluto Press.

Gardiner, J. 1975. "Women's Domestic Labor." *New Left Review* 69: 47–58.

Gibson-Graham, J. K. 2008. "Diverse Economies: Performative Practices for 'Other' Worlds." *Progress in Human Geography* 32(5): 613–632.

Glenn, E. N. 1992. "From Servitude to Service Work: Historical Continuities in the Racial Division of Paid Reproductive Labor." *Signs: Journal of Women in Culture and Society* 18(1): 1–43.

Gutiérrez-Rodríguez, E. 2007. "Reading Affect-On the Heterotopian Spaces of Care and Domestic Work in Private Households." *Forum: Qualitative Social Research*. www.qualitative-research.net/index.php/fqs/article/view/240 (accessed June 5, 2016).

Hardt, M. and A. Negri. 2000. *Empire*. Cambridge, MA: Harvard University Press.

Hartmann, H. 1979. "The Unhappy Marriage of Marxism and Feminism." *Capital and Class* 3(2): 1–33.

Healy, S. 2008. "Caring for Ethics and the Politics of Health Care Reform." *Gender, Place and Culture* 15(3): 267–284.

Himmelweit, S. 1995. "The Discovery of 'Unpaid Work': The Social Consequences of the Expansion of 'Work'." *Feminist Economics* 1(2): 1–19.

Himmelweit, S. and S. Mohun. 1977. "Domestic Labour and Capital." *Cambridge Journal of Economics* 1(1): 15–31.

hooks, b. 1984. *Feminist Theory from Margin to Center*. Boston: South End Press.

Hoskyns, C. and S. Rai 2007. "Recasting the Global Political Economy: Counting Women's Unpaid Work." *New Political Economy* 12(3): 277–317.

Joseph, G. 1981. "The Incompatible Ménage-a-trois: Marxism, Feminism and Racism." In *Women and Revolution: A Discussion of the Unhappy Marriage of Marxism and Feminism*, L. Sargent, ed. Boston: South End Press.

Leacock, E. 1972. Introduction to Frederick Engels, *The Origin of the Family, Private Property and the State*. New York: International Publishers.

March, M. H. and A. S. Runyon. 2000. *Gender and Global Restructuring: Sightings, Signs, Resistances*. New York: Routledge.

Marx, K. 1976. *Capital*, Volume 1. Trans. by B. Fowkes. Hardmonsworth: Penguin Books.

Marx, K., F. Engels, and E. J. Hobsbawm. 1998. *The Communist Manifesto: A Modern Edition*. London: Verso.

McKay, A. and J. Vanevery. 2000. "Gender, Family, and Income Maintenance: A Feminist Case for Citizens Basic Income." *Social Politics: International Studies in Gender, State & Society* 7(2): 266–284.

McKay, D. 2004. "Performing Identities, Creating Cultures of Circulation: Filipina Migrants Between Home and Abroad." Paper presented at the 15th Biennial Conference of the Asian Studies Association of Australia, Canberra.

Molyneux, M. 1979. "Beyond the Domestic Labor Debate." *New Left Review* 116(3): 3–27.

Nakano Glenn, E. 1992. "From Servitude to Service Work: Historical Continuities in the Racial Division of Paid Reproductive Labor." *Signs* 18(1): 1–43.

Oakley, A. 1974. *The Sociology of Housework*. New York: Pantheon.

Peterson, V. S. 2003. *A Critical Re-Writing of Global Political Economy: Integrating Reproductive, Productive and Virtual Economies*. New York: Routledge.

Resnick, S. A. and R. D. Wolff. 1987. *Knowledge and Class: A Critique of Political Economy*. Chicago: University of Chicago Press.

Roberts, A. 2013. "Financing Social Reproduction: The Gendered Relations of Debt and Mortgage Finance in Twenty-First-Century America." *New Political Economy* 18(1): 21–42.

Rubin, G. 1975. "The Traffic in Women: Notes on the Political Economy of Sex." In *Toward an Anthropology of Women*, R. R. Reiter, ed., 157–210. New York: Monthly Review Press.

Safri, M. 2009. "Economic Effects of Remittances on Immigrant and Non-Immigrant Households." In *Class Struggle on the Homefront Work, Conflict, and Exploitation in the Household*, G. Cassano, ed., 176–196. New York: Palgrave Macmillan.

Safri, M. and J. Graham. 2010. "The Global Household: Toward a Feminist Postcapitalist International Political Economy." *Signs* 36(1): 99–125.

Seccombe, W. 1974. "Housework under Capitalism." *New Left Review* 83: 85–96.

Spelman, E. V. 1988. *Inessential Woman: Problems of Exclusion in Feminist Thought*. Boston: Beacon Press.

Vastri, W. 2016. "Reproducing Movements and the Enduring Challenges of Materialist Feminism." In *Scandalous Economics*, A. A. Hozić and J. True, eds., 248–265. New York: Oxford University Press.

Vogel, L. 2000. "Domestic Labor Revisited." *Science & Society* 64(2): 151–170.

Weeks, K. 1978. "Life Within and Against Work: Affective Labor, Feminist Critique, and Post-Fordist Politics." *Ephemera* 7(1): 233–249.

———. 2011. *The Problem with Work: Feminism, Marxism, Antiwork Politics, and Postwork Imaginaries*. Durham: Duke University Press.

37

MARXISM AND ECOLOGY

Brett Clark and Stefano B. Longo

Following the Second World War, the scale and rate of human disruption of the planetary system dramatically increased, contributing to what is now called the "Great Acceleration" in the modern ecological crisis (Angus 2016; Hamilton and Grinevald 2015; Steffen et al. 2015; Waters et al. 2016). In response, a global environmental movement protested the proliferation of pollution, the intensification of demands placed on natural resources, the degradation of ecosystems and the risks associated with atomic and nuclear weapons. In the 1960s and 1970s, the environmental movement gained traction, demanding fundamental changes in society.

During this period, many critical assessments presented analyses that detailed how social processes, especially capitalist economic growth, contributed to environmental problems. Rachel Carson (1962) provided an in-depth account of the dangers and deaths associated with the bioaccumulation of pesticides throughout the food web. She insisted that the principal causes of ecological degradation were "the gods of profit and production" (Carson 1998, 210). Her assessment of the ecological circumstances led her to conclude that corporate enterprise "worships the gods of speed and quantity, and of the quick and easy profit, and out of this idolatry monstrous evils have arisen" (Carson 1998, 194). Barry Commoner (1967; 1971) examined the environmental and health hazards associated with radioactive fallout and chemical pollution. He proposed that the capitalist productive system, especially following the Second World War, given the expansion of synthetic chemicals, had contributed to a fundamental break in the human relationship with the planet, accelerating the degradation of ecological conditions. Club of Rome analysts, utilizing a series of statistical models assessing the relationship between population growth, economic development and availability of natural resources, warned that there are distinct natural limits to social systems, which if surpassed would exceed Earth's carrying capacity and cause serious ecological deterioration and harmful human impacts (Meadows et al. 1972). Murray Bookchin detailed a broad range of environmental concerns, including soil degradation, urban decay, food contamination, and air, water and land pollution. He warned of an "environmental breakdown" that "stems not merely from greed but from a market-oriented system in which everything is reduced to a commodity, in which everyone is reduced to a mere buyer or seller, and in which every economic dynamic centers on capital accumulation. Hence the prevailing society is *inherently* antiecological" (Bookchin 1974, xxxiii). These classic studies contributed to an awareness of ecological limits and problems, while raising critical questions regarding unfettered economic growth.

Furthermore, there has been a revival of Marxian scholarship related to ecological thought within most disciplines, addressing such issues as the domination of nature, natural limits, the dialectical relationship between humans and nature, green politics, sustainable development and productivism (see Benton 1989; Gareau 2008; Gorz 1983; 1994; Hughes 2000; Kovel 2002; Leiss 1974; Schmidt 1970; Vlachou 2005). In what follows, we outline three distinct, yet overlapping, approaches in ecological Marxism. We limit our discussion to these political-economic perspectives—namely the treadmill of production, the second contradiction of capitalism and metabolic analysis—because of their assessments of the dynamics of capitalism in relation to the biophysical world and their influential role in the advance of ecological Marxism.

Capitalism: Endless Accumulation

Influenced by Karl Marx and writing during the Second World War, Karl Polanyi—in *The Great Transformation* (first published in 1944)—describes how the emergence of market-based societies transformed social and ecological relationships. He indicates that prior to the rise of capitalism, economic systems of production and consumption were embedded within the institutions and cultural practices of societies as well as the larger ecological complex. Labor and distributional activities had previously been more likely influenced by principles of behavior, including householding, reciprocity and redistribution, that tended to increase social cohesion and solidarity. In other words, societies through various social norms and customs regulated economic activities, directing them to serve particular ends, such as human needs. As a result, "the economic system is run on non-economic motives ... as a mere function of social organization," which helps keep most impulses to gain in check (Polanyi 1957, 49, 74–5).

The advent and expansion of capitalism progressively changed human and ecological relationships. Polanyi, similar to Marx, explains that under a capitalist market economy social life becomes subordinated to the requirements of the economic realm. He indicates that "all transactions are turned into money transactions"—in order to meet the needs of capital (Polanyi 1957, 44, 132; see also Marx 1976). The new self-regulated economy becomes "disembedded" from social, cultural and ecological relations, which had previously regulated and constrained its operations. The capitalist economy imposes a novel order, or system of operation, because "a market economy can exist only in a market society." It expands and intensifies the commodification process. All aspects of the social and natural world—"the substance of society"—are subordinated "to the laws of the market" (Polanyi 1957, 49, 74–5). Rather than an emphasis on the exchange of qualities, social production and consumption activities are geared toward an exchange of quantities. Polanyi (1957, 165) explains that during the transformation toward capitalist social relations "it was necessary to liquidate organic society." This "divorcedness of a separate economic motive," which is unique to capitalism, and therefore relatively new in human history, became commonplace (Polanyi 1957, 54). In this, production is primarily geared to endless gain, rather than determined by social needs and use. This "boundless and limitless" production deepens alienation and increases the overall pressures placed on the biophysical world (Polanyi 1957, 57).

Paul Sweezy, reflecting upon the unique character of the capital system and its consequences, explains:

It is this obsession with capital accumulation that distinguishes capitalism from the simple system for satisfying human needs [as] it is portrayed ... in mainstream economic theory. And a system driven by capital accumulation is one that never stands still, one that is forever changing, adopting new and discarding old methods of production and distribution, opening up new territories, subjecting to its purposes societies too weak to protect themselves. Caught up in this process of restless innovation and expansion, the system rides roughshod over even its own beneficiaries if they get in its way or fall by the roadside. As far as the natural environment is concerned, capitalism perceives it not as something to be cherished and enjoyed but as a means to the paramount ends of profit-making and still more capital accumulation.

(Sweezy 2004, 92)

Capitalism is a dynamic system, premised on endless accumulation. As a grow-or-die system, capitalist development must expand exchange value, which is seen purely as a quantitative measure (Burkett 1999; Mészáros 1995). Qualitative relations, such as the conditions of life, are not a primary part of capitalist accounting. Marx famously explained this in terms of his M-C-M' formula. Capital is understood as the "continuous transformation of capital-as-money into capital-as-commodities, followed by a retransformation of capital-as-commodities into capital-as-more-money" (Heilbroner 1985, 36). It is exchange value, which knows only quantitative increase—not use value, which relates to the qualitative aspects of production—which drives the system (Burkett 1999; Foster et al. 2010; Kovel 2002). Thus capital constantly metamorphosizes into more capital, which includes surplus value, or profits, the generation of which is "the absolute law of this mode of production" (Marx 1976, 769). This foundational tendency towards expansion pushes the economic system onward, increasing the scale and breadth of its impacts upon the biophysical world (Foster 2000; Li 2009; Marx 1976).

Treadmill of Production

The treadmill of production is a political-economic perspective that was developed to better understand why environmental degradation had increased so quickly following the Second World War. Allan Schnaiberg (1980), the original developer of the treadmill of production approach, was influenced by the work of Marxist political econo-mists such as Charles Anderson, Paul Baran, Harry Braverman, Harry Magdoff, James O'Connor, and Paul Sweezy, as well as scholars such as John Kenneth Galbraith and Gabriel Kolko.

Schnaiberg (1980) emphasized that the growth imperative of capitalism generates a type of path dependency that creates an "enduring conflict" with the environment (see also Schnaiberg and Gould 1994). He contended that "the basic social force driving the treadmill is the inherent nature of competition and concentration of capital" (Schnaiberg 1980, 230). Capitalists constantly strive to increase profits, which are reinvested and employed to support technological innovation and commodity development to enlarge and intensify production. Accumulation takes precedence and drives a cycle of growth that necessitates ever-greater production (Schnaiberg 1980). Newer technologies generally displace workers, decreasing labor costs, while also increasing the overall efficiency of commodity production. Governments—dependent on taxes—often act on behalf of capital to further "national development" and/or ensure "social security." The development project, through the

Marshall Plan and the Bretton Woods system that followed the Second World War, helped expand the global capitalist economy, increasing access to mineral and energy resources in the global South and creating new markets.

The constant pursuit of profit and expansion of capitalist commodity production has direct implications related to natural resource extraction, pollution generation and overall environmental conditions. "For ecosystems, each level of resource extraction became commodified into new profits and new investments, which led to still more rapid increases in demand for ecosystem elements" (Gould et al. 2004, 297). As a result, capitalist growth requires an ever-increasing expansion of resources (i.e., matter and energy) to meet its insatiable appetite. The consequences of this growth manifest in a general disorganization of the environment, via withdrawals and additions (Schnaiberg 1980). Withdrawals refer to extracting and consuming natural resources, such as fossil fuels, trees, nutrients and minerals. Additions include the production of wastes that are not readily incorporated and/or broken down within ecosystems. These additions can include synthetic chemicals, the accumulation of nutrients in waterways and the increasing concentration of carbon dioxide in the atmosphere. The main point of the analysis is that increasing requirements are placed on the Earth system, using matter and energy and depositing wastes, to support commodity production. Each expansion in the production process raises the demands, increasingly at a scale and rate that can exceed the ecosystem's regenerative capacity (Burkett 1999; Foster et al. 2010; Schnaiberg 1980).

K. William Kapp (1971, 231) explains that capitalism is necessarily "an economy of unpaid costs." In other words, the capitalist economic system generates an array of negative externalities—these are social and environmental costs associated with production, such as water pollution, that are displaced onto other parties (generally the public) and the natural world (see also Anderson 1976). These costs are regarded as external to market transactions. As a result, capitalist enterprises are able to increase their profit margins.

This trend has only become more pronounced as more energy-intensive materials, such as plastics and synthetic chemicals, are incorporated into manufacturing, generating widespread waste and pollution that producers externalize (Schnaiberg and Gould 1994; Pellow 2007). To make matters worse, as Thorstein Veblen (1964) as well as Paul Baran and Paul Sweezy (1966) explained, the rise of monopoly capital contributed to the creation of modern marketing, in order to create consumers for the commodities produced, further reproducing and expanding capitalism. The packaging industry, which is linked to marketing, is the third largest industry in the world after food and energy (Foster and Clark 2012; Moore 2011). This industry produces items that are almost immediately discarded upon purchase. Treadmill scholars conclude that such a society, dominated by the growth imperative of capitalism, is running endlessly, faster and faster, expending energy and resources and producing pollution and wastes at an accelerating pace.

Second Contradiction of Capitalism

The second contradiction of capitalism perspective also recognizes that capitalism is a growth-dependent economic system, predicated on constant expansion. James O'Connor, the principal proponent of this approach, focuses primarily on the inherent crises of the capitalist system. His earlier work on the fiscal crisis of the state and accumulation crises in general influenced Schnaiberg's conception of the treadmill of production (O'Connor 1973; 1984). With the second contradiction of capital, O'Connor (1998) incorporates environmental conditions into an analysis of economic crisis.

Similar to treadmill of production scholars, O'Connor (1998) argues that capitalism systematically degrades and exploits the natural environment and labor. As part of its historic development, it creates patterns of polarization and uneven development. Through imperial and colonial relationships, resources such as food and other resources were funneled from the global South to the global North, enhancing the accumulation process in the latter and the immiseration of the peoples in the former. Over time, O'Connor (1998, 189) argues, the position of the South became more complicated, as many nations in the periphery "remained raw material suppliers, some became profitable markets for the cores' surplus manufactured good, and all of them became more or less important outlets for surplus capital in the North." In some cases, capital from the North combined "advanced technology" with low-wage labor in the South in order to expand profits. One of the consequences of this pattern of uneven development is that "the worst human ecological disasters as a rule occur in the South," where pollution is geographically concentrated. Here global capital exploits natural resources, concentrates wastes and externalizes social and environmental costs to vulnerable populations, deepening inequalities throughout the world (see also Guha and Martinez-Alier 1997; Wall 2005).

Within his analysis of the global capitalist system, O'Connor (1998, 176) notes that "the first contradiction of capitalism is internal to the system; it has nothing to do with the conditions [which include natural conditions] of production." It is characterized by capital overproduction, originating out of the class struggle and the overexploitation of labor, where capital extracts added surplus by restraining labor's wages and introducing new technologies to displace labor. As a result, capital expands its production of commodities, but there is not enough money among the laboring population to consume the goods. This contradiction, it is argued, confronts capital on the demand side.

The second contradiction of capitalism, according to O'Connor, produces an economic crisis due to the underproduction of capital, which involves the degradation of the external conditions of production. The conditions of capital include the personal world of laborers insofar as they are able to reproduce their capacity to work, natural conditions, and public institutions and infrastructure that aid in the operations of society. In the endless pursuit of growth, O'Connor (1998, 165) argues, capital impairs and destroys "rather than reproducing [its] own conditions." Natural conditions, on which capital depends for raw materials, are degraded. The health of workers is diminished. An expanding economic system that plunders the environment "self-destructively" undermines the natural conditions on which it depends and produces natural barriers to further expansion, negatively affecting profitability (Kovel 2002, 39–40; O'Connor 1998, 177). As a result, it is argued, capital confronts increasing production costs to its operations, given the degeneration of natural conditions. The worsening environmental conditions are seen as a spark to ignite the environmental movements (in which class does not figure as a primary force—rather these are seen in terms of "new social movements"), which will help usher in transformations to the economic system.

Metabolism and the Metabolic Rift

Proponents of metabolic analysis returned to Marx to draw upon the ecological foundations of classical historical materialism to develop a unified socio-ecological critique. In particular, Paul Burkett (1999) and John Bellamy Foster (1999; 2000) forged a groundbreaking analysis, combined with insights from the larger political-economy tradition, regarding Marx's ecology. This approach elaborated Marx's triadic scheme of "the universal metabolism of nature," the "social metabolism" and the metabolic rift (see also Foster and Clark 2016).

Burkett (1999) revealed the "ecological value-form analysis" that is present within Marx's work, whereby a distinction is made between wealth (which for Marx includes nature as well as labor) and value (which is based on labor alone). Marx outlined the one-sidedness of value-form in capitalism. Classical political economists viewed nature as a "free gift" to capital. Thus capitalist accounting does not take into account the contributions of nature, allowing for the systemic "robbing" of nature, the invisibility of natural limits and externalization of costs to society and nature. At the center of Marx's critique of capitalism is the contradiction between wealth and value. For him, nature constitutes, along with labor, one of the two sources of all wealth. For capital, nature is not part of the value calculus, so the endless drive to accumulation results in a destructive tendency to override natural limits (Burkett 1999; Marx 1967, 745).

Marx embedded socioeconomic systems in the larger biophysical world and explicitly studied the interchange of matter and energy between the environment and society (Foster 2000; Foster and Burkett 2016). Following scientific debates and discoveries, Marx incorporated the concept of metabolism into his critique of political economy, explaining that he employed the word to denote "the 'natural' process of production as the material exchange [*Stoffwechsel*] between man and nature" (Marx 1975, 209; see also Marx and Engels 1975, 553). He detailed how there is a necessary "metabolic interaction" between humans and the earth and that labor serves as "a process between man and nature, a process by which man, through his own actions, mediates, regulates and controls the metabolism between himself and nature" (Marx 1976, 283). At the same time, capitalism is recognized as a historically specific regime of accumulation that drives the growth imperative. In this, it is a distinct social-metabolic order that operates in accord with its own logic, defining what Marx saw as the social metabolism (Mészáros 1995).

Marx contended that the social metabolism operates within the "universal metabolism of nature," which stands for the broader biophysical world with its specific cycles and processes that produce and regenerate ecological conditions (Foster 2013, 8; Marx and Engels 1988, 54–66). Under capitalist commodity production, this relationship takes on such an alienated form that it generates ecological crises, manifesting as a "rift" in the socio-ecological metabolism between society and nature. With this conception, Marx avoided subordinating nature to society, or vice versa, allowing him to elude "the pitfalls of both absolute idealism and mechanistic science" (Foster 2013, 8). His metabolic analysis recognizes that humans and the rest of nature are in constant interaction, resulting in reciprocal influences, consequences and dependencies.

The social metabolism under capitalism materializes in a manner unlike previous socio-ecological systems. The practical activities of life are shaped by the expansion and accumulation of capital. As Sweezy (2004, 86–93) explained, in their "pursuit of profit … capitalists are driven to accumulate ever more capital, and this becomes both their subjective goal and the motor force of the entire economic system." The demands of capital are imposed on nature, increasing the burdens placed on ecological systems and the production of wastes.

Marx demonstrated this social-metabolic analysis in his assessment of the transformations associated with changes in agricultural production. Studying the work of his contemporary scientists, he noted that the soil required nitrogen, phosphorus and potassium to maintain its ability to produce crops, since plants take up these nutrients as they grow. The enclosure movement and the concentration of land that accompanied the rise of capitalism resulted in a division between town and country, causing the urban population to grow. Intensive industrial agricultural techniques were introduced to increase profits from crop production. This form of agriculture produced more food on less land, and urban centers expanded. Food and fiber were shipped to distant markets, transferring the nutrients of the soil from the country to the city (as well as from the global South to the global North). After being consumed, the nutrients in these goods accumulated as waste, rather than being returned to the countryside to enrich the land. Marx (1976, 637) explained that this type of production "disturbs the metabolic interaction between man and the earth," causing a rift in the soil nutrient cycle that undermines "the operation of the eternal natural condition for the lasting fertility of the soil." Here, the social metabolism of capital violated the universal metabolism associated with the soil nutrient cycle (also conceived as a law of restitution), undermining the conditions that supported human society.

Metabolic scholars illuminate how the transfer of energy and nutrients is tied to the accumulation process and increasingly takes place at the national and international level, as the bounty of the countryside and distant lands has been transferred to urban centers of the global North. Industrial capitalist agricultural practices that increase the yield of food and fiber tend to exacerbate the metabolic rift in the nutrient cycle, squandering the riches of the soil. For example, in the 1800s, massive quantities of guano were shipped from Peru to the global North to enrich depleted soils (Clark and Foster 2009; Foster 2000). Eventually artificial fertilizers were developed and used for this purpose. But given the town and country divide and the drive to accumulate capital, the metabolic rift in the nutrient cycle persists (Magdoff 2011; Mancus 2007).

In *The Political Economy of Global Warming*, Del Weston (2014, 66) contends that the "metabolic rift is at the crux of Marx's ecological critique of capitalism, denoting the disjuncture between social systems and the rest of nature." Metabolic scholars have examined how the social metabolism of capitalism as a global system has created specific environmental problems in the modern era by transgressing the universal metabolism of nature. For example, capitalist growth has been dependent on burning massive quantities of coal, natural gas and oil (Clark and York 2005; Foster and Clark 2012). This process has resulted in breaking the solar income budget, releasing enormous quantities of carbon that had been sequestered. At the same time, consequent growth-driven ecological degradation (e.g., deforestation) substantially reduces carbon sinks, further contributing to the accumulation of atmospheric carbon dioxide, resulting in a carbon rift that exacerbates human-caused climate change. As the growth imperative of capitalism intensifies the social metabolism without any regard for natural limits, socio-ecological rifts are created within specific natural cycles and systems. Even in overlooked realms, such as marine systems, the social metabolism of capitalism is altering ecosystem dynamics and life cycles. For instance, capital accumulation processes have been demonstrated to play a primary role in the structure and function of the fishing industry on a global scale. Capitalist economic forces have led to fish being harvested at a rate faster than they can reproduce and, at times, to the collapse of fisheries (Longo 2010; Longo et al. 2015).

The intensification of the social metabolism demands more energy and raw materials, generating an array of ecological contradictions and rifts (Burkett 2006; Foster et al. 2010). Metabolic scholars, along with treadmill proponents, argue that technological innovation plays a crucial role in capitalist development as it helps rationalize the labor process and reduce costs via automation. New technologies often make energy and raw material usage more efficient, but this innovation does not necessarily lower the overall demands placed on the biophysical world. In fact, more efficient resource usage often increases aggregate consumption of that particular resource—creating a socioeconomic dynamic known as the Jevons paradox, named after the nineteenth-century economist William Stanley Jevons (Clark and Foster 2001; Jevons 1906; Polimeni et al. 2008). In *The Coal Question*, Jevons noted this paradoxical relationship, whereby increased consumption outstrips gains made in energy efficiency. He did not, however, provide a full explanation for why this occurred. Marxists in the metabolic tradition explain that efficient operations produce savings, which are used to expand investment in production and thereby promote increased production and consumption, and accordingly total energy consumed, raw materials used and carbon dioxide produced (Foster et al. 2010; York 2010). This dynamic has led to situation where the most efficient nations are often found to be largest consumers of natural resources (York et al. 2004). To understand why this paradox arises, it is necessary to consider how the growth imperative of capital and processes of accumulation influence these dynamics. The Jevons paradox is a product of capitalist social relations. Notably, it illustrates that purely technological means cannot solve ecological problems.

The constant drive to accumulate capital creates distinct socio-ecological rifts and crises. Burkett (1999) discusses two different conceptions of ecological crisis within Marx's critique of capital. First, an environmental crisis of capital accumulation is caused by resource scarcity, which—as in O'Connor's second contradiction thesis—can increase the costs of operation for individual capitalists and capital as a whole. Such events have periodically occurred, such as the British cotton crisis created by the Civil War in the United States. Second, and perhaps more significant, is an ecological crisis proper, whereby the accumulation process results in general degradation of the conditions of life. In this case, the deterioration is not necessarily registered by capital due to the externalization of costs. Global climate change, in many ways, is an example of this. In such a case, there are negligible feedback mechanisms from rising ecological costs to economic crisis that can be counted on to check capitalism's destruction of the conditions that support life. To make matters worse, to the extent that a problem is recognized, capital's tendency toward commodification drives the growth of new industries and/or markets that can profit from environmental destruction, such as waste management, aquaculture and carbon trading (Foster 2009; Foster et al. 2010; Longo et al. 2015).

As a dynamic system, capitalism confronts environmental obstacles—such as a shortage or exhaustion of particular resources—through a series of shifts and technological fixes to maintain its expansion. Here environmental constraints are addressed by incorporating new resources into the production process, changing the location of production or developing new technologies to increase efficiency. Rather than solving ecological rifts, such shifts generally create new cumulative problems, generating additional disruptions in the conditions of life, often on a larger scale (Foster et al. 2010). Today the drive to capital accumulation is disrupting the planetary metabolism at cumulatively higher levels, threatening irreversible, catastrophic impacts for countless species, including our own.

Conclusion

In this chapter, we briefly discussed how the rise and expansion of capitalism fundamentally transformed social and ecological relationships. We also outlined the general foci and arguments of three prominent political-economic perspectives—the treadmill of production, the second contradiction of capitalism, and metabolic analysis. Each of these approaches addresses specific dynamics within the capitalist system that contribute to various forms of environmental degradation. As is expected, aspects of the distinct perspectives are complementary and overlapping. Metabolic analysis, the most recent of the three, explicitly analyzes the interchange and interpenetration between society and nature. In many ways, social metabolic analysis can serve as a bridge between the natural and social sciences

(Fischer-Kowalski 1998). Nevertheless, it is clear from all of these perspectives that the array of environmental problems, such as global climate change, the decline of freshwater and the loss biodiversity, are in part a consequence of the inherent drive of capital to increase accumulation. Each of these approaches contends that capitalism is an unsustainable socio-economic system, generating widespread ecological degradation. Thus, systemic change is necessary to create a socioeconomic order premised on meeting human needs (instead of capital needs) while protecting the conditions that support life.

References

Anderson, C. H. 1976. *The Sociology of Survival*. Homewood, IL: Dorsey Press.

Angus, I. 2016. *Facing the Anthropocene*. New York: Monthly Review Press.

Baran, P. and P. Sweezy. 1966. *Monopoly Capital*. New York: Monthly Review Press.

Benton, T. 1989. "Marxism and Natural Limits." *New Left Review* 178: 51–86.

Bookchin, M. 1974. *Our Synthetic Environment*. New York: Harper Colophon Books.

Burkett, P. 1999. *Marx and Nature*. New York: St. Martin's Press.

——. 2006. *Marxism and Ecological Economics*. Leiden: Brill.

Carson, R. 1962. *Silent Spring*. Boston: Houghton Mifflin.

——. 1998. *Lost Woods*. Boston: Beacon Press.

Clark, B. and J. B. Foster. 2001. "William Stanley Jevons and the Coal Question." *Organization & Environment* 14: 93–98.

——. 2009. "Ecological Imperialism and the Global Metabolic Rift." *International Journal of Comparative Sociology* 50(3–4): 311–334.

Clark, B. and R. York. 2005. "Carbon Metabolism." *Theory and Society* 34: 391–428.

Commoner, B. 1967. *Science and Survival*. New York: Viking Press.

——. 1971. *The Closing Circle*. New York: Alfred A. Knopf.

Fischer-Kowalski, M. 1998. "Society's Metabolism." *Journal of Industrial Ecology* 2(1): 61–78.

Foster, J. B. 1999. "Marx's Theory of Metabolic Rift." *American Journal of Sociology* 105(2): 366–405.

——. 2000. *Marx's Ecology*. New York: Monthly Review Press.

——. 2009. *The Ecological Revolution*. New York: Monthly Review Press.

——. 2013. "Marx and the Rift in the Universal Metabolism of Nature." *Monthly Review* 65(7): 1–19.

Foster, J. B. and P. Burkett. 2016. *Marx and the Earth*. Leiden: Brill.

Foster, J. B. and B. Clark. 2012. "The Planetary Emergency." *Monthly Review* 64(7): 1–25.

——. 2016. "Marx's Ecology and the Left." *Monthly Review* 68(2): 1–25.

Foster, J. B., B. Clark, and R. York. 2010. *The Ecological Rift*. New York: Monthly Review Press.

Gareau, B. 2008. "Class Consciousness or Natural Consciousness? Socionatural Relations and the Potential for Social Change." *Rethinking Marxism* 20(1): 120–141.

Gorz, A. 1983. *Ecology as Politics*. London: Pluto.

——. 1994. *Capitalism, Socialism, Ecology*. London: Verso.

Gould, K. A., D. N. Pellow, and A. Schnaiberg. 2004. "Interrogating the Treadmill of Production." *Organization & Environment* 17(3): 296–316.

Guha, R. and J. Martínez-Alier. 1997. *Varieties of Environmentalism*. London: Earthscan.

Hamilton, C. and J. Grinevald. 2015. "Was the Anthropocene Anticipated?" *The Anthropocene Review* 2(1): 59–72.

Heilbroner, R. 1985. *The Nature and Logic of Capital*. New York: W.W. Norton.

Hughes, J. 2000. *Ecology and Historical Materialism*. Cambridge: Cambridge University Press.

Jevons, W. S. 1906 [1865]. *The Coal Question*. London: Macmillan.

Kapp, K. W. 1971. *The Social Costs of Private Enterprise*. New York: Schocken.

Kovel, J. 2002. *The Enemy of Nature*. London: Zed Books.

Leiss, W. 1974. *The Domination of Nature*. Boston: Beacon Press.

Li, M. 2009. "Capitalism, Climate Change, and the Transition to Sustainability." *Development and Change* 40: 1039–1062.

Longo, S. B. 2010. "Mediterranean Rift: Socio-Ecological Transformations in the Sicilian Bluefin Tuna Fishery." *Critical Sociology* 38(3): 417–436.

Longo, S. B., R. Clausen, and B. Clark. 2015. *The Tragedy of the Commodity*. New Brunswick: Rutgers University Press.

Magdoff, F. 2011. "Ecological Civilization." *Monthly Review* 62(8): 1–25.

Mancus, P. 2007. "Nitrogen Fertilizer Dependency and its Contradictions." *Rural Sociology* 72(2): 269–288.

Marx, K. 1967. *Capital*, Volume 3. New York: International Publishers.

———. 1975. *Texts on Method*. Oxford: Blackwell.

———. 1976. *Capital*, Volume 1. New York: Vintage.

Marx, K. and F. Engels. 1975. *Collected Works*, Volume 24. New York: International Publishers.

———. 1988. *Collected Works*, Volume 30. New York: International Publishers.

Meadows, D. H., D. L. Meadows, J. Randers, and W. W. Behrens III. 1972. *The Limits to Growth*. New York: Universe Books.

Mészáros, I. 1995. *Beyond Capital*. New York: Monthly Review Press.

Moore, C. 2011. *Plastic Ocean*. New York: Avery.

O'Connor, J. 1973. *The Fiscal Crisis of the State*. New York: St. Martin's Press.

———. 1984. *Accumulation Crisis*. New York: Blackwell.

———. 1998. *Natural Causes*. New York: Guilford Press.

Pellow, D. 2007. *Resisting Global Toxins*. Cambridge, MA: MIT Press.

Polanyi, K. 1957. *The Great Transformation*. Boston: Beacon Press.

Polimeni, J. M., K. Mayumi, M. Giampietro, and B. Alcott. 2008. *The Jevons Paradox and the Myth of Resource Efficiency Improvements*. London: Earthscan.

Schmidt, A. 1970. *The Concept of Nature in Marx*. London: New Left Books.

Schnaiberg, A. 1980. *The Environment*. New York: Oxford University Press.

Schnaiberg, A. and K. A. Gould. 1994. *Environment and Society*. New York: St. Martin's Press.

Steffen, W., W. Broadgate, L. Deutsch, O. Gaffney, and C. Ludwig. 2015. "The Trajectory of the Anthropocene: The Great Acceleration." *Anthropocene Review* 2(1): 81–98.

Sweezy, P. 2004. "Capitalism and the Environment." *Monthly Review* 56(5): 86–93.

Veblen, T. 1964. *Absentee Ownership and the Business Enterprise in Modern Times*. New York: Augustus M. Kelley.

Vlachou, A. 2005. "Debating Sustainable Development." *Rethinking Marxism* 17(4): 627–638.

Wall, D. 2005. *Babylon and Beyond*. London: Pluto Press.

Waters, C. N., J. Zalasiewicz, C. Summerhayes, A.D. Barnosky, C. Poirier, A. Gałuszka, A. Cearreta, M. Edgeworth, E. C. Ellis, M. Ellis, C. Jeandel, R. Leinfelder, J. R. McNeill, D. deB. Richter, W. Steffen, J. Syvitski, D. Vidas, M. Wagreich, M. Williams, A. Zhisheng, J. Grinevald, E. Odada, N. Oreskes, and A. P. Wolfe. 2016. "The Anthropocene Is Functionally and Stratigraphically Distinct from the Holocene." *Science* 351(6269): 137–147.

Weston, D. 2014. *The Political Economy of Global Warming*. New York: Routledge.

York, R. 2010. "The Paradox at the Heart of Modernity." *International Journal of Sociology* 40: 6–22.

York, R., E. A. Rosa, and T. Dietz. 2004. "The Ecological Footprint Intensity of National Economies." *Journal of Industrial Ecology* 8: 139–154.

INDEX

Alstott, Anne 287–88
Althusser, Louis 3, 7–10, 20, 341; accumulation
  and 202; alienation and 136, 141; ancient
  modes of production and 272–73; articulation
  approach and 311; dialectical materialism and
  326–27; Hegel and 209n11; knowledge effects
  and 24; knowledge production and 22–23;
  overdetermination and 275n2;
  overdetermination's definition and 334n4;
  postmodernism and 343; primitive
  accumulation and 148; Spinoza and 24; SSA
  theory and 375; transition theory and 323
"amalgamate and allocate" procedure 65
Amariglio, Jack 20, 203, 205; class process and
  210n15; communism and 279
American Path 303; peasantry and 308n1
Amherst school 279. *See also* Resnick, Wolff
Amin, Samir 385
analytical marxism 350–54; falling rate of profit
  theories and 359n3; methodology of 354–58;
  positivism and 359n8
analytical philosophy 350; analytical marxism
  and 352, 354–56
anarchy 339
ancient class production: enterprise theory and
  175; family farms and 308n5
ancient modes of production 269–73
Anderson, Charles 401–2
Andreasson, Stefan 149
Anglo-Saxon Marxism 69
animal spirits 102
antagonism of interests 127; *Empire* and 210n22;
  globalization and 195n9; labor movement and
  293; neoliberalism and 250; non-productive
  labor and 129; revolution and 206;
  structuredness of 189
anthropocentrism 16
Anti-Dühring (Engels) 15
anti-essentialism 23; ancient modes of production
  and 272; communism and 279, 282;
  essentialism and 119–20; feminism and 392,
  395; postmodernism and 345; primitive
  accumulation and 148. *See also* essentialism
anti-semitism 279n11
apartheid 374
Appadurai, Arjun 16
appearance 22. *See also* essentialism
Apple 193
appropriability framework 193
appropriation of surplus: accumulation and 205;
  alienation and 141; ancient modes of
  production and 271–72; antagonism of
  interests and 195n9; circuit of capital and 98;
  communism and 35, 280–83; coupon stock
  market and 289n1; democracy and 34–35, 38;
  development and 313, 315, 318, 320; feminism
  and 392; financialization and 259; formal-

informal divide and 316; globalization and
  193; household surplus and 37; income and 39;
  mobility and 296n4; neoliberalism and 249;
  non-determinism and 329; postmodernism and
  340, 343, 345; price theory and 80, 83; self-
  employment and 269; socialism and 284–88;
  transition theory and 273–75
Arab Spring 252
arbitrage 257, 385
archaeology of knowledge 16–17, 340
Aristotle 131n1, 138; alienation and 141; goods
  and 142n26
Arkwright, Richard 52–53
Arthur, Chris 47
artisans. *See* craft labor
Asian crisis of 1997 149
Asiatic mode of production 334n2
Asimakopoulos, John 375
assemblage 205, 210n20
Association for Economic and Social Analysis
  (AESA) 241n1
Athenian society 138
Australia 395
Austrian school 71, 77n2, 245, 247
autonomy of migration approach 292

bailouts 251
Bakir, Erdogan 240, 242n10; business cycles and
  237–39
Balibar, Etienne 8; migration and 294
Bank for International Settlements 258
bankruptcy 261
banks 75, 258, 263, 366; accumulation and 207;
  Keynes on 367n14; monetary theory and 72;
  reproduction and 221; savings and loan crisis
  and 251
Baran, Paul 372, 382; accumulation and 199, 204;
  development and 310; ecology and 401;
  enterprise theory and 177; financialization and
  386; monopoly capital and 379, 383–85, 387;
  non-productive labor and 129; profit-rate trends
  and 210n25; rationality and 209n5; SSA theory
  and 371; treadmill of production and 402
Bardhan, Pranhab 358n2
Barlow, David E. 374
Barlow, Melissa H. 374
barter 71, 363–64; Ricardo and 367n5
Baseball, Major Leagues of 177
basic income 281, 283; feminism and 394
Basole, Amit 186n1
Basu, Pranab 150, 239–40
Baumol, William 130
Bautista, Juan José 151n1
Becker, Gary 246; labor movement and 293; non-
  productive labor and 125–26
being 3–5, 7
"being-becoming" 147, 149

411

Taylor & Francis eBooks

Helping you to choose the right eBooks for your Library

Add Routledge titles to your library's digital collection today. Taylor and Francis ebooks contains over 50,000 titles in the Humanities, Social Sciences, Behavioural Sciences, Built Environment and Law.

Choose from a range of subject packages or create your own!

Benefits for you

» Free MARC records
» COUNTER-compliant usage statistics
» Flexible purchase and pricing options
» All titles DRM-free.

Benefits for your user

» Off-site, anytime access via Athens or referring URL
» Print or copy pages or chapters
» Full content search
» Bookmark, highlight and annotate text
» Access to thousands of pages of quality research at the click of a button.

REQUEST YOUR FREE INSTITUTIONAL TRIAL TODAY

Free Trials Available
We offer free trials to qualifying academic, corporate and government customers.

eCollections – Choose from over 30 subject eCollections, including:

Archaeology	Language Learning
Architecture	Law
Asian Studies	Literature
Business & Management	Media & Communication
Classical Studies	Middle East Studies
Construction	Music
Creative & Media Arts	Philosophy
Criminology & Criminal Justice	Planning
Economics	Politics
Education	Psychology & Mental Health
Energy	Religion
Engineering	Security
English Language & Linguistics	Social Work
Environment & Sustainability	Sociology
Geography	Sport
Health Studies	Theatre & Performance
History	Tourism, Hospitality & Events

For more information, pricing enquiries or to order a free trial, please contact your local sales team:
www.tandfebooks.com/page/sales

 Routledge
Taylor & Francis Group

The home of Routledge books

www.tandfebooks.com

Printed in the United States
by Baker & Taylor Publisher Services